ACT® Total Prep 2026

ACT® is a registered trademark of ACT, Inc., which is not affiliated with Kaplan and was not involved in the production of, and does not endorse, this product.

Lead Editor
Heather Waite

Contributing Editors
Melissa McLaughlin; Ethan Weber; J. Scott Mullison

Special thanks to our writers and reviewers:
Steve Cisar, Marilyn Engle, Deborah Osborn, Bird Marathe, Aisa Diaz, Thomas Darragh, Karen McCulloch, Michael Collins, Boris Dvorkin, Mark Feery, Jo L'Abbate, Gordon Spector, Caroline Sykes, and Bonnie Wang.

Additional special thanks to
Jason Bedford, Sarah Seymour, Amy Zarkos, Megan Buckman, Subitha R. K., Joanna Graham, Mary Jo Rhodes, Michael Wolff, and the countless others who made this project possible.

ACT® is a registered trademark of ACT, Inc., which is not affiliated with Kaplan and was not involved in the production of, and does not endorse, this product.

This publication is designed to provide accurate and authoritative information in regard to the subject matter covered. It is sold with the understanding that the publisher is not engaged in rendering legal, accounting, or other professional service. If legal advice or other expert assistance is required, the services of a competent professional should be sought.

© 2025 Kaplan North America, LLC

Published by Kaplan North America, LLC dba Kaplan Publishing
1515 W. Cypress Creek Road
Fort Lauderdale, Florida 33309

ISBN: 978-1-5062-9759-0
10 9 8 7 6 5 4 3 2 1

All rights reserved. This material is protected under International and Pan-American Copyright Conventions. No part of this publication may be reproduced, distributed, or transmitted in any form or by any means—including photocopying, recording, or other electronic or mechanical methods, now known or hereinafter invented—duplicated, resold, stored in, introduced into, or incorporated into any information storage or retrieval system, or used in any artificial intelligence analysis software, such as generative AI systems or machine learning models, without the express written permission of Kaplan North America, LLC.

Kaplan North America, LLC print books are available at special quantity discounts to use for sales promotions, employee premiums, or educational purposes. For more information or to purchase books, please call the Simon & Schuster Special Sales department at 866-506-1949.

TABLE OF CONTENTS

OVERVIEW v

PART 1: THE ACT AND YOU 1
   CHAPTER 1: INSIDE THE ACT 3

PART 2: ACT ENGLISH. 11
   CHAPTER 2: THE METHOD FOR ACT ENGLISH 13
   CHAPTER 3: SPOTTING AND FIXING ERRORS: SENTENCE STRUCTURE, PUNCTUATION, AND AGREEMENT. 29
   CHAPTER 4: SPOTTING AND FIXING ISSUES: CONCISENESS, ORGANIZATION, AND DEVELOPMENT 75
   CHAPTER 5: ACT ENGLISH: TIMING AND SECTION MANAGEMENT STRATEGIES . . . 133
   TEST YOURSELF: ACT ENGLISH. 141

PART 3: ACT MATH 167
   CHAPTER 6: PREREQUISITE SKILLS AND CALCULATOR USE 169
   CHAPTER 7: THE METHOD FOR ACT MATH QUESTIONS. 179
   CHAPTER 8: NUMBER AND QUANTITY. 193
   CHAPTER 9: RATES, RATIOS, PROPORTIONS, AND PERCENTS 225
   CHAPTER 10: ALGEBRA. 249
   CHAPTER 11: TABLES, GRAPHS, STATISTICS, AND PROBABILITY 297
   CHAPTER 12: FUNCTIONS 327
   CHAPTER 13: GEOMETRY. 359
   CHAPTER 14: ACT MATH: TIMING AND SECTION MANAGEMENT STRATEGIES 415
   TEST YOURSELF: ACT MATH. 423

▶ **GO ONLINE**
www.kaptest.com/moreonline

PART 4: ACT READING 443

    CHAPTER 15: THE METHOD FOR ACT READING 445

    CHAPTER 16: ACT READING PASSAGE STRATEGIES 467

    CHAPTER 17: IDENTIFYING QUESTION TYPES 493

    CHAPTER 18: ANSWERING READING QUESTIONS 507

    CHAPTER 19: LITERATURE PASSAGES 533

    CHAPTER 20: PAIRED PASSAGES 559

    CHAPTER 21: ACT READING: TIMING AND SECTION MANAGEMENT
                     STRATEGIES 587

    TEST YOURSELF: ACT READING 599

PART 5: COUNTDOWN TO TEST DAY 621

    CHAPTER 22: COUNTDOWN TO TEST DAY .623

PART 6: PRACTICE TESTS 625

    PRACTICE TEST 1 629

    PRACTICE TEST 2 695

ONLINE

PART 7: ACT SCIENCE . . . . .ONLINE

    CHAPTER 23: THE METHOD FOR ACT SCIENCE . . . . .ONLINE

    CHAPTER 24: DATA . . . . .ONLINE

    CHAPTER 25: EXPERIMENTS . . . . .ONLINE

    CHAPTER 26: THINKING LIKE A SCIENTIST . . . . .ONLINE

    CHAPTER 27: ACT SCIENCE: TIMING AND SECTION
                    MANAGEMENT STRATEGIES .ONLINE

    TEST YOURSELF: ACT SCIENCE . . . . .ONLINE

PART 8: ACT WRITING . . . . .ONLINE

    CHAPTER 28: THE METHOD FOR THE ACT WRITING TEST . . . . .ONLINE

Overview

Three Tips for ACT Success

Most colleges will consider your ACT score as part of your application, so it's no surprise that it's a challenging test. It can feel intimidating, like a barrier you need to climb over. At Kaplan, it's our goal to help you look at the ACT as an opportunity—a chance to demonstrate your knowledge, as well as your critical thinking skills, which will be key to your success as a college student. Looking at the ACT as an opportunity will help you do better on the test.

Besides committing to a positive attitude toward the test, give yourself a head start with these tips:

- The ACT is a standardized test, meaning that scores for every testing administration mean the same thing. To achieve this reliability, the test maker must always ask questions on the same topics and in the same way. This makes the test predictable and, therefore, easier to prepare for. We've distilled how high-scoring students approach each section into Kaplan Methods. In fact, each method gets its own chapter. Learn these simple, step-by-step methods, and you'll approach questions like an expert.
- The ACT is not like the tests you take in school. When colleges want to know how you do on tests in school, they look at your transcript. Acing the ACT requires different skills. This book highlights these skills, from taking math shortcuts to avoiding incorrect-answer "traps" to managing your time. By studying this book, you'll learn to think like the maker of the test does.
- Your skill level now has nothing to do with your skill level on test day. Getting some questions incorrect? Having trouble with a specific topic? That just means you've found an opportunity to raise your score. Be patient with yourself! In your life so far, you've already learned thousands of things. You can learn a few more things to succeed on the ACT.

Read on to learn how your book and online resources are organized and how to make the best use of them. Good luck on the test—you're going to nail it!

Welcome to Kaplan!

Congratulations on taking this important step in your college admissions process! By studying with Kaplan, the official partner of live instruction for the ACT®, you'll maximize your score on the ACT, a major factor in your overall application.

Our experience shows that the greatest ACT score increases result from active engagement in the preparation process. Kaplan will give you direction, focus your preparation, and teach you the specific skills and effective test-taking strategies you need to know for the ACT. We will help you achieve your top performance on test day, but your effort is crucial. The more you invest in preparing for the ACT, the greater your chances of achieving your target score and getting into your top-choice college.

Are you registered for the ACT? Kaplan cannot register you for the official ACT. If you have not already registered for the upcoming ACT, visit the official website at **www.act.org** to register online and for information on registration deadlines, test sites, accommodations, fees, and test updates.

Chapter Organization

The chapters in this book follow a standard format to make this book as easy to use as possible.

How Much Do You Know?

At the beginning of most chapters, you have an opportunity to assess how much you already know about the topics by answering a set of test-like questions. If you answer most or all of the questions in a set correctly and in the most efficient way, you may want to skip one or more lessons in that chapter. If you answer some or all of the questions in a set incorrectly or in an inefficient way, you will want to review most or all of the lessons in that chapter. The answers and explanations for these sections are provided in the "Check Your Work" section immediately after the question set.

Try on Your Own

The lessons within each chapter start with a question (or passage) typical of the way the ACT tests a given topic and ends with a set of practice questions called "Try on Your Own." These sections are designed to provide immediate, targeted practice. Complete these questions and review their explanations at least once after reviewing the lesson. You might consider completing these questions multiple times if you are preparing for the ACT over an extended period of time. The answers and explanations for these sections are provided at the end of each chapter.

On Test Day

Most of the Math chapters include an "On Test Day" section that highlights one or more ways a question can be approached strategically. Complete these sections after you have reviewed the lessons but before you complete the "How Much Have You Learned?" question set.

How Much Have You Learned?

You need to reinforce what you learn in each chapter by practicing the Kaplan methods and strategies. Most chapters include a section called "How Much Have You Learned?" that features additional practice questions reinforcing the concepts explained in that chapter. The answers and explanations for these sections are provided at the end of each chapter.

Reflect

These sections can be completed during or after a chapter's completion. You might prefer to use the "Reflect" sections to evaluate your retention over time or reflect on the chapter as a whole when you complete all of the lessons. However you choose to reflect on your ACT studying, what's important is taking the time to do so.

Test Yourself

After all the chapters on each test—English, Math, Reading—you have an opportunity for section practice. Apply what you've learned to a test-like mix of questions. Use your results to determine what you've mastered and which chapters, if any, you should review.

Practice Tests

Kaplan's practice tests are designed to mimic the actual ACT. By taking practice tests, you will prepare yourself for the actual test day experience.

We recommend you complete your in-book and online practice tests as you make your way through the content of this book. You can score your in-book practice tests by hand using the score conversion tables in this book. Your online practice tests can be easily scored online, and Kaplan will provide you with a detailed score report. Use this summary to help you focus and review the content areas that comprise your greatest areas of improvement.

Online Resources

Your online resources are a very important part of this book's intended study plan. Additional study material, quizzes, practice tests, coverage for the optional ACT test sections (Science and Writing), and any last-minute updates will be there for you.

To access the online resources that are included with the book at no additional cost, follow the steps below.

1. Go to **kaptest.com/moreonline.**
2. Search for your book with its ISBN and title, or simply type "ACT" into the search bar.
3. Have this book available as you complete the on-screen registration instructions.

Then, whenever you want to use your online resources, go to **kaptest.com/login** and log in using the email address and password you used to register your book.

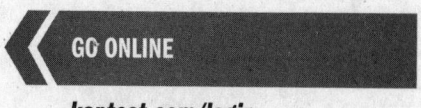

Your book's online resources include:

- ACT Science—bonus material that will answer your questions about the optional ACT Science Test. This material covers the Kaplan Method for ACT Science.
- ACT Writing—a bonus chapter that will answer your questions about the optional ACT Writing Test. The chapter covers the Kaplan Method for ACT Writing and provides a simple essay template that you can use on test day.
- Practice tests—more Kaplan practice tests, plus easy online scoring and detailed score reports.

If you have any trouble accessing your online resources, please email **book.support@kaplan.com** for assistance.

[PART 1]

THE ACT AND YOU

[CHAPTER 1]

INSIDE THE ACT

> **LEARNING OBJECTIVES**
>
> After completing this chapter, you will be able to:
> - Recall the timing and scope of each ACT test in anticipation of section management
> - State what the ACT scoring system means for you as a test taker

ACT Structure

An Enhanced ACT

The ACT has recently gone through some important changes, but there's no need to worry. Most students will find all of these changes beneficial, and for those of you who have already taken a previous version of the ACT, you'll find that much has stayed the same. This book has the resources to help you succeed on this enhanced ACT.

The ACT is now shorter with fewer questions, and you'll have more time on average to tackle each question. The Science Test is now optional; however, since some schools will want to see Science scores, make sure you know if you want, or need, to take this test. There will also be a few more questions that require basic knowledge of scientific topics, as well as a possible passage with engineering or design topics. Likewise, the Writing Test is optional. One of the most noticeable changes that you'll see involves the required Math Test. Instead of 5 answer choices, each question will now have 4. The required Reading Test features shorter passages and fewer questions per passage. The required English Test also features shorter passages with fewer questions and prominently adds a specific question stem to each question that will help you focus on the issue that is being tested.

The enhanced ACT features more choice for you as the test taker. You'll be able to choose to take the exam, with all of its test options, on the computer. If you prefer, you'll still be able to go with the traditional paper-and-pencil route for taking the test too.

If you choose the computer-based option, it'll still be taken at a testing center. It will not be a home-based exam with virtual proctoring. The testing devices (computers) will be

Part 1
THE ACT AND YOU

provided by the testing center. On the computer-based exam, you'll be able to highlight sections of passages yourself, and you'll be able to use a built-in calculator application. (You'll still be able to use your own permissible calculator on either version, paper or computer-based! In fact, we recommend that you use the test-legal calculator that you are most comfortable with.) The computer-based test will also have enhanced accessibility features, such as screen reader support, zoom, and answer masking.

The general nature of the testing format is not changing. The enhanced ACT is not an adaptive test: you'll have a given set of questions to answer for each test, and those won't change based on how well (or poorly) you do on previous questions. There will, however, be experimental questions that do not count toward your score. In the past, some students might have received an additional section, known as the "fifth" section, at the end of their exam that accounted for the experimental questions that the ACT used for research purposes. These experimental questions will now be included with every test section and with every administration. They are not marked, so test takers should have the mindset that every question is equally important.

When you take the ACT on a computer, the questions will look slightly different. Instead of a line reference in a question, you'll see the relevant content highlighted in the passage. However, in this book, we'll generally present the questions as they would look on the paper test.

While the experience of testing on paper or on a computer is different, there are more similarities than differences between the two formats. The ACT plans for the computer-based and paper-and-pencil exams to cost the same. Scratch paper is also allowed on either version of the exam, so it's truly a matter of your personal test-taking preference.

ACT Structure

The ACT, like any standardized test, is predictable. The more comfortable you are with the test structure, the more confidently you will approach each question type, thus maximizing your score.

The ACT is 2 hours and 5 minutes long and is made up of multiple-choice questions that test three subject areas: English, Math, and Reading. The optional Writing section is 40 minutes, and the optional Science section is 40 minutes.

Test	Allotted time (minutes)	Question count
English	35	50
Math	50	45
Reading	40	36
Science (optional)	40	40
Writing (optional)	40	1

ACT Scoring

ACT scoring can seem a bit complex. You will receive one scaled score ranging from 1 to 36 for each required test, and these scores will be averaged to calculate your composite score. You will receive a separate score for the optional Science and Writing tests, if you choose to take either.

In addition to your overall scores, you will receive subscores that provide a deeper analysis of your ACT performance, including a STEM and/or an ELA score if you take the optional test(s). The ACT also gives you a percentile ranking, which allows you to compare your scores with those of other test takers. For example, a student who scored in the 63rd percentile did better than 63 percent of all others who took that test.

The scores you need depend primarily on which colleges you are planning to apply to. For example, if you want to attend an engineering school, you'll typically need a higher math score than if you want to attend a liberal arts college. Research the colleges you are interested in, find out what scores they require, and structure your ACT studying accordingly.

Superscoring

The score reports sent to colleges for students who have taken the ACT more than once will include superscores. A superscore is like a composite score in that it is an average of your subject scores, but for the superscore, ACT selects your best subject score from every test administration. Therefore, your superscore is never lower than any composite score, and it is often higher than each of your composite scores. Not all schools consider the superscore in admissions, but many do, so check out the superscore policies of the colleges to which you plan to apply.

Since you can only get a superscore after you've taken more than one ACT, it's important to study for the entire test the first time around and work through as much of this book as you can before test day. However, if you're focused on specific sections in an effort to raise your superscore, just use those units of this book.

How to Maximize Your Score

The most important thing to remember while taking the test is that maximizing all the various scores and subscores depends on earning as many points as possible in every section. You'll find advice on test-taking strategies below and in the section management chapters at the end of the English, Math, and Reading sections of this book. However, if you still have a substantial amount of time to prepare for the ACT, the best advice we can give you is to improve the specific skills you need to answer math, English, and reading questions correctly and efficiently. That's what this book is for. You can work through the chapters and sections in any order you like, and you can skip the lessons you don't need. You don't need to start with English or answer every single question; just use the book in a way that works for you. Pick a lesson, read the instructional text, and work your way through the practice questions. There are hundreds of them in this book and its online resources, and they are very similar to those that you will see on test day. Practice will not only improve your skills but will also raise your confidence, and that's very important for test day success.

If you've already registered your book, go online (**kaptest.com/login**) and log in. There will be additional practice and advice for you there.

kaptest.com/login

When and Where to Take the ACT

For students testing in the United States or US territories, the ACT is offered each school year on seven Saturday test dates. Typically, exams are offered in September, October, December, February, April, June, and July. You can take the ACT up to 12 times. Some states offer special administrations of the ACT on different dates. Non-Saturday testing is available by request for students requiring religious or other exemptions.

The ACT is administered at schools around the country that serve as testing centers. Your high school may or may not be a testing center. Go to **www.act.org** for a list of testing centers near you and up-to-date information about the test. Historically, students have needed to register for the ACT approximately one month in advance to avoid paying a late fee.

Students who are testing outside of the United States or US territories should visit the ACT website for test date and test center information.

Part 1
THE ACT AND YOU

The ACT English Test

The ACT English Test will focus on your ability to revise and edit text from a range of content areas.

ACT English Test Overview	
Timing	35 minutes
Questions	50 passage-based multiple-choice questions
Passages	6 single passages with 5–10 questions each
Passage length	~200–400 words per passage

The ACT English Test will contain six single passages of different genres with a variety of rhetorical situations. A passage could be an argument, an informative or explanatory text, or a narrative.

The most prevalent question format on the ACT English Test will ask you to choose the best of three alternatives to an underlined portion of the passage or to decide that the current version is already the best option. You will be asked to improve the development, organization, and diction in the passages to ensure they conform to conventional standards of English grammar, usage, and style. There are three English Test reporting categories.

Skills Tested by English Test Questions	
Production of Writing	Topic development and organization, unity, and cohesion
Knowledge of Language	Precision and conciseness in word choice and consistency in style and tone
Conventions of Standard English	Sentence structure and formation, punctuation, and usage

The ACT Math Test

The ACT Math Test will focus on mathematical skills typically learned in required math courses before the beginning of 12th grade.

ACT Math Test Overview	
Timing	50 minutes
Questions	45 multiple-choice questions

All ACT math questions are multiple-choice questions with four answer choices. The Math Test is divided into three reporting categories.

Skills Tested by Math Test Questions	
Preparing for Higher Mathematics	Using higher-level math to answer questions in five domains: • Number and Quantity • Algebra • Functions • Geometry • Statistics and Probability
Integrating Essential Skills	Using essential concepts and skills to solve more complex problems, including: • Rates and percentages • Area, surface area, and volume • Solving problems using a chain of steps
Modeling (all questions counted within one of the two categories above)	Producing, interpreting, evaluating, and improving models

The ACT Reading Test

The ACT Reading Test will focus on your comprehension and reasoning skills when you are presented with challenging extended passages taken from a variety of content areas.

ACT Reading Test Overview	
Timing	40 minutes
Questions	36 passage-based multiple-choice questions
Passages	3 independent passages and 1 set of paired passages or 4 independent passages
Passage length	~650–900 words

Each passage is preceded by a heading that names the passage type, author, and source; this heading may also include important background information related to the passage.

The ACT Reading Test includes four types of passages: literary narrative, social science, humanities, and natural science. The blurb before the passage will identify literary narrative passages as "LITERARY NARRATIVE," but the social science, humanities, and natural science passages are all identified as "INFORMATIONAL." Often, one of the four passages will consist of two shorter prose passages that are related in some way. There are three reporting categories for the Reading Test.

Part 1
THE ACT AND YOU

Skills Tested by Reading Test Questions	
Key Ideas and Details	Determining central ideas and themes, summarizing information and ideas, understanding relationships between ideas, and drawing conclusions from facts stated in a passage
Craft and Structure	Determining word and phrase meanings, analyzing rhetorical word choice, analyzing text structure, and understanding and analyzing purpose and point of view
Integration of Knowledge and Ideas	Understanding author's claims, differentiating between facts and opinions, using evidence to make connections, analyzing how authors construct arguments, and evaluating reasoning and evidence from various sources

The ACT Science Test (Optional)

The ACT Science Test will generally focus on your scientific reasoning ability, but some questions will require knowledge of basic scientific principles.

ACT Science Test Overview	
Timing	40 minutes
Questions	40 passage-based multiple-choice questions
Passages	7 passages with 5–6 questions each
Passage length	~100–300 words depending on passage type

There are three passage types on the ACT Science Test:

ACT Science Test Passage Types	
Data Representation	Each passage has multiple figures and/or tables
Research Summaries	Each passage describes one or more experiments or studies and usually at least one figure and/or table
Conflicting Viewpoints	A passage with at least two viewpoints related to a theory or phenomenon

The ACT Science Test provides three reporting categories:

Skills Tested by Science Test Questions	
Interpretation of Data	Manipulating and analyzing data in tables, graphs, and diagrams
Scientific Investigation	Understanding experimental tools, procedures, and design and comparing, extending, and modifying experiments
Evaluation of Models, Inferences, and Experimental Results	Judging the validity of scientific information and formulating conclusions and predictions based on that information

The ACT Writing Test (Optional)

The ACT Writing Test assesses your writing skills. The Writing Test includes one prompt describing a complex issue and three perspectives related to that prompt. Your goal is to write an essay in which you present your own reasoned perspective; this perspective might—but does not need to—relate to one or more of the three perspectives in the prompt, but your essay must include a discussion of both your own perspective and at least one other. The specific perspective you decide to take will not affect your final score.

The issue discussed in the prompt might be a familiar one, but it might also be completely new to you. The Writing Test will always include a paragraph providing background on the issue because prior knowledge is not required.

The ACT Writing Test will be broken down into four categories for scoring: Ideas and Analysis, Development and Support, Organization, and Language Use and Conventions. Each of these elements will be scored on a scale of 2 to 12, and you will receive a single subject-level writing score, also on a scale of 2 to 12.

To help you prepare for the ACT Writing Test, check out the bonus chapter "The Method for the ACT Writing Test" in your online resources (**kaptest.com/login**). This chapter will help you decide whether to take this optional test. The chapter also covers the Kaplan Method for ACT Writing, provides a simple essay template that you can use on test day, and includes sample essay prompts and responses.

kaptest.com/login

Test-Taking Strategies

The ACT is different from the tests you are used to taking in school. For example, on a test given in school, you probably go through the questions in order. You spend more time on the harder questions than on the easier ones because harder questions are usually worth more points. You also probably show your work because your teacher tells you that how you approach a question is as important as getting the correct answer.

This approach is not optimal for the ACT. On the ACT, you benefit from moving around within a section if you come across tough questions because the harder questions are worth the same number of points as the easier questions. Similarly, showing your work is unimportant. It doesn't matter how you arrive at the correct answer—only that you answer the questions correctly.

The good news is that you can use the ACT's particular structure to your advantage. You have already learned about the overall structure of the ACT as well as the structures of each of the individual tests. The strategies outlined in this section can be applied to any of these tests.

Strategy #1: Triage the Test

You do not need to complete questions on the ACT in order. Every student has different strengths and should attack the test with those strengths in mind. Your main objective on the ACT should be to score as many points as you can. While approaching questions out of order may seem counterintuitive, it is a surefire way to achieve your best score.

Just remember, you can skip around within each test, but you cannot work on any test other than the one you've been instructed to work on.

To triage a test effectively, do the following:

1. Work through all the low-difficulty questions that you can do quickly. Skip questions that are hard or time-consuming.
   - For the Reading Test, start with the passage you find most manageable and work toward the one you find most challenging. You do not need to go in order.

2. Work through the questions that are doable but time-consuming.
3. Work through the high-difficulty questions.

Strategy #2: Eliminate

Even though there is no incorrect-answer penalty on the ACT, elimination is still a crucial strategy. If you can determine that one or more answer choices are definitely incorrect, you can increase your chances of getting the correct answer by paring the selection down.

To eliminate answer choices, do the following:

- Read each answer choice.
- Eliminate answer choices that you know are incorrect.
- Because there is no incorrect-answer penalty, take your best guess from the remaining choices.

Strategy #3: Guess

Multiple-choice questions on the ACT have four answer choices and no incorrect-answer penalty. That means if you have no idea how to approach a question, you have a 25 percent chance of randomly choosing the correct answer. Even though there's a 75 percent chance of selecting the incorrect answer, you won't lose any points for doing so. The worst that can happen on the ACT is that you'll earn zero points on a question, which means you should always at least take a guess, even when you have no idea what to do.

When guessing on a question, do the following:

- Try to strategically eliminate answer choices before guessing.
- If you run out of time, or have no idea what a question is asking, pick a Letter of the Day.

A "Letter of the Day" is an answer choice letter [A/F, B/G, C/H, or D/J] that you choose before test day to select for questions you guess on. You can use the same Letter of the Day for the entire ACT or change it depending on the section, but you should always use the same Letter of the Day within an individual section.

[PART 2]

ACT ENGLISH

[CHAPTER 2]

THE METHOD FOR ACT ENGLISH

> **LEARNING OBJECTIVE**
>
> After completing this chapter, you will be able to:
> - Effectively and efficiently apply the ACT English Method

How to Do ACT English

The English Test of the ACT tests a limited number of grammar errors and style or logic issues. You should feel empowered by familiarizing yourself with these recurring errors and issues and learn to spot them and address them quickly and efficiently. We'll describe the issues that you're likely to see on test day and how to deal with them in the next two chapters. In this chapter, we'll present a simple series of steps for tackling English questions.

Take a look at the passage and questions below and think about how you would approach them on test day. Then compare your approach to the recommendations that follow.

Gregory Hines, a Beloved Icon

During the last five decades of the 20th century; Gregory Hines enriched musical theater with his performances as a star of the Broadway stage. A multitalented artist, he was also employed as an actor, a director, and a producer in television and film.

He had the experience of earning and receiving numerous awards, including a Tony and a Daytime Emmy.

Hines began performing as a dancer when he was five, touring professionally in nightclubs across the country with his older brother, Maurice, as a duo. Hines found inspiration in watching fellow performers such as the Nicholas Brothers and Sandman Sims. At eight, he made his Broadway debut and remained a star of the stage in a variety of musicals, including *Eubie!*, *Sophisticated Ladies*, and *Jelly's Last Jam*.

1. Which choice makes the sentence most grammatically acceptable?
   A. **No Change**
   B. century, Gregory
   C. century. Gregory
   D. century, from the 1950s to the late 1990s,

2. Which choice makes the sentence most grammatically acceptable?
   F. **No Change**
   G. had the experience of earning
   H. had the experience of receiving
   J. earned

3. The writer wants to provide specific information regarding Hines's Broadway performances. Which choice best accomplishes that goal?
   A. **No Change**
   B. which debuted at various locations among the many venues of Broadway.
   C. which opened at different times throughout Hines's considerably long career.
   D. all of which were evaluated by the rotating group of dozens of theater professionals who are selected by the Tony Awards Administration Committee.

Chapter 2
The Method for ACT English

There is no need to read the entire passage before you start to answer questions. Instead, answer them as you read. When you see a number, finish the sentence you are reading and then look at the corresponding question. If you can answer the question based on what you've read so far, do so—this will likely be the case if the question is testing grammar. If you need more information—which may happen if the question is testing organization or relevance—keep reading until you have enough context to answer the question.

The new ACT makes determining what issue is being tested on each English question much easier that in the past. Every question now has a question stem that will directly tell you at least the general category of what is being tested. Sometimes, however, a detailed knowledge of the issue being tested will be obvious to you when you look at the underlined segment, even without looking at the question. (If it isn't, glance at the answer choices as well as the question stem to help you determine what the test maker is after.) For instance, in question 1 above, a semicolon is underlined, and you might correctly surmise that punctuation is being testing. Looking at the question "Which choice makes the sentence most grammatically acceptable?" and then taking a quick glance at the choices showing that most of them have the same words, in the same order, with only the punctuation marks being different, will confirm that punctuation is, indeed, being tested. **Identify the issue**, using the choices if helpful, is step 1 of the English Method.

To determine the correct punctuation, use the surrounding text. "During the last five decades of the 20th century" is an introductory phrase and cannot stand on its own, so A and C are incorrect; what comes before and after either a period (choice C) or a semicolon (choice A) must be able to stand on its own as a complete sentence. **Eliminate answer choices that do not address the issue** is step 2 of the English Method.

There may be more than one choice that addresses the issue. The two remaining choices are both grammatically correct and relevant to the surrounding context. However, (B) is more concise and therefore the correct answer. Choice D can be eliminated because "from the 1950s to the late 1990s" is redundant; the sentence already says "the last five decades of the 20th century." **Plug in the answer choices and choose the correct one** is step 3 of the English Method. Many students find the mnemonic *C C R* helpful with this step: the first *C* is for grammatically correct, the second *C* is for the most concise without losing any meaning, and the *R* is for the most relevant answer to the question that is being asked.

Here's what we did:

ACT ENGLISH METHOD

Step 1. Identify the issue (use the choices if need be)

Step 2. Eliminate answer choices that do not address the issue

Step 3. Plug in the remaining answer choices and select the correct one

---

Some questions include errors that may not seem apparent. For example, the underlined segment in question 2 is grammatically correct but wordy. Start by **identifying the issue**, using the choices if necessary. The answer choices are shorter than the original text, so conciseness is likely the issue being tested. **Eliminating answer choices that do not address the issue** is next, and F can definitely be eliminated due to wordiness. **Finally, plugging in the remaining choices and choosing the correct one** points you to (J): the single word *earned* expresses the same information as the much longer phrase "had the experience of earning and receiving." Choices G and H are shorter than the original, but they are not nearly as concise as (J).

Other questions may ask you to determine which answer choice provides the most specific description of a particular aspect of the passage. In those instances, **identifying the issue** is straightforward. **Eliminating answer choices that do not address the issue** is essential to answering this type of question. Question 3 requires you to determine which option provides the most specific information about Hines's Broadway

Part 2
ACT ENGLISH

performances. Eliminate B and C because they do not include specific details. **Plug in the remaining choices** and eliminate D because the process by which plays are evaluated by the Tony Awards Administration Committee is not relevant to the passage. Choice (A) is the correct answer.

A correct answer:

- has no grammatical errors
- is as short as possible while retaining the writer's intended meaning
- is relevant to the paragraph and the passage as a whole

Correct answers do NOT:

- provide information that contradicts or is irrelevant to the ideas developed by the original sentence, paragraph, or passage
- introduce new grammatical errors

Chapter 2
The Method for ACT English

How Much Have You Learned?

Directions: Take as much time as you need on these questions. Work carefully and methodically. Practice using the steps that you just learned.

PASSAGE I

Liberal Arts Education

[1]

The concept of liberal arts has existed since the time of ancient Greece, and the parameters of this discipline have largely remained <u>over the centuries</u> unchanged.
[A] In medieval times, the seven liberal arts were split into the Trivium (grammar, rhetoric, and logic) and the Quadrivium (arithmetic, geometry, astronomy, and music) and focused on providing students with a well-rounded education. [B]

1. The best placement for the underlined portion would be:
   A. where it is now.
   B. after the word *concept*.
   C. after the word *arts*.
   D. after the word *unchanged*.

[2]

Today's dictionaries define the liberal arts as "any study given to reflection and free inquiry," which is a <u>lengthy</u> category that has included various subjects throughout its history. Most modern liberal arts colleges have <u>consistent mirrored</u> the fundamental philosophy of ancient times.

2. Which choice best helps indicate that the liberal arts include many disciplines?
   F. **No Change**
   G. broad
   H. challenging
   J. perplexing

3. Which choice makes the sentence most grammatically acceptable?
   A. **No Change**
   B. consistently mirrored
   C. mirrored in a consistent fashion
   D. mirrored in a consistently fashion

In addition, most modern liberal arts colleges award
                        ⎯⎯⎯⎯⎯⎯⎯⎯⎯⎯⎯⎯⎯⎯⎯⎯⎯⎯⎯⎯⎯⎯⎯⎯⎯⎯⎯⎯⎯⎯⎯⎯
                                            4
master's and doctoral degrees.
⎯⎯⎯⎯⎯⎯⎯⎯⎯⎯⎯⎯⎯⎯⎯⎯⎯⎯⎯⎯⎯⎯⎯⎯⎯⎯
            4

4. The writer is considering deleting the underlined sentence. Should the writer make this deletion?

F. Yes, because it contradicts information earlier in the paragraph.
G. Yes, because it interrupts the writer's discussion of modern liberal arts education with irrelevant information.
H. No, because it provides an example showing how liberal arts education is still relevant.
J. No, because it makes a claim important to the writer's overall argument.

Liberal arts study still focuses on the arts, humanities, and sciences, and the basic notion of forming well-rounded
                                           ⎯⎯⎯⎯⎯⎯⎯⎯⎯⎯
                                                5
students in these areas is still

5. Which choice makes the sentence most grammatically acceptable?

A. **No Change**
B. sciences; and
C. sciences. And
D. sciences: and

the goal. [C] However, there is some concern that the
            ⎯⎯⎯⎯⎯⎯⎯⎯⎯
                6
philosophy behind liberal arts education

6. Which transition word or phrase is most logical in context?

F. **No Change**
G. As a result,
H. Furthermore,
J. Indeed,

does not reflect the current times in which today's students are living.
₇

7. Which choice is least redundant in context?

   A. **No Change**
   B. does not reflect the latest trends in education and the current times in which today's students are living.
   C. does not reflect the times in which today's students are living or the times in which future students will live.
   D. does not reflect the times in which today's students are living.

Responding to this concern, courses in computer science and information technology have been added to the curricula of many colleges and universities. [D]
₈

8. Which choice makes the sentence most grammatically acceptable?

   F. **No Change**
   G. computer science and information technology courses have been added to the curricula of many colleges and universities.
   H. computer science and information technology are the subject of courses that have been added to the curricula of many colleges and universities.
   J. many colleges and universities have added courses in computer science and information technology to their curricula.

[3]

The study of liberal arts may have evolved with the times, but its basic premise—that well-rounded students are well-educated students—remain as valid today as it was in ancient times.
₉

9. Which choice makes the sentence most grammatically acceptable?

   A. **No Change**
   B. remaining
   C. remains
   D. remained

Part 2
ACT ENGLISH

> Question 10 asks about the preceding passage as a whole.

10. The writer wants to add the following sentence to the essay:

    The late 1800s saw the rise of research universities that emphasized original research and practical applications over that traditional liberal arts focus.

    The sentence would most logically be placed at:

    F. Point A in Paragraph 1.
    G. Point B in Paragraph 1.
    H. Point C in Paragraph 2.
    J. Point D in Paragraph 2.

PASSAGE II

Clara Peeters, Female Pioneer

Clara Peeters was a pioneering Flemish painter celebrated for her exquisite still-life compositions. She is one of the few known female artists of the 17th century, and a trailblazer in a male-dominated field.
                              11

Peeters works often depicted lavish table settings
    12
and were characterized by

meticulous detail, rich textures, and an extraordinary
                        13
ability to render materials like glass, metal, and food with
                        13
striking realism. These paintings not only showcased her technical skill but also reflected themes of abundance, transience, and luxury.

11. Which choice makes the sentence most grammatically acceptable?

   A. **No Change**
   B. 17th century and a trailblazer,
   C. 17th century, and a trailblazer,
   D. 17th century and a trailblazer

12. Which choice makes the sentence most grammatically acceptable?

   F. **No Change**
   G. Peeters' works
   H. Peeters' work's
   J. Peeters work's

13. If the writer were to delete the underlined portion (adjusting the punctuation as needed), the paragraph would primarily lose:

   A. information about the style of paintings common in the 17th century.
   B. details that describe the components of the table settings that Peeters painted.
   C. details that typify Peeters' still-life paintings.
   D. information about the author's opinion of still-life paintings.

One of Peeters' notable contributions to art history is her inclusion of self-portraits, subtly reflected in polished surfaces like goblets or pewter plates. This clever device asserted it's presence and authorship in an
                                                14
era when women were often marginalized in the arts.
                                         15

Today, Clara Peeters' paintings are preserved in prominent museums, including the Prado in Madrid, underscoring her enduring legacy.

14. Which choice makes the sentence most grammatically acceptable?

    F. **No Change**
    G. her
    H. its
    J. their

15. Which choice most effectively maintains the essay's tone?

    A. **No Change**
    B. given the cold shoulder in
    C. shut out of
    D. left on the sidelines in

Reflect

Directions: Take a few minutes to recall what you've learned and what you've been practicing in this chapter. Consider the following questions, jot down your best answer for each one, and then compare your reflections to the expert responses on the following page. Use your level of confidence to determine what to do next.

1. What does an ACT expert look for when answering an ACT English question?

   _____
   _____
   _____

2. Describe at least three types of issues that could be present in English questions.

   _____
   _____
   _____

3. How does eliminating choices that do not address the issue make it easier to identify the correct answer?

   _____
   _____
   _____

Responses

1. What does an ACT expert look for when answering an ACT English question?

ACT experts look for clues in the passage, question stem, and answer choices to help identify the issue and determine which choices are correct and which are incorrect. These include punctuation marks, answer choice lengths, and words such as "relevant" in the question stem.

2. Describe at least three types of issues that could be present in English questions.

Punctuation issues could involve commas, colons, parentheses, and other punctuation marks. Correct answers should be concise, so incorrect choices could use more words than necessary. Correct answers should not add information that contradicts or is irrelevant to the rest of the passage.

3. How does eliminating choices that do not address the issue make it easier to identify the correct answer?

When you identify choices that must be incorrect because they don't address the issue, you save time by eliminating them without plugging them in and checking for correctness, conciseness, and relevance.

Next Steps

If you answered most questions correctly in the "How Much Have You Learned?" section, and if your responses to the Reflect questions were similar to those of the ACT expert, then consider the ACT English Method an area of strength and move on to the next chapter. Do keep using the method as you work on the questions in future chapters.

If you don't yet feel confident, review those parts of this chapter that you have not yet mastered and try the questions you missed again. As always, be sure to review the explanations closely. Also, go online (**kaptest.com/login**) for more practice. If you haven't already registered your book, do so at **kaptest.com/moreonline**.

GO ONLINE

kaptest.com/login

Chapter 2
The Method for ACT English

Answers and Explanations

How Much Have You Learned?

1. D
Difficulty: Medium
Category: Sentence Structure
Getting to the Answer: The phrase "over the centuries" must be placed logically and punctuated properly. Its original position interrupts the phrase "largely unchanged," so A is incorrect. Choices B and C are incorrect because placing the phrase at the beginning of the sentence is not logical; "over the centuries" is not referring to the concept of liberal arts but rather to the parameters of the discipline. Placing the phrase at the end of the sentence is logical and does not require additional punctuation, so (D) is correct.

2. G
Difficulty: Medium
Category: Development
Getting to the Answer: The word *broad* means "covering a large number of subjects or areas," so (G) is correct. Choices F, H, and J are incorrect because they do not clearly express the idea that liberal arts include a variety of subjects.

3. B
Difficulty: Low
Category: Agreement
Getting to the Answer: Adjectives can modify only nouns and pronouns; all other parts of speech are modified by adverbs. As written, the sentence uses the adjective *consistent* to modify the verb *mirrored*, so A is incorrect. Both (B) and C correct the error, but C is unnecessarily wordy, so (B) is correct. Choice D incorrectly uses the adverb *consistently* to modify the noun *fashion*.

4. G
Difficulty: Medium
Category: Development
Getting to the Answer: When deciding whether to delete a sentence, identify the purpose of the paragraph and determine whether the sentence supports it. This paragraph discusses concerns about liberal arts education in modern times. The sentence states that liberal arts schools also offer advanced degrees, which is not pertinent to the paragraph. Eliminate H and J. There is no contradiction, so eliminate F. Choice (G) correctly identifies the sentence as an irrelevant interruption.

5. A
Difficulty: Medium
Category: Sentence Structure
Getting to the Answer: When in doubt about the issue being tested, look at the answer choices. Here, the choices have different ways of joining two clauses. In the passage, the comma is used together with a coordinating conjunction to join two independent clauses, so (A) is correct. Although the semicolon in B can join two independent clauses, it cannot be used together with a coordinating conjunction. The period in C creates a sentence fragment. Finally, D is incorrect because a colon should not be followed by a coordinating conjunction.

6. F
Difficulty: Medium
Category: Organization
Getting to the Answer: When a question specifically asks for the most logical transition word, check that it correctly represents the relationship between the ideas it connects. In this sentence, the transition needs to connect the idea that some aspects of liberal arts study are the same as they were in ancient times with the idea that now there is some concern that these aspects don't reflect current needs. These two ideas contrast with each other. *However* does exactly that, so choice (F) is correct. Choices G, H, and J all incorrectly change the relationship between the ideas.

7. D
Difficulty: Medium
Category: Conciseness
Getting to the Answer: As written, the underlined portion includes a redundancy with the words *current* and *today's*. Choice (D) corrects this error by omitting the word *current*. Choices B and C are incorrect because they are even wordier than the original.

Part 2
ACT ENGLISH

8. J
Difficulty: Medium
Category: Sentence Structure
Getting to the Answer: An introductory clause should modify the noun that immediately follows it. As written, this sentence says that "courses in computer science and information technology" are "Responding to this concern." Choice F is incorrect. Choice (J) correctly puts the noun phrase, "many colleges and universities," immediately after the modifying clause. Choices G and H do not address the error.

9. C
Difficulty: Medium
Category: Agreement
Getting to the Answer: A check of the answer choices reveals that verb agreement is being tested. A verb must agree with its subject, which may not be the noun closest to it in the sentence. Although the plural noun *students* is the closest noun to the verb *remain*, the verb's subject is actually the singular noun *premise*, so A is incorrect. Choice (C) corrects the agreement error. Choice B creates a sentence fragment, and D uses a past-tense verb that does not match the surrounding verbs, which are in present tense.

10. G
Difficulty: Medium
Category: Development
Getting to the Answer: Consider where in the essay a reference to "The late 1800s" would fit best. Choice (G) correctly places the sentence between a reference to "In medieval times" and "Today's dictionaries." Choices F, H, and J position the sentence illogically within the essay, either too early or too late in the history of liberal arts education.

11. D
Difficulty: High
Category: Sentence Structure
Getting to the Answer: A glance at the answer choices reveals that the issue is punctuation. In the passage, a comma is used together with a coordinating conjunction to join an independent clause and a noun phrase. No comma is necessary to join an independent clause and a noun phrase when *and* is being used, so A is incorrect. Both B and C unnecessarily use a comma after the word "trailblazer," so eliminate them. Finally, (D) correctly includes no punctuation because none is necessary.

12. G
Difficulty: Medium
Category: Agreement
Getting to the Answer: The answer choices show that apostrophes are being tested. Apostrophes show either a contraction or possession. There is no contraction here, so examine whether possession is the issue. The phrase "Peeters works ... depicted" indicates that *works* is the subject of the sentence, since it is the thing doing the depicting. No apostrophe is needed for the subject, so eliminate H and J. *Peeters* is the artist who owns the works, so to show possession, an apostrophe should be used, so eliminate F and choose (G), the correct answer.

13. C
Difficulty: Medium
Category: Development
Getting to the Answer: First, identify the function of the underlined portion; this will show what the text would lose if it were left out. The "works ... were characterized by" the information in the underlined portion, so realize that the function of the underlined text is to give a description of characteristics of Peeters' art. Choice (C) is the correct answer. The underlined selection does not mention common styles of paintings in the 17th century, as in A, or the author's opinion about still-life paintings in general, as in D. Choice B is tempting, but the underlined portion is not describing what was contained in the table settings, but rather the style in which they were painted; it is incorrect.

14. G
Difficulty: High
Category: Agreement
Getting to the Answer: The answer choices contain pronouns, so look for the noun that the pronoun represents. The closest noun, *device*, cannot logically assert "presence and authorship" in a piece of art; only a person can assert authorship. Thus, *Peeters* must be the noun that the pronoun represents. The correct answer is (G). Choices F and H contain an incorrect pronoun; furthermore, F is a contraction of *it is*, which makes no sense in context. Choice J is plural, but a singular pronoun is required, so it is also incorrect.

15. A
Difficulty: Low
Category: Style and Tone
Getting to the Answer: This question is testing your ability to identify the author's tone, so look at the kind of words the author is using around the underlined portion. The words *notable* and *asserted* are used instead of words like "important" and "showed," so you can conclude that the tone is formal. Answer choice (A) is the most formal way of expressing the discrimination of women; all the other choices use casual idioms to express that idea.

[CHAPTER 3]

SPOTTING AND FIXING ERRORS: SENTENCE STRUCTURE, PUNCTUATION, AND AGREEMENT

LEARNING OBJECTIVES

After completing this chapter, you will be able to:

- Determine the correct punctuation and/or conjunctions to form a complete sentence
- Identify and correct inappropriate uses of semicolons
- Set off simple parenthetical elements using punctuation
- Identify and correct inappropriate uses of commas, dashes, and colons
- Identify and correct verb agreement issues
- Identify and correct pronoun agreement issues
- Identify and correct modifier agreement issues
- Identify and correct inappropriate uses of apostrophes
- Identify and correct expressions that deviate from idiomatic English

Part 2
ACT ENGLISH

How Much Do You Know?

Directions: Try out the questions below. The "Category" heading in the explanation for each question gives the title of the lesson that covers how to answer it. If you answered the question(s) for a given lesson correctly, you may be able to move quickly through that lesson. If you answered incorrectly, you may want to take your time on that lesson.

The Bebop Movement

For a jazz musician in New York City in the 1940s. The most interesting place to spend the hours between midnight and dawn was likely a Harlem nightclub called Minton's. After finishing their jobs at other clubs, young musicians like Charlie Parker, Dizzy Gillespie, Kenny Clarke, and Thelonious Monk would gather at Minton's and have "jam" sessions, or informal performances featuring lengthy group and solo improvisations, the all-night sessions resulted in the birth of modern jazz as these African American artists together forged a new sound, known as bebop.

Unlike "swing," the enormously popular jazz played in the 1930s, bebop was not dance music. Often it had been blindingly fast, incorporated irregular rhythms, and featured discordant sounds that jazz audiences had never heard before. The harmonic complexity of bebop distinguished it from other forms of jazz at the time. Bebop, unlike other forms of jazz, was based on a 12-note scale, thereby opening up vast new harmonic opportunities for musicians.

1. Which choice makes the sentence most grammatically acceptable?

   A. **No Change**
   B. 1940s; the
   C. 1940s, the
   D. 1940s, it was when the

2. Which choice makes the sentence most grammatically acceptable?

   F. **No Change**
   G. improvisations and the all-night sessions
   H. improvisations, the all-night sessions,
   J. improvisations. The all-night sessions

3. Which choice makes the sentence most grammatically acceptable?

   A. **No Change**
   B. was going to be blindingly fast, incorporated irregular rhythms, and featured discordant sounds
   C. was blindingly fast, incorporated irregular rhythms, and featured discordant sounds
   D. was blindingly fast, incorporated irregular rhythms, and featuring discordant sounds

The musicians who pioneered bebop shared, two common elements, a vision of the new music's possibilities and astonishing improvisational skill. Of these qualities, improvisation—the ability to play or compose a musical line on the spur of the moment—most enthralled the members of the bands that played at Minton's. As the essence of jazz, providing the context of a group setting for improvisation is paramount. Parker, perhaps the greatest instrumental genius jazz has known, was a brilliant improviser. He often played twice as fast as the rest of the band, but his solos, infused with creativity, was always in rhythm and exquisitely shaped, revealing a harmonic imagination that enthralled his listeners.

Unfortunately, the bebop movement, like many revolutions that fought its way into mainstream culture, initially encountered heavy resistance. Opposition came not only from older jazz musicians initially, but also, later and more lastingly from a general public alienated

4. Which choice makes the sentence most grammatically acceptable?
   F. No Change
   G. shared two common elements: a vision
   H. shared, two common elements a vision
   J. shared two common elements a vision

5. Which choice makes the sentence most grammatically acceptable?
   A. No Change
   B. improvisation within the context of a group setting is paramount.
   C. paramount is improvisation within the context of a group setting.
   D. paramount is the context of a group setting for improvisation.

6. Which choice makes the sentence most grammatically acceptable?
   F. No Change
   G. is
   H. are
   J. were

7. Which choice makes the sentence most grammatically acceptable?
   A. No Change
   B. it's
   C. their
   D. there

8. Which choice makes the sentence most grammatically acceptable?
   F. No Change
   G. but, later and more lastingly
   H. but, later and more lastingly—
   J. but also—later and more lastingly—

by the music genre's complexity and sophistication. Furthermore, due to the significant drop in music recordings during the musicians' strike, that was, in effect, from 1942 through 1944, the creative ferment that first produced bebop remains mostly undocumented today.

9. Which choice makes the sentence most grammatically acceptable?

   A. **No Change**
   B. genres'
   C. genres's
   D. genres

10. Which choice makes the sentence most grammatically acceptable?

    F. **No Change**
    G. strike that was in effect
    H. strike that was; in effect
    J. strike—that was in effect

Chapter 3
Spotting and Fixing Errors: Sentence Structure, Punctuation, and Agreement

Answers and Explanations

How Much Do You Know?

1. C
Difficulty: Low
Category: Sentence Structure
Getting to the Answer: As written, the phrase before the period is a sentence fragment, so A is incorrect. Replacing the period with a semicolon does not address this issue, so B is also incorrect. Choice (C) fixes the fragment by joining the dependent clause "For a jazz musician in New York City in the 1940s" and the independent clause "the most interesting place to spend the hours between midnight and dawn was likely a Harlem nightclub called Minton's" with a comma. Choice D both creates an illogical sentence structure and is unnecessarily wordy. Choice (C) is correct.

2. J
Difficulty: Low
Category: Sentence Structure
Getting to the Answer: As written, the underlined portion creates a run-on sentence, so F is incorrect. Eliminate G because replacing the comma with a coordinating conjunction (in this case, the word *and*) does not fix the run-on. Adding a comma after *sessions* does not fix the run-on either, so H is also incorrect. Choice (J) correctly separates the two independent clauses with a period.

3. C
Difficulty: Medium
Category: Agreement
Getting to the Answer: As written, the sentence includes a list of three verbs that are not in parallel form. A is incorrect. Eliminate B and D, since their verbs are also not in parallel form. Choice (C) correctly uses three past-tense verb phrases.

4. G
Difficulty: Medium
Category: Sentence Structure
Getting to the Answer: Colons are used to introduce lists or short phrases, so a colon is appropriate to use after *elements*. (G) is correct. Choice F is incorrect because the phrase "two common elements" is essential to the sentence, so it should not be surrounded by commas. Choice H incorrectly separates a verb from its object, and J incorrectly omits punctuation altogether.

5. B
Difficulty: High
Category: Agreement
Getting to the Answer: "As the essence of jazz" is an introductory modifying phrase, so the word(s) that immediately follow the comma must be the item(s) being modified. The word *improvisation* must come after the comma because the passage indicates that "jam" sessions, or informal performances, are the essence of jazz. (B) is correct. Choices A, C, and D do not put the word *improvisation* after the comma, so they all display modification errors.

6. J
Difficulty: Medium
Category: Agreement
Getting to the Answer: If a verb is underlined, make sure that it agrees with its subject. The subject, *solos*, is plural, and the verb *was* is singular, so F is incorrect. Eliminate G because it is also singular. Choice H is plural but in the present tense. Choice (J) is plural and correctly uses the past tense, which matches the tense of the rest of the paragraph.

7. C
Difficulty: Medium
Category: Agreement
Getting to the Answer: When a pronoun is underlined, check that it agrees with its antecedent, the noun to which it refers. The antecedent is the plural noun *revolutions*, so the plural pronoun *their* is needed; (C) is correct. Choice A is incorrect because *its* is singular. Choices B and D do not make sense in context: *it's* means "it is," and *there* indicates location, not possession.

8. J
Difficulty: High
Category: Sentence Structure
Getting to the Answer: The phrase "later and more lastingly" is a parenthetical phrase that must be properly punctuated. Only (J) correctly sets it off from the rest of the sentence with two matching punctuation marks. In addition, F and H incorrectly omit the word *also*, which must be included because the sentence includes the first part of the idiomatic phrase "not only…but also."

9. A

Difficulty: Medium
Category: Agreement
Getting to the Answer: The word *genre's* is a singular possessive noun. It makes sense in context because the sentence is describing the "complexity and sophistication" of a single genre of music. (A) is correct. Choices B and C are possessive, but they are both plural. In addition, C incorrectly adds an extra *s* after the apostrophe; *genres's* is considered grammatically incorrect in any context. Finally, choice D does not show possession at all.

10. G

Difficulty: Medium
Category: Sentence Structure
Getting to the Answer: When a punctuation mark is underlined, make sure that it is actually necessary. Commas, semicolons, and dashes all separate elements of the sentence into different logical units. Since the phrase "strike that was in effect" is one cohesive phrase, no punctuation of any sort should be used. Choice (G) is correct.

Chapter 3
Spotting and Fixing Errors: Sentence Structure, Punctuation, and Agreement

SENTENCE STRUCTURE: THE BASICS

LEARNING OBJECTIVES

After this lesson, you will be able to:

- Determine the correct punctuation and/or conjunctions to form a complete sentence
- Identify and correct inappropriate uses of semicolons

To answer a question like this

Women's Suffrage

The struggle for women's suffrage in the United States began several decades before national legislation was <u>enacted and the</u>[1] movement included a myriad of efforts that culminated in nationwide voting rights nearly fifty years after the birth of the women's suffrage movement.

1. Which choice makes the sentence most grammatically acceptable?

   A. **No Change**
   B. enacted, the
   C. enacted; the
   D. enacted but the

You need to know this

Fragments and Run-ons

A complete sentence must express a complete thought and have both a subject and a verb. If any one of these elements is missing, the sentence is a **fragment**. You can recognize a fragment because the sentence will not make sense as written.

Missing element	Example	Corrected sentence
Subject	*Ran a marathon.*	*Lola ran a marathon.*
Verb	*Lola a marathon.*	
Complete thought	*While Lola ran a marathon.*	*While Lola ran a marathon, her friends cheered for her.*

The fragment "While Lola ran a marathon" is an example of a dependent clause: it has a subject (Lola) and a verb (ran), but it does not express a complete thought because it starts with a subordinating conjunction (while). Notice what the word *while* does to the meaning: While Lola ran a marathon, what happened? To fix this type of fragment, eliminate the subordinating conjunction or join the dependent clause to an independent clause using a comma. Subordinating conjunctions are words and phrases such as *since, because, therefore, unless, although,* and *due to*.

Unlike a dependent clause, an independent clause can stand on its own as a complete sentence. If a sentence has more than one independent clause, those clauses must be properly joined. If they are not, the sentence is a **run-on**: *Lucas enjoys hiking, he climbs a new mountain every summer.* There are several ways to correct a run-on:

To correct a run-on	Example
Use a period	*Lucas enjoys hiking. He climbs a new mountain every summer.*
Use a semicolon	*Lucas enjoys hiking; he climbs a new mountain every summer.*
Make one clause dependent	*Since Lucas enjoys hiking, he climbs a new mountain every summer.*
Use a comma and a FANBOYS conjunction: For, And, Nor, But, Or, Yet, So	*Lucas enjoys hiking, so he climbs a new mountain every summer.*
Use a colon or a dash	*Lucas enjoys hiking: he climbs a new mountain every summer.* *Lucas enjoys hiking—he climbs a new mountain every summer.*

Semicolons

Semicolons are used in a specific way on the ACT:

Use a semicolon to . . .	Example
Join two independent clauses that are not connected by a comma and a FANBOYS conjunction	*Gaby knew that her term paper would take at least four hours to write; she got started in study hall and then finished it at home.*

You need to do this

To recognize and correct errors involving fragments, run-ons, and semicolons, familiarize yourself with the ways in which they are tested.

- Fragments
  - If a sentence is missing a subject, a verb, or a complete thought, it is a fragment.
  - Correct the fragment by adding the missing element.
- Run-ons
  - If a sentence includes two independent clauses, they must be properly joined:
    - Use a period
    - Use a semicolon
    - Make one clause dependent by using a subordinating conjunction (since, because, therefore, unless, although, due to, etc.)
    - Use a comma and a FANBOYS (For, And, Nor, But, Or, Yet, So) conjunction
    - Use a colon or a dash
- Semicolon use
  - A semicolon is used to join two independent clauses that are not connected by a comma and a FANBOYS conjunction.

Chapter 3
Spotting and Fixing Errors: Sentence Structure, Punctuation, and Agreement

Explanation
The clauses before and after the word *and* are independent clauses and must be punctuated properly. Choice (C) correctly uses a semicolon to join the two clauses. Choices A, B, and D include either a comma or a coordinating conjunction but not both, so they are incorrect.

Drills
If sentence formation or semicolons give you trouble, study the information above and try out these drill questions before completing the Try on Your Own questions below. Drill answers can be found in Answers and Explanations.

a. Correct the fragment by adding a subject: Volunteered to organize the upcoming fundraiser.

b. Correct the fragment by completing the thought: Upon finding the misplaced house keys.

c. Correct the run-on sentence by adding a punctuation mark: The historic center of town was restored it once again bustled with activity.

d. Correct the run-on sentence by adding a punctuation mark: Logical thinking is essential to scientific research the irony is that scientists who make important discoveries often do so on a hunch.

e. Make one clause dependent to correct the run-on sentence: The local farms had a poor harvest last year, the price of produce at the market has risen dramatically.

Try on Your Own
Directions: Take as much time as you need on these questions. Work carefully and methodically. There will be an opportunity for timed practice at the end of the chapter.

Espresso 89

For what seemed like eons; people in my neighborhood complained about the lack of coffee shops in our community. The discussions at times became passionate, and it seemed that my neighbors believed that a coffee shop would cure just about any problem our suburban neighborhood faced. Not a coffee drinker, I remained unconvinced that a venue to purchase coffee would make a significant difference. However, when a

2. Which choice makes the sentence most grammatically acceptable?
   F. **No Change**
   G. eons, people
   H. eons, and people
   J. eons. People

3. Which choice makes the sentence most grammatically acceptable?
   A. **No Change**
   B. passionate it
   C. passionate and it
   D. passionate; and it

Part 2
ACT ENGLISH

coffee shop did open nearby. I discovered that it offered
much more than warm beverages and convenient
snacks. Ingrid and Gus, the owners of Espresso 89, work

diligently to create an inclusive atmosphere thanks to
their dedication, their shop serves as a community center
for the area.

    Espresso 89 began by inviting a local artist to display
her paintings on the walls of the shop and holding a
"gallery" opening for the occasion. Ingrid and Gus
encouraged other local artists to sign up for future
opportunities to share their work with the coffee-
drinking public. Two or three nights a week, Espresso 89
hosts music or literary events that provide entertainment
and the opportunity for local artists to showcase their
talent. A retired elementary school teacher conducts
a weekly children's story hour she offers storybook
after storybook to delighted children and their grateful
parents.

4. Which choice makes the sentence most grammatically acceptable?
   F. **No Change**
   G. nearby, I
   H. nearby and
   J. nearby, and also I

5. Which choice makes the sentence most grammatically acceptable?
   A. **No Change**
   B. atmosphere, thanks
   C. atmosphere—thanks
   D. atmosphere so thanks

6. Which choice makes the sentence most grammatically acceptable?
   F. **No Change**
   G. hour, she offers
   H. hour; offering
   J. hour, offering

SENTENCE STRUCTURE: PARENTHETICAL ELEMENTS

> **LEARNING OBJECTIVE**
>
> After this lesson, you will be able to:
> - Set off simple parenthetical elements using punctuation

To answer a question like this

The Nineteenth <u>Amendment which granted all American women the right to vote, was</u> passed by Congress on June 4, 1919.

1. Which choice makes the sentence most grammatically acceptable?

   A. **No Change**

   B. Amendment, which granted all American women the right to vote, was

   C. Amendment which granted all American women the right to vote was

   D. Amendment which granted all American women the right to vote—was

You need to know this

Answer choices often move punctuation marks around, replace them with other punctuation marks, or remove them altogether. A question may even ask you for the proper placement of a parenthetical element. When underlined portions include commas, dashes, or parentheses, check to make sure the punctuation is used correctly in context.

Parenthetical Elements

Parenthetical elements may appear at the beginning, in the middle, or at the end of a sentence. They must be properly punctuated with parentheses, commas, or dashes for the sentence to be grammatically correct. A phrase such as *the capital of France* is considered parenthetical if the rest of the sentence is grammatically correct when it is removed. Notice that the parenthetical phrase is placed right next to what it's explaining or qualifying: *Paris*. Do not mix and match punctuation; a parenthetical element must begin and end with the same type of punctuation.

Part 2
ACT ENGLISH

Parenthetical element placement	Parentheses	Comma(s)	Dash(es)
Beginning	N/A	The capital of France, Paris is a popular tourist destination.	N/A
Middle	Paris (the capital of France) is a popular tourist destination.	Paris, the capital of France, is a popular tourist destination.	Paris—the capital of France—is a popular tourist destination.
End	A popular tourist destination is Paris (the capital of France).	A popular tourist destination is Paris, the capital of France.	A popular tourist destination is Paris—the capital of France.

You need to do this
If the underlined portion includes punctuation, ask yourself:

- Is the punctuation used correctly?

    The commas, dashes, or parentheses need to set off a parenthetical element, be used consistently, and be placed in the correct location.

- Is the punctuation necessary?

    If you cannot identify a reason why the punctuation is included, the punctuation should be removed.

- Is the phrase placed properly?

    A parenthetical phrase should be next to what it's explaining or qualifying for clarity.

Explanation
The phrase "which granted all American women the right to vote" is a parenthetical element that must be set off from the rest of the sentence with either two commas or two dashes. Choice (B) is correct.

Drills
If parenthetical elements give you trouble, study the information above and try out these drill questions before completing the Try on Your Own questions below. Drill answers can be found in Answers and Explanations.

a. Use a comma to correctly punctuate the parenthetical element at the beginning of the sentence: Delayed for two hours due to a thunderstorm the baseball game started much later than fans had expected.

b. Use parentheses to correctly punctuate the parenthetical element in the middle of the sentence: *The Heart of a Woman* originally published in 1981 is one of Maya Angelou's most popular books.

c. Use commas to correctly punctuate the parenthetical element in the middle of the sentence: The architect a keen observer known for her meticulous attention to detail gently pointed out the error in her coworker's design.

d. Use dashes to correctly punctuate the parenthetical element in the middle of the sentence: Contemporary Hawaiian quilts which are often featured at the Mokupāpapa Discovery Center reflect an eclectic blend of Hawaiian tradition and modern vision.

e. Use a comma to correctly punctuate the parenthetical element at the end of the sentence: A hurricane's strength is rated on a scale of 1 to 5 depending on the speed of sustained winds.

Try on Your Own

Directions: Take as much time as you need on these questions. Work carefully and methodically. There will be an opportunity for timed practice at the end of the chapter.

Medusa

For more than two thousand <u>years; Medusa</u> has been a prominent image in the world of art and the world of myth. As far back as 200 BCE, images of <u>Medusa—the defeated Gorgon, abounded.</u> For instance, the shield of Alexander the Great was graced with an image of the mythical Medusa. It was said that her hair was writhing <u>serpents and—</u>her gaze turned onlookers to stone.

Medusa was surely one of the most threatening figures of ancient Greek mythology. One of the three

2. Which choice makes the sentence most grammatically acceptable?

    F. **No Change**
    G. years, Medusa
    H. years Medusa
    J. years. Medusa

3. Which choice makes the sentence most grammatically acceptable?

    A. **No Change**
    B. Medusa the defeated Gorgon, abounded.
    C. Medusa the defeated Gorgon abounded.
    D. Medusa—the defeated Gorgon— abounded.

4. Which choice makes the sentence most grammatically acceptable?

    F. **No Change**
    G. serpents,
    H. serpents, and,
    J. serpents—and

Part 2
ACT ENGLISH

Gorgon <u>sisters</u> Medusa had been known for her beauty. However, she aroused the anger of the goddess Athena,
₅

who turned <u>Medusa's, once lovely hair,</u> to snakes. With
₆
the power to petrify anyone who looked upon her, Medusa was feared and thought impossible to defeat. The hero Perseus finally managed to do so only with the aid of the gods, using a mirror-like shield from Athena to avoid having to look directly upon Medusa and later donning the Helm of Hades <u>(a cap which granted the wearer invisibility)</u> to flee from the other two
₇
Gorgons.

5. Which choice makes the sentence most grammatically acceptable?
   A. **No Change**
   B. sisters,
   C. sisters because
   D. sisters was because

6. Which choice makes the sentence most grammatically acceptable?
   F. **No Change**
   G. Medusa's once lovely hair
   H. Medusa's once, lovely hair
   J. Medusa's—once lovely hair

7. The best placement for the underlined portion would be:
   A. where it is now.
   B. after the word *gods*.
   C. after the word *shield*.
   D. after the word *Helm*.

SENTENCE STRUCTURE: COMMAS, DASHES, AND COLONS

LEARNING OBJECTIVE

After this lesson, you will be able to:
- Identify and correct inappropriate uses of commas, dashes, and colons

To answer a question like this

In 1848, suffragists at the Seneca Falls Convention developed a wide array of demands, many of which were eventually considered too radical to be feasible. As a way of gaining broader support, these suffragists found it necessary to streamline and slightly alter their positions. The process was <u>tedious, but</u> necessary.
₁

1. Which choice makes the sentence most grammatically acceptable?
   A. **No Change**
   B. tedious: but
   C. tedious; but
   D. tedious but

Chapter 3
Spotting and Fixing Errors: Sentence Structure, Punctuation, and Agreement

You need to know this

Answer choices often move punctuation marks around, replace them with other punctuation marks, or remove them altogether. When underlined portions include commas, dashes, or colons, check to make sure the punctuation is used correctly in context.

Commas

There are two situations in which commas are not interchangeable with any other punctuation: when listing a series of items and when separating introductory words or phrases from the rest of the sentence.

Use commas to . . .	Comma(s)
Set off three or more items in a series	*Jeremiah packed a sleeping bag, a raincoat, and a lantern for his upcoming camping trip.*
Separate an introductory word or phrase from the rest of the sentence	*For example, carrots are an excellent source of several vitamins and minerals.*

Commas and Dashes

In many cases, either a comma or a dash may be used to punctuate a sentence.

Use commas or dashes to . . .	Comma(s)	Dash(es)
Separate independent clauses connected by a FANBOYS conjunction (For, And, Nor, But, Or, Yet, So)	*Jess finished her homework earlier than expected, so she started an assignment that was due the following week.*	*Jess finished her homework earlier than expected—so she started an assignment that was due the following week.*
Separate an independent and dependent clause	*Tyson arrived at school a few minutes early, which gave him time to organize his locker before class.*	*Tyson arrived at school a few minutes early—which gave him time to organize his locker before class.*
Separate parenthetical elements from the rest of the sentence (use either two commas or two dashes, not one of each)	*Professor Mann, who is the head of the English department, is known for assigning extensive projects.*	*Professor Mann—who is the head of the English department—is known for assigning extensive projects.*

Part 2
ACT ENGLISH

Colons and Dashes

Colons and dashes are used to include new ideas that introduce or explain something or that break the flow of the sentence. Note that the clause before the colon or dash must be able to stand on its own as a complete sentence.

Use colons and dashes to...	Colon	Dash
Introduce and/or emphasize a short phrase, quotation, explanation, example, or list that follows an independent clause	Sanjay had two important tasks to complete: a science experiment and an expository essay.	Sanjay had two important tasks to complete—a science experiment and an expository essay.
Separate two independent clauses when the second clause explains, illustrates, or expands on the first sentence	Highway 1 in Australia is one of the longest national highways in the world: it circles the entirety of the continent and connects every mainland state capital.	Highway 1 in Australia is one of the longest national highways in the world—it circles the entirety of the continent and connects every mainland state capital.

Unnecessary Punctuation

Knowing when punctuation should *not* be used is equally important. If an underlined portion includes punctuation, take time to consider whether it should be included at all.

Do NOT use punctuation to...	Incorrect	Correct
Separate a subject from its verb	The diligent student council, meets every week.	The diligent student council meets every week.
Separate a verb from its object or a preposition from its object	The diligent student council meets, every week.	The diligent student council meets every week.
Set off elements that are essential to a sentence's meaning	The, diligent student, council meets every week.	The diligent student council meets every week.
Separate adjectives that work together to modify a noun	The diligent, student council meets every week.	The diligent student council meets every week.

You need to do this

If the underlined portion includes punctuation, ask yourself:

- Is the punctuation used correctly?

  The punctuation needs to be the correct type (comma, dash, or colon) and in the correct location.

- Is the punctuation necessary?

  If you cannot identify a reason why the punctuation is included, the punctuation should be removed.

Chapter 3
Spotting and Fixing Errors: Sentence Structure, Punctuation, and Agreement

Explanation

A comma must be placed before *but* only if the words that follow form an independent clause. Here, only the word *necessary*, which is not an independent clause, appears after *but*, so no punctuation is needed. Choice (D) is correct.

Drills

If commas, colons, and dashes give you trouble, study the information above and try out these drill questions before completing the Try on Your Own questions below. Drill answers can be found in Answers and Explanations.

Edit each sentence to correct the punctuation issue.

a. The recipe includes my favorite fruit sweet red cherries.

b. Historically popular sayings are transferred by word of mouth and rarely found in written records so there is often no definite answer to the question of their origin.

c. Paradise tree snakes subsist mostly on lizards and bats which they immobilize with mild venom.

d. As a result the United States entered an isolationist period after World War I.

e. *Hamlet* begins with two of Shakespeare's favorite ways to grab an audience's attention a supernatural phenomenon and a murder plot.

Try on Your Own

Directions: Take as much time as you need on these questions. Work carefully and methodically. There will be an opportunity for timed practice at the end of the chapter.

Music in the Park

Some people think of classical music as tedious, and
                                                  2
unimaginative. They feel that music without lyrics is lacking in emotion or simply too complex to fully appreciate. For many years, I was among those who thought that listening to classical music was an abysmal experience. However when a friend convinced me to
              3
attend the New York Philharmonic performance in Central Park, a free event usually scheduled twice each summer, my entire perception of orchestras and classical music changed.

2. Which choice makes the sentence most grammatically acceptable?

   F. **No Change**
   G. tedious; and
   H. tedious, and,
   J. tedious and

3. Which choice makes the sentence most grammatically acceptable?

   A. **No Change**
   B. However,
   C. However;
   D. However:

Part 2
ACT ENGLISH

I knew that there would be a large audience for the performance, but I didn't think the atmosphere would be festive. Thousands of people had spread out blankets to relax and experience the music. By the end of the first
₄

piece: Mendelssohn's Symphony No. 4 in A Major—I
₅
was enthralled. The second piece was Tchaikovsky's 1812 Overture, and the audience hushed their already whispered conversations to hear the work's interplay among the brass, strings, woodwinds, and percussion instruments. The emotional ending, punctuated with booming cannons and lyrical, church bells, provided the
₆
opportunity for me to genuinely enjoy classical music, albeit for the very first time.

4. Which choice makes the sentence most grammatically acceptable?

   F. **No Change**
   G. performance; but
   H. performance; so
   J. performance, so

5. Which choice makes the sentence most grammatically acceptable?

   A. **No Change**
   B. piece, Mendelssohn's
   C. piece—Mendelssohn's
   D. piece Mendelssohn's

6. Which choice makes the sentence most grammatically acceptable?

   F. **No Change**
   G. lyrical church
   H. lyrical—church
   J. lyrical: church

AGREEMENT: VERBS

> **LEARNING OBJECTIVE**
>
> After this lesson, you will be able to:
> - Identify and correct verb agreement issues

To answer a question like this

Instead of arguing for equality based on principle, suffragists insisted that the difference between the two genders <u>were</u> precisely why women must be allowed
₁
to participate in government. In an attempt to appease opponents, suffragists insisted that the female vote would aid in purifying politics, enacting reforms, and outweighing less-desirable votes. The positive outcome of a female voting bloc, suffragists posited, would be a government that reflected a woman's position as protector of the home, family, and society.

1. Which choice makes the sentence most grammatically acceptable?

   A. **No Change**
   B. was
   C. will be
   D. was exactly and

You need to know this

Verb Tense

Verb tense indicates when an action or state of being took place: past, present, or future. The tense of the verb must fit the context of the passage. Each tense can express three different types of action.

Type of action	Past	Present	Future
Single action occurring only once	Connor **planted** vegetables in the community garden.	Connor **plants** vegetables in the community garden.	Connor **will plant** vegetables in the community garden.
Action that is ongoing at some point in time	Connor **was planting** vegetables in the community garden this morning before noon.	Connor **is planting** vegetables in the community garden this morning before noon.	Connor **will be planting** vegetables in the community garden this morning before noon.
Action that is completed before some other action	Connor **had planted** vegetables in the community garden every year until he gave his job to Jasmine.	Connor **has planted** vegetables in the community garden since it started five years ago.	Connor **will have planted** vegetables in the community garden by the time the growing season starts.

Part 2
ACT ENGLISH

Subject-Verb Agreement

A verb must agree with its subject in person and number:

- Person (first, second, or third)
  - First: **I ask** a question.
  - Second: **You ask** a question.
  - Third: **She asks** a question.
- Number (singular or plural)
  - Singular: **The apple tastes** delicious.
  - Plural: **Apples taste** delicious.

The noun closest to the verb is not always the subject. Take the following sentence as an example: *The chair with the lion feet is an antique.* The singular verb in this sentence, *is*, is closest to the plural noun *feet*. However, the verb's actual subject is the singular noun *chair*, so the sentence is correct as written.

When a sentence includes two nouns, only the conjunction *and* forms a compound subject requiring a plural verb form:

- Plural: *Saliyah **and** Taylor **are** in the running club.*
- Singular: ***Either** Saliyah **or** Taylor **is** in the running club.*
- Singular: ***Neither** Saliyah **nor** Taylor **is** in the running club.*

Collective nouns are nouns that name entities with more than one member, such as *group*, *team*, and *family*. Even though these nouns represent more than one person, they are grammatically singular and require singular verb forms:

- **The collection** of paintings **is** one of the most popular art exhibits in recent years.
- **The team looks** promising this year.

Parallelism

Verbs in a list, a compound, or a comparison must be parallel in form:

Feature	Example	Parallel form
A list	Chloe **formulated** a question, **conducted** background research, and **constructed** a hypothesis before starting the experiment.	3 simple past verb phrases
A compound	**Hunting** and **fishing** were essential to the survival of Midwestern Native American tribes such as the Omaha.	2 –ing verb forms
A comparison	Garrett enjoys **sculpting** as much as **painting**.	2 –ing verb forms

Chapter 3
Spotting and Fixing Errors: Sentence Structure, Punctuation, and Agreement

Note that parallelism may be tested using other parts of speech besides verbs. In general, any items in a list, compound, or comparison must be in parallel form. For example, if a list starts with a noun, the other items in the list must also be nouns; if it starts with an adjective, the other items must be adjectives, etc.:

Incorrect	Correct alternatives
Naomi likes **pumpkin pie and to drink coffee** on chilly weekend afternoons.	Naomi likes **pumpkin pie and coffee** on chilly weekend afternoons.
	Naomi likes **to eat pumpkin pie and to drink coffee** on chilly weekend afternoons.
Which of the dogs is the **most** docile and **better** behaved?	Which of the dogs is the **most** docile and **best** behaved?
	Which of the dogs is the **more** docile and **better** behaved?

You need to do this

If the underlined portion includes a verb, check that the verb:

- Reflects the correct tense: Does it fit the context?
- Agrees with the subject in person and number
- Is parallel in form with other verbs in a series, list, or compound if there is one in the sentence

Explanation

A verb must agree with its subject. In this case, the plural verb *were* does not agree with its singular subject *difference*; eliminate A. Eliminate C because the future tense does not make sense in context. The remaining choices both use the past-tense singular verb *was*, but D is unnecessarily wordy. Choice (B) is correct.

Drills

If verbs give you trouble, study the information above and try out these drill questions before completing the Try on Your Own questions below. Drill answers can be found in Answers and Explanations.

Edit each sentence to correct the verb issue.

a. Pablo present his experiment at the science fair last week.

b. The movie, with its complex plot and stirring themes, were critically acclaimed.

c. Neither the director nor the lead actor are at rehearsal today.

d. The park and the adjacent wildlife refuge encompasses more than 800 acres of mountains, lakes, and forests.

e. In order to pass the foreign language proficiency exam, you must be both a fluent speaker and able to read it as well.

Part 2
ACT ENGLISH

Try on Your Own

Directions: Take as much time as you need on these questions. Work carefully and methodically. There will be an opportunity for timed practice at the end of the chapter.

Mia's Attic

I thought the tour of my friend's new house was finished as we came to a halt outside her bedroom on the third floor. However, Mia had something else in mind. "Do you want to go up to the attic?" she asked me, her eyes sparkling with mischief. "When my mom <u>inherited</u>
2
the house from my grandmother last year, she told me that no one had gone up there for forty years!" In past

2. Which choice makes the sentence most grammatically acceptable?

   F. **No Change**
   G. inherits
   H. had inherited
   J. would have inherited

situations, either Mia's mom or older brother <u>were</u>
3
available to help me convince Mia that her latest plan was inadvisable. Unfortunately, they were both at work and unavailable to assist me in pleading my case.

I wasn't thrilled about the idea of exploring the dark, musty space overhead. In the past, I'd hesitated whenever Mia suggested risky or dangerous activities, but this time I just nodded, trying to appear nonchalant. Mia yanked on the cord dangling from the wooden door; a staircase unfolded, the bottom step landing directly in front of my feet. I looked up, acknowledging that seemingly endless darkness, quite possibly replete with eight-legged monsters, often <u>teem</u> with a myriad of
4
unexpected unpleasantries.

3. Which choice makes the sentence most grammatically acceptable?

   A. **No Change**
   B. was
   C. would be
   D. will have been

4. Which choice makes the sentence most grammatically acceptable?

   F. **No Change**
   G. will have teemed
   H. teems
   J. to teem

Hoping Mia wouldn't notice, I took a deep breath and grip the ladder. As I placed my foot on the bottom rung, I wondered how my best friend had failed to take my considerable fear of spiders into account. I like arachnids about as much as I enjoy watching gory movies, enduring frightening pranks, and dental appointments. "The sooner you get this over with, the better," I whispered to myself, trying to exude as much courage as possible.

5. Which choice makes the sentence most grammatically acceptable?

    A. **No Change**
    B. grips
    C. would grip
    D. gripped

6. Which choice makes the sentence most grammatically acceptable?

    F. **No Change**
    G. going to the dentist.
    H. trips to the dentist.
    J. dental appointments for a root canal.

AGREEMENT: PRONOUNS

LEARNING OBJECTIVE

After this lesson, you will be able to:
- Identify and correct pronoun agreement issues

To answer a question like this

Despite anti-suffragist objections, the suffrage movement finally achieved its' ultimate goal, but only after offering its participants a political education and a sense of taking an active role in the nation's history, which in turn helped to convince the rest of the country of the worth of the woman's vote.

1. Which choice makes the sentence most grammatically acceptable?

    A. **No Change**
    B. their
    C. they're
    D. its

You need to know this

Pronoun Forms

A pronoun is a word that takes the place of a noun. Pronouns can take three different forms, each of which is used based on the grammatical role it plays in the sentence.

Form	Pronouns	Example
Subjective: The pronoun is used as the subject	I, you, she, he, it, we, they, who	*Rivka is the student **who** will lead the presentation.*
Objective: The pronoun is used as the object of a verb or a preposition	me, you, her, him, it, us, them, whom	*With **whom** will Rivka present the scientific findings?*
Possessive: The pronoun expresses ownership	my, mine, your, yours, his, her, hers, its, our, ours, their, theirs, whose	*Rivka will likely choose a partner **whose** work is excellent.*

Note that a pronoun in subjective form can, logically, be the subject in a complete sentence. Pronouns that are in objective form cannot function as the subject.

When there are two pronouns or a noun and a pronoun in a compound structure, drop the other noun or pronoun to tell which form to use. For example: Leo and me walked into town. If you were talking about yourself only, you would say, "I walked into town," not "Me walked into town." Therefore, the correct form is subjective, and the original sentence should read: Leo and I walked into town.

Pronoun-Antecedent Agreement

A pronoun's antecedent is the noun it logically represents in a sentence. If the noun is singular, the pronoun must be singular; if the noun is plural, the pronoun must be plural.

Antecedent	Incorrect	Correct
selection	The selection of books was placed in **their** designated location.	The selection of books was placed in **its** designated location.
girls	The girls fed the giraffes all of the lettuce **she** had purchased.	The girls fed the giraffes all of the lettuce **they** had purchased.
sapling	The sapling, along with dozens of flowers, was relocated to where **they** would thrive.	The sapling, along with dozens of flowers, was relocated to where **it** would thrive.

You need to do this

If the underlined portion includes a pronoun, find the logical antecedent. Check that the pronoun:

- Uses the correct form
    - If the pronoun is the subject of the sentence, use a subjective pronoun such as *I, you, she, he, it, we, they,* or *who*.
    - If the pronoun is an object within the sentence, use an objective pronoun such as *me, you, her, him, it, us, them,* or *whom*.

Chapter 3
Spotting and Fixing Errors: Sentence Structure, Punctuation, and Agreement

- If the pronoun indicates possession, use a possessive pronoun such as *my, mine, your, yours, his, her, hers, its, our, ours, their, theirs,* or *whose*.
  - Agrees with its antecedent
    - A singular antecedent requires a singular pronoun; a plural antecedent requires a plural pronoun.

Explanation

Eliminate A immediately because the word *its'* is not correct in any context. The pronoun's antecedent, the noun to which the pronoun is referring, is "the suffrage movement," which is singular. Choice (D) correctly uses the singular possessive pronoun *its*. Choice B incorrectly uses a plural possessive pronoun, and C means *they are*, which does not make sense in context.

Drills

If pronouns give you trouble, study the information above and try out these drill questions before completing the Try on Your Own questions below. Drill answers can be found in Answers and Explanations.

Edit each sentence to correct the pronoun issue.

a. The scientist, about who I had read, was more charismatic in person than I had expected.

b. Between you and I, you are the better singer.

c. A jaguar, with its keen senses and sharp teeth and claws, is known for their ability to dominate prey.

d. The jar of olives is not in their regular location on the shelf.

e. One cannot help but be amazed by the scientific advances in the past century, especially if you study the history of science.

Try on Your Own

Directions: Take as much time as you need on these questions. Work carefully and methodically. There will be an opportunity for timed practice at the end of the chapter.

Galloping Gertie

For four months in the fall of 1940, citizens of the Puget Sound area of Washington used one of the most illustrious, and most dangerous, suspension bridges ever built; it had the opportunity to travel across the Tacoma Narrows Bridge, or "Galloping Gertie," which enjoyed a relatively short life compared to similar structures in the United States. "Gertie" taught important lessons on what to do—and what not to do—when building a suspension bridge.

2. Which choice makes the sentence most grammatically acceptable?

F. **No Change**
G. their
H. them
J. they

Part 2
ACT ENGLISH

State officials in Washington were the ones whom
                                                 ―――
                                                  3
identified a need for a bridge across Puget Sound.
The closest point was the Tacoma Narrows, a windy
2,800-foot gap. Construction began in November of
1938, and the bridge was officially opened on July 1,
1940. Although they knew about form and structure,
the bridge's engineers failed to take into account
aerodynamic components, particularly the wind, and
it's effect on the roadway. Because the roadbed was
―――
 4
constructed with rigid plate girders, it could not absorb
                                       ――
                                        5
the winds of Puget Sound. Consequently, on any windy
day, the roadway buckled and contorted, or "galloped"—
hence, the nickname. The undulation became so severe

that the bridge, as you would hope, was eventually closed
                   ―――
                    6
to traffic.

3. Which choice makes the sentence most grammatically acceptable?

   A. **No Change**
   B. who
   C. that
   D. that spoke up and

4. Which choice makes the sentence most grammatically acceptable?

   F. **No Change**
   G. its
   H. its'
   J. their

5. Which choice makes the sentence most grammatically acceptable?

   A. **No Change**
   B. they
   C. those
   D. these

6. Which choice makes the sentence most grammatically acceptable?

   F. **No Change**
   G. we
   H. it
   J. one

Chapter 3
Spotting and Fixing Errors: Sentence Structure, Punctuation, and Agreement

AGREEMENT: MODIFIERS

> **LEARNING OBJECTIVES**
>
> After this lesson, you will be able to:
> - Identify and correct modifier agreement issues
> - Identify and correct inappropriate uses of apostrophes

To answer a question like this

Much to their surprise, <u>it was quickly apparent to anti-suffragists</u>[1] that women, in fact, did not vote together as a bloc. Women voted as individuals and in smaller proportions than men.

1. Which choice makes the sentence most grammatically acceptable?

   A. **No Change**
   B. it was quick apparent to anti-suffragists
   C. anti-suffragists quick found
   D. anti-suffragists quickly found

You need to know this

A modifier is a word or phrase that describes, clarifies, or provides additional information about another part of the sentence. Modifier questions require you to identify the part of a sentence being modified and use the appropriate modifier in the proper place.

In order to be grammatically correct, the modifier must be placed as close to the word it describes as possible. Use context clues in the passage to identify the correct placement of a modifier; a misplaced modifier can cause confusion and is always incorrect on test day.

Note that a common way the ACT tests modifiers is with modifying phrases at the beginning of a sentence. Just like any other modifier, the modifying phrase grammatically modifies whatever is right next to it in the sentence. For example, consider the sentence, "While walking to the bus stop, the rain drenched Bob." The initial phrase, "While walking to the bus stop," grammatically modifies "the rain," creating a nonsense sentence; the rain can't walk to the bus stop. The writer meant that Bob was walking to the bus stop, so the sentence should read, "While walking to the bus stop, Bob was drenched by the rain."

Modifier/Modifying phrase	Incorrect	Correct
nearly	Andre **nearly** watched the play for four hours.	Andre watched the play for **nearly** four hours.
in individual containers	The art teacher handed out paints to students **in individual containers**.	The art teacher handed out paints **in individual containers** to students.
A scholar athlete	**A scholar athlete**, maintaining high grades in addition to playing soccer was expected of Maya.	**A scholar athlete**, Maya was expected to maintain high grades in addition to playing soccer.

Part 2
ACT ENGLISH

Adjectives and Adverbs

Use adjectives only to modify nouns and pronouns. Use adverbs to modify everything else.

- Adjectives are single-word modifiers that describe nouns and pronouns: *Ian conducted an **efficient** lab experiment.*
- Adverbs are single-word modifiers that describe verbs, adjectives, or other adverbs: *Ian **efficiently** conducted a lab experiment.*

Note that nouns can sometimes be used as adjectives. For example, in the phrase "the fashion company's autumn line," the word *fashion* functions as an adjective modifying *company*, and the word *autumn* functions as an adjective modifying *line*.

Comparative/Superlative

When comparing similar things, use adjectives that match the number of items being compared. When comparing two items or people, use the comparative form of the adjective. When comparing three or more items or people, use the superlative form.

Comparative (two items)	Superlative (three or more items)
better, more, newer, older, shorter, taller, worse, younger	best, most, newest, oldest, shortest, tallest, worst, youngest

Possessive Nouns and Pronouns

Possessive nouns and pronouns indicate that something belongs to someone or something. In general, possessive nouns are written with an apostrophe, while possessive pronouns are not.

To spot errors in possessive noun or pronoun construction, look for...	Incorrect	Correct
Two nouns in a row	The **professors lectures** were both informative and entertaining.	The **professor's lectures** were both informative and entertaining.
Pronouns with apostrophes	The book is **her's**.	The book is **hers**.
Words that sound alike	The three friends decided to ride **there** bicycles to the park over **they're** where **their** going to enjoy a picnic lunch.	The three friends decided to ride **their** bicycles to the park over **there** where **they're** going to enjoy a picnic lunch.

Apostrophes

Use an apostrophe to...	Example
Indicate the possessive form of a single noun	My oldest **sister's soccer game** is on Saturday.
Indicate the possessive form of a plural noun	My **two** older **sisters' soccer games** are on Saturday.
Indicate a contraction (e.g., don't, can't)	**They've** won every soccer match this season.

Note that plural nouns are formed without an apostrophe.

Incorrect	Correct
Sting ray's are cartilaginous fish related to **shark's**.	**Sting rays** are cartilaginous fish related to **sharks**.
There are many **carnival's** in this area every summer.	There are many **carnivals** in this area every summer.

To check whether *it's* is appropriate, replace it in the sentence with *it is* or *it has*. If the sentence no longer makes sense, *it's* is incorrect. The following sentences are correct:

The tree frog blends perfectly into its surroundings. When it holds still, it's nearly invisible.

Note that *its'* and *its's* are never correct.

You need to do this

If the underlined portion includes a modifier, determine whether the modifier:

- Is placed correctly
  - Is it as near as possible to the word it logically modifies?
  - If it is not in the correct place, where should it be moved?
- Agrees with the word or words it is describing
  - Does the sentence require an adjective or an adverb?
  - Does the noun or pronoun show proper possession?

If the underlined portion includes an apostrophe, make sure it correctly indicates either possession or a contraction. If an apostrophe is missing, select the answer choice that places it in the correct location.

Explanation

"Much to their surprise" is an introductory modifying phrase, so the noun that the phrase is modifying must come immediately after the comma. Eliminate A and B because "much to their surprise" is not modifying "it." Choice C introduces a new error by changing the adverb *quickly* to *quick*, which cannot be used to modify the verb *found*. Choice (D) places the correct phrase after the comma and does not introduce any new errors.

Drills

If modifiers give you trouble, study the information above and try out these drill questions before completing the Try on Your Own questions below. Drill answers can be found in Answers and Explanations.

Edit each sentence to correct the modifier or apostrophe issue.

a. A more safely approach is to test the temperature of the water before entering.

b. Jonas had to run to the store real quick before it closed.

c. The new student is the better speller in the class.

d. It took the chameleon a few weeks to acclimate to its' new habitat.

Try on Your Own

Directions: Take as much time as you need on these questions. Work carefully and methodically. There will be an opportunity for timed practice at the end of the chapter.

Basketry

Basketry may be the world's oldest handicraft. The earlier examples of basketry are 10,000 years old. These
          2

ancient fragments, which have been preserved good by
                                                 3
the dry environment of Danger Cave, Utah, show that early Native Americans mastered the art of weaving semi-rigid materials into useful objects. Notably, the

remains of baskets like the ones discovered in Utah have
     4
been found on nearly every continent.

   Materials, rather than technique or decoration, are oftentimes most useful in identifying a basket's origin. Willow, just pliant enough to be either woven or plaited, is the favored basket-making material of northern Europe. Opting for rigid materials, bamboo and rattan
                                              5
have been used by basket makers to create sturdy baskets
                       5
in other regions. Africa has yielded many basket-making materials, including palm leaves, tree roots, and grasses.

   The materials chosen by ancient basket makers also hint at the function of the baskets within a culture. Indigenous Canadian artisans used stiff, sturdy materials

2. Which choice makes the sentence most grammatically acceptable?

   F. No Change
   G. more earlier
   H. most earliest
   J. earliest

3. Which choice makes the sentence most grammatically acceptable?

   A. No Change
   B. very good
   C. quite well and thoroughly
   D. well

4. Which choice makes the sentence most grammatically acceptable?

   F. No Change
   G. remains' of baskets
   H. remain's of baskets
   J. remains of baskets'

5. Which choice makes the sentence most grammatically acceptable?

   A. No Change
   B. bamboo and rattan are used to create sturdy baskets by basket makers
   C. basket makers use bamboo and rattan to create sturdy baskets
   D. sturdy baskets are made by basket makers out of bamboo and rattan

Chapter 3
Spotting and Fixing Errors: Sentence Structure, Punctuation, and Agreement

like cedar root <u>designed to carry heavy loads</u> for baskets.
                                6
Nearby, the Tinglit culture in southeast Alaska used flexible materials like spruce root for baskets meant to fold flat for easy transport.

Not surprisingly, the materials used in basketry not only reflect the practical needs of different cultures but also highlight the enduring ingenuity and adaptability of this ancient craft.

6. The best placement for the underlined portion would be:

F. where it is now.
G. after the word *artisans*.
H. after the word *materials*.
J. after the word *baskets*.

AGREEMENT: IDIOMS

LEARNING OBJECTIVE
After this lesson, you will be able to:
- Identify and correct expressions that deviate from idiomatic English

To answer a question like this

Early 20th-century women did not necessarily vote as a united caucus, but they did feel a new sense of empowerment. They were, by law, participants in a democracy that <u>couldn't hardly</u> ignore them.
                                        1

1. Which choice makes the sentence most grammatically acceptable?

   A. **No Change**
   B. would not hardly
   C. wouldn't hardly
   D. could hardly

You need to know this

An idiom is a combination of words that must be used together to convey either a figurative or literal meaning. Idioms are often tested in the following ways:

1. Proper preposition use in context: The preposition must reflect the writer's intended meaning.
   - She waits **on** customers.
   - She waits **for** the bus.
   - She waits **with** her friends.

Part 2
ACT ENGLISH

2. Idiomatic expressions: Some words or phrases must be used together to be correct.
   - Simone will **either** bike **or** run to the park.
   - **Neither** the principal **nor** the teachers will tolerate tardiness.
   - This fall, Shari is playing **not only** soccer **but also** field hockey.

3. Implicit double negatives: Some words imply a negative and therefore cannot be paired with an explicit negative. The words *barely*, *hardly*, and *scarcely* fall into this category.
   - Incorrect: Janie **can't hardly** wait for vacation.
   - Correct: Janie **can hardly** wait for vacation.

Frequently tested prepositions	Idiomatic expressions	Words that can't pair with negative words
at	as…as	barely
by	between…and	hardly
for	both…and	scarcely
from	either…or	
of	neither…nor	
on	just as…so too	
to	not only…but also	
with	prefer…to	

You need to do this
- If the underlined portion includes a preposition, a conjunction, or *barely/hardly/scarcely*, look for a common idiom error.
- If the underlined segment includes a commonly misused word, check the context to determine whether it is used properly.

Explanation
Since *hardly* is implicitly negative, it cannot be paired with *not*; (D) is correct. Choices A and C include the words *couldn't* and *wouldn't*, respectively, which mean *could not* and *would not*. Choice B explicitly pairs the word *not* with *hardly*, so it is incorrect.

Drills
If idioms give you trouble, study the information above and try out these drill questions before completing the Try on Your Own questions below. Drill answers can be found in Answers and Explanations.

Edit each sentence to correct the idiomatic issue.

a. Straining to hear the bird perched in the tree, Jessa stood completely still, waiting with the sound to reach her.

b. The engineer examined the malfunctioning machine closely for evidence to missing components or worn elements.

Chapter 3
Spotting and Fixing Errors: Sentence Structure, Punctuation, and Agreement

c. The protestors' bold slogans not only angered the opposition, but elicited loud reactions from bystanders.

d. Given the cold climate, farmers quickly found that they could grow neither dates or figs.

e. The writing was nearly barely legible after the rain soaked through Tia's backpack and saturated her notebook.

Try on Your Own

Directions: Take as much time as you need on these questions. Work carefully and methodically. There will be an opportunity for timed practice at the end of the chapter.

Alfred Nobel

Given that few people have had the opportunity to read their own obituaries, scientist Alfred Nobel <u>couldn't scarcely</u> believe that, in 1888, his obituary was in the daily newspaper. Alfred surmised that the newspaper editor had been either grossly <u>misinformed, and</u> confused by a misidentification. In actuality, Alfred's brother Ludvig had died, and Ludvig was mistaken for Alfred. While Alfred was primarily known as an inventor and one of the richest people <u>in the world at the time</u>, the paper unapologetically gave him the moniker "Merchant of Death" because of the innumerable lives that his most notable invention, dynamite, had taken.

2. Which choice makes the sentence most grammatically acceptable?

   F. No Change
   G. could scarcely
   H. could not scarcely
   J. not scarcely

3. Which choice makes the sentence most grammatically acceptable?

   A. No Change
   B. misinformed and
   C. misinformed, or
   D. misinformed or

4. Which choice makes the sentence most grammatically acceptable?

   F. No Change
   G. in the world for the time being
   H. on the world for the time being
   J. on the world at the time

Part 2
ACT ENGLISH

Unable to accept that dynamite—which was widely used by warfare—would be his enduring legacy, Alfred crafted provisions in his will to create the Nobel Foundation upon his death. Nobel's foundation has not only acknowledged outstanding achievements in chemistry, economics, literature, medicine, peace, and physics, but raised awareness regarding crucial global issues.

5. Which choice makes the sentence most grammatically acceptable?

    A. **No Change**
    B. used with
    C. used in
    D. used to

6. Which choice makes the sentence most grammatically acceptable?

    F. **No Change**
    G. it
    H. but it
    J. but also

Chapter 3
Spotting and Fixing Errors: Sentence Structure, Punctuation, and Agreement

How Much Have You Learned?

Directions: For test-like practice, give yourself 8 minutes to complete this question set. Note that this is not a test-like mix of questions; rather, these 10 questions cover the sentence structure, punctuation, and agreement issues covered in this chapter.

Be sure to study the explanations, even for questions you got correct. They can be found at the end of this chapter.

The History of Marbles

It is impossible to pinpoint the exact date when the first marble was constructed, most likely out of <u>clay, it</u>[1] is a reasonable assumption to regard the concept of marbles as nearly as old as humankind. Marbles as we know them today, however, first originated in the middle of the 19th century when they were produced in mass quantities in Europe. Originating from their appearance, material, or use, <u>an important identifying factor is often indicated by marbles' names.</u>[2]

"<u>Alleys," for example were</u>[3] named for their composite material; the name indicates that they are made from alabaster. At least, that was the case for alleys produced at the turn of the last century. Nowadays, it's far more common for marbles to <u>consist: of</u>[4] glass, baked clay, steel, onyx, plastic, or agate.

1. Which choice makes the sentence most grammatically acceptable?
   A. No Change
   B. clay, nevertheless, it
   C. clay, but it
   D. clay; but it

2. Which choice makes the sentence most grammatically acceptable?
   F. No Change
   G. an important identifying factor is often indicated by the names of marbles.
   H. marble's names often indicate an important identifying factor.
   J. marbles' names often indicate an important identifying factor.

3. Which choice makes the sentence most grammatically acceptable?
   A. No Change
   B. "Alleys" for example, were
   C. "Alleys," for example: were
   D. "Alleys," for example, were

4. Which choice makes the sentence most grammatically acceptable?
   F. No Change
   G. consist of
   H. consist—of
   J. consist, of

63

Part 2
ACT ENGLISH

Regardless of the material with which they are made, marbles can be manipulated in a variety of ways. "Knuckling" is a <u>technique in which</u> the knuckles of the
                                          5
hand are balanced against the ground while a marble placed against the forefinger is shot outward by the thumb. Marbles may be thrown, rolled, and <u>players can even kick marbles.</u>
                                                                                              6
                                                                                              6

Not surprisingly, there <u>is near</u> as many varieties
                                   7
of marble games as there are ways to manipulate marbles. The most common American version involves winning opponents' marbles by knocking them out of a designated area with one's own marbles. Another popular game is <u>taw—also known as ringtaw, or ringer,</u>
                                   8
<u>the object</u> of which is to shoot marbles arranged like a
    8
cross out of a large ring. Players in a pot game such as moshie try to knock one another's marbles into a hole. In nineholes, or bridgeboard, players shoot their marbles through numbered arches on the board.

The popularity of marbles crosses cultural boundaries. The first marble games took place in <u>antiquity. Were</u> played with nuts, fruit pits, or pebbles.
    9
Even the great Augustus Caesar was known to have played marble games as a child. During Passover, Jewish children have customarily used filberts as marbles. Several traditional Chinese games are also played with

5. Which choice makes the sentence most grammatically acceptable?
   A. **No Change**
   B. technique, in which,
   C. technique in, which
   D. technique in which;

6. Which choice makes the sentence most grammatically acceptable?
   F. **No Change**
   G. players can choose to kick marbles.
   H. kick.
   J. kicked.

7. Which choice makes the sentence most grammatically acceptable?
   A. **No Change**
   B. is nearly
   C. are near
   D. are nearly

8. Which choice makes the sentence most grammatically acceptable?
   F. **No Change**
   G. taw—also known as ringtaw—or ringer the object
   H. taw—also known as ringtaw or ringer—the object
   J. taw, also known as ringtaw, or ringer, the object

9. Which choice makes the sentence most grammatically acceptable?
   A. **No Change**
   B. antiquity and were
   C. antiquity, and were
   D. antiquity; were

marbles. Indeed, while many people consider the game of marbles to be simple, <u>they actually have</u> a complex history.
                                                               10

10. Which choice makes the sentence most grammatically acceptable?

   F. **No Change**
   G. they actually has
   H. it actually have
   J. it actually has

Reflect

Directions: Take a few minutes to recall what you've learned and what you've been practicing in this chapter. Consider the following questions, jot down your best answer for each one, and then compare your reflections to the expert responses on the following page. Use your level of confidence to determine what to do next.

1. Name at least three ways to correct a run-on sentence.
   _____
   _____
   _____

2. How does the ACT test subject-verb agreement and parallelism?
   _____
   _____
   _____

3. What are the three different pronoun forms? When do you use each one?
   _____
   _____
   _____

4. What is the difference between an adjective and an adverb?
   _____
   _____
   _____

5. What are the three ways that apostrophes are tested on the ACT?
   _____
   _____
   _____

Responses

1. Name at least three ways to correct a run-on sentence.

There are a number of ways to fix a run-on sentence on the ACT: 1) use a period to create two separate sentences, 2) use a semicolon between the two independent clauses, 3) use a colon between the two independent clauses, 4) make one clause dependent, 5) add a FANBOYS conjunction after the comma, or 6) use a dash between the two independent clauses.

2. How does the ACT test subject-verb agreement and parallelism?

A subject and a verb must always agree in person (first, second, or third) and number (singular or plural). You will need to be able to spot subject-verb mismatches and correct them. Parallelism requires that all items in a list, a compound, or a comparison be in parallel form. The ACT may test lists or comparisons in which one item is in the incorrect form.

3. What are the three different pronoun forms? When do you use each one?

The three forms are subjective (when the pronoun is the subject), objective (when the pronoun is the object of a verb or preposition), and possessive (when the pronoun expresses ownership).

4. What is the difference between an adjective and an adverb?

An adjective is a single word that modifies a noun or a pronoun, while an adverb is a single word that modifies a verb, an adjective, or another adverb.

5. What are the three ways that apostrophes are tested on the ACT?

Apostrophes on the ACT are used to: 1) indicate the possessive form of a singular noun ('s), 2) indicate the possessive form of a plural noun (s'), or 3) indicate a contraction (don't = do not).

Next Steps

If you answered most questions correctly in the "How Much Have You Learned?" section, and if your responses to the Reflect questions were similar to those of the ACT expert, then consider sentence structure, punctuation, and agreement areas of strength and move on to the next chapter. Come back to these topics periodically to prevent yourself from getting rusty.

If you don't yet feel confident, review those parts of this chapter that you have not yet mastered. Be especially sure to review the explanations closely. Then, go online (**kaptest.com/login**) for more practice. If you haven't already registered your book, do so at **kaptest.com/moreonline** first.

GO ONLINE

kaptest.com/login

Part 2
ACT ENGLISH

Answers and Explanations

Sentence Structure: The Basics

1. Review the Explanation portion of the Sentence Structure: The Basics lesson.

Drill Answers

Note: These are not the only ways to correct the sentences; your answers may differ.

a. **The student** volunteered to organize the upcoming fundraiser.

b. Upon finding the misplaced house keys, **Hannah locked the front door.**

c. The historic center of town was restored. **It** once again bustled with activity.

d. Logical thinking is essential to scientific research**;** the irony is that scientists who make important discoveries often do so on a hunch.

e. The local farms had a poor harvest last year, **so** the price of produce at the market has risen dramatically.

2. **G**
Difficulty: Medium
Category: Sentence Structure
Getting to the Answer: The phrase "For what seemed like eons" is a dependent clause that must be set off from the rest of the sentence with a comma, so (G) is correct. Choices F, H, and J all create sentence fragments, since the first part of the sentence cannot stand on its own.

3. **A**
Difficulty: Low
Category: Sentence Structure
Getting to the Answer: If a sentence includes two independent clauses, they must be properly combined. The independent clauses can be separated by a coordinating conjunction and a comma, as they currently are in the passage, making (A) correct. They could also be separated by a semicolon, separated into two sentences, or edited so that the first part of the sentence is a dependent clause. B is incorrect because it eliminates the conjunction and the punctuation, which creates a run-on. C is incorrect because it does not include the comma after the coordinating conjunction. D is incorrect because a semicolon cannot be used with a coordinating conjunction between the two independent clauses.

4. **G**
Difficulty: Medium
Category: Sentence Structure
Getting to the Answer: Choice F is incorrect because placing a period after *nearby* creates a sentence fragment. Changing the period to a comma creates a grammatically correct sentence with an introductory phrase followed by an independent clause. Choice (G) is correct. Choices H and J incorrectly use the coordinating conjunction *and*, which makes the resulting sentence an incomplete thought.

5. **C**
Difficulty: High
Category: Sentence Structure
Getting to the Answer: The sentence includes two independent clauses that must be properly combined. Choice A is incorrect because it includes no punctuation whatsoever. Choice (C) correctly uses a dash to join the two clauses. Choices B and D are incorrect because both a comma and a coordinating conjunction are required to join two independent clauses. Choice B omits the conjunction, while D omits the comma.

6. **J**
Difficulty: Medium
Category: Sentence Structure
Getting to the Answer: The underlined portion contains parts of two independent clauses that must be properly combined. Choice F includes no punctuation at all, and choice G incorrectly uses a comma without a coordinating conjunction. Both choices create a run-on sentence. Finally, eliminate H because *offering* makes the part that follows the semicolon a dependent clause. A semicolon cannot be used to separate an independent clause and a dependent clause. Choice (J) is correct because the comma properly joins the independent clause at the beginning of the sentence with the dependent clause after the comma.

Sentence Structure: Parenthetical Elements

1. Review the Explanation portion of the Sentence Structure: Parenthetical Elements lesson.

Drill Answers

Note: These are not the only ways to correct the sentences; your answers may differ.

a. Delayed for two hours due to a thunderstorm, the baseball game started much later than fans had expected.

b. *The Heart of a Woman* (originally published in 1981) is one of Maya Angelou's most popular books.

c. The architect, a keen observer known for her meticulous attention to detail, gently pointed out the error in her coworker's design.

d. Contemporary Hawaiian quilts—which are often featured at the Mokupāpapa Discovery Center—reflect an eclectic blend of Hawaiian tradition and modern vision.

e. A hurricane's strength is rated on a scale of 1 to 5, depending on the speed of sustained winds.

2. G
Difficulty: Low
Category: Sentence Structure
Getting to the Answer: The first part of the sentence is an introductory phrase. Thus, it must be set off from the rest of the sentence with a comma, making choice (G) correct. Incorrect punctuation is used in choices F and J, and choice H is incorrect because it omits punctuation altogether.

3. D
Difficulty: Medium
Category: Sentence Structure
Getting to the Answer: The underlined segment sets off the nonessential phrase "the defeated Gorgon" with one comma and one dash. Either two commas or two dashes must be used to set off this phrase; using one of each is not grammatically proper. Thus, choice A can be eliminated. Choices B and C do not provide punctuation on both sides of the nonessential phrase, so they can be eliminated as well. Choice (D) is correct as it uses two dashes.

4. J
Difficulty: High
Category: Sentence Structure
Getting to the Answer: A phrase is considered parenthetical if the rest of the sentence is grammatically correct when it is removed. As written, the dash creates an error, because it leaves an orphaned conjunction ("and") after being removed. Thus, choice (F) is incorrect. A comma alone cannot join two independent clauses; choice G is incorrect because it creates a run-on sentence. Choice H incorrectly uses two commas around "and." Choice (J) is correct because it shifts the parenthetical to before the conjunction "and," meaning the rest of the sentence is grammatically correct even after the parenthetical is removed.

5. B
Difficulty: Medium
Category: Sentence Structure
Getting to the Answer: "One of the three Gorgon sisters" is an introductory modifying phrase that must be followed by a comma; (B) is correct. Choice A omits the comma, while C and D add unnecessary words that do not fix the original error.

6. G
Difficulty: High
Category: Sentence Structure
Getting to the Answer: The phrase "once lovely hair" is essential to the meaning of the sentence, so it should not be separated from the surrounding text with commas or dashes, as in choices F and J. Choice (G) is correct because no punctuation is needed. Choice H incorrectly inserts a comma into the phrase "once lovely hair." Since this phrase is one logical unit, it should not be broken up by a punctuation mark.

7. A
Difficulty: Low
Category: Sentence Structure
Getting to the Answer: The phrase "a cap which granted the wearer invisibility" explains the powers of the "Helm of Hades." Such an explanation is best placed next to the word or phrase that it explains, so choice (A) is correct. Choices B and C place the definition next to the wrong item. Choice D incorrectly inserts the definition midway through "Helm of Hades" rather than afterward.

Sentence Structure: Commas, Dashes, and Colons

1. Review the Explanation portion of the Sentence Structure: Commas, Dashes, and Colons lesson.

Drill Answers

Note: These are not the only ways to correct the sentences; your answers may differ.

a. The recipe includes my favorite fruit: sweet red cherries.

b. Historically popular sayings are transferred by word of mouth and are rarely found in written records, so there is often no definite answer to the question of their origin. OR Historically popular sayings are transferred by word of mouth and are rarely found in written records—so there is often no definite answer to the question of their origin.

c. Paradise tree snakes subsist mostly on lizards and bats, which they immobilize with mild venom.

d. As a result, the United States entered an isolationist period after World War I.

e. *Hamlet* begins with two of Shakespeare's favorite ways to grab an audience's attention—a supernatural phenomenon and a murder plot. OR *Hamlet* begins with two of Shakespeare's favorite ways to grab an audience's attention: a supernatural phenomenon and a murder plot.

2. **J**
Difficulty: Medium
Category: Sentence Structure
Getting to the Answer: When a comma is underlined, check to make sure it is necessary. The phrase "tedious and unimaginative" is one logical unit and should not be broken up by any sort of punctuation; (J) is correct.

3. **B**
Difficulty: Low
Category: Sentence Structure
Getting to the Answer: *However* is a transition word that needs to be separated from the rest of the sentence with a comma; (B) is correct.

4. **F**
Difficulty: Medium
Category: Sentence Structure
Getting to the Answer: The sentence includes two independent clauses properly joined with a comma

and a FANBOYS (For, And, Nor, But, Or, Yet, So) conjunction, so no change is needed. Choice (F) is correct. Choice G incorrectly uses a semicolon to separate two independent clauses with a FANBOYS conjunction between them. Choices H and J are incorrect because the ideas in the two independent clauses contrast with each other. The transition word *so* indicates cause-and-effect, not contrast.

5. **C**
Difficulty: Medium
Category: Sentence Structure
Getting to the Answer: The phrase "Mendelssohn's Symphony No. 4 in A Major" is a parenthetical phrase that must be set off by either two commas or two dashes. Since a dash is used at the end of the phrase, (C) is correct.

6. **G**
Difficulty: High
Category: Sentence Structure
Getting to the Answer: When a comma is underlined, check to make sure it is necessary. The phrase "lyrical church bells" is one logical unit and should not be broken up by any sort of punctuation; (G) is correct.

Agreement: Verbs

1. Review the Explanation portion of the Agreement: Verbs lesson.

Drill Answers

Note: These are not the only ways to correct the sentences; your answers may differ.

a. Pablo present**ed** his experiment at the science fair last week.

b. The movie, with its complex plot and stirring themes, **was** critically acclaimed.

c. Neither the director nor the lead actor **is** at rehearsal today.

d. The park and the adjacent wildlife refuge **encompass** more than 800 acres of mountains, lakes, and forests.

e. In order to pass the foreign language proficiency exam, you must be both a fluent speaker and **reader**.

2. **F**

Difficulty: Low
Category: Agreement
Getting to the Answer: When a verb is underlined, look for context clues that indicate which tense is needed. The sentence includes the phrase *last year*, so the simple past tense is appropriate; (F) is correct. Choice H is incorrect because it is in the past perfect form. This tense is used to indicate that one action happened *before* another action in the past. However, in this paragraph, the two verbs *inherited* and *told* occur at the same time. Finally, choice J contains the auxiliary verb *would*. This form is appropriate to use only when the sentence contains another clause starting with *if*.

3. **B**

Difficulty: High
Category: Agreement
Getting to the Answer: The idiomatic expressions *either . . . or* and *neither . . . nor* create singular subjects, and the phrase *past situations* indicates that past tense is required. Choice (B) is correct because it is the only option that uses the singular past-tense verb *was*.

4. **H**

Difficulty: High
Category: Agreement
Getting to the Answer: When a verb is underlined, identify its subject. The subject is *darkness*, which is singular. The singular present tense verb *teems* is needed; (H) is correct. Choice F is present tense but plural. Choices G and J are incorrect because the future perfect tense and the infinitive form of the verb *teem* do not make sense in context.

5. **D**

Difficulty: Medium
Category: Agreement
Getting to the Answer: Since the verb *grip* is part of the compound verb phrase "took a deep breath and grip the ladder," the verbs *took* and *grip* must match. As written, *took* is past tense and *grip* is present tense; eliminate A. Choice (D) corrects the error by changing *grip* to *gripped*.

6. **G**

Difficulty: High
Category: Agreement
Getting to the Answer: All items in a list must be parallel in structure. The first two items are verb phrases, so the last item must also be a verb phrase; (G) is correct. Choices F, H, and J are all noun phrases, not verb phrases.

Agreement: Pronouns

1. Review the Explanation portion of the Agreement: Pronouns lesson.

Drill Answers

Note: These are not the only ways to correct the sentences; your answers may differ.

a. The scientist, about **whom** I had read, was more charismatic in person than I had expected.

b. Between you and **me**, you are the better singer.

c. A jaguar, with its keen senses and sharp teeth and claws, is known for **its** ability to dominate prey.

d. The jar of olives is not in **its** regular location on the shelf.

e. One cannot help but be amazed by the scientific advances in the past century, especially if **one studies** the history of science.

2. **J**

Difficulty: Low
Category: Agreement
Getting to the Answer: When a pronoun is underlined, identify its antecedent, the noun to which it refers. The antecedent is *citizens*, so the subjective plural pronoun *they* is needed; (J) is correct. Choice F is incorrect because *it* is singular. Choices G and H are plural, but *their* is possessive and *them* is objective.

3. **B**

Difficulty: High
Category: Agreement
Getting to the Answer: When deciding between *who* and *whom*, see if there is a preposition in front of the word in question. If there is, then you need the objective case *whom*. In this sentence, there is no preposition, so the subjective case *who* is required; (B) is correct. On the ACT, the word *that* will not be used to refer to people, so C and D are incorrect.

Part 2
ACT ENGLISH

4. J
Difficulty: Medium
Category: Agreement
Getting to the Answer: The antecedent, the noun to which the pronoun refers, is *components*, so a plural pronoun is required; (J) is correct. Choice F means *it is* and H is not grammatically correct in any context. While G is a correctly written possessive pronoun, it is singular, not plural.

5. A
Difficulty: Medium
Category: Agreement
Getting to the Answer: Choice (A) is correct. The underlined pronoun refers to *the roadbed*, which is singular, so the singular pronoun *it* is correct as written.

6. J
Difficulty: Medium
Category: Agreement
Getting to the Answer: Throughout the passage, the writer does not address the reader directly, so F and G are incorrect. Choice H does not make sense in context. Choice (J) correctly uses the more formal indefinite pronoun *one*, which is grammatically correct and matches the writer's tone.

Agreement: Modifiers

1. Review the Explanation portion of the Agreement: Modifiers lesson.

Drill Answers

Note: These are not the only ways to correct the sentences; your answers may differ.

a. A **safer** approach is to test the temperature of the water before entering.

b. Jonas had to run to the store **really quickly** before it closed.

c. The new student is the **best** speller in the class.

d. It took the chameleon a few weeks to acclimate to **its** new habitat.

2. J
Difficulty: Medium
Category: Agreement
Getting to the Answer: The underlined segment includes the comparative adjective *earlier*. The comparative form is used only when discussing exactly two items or people. This sentence is about all examples of basketry, so F is incorrect. Choices G and H are incorrect because the phrases *more early* and *most early* are not as concise as *earliest*. Choice (J) correctly uses the superlative adjective *earliest*.

3. D
Difficulty: Low
Category: Agreement
Getting to the Answer: The verb phrase "have been preserved" must be modified by an adverb; eliminate A and B, which contain adjectives. Choice C is unnecessarily wordy. Choice (D) is both correct and concise.

4. F
Difficulty: Medium
Category: Agreement
Getting to the Answer: If the sentence had used the phrase "baskets' remains," an apostrophe would be needed. However, the preposition *of* makes punctuation unnecessary; G, H, and J are incorrect. Choice (F) correctly omits all apostrophes.

5. C
Difficulty: High
Category: Agreement
Getting to the Answer: "Opting for rigid materials" is an introductory modifying phrase, so the noun that the phrase is modifying must come immediately after the comma. Choice (C) correctly places *basket makers* after the comma. Choices A, B, and D do not feature the correct noun after the comma.

6. J
Difficulty: High
Category: Agreement
Getting to the Answer: The underlined portion of the sentence is a modifying phrase, so determine the noun that is "designed to carry heavy loads." The only noun that could logically be "designed" for a purpose is the baskets, so the phrase must be moved immediately after that word. Choice (J) is correct. *Root* (choice F), *artisans* (choice G), and natural *materials* (choice H) would not logically be "designed," so to place the modifying phrase next to any of these words would be incorrect.

Chapter 3
Spotting and Fixing Errors: Sentence Structure, Punctuation, and Agreement

Agreement: Idioms

1. Review the Explanation portion of the Agreement: Idioms lesson.

Drill Answers

Note: These are not the only ways to correct the sentences; your answers may differ.

a. Straining to hear the bird perched in the tree, Jessa stood completely still, waiting **for** the sound to reach her.

b. The engineer examined the malfunctioning machine closely for evidence **of** missing components or worn elements.

c. The protestors' bold slogans not only angered the opposition, but **also** elicited loud reactions from bystanders.

d. Given the cold climate, farmers quickly found that they could grow neither dates **nor** figs.

e. The writing was **barely** legible after the rain soaked through Tia's backpack and saturated her notebook.

2. **G**
Difficulty: Medium
Category: Agreement
Getting to the Answer: Since *scarcely* is implicitly negative, it cannot be paired with *not*; (G) is correct. Choice F includes *couldn't*, which means *could not*. Choices H and J also pair the word *not* with *scarcely*, so they are incorrect.

3. **D**
Difficulty: Medium
Category: Agreement
Getting to the Answer: The word *either* must be paired with *or*, not *and*; eliminate A and B. The phrase "confused by a misidentification" is not an independent clause, so a comma is not needed before *or*; (D) is correct.

4. **F**
Difficulty: Medium
Category: Agreement
Getting to the Answer: When prepositions such as *in* and *at* are underlined, make sure they are idiomatically correct. The phrase "in the world" is correct because Alfred was a part of the world population rather than an object placed upon the Earth's surface. In addition, "at the time" is correct because the context indicates that Alfred was one of the richest people in the world during that time period. Choice (F) is correct. The phrase "for the time being" doesn't make sense because the passage is describing past events, so G and H are incorrect. While J correctly includes "at the time," it incorrectly uses the preposition *on* instead of *in*.

5. **C**
Difficulty: Medium
Category: Agreement
Getting to the Answer: When a preposition is underlined, make sure that it is idiomatically correct. Warfare is an abstract concept and cannot use dynamite, so eliminate A. People use dynamite *in* war, so (C) is correct. Choice B is incorrect because dynamite is used as part of war, not alongside it. Choice D is incorrect because *used to* must be followed by a verb, which does not happen in this sentence.

6. **J**
Difficulty: High
Category: Agreement
Getting to the Answer: When a sentence includes the words *not only*, it must include *but also* as well. Only (J) includes *also*, so it is correct.

How Much Have You Learned?

1. **C**
Difficulty: Medium
Category: Sentence Structure
Getting to the Answer: As written, the sentence is a run-on, so A is incorrect. Choices B, (C), and D all attempt to fix the run-on error. Choice B is incorrect because the word *nevertheless* is not a coordinating conjunction and cannot join two sentences unless a semicolon is used as well. Choice D suffers from the opposite problem; it uses a coordinating conjunction with a semicolon instead of a comma. Only (C) corrects the run-on and does not introduce new errors.

2. **J**
Difficulty: High
Category: Agreement
Getting to the Answer: "Originating from their appearance, material, or use," is an introductory modifying phrase, so the item(s) that the phrase is modifying must immediately follow the comma after *use*. Eliminate F and G because the phrase is describing marbles'

names, not "an important identifying factor." Choice H is incorrect because it uses the singular possessive *marble's*, which does not match the plural noun *names*. Choice (J) correctly places *marbles' names* after the modifying phrase and does not introduce new errors.

3. D
Difficulty: Medium
Category: Sentence Structure
Getting to the Answer: Parenthetical information includes words or phrases that aren't essential to the sentence structure or content and must be set off with commas. Choices A and B are incorrect because they do not include commas on both sides of the parenthetical phrase *for example*. Choice C misuses the colon, which is used to introduce a short phrase, quotation, explanation, example, or list. Choice (D) correctly sets off the nonessential phrase *for example* with two commas.

4. G
Difficulty: Medium
Category: Sentence Structure
Getting to the Answer: Since the verb *consist* and the preposition *of* form one logical unit, they should not be separated by punctuation of any sort; (G) is correct.

5. A
Difficulty: Medium
Category: Sentence Structure
Getting to the Answer: Determine whether any of the tested comma rules apply to the underlined segment. Two commas are used to set off a nonessential phrase, so read the sentence without *in which* to see if the sentence still makes sense. Choice B is incorrect because the phrase *in which* is essential and thus should not be set off with commas. Choice C mistakenly places a comma between the preposition *in* and its object *which*. Finally, choice D is incorrect because the semicolon here is not joining two independent clauses. Choice (A) is correct.

6. J
Difficulty: Low
Category: Agreement
Getting to the Answer: The sentence includes items in a list that are not in parallel form, so F, G, and H are incorrect. Choice (J) fixes the issue by using the past-tense *kicked*, which matches the other past-tense verbs in the list.

7. D
Difficulty: High
Category: Agreement
Getting to the Answer: The underlined portion has two issues. The verb *is* does not agree with its subject *varieties*, and the adverb *nearly*, not the adjective *near*, is needed. Choice (D) fixes both mistakes. None of the other options corrects both errors.

8. H
Difficulty: Medium
Category: Sentence Structure
Getting to the Answer: Although a parenthetical phrase may appear in the beginning, middle, or end of a sentence, punctuation will always separate it from the rest of the sentence. Because the sentence makes logical sense without the phrase "also known as ring-taw, or ringer," two commas or two dashes are needed to set it off from the rest of the sentence. Eliminate F because using one dash and one comma is not acceptable. Eliminate G because the second dash is incorrectly placed in the middle of the parenthetical phrase. Choice J uses two commas correctly but includes an unnecessary comma after *ringtaw*. Choice (H) is correct, since it uses two dashes to offset the parenthetical phrase and excludes unnecessary punctuation.

9. B
Difficulty: Low
Category: Agreement
Getting to the Answer: The sentence that appears after the underlined period is a fragment, so A is incorrect. Choice (B) fixes the fragment by using the conjunction *and* to join the verb phrase after the period with the independent clause before the period. Choices C and D are incorrect because a semicolon or a comma and a coordinating conjunction are used to join two independent clauses, not an independent clause and a verb phrase.

10. J
Difficulty: Medium
Category: Agreement
Getting to the Answer: The underlined portion includes a pronoun and a verb. The phrase is referring to *the game*, so a singular pronoun and a singular verb are needed; (J) is correct. None of the other choices includes singular forms of both the pronoun and the verb.

[CHAPTER 4]

SPOTTING AND FIXING ISSUES: CONCISENESS, ORGANIZATION, AND DEVELOPMENT

> **LEARNING OBJECTIVES**
>
> After completing this chapter, you will be able to:
> - Revise wordy writing
> - Identify which choice most effectively matches a text's style and maintains its tone
> - Determine the appropriate transition word or phrase to establish logical relationships within and between sentences
> - Determine the appropriate transition sentence to establish logical relationships between paragraphs
> - Determine the most logical place for a sentence in a paragraph or passage
> - Identify the word that accomplishes the appropriate purpose within a sentence
> - Provide an introduction or conclusion to a paragraph or passage
> - Revise a sentence to accomplish a specific purpose
> - Determine the relevance of a sentence within a passage
> - Determine whether a passage has met a goal and state why or why not

How Much Do You Know?

Directions: Try out the questions below. The "Category" heading in the explanation for each question gives the title of the lesson that covers how to answer it. If you answered the question(s) for a given lesson correctly, you may be able to move quickly through that lesson. If you answered incorrectly, you may want to take your time on that lesson.

A Note About the Passages in This Chapter

Due to the more global nature of Organization and Development questions, you may see the same passages intentionally used multiple times throughout this chapter. Each lesson will present the portion of the passage needed to answer the question(s). On test day, the various question types will be spaced throughout the passage, so you should prepare to review the entire passage, not just the underlined segments or only one or two paragraphs.

Eva Salazar: Master Weaver

The Kumeyaay are a Native American people who have developed[1] in the area now known as San Diego, California, for 12,000 years. They have retained a rich cultural and social life despite a forced split in 1875, when many Kumeyaay were driven across the border into Mexico. Now resettled in small farming communities, such as San José de la Zorra, the families have preserved their traditional way of life.

It is in this remote valley that Eva Salazar learned the ancient art of basket weaving from her tribal elders. Traditionally, Kumeyaay women have the crucially necessary[2] responsibility of making baskets, which are important artifacts of everyday life. Kumeyaay baskets are tightly woven with expressive designs. They are made mostly for utilitarian purposes: cooking, storing food products, and gathering ingredients. As traditional objects of art, they are also valued for their aesthetic beauty.

1. Which choice is clearest and most precise in context?

   A. **No Change**
   B. blossomed
   C. thrived
   D. withered

2. Which choice is least redundant in context?

   F. **No Change**
   G. crucial
   H. necessary and crucial
   J. fundamentally crucial

Underline{Following in her ancestors' footsteps,} Eva Salazar uses native materials to weave her intricate baskets, primarily the strong, sharp reed known as juncus, as well as yucca, sumac, and other native plants. She colors the reeds with black walnut, elderberry, and other natural dyes. Eva specializes in coiled baskets, and her shapes and decorations echo traditional forms.

Though she is best known for her baskets, Eva Salazar also makes dolls, willow bark skirts, nets, and shell necklaces. Her most ambitious work is a basket measuring almost three feet in diameter. The basket took her two years to weave and represents a masterpiece of Native American art.

Today, Eva is heralded as a master weaver. Now an American citizen living in San Diego, she remains focused on traditional tribal arts and teaches basket weaving at local reservations and colleges. Her baskets continue to represent the height of Kumeyaay basket-weaving artistry.

3. If the author were to delete the underlined portion, the sentence would primarily lose:

   A. a counterargument regarding the authenticity of modern crafts.
   B. a key detail that explains Eva Salazar's relationship to the Kumeyaay.
   C. a claim that Eva Salazar will develop her own basket-weaving methods in the future.
   D. a suggestion that the Kumeyaay should place greater value on Eva Salazar's work.

4. Given that all the choices are accurate, which one provides the best transition from the preceding paragraph to this paragraph?

   F. **No Change**
   G. Because
   H. Nonetheless
   J. On the other hand

5. Which choice most effectively concludes the passage?

   A. **No Change**
   B. She is famous for not letting the Kumeyaay traditions be lost.
   C. Her work has inspired countless artists to follow in her footsteps, ensuring that Kumeyaay basket weaving continues to thrive.
   D. She will be remembered for her unique adaptations of the Kumeyaay traditions.

Sweat Lodges

The 21st century has seen a marked increase in the popularity of natural medicines and therapies. Among the most common of these is the sweat lodge, a practice established by some groups of indigenous peoples of the Americas. Because of the benefits this practice offers, many cultures independently evolved similar traditions, including the Finnish sauna and the Turkish steam room. The basic purpose of these therapies is to raise the body's core temperature to between 102 and 106 degrees Fahrenheit. At this temperature, bacterial and viral infections within the body cannot easily survive. The heat can also ease muscle tension and soreness, and the resulting perspiration flushes the system of toxins.

[1] In other designs, an altar barrier is positioned between the fire and the entrance to prevent participants from accidentally falling into the fire pit when they emerge from the lodge. [2] A traditional sweat lodge may be built from willow, as its bark is considered medicinal and, indeed, contains the same analgesic as aspirin. [3] Other lodges are made using a few different materials, including blankets, animal skins, and canvas. [4] In some traditions, the entrance of the sweat lodge faces east, with a clear and unobstructed view of a sacred fire pit where the stones are heated before being brought inside the lodge. [7]

6. Which choice provides the best transition from the start of the paragraph into the information that follows?

   F. **No Change**
   G. Nearly every culture has adopted this practice in some form,
   H. The benefits this practice offers have led many other cultures to adapt it in forms more suited to their own resources,
   J. The popularity of the practice is well-earned by the many health benefits it grants to participants,

7. For the sake of the logic and coherence of this paragraph, Sentence 1 should be placed:

   A. where it is now.
   B. after Sentence 2.
   C. after Sentence 3.
   D. after Sentence 4.

The exact ceremonial process will vary, but prior to entering the lodge, <u>participants usually change into simple, traditional clothing.</u> In some versions of the ceremony, the
                                      8
Stone People spirits are called upon and the sweat leader sounds the Water Drum once all participants have entered the lodge. A sweat might include more than one session, each lasting 30 to 45 minutes and focused on one of four distinct themes: the spirit world, cleanliness and honesty, individual prayer, and growth and healing.

Traditional sweat lodge ceremonies, which often included songs, prayers, and chants, were believed to purify not only the body <u>but also the mind as well.</u> "Healing comes
                                      9
on a spiritual level," wrote Dr. Lewis Mehl-Madrona in his book *Coyote Medicine*. "Ceremony and ritual provide the means of making ourselves available."

8. The writer wants to emphasize the spiritual aspects of the sweat lodge tradition. Which choice best accomplishes this goal?

   F. **No Change**
   G. the sweat leader must complete years of intense training to be entrusted with the role.
   H. it is important to ensure that all participants are healthy, since otherwise the intense conditions of a sweat can be harmful.
   J. participants are often smudged with the smoke of burning sage, sweetgrass, or cedar to signify ritual cleanliness.

9. Which choice is least redundant in context?

   A. **No Change**
   B. but also the mind in addition.
   C. but also the mind.
   D. but also additionally the mind.

Question 10 asks about the preceding passage as a whole.

10. Suppose the author's main goal had been to write an essay describing a personal experience with a sweat lodge. Would this passage accomplish the purpose?

    F. Yes, because the passage tells about the process a person goes through in a sweat.
    G. Yes, because the passage explains how Dr. Lewis Mehl-Madrona feels about the ceremony.
    H. No, because only the last two paragraphs discuss what happens at a sweat lodge.
    J. No, because the passage describes general information about sweat lodge ceremonies, not one specific experience.

Part 2
ACT ENGLISH

Answers and Explanations

How Much Do You Know?

1. C
Difficulty: Medium
Category: Development: Precision
Getting to the Answer: This question tests precise word choice. The sentence says that the Kumeyaay have lived in southern California for millennia; moreover, the sentence that follows says they maintained "a rich cultural and social life," so the correct answer must reflect that. Choices A and B both incorrectly suggest a process or change, and D is the opposite of the author's meaning. Only (C) correctly expresses the intended meaning.

2. G
Difficulty: Low
Category: Conciseness
Getting to the Answer: *Crucially necessary* is redundant. Choices F and H both include these words in different forms, so eliminate them. Choice J includes a word with a similar meaning in context, *fundamentally*, so it is also redundant. Only (G) eliminates the redundancy.

3. B
Difficulty: Medium
Category: Development: Revising Text
Getting to the Answer: The underlined portion details the relationship between Eva Salazar and the Kumeyaay. Deleting this would take away a key detail explaining her ties to the native community whose traditions she carries on through her art. Choice (B) is correct. Since the underlined segment does not provide a counterargument, claim, or suggestion, A, C, and D are incorrect.

4. F
Difficulty: Medium
Category: Organization: Transitions
Getting to the Answer: Transitions must accurately convey the relationship between ideas. The underlined transition correctly shows a contrast between what Eva is primarily known for and her other artistic creations. Choice (F) is correct. Choice G is not a contrast transition. The contrast transitions in H and J both make the first clause independent rather than dependent, turning the sentence into a run-on. Since they introduce a grammatical error, they are incorrect.

5. C
Difficulty: High
Category: Development: Introductions and Conclusions
Getting to the Answer: The final sentence must effectively conclude both the passage and the paragraph. The passage discusses Eva Salazar's dedication to preserving Kumeyaay traditions. According to the final paragraph, she has done this through learning her craft and passing her knowledge on to other artists. Choice (C) conveys how she has kept basket-weaving traditions alive through her own work and through teaching others. You may hesitate to choose this answer because it is noticeably less concise than the other options, but sometimes a long sentence is needed to convey complex ideas. Always think carefully about what a question asks to make sure the answer fulfills it. Choices B and D are incorrect because both bring up ideas outside the scope of the passage; Salazar's fame or unique adaptations of traditional art are never discussed. Choice A is factually correct but not a good conclusion because it does not emphasize the preservation of Kumeyaay artistic traditions.

6. F
Difficulty: High
Category: Organization: Transitions
Getting to the Answer: An effective transition must show the relationship between the ideas it connects. The beginning of this paragraph introduces the popularity of natural medicine, particularly sweat lodges. The information that follows briefly mentions similar practices elsewhere but primarily discusses the health benefits of such practices. Choice G does not connect sweat lodges to health benefits, so eliminate it. Choice H does connect the two, but it also brings up the topic of resources, which is not mentioned in the paragraph at all. Choice J may be tempting because it neatly connects the popularity of sweat lodges to their health benefits. However, when plugged into the sentence, it creates a modifier error in which the phrase "including the Finnish sauna and the Turkish steam room" describes *participants* instead of *examples* of similar practices. Only (F) connects sweat lodges with similar practices and with health benefits.

Chapter 4
Spotting and Fixing Issues: Conciseness, Organization, and Development

7. D
Difficulty: Medium
Category: Organization: Sentence Placement
Getting to the Answer: Sentence 1 does not fit well where it is now, since it jumps right into the middle of an ongoing description with specific details that have not yet been discussed, like the fire and the entrance. The paragraph would be clearer and more logical if Sentence 1 were placed after those details have been introduced in Sentence 4. Thus, (D) is the correct answer.

8. J
Difficulty: Medium
Category: Development: Revising Text
Getting to the Answer: This question asks about how an author would emphasize the spiritual aspects of the sweat lodge. Choice H discusses purely practical concerns and can be quickly eliminated. Choices F and G do not make clear whether the preparations they describe have spiritual significance or not. Choice (J) is the only answer that explicitly states that an action is undertaken for ritual, symbolic reasons, so (J) is correct.

9. C
Difficulty: Low
Category: Conciseness
Getting to the Answer: Including both *also* and *as well* makes this phrase redundant. Choices A, B, and D all include similarly redundant transition words, so (C) is correct.

10. J
Difficulty: Medium
Category: Development: Purpose
Getting to the Answer: To answer this type of question, first determine the primary purpose of the passage. This passage describes the physical and spiritual elements of Native American sweat lodge traditions. If the author's goal were to focus on an individual's experience, this passage would not be successful. Eliminate F and G. Choice H gives an incorrect reason why the passage does not fulfill the author's goal. Only (J) correctly identifies that the passage does not succeed because it gives a general description rather than tells an individual's story.

Part 2
ACT ENGLISH

CONCISENESS

> **LEARNING OBJECTIVE**
>
> After this lesson, you will be able to:
> - Revise wordy writing

To answer a question like this

Sweat Lodges

Traditional Native American sweat lodges focus on both physical and spiritual healing. <u>Sometimes,</u> a sweat might include more than one session, each lasting 30 to 45 minutes and focused on one of four distinct themes: the spirit world, cleanliness and honesty, individual prayer, and growth and healing.

1. Which choice is least redundant in context?

    A. **No Change**
    B. More often,
    C. Occasionally,
    D. DELETE the underlined portion and capitalize the word *A*.

You need to know this

Conciseness

A concise sentence does not include any unnecessary words. An ACT test question may ask you to revise wordy phrasing. Each word must contribute to the meaning of the sentence; otherwise, it should be eliminated.

A *redundant* sentence says something twice: "The new policy precipitated a crisis situation." A crisis is a type of situation, so there is no need to include both *crisis* and *situation*. The sentence should be rephrased as, "The new policy precipitated a crisis." Redundancy is always incorrect on the ACT.

Wordy/Redundant sentence	Concise sentence
The superb musical score **added enhancement to the experience of** the play's development.	The superb musical score **enhanced** the play's development.
I **did not anticipate** the **surprising, unexpected** plot twist.	I **did not anticipate** the plot twist.
The students **increased some of their knowledge of** Tuscan architecture.	The students **learned about** Tuscan architecture.

Chapter 4
Spotting and Fixing Issues: Conciseness, Organization, and Development

You need to do this

Choose the most concise, grammatically correct option that conveys the writer's intended meaning. When answering questions about conciseness:

- Consider selecting the "DELETE the underlined portion" answer choice, if there is one, according to the following guidelines: If the underlined portion is wordy or redundant, delete it.
  - If the underlined portion does not enhance the intended meaning or clarity of the passage, delete it.
  - Each of the four answer choices is equally likely, so give the delete option the same weight as the others.
- Identify the shortest answer choice (it will not always be the correct answer, but it is an efficient place to start).
- Identify words and phrases that have the same meaning, e.g., *thoughtful* and *mindful* or *end result* and *final outcome*. Find a choice that deletes one of the redundant expressions.

Explanation

When "DELETE the underlined portion" is an option, check whether the underlined portion contributes to the meaning of the passage. Eliminate A because the word *might* already shows that multi-session sweats do not occur all the time. *More often* and *occasionally* introduce information about frequency that is not supported by the passage, so B and C are incorrect. Because none of the other answer choices adds to the meaning of the sentence, (D) is the correct answer.

Drills

If conciseness gives you trouble, study the information above and try out these drill questions before completing the Try on Your Own questions below. Drill answers can be found in Answers and Explanations.

Eliminate word(s) to make the sentences more concise without losing meaning.

a. The school was founded and established in 1906.

b. I felt a sense of nervous anxiety before the curtain rose.

c. We were in agreement with each other that Naomi should be captain.

d. After a job interview, make sure to send a note of gratitude expressing thanks to your interviewer.

e. Not long after he graduated from Oxford, Oscar Wilde moved to London, a place in which he embarked on his literary career in earnest.

Part 2
ACT ENGLISH

Try on Your Own

Directions: Take as much time as you need on these questions. Work carefully and methodically. There will be an opportunity for timed practice at the end of the chapter.

International Model United Nations

For many years, The Hague has been the stage of The European International Model United Nations (TEIMUN), which is a model of the United Nations.
                                              2
TEIMUN started in 1987, when a group of American students on an exchange program in the Netherlands organized the first conference as a part of their focus on international relations. The organizers hoped to educate participants about the workings of an international organization in order to combat a growing sense of
                                                    3
isolationism among European youth.
    3
There were many hurdles to overcome, for students' attitudes in Europe toward simulations of the United Nations were not favorable. Hence, drumming up interest was a struggle. The Americans also wanted to ensure that this new model UN would have a plan to
                  4
help students from less-developed European countries
              4
with their participation. Through the American students'
        4
hard work, TEIMUN prospered and attracted more participants. Over the years, the TEIMUN conference has become one of the biggest and most important model United Nations on the European continent, with participants from over 65 countries.

2. Which choice is least redundant in context?

   F. **No Change**
   G. being a model of the United Nations.
   H. which is a model UN.
   J. DELETE the underlined portion and change comma after *(TEIMUN)* to a period.

3. Which choice is least redundant in context?

   A. **No Change**
   B. the increasing and growing isolationism
   C. a growing feeling of isolationism and separation
   D. the increasing isolationism and sense of alienation

4. Which choice is least redundant in context?

   F. **No Change**
   G. their new model United Nations had systems in place to help students from less-developed European countries participate.
   H. there were rules built in to the system with the purpose of helping students from less-developed countries in their participation.
   J. there were methods for helping students from less-developed countries to participate.

Chapter 4
Spotting and Fixing Issues: Conciseness, Organization, and Development

STYLE AND TONE

LEARNING OBJECTIVE
After this lesson, you will be able to:
- Identify which choice most effectively matches a text's style and maintains its tone.

To answer a question like this

The Odyssey

In Homer's epic poem, *The Odyssey*, the protagonist, Odysseus, undertakes a torturous journey home after ten years of fighting the Trojan War. He and his crew encounter numerous perils along their voyage. The adventures of Odysseus <u>explore themes</u> of wandering,
1
homecoming, and the host-guest relationship.

1. Which choice most closely maintains the stylistic pattern established in the preceding two sentences?

   A. **No Change**
   B. take a crack at ideas
   C. dabble with themes
   D. play around with concepts

You need to know this

Style and Tone

When authors write a text, they intend to make a particular point. Their word choice and their writing style help to convey that point to the reader. Every sentence contributes to that goal. Any sentence that undermines that goal should be rephrased.

Style is the way an individual author expresses an idea. Sometimes, a single word might be the only clue needed to keep a consistent style, such as when an author sprinkles their writing with descriptors that evoke strong images in the reader's mind. *Tone* can be thought of as the author's voice. Is the author conveying a casual vibe, like a friend talking to you over lunch? Or are they aiming for a formal, scholarly feeling?

The intersection between style and tone defines this lesson. For example, two scholarly texts might use different styles to express their ideas. One might be dryly worded, expressing facts without judgment. Another text might use moralistic language while educating the reader. Remember, Style and Tone questions require the reader to closely read the text to pay attention to word choice and context clues.

Part 2
ACT ENGLISH

Clashing Style and Tone	Consistent Style and Tone
Remaining neutral is sometimes incorrect. *Impartiality does not mean neutrality. Impartial justice consists not in being neutral between right and wrong, but in finding out the right and virtuously upholding it, wherever found, against the wrong.*	***It is a wicked thing to be neutral between right and wrong.*** *Impartiality does not mean neutrality. Impartial justice consists not in being neutral between right and wrong, but in finding out the right and virtuously upholding it, wherever found, against the wrong.*
We may now picture this great Fleet, with its flotillas and cruisers, **leaving** *Portland Harbour, squadron by squadron, scores of gigantic castles of steel wending their way across the misty, shining sea, like giants bowed in anxious thought.*	*We may now picture this great Fleet, with its flotillas and cruisers,* **steaming slowly out of** *Portland Harbour, squadron by squadron, scores of gigantic castles of steel wending their way across the misty, shining sea, like giants bowed in anxious thought.*

You need to do this

Choose the option that conveys the author's intended meaning. When answering questions about Style and Tone:

- Determine the author's goal with their writing. For instance, are they trying to entertain or to educate the reader?
- Pay attention to the author's word choice. Is there a trend in the type of words they are using? For example, colorful descriptors, positive language, or even just concise phrasing with no embellishments could indicate the style of the author.
- If you are ever unsure of what the author intended, then reread the two sentences preceding the sentence with the Style and Tone question. Ask yourself what trends you notice in the text.

Explanation

If the question stem asks you which choice "most closely maintains the stylistic pattern," then it is a Style and Tone question. As you read the passage, pay attention to the word choice. If you are unsure of what the author intended, then carefully review the two sentences preceding the sentence with the Style and Tone question. Try to paraphrase what the author intends in your own words, then review the answer choices and eliminate as you go. In this passage, the author intends a scholarly tone. Choice (A) is the best option, as the existing text fits the rest of the passage; B, C, D are all too casual in tone.

Try on Your Own

Directions: Take as much time as you need on these questions. Work carefully and methodically. There will be an opportunity for timed practice at the end of the chapter.

The Long Voyage of Oguri Jukichi

Oguri Jukichi (1785–1853) wrote one of the most harrowing tales of a ship adrift at sea. On November 4th, 1813, the merchant vessel he was aboard, the *Tokujomaru*, sailed for Edo (modern-day Tokyo). However, that day a terrible storm came upon the ship, washing one sailor overboard. The wind was so terrible that even lowering their sail was insufficient, and the crew decided to chop down their own mast. They also dropped anchor to avoid being pulled out to sea, but the seafloor was further down than their 1,800-foot rope. Once the storm passed, the *Tokujomaru* was damaged and adrift.

Because she was a merchant vessel, the *Tokujomaru* carried a hefty cargo of rice, soybeans, and oil. The rice and soybeans fed the hungry crew as they drifted aimlessly on the open ocean. However, a lack of fresh water created a punishing thirst. Jukichi realized they could use their cargo of oil to boil seawater underneath an overturned cauldron, providing water. To improve morale, Jukichi led the beleaguered crew in 10,000 recitations to the Buddha every day. Sharks swarmed the boat, and the fearful men fended them off with boiling water. However, after 484 days at sea, scurvy had afflicted the crew, and only three men survived.

Finally, another ship finally came across it, the American merchant ship *Forester*. The *Tokujomaru* had undertaken a delightful adventure, ending up some 300 miles off the California coastline, near modern-day Santa Barbara County. Jukichi and the two other survivors eventually made their way back to Japan, where Jukichi wrote about the ordeal.

2. Which choice most closely maintains the stylistic pattern established in the preceding two sentences?

F. **No Change**
G. resorted to chopping down
H. went ahead and chopped down
J. did something to

3. Which choice most effectively maintains the essay's tone?

A. **No Change**
B. gathering the dihydrogen monoxide that ran down
C. collecting the condensation that dripped down
D. offering sweet relief from dehydration

4. Which choice most effectively maintains the essay's tone?

F. **No Change**
G. finally made its long-delayed landfall
H. drifted across the Pacific Ocean
J. traveled for some time

ORGANIZATION: TRANSITIONS

LEARNING OBJECTIVES

After this lesson, you will be able to:

- Determine the appropriate transition word or phrase to establish logical relationships within and between sentences
- Determine the appropriate transition sentence to establish logical relationships between paragraphs

To answer a question like this

International Model United Nations

Students still direct and organize each yearly conference. They seek new ways to attract enthusiastic participants, <u>since students from less-developed nations are still underrepresented.</u> Countless alumni have gone on to pursue careers in international policy after first encountering the art of diplomacy during their years in TEIMUN.

1. Which choice most effectively leads the reader from the first sentence of this paragraph to the information that follows in the rest of the paragraph?

   A. **No Change**
   B. and they strongly believe that TEIMUN is a powerful avenue for fostering an interest in diplomacy among Europe's youth.
   C. even working to expand recruitment outside of Europe.
   D. and they closely follow the policies of individual countries as well as international relations in order to keep the conference up to date.

You need to know this

Writers use transitions to show relationships such as contrast, cause and effect, continuation, emphasis, and chronology (order of events). Knowing which words indicate which type of transition will help you choose the correct answer on test day.

Contrast transitions	Cause-and-effect transitions	Continuation transitions	Emphasis transitions	Chronology transitions
although, but, despite, even though, however, in contrast, nonetheless, on the other hand, rather than, though, unlike, while, yet	as a result, because, consequently, since, so, therefore, thus	also, furthermore, in addition, moreover	certainly, in fact, indeed, that is	before, after, first (second, etc.), then, finally

Chapter 4
Spotting and Fixing Issues: Conciseness, Organization, and Development

You need to do this
If a transition word is underlined, you must determine the writer's intended meaning and find the transition that best conveys this meaning. Use the surrounding text to pinpoint the appropriate word.

Explanation
The underlined portion needs to connect the beginning of the paragraph, which discusses student organizers recruiting participants, with the last sentence, which discusses TEIMUN alumni inspired to pursue diplomatic careers. The only answer choice that does so effectively is (B).

Drills
If transitions give you trouble, study the information above and try out these drill questions before completing the Try on Your Own questions below. Drill answers can be found in Answers and Explanations.

Choose the correct transition word for each sentence.

a. (Due to/Despite) its impressive technical innovations, the small start-up thrived.

b. Cashew nuts are a popular snack worldwide; (however/moreover), they can be difficult to harvest because their shells contain a toxic resin.

c. Izdehar is the most level-headed of my friends—(in fact/next), I think she's more reliable than some adults I know.

d. After days of hard work, we (finally/nonetheless) finished our science fair project.

e. The actor won an award for best supporting role this year (consequently/in addition to) releasing her first pop music album.

Try on Your Own
Directions: Take as much time as you need on these questions. Work carefully and methodically. There will be an opportunity for timed practice at the end of the chapter.

The Victorian Way of Life

The Victorian Era stretched from the coronation of Queen Victoria in 1837 to her death in 1901. Over her 63-year reign, her influence on Britain was profound. Politics and international affairs aside, manners, morals, and even dress conformed to Victoria's straightlaced concepts of what was and was not acceptable. Despite² the upper classes, propriety and reputation had to be spotlessly maintained.

2. Which transition word or phrase is most logical in context?

  F. No Change
  G. Especially for
  H. Regardless of
  J. Occasionally among

[3] In the 1840s, women's dresses were relatively simple, albeit with a number of stiff petticoats. Thirty years later, restricting corsets were worn to pull in the waist to the smallest width possible while still leaving the wearer room to breathe. Hats and gloves were expected for all occasions.

Most upper-class women were educated only to the point of literacy, with household management and domestic arts such as needlework heavily emphasized. Because of this, some women were quite well schooled, depending on their fathers' opinion about the propriety of educated females. Queen Victoria herself, unsurprisingly, fell on the more educated end of the spectrum; she spoke multiple languages and studied law and ethics as a teenager. However, her favorite subject was history.

It is a mark of the length, importance, and impact of Queen Victoria's reign that this period of British history is known as the Victorian Era. She left her indelible mark not only on society and culture but also on British influence throughout the world.

3. Given that all the choices are accurate, which one provides the most effective transition from the previous paragraph to this paragraph?

A. Victoria believed modesty was particularly important for women.
B. Lower classes were less constrained.
C. Fashion styles were among the prescribed customs.
D. The period's fashion innovations remain famous to this day.

4. Which transition word or phrase, if any, is most logical in context?

F. **No Change**
G. rather than
H. therefore
J. **Delete** the underlined portion.

5. Which transition word or phrase is most logical in context?

A. **No Change**
B. Therefore,
C. Indeed,
D. On the other hand,

6. Given that all the choices are accurate, which one provides the best transition from the information in this paragraph to the information in the next paragraph?

F. **No Change**
G. This background both prepared her to be a world leader and influenced her royal policy.
H. Her governess and varied tutors found her a bright but willful student.
J. In fact, she was better educated than many of her prime ministers.

ORGANIZATION: SENTENCE PLACEMENT

LEARNING OBJECTIVE

After this lesson, you will be able to:
- Determine the most logical place for a sentence in a paragraph or passage

To answer a question like this

Symbiotic Relationships

In the natural world, when two or more different organisms coexist, they are involved in a symbiotic relationship. Sometimes these relationships are beneficial to both organisms; other times, these relationships are beneficial to only one organism and either have no effect or are harmful to the other organism. When both organisms benefit, their relationship is known as mutualism.

[1] A classic symbiotic relationship of this kind takes place in the digestive tract of Florida wood-eating termites. [2] The protozoa provide the termite with a service necessary to its survival: they digest the cellulose in the wood that the termite consumes. [3] We think of a termite as being able to digest wood, but, in fact, it cannot. [4] The termite plays host to the protozoa, single-celled organisms that live in the termite's gut. 1

1. For the sake of logic and cohesion, Sentence 2 should be placed:

   A. where it is now.
   B. before Sentence 1.
   C. after Sentence 3.
   D. after Sentence 4.

Part 2
ACT ENGLISH

You need to know this
Some Organization questions will ask you to check and potentially fix the placement of a sentence within a paragraph. Others will ask you for the best place to insert a new sentence. Your approach in both cases should be the same.

You need to do this
Look for specific clues that indicate the best organization. Common clues include:

- Chronology: If the information is presented in order by the time when it occurred, place the sentence within the correct time frame.
- Explanation of a term or phrase: If the passage features a term, such as nuclear fusion, the writer will explain what it is (in this case, the joining of two or more nuclei to form a heavier nucleus) before using the term in other contexts.
- Introduction of a person: If the passage introduces someone, such as Grace Hopper, the writer will first refer to the person by first and last name before referring to the person by either first name (Grace) or last name (Hopper) only.
- Examples: A general statement is often followed by support in the form of examples.
- Logic: Transition words such as "however," "also," "furthermore," and "therefore" may signal the logic of the paragraph. For example, the word "therefore" indicates that a conclusion is being drawn from evidence that should logically come before it.

Explanation
Sentence 2 discusses the function of the protozoa, but the protozoa haven't yet been introduced in the paragraph. Sentence 2 must be moved to follow the sentence that introduces the protozoa, which is Sentence 4. Choice (D) is correct.

Try on Your Own
Directions: Take as much time as you need on these questions. Work carefully and methodically. There will be an opportunity for timed practice at the end of the chapter.

Symbiotic Relationships

[1]

In the natural world, when two or more different organisms coexist, they are involved in a symbiotic relationship. Sometimes these relationships are beneficial to both organisms; other times, these relationships are beneficial to only one organism and either have no effect or are harmful to the other organism. [A] When both organisms benefit, their relationship is known as mutualism.

Chapter 4
Spotting and Fixing Issues: Conciseness, Organization, and Development

[2]

A classic symbiotic relationship of this kind takes place in the digestive tract of Florida wood-eating termites. We think of a termite as being able to digest wood, but, in fact, it cannot. The termite plays host to the protozoa, single-celled organisms that live in the termite's gut. The protozoa provide the termite with a service necessary to its survival: they digest the cellulose in the wood that the termite consumes.

[3]

That is far from the whole story, however. The only movement that protozoa are capable of on their own is spinning; they cannot move around inside the termite's intestine to reach the cellulose. This problem is solved by a third member of the partnership. [B] Each protozoan harbors a colony of thousands of bacteria attached to its surface. Whip-like tentacles on the bacteria (known as flagella) wave back and forth and propel each host protozoan forward. [C]

[4]

These bacteria may do more than just drive the protozoan around. Some bacteria can be found inside the protozoan and are thought to help with the digestion of tiny wood particles. [D] If this all sounds strange, consider the fact that humans have symbiotic relationships with bacteria of their own. [2]

> Question 2 asks about the passage as a whole.

2. The writer would like to add the following sentence to the essay:

   > This allows the protozoan to move around and to continue consuming cellulose within the termite.

   The sentence would most logically be placed at:

   F. Point A in Paragraph 1.
   G. Point B in Paragraph 3.
   H. Point C in Paragraph 3.
   J. Point D in Paragraph 4.

Early 19th-Century Women in New England

[1]

In the early 19th century, the market economy expanded, and the home became a haven from the developing commercialism. [A] With men working in factories, women were responsible for housekeeping, providing religious education, and raising children.

[2]

[B] In addition to running their households, women also had opportunities for wage work. This included producing goods, such as palm-leaf hats and straw-braided items, for wider consumption. [C] Wage work provided women with the ability to live at home while earning money to supplement the family's income. [D]

[3]

[1] Shoemaking was another source of income for women, but their work was socially and physically isolated from the shoe binding that took place in cobblers' shops. [2] However, when increased demand for shoes required the use of sewing machines to speed up the pace of production, women organized a small-scale movement that trained young women to use sewing machines in their homes. [3] Despite this move, women who worked at home as shoe binders remained isolated and vulnerable to competition from the more lucrative and efficient factories. [4] Women were also denied craft status and admission into unions, which limited their influence. 3

3. For the sake of logic and cohesion, Sentence 4 should be placed:

   A. where it is now.
   B. before Sentence 1.
   C. before Sentence 2.
   D. before Sentence 3.

[4]

[F] Women who worked in factories were also prohibited from joining unions, allowing factories such as the Lowell Mills to exploit their labor. [G] However, female factory workers were offered a type of work outside of the home and away from their families, which provided them with a new level of independence. [H]

[5]

For many women, the changes in women's roles during the first half of the 19th century were part of a positive and liberating transformation. [J] For others, though, either their roles remained quite traditional, or their new endeavors, such as working in factories, were not as freeing as they had hoped. Women's experiences with and reactions to the changes they encountered varied, but many were eager for the journey ahead.

[6]

[1] Women helped move the economy of the United States away from agriculture and towards manufacturing. [2] Women seeking their own forms of employment outside the house disrupted this model and paved the way for the diverse economy that we enjoy today. [3] Prior to woman taking an active role in the workforce, households were seen as an indivisible economic unit. [6]

Questions 4–5 ask about the preceding passage as a whole.

4. The writer wants to add the following sentence to the essay:

    During this time, middle-class wives and mothers in New England assumed the role of protectors and leaders of home life.

   The sentence would most logically be placed at:

   F. Point A in Paragraph 1.
   G. Point B in Paragraph 2.
   H. Point C in Paragraph 2.
   J. Point D in Paragraph 2.

5. The writer wants to add the following sentence to the essay:

    For example, they were paid half the wages given to men.

   The sentence would most logically be placed at:

   A. Point F in Paragraph 4.
   B. Point G in Paragraph 4.
   C. Point H in Paragraph 4.
   D. Point J in Paragraph 5.

6. Which sequence of sentences makes this paragraph most logical?

   F. **No Change**
   G. 1, 3, 2
   H. 3, 1, 2
   J. 3, 2, 1

Part 2
ACT ENGLISH

DEVELOPMENT: PRECISION

LEARNING OBJECTIVE

After this lesson, you will be able to:

- Identify the word or clause that accomplishes the appropriate purpose within a sentence

To answer a question like this

Humphrey Bogart

Although the screen appeal of Humphrey Bogart has grown immeasurably since his death in 1957, his early life was not filled with success. Born in New York City in 1899 as the son of a prominent surgeon, young Humphrey was quickly put on the track to medical school. After finishing his early schooling, he went to the prestigious Phillips Academy. Bogart, however, was not academically inclined, and during adolescence he was often described as a troublemaker. In 1918, Bogart entered the navy. It was during the service when he received an injury that partially paralyzed his upper lip, creating his <u>splendid</u> snarl.
1

1. Which choice best illustrates how the injury noticeably marked Bogart's appearance?

   A. **No Change**
   B. outrageous
   C. distinctive
   D. insignificant

Chapter 4
Spotting and Fixing Issues: Conciseness, Organization, and Development

You need to know this
Some questions test your knowledge of the correct word to use in context. You must identify which word(s) best convey the writer's intended meaning.

Incorrect	Correct
The initial reason the students gather in the auditorium is that it is the only location large enough for all of them.	The primary reason the students gather in the auditorium is that it is the only location large enough for all of them.
It is common for children to perform the actions of their parents.	It is common for children to mimic the actions of their parents.
Zeke apologized for overstepping when he walked into the crowded conference room.	Zeke apologized for intruding when he walked into the crowded conference room.

You need to do this
Read the surrounding text to deduce the author's intended meaning. Then evaluate all four answer choices. Eliminate the answer choices that:

- Create grammatical errors
- Do not make sense in context
- Do not convey the writer's intended meaning

If one or more of the words among the answer choices is unfamiliar, process of elimination can still help you get to the correct answer. If you recognize any of the options, decide whether to keep or eliminate them. For the words that remain, use roots, prefixes and suffixes, and word charge (whether a word feels positive, negative, or neutral) to make your decision. If all else fails, trust your instincts and guess; never leave a question blank.

Explanation
The question asks for a word that approximately means *noticeably marked*. Choice D is the exact opposite, and A and B are too strongly charged—*splendid* has a strong positive charge and *outrageous* has a strong negative charge. Choice (C) is correct.

Try on Your Own
Directions: Take as much time as you need on these questions. Work carefully and methodically. There will be an opportunity for timed practice at the end of the chapter.

The History of Advertising

Over the past few decades, advertising has changed radically. In the 1990s, large companies hoped to reach their target markets through advertisements in national magazines and network television, while smaller companies <u>promoted</u> local newspapers, phone books, and radio stations. Of course, companies large and small still buy advertisements in mass media outlets that reach large numbers of consumers. However, with a new

2. Which choice is clearest and most precise in context?

   F. **No Change**
   G. appropriated
   H. utilized
   J. manipulated

97

millennium came new competitors, including a larger media outlet than previously imagined: the internet.

3. Which choice best conveys the opportunity presented by the internet?
   A. No Change
   B. circumstances,
   C. occurrences,
   D. possibilities,

Thomas Paine

As a young man, Paine worked as a corsetmaker, sailor, and minister, but he only found his true calling when he moved to the British colonies in America. Paine first gained recognition as the editor of *Pennsylvania Magazine*, and as political turmoil engulfed the colonies, he became more vocal. In 1776, Paine anonymously published a pamphlet titled "Common Sense" that argued forcefully for American independence from Britain. The pamphlet was tremendously popular; soon there were 200,000 copies in circulation. Many historians credit the pamphlet with helping to convince the American people to fight for self-rule.

Thomas Paine's influence continued far beyond sparking the Revolutionary War. Once the war began, Paine published a series of pamphlets called *The American Crisis*, which, in the midst of a bloody war, helped keep the morale of the troops up. In addition to his achievements as a writer, Thomas Paine is credited with conceiving the name "The United States of America."

4. Which choice best specifies Paine's increased fame?
   F. No Change
   G. prominent.
   H. understandable.
   J. divisive.

5. Which choice is clearest and most precise in context?
   A. No Change
   B. tasked
   C. helped
   D. noted

Because Thomas Paine was a writer, Thomas Jefferson and John Adams drew heavily on his work when drafting the Declaration of Independence. Later in life, Paine wrote other highly controversial works. In 1797, Paine did his part to inspire what would become Social Security. He suggested a system of social insurance for the young and the elderly in his last great work, "Agrarian Justice."

6. Which choice best portrays Paine positively and describes why Jefferson and Adams used his work?

F. an extremely talented writer,
G. the best writer in the colonies,
H. an adequate author,
J. an author of controversial content,

DEVELOPMENT: INTRODUCTIONS AND CONCLUSIONS

LEARNING OBJECTIVE

After this lesson, you will be able to:
- Provide an introduction or conclusion to a paragraph or passage

To answer a question like this

Early Writing Careers

Many well-known writers began their careers while they were still teenagers. Stephen King, for example, began submitting stories to science fiction magazines when he was just thirteen years old. If you are serious about a writing career, you can submit work to many publications that accept unsolicited manuscripts. It is best, however, to send a query letter first.

A query letter is a one-page document in which you introduce yourself to the editors of the publication and ask if they would like to read your work. Begin by telling the editor a little bit about yourself. Include a paragraph or two outlining the story you've written or would like to write. If you've taken any creative writing courses, won prizes for your writing, or had any work published, tell the editor about that too. Don't forget to thank the editor for taking the time to read your letter.

Part 2
ACT ENGLISH

You probably won't sell your first story, but don't get discouraged. Stephen King didn't sell his first submission either—or dozens after that. <u>Nevertheless, he persisted, and he became a best-selling author.</u>
                                            1

1. Which choice best concludes the essay?

    A. **No Change**
    B. Eventually, he found an editor who liked his work, and the rest is history.
    C. Despite that, he didn't give up, and neither should you.
    D. Being a professional writer is a difficult career to break into.

You need to know this

Some questions ask you to improve the beginning or ending of a paragraph or passage.

- An introduction should:
    - Explain the topic and purpose of a paragraph
    - Include information discussed later in the paragraph
    - When applicable, provide an appropriate transition from the previous paragraph or into the next paragraph
- A conclusion should:
    - Summarize the topic and purpose of a paragraph/passage
    - Include information discussed earlier in the paragraph/passage
    - When applicable, provide an appropriate transition from the previous paragraph or into the next paragraph

Introduction and conclusion questions are not testing conciseness, even if they ask about deleting information. *Focus on relevance rather than conciseness.* You can save time by identifying the relevant choice without spending time considering the grammar of each choice.

You need to do this

- Determine the writer's intended purpose for the paragraph or essay as a whole.
- Read before and/or after the underlined segment, noting key transition words.
- Eliminate choices that do not provide an appropriate introduction or conclusion.
- For a question about the conclusion to the passage, eliminate choices that focus too much on the final paragraph and not enough on the passage as a whole or too much on the passage as a whole and not enough on the final paragraph.
- Choose the most relevant option.

Explanation

This passage focuses on advising and encouraging aspiring young writers. The last paragraph in particular discusses the importance of not giving up and cites the example of Stephen King. Choice (C) is correct because it references both ideas and ties them together. Choice A may be tempting, but it is incorrect because it refers only to Stephen King. It does not address young writers in general.

Chapter 4
Spotting and Fixing Issues: Conciseness, Organization, and Development

Try on Your Own

Directions: Take as much time as you need on these questions. Work carefully and methodically. There will be an opportunity for timed practice at the end of the chapter.

Community-Supported Agriculture

This spring, my family joined our local community-supported agriculture, or CSA, association. We wanted to eat more locally grown foods, and the CSA provided the perfect opportunity. Like other members, we bought a year's "share" of the farm's crop before the growing season began. Once it did, the farm delivered a box filled with freshly harvested fruits and vegetables every week.

We immediately discovered that fresh, in-season food is delicious. I had disliked broccoli previously, but one bunch that arrived in our second June box convinced me I'd been wrong. My younger brother, who is normally resistant to new foods, ventured to try both kale and turnips from the CSA and enjoyed both. <u>Of the four people in my family, my mother is definitely the most accomplished cook.</u>
                                          2

2. Given that all the choices are true, which one provides a conclusion to this paragraph that is most consistent with the other information in the paragraph?

   F. **No Change**
   G. Prior to our experience with the CSA, the most exotic vegetable he would willingly eat was a carrot—and only the orange kind.
   H. The cardboard boxes are recycled each week, and the CSA even provides composting services on-site.
   J. We pick up our vegetables every Thursday afternoon.

Furthermore, we've been vexed by the outlandish number of zucchini in our boxes. Each week in July, we received at least six. At first, we just grilled the zucchini. Then, we sautéed it with pasta. By the third week, when we opened our box to find ten more zucchini, we had to get inventive. We experimented with recipes for zucchini soup, casserole, bread, pizza, and even brownies. Though everything was tasty, we're all anticipating the end of zucchini season with relief. Of course, by then tomato season will have begun, and we'll be looking for ways to prepare a new vegetable deluge. I foresee more delicious experiments in the future.

3. Given that all the choices are accurate, which one best helps the sentence introduce the main focus of the paragraph?

A. **No Change**
B. We have, however, found a minor flaw in the CSA boxes: a profusion of zucchini.
C. The CSA has also encouraged creative cooking with unfamiliar produce.
D. Not all of the produce we've received has been good, however.

Early 19th-Century Women in New England

In the early 19th century, the market economy expanded, and the home became a haven from the developing commercialism. During this time, middle-class wives and mothers in New England assumed the role of protectors and leaders of home life. With men working in factories, women were responsible for housekeeping, providing religious education, and raising children.

In addition to running their households, women became deeply involved in the labor movements of the time. This included producing goods, such as palm-leaf hats and straw-braided items, for wider consumption. Wage work provided women with the ability to live at home while earning money to supplement the family's income.

4. Given that all the choices are accurate, which one best helps the sentence introduce the main focus of the paragraph?

F. **No Change**
G. women became some of the most important contributors to the industrial age.
H. women grew increasingly involved in politics.
J. women also had opportunities for wage work.

Shoemaking was another source of income for women, but their work was socially and physically isolated from the shoe binding that took place in cobblers' shops. However, when increased demand for shoes required the use of sewing machines to speed up the pace of production, women organized a small-scale movement that trained young women to use sewing machines in their homes. Despite this move, women who worked at home as shoe binders remained isolated and vulnerable to competition from the more lucrative and efficient factories. Women were also denied craft status and admission into unions, which limited their influence.

Francis Cabot Lowell employed women in a new kind of factory, where they were also prohibited from joining unions. This allowed factories such as the Lowell Mills to exploit women's labor. For example, they were usually paid half the wages given to men. However, female factory workers were offered a type of work outside of the home and away from their families, which provided them with a new level of independence.

For many women, the changes in women's roles during the first half of the 19th century were a part of a positive and liberating transformation. For others, though, either their roles remained quite traditional, or their new endeavors, such as working in factories, were not as freeing as they had hoped. Women's experiences with and reactions to the changes they encountered varied, but many were eager for the journey ahead.

5. Which of the following statements would best build on the ideas presented in this essay to introduce this paragraph?

A. **No Change**
B. A similar tension marked women's employment in factories,
C. Women attempted to reform laws governing factories,
D. Some women abandoned their responsibilities at home for jobs in factories,

6. Which of the following provides the best conclusion to the essay?

F. **No Change**
G. Unfortunately, discrimination and unfair work practices continue to plague women in the workplace to this day.
H. Decades passed before the societal changes of the 19th century were widely accepted.
J. This divide led to an alienation that plagued the women's movement of New England throughout the 19th and 20th centuries.

Part 2
ACT ENGLISH

DEVELOPMENT: REVISING TEXT

LEARNING OBJECTIVES

After this lesson, you will be able to:

- Revise a sentence to accomplish a specific purpose
- Determine the relevance of a sentence within a passage

To answer a question like this

Humphrey Bogart

When Bogart was released from the navy in 1920, he turned his attention toward the theater. A family friend in the business hired him to work in a theater office in New York. Bogart eventually became a stage manager and finally procured some minor roles on the stage. His inexperience showed, however, and he struggled to find any substantive parts. In the early 1930s, Bogart set out for Hollywood, and although he quickly signed a contract with Fox Pictures, he appeared, marginally, in only three films.

1. If the writer were to delete the underlined portion (adjusting capitalization as necessary), the sentence would primarily lose:

   A. details about Bogart's success.
   B. a warning against changing careers.
   C. an example illustrating Bogart's lack of expertise.
   D. a reason for Bogart's slow start in the theater.

You need to know this

Some Development questions focus on revising text in a way that affects the meaning of the passage. Most questions with this focus ask you to select the choice that:

- Accomplishes a unique, specified goal,
- Describes what would be lost if the underlined segment were deleted, or
- States why a sentence should or should not be added or deleted.

For these questions, all of the answer choices are grammatically and stylistically correct. Given this fact, your task is to determine which option provides information that is most pertinent to the passage. The correct choice will relate directly to the surrounding text and could serve as support for a point, a transition to a new idea, or some other purpose.

Chapter 4
Spotting and Fixing Issues: Conciseness, Organization, and Development

You need to do this

When a Development question focuses on revising text in a meaningful way, you should always consider both what information the question stem and/or underlined segment provides and whether that information (a) matches the writer's focus and (b) helps express the purpose of the sentence or paragraph. Then, refine your approach:

- When a question asks you which choice accomplishes a unique, specified goal, eliminate incorrect choices that do not accomplish this goal and confirm the correct choice using the passage. Incorrect choices:
  - Mention information that is beyond the scope of the writer's discussion,
  - Do not relate to the surrounding text, or
  - Do not help express the purpose of the sentence or paragraph.
- When a question describes what would be lost if the underlined segment were deleted, treat it like a Reading question: evaluate the passage and the underlined segment and predict the answer.
- When the answer choices state why a sentence should or should not be added or deleted, decide whether the answer should include Yes or No and eliminate the two choices that don't match; then, use the passage to determine the correct reasoning.

Be sure to plug the proposed revisions back into the passage and read the full sentence (or paragraph) to best assess the change in context.

Explanation

When asked what would be lost if a phrase were deleted, consider what the phrase adds to the surrounding text. The second half of the sentence says that Bogart "struggled to find any substantive parts," and the underlined portion supports that claim by citing his inexperience. Eliminate A because the underlined portion is about Bogart's early struggles rather than his success. Eliminate B because the paragraph describes Bogart's life without giving any advice to the reader. Choice C is incorrect because the underlined portion does not provide a specific example of Bogart's inexperience. Only (D) correctly characterizes the underlined portion and its relationship to the rest of the sentence.

Try on Your Own

Directions: Take as much time as you need on these questions. Work carefully and methodically. There will be an opportunity for timed practice at the end of the chapter.

Community Supported Agriculture

This spring, my family joined our local community-supported agriculture, or CSA, association. We wanted to eat more healthy foods, and the CSA provided the perfect opportunity. Like other members, we bought a year's "share" of the farm's crop before the growing season began. Once it did, the farm delivered a box filled with freshly harvested fruits and vegetables every week.

2. The writer wants to emphasize how the family's goal connects to their decision to join the CSA. Which choice best accomplishes the writer's goal?

   F. No Change
   G. more fruits and vegetables,
   H. more locally grown foods,
   J. more unfamiliar fruits and vegetables,

[3] We immediately discovered that fresh, in-season food is delicious. I had disliked broccoli previously, but one bunch that arrived in our second June box convinced me I'd been wrong. My younger brother, who showed little interest in the CSA at first, ventured to try both kale and turnips from the CSA and enjoyed both. Prior to our experience with the CSA, the most exotic vegetable he would willingly eat was a carrot—and only the orange kind.

The History of Advertising

Over the past few decades, advertising has changed radically. In the 1990s, large companies hoped to reach their target markets through advertisements in national magazines and network television, while smaller companies utilized local newspapers, phone books, and radio stations. Of course, companies large and small still buy advertisements in mass media outlets that reach large numbers of consumers. However, with a new millennium came new possibilities, including a larger media outlet than previously imagined: the internet.

3. At this point, the writer is considering dividing the paragraph into two. Should the writer begin a new paragraph here?

A. Yes, because doing so would separate the family's decision to join the CSA from the CSA's impact on the family.
B. Yes, because doing so would allow the author to contrast the family's goal with their actual experience with the CSA.
C. No, because doing so would disconnect details that support the same main point.
D. No, because doing so would make the resulting paragraphs too brief without reason.

4. Given that all the choices are accurate, which one most effectively supports the paragraph's main point by showing a contrast with the information that follows in the sentence?

F. **No Change**
G. who is usually the most adventurous member of the family,
H. who has never met a food he wasn't curious about,
J. who is normally resistant to new foods,

5. If the writer were to delete the underlined portion (adjusting the punctuation as needed), the sentence would primarily lose:

A. a connection between the advertising methods of small and large companies.
B. information about how companies can differ in size.
C. a description of what makes a company large or small.
D. a contrast between the advertising budgets of small and large companies.

Chapter 4
Spotting and Fixing Issues: Conciseness, Organization, and Development

The internet allowed businesses to use targeted advertising, including company websites, banner advertisements, and ads generated by search engines, to reach more specific audiences. Small, local businesses in particular benefited greatly from these new marketing opportunities. [6]

Thomas Paine

Compared to most of America's other Founding Fathers, Thomas Paine is not nearly as well known. In fact, there are many Americans who have either never even heard of him or cannot recall his significance in history. [7] Paine was born in 1737 as the son of a corsetmaker—a tailor specializing in corsets and other undergarments—and grew up in rural Thetford, England.

As a young man, Paine worked as a corsetmaker, sailor and minister, but he only found his true calling when he moved to the British colonies in America. Paine first gained recognition as the editor of *Pennsylvania Magazine*, and as political turmoil engulfed the colonies, he became more prominent. In 1776, Paine anonymously published a pamphlet titled "Common Sense" that argued forcefully for American independence from Britain. The pamphlet's popularity spread like

6. The writer is considering adding the following accurate sentence:

   Small specialty shops were once relatively limited to serving local populations of customers, but today those same shops can have customers from around the world.

   Should the writer make this addition here?

   F. Yes, because it clarifies the kind of advertising being discussed.
   G. Yes, because it explains why small businesses benefited from internet advertising.
   H. No, because it does not explain why small shops should use internet advertising.
   J. No, because it is unnecessarily specific.

7. If the writer were to delete the preceding sentence, the paragraph would primarily lose:

   A. an explanation for Paine's relative obscurity.
   B. a statement supporting and elaborating on the previous sentence.
   C. a claim the writer will prove in the rest of the paragraph.
   D. an expression of the writer's disappointment in Americans' ignorance.

wildfire; soon there were 200,000 copies in circulation. Many historians credit the pamphlet with helping to convince the American people to fight for self-rule. [8]

Thomas Paine's influence continued far beyond sparking the Revolutionary War. Once the war began, Paine published a series of pamphlets called *The American Crisis*, which, in the midst of a bloody war, helped keep the morale of the troops up. In addition to his achievements as a writer, Thomas Paine is credited with conceiving the name "The United States of America." Because Thomas Paine was an extremely talented writer, Thomas Jefferson and John Adams drew heavily on his work when drafting the Declaration of Independence. Later in life, Paine wrote other highly controversial works. He was even exiled from England and imprisoned in France for his writings. In 1797, Paine did his part to inspire what would become Social Security. He suggested a system of social insurance for the young and the elderly in his last great work, "Agrarian Justice."

8. The writer is considering deleting the preceding sentence. Should the sentence be kept or deleted?

F. Kept, because it offers a detail that demonstrates the impact of Paine's writings.
G. Kept, because it includes evidence that conflicts with information presented earlier in the passage.
H. Deleted, because it presents a description of the contents of Paine's pamphlet.
J. Deleted, because it is an elaboration of Paine's goals in writing "Common Sense."

Early 19th-Century Women in New England

In addition to running their households, women also had opportunities for wage work. This included producing goods, such as palm-leaf hats and straw-braided items, for wider consumption. Wage work provided women with the ability to live at home while earning money to supplement the family's income.

Chapter 4
Spotting and Fixing Issues: Conciseness, Organization, and Development

Shoemaking was another source of income for women, and, like wage work, it allowed them to earn money from home. However, when increased demand for shoes required the use of sewing machines to speed up the pace of production, many women had to turn to other sources of work and revenue. Despite this bold move, women who worked at home as shoe binders remained isolated and vulnerable to competition from the more lucrative and efficient factories. Women were also denied craft status and admission into unions, which limited their influence.

Women who worked in factories were also prohibited from joining unions, allowing factories such as the Lowell Mills to exploit their labor. However, female factory workers were offered a type of work outside of the home and away from their families, which provided them with a new level of independence.

9. Given that all the choices are accurate, which one best emphasizes the disadvantages experienced by women working from home?

   A. No Change
   B. though it required more specialized tools than other goods they could produce from home.
   C. but their work was socially and physically isolated from the shoe binding that took place in cobblers' shops.
   D. who often sought multiple sources of income they could fit around their household responsibilities.

10. Given that all of the choices are accurate, which of the following provides the most relevant information at this point in the essay?

    F. No Change
    G. few women could afford to make the switch because of the high cost of personal sewing machines.
    H. women had a difficult time keeping up in addition to their responsibilities at home.
    J. women organized a small-scale movement that trained young women to use sewing machines in their homes.

11. Given that all are accurate, which choice provides new information that helps emphasize the opportunity factory work offered for some women?

    A. No Change
    B. income in addition to that of their families,
    C. lower wages than their male counterparts,
    D. a part in the burgeoning Industrial Revolution,

DEVELOPMENT: PURPOSE

LEARNING OBJECTIVE

After this lesson, you will be able to:

- Determine whether a passage has met a goal and state why or why not

To answer a question like this

Humphrey Bogart

Although the screen appeal of Humphrey Bogart has grown immeasurably since his death in 1957, his early life was not marked by success. Born in New York City in 1899 as the son of a prominent surgeon, young Humphrey was quickly put on the track to medical school. After finishing his early schooling, he went to the prestigious Phillips Academy. Bogart, however, was not academically inclined, and during adolescence he was often described as a troublemaker. In 1918, Bogart entered the navy. It was in the service that he received an injury that partially paralyzed his upper lip, creating his distinctive snarl.

When Bogart was released from the navy in 1920, he turned his attention toward the theater. A family friend in the business hired him to work in a theater office in New York. Bogart eventually became a stage manager and finally worked himself into some minor roles on the stage. His inexperience showed, however, and he struggled to find any substantive parts. In the early 1930s, Bogart set out for Hollywood, and although he quickly signed a contract with Fox Pictures, he appeared, marginally, in only three films.

Frustrated with his stagnant career, he returned to the Broadway stage and finally caught his break as Duke Mantee in the play *The Petrified Forest*. Bogart's performance as the quintessential tough guy soon catapulted his career. Bogart consistently created rich and complex screen images punctuated by his hangdog expressions, perennial five o'clock shadow, and world-weary attitude. From his early gangster roles to his consummate portrayal of the reluctant hero, Bogart's performances came to personify male elegance on the screen, and it is unlikely that his illustrious career will ever be forgotten.

> Question 1 asks about the preceding passage as a whole.

1. Suppose the writer's primary purpose had been to describe the life of someone who struggled before finding success. Would this essay accomplish that purpose?

    A. Yes, because it describes Bogart's perseverance in response to people who doubted his talent.
    B. Yes, because it depicts several setbacks Bogart experienced before he found a lasting career.
    C. No, because it focuses mainly on the reasons for Bogart's success.
    D. No, because it does not describe Bogart's troubles in detail.

You need to know this

On the ACT, some Development questions will ask you to determine why an essay does or does not achieve a given purpose. Writers select particular wording and details to support the purpose of the passage while maintaining a consistent tone and focus, so determining why a given purpose is or is not appropriate will require use of the entire passage.

Chapter 4
Spotting and Fixing Issues: Conciseness, Organization, and Development

Only some passages will include these types of questions, but when one is present, it will usually be the last question in the set and preceded by a boxed-in instructional sentence such as this:

> Question 10 asks about the preceding passage as a whole.

You need to do this
- Determine the author's point of view and main topic and predict the purpose.
- Ask yourself whether the given purpose is close to your prediction (Yes, because . . .) or not (No, because . . .).
- Eliminate the two choices that do not match your Yes/No conclusion.
- Examine the reasoning in the two remaining answers and use the passage to determine which is correct.

Explanation
To determine the essay's primary purpose, summarize the passage as a whole. The passage describes Bogart's slow rise to fame, detailing the challenges he faced before and during his attempts to become a successful actor. This matches the purpose in the question stem, so eliminate C and D. The passage does not mention anyone doubting Bogart's talent, so A is incorrect. Choice (B) is correct because it accurately connects the features of the passage to the stated purpose.

Try on Your Own
Directions: Take as much time as you need on these questions. Work carefully and methodically. There will be an opportunity for timed practice at the end of the chapter.

Early Writing Careers

Many well-known writers began their careers while they were still teenagers. Stephen King, for example, began submitting stories to science fiction magazines when he was just thirteen years old. If you are serious about a writing career, you can submit work to many publications that accept unsolicited manuscripts. It is best, however, to send a query letter first.

A query letter is a one-page document in which you introduce yourself to the editors of the publication and ask if they would like to read your work. Begin by telling the editor a little bit about yourself. Include a paragraph or two outlining the story you've written or would like to write. If you've taken any creative writing courses, won prizes for your writing, or had any work published,

> Question 2 asks about the preceding passage as a whole.

2. If the writer's primary goal were to write an essay about a well-known author's path to success, would this essay accomplish that purpose?

F. Yes, because it discusses how Stephen King's career began.

G. Yes, because it tells about the writer's path to success.

H. No, because it doesn't give enough details about Stephen King's career path.

J. No, because it focuses on giving advice to aspiring authors.

tell the editor about that, too. Don't forget to thank the editor for taking the time to read your letter.

You probably won't sell your first story, but don't get discouraged. Stephen King didn't sell his first submission either—or dozens after that. Despite that, he didn't give up, and neither should you.

The History of Advertising

Over the past few decades, advertising has changed radically. In the 1990s, large companies hoped to reach their target markets through advertisements in national magazines and network television, while smaller companies utilized local newspapers, phone books, and radio stations. Of course, companies large and small still buy advertisements in mass media outlets that reach large numbers of consumers. However, with a new millennium came new possibilities, including a larger media outlet than previously imagined: the internet.

The internet allowed businesses to use targeted advertising, including company websites, banner advertisements, and ads generated by search engines, to reach more specific audiences. Small, local businesses in particular benefited greatly from these new marketing opportunities. Small specialty shops, previously limited to serving local populations of customers, were able to expand their clientele around the world.

Today, companies continue to develop ever more sophisticated methods to use the internet to reach their customers. Individually tailored advertisements appear on social media sites, in email inboxes, in the midst of streamed entertainment, and more. As internet use expands, so too will the ways businesses advertise through it.

Question 3 asks about the preceding passage as a whole.

3. Suppose the writer's goal had been to write an essay about how the internet has changed the world. Would this essay accomplish that goal?

    A. Yes, because it describes how businesses use the internet.
    B. Yes, because it emphasizes the broad impact the internet has had.
    C. No, because it focuses on advertising rather than the overall impact of the internet.
    D. No, because it suggests that companies would have changed without the internet.

Community-Supported Agriculture

This spring, my family joined our local community-supported agriculture, or CSA, association. We wanted to eat more locally grown foods, and the CSA provided the perfect opportunity. Like other members, we bought a year's "share" of the farm's crop before the growing season began. Once it did, the farm delivered a box filled with freshly harvested fruits and vegetables every week.

We immediately discovered that fresh, in-season food is delicious. I had disliked broccoli previously, but one bunch that arrived in our second June box convinced me I'd been wrong. My younger brother, who is normally resistant to new foods, ventured to try both kale and turnips from the CSA and enjoyed both. Prior to our experience with the CSA, the most exotic vegetable he would willingly eat was a carrot—and only the orange kind.

We have, however, found a minor flaw in the CSA boxes: a profusion of zucchini. Each week in July, we received at least six. At first, we just grilled the zucchini. Then, we sautéed it with pasta. By the third week, when we opened our box to find ten more zucchini, we had to get inventive. We experimented with recipes for zucchini soup, casserole, bread, pizza, and even brownies. Though everything was tasty, we're all anticipating the end of zucchini season with relief. Of course, by then tomato season will have begun, and we'll be looking for ways to prepare a new vegetable deluge. I foresee more delicious experiments in the future.

> Question 4 asks about the preceding passage as a whole.

4. If the writer's goal were to write a brief essay about the purpose and organization of community-supported agriculture, would this essay successfully accomplish that goal?

F. Yes, because it explains how community-supported agriculture works.

G. Yes, because it fully describes both the benefits and drawbacks of community-supported agriculture.

H. No, because it focuses instead on one family's experience with community-supported agriculture.

J. No, because it fails to provide an overview of how membership in a community-supported agriculture association works.

Thomas Paine

Compared to most of America's other Founding Fathers, Thomas Paine is not nearly as well known. In fact, there are many Americans who have either never even heard of him or cannot recall his significance in history. Paine was born in 1737 as the son of a corsetmaker—a tailor specializing in corsets and other undergarments—and grew up in rural Thetford, England.

As a young man, Paine worked as a corsetmaker, sailor and minister, but he only found his true calling when he moved to the British colonies in America. Paine first gained recognition as the editor of *Pennsylvania Magazine*, and as political turmoil engulfed the colonies, he became more vocal. In 1776, Paine anonymously published a pamphlet titled "Common Sense" that argued forcefully for American independence from Britain. The pamphlet's popularity spread like wildfire; soon there were 200,000 copies in circulation. Many historians credit the pamphlet with helping to convince the American people to fight for self-rule.

Thomas Paine's influence continued far beyond sparking the Revolutionary War. Once the war began, Paine published a series of pamphlets called *The American Crisis*, which, in the midst of a bloody war, helped keep the morale of the troops up. In addition to his achievements as a writer, Thomas Paine is credited with conceiving the name "The United States of America." Because Thomas Paine was an extremely talented writer, Thomas Jefferson and John Adams drew heavily on his work when drafting the Declaration of Independence. Later in life, Paine wrote other highly controversial works. In 1797, Paine did his part to inspire what would become Social Security. He suggested a system of social insurance for the young and the elderly in his last great work, "Agrarian Justice."

Given Thomas Paine's contributions to America, he deserves recognition as one of our most important Founding Fathers. Whether you think of him as a patriot who named an entire nation or a controversial activist who lobbied for socialist ideas, he should at the very least be remembered as a seminal figure in the development of a new, autonomous nation.

> Question 5 asks about the preceding passage as a whole.

5. Suppose the writer's primary purpose had been to advocate placing a greater emphasis on Thomas Paine's contributions to American history. Would this essay accomplish that purpose?

   A. Yes, because it praises Paine's influence.
   B. Yes, because it is a thorough treatise on American history.
   C. No, because it does not establish that Paine's contributions were beneficial.
   D. No, because it focuses too much on the American Revolution.

Chapter 4
Spotting and Fixing Issues: Conciseness, Organization, and Development

How Much Have You Learned?

Directions: For test-like practice, give yourself 11 minutes to complete this question set. Note that this is not a test-like mix of questions; rather, these 15 questions cover the conciseness, style and tone, organization, and development issues covered in this chapter.

Be sure to study the explanations, even for questions you got correct. They can be found at the end of this chapter.

PASSAGE I

The Library System

[1]

Since the turn of the century, library systems have undergone increasing computerization, a trend that has led to speculation about the future of libraries. Some people believe that not only the card catalog but also the library stacks themselves will eventually be rendered obsolete. <u>Many today have never even used a card catalog and hardly know what one is.</u>
　　　　　　　　　　1

[2]

This thought presents an interesting picture of the future. <u>Despite</u> spending a cozy evening with a good book,
　　　　　　　2
we may be curling up with a laptop computer. With all the intriguing possibilities the future holds, we are inclined

1. The writer wants to emphasize the changes technology is bringing to libraries. Which choice best accomplishes this goal?

   A. **No Change**
   B. It is quite likely, they say, that in the very near future, electronic data will replace books as we know them.
   C. Along with decreases in funding, this may spell trouble for libraries in the future.
   D. Young people, they say, are less and less interested in reading books, even on electronic devices like tablets.

2. Which transition word or phrase is most logical in context?

   F. **No Change**
   G. While
   H. Since
   J. Instead of

Part 2
ACT ENGLISH

to ignore the past. [A] <u>We should not ignore the past because it helps make us who we are.</u>
                                    3

[3]

Libraries may have originated as early as the third millennium BCE in Babylonia. There, clay tablets were used for record-keeping purposes and stored in <u>temples in ancient Babylonia.</u> [B] In the seventh century
                       4
BCE, the King of Assyria organized an enormous collection of records; approximately 20,000 tablets and fragments have been recovered. [5] In the second century CE, libraries were founded in monasteries. [C] It was not until the 13th century CE that university libraries were created.

3. Given that all the following sentences are accurate, which one would provide the most effective transition from this paragraph to the rest of the essay?

   A. No Change
   B. Libraries have a past as well as a future, both of which are important to keep in mind when thinking about them.
   C. The future of libraries is something perhaps none of us can fully predict, and we shouldn't try.
   D. While the future of libraries is an interesting topic, the library system's rich history is also quite intriguing.

4. Which choice is least redundant in context?

   F. No Change
   G. temples millennia ago in a country called Babylonia.
   H. temples.
   J. temples located in Babylonia.

5. At this point, the writer is considering adding the following accurate sentence:

   The first libraries to store books were fourth-century BCE Greek temples established in conjunction with the various schools of philosophy.

   Should the writer make this addition?

   A. Yes, because it adds a relevant detail.
   B. Yes, because it supports the main idea of religious contributions to libraries.
   C. No, because it does not say where the temples were.
   D. No, because it distracts from the emphasis on books.

Chapter 4
Spotting and Fixing Issues: Conciseness, Organization, and Development

[4]

The institution of the library continued to change
over time. The emergence of a middle class, a growth in
literacy, and the invention of the printing press all played a
role. [D] However, wars and revolutions served to hinder
the development of the library system in England. For
example, Henry VIII ordered the destruction of countless
manuscripts and disbanded some monastic libraries during
the English Reformation.

[5]

In the days of King Henry, many English citizens were
pondering the fate of the nascent library system. Today's
societal changes are likewise causing some of us to consider

the same thing, although in ways that medieval readers

could never have imagined. Did we really swap clay tablets
to paperbacks just to ditch the books for microchips?

6. Given that all the following sentences are accurate, which one would most effectively introduces the paragraph?
   F. **No Change**
   G. Many societal changes occurred in the Renaissance.
   H. During the Renaissance, a series of societal changes began to transform the library system into the form we have today.
   J. The Renaissance was a rebirth of classical ideas and artistic styles.

7. Which choice is clearest and most precise in context?
   A. **No Change**
   B. futile
   C. delicate
   D. immature

8. Which transition word is most logical in context?
   F. **No Change**
   G. despite
   H. also
   J. consequently

9. Which choice most effectively maintains the essay's tone?
   A. **No Change**
   B. So we dumped clay tablets for paperbacks, and now we're tossing the paperbacks for microchips?
   C. Have we progressed from clay tablets to paperbacks only to trade our paperbacks in for microchips?
   D. Are we really so fickle that after we chucked clay tablets for paperbacks we will now get rid of paperbacks for microchips?

Question 10 asks about the preceding passage as a whole.

10. The writer wants to add the following accurate sentence to the essay:

    With the increased availability of books, patrons of scholarship founded libraries and academies of scholars in major cities throughout much of Europe.

    The sentence would most logically be placed at:

    F. Point A in Paragraph 2.
    G. Point B in Paragraph 3.
    H. Point C in Paragraph 3.
    J. Point D in Paragraph 4.

PASSAGE II

The Fate of the Mary Rose

The Mary Rose was a favorite warship of the Tudor King Henry VIII. After serving in the English navy for 33 years, she saw her last action in July of 1545. During the Battle of the Solent against the French fleet, the Mary Rose sank <u>in front of the very eyes of a distraught Henry VIII.</u>
                                    11

11. If the writer were to delete the underlined portion (adjusting the punctuation as needed), the paragraph would primarily lose:

    A. a clarification of Henry VIII's attitude toward the French fleet.
    B. a detail that emphasizes the personal connection between the king and the Mary Rose.
    C. a suggestion that the Mary Rose sank due to a combination of factors.
    D. a detail highlighting the writer's opinion of the Battle of Solent.

Though the exact cause of the Mary Rose's sinking remains a mystery, experts agree that it was likely due to a combination of factors—perhaps instability caused by heavy guns and an open gunport set low on the ship's side. Hence the impact of her loss is clear: her sinking was both
        12
an unexpected and costly blow for England, and a serious blow to the pride of Henry VIII.

For centuries, the Mary Rose laid submerged off the south coast of England, her precise location unknown. It wasn't until 1971 that the ship's remains were finally located, and in 1982, a significant portion was raised from the seabed. The artifacts preserved in the Mary Rose include wooden instruments like a fiddle and a still shawm, personal items like combs and shoes, and armaments,
                                                           13
all offering a vivid glimpse into Tudor life and naval warfare.

Today, the preserved timbers of the Mary Rose can be seen in a museum dedicated to her story as she deserves, alongside the other great ships of English
                14
maritime history.
     14

12. Which transition word or phrase is most logical in context?

    F. **No Change**
    G. Likewise,
    H. Finally,
    J. Nevertheless,

13. Which choice best maintains the stylistic pattern of descriptions established earlier in the sentence?

    A. **No Change**
    B. the era's most modern armaments
    C. the era's most modern weaponry such as swords and crossbows
    D. swords and crossbows

14. Which of the following choices best concludes the paragraph and the essay?

    F. **No Change**
    G. which is a popular place to visit in England.
    H. much like Isaac Allerton shipwreck which is preserved in the Key West Museum in the United States.
    J. where she still serves her country by providing valuable insights into Tudor maritime history.

Question 15 asks about the preceding passage as a whole.

15. Suppose the writer's primary purpose had been to provide an overview of maritime history during the reign of Henry VIII. Would this essay accomplish the purpose?

    A. Yes, because it explains how the Mary Rose was important to Henry VIII.
    B. Yes, because it describes how the legacy of the Mary Rose lives on in a museum.
    C. No, because it instead relates the history of only one ship.
    D. No, because it focuses on King Henry VIII's naval losses than on England's maritime history.

Chapter 4
Spotting and Fixing Issues: Conciseness, Organization, and Development

Reflect

Directions: Take a few minutes to recall what you've learned and what you've been practicing in this chapter. Consider the following questions, jot down your best answer for each one, and then compare your reflections to the expert responses on the following page. Use your level of confidence to determine what to do next.

1. When should you consider selecting "DELETE the underlined portion"?
   _____
   _____
   _____

2. How can transition words help you determine the most logical placement for a sentence?
   _____
   _____
   _____

3. Why is relevance important in determining whether a sentence should be revised, added, or deleted?
   _____
   _____
   _____

4. Name one goal of the introduction to a paragraph/passage. Name one goal of the conclusion to a paragraph/passage.
   _____
   _____
   _____

Responses

1. When should you consider selecting "DELETE the underlined portion"?

If the underlined portion is wordy/redundant, does not enhance the meaning of the sentence, or does not provide clarity, select "DELETE the underlined portion." Remember that "DELETE the underlined portion" is just as likely as any of the other three choices.

2. How can transition words help you determine the most logical placement for a sentence?

The kind of transition word that a sentence begins with (contrast, cause-and-effect, continuation, emphasis, chronology) determines the purpose the sentence should serve within the context. If the sentence serves that purpose within the context, it is logically placed.

3. Why is relevance important in determining whether a sentence should be revised, added, or deleted?

If a sentence is missing relevant information, it needs to be revised. If you are going to add a sentence, it should be relevant to the existing information in the passage. If information is not relevant to the passage, it should be deleted.

4. Name one goal of the introduction to a paragraph/passage. Name one goal of the conclusion to a paragraph/passage.

A good introduction should explain the topic and purpose and include information that will be discussed later in the paragraph/passage. A good conclusion should summarize the topic and purpose and include information that was discussed earlier in the paragraph/passage.

Next Steps

If you answered most questions correctly in the "How Much Have You Learned?" section, and if your responses to the Reflect questions were similar to those of the ACT expert, then consider conciseness, organization, and development areas of strength and move on to the next chapter. Come back to these topics periodically to prevent yourself from getting rusty.

If you don't yet feel confident, review those parts of this chapter that you have not yet mastered. Then, try the questions you missed again. As always, be sure to review the explanations closely. Then go online (**kaptest.com/login**) for more practice. If you haven't already registered your book, do so at **kaptest.com/moreonline**.

GO ONLINE

kaptest.com/login

Chapter 4
Spotting and Fixing Issues: Conciseness, Organization, and Development

Answers and Explanations

Conciseness

1. Review the Explanation portion of the Conciseness lesson.

Drill Answers

Note: These are not the only ways to correct the sentences; your answers may differ.

a. The school **was founded** in 1906.

b. I felt **anxious** before the curtain rose.

c. We **agreed** that Naomi should be captain.

d. After a job interview, make sure to send a note **thanking** your interviewer.

e. Not long after he graduated from Oxford, Oscar Wilde moved to London, **where** he embarked on his literary career in earnest.

2. **J**
Difficulty: Low
Category: Conciseness
Getting to the Answer: The underlined portion in F repeats information that is already included in the name of TEIMUN. Choices G and H do so as well; (J) is the only choice that eliminates the redundancy.

3. **A**
Difficulty: Low
Category: Conciseness
Getting to the Answer: Choices B, C, and D all introduce redundant language. Thus, (A) is the correct answer.

4. **J**
Difficulty: Medium
Category: Conciseness
Getting to the Answer: The underlined portion uses more words than is necessary to convey its meaning, as do G and H. Choice (J) is less wordy while still being clear, so it is correct.

Style and Tone

1. Review the Explanation portion of the Conciseness lesson.

2. **G**
Difficulty: Medium
Category: Style and Tone
Getting to the Answer: If the question stem asks you which choice "most closely maintains the stylistic pattern," then it is a Style and Tone question. As you read the passage, pay attention to the word choice. Is the author creating a casual tone of voice? Or a formal, scholarly tone? Do they skim over the fine details or do they want to convey specific, perhaps even technical, information? If you are unsure of what the author intended, then carefully review the two sentences preceding the sentence with the Style and Tone question. Try to paraphrase what the author intends in your own words, then review the answer choices and eliminate as you go.

In this passage, the author intends a formal and detailed but somewhat dramatic tone. This style is intended to convey the scope and feeling of Oguri Jukichi's 484 days adrift on the sea. Eliminate F, as "decided to chop down" implies with the word "decided" that chopping down the mast was a voluntary choice, which does not suit the extreme situation. Choice (G), "resorted to chopping down," conveys the same idea but with more of a sense of desperation, which matches the authorial tone from the earlier sentences. Choice H is too casual in tone, and Choice J is too vague in tone.

3. **D**
Difficulty: Low
Category: Style and Tone
Getting to the Answer: In this passage, the author intends a formal and detailed but somewhat dramatic tone. This style is intended to convey the scope and feeling of Oguri Jukichi's 484 days adrift on the sea.

Eliminate A, as it lacks the detail and somewhat dramatic tone of the preceding sentences. Eliminate B, as it is overly detailed and clinical. Eliminate C because, while it fits the detailed tone of the rest of the passage, it lacks the emotional sensory details of (D). Remember, sometimes a single word might be the only clue needed to keep a consistent style. Notice how the second paragraph in the passage mentions "hefty cargo," "hungry crew," "punishing thirst," "fearful men." The phrase "sweet relief" fits that stylistic quirk.

4. **H**
Difficulty: Hard
Category: Style and Tone
Getting to the Answer: In this passage, the author intends a formal and detailed but somewhat dramatic tone. This style is intended to convey the scope and color of Oguri Jukichi's 484 days adrift on the sea.

Eliminate F, as the word choice of "delightful adventure" does not suit the passage, given the hardships described within it. Eliminate G, as it does not fit the context of the passage, as the *Tokujomaru* did not make "landfall." The passage states that the ship was found "some 300 miles off the California coastline" by the Forester. Choice (H) is formal and detailed, fitting the revelation that the *Tokujomaru* had journeyed across the Pacific Ocean. Choice J is imprecise and does not fit the detailed, formal style of the passage.

Organization: Transitions

1. Review the Explanation portion of the Organization: Transitions lesson.

Drill Answers

a. **Due to** its impressive technical innovations, the small start-up thrived.

b. Cashew nuts are a popular snack worldwide; **however**, they can be difficult to harvest because their shells contain a toxic resin.

c. Izdehar is the most level-headed of my friends—**in fact**, I think she's more reliable than some adults I know.

d. After days of hard work, we **finally** finished our science fair project.

e. The actor won an award for best supporting role this year **in addition to** releasing her first pop music album.

2. **G**
Difficulty: Medium
Category: Organization
Getting to the Answer: Transitions must accurately reflect the writer's purpose. Here, the writer's goal is to emphasize how important good manners were for the upper classes. The word *Despite* is a contrast transition, which is the opposite of the writer's intent. Eliminate F and H because they are both contrast transitions. Choice J is incorrect because good manners were important at all times, not just occasionally. Choice (G) is correct, since *Especially for* emphasizes the point the writer is making.

3. **C**
Difficulty: Medium
Category: Organization
Getting to the Answer: This question asks for a transition sentence connecting the first and second paragraphs. The first is about Queen Victoria's ideas of propriety impacting culture; the second is about period fashion. The correct answer will include both ideas, and only (C) does so.

4. **F**
Difficulty: High
Category: Organization
Getting to the Answer: This sentence presents a contrast between two ideas: the desire to cinch the waist as much as possible and the fact that women still needed to breathe. Therefore, a contrast transition word is needed. Choice (F) is correct. Choice H is incorrect because it is a cause-and-effect transition word. Choice G is incorrect because *rather than* is idiomatically incorrect in this context. The phrase *rather than* sets up a comparison. Comparisons must be between like terms. As it stands, the sentence is comparing "to pull" with "leaving." These verbs are not in the same form, so the comparison is illogical and thus incorrect. Choice J is incorrect because the contrast transition word is grammatically and logically needed to connect the ideas.

5. **D**
Difficulty: Medium
Category: Organization
Getting to the Answer: The preceding sentence discusses the limited education that many women received during the Victorian Era. Then the paragraph states that a minority of women were educated

more fully. The difference between the two requires a contrast transition, and the current transition word does not serve this purpose. Choice B indicates cause and effect and C emphasizes a point, so the correct answer is (D).

6. **G**
Difficulty: High
Category: Organization
Getting to the Answer: This question asks for a transition sentence from the third paragraph into the fourth paragraph. The third paragraph discusses women's education in the Victorian era, including Victoria's own, while the fourth paragraph discusses Victoria's lasting impact. Choices F, H, and J all focus on her education alone and offer specific details rather than showing a connection between ideas. Choice J may be tempting because it compares her education to her prime ministers', which indirectly suggests the topic of government policy. However, the final paragraph does not mention her prime ministers, so J does not actually show the connection between these two paragraphs. Choice (G), on the other hand, clearly states the relationship between Victoria's education and her reign, so it is correct.

Organization: Sentence Placement

1. Review the Explanation portion of the Organization: Sentence Placement lesson.

2. **H**
Difficulty: Medium
Category: Organization
Getting to the Answer: When looking for the correct location to add a sentence, first consider the content of the sentence to be added. The pronoun *This* at the beginning of the sentence shows that the previous sentence must reference something that "allows the protozoan to move." Choice (H) would place the new sentence after one about flagella propelling the protozoan; thus, it is correct.

3. **A**
Difficulty: Medium
Category: Organization
Getting to the Answer: Sentence 4 contains the continuation transition *also*. This shows that it is a logical extension of the sentence that comes immediately before it. Since Sentence 4 references craft status and unions, the sentence before Sentence 4 must also discuss these or other closely related topics. Use this to determine where Sentence 4 should go. Choice B is clearly incorrect because then the transition word *also* would have nothing from which to transition. Choices C and D are incorrect because neither contains references to anything remotely similar to craft status and unions. Thus, (A) is correct.

4. **F**
Difficulty: High
Category: Organization
Getting to the Answer: The sentence the writer wants to add discusses women and home life. It also starts with the phrase "During this time," which needs to make sense as a transition from the previous sentence. Choice (F) places the sentence correctly in a paragraph discussing women and home life in the 19th century. Choices G, H, and J all place it in a paragraph about women and wage work, which doesn't fit the content of the sentence.

5. **B**
Difficulty: Medium
Category: Organization
Getting to the Answer: The new sentence provides an example of women being treated unfairly, so it must follow and support a sentence about problems women faced at work. Choice A is incorrect because it places the example at the very beginning of the paragraph where it would not follow or support any sentence. Choices C and D place the example after sentences that describe some of the benefits of women working outside of the home. The new sentence details some of the injustices that women faced, so the two ideas do not logically belong together. Choice (B) is the only option that places the new sentence after one about difficulties women encountered, so it is correct.

6. **G**
Difficulty: Medium
Category: Organization
Getting to the Answer: Sentence 2 references "this model." Sentence 3 makes this reference clear: households were no longer seen as indivisible economic units. Since Sentence 2 must come right after Sentence 3, eliminate F and H. The "diverse economy" of "today" shows the present ramifications of the history described in the passage. Sentence 2 looks ahead

and attempts to show how the ideas discussed in the passage are relevant to their readers' lives. Therefore, it is best positioned as a conclusion. Choice (G) is correct.

Development: Precision

1. Review the Explanation portion of the Development: Precision lesson.

2. **H**
Difficulty: Medium
Category: Development
Getting to the Answer: The sentence sets up a parallel between large companies using certain outlets to advertise and small companies using others, so the underlined word needs to mean *use*. Only (H) conveys this meaning.

3. **D**
Difficulty: Medium
Category: Development
Getting to the Answer: While all of the answers might seem like they could fit, the question asks for one that conveys opportunity, or positive potential. Choice A, *competitors*, is too negative, while B and C are both neutral. Choice (D) highlights the positive potential of the internet and is correct.

4. **G**
Difficulty: High
Category: Development
Getting to the Answer: While each answer choice is grammatically correct, only (G) expresses Paine's celebrity status.

5. **A**
Difficulty: Low
Category: Development
Getting to the Answer: When the underlined portion is a single word, make sure the word fits in the context. Because Paine lived hundreds of years ago, it does not make sense to say that he is *tasked* or is *helped* with something, so eliminate B and C. Choice D creates the phrase *is noted with*. *With* is not the correct preposition to use with this verb, so D is incorrect. Choice (A) is correct.

6. **F**
Difficulty: Medium
Category: Development
Getting to the Answer: Consider both the surrounding details and the author's tone to determine which phrase fits the context of the essay. Throughout, the author describes increased recognition of Paine's achievements. Eliminate H because it is too neutral and J because it is too negative. While G is certainly positive in tone, it goes beyond what is stated in the passage. The author says that Paine was a good writer, but this does not necessarily mean that he was the best in the colonies. Choice (F) is correct because it perfectly matches the author's positive tone regarding Paine and accurately describes why Paine's work would be used by Jefferson and Adams.

Development: Introductions and Conclusions

1. Review the Explanation portion of the Development: Introductions and Conclusions lesson.

2. **G**
Difficulty: Medium
Category: Development
Getting to the Answer: On the ACT, a strong concluding sentence will not introduce a new topic. The correct answer choice will be clearly connected to the other details in the paragraph and function as an effective summary. The paragraph describes how the narrator's family reacted positively to the CSA. Choice (G) is correct; it follows naturally from the information about the new vegetables the brother has eaten because of the family's CSA membership. The other choices are not connected to the topic of the family's positive experience with the new food from the CSA.

3. **B**
Difficulty: High
Category: Development
Getting to the Answer: This paragraph describes a small problem the narrator's family has encountered with the CSA, although the narrator presents it with humor and maintains a positive tone. Choices A and D are both too negative, so eliminate them. Choice C is true but does not accurately capture the main point of the paragraph. The correct answer is (B).

4. J
Difficulty: Medium
Category: Development
Getting to the Answer: The paragraph is primarily about women's ability to earn money by producing goods from home. Choice F, while it is about women in the workforce, brings up a topic outside the scope of the paragraph. Likewise, G makes a claim much stronger than the paragraph can actually support. Finally, H isn't about labor at all. The correct answer is (J), which introduces wage work as an opportunity for women.

5. B
Difficulty: Medium
Category: Development
Getting to the Answer: This paragraph discusses both the negative and positive aspects of factory jobs for women. Choices A and C bring in ideas outside the scope of the paragraph and passage and are thus incorrect. Choice D, while it does discuss women working at factories, has a strong negative tone that is incompatible with the rest of the passage. On the other hand, (B) acknowledges that factory work was a mixed blessing for women, which fits well with the rest of the paragraph. The correct answer is (B).

6. F
Difficulty: High
Category: Development
Getting to the Answer: The concluding sentence must effectively summarize both the final paragraph and the passage as a whole. The main topic of the passage is the positive and negative changes in women's roles, and the final paragraph is a broad retrospective on those developments. Choice (F) provides the best conclusion by focusing on women's roles in the early 19th century. The other choices, G, H, and J, either bring up new ideas or look beyond the early 19th century.

Development: Revising Text

1. Review the Explanation portion of the Development: Revising Text lesson.

2. H
Difficulty: High
Category: Development
Getting to the Answer: Look for a choice that meets the author's goal for the underlined phrase. Choices F, G, and J all suggest general goals that could be easily addressed without using the CSA. Only (H) includes *locally grown foods*, which is a precise goal that would be most effectively achieved through the CSA.

3. A
Difficulty: High
Category: Development
Getting to the Answer: The question asks whether this paragraph should be broken at this point. Look at the sentences before the point and after the point. Since they do not have the same purpose or main idea, they should not be included in the same paragraph. Eliminate choices C and D. Choice (A) includes the reason why there should be a paragraph break and is correct. Choice B is incorrect because there is not a contrast between what comes before and what comes after the new paragraph break.

4. J
Difficulty: High
Category: Development
Getting to the Answer: The paragraph's main point is that the produce from the CSA is especially delicious, and the latter part of the sentence supports this by saying that the narrator's brother tried and liked vegetables that the CSA supplied. The question asks for a contrast with the rest of the sentence that will support the paragraph as a whole, so the correct answer will provide information that conflicts with the brother liking the vegetables from the CSA. Choice (J) is correct.

5. A
Difficulty: Low
Category: Development
Getting to the Answer: In the previous sentence, the author discussed how large companies advertise differently than small companies. This sentence describes what is common to both, and the underlined portion makes the connection explicit. Choice (A) is correct.

6. G
Difficulty: Medium
Category: Development
Getting to the Answer: When a question asks about adding a sentence, consider what the sentence contributes to the paragraph as a whole. This paragraph describes the advantages of internet advertising, focusing particularly on the benefits for small businesses. The additional sentence illustrates this benefit, so it

should be added. Eliminate H and J. Choice F advocates adding the sentence, but for the incorrect reason. The correct answer is (G).

7. B
Difficulty: High
Category: Development
Getting to the Answer: The first sentence in the paragraph says that Paine is not widely known. The sentence in question supports this claim by stating that few people today are aware of him. Choice (B) is correct. Choice A is incorrect because the sentence does not provide an explanation, only an elaboration. Choice C is incorrect because the rest of the paragraph is not devoted to proving this claim. Finally, D is incorrect because the author's tone is neutral, not judgmental.

8. F
Difficulty: Medium
Category: Development
Getting to the Answer: The question asks if the writer should keep or delete the preceding sentence. First, decide if it should be kept or deleted by looking at the context. The sentence in question is preceded by a sentence describing the popularity of Paine's pamphlet "Common Sense"; the sentence being considered for deletion explains the importance of that popularity by describing its influence on historical events. It should be kept, so Choices H and J can be eliminated. The correct answer is (F) because it offers the correct reason for keeping the sentence. Choice G is incorrect because the reasoning is not relevant.

9. C
Difficulty: Medium
Category: Development
Getting to the Answer: The question specifically asks for a choice that emphasizes the disadvantages of working from home. Choice (C) describes how women were isolated as a result, whereas the other choices focus on positive or neutral aspects of such work. The correct answer is (C).

10. J
Difficulty: High
Category: Development
Getting to the Answer: This sentence starts out describing a change in the shoemaking industry that affected women. The following sentence begins with "Despite this bold move" and goes on to describe how women still struggled to compete with factories. The underlined portion must describe a bold move intended to help women keep up with changes in the shoemaking industry. Choice (J) is correct.

11. A
Difficulty: High
Category: Development
Getting to the Answer: This question asks for new information that emphasizes how factory work was beneficial for women. Choices B and D both present information included earlier in the passage. Choice C gives new information, but it focuses on the downsides of factory work. Only (A) gives new information that shows how factory work could be an opportunity, so (A) is correct.

Development: Purpose

1. Review the Explanation portion of the Development: Purpose lesson.

2. J
Difficulty: Medium
Category: Development
Getting to the Answer: First determine the main idea of the passage. This passage is focused on giving advice to aspiring authors, occasionally using an established author as an example. This does not match the purpose described in the question stem, so eliminate F and G. Choice H does not accurately state why the passage does not match the described purpose. The correct answer is (J).

3. C
Difficulty: Medium
Category: Development
Getting to the Answer: This passage focuses on how advertising has changed over time, particularly with the arrival of the internet. The question's description of "how the internet has changed the world" is much more broad, so it does not match the passage. Eliminate A and B. The passage does not make the suggestion described in D, so choice (C) is correct.

Chapter 4
Spotting and Fixing Issues: Conciseness, Organization, and Development

4.   H
Difficulty: Medium
Category: Development
Getting to the Answer: Begin by identifying the main idea of the passage. The main idea is that one family has enjoyed its experience with a CSA membership but has also experienced some drawbacks. This main idea does not match the much more general purpose given in the question, so eliminate F and G. Choice J contradicts the essay, which does provide some information on membership. Choice (H) correctly identifies the focus of the essay.

5.   A
Difficulty: Medium
Category: Development
Getting to the Answer: When asked whether a passage accomplishes a particular purpose, consider the scope and tone of the passage. The passage focuses on Paine's influence on the founding of the United States, and the final paragraph says that he deserves more recognition. This matches the purpose in the question stem, so eliminate C and D. Eliminate B because this short passage is not a "thorough treatise." Choice (A) accurately reflects the scope and tone of the passage and is therefore correct.

How Much Have You Learned?

1.   B
Difficulty: High
Category: Development
Getting to the Answer: The question asks for a sentence that emphasizes the changes technology is bringing to libraries. Choice A is about a change that has already happened. Choice C refers to funding, not technology. Choice D mentions electronic devices and people reading less, but technology is not cited as the cause of the change. Choice (B) is correct because it discusses how electronic data may replace physical books.

2.   J
Difficulty: Medium
Category: Organization
Getting to the Answer: When the question asks about a transition, identify what ideas it connects and determine their relationship. In this sentence, the first part is about reading a book, and the second part is about using a laptop. Given the context of the passage so far, these two are likely meant to be in contrast. Eliminate H because it is a cause-and-effect transition. *Despite* and *While*, although contrast words, do not reflect the author's intended meaning that people are using laptops as an alternative to reading books, so eliminate F and G. *Instead of* is a contrast transition that makes sense in context, so (J) is correct.

3.   D
Difficulty: Medium
Category: Development
Getting to the Answer: The current paragraph speculates about the future of libraries, and the following paragraph discusses the origin and development of libraries. The transition sentence should connect these two topics. Eliminate A because it does not discuss libraries. Choice B connects the past and the future, but it does not provide any reason to begin discussing the history of libraries. Choice C focuses only on the future, so it is not an appropriate transition. Choice (D) connects the future of libraries with their past, while giving the reader a reason to want to know more about their history, so it is correct.

4.   H
Difficulty: Medium
Category: Conciseness
Getting to the Answer: The underlined phrase includes information that is already stated earlier in the paragraph. The only answer choice that eliminates all redundancy is (H).

5.   A
Difficulty: High
Category: Development
Getting to the Answer: A sentence should be added only if it is relevant to the main point of the paragraph and fits well in context. The additional sentence is relevant to the discussion about the history of libraries because it helps fill in the timeline of library development. Since it should be added, eliminate C and D. While B may be tempting, the paragraph does not emphasize religious contributions to libraries; it merely mentions that a few of the developments took place in temples and monasteries. Choice (A) correctly states the reason for adding the sentence.

6. H
Difficulty: Medium
Category: Development
Getting to the Answer: An introductory sentence should give the reader a broad idea of the paragraph's topic and flow well into the sentence that immediately follows it. Because the next sentence lists societal factors that "played a role," the introductory sentence should relate these factors to the history of libraries. Choice (H) is correct because it both introduces the societal changes and continues the timeline of library development from the preceding paragraph.

7. A
Difficulty: High
Category: Development
Getting to the Answer: This question tests precision. The rest of the sentence states that the fate of the library system was in question, and the previous paragraph describes circumstances that hindered its growth and development. The correct answer will reflect this context. Choice B, *futile*, is too strongly negative. Choice C, *delicate*, does not capture the idea that the library system was growing and changing. Finally, D, *immature*, is used to describe a person's emotional state and cannot be meaningfully used to describe an inanimate object. *Nascent* captures the meaning that the library system was just beginning and the course of its development was still unknown; (A) is correct.

8. F
Difficulty: Medium
Category: Organization
Getting to the Answer: When transition words are being tested, first identify the relationship between the ideas before and after the underlined portion. Logically, the pair of ideas in the text are in contrast. People may consider questions similar to those considered by English citizens under Henry VIII, but they think about these questions in very different ways. Eliminate H and J. Since the word *despite* can introduce only a noun phrase, G is incorrect. Choice (F) fits with both the logic and grammatical structure of the sentence, so it is correct.

9. C
Difficulty: Low
Category: Style and Tone
Getting to the Answer: When the question asks about the essay's tone, find words in the passage in which the author could have used positively or negatively charged words but chose not to, or vice versa. In addition, find words that the author could have used in a more formal way but chose not to, or vice versa. In the second paragraph, the author chooses mildly positive words like *interesting* and *intriguing* instead of strongly charged words like *awful* or *wonderful*. The author also equates the experience of books and laptops, writing "spending a cozy evening with a good book . . . curling up with a laptop computer." This suggests that the author isn't choosing one option over another. The author also uses formal vocabulary instead of casual—for example, using *rendered obsolete* instead of *a thing of the past* in the first paragraph. The author is using a formal, relatively neutral tone in the essay, so eliminate the choices that don't reflect that. Choices A, B, and D are all too casual, using informal and somewhat negatively charged words *dumped, tossing,* and *chucked* for *trade* as used in (C), the correct choice.

10. J
Difficulty: Medium
Category: Organization
Getting to the Answer: When considering where to add a sentence, first examine its content. This sentence says that books became more available and patrons founded libraries throughout Europe, so it must go in one of the paragraphs about the history of libraries. Paragraph 2 does not discuss this topic, so eliminate F. Paragraph 3 is about the historical development of the first libraries, but Paragraph 4 describes their proliferation, so both G and H can be eliminated. Choice (J) correctly places the new sentence in the paragraph discussing the development of libraries in Europe, including the invention of the printing press.

11. B
Difficulty: Medium
Category: Development
Getting to the Answer: To determine what the paragraph would lose, first determine what the function of the underlined portion is. The phrase "in front of the very eyes of a distraught Henry VIII" is a detail that shows how much Henry cared about his favorite warship. Choice (B) is correct. Choice A is incorrect because the phrase does not clarify Henry's attitude about the French; it is only in reference to the loss of the Mary Rose. Choice C is incorrect because this paragraph does not contain information about the reasons why the Mary Rose sank; that information is in the next

paragraph. Finally, D is incorrect because the author's tone is factual; there are no words that imply the author's opinion of this topic.

12. J
Difficulty: High
Category: Organization
Getting to the Answer: When the question asks about a transition, identify what ideas it connects and determine their relationship. In the text, the transition contrasts the mystery of the cause of the sinking and the clarity of the impact. Choice (J), *Nevertheless*, is the only contrast transition, so it is correct. But if you are stuck, use elimination. Eliminate A because *Hence* is a cause-and-effect word meaning *consequently*. Though the impact of the sinking was a consequence of the sinking, it wasn't the consequence of the mystery surrounding why the Mary Rose sank, so F is incorrect. Choice G, *Likewise*, is a continuation transition that implies a similarity between the ideas; that relationship is not true in context, so B is incorrect. Choice H, *Finally*, implies that the impact is the final step of a sequence, but the story of the Mary Rose continues, so H is incorrect.

13. C
Difficulty: Medium
Category: Style and Tone
Getting to the Answer: If the question stem asks you which choice "most closely maintains the stylistic pattern," then it is a Style and Tone question. As you read the sentence, pay attention to the word choice. The author is listing items found in the Mary Rose that "[offer] a vivid glimpse in Tudor life and naval warfare." Each item in the list describes a general category followed by examples.

Eliminate A and B, as each doesn't include examples. Eliminate D since it only lists examples. Choice (C) is correct, as it lists both the category ("the era's most modern weaponry") and examples ("swords and crossbows").

14. J
Difficulty: Medium
Category: Development
Getting to the Answer: The concluding sentence must effectively summarize both the final paragraph and the passage as a whole. The main topic of the passage is the history of the Mary Rose, and the final paragraph details where the Mary Rose is today. Choice (J) provides the best conclusion by connecting the Mary Rose's history of service to how she still serves England today. The other choices, F, G, and H, bring up irrelevant details about the current location of the museum, or make an irrelevant comparison to another preserved shipwreck.

15. C
Difficulty: Medium
Category: Development
Getting to the Answer: When considering the purpose of an essay, first determine the main idea of the passage. This passage is focused on the history of the Mary Rose, a particular ship of King Henry VIII's navy. It is not an *overview* as the purpose is described in the question stem, so eliminate A and B. Choice D does not accurately state why the passage does not match the described purpose: the passage does not focus on naval losses in general. The correct answer is (C).

[CHAPTER 5]

ACT ENGLISH: TIMING AND SECTION MANAGEMENT STRATEGIES

> **LEARNING OBJECTIVE**
>
> After completing this chapter, you will be able to:
> - Move quickly and efficiently through the English Test so that you have a fair chance at every question

Timing

You have 35 minutes to complete 50 questions, so, on average, you should take about 7 minutes per 10 questions. Those questions will come in 6 passages of either 5 or 10 questions each.

Section Management

You do not need to spend the same amount of time on each question. Every question counts for the same number of points, so be sure to complete the questions you find easiest to answer first. If a particular question is challenging, take a guess and come back to it if you have time. The test rewards students for conciseness, so when you guess, choosing the shortest option is a good idea. It won't always be the correct answer, but it certainly is a good guess.

Moving efficiently through this section is important, but that does not mean that you should skip over most of the text that isn't underlined. Even if sections of a passage are not underlined, you should still read everything because an understanding of the passage as a whole is often necessary to answer certain questions. Reading all of the text in the passage is essential to answering questions efficiently and accurately.

There are full-length English passages in the "How Much Have You Learned?" section that comes next (one 10-question passage and one 5-question passage). Use them to practice timing: skip questions you find too time-consuming, return to them if you have time, and keep an eye on the clock. When you are finished, check your work—and reflect on how well you managed the timing. Then keep practicing these timing strategies when you take full-length tests, both in your book and online.

Part 2
ACT ENGLISH

How Much Have You Learned?

Directions: For test-like practice, give yourself 11 minutes to complete these 15 questions. Be sure to study the explanations, even for questions you got correct. They can be found at the end of this chapter.

PASSAGE I

Frankenstein

The character of Frankenstein did not originate in Hollywood. Rather, the legendary mad scientist <u>whom sought to reanimate</u> lifeless bodies was
                                 1
the creation of Mary Wollstonecraft Shelley, who was married to famed poet Percy Bysshe Shelley. *Frankenstein: The Modern Prometheus*, Mary Shelley's novel published in 1818, is considered one of the greatest horror tales of all time.

Mary Shelley created her <u>desperate</u> subject in
                                         2
response to a bet. [A] She, her husband—Lord Byron— and Byron's physician had a contest to see who could write the best ghost story. Although <u>the writing project</u>
                                                                                3
<u>began whimsical,</u> her tale became a serious examination
        3
of the fate of an individual who decides to overstep moral and social bounds. [B]

Shelley's novel tells the story of a scientist, Dr. Victor <u>Frankenstein, who</u> discovers the secret of
                                        4
bringing corpses back to life and creates a monster

1. Which choice makes the sentence most grammatically acceptable?

   A. **No Change**
   B. whom seeks to reanimate
   C. who sought in reanimating
   D. who sought to reanimate

2. The writer wants to emphasize that the work is a horror story. Which choice best accomplishes this goal?

   F. **No Change**
   G. offensive
   H. nightmarish
   J. dangerous

3. Which choice makes the sentence most grammatically acceptable?

   A. **No Change**
   B. the writing project was begun whimsical,
   C. the writing project began whimsically, but
   D. the writing project began whimsically,

4. Which choice makes the sentence most grammatically acceptable?

   F. **No Change**
   G. Dr. Victor Frankenstein—who
   H. Dr. Victor Frankenstein: who
   J. Dr. Victor Frankenstein, he

Chapter 5
ACT English: Timing and Section Management Strategies

with material from graveyards, dissecting rooms, and slaughterhouses.
    5

5. If the writer were to delete the underlined portion, the paragraph would primarily lose:

   A. information that emphasizes the grisliness of how Frankenstein acquired his materials.
   B. details about the sources from which Mary Shelley drew inspiration for her story.
   C. an explanation of why Frankenstein's monster ultimately became dangerous.
   D. a description that shows Frankenstein's dedication to his work.

Similar to his gruesome appearance, the
    6
monster is basically good. [C] After being rejected by Dr. Frankenstein and all other people with whom he comes into contact, the monster becomes violent.

One by one, the monster murders the people Dr. Frankenstein cares for the most: his younger brother, and his best friend, and he even killed his wife. [D] The
    7
tale ends with Dr. Frankenstein chasing the monster to the North Pole, where each of them eventually dies.

6. Which transition word is most logical in context?

   F. **No Change**
   G. Although
   H. Despite
   J. Because of

7. Which choice makes the sentence most grammatically acceptable?

   A. **No Change**
   B. his younger brother, and his best friend, and his wife.
   C. his younger brother, best friend, and his wife.
   D. his younger brother, his best friend, and his wife.

It is a horror story, Mary Shelley's *Frankenstein*
    8
is respected by many as a literary classic. The critical acclaim and continued popularity of the story are also evidenced by the numerous films that have been based on it. Some versions, like *Young Frankenstein*, provide a humorous retelling of the story. Other versions,

8. Which choice makes the sentence most grammatically acceptable?

   F. **No Change**
   G. Although it is a horror story,
   H. It is a horror story, for
   J. The horror story,

Part 2
ACT ENGLISH

like the 1994 *Mary Shelley's Frankenstein*, attempt to be faithful and true to the original.
9

9. Which choice is least redundant in context?

   A. No Change
   B. faithful to
   C. faithful and closely follow
   D. accurate and faithful reproductions of

> Question 10 asks about the preceding passage as a whole.

10. The writer wants to add the following sentence to the essay:

    > The monster, who is nameless, only becomes evil when his creator refuses to accept and care for him.

    The sentence would most logically be placed at:

    F. Point A in Paragraph 2.
    G. Point B in Paragraph 2.
    H. Point C in Paragraph 3.
    J. Point D in Paragraph 3.

PASSAGE II

Medieval Illuminations

In medieval times, the term illumination originally,
                                        11
described the embellishments of text in a hand-crafted
11
book, using gold or silver to make the text appear illuminated. There were two categories of the artists who created the illuminations. Some artists illustrated

11. Which choice makes the sentence most grammatically acceptable?

    A. No Change
    B. illumination, originally, described
    C. illumination originally described
    D. illumination originally; described

the texts with relevant paintings, while <u>others decorated the text by embellishing initial capital letters and the margins.</u>
                                                                 12

Traditionally, scholars believed that only monks created illuminations as they copied books to use in worship in medieval times. <u>Images of monks sitting in a well-lit room at large tilted desks, working to copy text and add embellishments, have even appeared in films such as 1998's *Ever After*.</u> However, scholars have
                                                                 13
recently discovered that nuns also illuminated texts for study and worship, beginning in the 10th century.

<u>Monasteries and convents offered their residents education and training in hand-crafting religious texts.</u>
                                                                 14

More medieval nuns have gained recognition for the content of their illuminations. For instance, in 12th-century Germany, Guda was one of the first female artists to craft a self-portrait as part of her illuminations. In her manuscript *MS. Barth. 42*, Guda was both a writer

12. Which choice is least redundant in context?

F. No Change
G. others embellished the initial capital letters and the margins.
H. other artists added decorations to the text by embellishing the initial capital letters and the margins.
J. others decorated the pages of the texts with embellishments in the initial capital letters and the margins.

13. The writer is considering deleting the underlined sentence. Should the sentence be kept or deleted?

A. Kept, because it allows the reader to imagine the monks and how the illuminations were created.
B. Kept, because it shows how films have been influenced by the history of illuminated manuscripts.
C. Deleted, because it removes irrelevant information about the portrayal of the creation of illuminated manuscripts in film.
D. Deleted, because it doesn't include a description for both monks and nuns creating illuminated manuscripts.

14. Given that all the choices are accurate, which one provides the best transition from this paragraph to the subsequent paragraph?

F. No Change
G. So many of these nuns remained unknown because some convents closed and the libraries were lost.
H. Illuminated manuscripts have been found to be more fanciful when the nuns completed them.
J. Some of these nuns have since been recognized as brilliant artists.

Part 2
ACT ENGLISH

and artist. She <u>drew pretty pictures</u>, including her self-
                          15
portrait, and embellished the margins. Some scholars believe the self-portrait was her signature or a way to give power to her words.

15. Which choice most effectively maintains the essay's tone?

A. **No Change**
B. painted elaborate images within the initial capital letters
C. added amazingly detailed pictures
D. painted unimaginative scenes

Answers and Explanations

Passage I

1. D
Difficulty: Medium
Category: Agreement
Getting to the Answer: A subjective pronoun performs the action in a sentence; an objective pronoun is the receiver of the action in a sentence. The pronoun in the underlined segment, *whom*, is an objective pronoun. However, the verbs in the answer choices require the subjective pronoun *who*. Eliminate A and B. Choice C introduces an idiom error, since "sought in reanimating" is not grammatically correct English. The correct answer is (D).

2. H
Difficulty: Medium
Category: Development
Getting to the Answer: This question tests precision. Although all of the answer choices are grammatically correct, the question asks for one that particularly emphasizes horror. *Desperate*, *offensive*, or *dangerous* subjects do not necessarily inspire horror, so F, G, and J are incorrect. Only *nightmarish* has connotations of horror, so the correct answer is (H).

3. D
Difficulty: Medium
Category: Agreement
Getting to the Answer: Recall that adverbs modify verbs, while adjectives modify nouns. Since the word being modified is the verb *began*, it must be modified by an adverb. The word *whimsical* is an adjective, so eliminate A and B. Choice C correctly contains an adverb but disrupts the structure of the sentence with the extra conjunction *but*. The correct answer is (D).

4. F
Difficulty: Medium
Category: Sentence Structure
Getting to the Answer: The underlined section includes a comma that sets off nonessential information—the name of the scientist. The punctuation at the beginning and end of the nonessential information must match. Since the opening punctuation is a comma, the closing punctuation must be a comma as well; eliminate G and H. Choice J keeps the comma, but introduces a new error by changing *who* to *he*, which makes the sentence a run-on. The sentence is correct as written, so (F) is the answer.

5. A
Difficulty: High
Category: Development
Getting to the Answer: This question asks what would be lost if the underlined portion were deleted. The underlined portion is a list of places from which Dr. Frankenstein gathered body parts. Including these details emphasizes the morbid nature of the story. Choice (A) is correct. There is nothing in the passage that suggests that Mary Shelley was inspired by these locations or that the monster became dangerous because of his origins; in fact, evidence elsewhere in the passage contradicts both B and C. Choice D is incorrect because showing Frankenstein's dedication to his work is not the primary effect of the underlined portion.

6. H
Difficulty: Medium
Category: Organization
Getting to the Answer: This sentence asks for a transition word that contrasts the monster's *gruesome appearance* with his good nature. The transitions *Similar to* and *Because of* do not convey this contrast, so eliminate F and J. Choice G contains the contrast word *Although*, but it creates a fragment when plugged back into the original sentence. The correct answer is (H).

7. D
Difficulty: Low
Category: Sentence Structure
Getting to the Answer: When a list is underlined, ensure that all items of the list have parallel structure. Choices A and C both contain elements that do not match each other, so they are incorrect. The list items in choice B match, but the *and* before the phrase "his best friend" is unnecessary. The correct answer is (D).

8. G
Difficulty: Medium
Category: Sentence Structure
Getting to the Answer: This sentence includes two independent clauses incorrectly joined with a comma, forming a run-on sentence. Eliminate F. Choice H correctly contains a coordinating conjunction that joins the two independent clauses, but it creates an incorrect logical relationship between the clauses—being a horror story is not a result of the book being viewed as a classic. Choice J changes the sentence structure

completely and introduces a comma error. Choice (G) makes the first clause dependent by using a subordinating conjunction that correctly captures the logical relationship between the clauses. The correct answer is (G).

9. B
Difficulty: Low
Category: Conciseness
Getting to the Answer: The underlined phrase is redundant. Eliminate A. Choices C and D are also unnecessarily wordy, so eliminate them, too. Only (B) is free of redundancy, so (B) is correct.

10. H
Difficulty: High
Category: Organization
Getting to the Answer: This sentence focuses on the monster's transition from good to evil. Paragraph 2 does not discuss the monster at all, so you can eliminate F and G. Choice J would put the sentence too late in Paragraph 3, after the monster has already committed evil acts. Choice (H) is the correct answer.

Passage II

11. C
Difficulty: Medium
Category: Sentence Structure
Getting to the Answer: Peek at the choices to see what the specific issue might be. All the answers have the same words but different possibilities for the comma between *illumination* and *originally* from the passage. Consider whether the commas are necessary. The original phrase has a comma between *illumination* and *originally*. This inserts a break between the subject of the sentence and the modified verb *described*. Eliminate choices A and B. Choice (C) removes the unnecessary comma and is correct. Choice D replaces the comma with a semicolon, but the phrase before the semicolon is not an independent clause and is incorrect.

12. G
Difficulty: Medium
Category: Conciseness
Getting to the Answer: The underlined portion uses more words than necessary to convey its meaning, as do H and J. Choice (G) is less wordy while still being clear, so it is correct.

13. C
Difficulty: Medium
Category: Development
Getting to the Answer: To answer this question, decide first whether the sentence should be kept or deleted. The sentence seems off-topic, discussing illuminated manuscripts in film. Eliminate choices A and B. Choice D offers the wrong reason for deleting the sentence. Choice (C) is correct.

14. J
Difficulty: High
Category: Organization
Getting to the Answer: When asked for the best transition from one paragraph to the next, look at the sentence preceding the underlined one and the sentence at the beginning of the next paragraph. The correct answer needs to connect the nuns who illuminated texts with one specific example. Eliminate choices F, G, and H because they don't act as a connector between the nuns in general and one specific nun. So choice (J) is correct.

15. B
Difficulty: Medium
Category: Style and Tone
Getting to the Answer: This essay is written in an objective, academic tone that includes more formal language. Choice A is too casual and should be eliminated. Choice (B) uses more formal language and offers details similar to the underlined phrase. Choice C is incorrect because it offers a very positive assessment of the pictures, which doesn't match the neutral tone of the rest of the essay. Choice D is incorrect because it offers a criticism of the illustrations.

TEST YOURSELF: ACT ENGLISH

Directions: For test-like timing, give yourself 35 minutes to complete the following 50 questions.

PASSAGE I

Television Displays

When most people watch their favorite shows, they probably don't stop to think about how the television set or computer screen works. All such displays, as well as film projectors, depend on an optical illusion called the phi phenomenon. If a human eye sees a series of related <u>snapshots quickly</u> enough, one after the other, the brain
1
perceives motion. Flipping through pages of similar

doodles <u>offered</u> a simple demonstration of
2

1. Which choice makes the sentence most grammatically acceptable?

   A. **No Change**
   B. snapshots, quickly
   C. snapshots quickly,
   D. snapshots; quickly

2. Which choice makes the sentence most grammatically acceptable?

   F. **No Change**
   G. offers
   H. offer
   J. has offered

this thing.
   3

For television screens, the technical challenge is how to change images quickly: the display has to present each image, hold it for a split second, and then replace it with the next image. To achieve the illusion of motion, television shows are typically displayed at thirty images, or frames—per second.
                                   4

For decades after the birth of television, a more controversial event than many people realize, these images were primarily created using a beam of electrons, or cathode ray. [5] In cathode ray tubes, or CRTs, this beam sweeps over an array of dots that glow when the

3. Which choice is clearest and most precise in context?

   A. **No Change**
   B. this effect.
   C. all that.
   D. DELETE the underlined portion and end the sentence with a period.

4. Which choice makes the sentence most grammatically acceptable?

   F. **No Change**
   G. images, or frames
   H. images or frames
   J. images—or frames—

5. The writer is considering deleting the following phrase from the preceding sentence:

   > a more controversial event than many people realize,

   Should the writer make this deletion?

   A. Yes, because the phrase is irrelevant to the paragraph's discussion of the technical details of how certain televisions work.
   B. Yes, because the phrase suggests that the controversy surrounding television contributed to the challenges of creating it.
   C. No, because the phrase offers additional information about the birth of television that gives context to the details that follow.
   D. No, because the phrase makes clear that people's views about television have changed alongside the physical challenges of making television.

beam strikes it. The television signal rapidly turns the
          6
beam on and off, synchronizing the electrons to hit
exactly the dots that make up the proper picture. As the
glow from one sweep fades, another sweep begins.

   In consumer applications, cathode ray tubes have
been replaced by liquid crystal displays (LCDs), which
are thinner, lighter, and potentially bigger. [A] Unlike
CRTs, LCDs work by selectively blocking light rather
than emitting it: the entire screen is backlit, with layers
of filters determining the quantity and color of light that
                                                        7
reaches the screen. [B] One of these filters, the liquid
    7
crystal from which the technology takes its name, can be
turned on or off electronically, allowing the image to

change quick as electricity passes through the screen. [C]
       8
However, as technology marches on, these displays may
in turn be surpassed by organic light-emitting diodes

or the more mysteriously named "quantum dots." [D]
              9
CRTs dominated television for five decades; in five more,

6. Which choice makes the sentence most grammatically acceptable?

   F. No Change
   G. these.
   H. that.
   J. them.

7. Which choice is least redundant in context?

   A. No Change
   B. light that reaches the screen through the filters.
   C. light that passes through and reaches the screen.
   D. light that is filtered out or allowed to reach the screen.

8. Which choice makes the sentence most grammatically acceptable?

   F. No Change
   G. quickly
   H. quickest
   J. more quickly

9. Which choice provides the most interesting description of the "quantum dots"?

   A. No Change
   B. confusingly
   C. secretively
   D. intriguingly

who knows how we will watch TV? [10]

10. The writer wants to divide this paragraph into two in order to separate discussion of current television displays from speculation about future television displays. The best place to begin the new paragraph would be at:

    F. Point A.
    G. Point B.
    H. Point C.
    J. Point D.

PASSAGE II

Turning Eight

The scent of freshly mown grass and vanilla frosting still lingers in my memory. It was the day of my birthday party, and the backyard had been transformed into a wonderland of balloons, streamers, and laughter from my classmates <u>who had</u> been exuberantly greeting each other.
                    11

11. Which choice makes the sentence most grammatically acceptable?

    A. **No Change**
    B. whom had
    C. whose
    D. they had

The cake was shaped like a castle, complete with novelty candles that <u>lit up and burned</u>, mirroring my
                                   12
excitement as everyone sang. I remember standing at the table decorated with a red tablecloth, with a too-big plastic crown on my head, trying to blow out all eight candles in one breath. I only managed six.

12. Which choice best illustrates the joy and excitement that the narrator is feeling?

    F. **No Change**
    G. glowed and lighted
    H. flashed and sparked
    J. scorched and blackened

After the cake, it was time for the piñata a papier-mâché monster head that Mom had made. Each swing of the bat felt like an epic sword fight, and when the candy finally rained down, we scrambled after the treasure.

But it wasn't just the games or the gifts that stayed with me. It was the warmth of my friends and family, their joy wrapped around me like a second skin.

Now, as the years stretch behind me, I let my eyes fall closed, and I smile. That little kid didn't know it then, but he was living the dream.

13. Which choice makes the sentence most grammatically acceptable?

    A. **No Change**
    B. piñata; a papier-mâché monster head that
    C. piñata—a papier-mâché monster head that
    D. piñata: a papier-mâché monster head, that

14. If the writer were to delete the underlined portion, the paragraph would primarily lose:

    F. a detail emphasizing the joy that the narrator feels while remembering the games and gifts.
    G. an image that suggests the emotions of the narrator's friends and family as they remember the party years later.
    H. a detail revealing that the narrator feels the affection of his family and friends is somewhat lacking.
    J. an image that enhances emotional impact by comparing the narrator's feelings of close, warm relationships to a physical object.

15. Which choice is least redundant in context?

    A. **No Change**
    B. as the years stretch behind me, I let my eyes fall closed as a smile rises to my lips.
    C. many years later, I find myself closing my eyes and smiling.
    D. years later, I close my eyes and smile.

Part 2
ACT ENGLISH

PASSAGE III

A Prima Ballerina

[1]

Until the late 1940s, no ballerinas in the world were as prominent <u>than</u> the best Europeans, particularly the Russians. In 1949, however, American Maria Tallchief danced the lead in *The Firebird*, staged by celebrated choreographer George Balanchine for the New York City Ballet. With this performance, Tallchief <u>vaulted</u> to international stardom.

[2]

Born in 1925 to a Native American father of the Osage Nation and a Scots-Irish mother, Tallchief began dancing ballet at the age of three. Elizabeth Marie Tall Chief, as she was then named, also studied <u>other subjects,</u> while her grandmother took her to traditional Osage dance ceremonies. These experiences probably provided <u>for Tallchief's later belief</u> the basis that ballet should be grounded in movement and musicality.

16. Which choice makes the sentence most grammatically acceptable?
    F. **No Change**
    G. as
    H. then
    J. of

17. Which choice makes the sentence most grammatically acceptable?
    A. **No Change**
    B. vaults
    C. vaulting
    D. had vaulted

18. Given that all the choices are accurate, which one provides the most relevant information at this point in the essay?
    F. **No Change**
    G. gymnastics and piano,
    H. reading and math,
    J. academic topics,

19. The best placement for the underlined portion would be:
    A. where it is now.
    B. after the word *experiences*.
    C. after the word *basis*.
    D. after the word *grounded*.

[3]

Moving to Los Angeles to further her studies, Tallchief resolved in her teenage years devoted her life to the craft of ballet. She moved again in 1942, this time to
                                                        20

New York City. Soon despite her relative inexperience,
                  21
she was accepted into the prestigious Ballet Russe de Monte Carlo. As a newcomer, Tallchief resisted

pressure to "Russify" her name to "Tallchieva" and
                                                  22
appeared in seven different ballets within two months.
                        22

[4]

When Balanchine began to coach the company, he and Tallchief clicked artistically. He designed ballets to highlight her technical prowess, easy energy, and

regal grace through his designs. In response, she
      23
worked relentlessly to improve her skills, actually lengthening her limbs over time. When Balanchine left the Ballet Russe in 1946 to found the New York City

20. Which choice makes the sentence most grammatically acceptable?

    F. No Change
    G. that would devote
    H. to devote
    J. devoting

21. Which choice makes the sentence most grammatically acceptable?

    A. No Change
    B. Soon, despite her relative inexperience
    C. Soon, despite her relative inexperience,
    D. Soon—despite her relative inexperience,

22. Given that all the choices are accurate, which one best builds on the beginning of the sentence to emphasize the pressure Tallchief was under to imitate the contemporary stars of ballet?

    F. No Change
    G. but strove to match the skill of first ballerina Nathalie Krassovska.
    H. and lost weight due to poor nutrition and stress.
    J. but went by Maria and combined the words Tall and Chief.

23. Which choice is least redundant in context?

    A. No Change
    B. grace that she would show.
    C. grace, all qualities of hers.
    D. grace.

Part 2
ACT ENGLISH

Ballet. Tallchief followed in order to continue their
artistic collaboration. This relationship continued

for over a decade, resulting in productions such as *The Nutcracker*. Tallchief retired as a ballerina in 1965 and is remembered as a woman who shattered stereotypes and broadened the field of ballet.

24. Which choice makes the sentence most grammatically acceptable?

   F. **No Change**
   G. Ballet, Tallchief
   H. Ballet; Tallchief
   J. Ballet—Tallchief

25. Which choice provides the most effective description of Tallchief's successful artistic partnership with Balanchine?

   A. **No Change**
   B. performances
   C. triumphs
   D. works

PASSAGE IV

Stax Records

[1]

In the 1960s, Stax Records stood at the forefront of new and evolving musical genres. It did not give its name to an entire trend in popular music, as its rival Motown Records did. However, Stax arguably influenced the development of rhythm and blues just as extensively. [A] There, luminaries such as Otis Redding and Isaac Hayes recorded numerous songs that become radio sensations during Stax's heyday.

26. Which choice makes the sentence most grammatically acceptable?

   F. **No Change**
   G. music. As
   H. music; as
   J. music, and as

27. Which choice makes the sentence most grammatically acceptable?

   A. **No Change**
   B. have become
   C. became
   D. had become

[2]

Many credit the session musicians at Stax with the achievements of the record label. However, these
musicians, several of whom formed the successful band Booker T. & the M.G.'s, were renowned within the industry for their skill. Regrettably, the performers were underappreciated and underpaid, even as they recorded

dozens and dozens of hits of the era.

[3]

[B] Another reason Stax found success is that partial owner and entrepreneur Estelle Axton also ran a record store. Playing rough drafts of songs for her teenaged customers and observing their reactions, Axton quickly discovered what would sell and what would not. [30]

28. Which transition word or phrase is most logical in context?

F. **No Change**
G. Thus, these
H. At first, these
J. These

29. Which choice is least redundant in context?

A. **No Change**
B. dozens of hits, maybe fifty or sixty, or even more.
C. multiple dozen hits.
D. dozens of hits.

30. If the writer were to delete the preceding sentence, the paragraph would primarily lose:

F. an explanation of how the store added to the label's success.
G. background information about one of the owners of Stax.
H. an overview of typical leisure activities of teenagers at the time.
J. an observation that weighs against a claim made earlier.

Part 2
ACT ENGLISH

[4]

Atlantic Records was another successful record label
of the time. Stax had signed a distribution deal with
Atlantic Records, but the arrangement ended bitterly
in 1968. The legal rights for almost all the hits went
to Atlantic, leading to a devastating decline for Stax.
In 1975, the label declared bankruptcy. Even after its
corporate rebirth shortly afterward, Stax struggled for
decades, surviving only by reissuing the few songs still
under its control. [C]

[5]

In recent years, however, a floundering Stax Records
has signed new artists and begun recording hits again.
[D] In 2013, several Stax musicians even performed at

the White House in an event that showcased Memphis

31. Given that all the choices are accurate, which one provides the most effective transition between the last sentence of the previous paragraph and the first sentence of this paragraph?

   A. **No Change**
   B. Unfortunately, this golden age did not last.
   C. Legal ownership of songs is a prime component of music law.
   D. Stax Record's business relationship with Atlantic Records also benefited Stax.

32. Which choice provides the most specific indication that Stax is making a comeback?

   F. **No Change**
   G. a fledgling
   H. an outdated
   J. a rejuvenated

33. Which choice is clearest and most precise in context?

   A. **No Change**
   B. supplied
   C. uncovered
   D. unified

soul music. Back in Memphis, dedicated to
American soul music, the site where the legendary
recording studio once stood is now occupied by a
museum.
34

34. Which choice makes the sentence most grammatically acceptable?

F. No Change
G. a museum dedicated to American soul music now occupies the site where the legendary recording studio once stood.
H. dedicated to American soul music, the legendary recording studio once stood on a site now occupied by a museum.
J. an American soul music museum now occupies the dedicated site where the legendary recording studio once stood.

Question 35 asks about the preceding passage as a whole.

35. The writer is considering adding the following sentence to the essay:

   Indeed, the sound of Southern soul was largely born at the Stax studio in Memphis, Tennessee.

If the writer were to add this sentence, it would most logically be placed at:

A. Point A in Paragraph 1.
B. Point B in Paragraph 3.
C. Point C in Paragraph 4.
D. Point D in Paragraph 5.

Part 2
ACT ENGLISH

PASSAGE V

The Bluehead Chubs' Rocky Nest

In the sandy, rock-lined shores of the Rapidan River in north-central Virginia, fish known as bluehead chubs construct temporary nests for fertilized eggs and larvae. Built in as little as a day, these nests—which can span as wide as three feet and as tall as two feet—are made with up to 7,000 pieces of gravel gathered from up to 25 yards away by a fish only the size of your hand. [36]

Though referred to as nests, which commonly evokes thoughts of bowl-shaped tangles of sticks, strings, and other found materials, these sanctuaries are dome-like structures that stand out against a backdrop of the river's algae-covered substrate. Primarily used to attract egg-laying female chubs, the nests also house other

36. If the writer were to delete the phrase "which can span as wide as three feet and as tall as two feet" from the preceding sentence (adjusting the punctuation as needed), the sentence would primarily lose:

F. specific information that illustrates the unique dimensions of the largest nest built by a bluehead chub.
G. specific information that emphasizes the significant size of the bluehead chubs' nests.
H. details that clarify how the chubs can thrive in the Rapidan River.
J. details that underscore how the chubs' nests are similar to the nests of other fish.

37. The writer wants to emphasize the details of the chubs' nesting location by using vivid language to evoke a specific image. Which choice best accomplishes this goal?

A. **No Change**
B. riverbed rocks.
C. assorted green gravel.
D. shimmering plant-slicked stones.

fishes, or "nest associates," they search for sanctuary in
                              38
which to lay their own offspring. Many minnow species
also spawn in the bluehead architecture, taking

advantage of the protection provided to all the fish
                                     39
hidden from predators.
       39

   While other fish, such as trout, may craft nests using
their fins and tails, the bluehead chub and other fish in
the *Cyprinidae* family are unique in that they carry the
rocks in their mouth. In fact, most mature males have
keratin on the inside of it's mouths that acts as a sort of
                         40
callus, protecting them from harm.

38. Which choice makes the sentence most grammatically acceptable?

   F. **No Change**
   G. searches
   H. searching
   J. searched

39. Which choice is least redundant in context?

   A. **No Change**
   B. that all the groups of fish benefit from together.
   C. from the predators who hunt all the fish grouped together.
   D. provided by the shared space in which the different groups of fish huddle.

40. Which choice makes the sentence most grammatically acceptable?

   F. **No Change**
   G. of their
   H. of its
   J. of there

PASSAGE VI

Dropping an Egg

<u>My freshman teacher, Ms. Windham, of physics,</u>
              41
did not like sitting down. After greeting us at the door,
she <u>sprang</u> around the room, acting out the motion of
       42
a projectile according to Newton's laws or the behavior
of gas particles under pressure. Even when we were
taking a test, she moved quietly and actively among our
desks, as if eager for the class to return to more energetic
activities.

With her <u>infectious enthusiasm that was contagious</u>
                                    43
<u>among the students,</u> Ms. Windham did not want us to
      43

be sitting for long, either. <u>They themselves</u> were often
                                      44
the gas particles or the projectiles—although not
literally, of course. We built various devices to accelerate
small steel balls, including painstakingly calibrated
catapults and cartoonishly twisted rolling tracks. In the
gymnasium, we floated on a noisy hovercraft that she
and the rest of the science department had constructed,
a contraption of plywood and garbage bags powered by

41. Which choice makes the sentence most grammatically acceptable?

A. **No Change**
B. Ms. Windham my freshman teacher of physics
C. My freshman physics teacher, Ms. Windham,
D. My physics teacher, Ms. Windham, for freshmen,

42. Which choice best illustrates the high level of energy with which Ms. Windham taught?

F. **No Change**
G. twitched
H. sauntered
J. tottered

43. Which choice is least redundant in context?

A. **No Change**
B. infectious zeal that spread from person to person,
C. zealous, eager enthusiasm that infected us all,
D. contagious enthusiasm,

44. Which choice makes the sentence most grammatically acceptable?

F. **No Change**
G. You yourselves
H. We ourselves
J. They and I

leaf blowers. That occasion was one of the few times I saw Ms. Windham seated, smiling as she glided across the gym floor.

The highlight of the year was the springtime egg drop. Much prestige was associated at this contest, which involved building a capsule that, when dropped from the roof of the science wing, would protect a raw egg nestled inside it. As Ms. Windham explained, the top <u>prize was for a combination of speed and accuracy would</u> be
             45
awarded to the capsule that fell fastest and landed closest to the target while still preserving its egg.

Another prize <u>went</u> to the pod that took the longest
              46
to land. The Disaster Miracle trophy would be for the capsule that broke apart most dramatically—in Ms. Windham's judgment—but nevertheless kept the egg inside safe.

<u>Before this class, I had never operated power tools.</u>
                       47
My lab partner and I ultimately chose to aim for the Disaster Miracle: we thought it would be the most fun to design and especially to deploy. On the day of the drop,

45. Which choice makes the sentence most grammatically acceptable?

   A. No Change
   B. prize was for a combination of speed and accuracy, would
   C. prize, for a combination of speed and accuracy, to
   D. prize, for a combination of speed and accuracy, would

46. Which choice makes the sentence most grammatically acceptable?

   F. No Change
   G. goes
   H. would go
   J. has gone

47. Given that all the choices are accurate, which one provides the best transition from the preceding paragraph to this paragraph?

   A. No Change
   B. On the day of the drop, the weather was gorgeous.
   C. Earlier in the spring, I had read my first book about engineering.
   D. Deciding which prize to strive for was far from straightforward.

my "Egg-splorer" module shattered beautifully
48

on impact, and the egg survived. Years later, the photo
                                    49
of my partner and me holding our trophy over our heads still makes me smile, even as I prepare to pursue my undergraduate degree in mechanical engineering.

The photo has a special spot in my scrapbook of high
                                        50
school memories.
     50

48. Which choice makes the sentence most grammatically acceptable?

   F. **No Change**
   G. their
   H. whose
   J. our

49. Which transition word or phrase is most logical in context?

   A. **No Change**
   B. Next,
   C. In the meantime,
   D. So far,

50. Which choice most effectively concludes the paragraph and the essay?

   F. **No Change**
   G. I credit Ms. Windham and her engaging approach to teaching physics with sparking my passion for science.
   H. Ms. Windham still conducts the popular egg drop event, with its humorous Disaster Miracle prize, every spring.
   J. Ms. Windham, in her true energetic style, would literally jump with excitement when viewing the egg drops.

Answers and Explanations

Passage I

1. A
Difficulty: Low
Category: Sentence Structure: Commas, Dashes, and Colons
Getting to the Answer: This question tests correct usage of commas and semicolons. *Snapshots* is part of the object of the verb *sees*, and *quickly* is an adverb describing the verb; neither of them should be separated from another part of the sentence, so no punctuation is needed here. The correct answer is (A).

For the record: putting a comma between *snapshots* and *quickly* separates *quickly* from the verb it describes, so B is incorrect. In C, the comma is separating the words *quickly* and *enough*, but since *enough* is describing *quickly*, the two words should not be separated. Finally, the semicolon in D does not separate two independent clauses, so it is incorrect.

2. G
Difficulty: High
Category: Agreement: Verbs
Getting to the Answer: Although this sentence may seem grammatically correct on its own, the underlined verb is in past tense, while the rest of the paragraph is in simple present tense. Eliminate F and J since neither matches the tense of the rest of the paragraph. Choice H is in the correct tense, but it introduces a new error: *offer* is a plural verb, but the subject of the verb is the act of flipping, which is singular. Thus, it requires the singular present tense verb *offers*. Choice (G) is correct.

3. B
Difficulty: Medium
Category: Development: Precision
Getting to the Answer: The phrase *this thing* is vague; more specific wording is necessary. Eliminate A. Choice C is just as vague, so eliminate it as well. Choice D may be tempting, since deleting the phrase would fix the vagueness problem and make the sentence more concise, but when this option is plugged into the sentence, the result is "a simple demonstration of." Since *of* has no object, this is incorrect, eliminate it. Choice (B) clearly and specifically refers to the phi phenomenon, so it is the correct answer.

4. J
Difficulty: Low
Category: Sentence Structure: Parenthetical Elements
Getting to the Answer: Parenthetical elements, like the phrase *or frames*, must be set off by matching punctuation, whether commas, dashes, or parentheses. Eliminate F because the punctuation does not match. Eliminate G because only one punctuation mark is present. Eliminate H because it has no punctuation at all. Choice (J) is the only answer to use matching punctuation to set off nonessential information, so it is correct.

5. A
Difficulty: Medium
Category: Development: Revising Text
Getting to the Answer: First, determine whether the line in question should be deleted. In this case, the phrase is unrelated to the sentence and paragraph it is in, so it should be cut. Eliminate C and D. Then, check the "Yes" choices for the one that matches your reasoning. Choice (A) matches and is correct.

6. J
Difficulty: High
Category: Agreement: Pronouns
Getting to the Answer: When a pronoun is underlined, check that it is in the correct form and matches the noun it refers to. Here, the pronoun must be plural because it is the *dots* that are lighting up—you can tell because the verb *glow* is plural, so its subject must be the plural *dots* rather than the singular *array*. Eliminate F. *That* is also singular, so eliminate H. *These*, while plural, is not in the correct form to fit in the sentence, so eliminate G. *Them* is plural and in the right form, so (J) is correct.

7. A
Difficulty: Medium
Category: Conciseness
Getting to the Answer: When the underlined portion seems to be grammatically correct, check the choices to see if there is another issue. Here, the problem is wordiness. Since the sentence discusses filters earlier, B and D are redundant. In C, "passes though" and "reaches" mean the same thing. Choice (A) conveys the writer's meaning most concisely, so it is correct.

8. G
Difficulty: Low
Category: Agreement: Modifiers
Getting to the Answer: In this sentence, *quick* is describing the verb *change*, so it should be an adverb rather than an adjective. Eliminate F. *Quickly* is the correct form, so (G) is correct.

Choices H and J are incorrect because these are comparison words and nothing is being compared.

9. D
Difficulty: Medium
Category: Development: Precision
Getting to the Answer: Since the question stem asks for a word that shows quantum dots are *interesting*, look for a choice that means *interesting*. Choice (D) fits well and is correct.

Mysteriously describes something that is unknown; *confusingly* describes something that is not understood; and *secretively* describes something that is deliberately hidden. These things do not necessarily have to be *interesting*, however, so A, B, and C are incorrect.

10. H
Difficulty: Medium
Category: Development: Revising Text
Getting to the Answer: To answer a question like this, look for where the paragraph shifts its focus. The transition word *However* is a good clue, and the sentence continues with "as technology marches on." Furthermore, the sentence immediately before this one describes the liquid crystal filter in LCD televisions. Point C is where the paragraph changes from discussing current television displays to speculating about future ones, so (H) is correct.

Passage II

11. A
Difficulty: High
Category: Agreement
Getting to the Answer: A quick glance at the answer choices reveals the issue to be pronouns. Look for the antecedent of the pronoun; the pronoun *who* is standing in for *classmates*, which is the subject of the relative clause. In the subjective case, *who* is the correct pronoun, so (A) is correct. Choice B is incorrect; *whom* would be the pronoun if *classmates* was the object of the clause. Choice C is a possessive pronoun, which does not make sense in this context. Choice D is incorrect because it would introduce another error by making the sentence a run-on.

12. H
Difficulty: Medium
Category: Development
Getting to the Answer: This question is testing precision, as it asks which choice describes candles burning in a way that conveys joy and excitement. Choices F and G are too neutral and too calm, respectively. Choice (H) is correct; "flashed and sparked" convey the appropriate sense of energy and delight that a kid would feel at a birthday party. Choice J is incorrect because the negative connotations of "scorched and blackened" do not convey joy.

13. C
Difficulty: High
Category: Sentence Structure
Getting to the Answer: This question is testing sentence structure; all the choices contain ways to join these clauses. Start by determining that "After the cake, it was time for the piñata" is an independent clause, and "a papier-mâché monster head that Mom had made" is a dependent clause. Eliminate A because it results in a run-on. Eliminate B since a semicolon cannot properly connect an independent clause and a dependent clause. The last two choices correctly use a dash and a colon, respectively, to separate these two clauses, but D incorrectly places a comma before the word *that*, which begins an essential phrase. Choice (C) is correct.

14. J
Difficulty: Medium
Category: Development
Getting to the Answer: To determine what the paragraph would lose, first determine what the function of the underlined portion is. The phrase "like a second skin" is imagery that helps the reader understand how the narrator is feeling surrounded by friends and family. The best match is (J), the correct answer. Choices F and G are distortions; both are incorrect. According to the first sentence in the paragraph, the narrator remembers joy not from the gifts and games as mentioned in F, but from friends and family. Similarly, G is incorrect because the family and friends are not remembering

the party; the narrator is. Choice H is incorrect because it is opposite; the narrator does not find the affection of his family and friends lacking at all.

15. D
Difficulty: Low
Category: Conciseness
Getting to the Answer: The phrase "least redundant" indicates this is a Conciseness question. Examine the shortest choice, (D), and compare it to the text to make sure no essential information has been left out. The choice has all the essential information in the fewest words, so (D) is correct. All the other choices have the same meaning but use more words.

Passage III

16. G
Difficulty: Low
Category: Agreement: Idioms
Getting to the Answer: As written, "as prominent than" is idiomatically incorrect. To complete the idiom, the underlined word should be *as*. Choice (G) is correct.

17. A
Difficulty: Low
Category: Agreement: Verbs
Getting to the Answer: To fit with the other verbs in this paragraph, the underlined word should be in simple past tense. It is correct as written, so the correct choice is (A).

Choices B and C are in present tense, so they are incorrect. Choice D may be more tempting, because it uses past tense. However, the helping verb *had* suggests that Tallchief had already achieved fame before some other past event occurred. Because the passage does not mention such an event, D is incorrect as well.

18. G
Difficulty: High
Category: Development: Revising Text
Getting to the Answer: The question asks for the most relevant information. Choices F and J are too vague to be the most relevant, so eliminate them. Choice H, "reading and math," has little to do with Tallchief's dancing studies, so eliminate it. Additionally, the next sentence discusses Tallchief's belief in the importance of "movement and musicality," which parallels nicely with "gymnastics and piano." Choice (G) is correct.

19. C
Difficulty: Medium
Category: Agreement: Modifiers
Getting to the Answer: As written, this sentence has a placement issue. The underlined phrase ought to immediately follow the word it is describing, so think about what word in the sentence "for Tallchief's later belief" logically follows. Because Tallchief's experiences gave her a *basis for* her belief, (C) is correct. Choices A, B, and D all incorrectly place the underlined phrase.

20. H
Difficulty: Medium
Category: Agreement: Verbs
Getting to the Answer: As written, the underlined verb's tense is idiomatically incorrect. This is clear if you remove the phrase "in her teenage years": saying she "resolved *devoted* her life to ballet" is incorrect. Eliminate F. Plug in the remaining choices to see which one results in an idiomatically correct construction. Choice J does not provide an acceptable verb form—"resolved *devoting* her life to ballet" is no better than F—so eliminate J. Choice G creates a subordinate clause by introducing the word *that*. The verb *would devote* is in an acceptable form for this new clause, but it lacks a subject; therefore, G is also incorrect. Choice (H) fixes the problem without introducing any new errors, so it is correct.

21. C
Difficulty: Medium
Category: Sentence Structure: Parenthetical Elements
Getting to the Answer: *Soon* is nonessential information that must be set off from the rest of the sentence with punctuation. Because A lacks punctuation after *Soon*, eliminate it. Choice D inserts a dash, but parenthetical elements at the beginning of sentences cannot be set off with dashes, so eliminate D. Choice B correctly uses a comma after *Soon*, but it omits the comma after *inexperience*. Because "despite her relative inexperience" is also parenthetical information that should be separated from the rest of the sentence, B is incorrect. Choice (C) fixes the initial error by inserting a comma after *Soon* and does not create any new issues, so (C) is correct.

Part 2
ACT ENGLISH

22. J
Difficulty: High
Category: Development: Revising Text
Getting to the Answer: Think carefully about which choice would best accomplish the purpose given in the question. The first paragraph states that the most famous ballerinas of the time were Russian, and the first half of this sentence describes how Tallchief refused to "Russify" her name. Dancing in many ballets does not show that she was pressured to imitate Russian ballerinas, so eliminate F. Tallchief might easily have wished to be as skilled as the first ballerina without any external pressure, so eliminate G. Similarly, although the mention of *stress* in H may be tempting, there is no evidence that pressure to imitate others caused the stress. Eliminate H. Choice (J) fits, showing that although Tallchief did not want to use a Russian version of her name, she did partially alter it when pressured to do so.

23. D
Difficulty: Low
Category: Conciseness
Getting to the Answer: The first part of the sentence states that Balanchine designed ballets with Tallchief in mind, so the phrase "through his designs" is redundant. Eliminate A. Choices B and C are unnecessarily wordy, so eliminate them also. Choice (D) is the most concise choice and therefore correct.

24. G
Difficulty: Low
Category: Sentence Structure: The Basics
Getting to the Answer: The phrase before the period in the underlined portion is a fragment. It cannot stand alone and needs to be connected to the following sentence, so eliminate F. A semicolon connects two independent clauses, so eliminate H. When a dash is used between two clauses, both must be independent, so J is also incorrect. A comma is used to connect a dependent to an independent clause, so (G) is correct.

25. C
Difficulty: Medium
Category: Development: Precision
Getting to the Answer: While all of the choices could fit grammatically in the sentence, the question specifically asks for one that conveys an artistic partnership. Choices A, B, and D are all too neutral; *productions, performances,* and *works* can all be victories or failures.

Triumphs clearly shows that Tallchief and Balanchine achieved success by working together, so (C) is correct.

Passage IV

26. F
Difficulty: Low
Category: Sentence Structure: The Basics
Getting to the Answer: The underlined portion connects two clauses. The word *as* makes the second clause dependent, meaning that the clause cannot function as a stand-alone sentence. Eliminate G, which turns the second clause into a fragment. Also eliminate H and J, which are ways of joining two independent clauses, not an independent and a dependent clause. Choice (F) is correct because a comma can be used to join a subordinate clause to an independent clause.

27. C
Difficulty: Low
Category: Agreement: Verbs
Getting to the Answer: Use context to determine the appropriate tense for the underlined verb. In the same sentence as the underline, the verb *recorded* appears in past tense. Therefore, the action described by the underlined verb should also be in the past—something that occurred back in *Stax's heyday*. The simple past tense (C) is correct.

Choice A is incorrect because it is present tense. Choices B and D are incorrect because they use tenses that are too complex for this context. (For the record, B indicates a past action that continues into the present time, and D indicates an action that occurred before another past action.)

28. J
Difficulty: Medium
Category: Organization: Transitions
Getting to the Answer: The underlined word *However* indicates a contrast, so determine whether this type of transition is appropriate in context. The previous sentence attributes the *achievements* of Stax to its *musicians*. The sentence with the underline builds on this idea by claiming the musicians were "renowned within the industry for their skill." These ideas do not contrast, so eliminate F. Eliminate the cause-and-effect transition in G because the achievements of the label are not the cause of the musicians' renown. The sentence is not part of a chronological narrative, so

eliminate H. Getting rid of the transition word entirely, (J), maintains the appropriate logic between the ideas in the paragraph.

29. D
Difficulty: Low
Category: Conciseness
Getting to the Answer: The underlined portion repeats the word *dozens* and the answer choices are of varying lengths, so check to see if there is an issue with conciseness. Indeed, repeating *dozens* is unnecessary, as is specifying that the hits were during the era in which the performers recorded them. Eliminate A. Eliminate B, which is even wordier. The phrase *multiple dozen* in C is still redundant. Choice (D) is correct because it most concisely expresses the writer's intended meaning: the performers recorded *many* hits.

30. F
Difficulty: Medium
Category: Development: Revising Text
Getting to the Answer: Consider the relevance of the sentence in the context of the paragraph. The first sentence of the paragraph identifies the topic: Axton running a record store was an additional reason for Stax's success. The sentence in question explains why this was the case: she was able to discover "what would sell and what would not." Choice (F) is correct because it accurately identifies the sentence as an explanation of how the store contributed to Stax's success.

The other choices are incorrect because they do not identify the sentence as support for the paragraph's topic. Furthermore, G and H are incorrect because the sentence provides little background about Axton or teenagers. Choice J is incorrect because the sentence does not counter any previous claim.

31. B
Difficulty: High
Category: Development: Introductions and Conclusions
Getting to the Answer: Understand the previous paragraph and then read the paragraph and paraphrase its main idea before looking at the answer choices. The paragraph begins by mentioning a deal between Stax and Atlantic Records that ended badly. The remainder of the paragraph focuses on what happened to Stax afterward: losing the rights to hit songs, filing bankruptcy, and going through decades of struggle. The paragraph focuses on the decline of Stax from the success described in the previous paragraph, so (B) is correct.

Choice A is incorrect because the paragraph's main focus is Stax, not Atlantic Records. Choice C is incorrect because it focuses too broadly on overall music law. Choice D is incorrect because the paragraph is about Stax's decline, not its success.

32. J
Difficulty: Medium
Category: Development: Precision
Getting to the Answer: Analyze the choices to determine which word best indicates that Stax is undergoing a *comeback*—a change from struggle to success. Eliminate F, *floundering*, which indicates struggle only. Choice G, *fledgling*, means something that is young and inexperienced, which does not describe a decades-old music label. Choice H, *outdated*, would mean that Stax is old-fashioned, not that it is achieving new success. Choice (J), *rejuvenated*, means to make new or fresh and thus correctly captures the idea of a comeback.

33. A
Difficulty: Medium
Category: Development: Precision
Getting to the Answer: When the answer choices contain various word choices, first make a prediction for the intended meaning of the underlined word. The sentence describes an *event* at the White House that did something to Memphis soul music. Predict that an event likely had the purpose of positively *featuring* or *celebrating* or *highlighting* the music style. This matches (A), *showcased*.

Music is not usually said to be *supplied*, so B is incorrect. Nothing in the context indicates that Memphis soul music was previously hidden or disunited, so C and D are incorrect.

34. G
Difficulty: High
Category: Agreement: Modifiers
Getting to the Answer: The answer choices place the modifying phrase "dedicated to American soul music" in various locations. The phrase describes *a museum*, so it should be adjacent to *a museum*. Eliminate F, in which the phrase describes *the site*, and H, in which the phrase describes "the legendary recording studio." Choice J changes the meaning of the sentence by using *dedicated* to describe *site*. Choice (G) is correct because it places the modifying phrase next to *a museum*.

35. A

Difficulty: Medium
Category: Organization: Sentence Placement
Getting to the Answer: The new sentence begins with the transition word *Indeed*, indicating that the detail about Southern soul developing at Stax should build upon a related idea in the previous sentence. The new sentence also identifies Stax studio's location in Memphis. Test the potential placements for the sentence to determine where these details logically fit. Choice (A) is correct because the new sentence ties together the ideas before and after Point A. The previous sentence identified Stax's strong influence on rhythm and blues, and the new sentence identifies this type of music as "the sound of Southern soul." The new sentence's detail that the studio was in Memphis anchors the *There* in the sentence that follows Point A.

Choices B and C are incorrect because the new sentence does not match the topics of Paragraphs 3 and 4, which discuss Estelle Axton's contribution to the success of Stax and Stax's decline, respectively. Choice D is incorrect because placing the sentence at Point D would interrupt the discussion of Stax's successes in recent years.

Passage V

36. G

Difficulty: Medium
Category: Development: Revising Text
Getting to the Answer: Consider the relevance of the phrase in the context of the sentence. The first part of the sentence explains that the nest can be built in just a day. The idea after the parenthetical information is that it has thousands of pebbles and is assembled by a small fish. The offset phrase is about the size of the structure, which, when compared to the time frame and fish's size, is quite impressive. Choice (G) is correct because it accurately identifies that the phrase highlights the significant size of the nest.

Choice F can be eliminated because nothing in the sentence suggests that the nests' dimensions are "unique" or the "largest." Incorrect choice H brings in details outside of the text: there is nothing about the nests' size contributing to the fish *thriv[ing]*. Choice J is incorrect because there are no comparisons with other fish until the third paragraph.

37. D

Difficulty: Medium
Category: Development: Revising Text
Getting to the Answer: This question is looking for *vivid* language that brings out a certain image, so look for words in the answer choices that help the reader imagine the nesting with vivid, or intense, language. Choice A employs very technical language; eliminate it. Choice B has plain, direct language and is incorrect. Choice C uses a descriptor that could paint a picture, *green*, but it is not really a fanciful word. Choice H can be eliminated. This leaves choice (D) as correct. On test day, select this answer with confidence and move on. For reference, *shimmering* has an intense quality, and *plant-slicked* helps draw a specific image.

38. H

Difficulty: Hard
Category: Agreement: Verbs
Getting to the Answer: Use context to determine the appropriate tense for the underlined verb or verb phrase. The sentence starts with a modifying phrase that sets up a complete idea about the nests (the nests . . . house), so the verb *search* must be used to create a subordinate sentence. Choice F is incorrect because "the nests also house other fishes . . . [they search]" creates a sentence error by having two complete thoughts without the correct punctuation to separate them. Eliminate choice G because *searches* would create two independent clauses ("the nests also house other fishes . . . [search]") in a sentence that does not have punctuation to correctly separate them. Choice (H) correctly creates a supplemental idea that supports the main idea: "the nests also house other fishes . . . searching for sanctuary."

On test day, select that choice and move on. For further development, note that choice J is incorrect because nothing in the sentence supports a past tense verb.

39. A

Difficulty: High
Category: Conciseness
Getting to the Answer: The question is testing wordiness. The sentence that contains the underlined phrase explains that many minnows take advantage of the protection offered by the nest. There is no redundancy, so (A) is correct.

Choice B is incorrect because *all*, *groups of fish*, and *together* repeat a idea of *many*, which could be communicated with fewer words. Incorrect choice C would be eliminated for similar repetition. Choice D is also incorrect because it includes excessive words and phases that signal *multitude: shared, different,* and *groups of fish.*

40. G
Difficulty: Low
Category: Agreement: Pronouns
Getting to the Answer: When a pronoun is underlined, check that it is in the correct form and matches the noun to which it refers. Here, the pronoun must be plural because the keratin is in the mouths of *males*. Eliminate F and H because the former is the contraction of *it is* and the latter is singular possessive. Eliminate J, *there*, because it is not a possessive plural pronoun. Choice (G) is correct.

Passage VI

41. C
Difficulty: Medium
Category: Sentence Structure: Parenthetical Elements
Getting to the Answer: Either *Ms. Windham* or some form of "my freshman physics teacher" could be the subject of the sentence. Either phrase by itself would sufficiently specify the person being described, so the other phrase, if also included, would be parenthetical information added to the sentence to provide additional detail. Keeping in mind that parenthetical elements must be set off from the rest of the sentence, look for the choice that punctuates the phrases correctly. Choice A does set off the phrase *Ms. Windham* with commas, but it is incorrect because it inserts the phrase in the middle of "My freshman teacher of physics" and adds an unnecessary comma after *physics*, separating the subject and verb of the sentence. Choice B fails to use commas to set off the nonessential phrase "my freshman teacher of physics," so it is incorrect. Choice (C) is correct because it sets off the nonessential phrase *Ms. Windham* without adding unneeded punctuation. Choice D introduces the same issues as A, inserting the phrase *Ms. Windham* in an illogical spot and adding a comma between the sentence's subject and verb.

42. F
Difficulty: Medium
Category: Development: Precision
Getting to the Answer: Evaluate the answer choices to see which one conveys a high level of energy. As written, *sprang* can mean to move suddenly or quickly, which certainly conveys movement with a high level of energy; (F) is correct. Choice G, *twitched*, could describe quick movement, but the word implies a sudden jerking motion that does not necessarily convey the idea of moving energetically around a classroom. Choice H is incorrect because *sauntered* means to walk slowly, which is the opposite of the intended meaning. Choice J is incorrect because *tottered* means to move unsteadily, not energetically.

43. D
Difficulty: Medium
Category: Conciseness
Getting to the Answer: In context, *infectious* and *contagious* are redundant, so eliminate A. Choices B and C are also unnecessarily wordy ways to express the idea that Ms. Windham's enthusiasm spread to others. For B, *infectious* means the same as "spread from person to person," and for C, *zealous* and *eager* are redundant. Choice (D) is correct because it most concisely conveys the writer's intended meaning.

44. H
Difficulty: Medium
Category: Agreement: Pronouns
Getting to the Answer: When a pronoun is underlined, find its antecedent to determine whether they are in agreement. In this sentence, the pronoun refers to whoever were the "gas particles or the projectiles." The previous sentence provides the context: "Ms. Windham did not want *us* to be sitting for long." The pronoun refers to the group of students that includes the narrator, so eliminate choices F and G, which do not include the narrator. In context, J is an unnecessarily wordy way of saying *we*, so J is incorrect. Choice (H) is correct.

45. D
Difficulty: High
Category: Sentence Structure: Parenthetical Elements
Getting to the Answer: As written, the parts of the sentence run together. Two verbs (*was . . . would be*) apply to the subject *the top prize*, but there isn't an *and* to correctly set up this compound predicate. Eliminate A. Eliminate B as well; merely placing a comma before the second verb does not correct the original error. Choice C is incorrect because it removes all predicate verbs from the sentence, resulting in a fragment. Choice (D) fixes the error by making the phrase "for a combination of speed and accuracy" parenthetical and deleting the verb *was*, resulting in a sentence with *would be* as the main verb. Choice (D) is correct.

46. H
Difficulty: Low
Category: Agreement: Verbs
Getting to the Answer: When a verb is underlined, always check that it both agrees with its subject and matches the surrounding verb forms. The paragraph is describing prizes for the upcoming egg drop, so the conditional verb *would be* is used in the second sentence of the paragraph. Only (H), *would go*, matches the rest of the paragraph.

The other choices do not match the conditional verbs used in the rest of the paragraph: F is past tense, G is present tense, and J is present perfect tense.

47. D
Difficulty: Medium
Category: Organization: Transitions
Getting to the Answer: Because you are asked to make a transition, consider both what was occurring at the end of the previous paragraph and what is happening in this paragraph. The previous paragraph describes the various possible prizes for the egg drop, and this paragraph begins by stating that the narrator and their partner chose to try to win the *Disaster Miracle* prize. The correct choice should provide a link between the general description of the contest to the narrator's particular experience. This is best accomplished by (D).

None of the other choices provides this transition. Choice A is entirely off-topic. Choice B introduces the day of the egg drop but does not logically fit between sentences about making the choice of which prize to pursue. Choice C connects to ideas later in the last paragraph, but, like B, interrupts the flow of the ideas about the egg drop prizes.

48. J
Difficulty: Medium
Category: Agreement: Pronouns
Getting to the Answer: Make sure that an underlined pronoun both matches its antecedent and is in the correct form. The pronoun here should be possessive, because the "Egg-splorer" belongs to the pronoun. All of the choices are possessive, so now consider the pronoun's antecedent. The previous sentence makes it clear that the Egg-splorer belongs to "My lab partner and I" and uses the pronoun *we*. The underlined pronoun should include both the narrator and the lab partner, so (J) is correct.

Choice F is incorrect because *my* excludes the lab partner. Choice G is incorrect because *their* excludes the narrator. Choice H is incorrect because *whose* would change the structure of the sentence, implying that the Egg-splorer belongs to the "day of the drop."

49. A
Difficulty: Medium
Category: Organization: Transitions
Getting to the Answer: Consider the sequence of events in the surrounding context to determine which transition phrase is appropriate. The previous sentence describes what happens on "the day of the drop." The sentence with the underline indicates that the photo *still* makes the narrator smile while preparing for college. The transition phrase should link this past event to the present, which is best accomplished by (A).

Choice B is incorrect because *Next* indicates sequential events, which is not appropriate for the timeline described in the passage. Choice C, *in the meantime*, describes two concurrent events. Choice D is incorrect because the author does not make any indication that the photo has only made her smile *so far* and will stop making her smile in the future.

50. G
Difficulty: High
Category: Development: Introductions and Conclusions
Getting to the Answer: Review the main ideas of the essay so you can determine the best conclusion. The first two paragraphs describe the active teaching style of the narrator's physics teacher. The third paragraph describes the annual spring egg drop. The focus of the last paragraph shifts to the narrator's particular experience of winning a prize at the egg drop, including the positive reaction the memory of the event continues to have on the narrator as she prepares for college. The last sentence should synthesize these ideas; (G) is correct because it connects Ms. Windham's teaching to its positive impact on the narrator.

Choice F is incorrect because it focuses too narrowly on photos, which are only referenced in a detail in the previous sentence. Choice H is incorrect because it omits any mention of Ms. Windham's teaching style in the first two paragraphs and any indication of her lasting impact on the narrator. Choice J is incorrect because Ms. Windham's immediate reaction to the egg drops does not logically fit after the narrator's reflection on the photo of the egg drop.

[PART 3]

ACT MATH

[CHAPTER 6]

PREREQUISITE SKILLS AND CALCULATOR USE

> **LEARNING OBJECTIVES**
>
> After completing this chapter, you will be able to:
>
> - Identify skills you need to develop to obtain the full benefits of the math sections of this book
> - Distinguish ACT questions on which a calculator will be helpful or unhelpful

MATH FUNDAMENTALS

> **LEARNING OBJECTIVE**
>
> After this lesson, you will be able to:
>
> - Identify skills you need to develop to obtain the full benefits of the math sections of this book

Course Prerequisites

This course focuses on the skills that are tested on the ACT. It assumes a working knowledge of arithmetic, algebra, and geometry. Before you dive into the subsequent chapters, where you'll try test-like questions, there are a number of concepts—ranging from basic arithmetic to geometry—that you should master. The following sections contain a brief review of these concepts.

Order of Operations

The **order of operations** is one of the most fundamental of all arithmetic rules. A well-known mnemonic device for remembering this order is PEMDAS: Please Excuse My Dear Aunt Sally. This translates to Parentheses, Exponents, Multiplication/Division, Addition/Subtraction. Perform multiplication and division from left to right (even if it means division before multiplication) and treat addition and subtraction the same way.

$$(14 - 4 \div 2)^2 - 3 + (2 - 1)$$
$$= (14 - 2)^2 - 3 + (1)$$
$$= 12^2 - 3 + 1$$
$$= 144 - 3 + 1$$
$$= 141 + 1$$
$$= 142$$

Subtracting a positive number is the same as adding its negative. Likewise, subtracting a negative number is the same as adding its positive.

$$r - s = r + (-s) \rightarrow 22 - 15 = 7 \text{ and } 22 + (-15) = 7$$
$$r - (-s) = r + s \rightarrow 22 - (-15) = 37 \text{ and } 22 + 15 = 37$$

Commutative, Associative, and Distributive Properties

Three basic properties of number (and variable) manipulation—commutative, associative, and distributive—will assist you with algebra on test day.

- **Commutative:** Numbers can swap places and still provide the same mathematical result. This is valid only for addition and multiplication.

$$a + b = b + a \rightarrow 3 + 4 = 4 + 3$$
$$a \times b = b \times a \rightarrow 3 \times 4 = 4 \times 3$$

  BUT: $3 - 4 \neq 4 - 3$ and $3 \div 4 \neq 4 \div 3$

- **Associative:** Different number groupings will provide the same mathematical result. This is valid only for addition and multiplication.

$$(a + b) + c = a + (b + c) \rightarrow (4 + 5) + 6 = 4 + (5 + 6)$$
$$(a \times b) \times c = a \times (b \times c) \rightarrow (4 \times 5) \times 6 = 4 \times (5 \times 6)$$

  BUT: $(4 - 5) - 6 \neq 4 - (5 - 6)$ and $(4 \div 5) \div 6 \neq 4 \div (5 \div 6)$

- **Distributive:** A number that is multiplied by the sum or difference of two other numbers can be rewritten as the first number multiplied by the two others individually. This does not work with division.

$$a(b + c) = ab + ac \rightarrow 6(x + 3) = 6x + 6(3)$$
$$a(b - c) = ab - ac \rightarrow 3(y - 2) = 3y + 3(-2)$$

  BUT: $12 \div (6 + 2) \neq 12 \div 6 + 12 \div 2$

  Note: When subtracting an expression in parentheses, such as in $4 - (x + 3)$, distribute the negative sign outside the parentheses first: $4 + (-x - 3) \rightarrow 1 - x$.

Prime Factorization

A **prime number** is a positive integer that is divisible without a remainder by only 1 and itself. The number 2 is the smallest prime number and the only even prime number; 1 is not considered prime.

To find the prime factorization of an integer, use a factor tree to keep breaking up the integer into factors until all the factors are prime numbers. To find the prime factorization of 36, for example, you could begin by breaking it into 4×9. Then break 4 into 2×2 and break 9 into 3×3. The prime factorization of 36 is $2 \times 2 \times 3 \times 3$.

Manipulating Fractions

You should be comfortable manipulating both proper and improper fractions.

- To add and subtract fractions, first find a common denominator, then add the numerators together.

$$\frac{2}{3} + \frac{5}{4} \rightarrow \left(\frac{2}{3} \times \frac{4}{4}\right) + \left(\frac{5}{4} \times \frac{3}{3}\right) = \frac{8}{12} + \frac{15}{12} = \frac{23}{12}$$

- Multiplying fractions is straightforward: multiply the numerators together, then repeat for the denominators. Cancel when possible to simplify the answer.

$$\frac{5}{8} \times \frac{8}{3} = \frac{5}{\cancel{8}} \times \frac{\cancel{8}}{3} = \frac{5 \times 1}{1 \times 3} = \frac{5}{3}$$

- Dividing by a fraction is the same as multiplying by its reciprocal. Once you've rewritten a division question as multiplication, follow the rules for fraction multiplication to simplify.

$$\frac{3}{4} \div \frac{3}{2} = \frac{\cancel{3}^1}{\cancel{4}_2} \times \frac{\cancel{2}^1}{\cancel{3}_1} = \frac{1 \times 1}{2 \times 1} = \frac{1}{2}$$

Evaluating Expressions and Equations

Whatever you do to one side of an equation, you must do to the other. For instance, if you multiply one side by 3, you must multiply the other side by 3 as well.

The ability to solve straightforward, one-variable equations is critical on the ACT. Here's an example:

$$\frac{4x}{5} - 2 = 10$$

$$\frac{4x}{5} = 12$$

$$\frac{5}{4} \times \frac{4x}{5} = 12 \times \frac{5}{4}$$

$$x = 15$$

Number Lines

Absolute value refers to the distance a number is from 0 on a number line. Because absolute value is a distance, it is always positive or 0. Absolute value can never be negative.

$$|-17| = 17, \ |21| = 21, \ |0| = 0$$

Fraction/Decimal/Percent Conversion

Percent means "out of a hundred." For example, $27\% = \frac{27}{100}$. You can also write percents as decimals, e.g., $27\% = 0.27$.

The ability to recognize a few simple fractions masquerading in decimal or percent form will save you time on test day, as you won't have to turn to your calculator to convert them. Memorize the content of the following table.

Fraction	Decimal	Percent
$\frac{1}{10}$	0.1	10%
$\frac{1}{5}$	0.2	20%
$\frac{1}{4}$	0.25	25%
$\frac{1}{3}$	$0.333\overline{3}$	$33.3\overline{3}\%$
$\frac{1}{2}$	0.5	50%
$\frac{3}{4}$	0.75	75%

You will encounter **irrational numbers**, such as common radicals and π, on test day. You can carry an irrational number through your calculations as you would a variable (e.g., $4 \times \sqrt{2} = 4\sqrt{2}$.) Only convert to a decimal when you have finished any intermediate steps and when the question asks you to provide an *approximate* value.

Part 3
ACT MATH

Graphing

Basic two-dimensional graphing is performed on a coordinate plane. There are two axes, x and y, that meet at a central point called the origin. Each axis has both positive and negative values that extend outward from the origin at evenly spaced intervals. The axes divide the space into four sections called quadrants, which are labeled I, II, III, and IV. Quadrant I is always the upper-right section, and the rest follow counterclockwise.

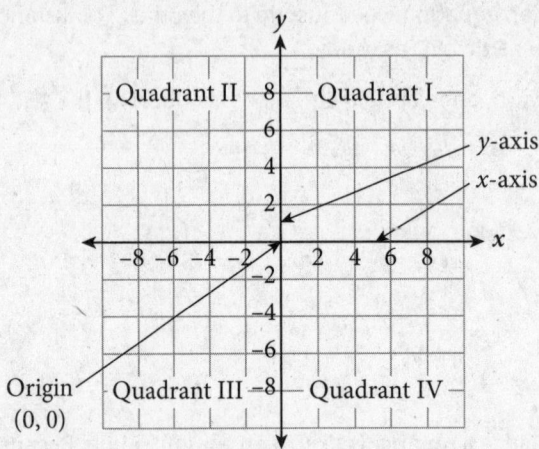

To plot points on the coordinate plane, you need their coordinates. The x-coordinate is where the point falls along the x-axis, and the y-coordinate is where the point falls along the y-axis. The two coordinates together make an ordered pair written as (x, y). When writing ordered pairs, the x-coordinate is always listed first (think alphabetical order). Four points are plotted in the following figure as examples.

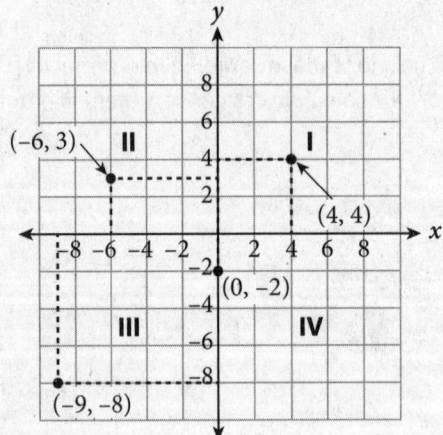

172

Chapter 6
Prerequisite Skills and Calculator Use

When two points are vertically or horizontally aligned, calculating the distance between them is easy. For a horizontal distance, only the *x*-value changes; for a vertical distance, only the *y*-value changes. Take the positive difference of the *x*-coordinates (or *y*-coordinates) to determine the distance—that is, subtract the smaller number from the larger number so that the difference is positive. Two examples are presented here:

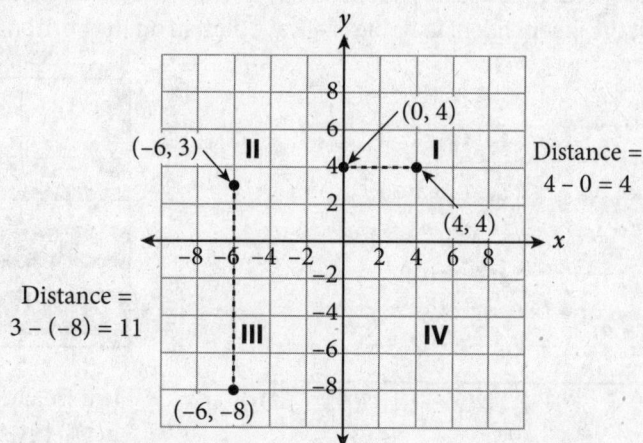

Two-variable equations have an independent variable (input) and a dependent variable (output). The dependent variable (often *y*) depends on the independent variable (often *x*). For example, in the equation $y = 3x + 4$, *x* is the independent variable; any *y*-value depends on what you plug in for *x*. You can construct a table of values for the equation, which can then be plotted.

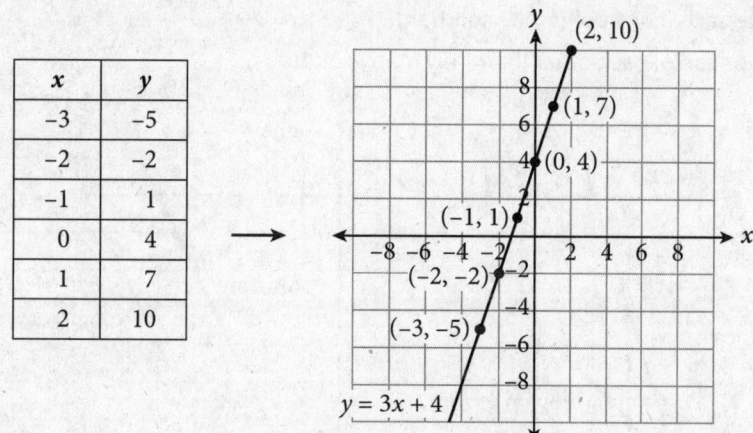

173

Part 3
ACT MATH

You may be asked to infer relationships from graphs. In the first of the following graphs, the two variables are time and population. Clearly the year does not depend on how many people live in the town; rather, the population increases over time and thus depends on the year. In the second graph, you can infer that plant height depends on the amount of rain; thus, rainfall is the independent variable. Note that the independent variable for the second graph is the vertical axis; this can happen with certain nonstandard graphs. On the standard coordinate plane, however, the independent variable is always plotted on the horizontal axis.

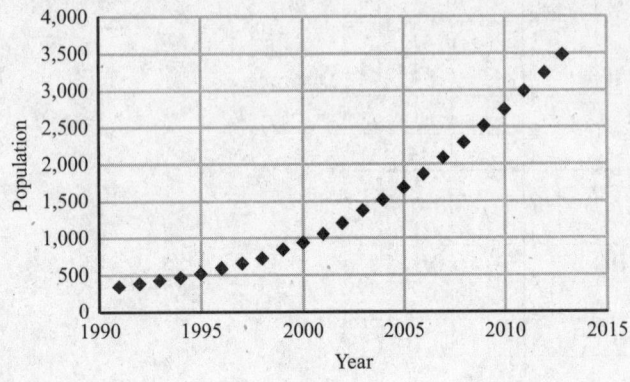
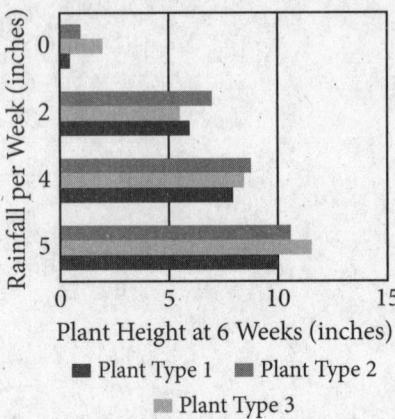

Lines and Angles

When two straight lines are graphed simultaneously, one of three possible scenarios will occur:

- The lines will not intersect at all (no solution).
- The lines will intersect at one point (one solution).
- The lines will lie on top of each other (infinitely many solutions).

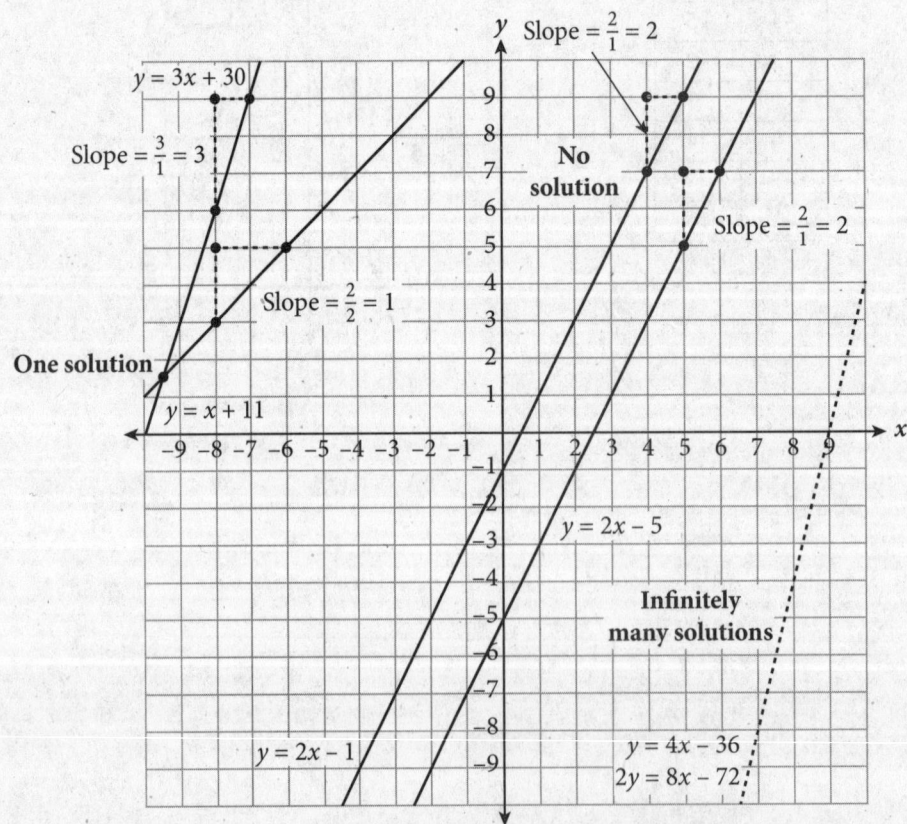

Chapter 6
Prerequisite Skills and Calculator Use

Adjacent angles can be added to find the measure of a larger angle. The following diagram demonstrates this:

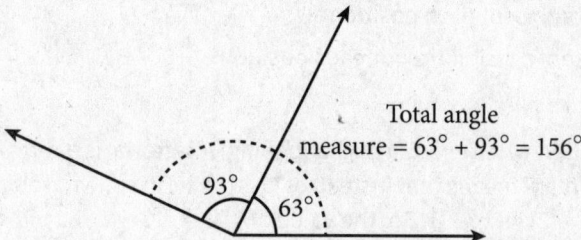

Two angles that sum to 90° are called complementary angles. Two angles that sum to 180° are called supplementary angles.

Two distinct lines in a plane will either intersect at one point or extend indefinitely without intersecting. If two lines intersect at a right angle (90°), they are perpendicular and are denoted with ⊥. If the lines never intersect, they are parallel and are denoted with ∥.

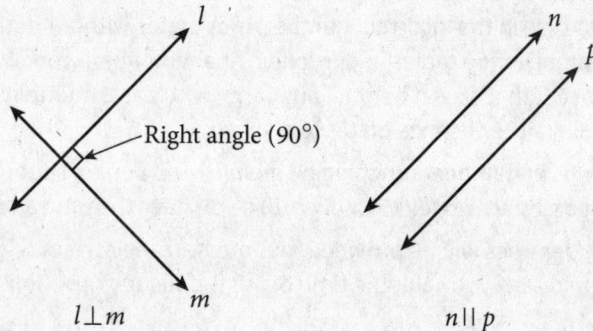

Radius and Diameter

A circle's perimeter is known as its circumference (C) and is found using $C = 2\pi r$, where r is the radius (distance from the center of the circle to its edge). The area of a circle is given by $A = \pi r^2$. The symbol is the lowercase Greek letter pi (π, pronounced "pie"), which is approximately 3.14. You should carry π throughout your calculations without rounding unless instructed otherwise.

A tangent line touches a circle at exactly one point and is perpendicular to a circle's radius at the point of contact.

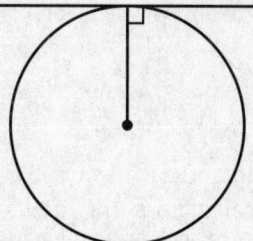

The presence of a right angle opens up the opportunity to draw otherwise hidden shapes, so pay special attention to tangents when they're mentioned.

Simple Counting Techniques

Counting techniques are used to find how many arrangements of something are possible.

When dealing with groups of numbers, keep in mind the Fundamental Counting Principle: if an event has m possible outcomes, and another independent event has n possible outcomes, then there are mn ways for the two events to occur together (multiply). You'll know to use this principle when you see phrases like "how many different" or "how many distinct."

Here's a good general strategy to follow:

- Step 1: Draw a blank to represent each position
- Step 2: Fill in the number of possibilities for each position
- Step 3: Multiply

Factorials (!) are sometimes used when counting is happening. A factorial is a term with an exclamation mark following it; the exclamation mark means that instead of just the term shown, you need to calculate the value of term $\times$ (term $-$ 1) $\times$ (term $-$ 2) $\times \ldots \times$ 1. So, the value of 4! is $4 \times 3 \times 2 \times 1 = 24$. On the ACT, factorials within a fraction are a clue that you can cancel common terms before multiplying.

Mental Math

Even if you're a math whiz, you need to adjust your thought process in regard to the ACT to give yourself the biggest advantage you can. Knowing a few extra things will boost your speed on test day.

- Don't misuse your calculator by using it to calculate basic results you can probably memorize, such as $15 \div 3$; it's far too easy to type in the incorrect number or operator without noticing. You can save time on test day by reviewing multiplication tables in particular. At a minimum, work up through the 10s. If you know them through 12 or 15, that's even better. Familiarity with basic multiplication can go a long way toward improving your overall confidence on test day.
- You can save a few seconds of number crunching by memorizing perfect squares. Knowing perfect squares through 10 is a good start; go for 15 or even 20 if you have the time and motivation.
- Advanced formulas and identities will be provided, but memorizing certain relationships, such as $\cos^2(x) + \sin^2(x) = 1$, could save you valuable time on high-difficulty questions.

If you're comfortable with these concepts, read on for tips on calculator use. If not, frequently review this lesson and remember to refer to it for help if you get stuck in a later chapter.

CALCULATOR USE

LEARNING OBJECTIVE

After this lesson, you will be able to:

- Distinguish ACT questions on which a calculator will be helpful or unhelpful

Calculators and the ACT

Educators and parents believe that calculators serve a role in solving math questions, but they are sometimes concerned that students rely too heavily on calculators. They believe this dependence weakens students' overall ability to think mathematically. While the ACT does have a calculator policy that prohibits some models of calculators, they do allow you to have access to a permissible calculator during the entire ACT Math Test.

However, just because you can use your calculator doesn't mean you should. Many students never stop to ask whether using a calculator is the most efficient way to solve a question. This chapter will show you how the strongest test takers strategically use their calculators; that is, they carefully evaluate when to use the calculator and when to skip it in favor of a more streamlined approach. As you will see, even though you can use a calculator, sometimes it's more beneficial to save your energy by approaching a question more strategically. Work smarter, not harder.

Chapter 6
Prerequisite Skills and Calculator Use

Which Calculator Should You Use?

The ACT allows most four-function, scientific, and graphing calculators, but you should visit the ACT's website for a list permissible calculators.

When given a choice, most students prefer using their own calculator that they are comfortable with over any other calculators that may be available to them. No matter which ACT-permissible calculator you choose, make sure that you can use it efficiently; you don't want to waste valuable time on test day looking for the exponent button or figuring out how to correctly graph equations.

A graphing calculator's capabilities extend well beyond what you'll need for the test, so don't worry about memorizing every function. The next few pages will cover which calculator functions you'll want to know how to use for the ACT. If you're not already familiar with your graphing calculator, you'll want to get the user manual; you can find this on the internet by searching for your calculator's model number. Identify the calculator functions necessary to answer various ACT Math questions, then write down the directions for each to make yourself a handy study sheet.

When Should You Use a Calculator?

Some ACT question types are designed based on the idea that students will do some or all of the work using a calculator. As a master test taker, you need to know what to look for so you can identify when calculator use is advantageous. Questions involving statistics, determining roots of complicated quadratic equations, and working with a few other topics are generally designed with calculator use in mind.

Other questions aren't intentionally designed to involve calculator use. Solving some with a calculator can save you time and energy, but you'll waste both if you go for the calculator on others. You will have to decide which method is best for you when you encounter the following topics:

- Graphing quadratics and circles
- Simplifying exponents and radicals and calculating roots
- Plane and coordinate geometry

Practicing long computations by hand and with the calculator will not only boost your focus and mental math prowess, but it will also help you determine whether it's faster to do the work for a given question by hand or reach for the calculator on test day.

Graphing quadratic equations may be a big reason you got that fancy calculator in the first place; it makes answering these questions a snap! This is definitely an area where you need to have an in-depth knowledge of your calculator's functions. The key to making these questions easier by using the calculator is to be meticulous when entering the equation. Also, be aware that some equations, such as the equation of a circle, might be more time-consuming to graph on your calculator than to sketch on paper.

Another stressful area for many students is radicals, especially when the answer choices are written as decimals. Those two elements are big red flags that trigger a reach for the calculator. Beware: not all graphing calculators have a built-in radical simplification function, so consider familiarizing yourself with this process.

Geometry can also be a gray area for students when it comes to calculator use. Consider working by hand when dealing with angles and lines, specifically when filling in information on complementary, supplementary, and congruent angles. You should be able to work fluidly through those questions without using your calculator, but feel free to reach for your calculator when operating on large numbers.

If you choose to use trigonometric functions to get to the answer on triangle questions, make sure you have your calculator set to degrees or radians as required by the question.

Part 3
ACT MATH

To Use or Not to Use?

A calculator is a double-edged sword on the ACT: using one can be an asset for verifying your work if you struggle when doing math by hand, but turning to it for the simplest computations will cost you time that you could devote to more complex questions. Practice solving questions with and without a calculator to get a sense of your personal preference as well as your strengths and weaknesses with and without one. Think critically about when a calculator saves you time and when mental math is faster. Use the exercises in this book to practice your calculations so that by the time test day arrives, you'll be in the habit of using your calculator as effectively as possible!

[CHAPTER 7]

THE METHOD FOR ACT MATH QUESTIONS

LEARNING OBJECTIVE

After completing this chapter, you will be able to:
- Effectively and efficiently apply the ACT Math Method

How to Do ACT Math

ACT Math questions can sometimes seem more difficult than they actually are, especially when you are working under time pressure. The method we are about to describe will help you answer ACT Math questions, whether you are comfortable with the math content or not. This method is designed to give you the confidence you need to get the correct answers on the ACT by helping you think through a question logically, one piece at a time.

Take a look at this question and spend a minute thinking about how you would attack it if you saw it on test day.

> A certain television set is discounted 20% on Monday and then discounted another 25% on Tuesday. What is the total percent discount applied to the price of the television on Monday and Tuesday?
>
> A. 22.5%
> B. 40%
> C. 45%
> D. 50%

Many test takers may see a question like this and panic. Others may waste a great deal of time reading and rereading without a clear goal. You want to avoid both of those outcomes.

Start by clearly defining for yourself **what the question is actually asking**. What do the answer choices represent? In this question, they represent total percent discount.

Next, **examine the information** that you have and organize it logically. The question asks about the total percent discount applied to the price of the television on Monday and Tuesday. You are given the percent discount on Monday (20%) and the discount on Tuesday (25%). However, you can't just add the two percents to get the total percent discount.

(Watch out for C, which is a distractor that does just that.) You need to use the discounted price on Monday to calculate the discounted price on Tuesday in order to calculate the total percent change.

Now, **make a strategic decision** about how to proceed. You aren't given the original price of the television set, so this is a perfect question for Picking Numbers. When Picking Numbers for percents questions for which the initial value is unknown, you should usually start with 100 to make your calculations easier: pick $100 as the original cost. Then Monday's price is 80% of that, or $100(0.8) = $80, and Tuesday's price is 75% of the new amount, or $80(0.75) = $60. The total amount of the discount is $100 − $60 = $40. Now use the percent change formula:

$$\text{percent change} = \frac{\text{amount of change}}{\text{original amount}} \times 100\%$$

$$= \frac{\$100 - \$60}{\$100} \times 100\%$$

$$= \frac{\$40}{\$100} \times 100\%$$

$$= 40\%$$

Finally, **confirm** that you answered the right question: you want the total percent discount *applied* to the price of the television on Monday and Tuesday. This means that the price was decreased by 40%. Great! You're done; the correct answer is (B).

Here's what we did:

ACT MATH METHOD

Step 1. State what the question is asking

Step 2. Examine the given information

Step 3. Choose your approach

Step 4. Confirm that you answered the right question

You can think of these steps as a series of questions to ask yourself:

1. What do they want?
2. What are they giving me to work with?
3. How should I approach this?
4. Did I answer the right question?

Not all ACT Math questions will require that you spend a lot of time on all the steps. The question above required a fair amount of analysis in steps 1 and 2 because it is a word problem. Other questions will require very little thought in steps 1 and 2. Carefully deciding on the appropriate strategy in step 3 will allow you to effectively answer questions. Step 4 is quick, but you should always do it: just make sure you answered the question that was actually asked before you select your response. Doing so will save you from rushed mistakes on questions that you know how to do and should be getting credit for.

There are several approaches you can choose from in step 3: Picking Numbers, Backsolving, doing the traditional math, Elimination, or taking a strategic guess.

Note that since the answer choices in the question above were numbers and did not contain variables, you were done once you found a match. However, when using the **Picking Numbers** strategy for questions with variables in the question stem *and* the answer choices, it is always possible that another answer choice can produce the same result, so check all the answer choices to be sure there isn't another match. Choose a number(s) to substitute for the variable(s) in the question and then substitute the same number(s) for the variable(s) in the choices to see which one matches. If there is more than one match, go back and pick another number to distinguish between the choices that match.

When using the Picking Numbers strategy, use numbers that are permissible and manageable. That is, use numbers that are allowed by the stipulations of the question and that are easy to work with. A small positive integer is usually the best choice in this situation. Here is an example:

Which of the following expressions will produce an odd number for any integer a?

F. a^2
G. $a^2 + 1$
H. $a^2 + 2$
J. $2a^2 + 1$

Step 1: What do they want? The choice that is always odd.

Step 2: What do they give you? The variable, a, is any integer.

Step 3: What approach will you use?

Rather than trying to think this one through abstractly, it may be easier to Pick Numbers for a. The question states that a is any integer, so it could be even or odd. Try an even value for a. Let $a = 2$ and plug the value into the answer choices. Eliminate choices that are not odd:

Choice F: $a^2 = 2^2 = 4$ Eliminate.

Choice G: $a^2 + 1 = 2^2 + 1 = 5$ Keep.

Choice H: $a^2 + 2 = 2^2 + 2 = 6$ Eliminate.

Choice J: $2a^2 + 1 = 2(2)^2 + 1 = 9$ Keep.

Choices G and J give an odd result. Go back and try an odd value for a, like 3, for the remaining choices.

Choice G: $a^2 + 1 = 3^2 + 1 = 10$ Eliminate.

Choice (J): $2a^2 + 1 = 2(3)^2 + 1 = 19$ Keep.

Only (J) is odd for any integer a, so (J) is correct.

Part 3
ACT MATH

In the next example, you'll see Backsolving in action:

A physics midterm has 60 questions. The test is scored as follows: for each correct answer, 2 points are awarded; for each incorrect answer, $\frac{2}{3}$ of a point is subtracted; for unanswered questions, points are neither added nor subtracted. If Denise scored a 68 and did not answer 2 of the questions, how many questions did she answer correctly?

A. 34
B. 36
C. 38
D. 40

Step 1: What do they want? The number of questions Denise answered correctly.

Step 2: What do they give you? The total number of questions answered ($60 - 2 = 58$), the number of points for correct (2) and incorrect $\left(-\frac{2}{3}\right)$ answers, and Denise's midterm score (68).

Step 3: What approach will you use?

Here's a chance to practice Backsolving: plug the choices in for the unknown and see which one works. It often makes sense to start with C when you can tell from the context whether you'll need a larger or smaller answer choice if the one you're testing fails. If the question asks for the smallest or largest value, start with A/F or D/J, respectively.

For this question, start with one of the middle answer choices, C. If Denise answered 38 of the questions correctly and skipped 2, then she answered $60 - 38 - 2 = 20$ questions incorrectly. She gets 2 points for every correct question and loses $\frac{2}{3}$ of a point for every incorrect question, so do the calculations to determine her total points:

$$38(2) - 20\left(\frac{2}{3}\right) = 76 - \frac{40}{3}$$
$$= \frac{228}{3} - \frac{40}{3}$$
$$= \frac{188}{3}$$
$$= 62\frac{2}{3}$$

This is less than 68, so 38 is too low: eliminate both A and B, leaving (D), the correct answer. On test day, select that choice and move on with confidence. But, to practice this skills, try the largest-value choice: 40. If Denise answered 40 questions correctly, she earned $40(2) - 18\left(\frac{2}{3}\right) = 80 - 12 = 68$ points.

Step 4: Did you solve for the right thing? You found the number of questions Denise answered correctly to earn a score of 68 points, so yes. Choice (D) is the correct answer. You do not need to evaluate the other answer choices.

Chapter 7
The Method for ACT Math Questions

Here's an example using the Elimination strategy:

Suppose line PQ is perpendicular to line RS and Q is a point on line RS. If point L is in the interior of ∠PQS, which of the following could be the measure of ∠LQR?

F. 110°
G. 90°
H. 70°
J. 50°

Step 1: What do they want? A possible measure of ∠LQR.

Step 2: What do they give you? PQ is perpendicular to RS and Q is a point on RS. Point L is in the interior of ∠PQS.

Step 3: What approach will you use?

When the question does not provide a figure, draw one yourself.

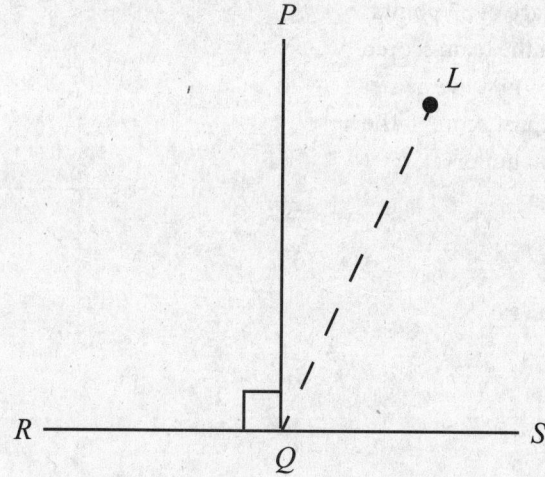

Because lines PQ and RS are perpendicular, ∠PQR must form a 90° angle. If point L is in the interior of ∠PQS, the measure of ∠LQR must be greater than 90°. You can eliminate all choices that are less than or equal to 90°. Only (F) is greater than 90°, so it is correct.

Step 4: Did you solve for the right thing? You found the measure of ∠LQR, so yes. Choose (F) and move on.

Now it's your turn. Be deliberate with the questions in the next section. If there is analysis to do up front, do it. If there is more than one way to do a question, consider carefully before choosing your approach, and be sure to check whether you answered the right question. Forming good habits now, in slow and careful practice, will set you up for confidence on test day.

Part 3
ACT MATH

How Much Have You Learned?

Directions: Take as much time as you need on these questions. Work carefully and methodically. There will be opportunities for timed practice in future chapters.

1. Let z equal $3x - 2y + 1$. If the value of x is increased by 2 and the value of y is decreased by 3, what will happen to the value of z?

    A. It will decrease by -13.
    B. It will decrease by -12.
    C. It will increase by 12.
    D. It will increase by 13.

2. A basketball team needs an average of 85 points to receive post-season honors. If the team scored 82, 78, 92, 80, and 83 points in its first five games, what is the minimum the team must score in the sixth game to receive post-season honors?

    F. 90
    G. 95
    H. 100
    J. 105

3. Which of the following is the graph for the function defined below?

    $$f(x) = \begin{array}{l} x^2 + 1 \text{ for } x \leq 2 \\ x - 4 \text{ for } 2 < x < 6 \\ 2 - x \text{ for } x \geq 6 \end{array}$$

    A.
    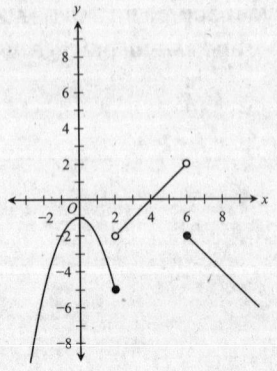

    B.
    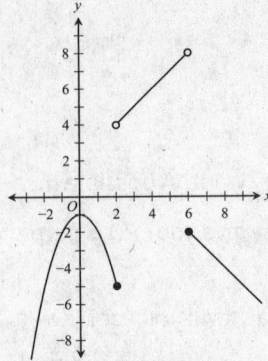

    C.
    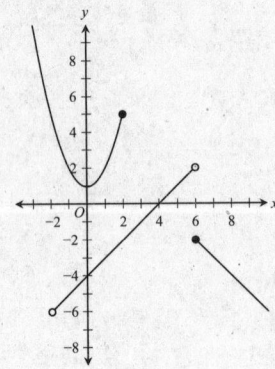

    D.
    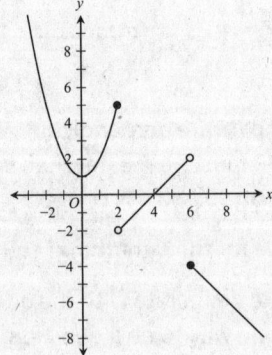

184

4. Which range of heights contains the median of the data?

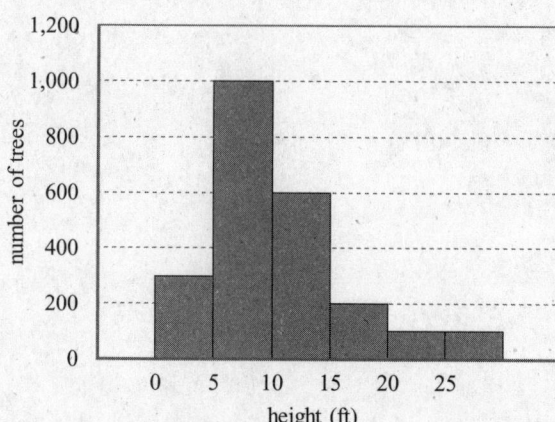

F. 0–4
G. 5–9
H. 10–14
J. 15–19

5. A certain high school class contains 5 students with red hair, 15 with brown hair, 20 with black hair, and 12 with blonde hair. If this data is plotted on a pie chart, what is the measure of the central angle of the sector of students with blonde hair? Round to the nearest degree.

A. 23°
B. 83°
C. 107°
D. 138°

6. On the number line below, point G is the midpoint of FH and $HJ = JK$. If $HK = 18$, what is the length of GJ?

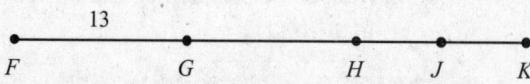

F. 18
G. 22
H. 26
J. 31

7. What is the period of the function $f(x) = 2\sin(3x - \pi)$?

A. $\dfrac{\pi}{3}$
B. $\dfrac{\pi}{2}$
C. $\dfrac{2\pi}{3}$
D. $\dfrac{5\pi}{6}$

8. In 1992, the cost of a school lunch was $1.20. In 2017, the cost of a school lunch was $2.90. Assuming the cost increased linearly, what was the cost of a school lunch in 2002?

F. $1.52
G. $1.70
H. $1.88
J. $2.20

9. Viktor owns a car dealership. The numbers of different types of vehicles on his car lot are given in the following table. If a vehicle is selected at random, what is the probability that it is NOT a luxury vehicle or SUV?

Vehicle type	Number on lot
Subcompact	64
Compact	35
Midsize	61
Full-size	58
Luxury	32
SUV	43
Truck	27
Total	320

A. $\frac{7}{32}$

B. $\frac{15}{64}$

C. $\frac{49}{64}$

D. $\frac{7}{8}$

10. If the sum of five consecutive even integers is equal to their product, what is the greatest of the five integers?

F. 4
G. 10
H. 14
J. 16

Chapter 7
The Method for ACT Math Questions

Reflect

Directions: Take a few minutes to recall what you've learned and what you've been practicing in this chapter. Consider the following questions, jot down your best answer for each one, and then compare your reflections to the expert responses on the following page. Use your level of confidence to determine what to do next.

1. Think about your current habits when attacking ACT questions. Are you a strategic test taker? Do you take the time to think through what would be the fastest way to the answer?
   _____
   _____
   _____

2. Do word problems give you trouble? If so, what can you do?
   _____
   _____
   _____

3. What are the steps of the ACT Math Method, and why is each step important?
   _____
   _____
   _____

Responses

1. Think about your current habits when attacking ACT questions. Are you a strategic test taker? Do you take the time to think through what would be the fastest way to the answer?

If yes, good for you! If not, we recommend doing questions more than one way whenever possible as part of your ACT prep. If you can discover now, while you're still practicing, that Picking Numbers is faster for you on certain types of questions but not on others, you'll be that much more efficient on test day.

2. Do word problems give you trouble? If so, what can you do?

If word problems are difficult for you, get into the habit of taking an inventory, before you do any math, of what the question is asking for and what information you have.

3. What are the steps of the ACT Math Method, and why is each step important?

Here are the steps:

Step 1. *State what the question is asking*

Step 2. *Examine the given information*
(Taking an inventory is especially important in word problems.)

Step 3. *Choose your approach*
(Taking a moment to decide what approach will be the fastest way to the answer will ultimately save you time.)

Step 4. *Confirm that you answered the right question*
(Making sure you solved for the right thing will save you from losing points to speed mistakes on questions that you know how to do and should be getting credit for.)

Next Steps

If you answered most questions correctly in the "How Much Have You Learned?" section, and if your responses to the Reflect questions were similar to those of the ACT expert, then consider the ACT Math Method an area of strength and move on to the next chapter. Do keep using the method as you work on the questions in future chapters.

If you don't yet feel confident, review those parts of this chapter that you have not yet mastered, and try the questions you missed again. As always, be sure to review the explanations closely. Then go online (**kaptest.com/login**) for more practice. If you haven't already registered your book, do so at **kaptest.com/moreonline**.

GO ONLINE

kaptest.com/login

Answers and Explanations

1. C
Difficulty: Medium
Category: Number and Quantity
Getting to the Answer: The question asks for the value of z after x is increased by 2 and y is decreased by 3. You are given $z = 3x - 2y + 1$. The new value of x is $x + 2$ and the new value of y is $y - 3$. Substitute these new values into the expression, $3x - 2y + 1$, to find the new value of z: $3(x + 2) - 2(y - 3) + 1$. This gives $3x + 6 - 2y + 6 + 1$, which equals $3x - 2y + 13$. Since the original value of z was $3x - 2y + 1$, this new expression is $13 - 1 = 12$ greater. Thus, the value of z will increase by 12. Choice (C) is correct.

Alternatively, you could Pick Numbers for x and y. If $x = 1$ and $y = 2$, then $z = 3(1) - 2(2) + 1 = 0$. Increasing x by 2 and decreasing y by 3 gives $x + 2 = 1 + 2 = 3$ and $y - 3 = 2 - 3 = -1$. Thus, the new value of z is $3(3) - 2(-1) + 1 = 9 + 2 + 1 = 12$. The change is $12 - 0 = 12$. Since the change is positive, z will increase by 12. This matches (C).

2. G
Difficulty: Medium
Category: Statistics and Probability
Getting to the Answer: The question gives the scores of the first 5 games and asks what score a team must get in the next game to attain an average score of 85 for 6 games. The average of a group of numbers is the sum of the values divided by the number of values. You can either set up an equation to solve for the missing score or use Backsolving to strategically test choices.

Backsolving is often a great way to solve questions about averages, especially ones that give you the average and ask for a missing number. Replace that missing number with a choice and find the average. If the average matches the desired average, you're done! If the average doesn't match, use your result to determine if you need a larger or smaller choice. In this question, because you need a minimum, start with the smallest number:

Choice F: $\dfrac{82 + 78 + 92 + 80 + 83 + 90}{6} = \dfrac{505}{6} = 84.17$

Because 84.17 is less than 85, try the next-largest number:

Choice (G): $\dfrac{82 + 78 + 92 + 80 + 83 + 95}{6} = \dfrac{510}{6} = 85$

This equals 85, so the team needs to score a minimum of 95 points on the sixth game to advance to the playoff round, and (G) is correct.

To answer the question algebraically, call the missing score x, set up the average equation, and solve for x:

$$\dfrac{82 + 78 + 92 + 80 + 83 + x}{6} = 85$$
$$415 + x = 510$$
$$x = 95$$

This approach also shows that (G) is correct.

Alternatively, if you know how to use the balance approach for averages, you could determine that the 82 score was 3 less than the desired average, the 78 score was 7 less, the 92 score was 7 greater, the 80 score was 5 less, and the 83 score was 2 less for a total of 10 less. Thus, the fourth score would need to be $85 + 10 = 95$ to raise the average to 85. Remember, step 3 is all about figuring out which approach works best for you, so be sure to practice approaching questions in multiple ways.

3. D
Difficulty: Medium
Category: Functions
Getting to the Answer: The question asks which of the graphs in the choices correctly shows the piecewise function given. To identify which graph matches the piecewise-defined function, evaluate each piece of the function for the given domain.

When $x \leq 2$, the function is $f(x) = x^2 + 1$. This is an upward-facing parabola since the coefficient of x^2 is positive. Eliminate A and B.

Evaluate the next piece of the function, $f(x) = x - 4$. Note that the domain of this piece of the function is $2 < x < 6$, which matches (D). Graph C does not match since the domain of the line $x - 4$ is $-2 < x < 6$. There is no need to consider the third piece of the function.

4. G
Difficulty: Medium
Category: Statistics and Probability
Getting to the Answer: The question asks which range of the histogram contains the median value. The median of a set of data is the middle value when the data is written in ascending order. This means that half of the data is less than the median and half is greater.

The total number of data values is the sum of the number of trees in each group: $300 + 1{,}000 + 600 + 200 + 100 + 100 = 2{,}300$. Half of that is 1,150. From left to right, the first bar contains 300 data values and the second bar contains 1,000 more, for a total of 1,300 data values. The middle value for all the data must therefore lie within the interval represented by the second bar, making (G) correct. Note that it is not possible to determine the exact median, only the interval within which it lies. Be certain that you used the correct total when determining the median.

5. B
Difficulty: Medium
Category: Geometry
Getting to the Answer: There are a total of $5 + 15 + 20 + 12 = 52$ students. Out of these, $\frac{12}{52} = \frac{3}{13}$ have blonde hair. There are 360° in a pie chart because it forms a circle. To find the measure of the central angle of the sector for the blonde group, multiply 360° by the fraction above: $360°\left(\frac{3}{13}\right) \cong 83.07°$. Choice (B) is correct.

6. G
Difficulty: Medium
Category: Number and Quantity
Getting to the Answer: The question asks for the length of segment *GJ* on the line segment shown. Point *G* bisects segment *FH* and point *J* bisects segment *HK*. The length of *FG* is 13 and the length of *HK* is 18.

Since *G* is the midpoint of *FH*, $GH = FG = 13$. Also, since $HK = 18$ and $HJ = JK$, $HJ = JK = 9$. Line segment $GJ = GH + HJ$, which is $13 + 9 = 22$. The correct choice is (G). Check that you answered the question that was asked; F is *HK*, H is *FH*, and J is *GK*.

7. C
Difficulty: High
Category: Functions
Getting to the Answer: The question asks for the period of the function $2\sin(3x - \pi)$. Recall that the period of sin, cos, sec, and csc graphs is 2π, which means that the function values repeat themselves every full rotation around a circle, which is 2π radians.

For the general function $a\sin(bx - c) + d$, *a* affects the amplitude or vertical stretch, *b* affects the period or horizontal stretch, *b* and *c* together affect the horizontal shift, and *d* affects the vertical shift.

Since only *b* affects the period, you can think of this function as just sin(3*x*). Multiplying the value inside the parentheses "speeds up" the process of completing the full circle, which shortens the period and results in a horizontal contraction. Thus, multiplying the *x* by 3 means that the function will cycle through its values 3 times as quickly as sin(*x*). The function will make three cycles every 2π radians, or one cycle every $\frac{2\pi}{3}$ radians. Choice (C) is correct.

8. H
Difficulty: Medium
Category: Algebra
Getting to the Answer: The question asks for the cost of a school lunch in 2002. You are given the costs in 1992 and 2017 and the fact that the cost increased linearly during that time span. Since the cost increased linearly, determine the constant rate at which the cost of a school lunch increased per year. The constant rate, or slope, is $\frac{\$2.90 - \$1.20}{2017 - 1992} = \frac{\$1.70}{25} = \$0.068$ per year. Thus, the cost in 2002 (10 years after 1992) is $\$1.20 + \$0.068(10) = \$1.88$. Choice (H) is correct.

9. C
Difficulty: Medium
Category: Statistics and Probability
Getting to the Answer: The question asks for the probability that a vehicle selected at random from the cars shown in the table will not be either a luxury vehicle or an SUV. Recall the fundamental probability formula: $\text{probability} = \frac{\text{number of desired outcomes}}{\text{number of total possible outcomes}}$. Also remember that the probability of an event NOT occurring is 1 minus the probability of that event occurring. Since calculating the probability of selecting a luxury vehicle or SUV involves less number-crunching, determine that probability and then subtract it from 1 to find the probability of NOT selecting a luxury vehicle or SUV:

Viktor has 320 cars in his lot. The probability of selecting a luxury vehicle or SUV is $\frac{32 + 43}{320} = \frac{75}{320} = \frac{15}{64}$.
Thus, the probability of NOT selecting a luxury vehicle or SUV is $1 - \frac{15}{64} = \frac{64}{64} - \frac{15}{64} = \frac{49}{64}$. Choice (C) is correct.

10. F

Difficulty: Medium

Category: Number and Quantity

Getting to the Answer: The question asks for the greatest of five consecutive even integers whose product is equal to their sum. First, put the question into words you can more easily understand. It says that when you add up the five consecutive even integers, you get the same thing as when you multiply them. The word *even* tells you that the difference between each integer in the sequence is 2. Finally, the answer choices themselves represent numbers that could be the final term of this sequence.

You could model the situation with an equation: $x + (x-2) + (x-4) + (x-6) + (x-8) = x(x-2)(x-4)(x-6)(x-8)$. However, that's a very difficult equation to solve algebraically; try Backsolving instead. The question asks for the greatest of the integers, so you have to start with the greatest answer choice, J. If you start with any other, you won't know whether it's actually the correct answer, even if it works, as the next largest answer choice may *also* work.

Choice J: $16 + 14 + 12 + 10 + 8 = 60$. Unfortunately, $16 \times 14 \times 12 \times 10 \times 8$ is way too big.

Choice H: $14 + 12 + 10 + 8 + 6 = 50$. The product $14 \times 12 \times 10 \times 8 \times 6$ is still too large.

Choice G: $10 + 8 + 6 + 4 + 2 = 30$. But as before, the product $10 \times 8 \times 6 \times 4 \times 2$ is much greater than the sum.

Choice (F): $4 + 2 + 0 + (-2) + (-4) = 0$ and the product $4 \times 2 \times 0 \times -2 \times -4 = 0$.

Choice (F) is correct.

[CHAPTER 8]

NUMBER AND QUANTITY

LEARNING OBJECTIVES

After completing this chapter, you will be able to:

- Apply exponent rules
- Add, subtract, multiply, and divide numbers written in scientific notation
- Apply radical rules
- Solve absolute value equations
- Identify a specific term in an arithmetic or geometric sequence
- Perform arithmetic operations on imaginary and complex numbers
- Perform arithmetic operations using matrices

Part 3
ACT MATH

How Much Do You Know?

Directions: Try out the questions below. Show your work so that you can compare your solutions to the ones found on the next page. The "Category" heading in the explanation for each question gives the title of the lesson that covers how to solve it. If you answered the question(s) for a given lesson correctly, and if your scratchwork looks like the explanations, you may be able to move quickly through that lesson. If you answered incorrectly or used a different approach, you may want to take your time on that lesson.

1. What is the value of $\dfrac{10^5 \times 100^7}{1{,}000^6}$?

   A. 1
   B. 10
   C. 100
   D. 1,000

2. Which of the following is equivalent to $\sqrt{24} + \sqrt{150}$?

   F. $\sqrt{174}$
   G. $7\sqrt{6}$
   H. $29\sqrt{6}$
   J. $36\sqrt{29}$

3. If $x = 4$, evaluate $\left|\dfrac{x-8}{2x+2}\right|$.

   A. $-\dfrac{1}{2}$
   B. $-\dfrac{2}{5}$
   C. $\dfrac{2}{5}$
   D. $\dfrac{1}{2}$

4. If the first term in a geometric sequence is 4 and the third term is 100, what is the common ratio (r)?

   F. 3
   G. 4
   H. 5
   J. 6

5. Write $(3i + 4) - (5i + 3)$ in $a + bi$ form.

   A. $1 - 2i$
   B. $7 - 2i$
   C. $7 + 8i$
   D. $5 + 2i$

Answers and explanations are on the next page. ▶ ▶ ▶

Answers and Explanations

How Much Do You Know?

1. B
Difficulty: Low
Category: Number and Quantity: Exponents
Getting to the Answer: To perform the arithmetic efficiently, begin by rewriting every term in the expression as 10 raised to some power:

$$\frac{10^5 \times (10^2)^7}{(10^3)^6}$$

Apply exponent rules and simplify. Remember that when you divide, you subtract the exponents, and when you raise one exponent to another, you multiply:

$$\frac{10^5 \times 10^{14}}{10^{18}} = \frac{10^{19}}{10^{18}} = 10^{19-18} = 10$$

Therefore, (B) is correct.

2. G
Difficulty: Low
Category: Number and Quantity: Radicals
Getting to the Answer: Simplify each radical by looking for two numbers that multiply to equal the radicand (the number under the radical sign). Numbers that are perfect squares are optimal. Then combine like terms:

$$\sqrt{24} + \sqrt{150}$$
$$\sqrt{4}\sqrt{6} + \sqrt{25}\sqrt{6}$$
$$2\sqrt{6} + 5\sqrt{6}$$
$$7\sqrt{6}$$

Choice (G) is correct.

3. C
Difficulty: Low
Category: Number and Quantity: Absolute Value
Getting to the Answer: You need to find the value of the expression. To do so, plug in the given value for *x* and simplify. Remember that the final answer is positive since the entire expression is inside absolute value brackets:

$$\left|\frac{(4)-8}{2(4)+2}\right| = \left|\frac{-4}{10}\right|$$
$$= \frac{4}{10}$$
$$= \frac{2}{5}$$

Choice (C) is correct.

4. H
Difficulty: Medium
Category: Number and Quantity: Sequences
Getting to the Answer: The question asks for the common ratio in a sequence. Since the sequence is geometric, you multiply each term by some constant (*r*) to get to the next term. The best way to solve this question is to plug in the answer choices. Since the first and third terms of the sequence are given, multiply the first term by the common ratio given in each answer choice twice. Whichever choice results in 100 is the correct answer.

F) $4 \times 3 \times 3 = 36 \neq 100$ Eliminate
G) $4 \times 4 \times 4 = 64 \neq 100$ Eliminate
H) $4 \times 5 \times 5 = 100$

You can stop here: (H) is correct.

5. A
Difficulty: Low
Category: Number and Quantity: Imaginary Numbers
Getting to the Answer: Combine like terms, being careful to distribute the negative on the outside of the parentheses.

$$(3i + 4) - (5i + 3)$$
$$3i + 4 - 5i - 3$$
$$-2i + 1$$
$$1 - 2i$$

Choice (A) is correct.

EXPONENTS

> **LEARNING OBJECTIVES**
>
> After this lesson, you will be able to:
> - Apply exponent rules
> - Add, subtract, multiply, and divide numbers written in scientific notation

To answer a question like this

Which of the following is equivalent to $\dfrac{(3.0 \times 10^4)(8.0 \times 10^9)}{1.2 \times 10^6}$?

A. 2.0×10^6
B. 2.0×10^7
C. 2.0×10^8
D. 2.0×10^9

You need to know this

Exponents

Rule	Example
When multiplying two terms with the same base, add the exponents.	$a^b \times a^c = a^{(b+c)} \to 4^2 \times 4^3 = 4^{(2+3)} = 4^5$
When dividing two terms with the same base, subtract the exponents.	$\dfrac{a^b}{a^c} = a^{(b-c)} \to \dfrac{4^3}{4^2} = 4^{(3-2)} = 4^1$
When raising a power to another power, multiply the exponents.	$(a^b)^c = a^{(bc)} \to (4^3)^2 = 4^{(3 \times 2)} = 4^6$; $(y^2)^3 = y^{(2 \times 3)} = y^6$
When raising a product to a power, apply the power to all factors in the product.	$(2m)^3 = 2^3 \times m^3 = 8m^3$
Any nonzero term raised to the zero power equals 1.	$a^0 = 1 \to 4^0 = 1$
A base raised to a negative exponent can be rewritten as the reciprocal raised to the positive of the original exponent.	$a^{-b} = \dfrac{1}{a^b} \to 4^{-2} = \dfrac{1}{4^2}$; $\dfrac{1}{a^{-b}} = a^b \to \dfrac{1}{5^{-3}} = 5^3$
A negative number raised to an even exponent will produce a positive result; a negative number raised to an odd exponent will produce a negative result.	$(-2)^4 = 16$, but $(-2)^3 = -8$

Part 3
ACT MATH

Scientific Notation

Scientific notation is used to express very large or very small numbers.

- A number written in scientific notation is a number that is greater than or equal to 1, but less than 10, raised to a power of 10.
  - 3.64×10^8 is written in scientific notation, while 36.4×10^7 is not.
  - The two numbers are equivalent, but the second doesn't meet the definition of scientific notation because 36.4 is not between 1 and 10.
- To write a number in scientific notation, move the decimal point (to the right or to the left) until the number is between 1 and 10.
  - Count the number of places you moved the decimal point—this tells you the power of 10 that you'll need.
  - If the original number was a tiny decimal number (which means you had to move the decimal to the right), the exponent will be negative.
  - If the original number was a large number (which means you had to move the decimal point to the left), the exponent will be positive.
- You can add and subtract numbers written in scientific notation as long as the power of 10 in each term is the same; simply add (or subtract) the numbers and keep the same power of 10.
- You can multiply and divide numbers written in scientific notation using rules of exponents; simply multiply (or divide) the numbers and add (or subtract) the powers of 10.

You need to do this

- Identify the appropriate rule by looking at the operation.
- Apply the rule.
- Repeat as necessary.

Straightforward ACT exponent questions should be quick points, but it's more likely you'll apply exponent rules as one step in solving a Medium or High difficulty question. Make sure you memorize the rules in the table on the previous page before test day.

Explanation

You'll need several exponent rules to answer the scientific notation question at the beginning of this lesson. Work through this question slowly and methodically.

First, simplify the numerator by multiplying the 3.0 and 8.0: $3 \times 8 = 24.0$. Then, determine the product of 10^4 and 10^9 by adding the exponents: $10^4 \times 10^9 = 10^{(4+9)} = 10^{13}$. Now, the numerator has a value of 24.0×10^{13}.

Since the values in both the numerator and the denominator are being multiplied, you can simplify the fraction by dividing the similar terms. First, divide the first terms of the expressions: $24.0 \div 1.2 = 20.0$. To find the value of $10^{13} \div 10^6$, subtract the exponents: $10^{(13-6)} = 10^7$. Combine these terms: 20.0×10^7.

Finally, convert the result into standard scientific notation. All of the choices start with 2.0, so factor out 10 from the first term ($20.0 \div 10 = 2.0$) and multiply the second term (10^7) by that 10, which can also be written as 10^1:

$$\frac{(3.0 \times 10^4)(8.0 \times 10^9)}{1.2 \times 10^6} = \frac{24.0 \times 10^{13}}{1.2 \times 10^6}$$
$$= 20.0 \times 10^7$$
$$= 2.0 \times 10^7 \times 10^1$$
$$= 2.0 \times 10^8$$

Therefore, (C) is correct.

Chapter 8
Number and Quantity

Drills

If exponents or scientific notation gives you trouble, study the information above and try out these drill questions before completing the Try on Your Own questions below. Simplify each expression, and if the answer involves numbers only, write your answer in scientific notation. Drill answers can be found in Answers and Explanations.

a. $820{,}000{,}000 + 500{,}000{,}000$

b. $(3.5 \times 10^5) \times (4.0 \times 10^3)$

c. $\dfrac{4.2 \times 10^8}{2.0 \times 10^5}$

d. $x^4 \times x^3$

e. $\dfrac{y^{10}}{y^4}$

Try on Your Own

Directions: Take as much time as you need on these questions. Work carefully and methodically. There will be an opportunity for timed practice at the end of the chapter.

1. What is the value of $\dfrac{3{,}200{,}000 - 2{,}300{,}000}{3{,}000}$?

    A. 3.0×10^2
    B. 3.0×10^3
    C. 3.0×10^4
    D. 3.0×10^5

2. Simplify $\dfrac{z^9 y^4 x^6}{x y^6 z^3}$.

    F. $\dfrac{y^2}{xz^6}$
    G. $\dfrac{x^5 z^6}{y^2}$
    H. $\dfrac{z^8 x^3}{y^2}$
    J. $z^8 y^2 x^3$

3. Evaluate $\dfrac{(2.0 \times 10^4)(6.0 \times 10^7)}{4.0 \times 10^2}$ and write in scientific notation.

    A. 3.0×10^8
    B. 3.0×10^9
    C. 4.0×10^8
    D. 4.0×10^9

4. Which of the following is equivalent to $\dfrac{a^{-7} c^2 b^{-4}}{b^2 c^{-3} a^{-3}}$?

    F. $\dfrac{c^5}{a^4 b^6}$
    G. $\dfrac{a^{-10} b^{-4}}{c^5}$
    H. $\dfrac{a^{10} b^6}{c^5}$
    J. $\dfrac{c^{-5}}{a^{-10} b^{-6}}$

HINT: For Q5, remember the definition of scientific notation. What must be true about the first part?

---

5. Write $\dfrac{2.1 \times 10^{-12}}{(2.0 \times 10^4)(5.0 \times 10^3)}$ in scientific notation.

    A. 0.21×10^{-5}
    B. 2.1×10^{-6}
    C. 2.1×10^{-19}
    D. 2.1×10^{-20}

Part 3
ACT MATH

RADICALS

LEARNING OBJECTIVE

After this lesson, you will be able to:

- Apply radical rules

To answer a question like this

Which of the following expressions is equivalent to $\dfrac{4x}{10 - \sqrt{5}}$?

A. $\dfrac{40x + 4x\sqrt{5}}{95}$

B. $\dfrac{40x + 4x\sqrt{5}}{105}$

C. $\dfrac{44x - 77}{95}$

D. $\dfrac{4x - 7}{10 + \sqrt{5}}$

You need to know this

Rule	Example
When a fraction is under a radical, you can rewrite it using two radicals: one containing the numerator and the other containing the denominator.	$\sqrt{\dfrac{a}{b}} = \dfrac{\sqrt{a}}{\sqrt{b}} \rightarrow \sqrt{\dfrac{4}{9}} = \dfrac{\sqrt{4}}{\sqrt{9}} = \dfrac{2}{3}$
Two factors under a single radical can be rewritten as separate radicals multiplied together.	$\sqrt{ab} = \sqrt{a} \times \sqrt{b} \rightarrow \sqrt{75} = \sqrt{3 \times 25}$ $= \sqrt{3} \times 5$ $= 5\sqrt{3}$
A radical can be written using a fractional exponent.	$\sqrt{a} = a^{\frac{1}{2}} \rightarrow \sqrt{289} = 289^{\frac{1}{2}} \quad \sqrt[3]{a} = a^{\frac{1}{3}} \rightarrow \sqrt[3]{729} = 729^{\frac{1}{3}}$
When you have a fractional exponent, the numerator is the power to which the base is raised, and the denominator is the root to be taken.	$a^{\frac{b}{c}} = \sqrt[c]{a^b} \rightarrow 5^{\frac{2}{3}} = \sqrt[3]{5^2}$
When a number is squared, the original number can be positive or negative, but the square root of a number can only be positive.	If $a^2 = 81$, then $a = \pm 9$, BUT $\sqrt{81} = 9$ only.
Cube roots of negative numbers are negative.	$\sqrt[3]{-27} = -3$

Chapter 8
Number and Quantity

To rationalize a fraction containing a radical combined with a number or variable in the denominator, multiply both the numerator and the denominator by the conjugate of the denominator. (The conjugate of a binomial uses the same terms but the opposite sign between them.)	$\dfrac{3}{2+\sqrt{5}}\ \rightarrow$ the conjugate of $(2+\sqrt{5})$ is $(2-\sqrt{5})$ $$\dfrac{3}{2+\sqrt{5}} \times \dfrac{2-\sqrt{5}}{2-\sqrt{5}} = \dfrac{3(2-\sqrt{5})}{(2+\sqrt{5})(2-\sqrt{5})}$$ $$= \dfrac{6-3\sqrt{5}}{4-2\sqrt{5}+2\sqrt{5}-\sqrt{5}\times 5}$$ $$= \dfrac{6-3\sqrt{5}}{4-\sqrt{25}}$$ $$= \dfrac{6-3\sqrt{5}}{4-5}$$ $$= \dfrac{6-3\sqrt{5}}{-1}$$ $$= -6+3\sqrt{5}$$

You need to do this

- Identify the appropriate rule by looking at the answer choices. What form do you need to get the expression into? What rule do you need to apply to get there?
- Apply the rule.
- Repeat as necessary.

Straightforward ACT radicals questions should be quick points. Before test day, make sure that you memorize the rules in the table shown.

Explanation

Notice that three of the answer choices have no radicals in the denominator; this suggests that the denominator most likely needs to be rationalized. Multiply both the numerator and denominator by the conjugate of the denominator since this will eliminate any radicals in the denominator.

$$\dfrac{(4x)(10+\sqrt{5})}{(10-\sqrt{5})(10+\sqrt{5})} = \dfrac{40x+4x\sqrt{5}}{100-5} = \dfrac{40x+4x\sqrt{5}}{95}$$

Choice (A) is correct.

Drills

If radicals give you trouble, study the information above and try out these drill questions before completing the Try on Your Own questions below. Drill answers can be found in Answers and Explanations.

a. $\dfrac{1}{\sqrt{3}} + \dfrac{8}{\sqrt{2}}$

b. $9^{-\frac{3}{2}}$

c. $\sqrt{0.0016x^2}$

d. $(5\sqrt{3})^2$

e. $13x\sqrt{5} - 4x\sqrt{5}$

Part 3
ACT MATH

Try on Your Own

Directions: Take as much time as you need on these questions. Work carefully and methodically. There will be an opportunity for timed practice at the end of the chapter.

1. What is the greatest integer smaller than $\sqrt{160}$?

   A. 12
   B. 13
   C. 14
   D. 15

2. Which of the following is equivalent to $(\sqrt{8} + \sqrt{6})(\sqrt{8} - \sqrt{6})$?

   F. 1
   G. 2
   H. $\sqrt{14}$
   J. 7

3. Which of the following is equivalent to the product $\sqrt{3} \times \sqrt[6]{3}$?

   A. $\sqrt[6]{3}$
   B. $\sqrt[7]{3}$
   C. $\sqrt[6]{6}$
   D. $\sqrt[3]{9}$

4. Which of the following values of n satisfies the inequality $\frac{4}{5} < n < 1$?

   F. $\frac{\sqrt{14}}{5}$
   G. $\frac{\sqrt{18}}{5}$
   H. $\frac{\sqrt{26}}{5}$
   J. $\frac{\sqrt{30}}{5}$

HINT: For Q5, is there an alternative to the radicals presented in the question stem and answer choices that could make the algebra easier to manage?

---

5. Which of the following is equivalent to $\dfrac{\sqrt[5]{x^3}\,\sqrt{z^5}\,\sqrt[3]{y^4}}{z^2\,\sqrt[3]{y}\,\sqrt[5]{x^2}}$?

   A. $\sqrt[3]{x^2}\,\sqrt[5]{y^3}\,\sqrt[5]{z^4}$
   B. $\dfrac{x^5}{zy^2\,\sqrt[4]{z}\,\sqrt[5]{y^3}}$
   C. $\dfrac{x\,\sqrt[6]{y^{17}}}{\sqrt[3]{z^{10}}}$
   D. $y\,\sqrt[5]{x}\,\sqrt{z}$

202

ABSOLUTE VALUE

> **LEARNING OBJECTIVE**
>
> After this lesson, you will be able to:
> - Solve absolute value equations

To answer a question like this

Evaluate $\left|\dfrac{5-9}{8-6}\right| - |4-8|$.

A. -4
B. -2
C. 2
D. 4

You need to know this

- Absolute value means the distance a number is from 0 on a number line.
- Because absolute value is a distance, it is always positive or 0.
- Absolute value symbols function as grouping symbols (like parentheses or brackets) in the order of operations.

You need to do this

- Follow the order of operations and simplify the expression from the inside set of parentheses or absolute value brackets out.
- Collect and combine like terms.
- Be careful with your positive and negative signs.

Explanation

There are two sets of absolute value brackets, but they are not nested, so you can calculate them independently. First, simplify the terms within the grouping symbols; then, determine the absolute value and complete the subtraction. To account for the absolute value brackets, make each term positive after you simplify it.

$$\left|\dfrac{5-9}{8-6}\right| - |4-8| = \left|\dfrac{-4}{2}\right| - |-4|$$
$$= |-2| - 4$$
$$= 2 - 4$$
$$= -2$$

Hence, (B) is correct.

Part 3
ACT MATH

Drills

If absolute values give you trouble, study the information above and try out these drill questions before completing the Try on Your Own questions below. Drill answers can be found in Answers and Explanations.

a. $||-4+3|-|7-10||$

b. $\left|\dfrac{-7 \times 4}{6 \times 2}\right|$

c. Given $x = -2$, evaluate $-|x-4| + 5x$.

d. Given $x = 3$, evaluate $-\left|\dfrac{4x-10}{-x-2}\right|$.

e. Given $x = -3$ and $y = 4$, evaluate $|xy + 5| - \left|\dfrac{y}{2} - 1\right|$.

Try on Your Own

Directions: Take as much time as you need on these questions. Work carefully and methodically. There will be an opportunity for timed practice at the end of the chapter.

1. What is the value of $\dfrac{|5-2x|-13}{-x}$ when $x = 3$?

   A. 3
   B. 4
   C. $\dfrac{14}{3}$
   D. 6

2. If $a = -2$, then which of the following is equivalent to $-2|5a - 4|$?

   F. -28
   G. -12
   H. 12
   J. 28

3. When $t = 8$, what is the value of $-4\left|\dfrac{t}{2} - 4\right| + 4$?

   A. -8
   B. -4
   C. 4
   D. 8

4. Which of the following is equivalent to $-\left|\dfrac{-4 \times 10}{3 \times 5}\right|$?

   F. $-\dfrac{8}{3}$
   G. $-\dfrac{4}{3}$
   H. $\dfrac{4}{3}$
   J. $\dfrac{8}{3}$

HINT: For Q5, take the time to familiarize yourself with both the question and the information provided. Which two answer choices can be marked incorrect without doing any substitution or algebra?

---

5. Given that $b = 3$ and $d = 1$, which of the following is equivalent to $\left|\dfrac{2b-3}{-4d+1}\right|$?

   A. -2
   B. -1
   C. 1
   D. 2

Chapter 8
Number and Quantity

SEQUENCES

> **LEARNING OBJECTIVE**
>
> After this lesson, you will be able to:
>
> - Identify a specific term in an arithmetic or geometric sequence

To answer a question like this

If the first term in a geometric sequence is 3, the third term is 48, and all the terms are positive integers, what is the ELEVENTH term?

- A. 228
- B. 528
- C. 3,145,728
- D. 12,582,912

You need to know this

A **sequence** is a list of numbers or expressions in which there is a pattern.

- Each number in a sequence is called a term and is named by, or is a function of, its position in the sequence.
- The first term in a sequence is called a_1, the nth term is called a_n, the term right after the nth term is called a_{n+1}, and so on. So a general sequence looks like $a_1, a_2, a_3, \ldots a_{n-1}, a_n, a_{n+1}, \ldots$.
- You can also write a sequence using function notation: $f(1), f(2), f(3), \ldots, f(n-1), f(n), f(n+1), \ldots$.
- A sequence can be arithmetic, geometric, or neither. For example, the sequence 1, 8, 27, 64, 125, ... has a pattern (perfect cubes) but is neither arithmetic nor geometric.

An **arithmetic sequence** is a sequence in which the same number is added to get from one term to the next.

- The difference between any two terms is called the common difference and is usually represented by the variable d.
- You can find the nth term in an arithmetic sequence using this formula: $a_n = a_1 + (n-1)d$.

A **geometric sequence** is a sequence in which the same number is multiplied to get from one term to the next.

- The number that you're multiplying by is called the common ratio and is usually represented by the variable r.
- You can find the nth term in a geometric sequence using this formula: $a_n = a_1 r^{(n-1)}$.

You need to do this

- Look for clues in the question stem to help you determine the type of sequence.
- Use any given terms to calculate the common difference or common ratio.
- Use Backsolving or the appropriate formula as needed to calculate the missing value.

Explanation

To find the next term in a geometric sequence, multiply the current term by a constant r. You are told that $a_1 = 3$ and $a_3 = 48$, so find r by creating the equation $a_1 \times r \times r = a_3$. Plugging in the given values yields $3 \times r \times r = 48$. Thus, $r^2 = 16$ and $r = 4$. Finally, use the general form of a geometric sequence, $a_n = a_1 r^{(n-1)}$, to solve for a_{11}.

$$a_{11} = a_1(r)^{(11-1)}$$
$$= 3(4^{10})$$
$$= 3{,}145{,}728$$

Choice (C) is correct.

Try on Your Own

Directions: Take as much time as you need on these questions. Work carefully and methodically. There will be an opportunity for timed practice at the end of the chapter.

1. Four numbers are in a sequence with 8 as the first term and 36 as the last term. The first three numbers form an arithmetic sequence with a common difference of -7. The last three numbers form a geometric sequence. What is the common ratio of the last three terms of the sequence?

   A. -10
   B. -6
   C. 10
   D. 32

   HINT: For Q2, how can you determine the common difference without consecutive terms?

2. What three numbers should be placed in the blanks below so that the difference between consecutive numbers is the same?

   $12, \_\_, \_\_, \_\_, 32$

   F. 16, 22, 28
   G. 17, 22, 27
   H. 22, 24, 30
   J. 23, 29, 31

3. If the first and second terms of a geometric sequence are 3 and 12, what is an expression for the value of the TWENTY-FOURTH (24th) term of the sequence?

   A. $a_{24} = 3^4 \times 12$
   B. $a_{24} = 3^4 \times 23$
   C. $a_{24} = 4^{23} \times 3$
   D. $a_{24} = 4^{24} \times 3$

4. If the first four terms of an arithmetic sequence are 25, 21, 17, and 13, respectively, what is the TWENTIETH (20th) term of the sequence?

   F. -55
   G. -51
   H. -47
   J. -43

5. If the fifth and the sixth terms of a geometric sequence are 3 and 1, respectively, what is the FIRST term of the sequence?

   A. -5
   B. 11
   C. 27
   D. 243

IMAGINARY NUMBERS

LEARNING OBJECTIVE

After this lesson, you will be able to:

- Perform arithmetic operations on imaginary and complex numbers

To answer a question like this

Given a positive integer n such that $i^n = -1$, which of the following statements about n must be true? (Note: $i^2 = -1$)

A. When n is divided by 4, the result is a multiple of 0.
B. When n is divided by 4, the result is a multiple of $\frac{1}{3}$.
C. When n is divided by 4, the result is a multiple of $\frac{1}{2}$.
D. When n is divided by 4, the result is a multiple of 2.

You need to know this

The square root of a negative number is not a real number but an **imaginary number**.

To take the square root of a negative number, use i, which is defined as $i = \sqrt{-1}$. For example, to simplify $\sqrt{-49}$, rewrite $\sqrt{-49}$ as $\sqrt{-1 \times 49}$, take the square root of -1 (which is by definition i), and then take the square root of 49, which is 7. The end result is $7i$.

When a number is written in the form $a + bi$, where a is the real component and b is the imaginary component (and i is $\sqrt{-1}$), it is referred to as a **complex number**.

Solving ACT questions that involve complex numbers in the denominator of a fraction will require the use of a conjugate number. Complex numbers and the conjugates that go with them are binomials, so you can use FOIL to multiply complex numbers by their conjugate numbers. Review this skill in chapter 10 if needed.

The powers of i follow a predictable pattern that can help you work more efficiently on the ACT.

When you have ...	... it becomes ...
i^1	i
i^2	$\sqrt{-1} \times \sqrt{-1} = -1$
i^3	$i^2 \times i = -1 \times i = -i$
i^4	$i^2 \times i^2 = -1 \times -1 = 1$

So, the cycles of i are $i, -1, -i, 1$, then repeat (try a few more if you're not convinced). When you have i raised to an exponent greater than 4, divide the exponent by 4. The remainder will dictate the final answer.

- Take i^{63} as an example.
- Divide 63 by 4 to get 15 with a remainder of 3.
- This means that $i^{63} = (i^4)^{15} \times i^3 = 1^{15} \times i^3$.
- Because $i^3 = -i$, i^{63} becomes $-i$.

Part 3
ACT MATH

You need to do this
Add, subtract, multiply, and divide complex numbers just as you do real numbers.

- To add (or subtract) complex numbers, simply add (or subtract) the real parts and then add (or subtract) the imaginary parts.
- To multiply complex numbers, treat them as binomials and use FOIL. To simplify the product, use the simplification $i^2 = -1$ and combine like terms.
- To divide complex numbers, write them in fraction form and multiply the numerator and denominator by the **conjugate** of the complex number in the denominator. To form the conjugate, change the sign in the complex number. For example, the conjugate of $2 + i$ is $2 - i$.
- Use FOIL as needed to multiply complex numbers by their conjugates.

Explanation
The statement $i^n = -1$ will be satisfied when $n = 2, 6, 10, 14, \ldots$ because there are four stages in the cycle of i and the definition of i is that $i^2 = -1$. Every answer asks what happens when n is divided by 4. Divide each of the values of n above by 4 and see if you can spot a pattern.

$\frac{n}{4} = \frac{1}{2}, \frac{3}{2}, \frac{5}{2}, \frac{7}{2}, \ldots$. All of these numbers are multiples of $\frac{1}{2}$, so (C) is correct.

Try on Your Own
Directions: Take as much time as you need on these questions. Work carefully and methodically. There will be an opportunity for timed practice at the end of the chapter.

HINT: For Q1, what quadratic process can help you multiply the complex numbers in the question?

1. Given that $i = \sqrt{-1}$, which of the following is equal to $(11 + 4i)(2 - 5i)$?

   A.   2
   B.   42
   C. $22 - 20i$
   D. $42 - 47i$

2. Which of the following is the correct simplification of the expression $(2 + 7i) - (4 - 3i)$?

   F. $-2 + 4i$
   G. $-2 + 10i$
   H. $2 - 4i$
   J. $2 + 10i$

3. The complex number i is defined such that $i^2 = -1$. What is the value of $(2i - 3)^2$?

   A. -13
   B.   5
   C. $9 + 4i$
   D. $5 - 12i$

4. If $i^2 = -1$, which of the following is a square root of $8 - 6i$?

   F. $3 + i$
   G. $3 - i$
   H. $4 + 3i$
   J. $4 - 3i$

5. Which of the following numbers is NOT a real number?

   A. $-\sqrt{9}$
   B. 3^{-2}
   C. $\sqrt{-9}$
   D. $(-3)^2$

Chapter 8
Number and Quantity

MATRICES

LEARNING OBJECTIVE

After this lesson, you will be able to:

- Perform arithmetic operations using matrices

To answer a question like this

If $\begin{bmatrix} 1 & 2 & 3 \end{bmatrix} \begin{bmatrix} x \\ 2x \\ 3x \end{bmatrix} = 42$, what is the value of x?

A. 2
B. 3
C. 4
D. 6

You need to know this

A **matrix** (*plural: matrices*) is a rectangular arrangement of numbers, symbols, or expressions, formatted in rows and columns.

- You can think of matrices as tables with no borders around the cells.
- The ACT tests matrices mostly in basic ways—addition, subtraction, and perhaps a multiplication question here or there.
- To add (or subtract) matrices, the matrices must be exactly the same size. Add (or subtract) the corresponding entries (the numbers that sit in the same spots).
- You can multiply an entire matrix by a number by multiplying each entry in the matrix by that number.
- Often, a high difficulty matrix question will appear as one of the final 10 questions.
  - These questions are more difficult because they typically require algebraic and critical thinking skills as opposed to straightforward calculations.
  - The definition of the determinant of matrix $\begin{bmatrix} a & b \\ c & d \end{bmatrix}$ (which is equal to $ad - bc$) will be provided when needed.

You need to do this

Carefully determine whether the question is asking for:

- a missing value within a matrix?
- the sum or difference of two or more matrices?
- the product of a matrix and a number?
- something else, potentially unfamiliar?

Examine the given information:

- How many matrices are there?
- Are you given a specified piece of information, such as the definition of the discriminant, to use in some way?
- How many variables are there? How many do you need?

Choose your approach:

- Can you Backsolve using the answer choices?
- Can you use algebra to find a requested combination?
- If so, what equation can you set up to find a missing value?
- If you're stuck or know the approach will take a long time, mark the question to return to it later if you have time remaining.

Explanation

When multiplying matrices, the number of columns in the first matrix must match the number of rows in the second matrix. Here, you are multiplying a 1×3 matrix and 3×1 matrix. These match up, so multiply the rows of the first matrix by the columns of the second matrix. This creates a simple equation in x.

$$(1)(x) + (2)(2x) + (3)(3x) = 42$$
$$x + 4x + 9x = 42$$
$$14x = 42$$
$$x = 3$$

Choice (B) is correct.

Try on Your Own

Directions: Take as much time as you need on these questions. Work carefully and methodically. There will be an opportunity for timed practice at the end of the chapter.

1. If $A = \begin{bmatrix} 4 & 0 & 3 \\ 0 & -2 & 1 \end{bmatrix}$ and $B = \begin{bmatrix} 1 & 5 & -2 \\ 0 & 0 & 4 \end{bmatrix}$, then $2A + B = ?$

   A. $\begin{bmatrix} 9 & 5 & 4 \\ 0 & -4 & 6 \end{bmatrix}$

   B. $\begin{bmatrix} 9 & 5 & 4 \\ 0 & 0 & 4 \end{bmatrix}$

   C. $\begin{bmatrix} 8 & 0 & 6 \\ 0 & -4 & 2 \end{bmatrix}$

   D. $\begin{bmatrix} 5 & 5 & 1 \\ 0 & -2 & 5 \end{bmatrix}$

2. From the four matrices shown below, which of the following products is NOT possible?

   $A = \begin{bmatrix} 1 & 2 \\ 3 & 4 \end{bmatrix} \quad B = \begin{bmatrix} 5 & 6 & 7 \\ 8 & 9 & 0 \end{bmatrix} \quad C = \begin{bmatrix} 2 \\ 4 \end{bmatrix} \quad D = \begin{bmatrix} 3 & 5 \end{bmatrix}$

   F. AB
   G. AC
   H. BC
   J. CD

3. Which of the following matrices is equal to the product of $\begin{bmatrix} 1 & 2 & 3 \end{bmatrix}$ and $\begin{bmatrix} -1 \\ -2 \\ -3 \end{bmatrix}$?

   A. -14
   B. 14

   C. $\begin{bmatrix} -1 & 0 & 0 \\ 0 & -4 & 0 \\ 0 & 0 & -9 \end{bmatrix}$

   D. $\begin{bmatrix} 0 & 1 & -1 \\ 2 & 0 & -2 \\ 3 & -3 & 0 \end{bmatrix}$

4. Evaluate $2x + y + 4z$, given $\begin{bmatrix} 4 & y & 8 \end{bmatrix} \begin{bmatrix} x \\ 2 \\ z \end{bmatrix} = 10.$

   F. 2
   G. 3
   H. 4
   J. 5

Chapter 8
Number and Quantity

> HINT: For Q5, how can you calculate the values of the four variables?

5. What is the value of $zy - xw$, given
$$\begin{bmatrix} 3x & 3 \\ 2w & 2z \end{bmatrix} + \begin{bmatrix} 6 & -2y \\ -4 & -6 \end{bmatrix} = \begin{bmatrix} 9 & 4 \\ 6 & 10 \end{bmatrix}?$$
    A. -9
    B. -1
    C. 6
    D. 7

Part 3
ACT MATH

On Test Day

Remember that the ACT doesn't ask you to show your work. If you find the math in a question challenging, there may be another way to get to the answer.

Try out this question first using straightforward math and then using the Backsolving strategy from earlier in this chapter. Which approach do you find easier? There's no right or wrong answer—just remember your preferred approach and try it first if you see a question like this on test day.

1. What is the largest integer less than $\sqrt{250}$?

    A. 15
    B. 16
    C. 17
    D. 19

The correct answer and both ways of solving can be found at the end of this chapter.

Chapter 8
Number and Quantity

How Much Have You Learned?

Directions: For test-like practice, give yourself 10 minutes to complete this question set. Be sure to study the explanations, even for questions you got correct. They can be found at the end of this chapter.

1. The number $5^{\frac{5}{2}}$ is equal to which of the following?

   A. 12.5
   B. 25
   C. $\sqrt[5]{25}$
   D. $\sqrt{5^5}$

2. If $i^2 = -1$, which of the following represents $\dfrac{1}{3-i}$ written in $a + bi$ form?

   F. $\dfrac{3}{10} + \dfrac{1}{10}i$
   G. $\dfrac{1}{3} - \dfrac{1}{i}$
   H. $3 + i$
   J. $3 - i$

3. Evaluate $\dfrac{|14 + |2x - 4||}{5x + 6}$ when $x = -2$.

   A. -12
   B. $-\dfrac{11}{2}$
   C. -2
   D. $\dfrac{9}{4}$

4. The first four terms of a geometric sequence are $-2, 4, -8,$ and 16. What is the NINTH term of the geometric sequence?

   F. -512
   G. -256
   H. 256
   J. 512

5. If $m = 2n$, then for what positive value of n does the determinant of $\begin{bmatrix} m & 8 \\ 4 & n \end{bmatrix}$ equal 0? (Note: The determinant of matrix $\begin{bmatrix} a & b \\ c & d \end{bmatrix}$ equals $ad - bc$.)

   A. 4
   B. $4\sqrt{2}$
   C. 8
   D. $8\sqrt{2}$

6. Which of the following is equivalent to $\dfrac{10}{7 - 2\sqrt{5}}$?

   F. $\dfrac{70 - 47\sqrt{55}}{29}$
   G. $\dfrac{70 + 20\sqrt{5}}{29}$
   H. $\dfrac{27 + \sqrt{5}}{45}$
   J. $\dfrac{25 - \sqrt{55}}{45}$

7. Which of the following is equivalent to $\dfrac{(xy^2)^{-4} z^3}{z^{-1} y^2 x^{-3}}$?

   A. $\dfrac{1}{z^4}$
   B. $\dfrac{x^3 y^2}{z^4}$
   C. $\dfrac{z^2}{x^4 y^3}$
   D. $\dfrac{z^4}{xy^{10}}$

Part 3
ACT MATH

8. When the imaginary number i is defined as $i = \sqrt{-1}$, it follows that $i^2 = -1$. Based on this information, which of the following is equivalent to $\dfrac{i^3 + 4i}{\sqrt{-9}}$?

F. -1
G. 1
H. 3
J. $3i$

9. Which of the following expresses the value of $530{,}000{,}000 - 442{,}000{,}000$ in scientific notation?

A. 8.8×10^6
B. 8.8×10^7
C. 8.8×10^8
D. 8.8×10^9

10. If $\begin{bmatrix} x & 6 \\ 13 & x \end{bmatrix} + \begin{bmatrix} 2 & 3y \\ 5 & y \end{bmatrix} = \begin{bmatrix} 6 & 12 \\ 18 & z \end{bmatrix}$, what is the value of z?

F. 6
G. 8
H. 22
J. 24

Chapter 8
Number and Quantity

Reflect

Directions: Take a few minutes to recall what you've learned and what you've been practicing in this chapter. Consider the following questions, jot down your best answer for each one, and then compare your reflections to the expert responses on the following page. Use your level of confidence to determine what to do next.

1. How do you add, subtract, multiply, and divide terms that involve exponents? What must be true in order to complete these operations?

   _____
   _____
   _____

2. How are exponents and radicals related?

   _____
   _____
   _____

3. When you answer questions involving absolute value, what is the most important thing to pay attention to?

   _____
   _____
   _____

4. How can the algebraic skill FOIL help you answer tough imaginary number questions?

   _____
   _____
   _____

Responses

1. How do you add, subtract, multiply, and divide terms that involve exponents? What must be true in order to complete these operations?

To combine terms that involve exponents, the terms must have the same base. To add or subtract, keep the base and the exponent the same and add or subtract the coefficients (e.g., $2x^2 + 3x^2 = 5x^2$). To multiply, keep the base the same and add the exponents (e.g., $x^2 x^3 = x^5$). To divide, keep the base the same and subtract the exponents (e.g., $x^8 \div x^2 = x^6$).

2. How are exponents and radicals related?

Radicals are fractional, or inverse, exponents.

3. When you answer questions involving absolute value, what is the most important thing to pay attention to?

When solving an equation like $|x| = 8$, there are two possibilities for x: 8 and −8. Do not forget that the answer could be negative!

4. How can the algebraic skill FOIL help you answer tough imaginary number questions?

To multiply two imaginary numbers in $a + bi$ form, you must FOIL. Simplify, collect like terms, and remember that $i^2 = -1$.

Next Steps

If you answered most questions correctly in the "How Much Have You Learned?" section, and if your responses to the Reflect questions were similar to those of the ACT expert, then consider number and quantity an area of strength and move on to the next chapter. Come back to this topic periodically to prevent yourself from getting rusty.

If you don't yet feel confident, review those parts of this chapter that you have not yet mastered. Then, try the questions you missed again. As always, be sure to review the explanations closely. Then go online (**kaptest.com/login**) for more practice. If you haven't already registered your book, do so at **kaptest.com/moreonline**.

GO ONLINE

kaptest.com/login

Answers and Explanations

Exponents

Drill Answers

a. 1.32×10^9

b. 1.4×10^9

c. 2.1×10^3

d. x^7

e. y^6

1. A
Difficulty: Low
Category: Number and Quantity
Getting to the Answer: Simplify the numerator and divide. Then convert into scientific notation.

$$\frac{3,200,000 - 2,300,000}{3,000} = \frac{900,000}{3,000}$$
$$300 = 3.0 \times 10^2$$

Choice (A) is correct.

2. G
Difficulty: Medium
Category: Number and Quantity
Getting to the Answer: Combine like terms and apply exponent rules to simplify. Remember that when you divide, you subtract the exponents.

$$\frac{x^6 \, y^4 \, z^9}{x \, y^6 \, z^3} = x^5 y^{-2} z^6 = \frac{x^5 z^6}{y^2}$$

Choice (G) is correct.

3. B
Difficulty: Low
Category: Number and Quantity
Getting to the Answer: First, simplify the numerator. Divide the numbers without exponents (12.0 and 4.0) first. Then, apply exponent rules to determine the correct power of 10: add the exponents when multiplying the same bases and subtract the exponents when dividing the same bases.

$$\frac{(2.0 \times 10^4)(6.0 \times 10^7)}{4.0 \times 10^2} = \frac{12.0 \times 10^{11}}{4.0 \times 10^2} = 3.0 \times 10^9$$

Choice (B) is correct.

4. F
Difficulty: Medium
Category: Number and Quantity
Getting to the Answer: Remember that you can make a term with a negative exponent have a positive exponent by taking the reciprocal of the term. To make this expression easier to understand, begin by making all the exponents positive. Then apply exponent rules to simplify.

$$\frac{a^{-7}c^2b^{-4}}{b^2c^{-3}a^{-3}} = \frac{a^3c^2c^3}{a^7b^2b^4} = \frac{c^5}{a^4b^6}$$

Choice (F) is correct.

5. D
Difficulty: Medium
Category: Number and Quantity
Getting to the Answer: Simplify the denominator and divide. Make sure that the answer is written in correct scientific notation.

$$\frac{2.1 \times 10^{-12}}{(2.0 \times 10^4)(5.0 \times 10^3)} = \frac{2.1 \times 10^{-12}}{10.0 \times 10^7}$$
$$\frac{2.1 \times 10^{-12}}{10^8} = 2.1 \times 10^{-20}$$

Choice (D) is correct.

Radicals

Drill Answers

a. $\dfrac{\sqrt{2} + 8\sqrt{3}}{\sqrt{6}}$

b. $\dfrac{1}{27}$

c. $\pm 0.04x$

d. 75

e. $9x\sqrt{5}$

Part 3
ACT MATH

1. A
Difficulty: Low
Category: Number and Quantity
Getting to the Answer: The best way to find the biggest integer smaller than $\sqrt{160}$ is to square each answer choice. The largest one that, when squared, is still smaller than 160 is correct.

$$A)\ 12^2 = 144$$
$$B)\ 13^2 = 169$$

Since the answer choices are listed in increasing order, all other choices will be even larger than 169. Thus, (A) is correct.

2. G
Difficulty: Medium
Category: Number and Quantity
Getting to the Answer: Use the FOIL method to simplify. Notice that the terms being multiplied are conjugates, which means that the cross terms will cancel out. If you observe this, you can save some time by multiplying only the First and Last terms.

$$(\sqrt{8} + \sqrt{6})(\sqrt{8} - \sqrt{6}) = 8 - \sqrt{48} + \sqrt{48} - 6 = 2$$

Choice (G) is correct.

3. D
Difficulty: Medium
Category: Number and Quantity
Getting to the Answer: Because the radicals have different roots, you can't use the basic radical properties. Instead, change each radical into exponent form. Since you are multiplying two terms with the same base, add the exponents. Finally, change the expression back into radical form.

$$\sqrt{3} \times \sqrt[6]{3} = 3^{\frac{1}{2}} \times 3^{\frac{1}{6}}$$
$$= 3^{\frac{3}{6}} \times 3^{\frac{1}{6}}$$
$$= 3^{\frac{4}{6}}$$
$$= 3^{\frac{2}{3}}$$
$$= \sqrt[3]{3^2}$$
$$= \sqrt[3]{9}$$

Choice (D) is correct.

4. G
Difficulty: Low
Category: Number and Quantity
Getting to the Answer: Your task is to find the fraction between $\frac{4}{5}$ and 1. Notice that all the answer choices have radicals in the numerator and 5 in the denominator. Manipulate the given inequality to get it into the same form.

$$\frac{4}{5} < n < 1$$
$$\frac{4}{5} < n < \frac{5}{5}$$
$$\frac{\sqrt{16}}{5} < n < \frac{\sqrt{25}}{5}$$

Since 18 is between 16 and 25, (G) is correct.

5. D
Difficulty: High
Category: Number and Quantity
Getting to the Answer: First, change the radicals into exponent form. Next, apply exponent rules to simplify, adding exponents when multiplying and subtracting exponents when dividing. Remember that you need common denominators to add or subtract fractions. Finally, convert the exponents back into radical form.

$$\frac{\sqrt[5]{x^3}\ \sqrt{z^5}\ \sqrt[3]{y^4}}{z^2\ \sqrt[3]{y}\ \sqrt[5]{x^2}} = \frac{x^{\frac{3}{5}} z^{\frac{5}{2}} y^{\frac{4}{3}}}{z^2 y^{\frac{1}{3}} x^{\frac{2}{5}}}$$

$$\frac{x^{\frac{3}{5}} y^{\frac{4}{3}} z^{\frac{5}{2}}}{x^{\frac{2}{5}} y^{\frac{1}{3}} z^2} = x^{\frac{1}{5}} y z^{\frac{1}{2}}$$

$$x^{\frac{1}{5}} y z^{\frac{1}{2}} = y \sqrt[5]{x}\ \sqrt{z}$$

Choice (D) is correct.

Absolute Value

Drill Answers

a. 2
b. $\frac{7}{3}$
c. -16
d. $-\frac{2}{5}$
e. 6

Chapter 8
Number and Quantity

1. B
Difficulty: Low
Category: Number and Quantity
Getting to the Answer: Plug in 3, the value given for x, and simplify. Remember that absolute value brackets change negative numbers into positive numbers.

$$\frac{|5-2x|-13}{-x} = \frac{|5-2(3)|-13}{-3}$$
$$= \frac{|5-6|-13}{-3}$$
$$= \frac{|-1|-13}{-3}$$
$$= \frac{1-13}{-3}$$
$$= \frac{-12}{-3}$$
$$= 4$$

Choice (B) is correct.

2. F
Difficulty: Medium
Category: Number and Quantity
Getting to the Answer: Start by plugging in -2, the given value. Simplify and make sure to utilize the absolute value.

$$-2|5a-4| = -2|5(-2)-4|$$
$$= -2|-14|$$
$$= -28$$

Thus, (F) is correct. Do not be tricked by choice J: this would be the answer without using the absolute value.

3. C
Difficulty: Medium
Category: Number and Quantity
Getting to the Answer: First, plug in the given value of 8 and simplify inside of the absolute value. Make sure the number inside the absolute value is not negative before moving on to the next simplifying steps.

$$-4\left|\frac{t}{2}-4\right|+4 = -4\left|\frac{(8)}{2}-4\right|+4$$
$$= -4|0|+4$$
$$= 4$$

Choice (C) is correct.

4. F
Difficulty: Medium
Category: Number and Quantity
Getting to the Answer: First, simplify the numerator and denominator, then reduce the resulting fraction. The fraction inside the absolute value will be positive. Then, multiply the negative outside of the absolute value.

$$-\left|\frac{40}{15}\right| = -\left|\frac{8}{3}\right| = -\frac{8}{3}$$

Choice (F) is correct. J is a trap answer; it is the expression's result if the absolute value were absent.

5. C
Difficulty: Medium
Category: Number and Quantity
Getting to the Answer: Plug in the given values ($b = 3$ and $d = 1$) and simplify the numerator and denominator. After you divide, make sure that the resulting number is positive because of the absolute value.

$$\left|\frac{2b-3}{-4d+1}\right| = \left|\frac{2(3)-3}{-4(1)+1}\right|$$
$$= \left|\frac{3}{-3}\right|$$
$$= |-1|$$
$$= 1$$

Choice (C) is correct. Be careful; B would be the answer if there were no absolute value brackets.

Sequences

1. B
Difficulty: Medium
Category: Number and Quantity
Getting to the Answer: Your task is to find r, the common ratio of a geometric sequence. Since you are told that the first three terms form an arithmetic sequence with a common difference of -7, you can find the second and third terms in the sequence by subtracting 7. So, $a_1 = 8$, $a_2 = 1$, and $a_3 = -6$. You are also told that $a_4 = 36$ and that the last three terms form a geometric sequence. $1 \times r = -6$ and $-6 \times r = 36$, so the ratio is -6. Choice (B) is correct.

Part 3
ACT MATH

2. G
Difficulty: Medium
Category: Number and Quantity
Getting to the Answer: The question gives you the first and fifth terms of an arithmetic sequence. The task is to figure out the middle three terms. Use the arithmetic sequence formula with $n = 5$, $a_1 = 12$, and $a_5 = 32$ to solve for the common difference.

$$a_5 = a_1 + (n - 1)d$$
$$32 = 12 + (5 - 1)d$$
$$32 = 12 + 4d$$
$$20 = 4d$$
$$5 = d$$

Starting at 12 and repeatedly adding 5 yields 12, 17, 22, 27, 32.

Hence, (G) is correct. Note that you can also solve this question by Backsolving. Choices H and J are themselves not arithmetic sequences, so they're incorrect. Choice F doesn't work because the difference between 12 and 16 is 4, whereas the difference between 16 and 22 is 6. This leaves (G) as the only choice that works.

3. C
Difficulty: Low
Category: Number and Quantity
Getting to the Answer: Since the first and second terms are given, find the common ratio r by setting $3r = 12$. This yields $r = 4$. The question asks for the 24th term, so plug $r = 4$, $n = 24$, and $a_1 = 3$ into the geometric sequence formula.

$$a_n = a_1 r^{(n-1)}$$
$$a_{24} = 3 \times 4^{(24-1)}$$
$$a_{24} = 3 \times 4^{23}$$

Terms can be multiplied in any order, so $a_{24} = 3 \times 4^{23} = 4^{23} \times 3$. Therefore, (C) is correct.

4. G
Difficulty: Low
Category: Number and Quantity
Getting to the Answer: It is too laborious to calculate the 20th term of this sequence by hand, so plug $d = -4$, $n = 20$, and $a_1 = 25$ into the arithmetic sequence formula.

$$a_n = a_1 + (n - 1)d$$
$$a_{20} = 25 + (20 - 1)(-4)$$
$$a_{20} = 25 - 76$$
$$a_{20} = -51$$

Therefore, (G) is correct.

5. D
Difficulty: Low
Category: Number and Quantity
Getting to the Answer: Since the fifth and sixth terms of the sequence are given, you can find the common ratio r by setting $3r = 1$. This yields $r = \frac{1}{3}$. Now plug $r = \frac{1}{3}$, $a_6 = 1$, and $n = 6$ into the geometric sequence formula and solve for a_1.

$$a_n = a_1 r^{(n-1)}$$
$$a_6 = a_1 \left(\frac{1}{3}\right)^{(6-1)}$$
$$1 = a_1 \left(\frac{1}{3}\right)^5$$
$$1 = a_1 \left(\frac{1}{243}\right)$$
$$243 = a_1$$

Therefore, (D) is correct.

Imaginary Numbers

1. D
Difficulty: Medium
Category: Number and Quantity
Getting to the Answer: FOIL the given expression and remember that $i^2 = -1$. Simplify by combining like terms. Finally, make sure that your answer is in $a + bi$ form.

$$(11 + 4i)(2 - 5i) = 22 - 55i + 8i - 20i^2$$
$$= 22 - 47i - 20(-1)$$
$$= 22 - 47i + 20$$
$$= 42 - 47i$$

Choice (D) is correct.

2. G

Difficulty: Low
Category: Number and Quantity
Getting to the Answer: Combine like terms, being careful to distribute the negative outside the parentheses.

$$2 + 7i - (4 - 3i) = 2 + 7i - 4 + 3i$$
$$= -2 + 10i$$

Choice (G) is correct.

3. D

Difficulty: Medium
Category: Number and Quantity
Getting to the Answer: Since the term in parentheses is squared, write out both terms and FOIL. Remember that $i^2 = -1$.

$$(2i - 3)(2i - 3) = 4i^2 - 6i - 6i + 9$$
$$= 4i^2 - 12i + 9$$
$$= 4(-1) - 12i + 9$$
$$= -4 - 12i + 9$$
$$= 5 - 12i$$

Choice (D) is correct.

4. G

Difficulty: Medium
Category: Number and Quantity
Getting to the Answer: The square root of n is a number that yields n when it is multiplied by itself. It is difficult to take the square root of $8 - 6i$ directly because the number has both a real and an imaginary component, so approach the question strategically. Backsolve by squaring each answer choice. The one that equals $8 - 6i$ is the square root:

(F) $(3 + i)(3 + i) = 9 + 3i + 3i + i^2$
$$= 9 + 6i - 1$$
$$= 8 + 6i$$
Eliminate

(G) $(3 - i)(3 - i) = 9 - 3i - 3i + i^2$
$$= 9 - 6i - 1$$
$$= 8 - 6i$$
Correct

There is no need to go any further. Choice (G) is correct.

5. C

Difficulty: Low
Category: Number and Quantity
Getting to the Answer: The imaginary number i is defined as $i = \sqrt{-1}$. The only answer that has a negative number under a radical sign is (C).

Matrices

1. A

Difficulty: Medium
Category: Number and Quantity
Getting to the Answer: To add or subtract matrices, both matrices need to have the same dimensions. Both A and B are 2×3 matrices, so they are compatible. To compute $2A$, multiply each entry in A by 2. To add A and B, add each corresponding component in A and B.

$$2\begin{bmatrix} 4 & 0 & 3 \\ 0 & -2 & 1 \end{bmatrix} + \begin{bmatrix} 1 & 5 & -2 \\ 0 & 0 & 4 \end{bmatrix}$$

$$\begin{bmatrix} 8 & 0 & 6 \\ 0 & -4 & 2 \end{bmatrix} + \begin{bmatrix} 1 & 5 & -2 \\ 0 & 0 & 4 \end{bmatrix}$$

$$\begin{bmatrix} 9 & 5 & 4 \\ 0 & -4 & 6 \end{bmatrix}$$

Thus, (A) is correct.

2. H

Difficulty: Low
Category: Number and Quantity
Getting to the Answer: When multiplying matrices, the number of columns of the first matrix must match the number of rows in the second matrix. BC is not possible because the 3 columns in B do not match the 2 rows in C.

Choice (H) is correct.

3. A

Difficulty: Low
Category: Number and Quantity
Getting to the Answer: When multiplying matrices, the number of columns in the first matrix must match the number of rows in the second matrix. Here, you are multiplying a 1×3 matrix and a 3×1 matrix. The product matrix will have the same number of rows as the first matrix and the same number of columns as the second matrix. This means that the resulting matrix is 1×1. Eliminate C and D immediately. Finally, multiply

the two matrices by multiplying the rows of the first matrix by the columns of the second matrix.

$$[1 \quad 2 \quad 3] \begin{bmatrix} -1 \\ -2 \\ -3 \end{bmatrix}$$

$$1(-1) + 2(-2) + 3(-3)$$
$$-1 - 4 - 9$$
$$-14$$

Choice (A) is correct.

4. J
Difficulty: Medium
Category: Number and Quantity
Getting to the Answer: Remember that you multiply two matrices by multiplying the columns of the first matrix by the rows of the second matrix.

$$[4 \quad y \quad 8] \begin{bmatrix} x \\ 2 \\ z \end{bmatrix} = 10$$

$$4(x) + 2(y) + z(8) = 10$$
$$4x + 2y + 8z = 10$$

Notice that your end goal is very similar to the equation above. Divide both sides by 2 to obtain $2x + y + 4z = 5$.

Thus, (J) is correct.

5. A
Difficulty: High
Category: Number and Quantity
Getting to the Answer: Matrices can be added only if their dimensions are the same. Here, all the matrices are 2×2, so add the matrices component-wise.

$$\begin{bmatrix} 3x+6 & 3-2y \\ 2w-4 & 2z+-6 \end{bmatrix} = \begin{bmatrix} 9 & 4 \\ 6 & 10 \end{bmatrix}$$

Next, write out four equations and solve for each variable.

$$3x + 6 = 9 \Rightarrow x = 1$$
$$2w - 4 = 6 \Rightarrow w = 5$$
$$3 - 2y = 4 \Rightarrow y = -\frac{1}{2}$$
$$2z + -6 = 10 \Rightarrow z = 8$$

Finally, plug these values into $zy - xw$.

$$zy - xw$$
$$8\left(-\frac{1}{2}\right) - 1(5)$$
$$-4 - 5$$
$$-9$$

Choice (A) is correct.

On Test Day

1. A
Difficulty: Low
Category: Number and Quantity
Getting to the Answer: Using straightforward math, you will use your calculator to approximate the square root of 250: 15.8114. This is between the integers 15 and 16, and 16 is not smaller than 15.8114, so (A) is correct.

Another way to find the biggest number smaller than $\sqrt{250}$ is to Backsolve and square each answer choice. The largest one that is still smaller than $\sqrt{250}$ is correct:

A) $15^2 = 225$
B) $16^2 = 256$

Since the answer choices are listed in increasing order, all other choices will be even larger than 256. Thus, (A) is correct.

How Much Have You Learned?

1. D
Difficulty: Medium
Category: Number and Quantity
Getting to the Answer: Recall that with a fractional exponent, the top number represents the power, while the bottom number represents the root. Thus, an exponent of $\frac{5}{2}$ involves raising a number to the 5th power and taking a square root. The base of the exponent is 5, so raise it to the 5th power and take the square root. The only choice that does this is (D), so (D) is correct.

2. F

Difficulty: Medium
Category: Number and Quantity
Getting to the Answer: For this question, you need to rearrange an expression, not solve an equation. When there are imaginary numbers in the denominator of a fraction, multiply both the numerator and denominator by the conjugate of the denominator to make sure all imaginary numbers are eliminated in the denominator.

$$\frac{1}{3-i} \frac{(3+i)}{(3+i)} = \frac{3+i}{9-i^2}$$

$$\frac{3+i}{10} = \frac{3}{10} + \frac{1}{10}i$$

Choice (F) is correct.

3. B

Difficulty: Medium
Category: Number and Quantity
Getting to the Answer: Plug in -2, the value for x, and simplify. Make sure that any number that comes out of an absolute value is positive.

$$\frac{|14+|2x-4||}{5x+6} = \frac{|14+|2(-2)-4||}{5(-2)+6}$$

$$= \frac{|14+|-4-4||}{-10+6}$$

$$= \frac{|14+8|}{-4}$$

$$= \frac{22}{-4}$$

$$= -\frac{11}{2}$$

Choice (B) is correct.

4. F

Difficulty: Medium
Category: Number and Quantity
Getting to the Answer: Since you are working with a geometric sequence, first find r by comparing the first and second terms.

$$-2r = 4$$
$$r = -2$$

Then plug $a_1 = -2$, $r = -2$, and $n = 9$ into the geometric sequence formula to solve for the ninth term, a_9.

$$a_n = a_1 r^{(n-1)}$$
$$a_n = -2r^{(n-1)}$$
$$a_9 = -2(-2)^{(9-1)}$$
$$= -2(-2)^8$$
$$= -2^9$$
$$= -512$$

Choice (F) is correct.

5. A

Difficulty: High
Category: Number and Quantity
Getting to the Answer: The question asks for the value of n that makes the determinant of the given matrix equal 0. You are given the formula for calculating the determinant. Substitute m for a, 8 for b, 4 for c, and n for d, and set the resulting expression equal to 0.

$$ad - bc = 0$$
$$mn - 8(4) = 0$$
$$mn - 32 = 0$$
$$mn = 32$$

The question states that $m = 2n$. Substitute $2n$ for m and solve for n:

$$(2n)n = 32$$
$$2n^2 = 32$$
$$n^2 = 16$$
$$n = \pm 4$$

The question asks for the positive value of n, so (A) is correct.

6. G

Difficulty: Medium
Category: Number and Quantity
Getting to the Answer: On the ACT, square roots normally do not appear in the denominators of fractions in answer choices. Rationalize the denominator by multiplying the top and bottom by the conjugate.

$$\frac{(10)}{(7-2\sqrt{5})} \times \frac{(7+2\sqrt{5})}{(7+2\sqrt{5})} = \frac{70+20\sqrt{5}}{49-4(5)}$$

$$= \frac{70+20\sqrt{5}}{29}$$

Choice (G) is correct.

Part 3
ACT MATH

7. D
Difficulty: Medium
Category: Number and Quantity
Getting to the Answer: Remember that when an exponent is raised to another exponent, the exponents are multiplied. Simplify and combine like terms.

$$\frac{(xy^2)^{-4}z^3}{z^{-1}y^2x^{-3}} = \frac{x^{-4}y^{-8}z^3}{z^{-1}y^2x^{-3}} = \frac{x^{-1}y^{-10}z^4}{1} = \frac{z^4}{xy^{10}}$$

Choice (D) is correct.

8. G
Difficulty: High
Category: Number and Quantity
Getting to the Answer: Rather than solving an equation, you are manipulating an expression using properties of i. Simplify the expression using the identities $i = \sqrt{-1}$ and $i^2 = -1$.

$$\frac{i^3 + 4i}{\sqrt{-9}} = \frac{i^2(i) + 4i}{\sqrt{9}\sqrt{-1}} = \frac{-i + 4i}{3i} = \frac{3i}{3i} = 1$$

Choice (G) is correct.

9. B
Difficulty: High
Category: Number and Quantity
Getting to the Answer: Your task is to select the answer choice that expresses the difference in scientific notation. Write each number in scientific notation, then solve.

$$530{,}000{,}000 = 5.3 \times 10^8$$
$$442{,}000{,}000 = 4.42 \times 10^8$$
$$5.3 \times 10^8 - 4.42 \times 10^8 = 0.88 \times 10^8$$

However, this is not the final answer. To be in scientific notation, the number before the multiplication sign must be between 1 and 10. In other words, you need to move the decimal to the right one place. When you move the decimal to the right, you multiply the number by 10. To keep the same overall value, you need to divide the power of 10 by 10, or decrease the power of 10 by 1. Rewriting 0.88×10^8 as 8.8×10^7, you find that the answer is (B).

10. F
Difficulty: Medium
Category: Number and Quantity
Getting to the Answer: Your task is to find z. Although writing an equation for z only involves the bottom right numbers in the matrices, doing so will give you $x + y = z$, so you will need the rest of the matrix to determine the missing variables.

First, add the two matrices. Remember that matrix addition is performed component-wise—add the numbers that sit in the same spots:

$$\begin{bmatrix} x & 6 \\ 13 & x \end{bmatrix} + \begin{bmatrix} 2 & 3y \\ 5 & y \end{bmatrix} = \begin{bmatrix} x+2 & 6+3y \\ 13+5 & x+y \end{bmatrix}$$

Next, set the matrix sum equal to the third matrix:

$$\begin{bmatrix} x+2 & 6+3y \\ 18 & x+y \end{bmatrix} = \begin{bmatrix} 6 & 12 \\ 18 & z \end{bmatrix}$$

You can now write out three equations and solve for each variable:

$$x + 2 = 6 \Rightarrow x = 4$$
$$6 + 3y = 12 \Rightarrow y = 2$$
$$x + y = z \Rightarrow z = 6$$

Choice (F) is correct.

[CHAPTER 9]

RATES, RATIOS, PROPORTIONS, AND PERCENTS

LEARNING OBJECTIVES

After completing this chapter, you will be able to:

- Solve math questions with real-world scenarios using one or more rates
- Create a ratio to represent the relationship between two numbers
- Set up a proportion and solve to find a missing value
- Calculate percents
- Calculate percent change

Part 3
ACT MATH

How Much Do You Know?

Directions: Try out the questions below. Show your work so that you can compare your solutions to the ones found on the next page. The "Category" heading in the explanation for each question gives the title of the lesson that covers how to solve it. If you answered the question(s) for a given lesson correctly, and if your scratchwork looks like ours, you may be able to move quickly through that lesson. If you answered incorrectly or used a different approach, you may want to take your time on that lesson.

1. Muna bikes to school every morning. It takes her 20 minutes to travel 3 miles. What is Muna's average speed, in miles per hour, on her trip to school?

   A. 8
   B. 9
   C. 10
   D. 11

2. The ratio of seniors to juniors in a class is 3:5. If the class has 32 total students who are exclusively juniors and seniors, how many more juniors are there than seniors?

   F. 5
   G. 8
   H. 12
   J. 20

3. Tyrone is reading a road map. On the map, $\frac{1}{4}$ inch represents 12 miles. How many miles apart are two cities that are $3\frac{1}{2}$ inches apart on Tyrone's map?

   A. 48
   B. 96
   C. 132
   D. 168

4. If 125% of a number is 470, what is 50% of the number?

   F. 168
   G. 188
   H. 208
   J. 228

5. There are green, red, and blue marbles in a bag in a ratio of 1:2:3. The total number of marbles in the bag is 42. All the red marbles are taken and moved into a new bag with different marbles. After the addition of the red marbles, the second bag contains 52 marbles. How many marbles were in the second bag before the addition of the red marbles?

   A. 24
   B. 31
   C. 38
   D. 45

Answers and explanations are on the next page. ▶ ▶ ▶

Part 3
ACT MATH

Answers and Explanations

How Much Do You Know?

1. B
Difficulty: Low
Category: Number and Quantity: Rates, Ratios, and Proportions
Getting to the Answer: The question asks for a bicyclist's average speed and provides distance in miles and time in minutes. Notice that all of the answer choices are in miles per hour, so start by converting the time from minutes into hours:

$$20 \text{ minutes} \times \frac{1 \text{ hour}}{60 \text{ minutes}} = \frac{20}{60} \text{ hours} = \left(\frac{1}{3}\right) \text{ hours}$$

Now use the formula $d = rt$ to solve for Muna's mile-per-hour rate, or r.

$$d = rt$$
$$3 = r\left(\frac{1}{3}\right)$$
$$9 = r$$

Choice (B) is correct.

2. G
Difficulty: Medium
Category: Number and Quantity: Rates, Ratios, and Proportions
Getting to the Answer: Read carefully; the question asks how many *more* juniors *than* seniors are in a class. The stem provides the number of *total* students and the ratio of seniors to juniors. Convert the part-to-part ratio to a part-to-whole ratio of seniors to total students: $\frac{3}{3+5} = \frac{3}{8}$. Then, set up a proportion and cross-multiply to solve for the number of seniors:

$$\frac{3}{8} = \frac{s}{32}$$
$$3(32) = 8s$$
$$96 = 8s$$
$$12 = s$$

Since there are 12 seniors in a class of 32 total students, there must be $32 - 12 = 20$ juniors. The question asks how many more juniors there are than seniors, so the correct answer is $20 - 12 = 8$, (G).

3. D
Difficulty: Medium
Category: Number and Quantity: Rates, Ratios, and Proportions
Getting to the Answer: The question asks you to determine the mileage between two cities. You are given their distance apart on a road map and the scale used for the map. Set up a proportion and cross-multiply. Convert $3\frac{1}{2}$ into the improper fraction $\frac{7}{2}$ to make the calculations easier.

$$\frac{\frac{1}{4} \text{ inch}}{12 \text{ miles}} = \frac{\frac{7}{2} \text{ inch}}{x \text{ miles}}$$
$$\frac{1}{4}x = 12\left(\frac{7}{2}\right)$$
$$\frac{1}{4}x = 42$$
$$x = 168$$

Since the question asks for how many miles the two cities are apart, which is x, choice (D) is correct.

4. G
Difficulty: Medium
Category: Number and Quantity: Percents
Getting to the Answer: This question asks for the value of 50% of a number given the value of 125% of that number. Translate carefully from English into math. In a word problem, "of" means multiply, "a number" means a variable, and "is" means equals. Translate the first part of the question and solve for x. Remember that $125\% = 1.25$.

$$1.25x = 470$$
$$x = 376$$

Finally, because it's what the question asks for, take 50% of x.

$$(0.50)x = (0.50)(376)$$
$$= 188$$

Choice (G) is correct.

Chapter 9
Rates, Ratios, Proportions, and Percents

5. C
Difficulty: Medium
Category: Number and Quantity: Rates, Ratios, and Proportions
Getting to the Answer: The question asks for the original number of marbles in the second bag. You are given the final number of marbles in that bag, the ratio of different colors of marbles, and the total number of marbles in the first bag from which the red marbles were taken. Use the ratio to find the number of red marbles and subtract that from the total number of marbles in the second bag.

Since the ratio of green to red to blue marbles in the first bag is 1:2:3, the ratio of red marbles to total marbles is 2:6. Set up a proportion and cross-multiply to solve for the number of red marbles in the first bag:

$$\frac{2}{6} = \frac{r}{42}$$
$$\frac{1}{3} = \frac{r}{42}$$
$$42 = 3r$$
$$14 = r$$

Since there are 52 marbles in the second bag after the addition of the red marbles from the first bag, there must have been $52 - 14 = 38$ marbles originally in the second bag. This is the value you need, so (C) is correct.

Part 3
ACT MATH

RATES, RATIOS, AND PROPORTIONS

LEARNING OBJECTIVES

After this lesson, you will be able to:

- Solve math questions with real-world scenarios using one or more rates
- Create a ratio to represent the relationship between two numbers
- Set up a proportion and solve to find a missing value

To answer a question like this

A construction team is building a house from blueprints that are made to scale. Every 0.5 inch on the blueprint corresponds to 5 feet that the construction team needs to build. One wall the team is currently working on is 4.5 inches tall in the blueprint. Approximately how many *feet* tall does the wall need to be?

A. 15
B. 27
C. 45
D. 63

You need to know this

A **rate** is any "something per something"—days per week, miles per hour, dollars per gallon, etc.

- Pay close attention to the units of measurement; the rate could be given in one measurement in the question and a different measurement in the answer choices.
    - This means you would need to convert the units in the first rate to the units in the desired rate before you answer the question.
    - On the ACT, unit conversion is usually tested in conjunction with geometry, so you should review chapter 13 for instruction on this skill.
- Rate questions will often use the DIRT formula: Distance Is Rate $\times$ Time, or $d = rt$. The rate will always be the something per something, the distance value will match the units in the first part of the rate ("something per . . ."), and the time value will match the units in the second part of the rate (". . . per something").

A **ratio** is a comparison of one quantity to another.

- When writing ratios, you can compare one part of a group to another part of that group, or you can compare a part of the group to the whole group.
    - If you have a bowl of apples and oranges, you can write ratios that compare apples to oranges (part to part), apples to total fruit (part to whole), and oranges to total fruit (part to whole).
- Ratios can be expressed using colons (3:5), fractions $\left(\frac{3}{5}\right)$, or words (3 to 5).
- Ratios are typically expressed in lowest terms and convey relative amounts—not necessarily actual amounts.
    - If there are 10 apples and 6 bananas in a bowl, the ratio of apples to bananas would likely be expressed as $\frac{5}{3}$ on the ACT rather than as $\frac{10}{6}$.
    - If you know the ratio of apples to bananas and either the actual number of apples or the total number of pieces of fruit, you can find the actual number of bananas by setting up a proportion, but if you only know ratios and no actual numbers, you cannot calculate any actual numbers.

Chapter 9
Rates, Ratios, Proportions, and Percents

- If the ratio of apples to bananas is $\frac{5}{3}$ and there are 10 apples, then you can use the common multiplier 2 (because $5 \times 2 = 10$) to determine that there must be $3 \times 2 = 6$ bananas.
- If the ratio of apples to bananas is $\frac{5}{3}$ and there are 16 pieces of fruit, you can set up a proportion to find the number of bananas:

$$\frac{3 \text{ bananas}}{5 \text{ apples}} \rightarrow \frac{3 \text{ bananas}}{8 \text{ total fruit}}$$

$$\frac{3 \text{ bananas}}{8 \text{ total fruit}} = \frac{b \text{ bananas}}{16 \text{ total fruit}}$$

$$3(16) = 8b$$
$$48 = 8b$$
$$6 = b$$

- If the only information provided is that the ratio of apples to bananas is $\frac{5}{3}$ and the ratio of apples to total fruit is $\frac{5}{8}$, then there is not enough information to determine the actual numbers of apples or bananas or the total number of fruit.

A **proportion** is simply two ratios set equal to each other, e.g., $\frac{a}{b} = \frac{c}{d}$.

- Proportions are an efficient way to solve certain questions, but you must exercise caution when setting them up.
- Noting the units of each piece of the proportion will help you put each piece of the proportion in the right place.
- Cross-multiplication allows you to easily convert a proportion into an often easy-to-solve equation:

$$\frac{a}{b} \times \frac{c}{d} \rightarrow ad = bc$$

- If you know any three numerical values in a proportion, you can solve for the fourth.
    - For example: say a fruit stand sells 3 peaches for every 5 apricots, and you need to calculate the number of peaches sold on a day when 20 apricots were sold.
    - You could use this information to set up a proportion and solve for the unknown:

$$\frac{3}{5} = \frac{p}{20}$$

    - You can now solve for the number of peaches sold, p, by cross-multiplying:

$$60 = 5p$$
$$p = 12$$

    - Alternatively, you could use the common multiplier to solve for p: the numerator and denominator in the original ratio must be multiplied by the same value to arrive at their respective terms in the new ratio.
    - To get from 5 to 20 in the denominator, you multiply by 4, so you also have to multiply the 3 in the numerator by 4 to arrive at the actual number of peaches sold: $4(3) = 12$.

You need to do this

- Identify the quantities and units used in any rates, ratios, or proportions in the question stem or answer choices.
- When needed, convert between part:part and part:whole ratios.
- When helpful, convert ratios that use colons into ratios that use fractions.

Part 3
ACT MATH

- Use common multipliers to calculate common ratios.
- Set up a proportion using two ratios and solve for the unknown either by cross-multiplying or by using the common multiplier.

Explanation

The question asks how many feet tall a wall must be and gives the blueprint scale in inches. Use the given information to set up a proportion to solve for the actual height of the wall. Make sure that the units on both sides of the equal sign match up:

$$\frac{0.5 \text{ inch}}{5 \text{ feet}} = \frac{4.5 \text{ inch}}{x \text{ feet}}$$

$$0.5x = 4.5(5)$$

$$0.5x = 22.5$$

$$x = 45$$

Thus, the wall must be 45 feet tall, and choice (C) is correct.

Drills

If rates, ratios, and proportions give you trouble, study the information above and try out these drill questions before completing the Try on Your Own questions that follow. Determine the value of the variable for each part. Drill answers can be found in Answers and Explanations.

a. $\frac{2}{10} = \frac{x}{15}$

b. $\frac{7}{2} = \frac{7}{x}$

c. $\frac{a}{12} = \frac{6}{8}$

d. $\frac{\frac{1}{2}}{w} = \frac{\frac{1}{4}}{\frac{5}{2}}$

e. $\frac{2.5}{5} = \frac{z}{4}$

Try on Your Own

Directions: Take as much time as you need on these questions. Work carefully and methodically. There will be an opportunity for timed practice at the end of the chapter.

1. Which of the following values of x satisfies the proportion $\frac{5(x-2)}{9} = \frac{4}{3}$?

   A. $\frac{33}{15}$

   B. $\frac{42}{15}$

   C. $\frac{51}{15}$

   D. $\frac{66}{15}$

> HINT: For Q2, fractions inside of fractions can look confusing, but the cross-multiplication still works the same way. Which terms should you multiply together?

2. What is the value of $x - y$ if $y = 4$ and $\frac{\frac{3}{5}}{\frac{1}{2}} = \frac{x}{10}$?

   F. 4

   G. 8

   H. 12

   J. 16

Chapter 9
Rates, Ratios, Proportions, and Percents

3. At the end of the season, a team's ratio of wins to losses was 3:5. If there were no ties, what percentage of its games did the team win?

   A. $37\frac{1}{2}\%$

   B. 40%

   C. $62\frac{1}{2}\%$

   D. 75%

4. Four liters of water are mixed with 6 juiced lemons to make lemonade. How many liters of water should be mixed with 10 juiced lemons to obtain the same result?

   F. $4\frac{2}{3}$

   G. $5\frac{1}{3}$

   H. $6\frac{2}{3}$

   J. $8\frac{1}{3}$

5. For a certain company, a train coming from New York to Washington, D.C., takes 3 hours to travel 228 miles. A new company's train is able to complete the same journey in only 2.5 hours. How much faster is the new company's train in terms of miles per hour (mph)?

   A. 11.7

   B. 15.2

   C. 17.3

   D. 21.4

6. Two packages of strawberries are sold for $10. How many packages could you buy with $25?

   F. 4

   G. 5

   H. 6

   J. 7

7. Which of the following is equivalent to $\frac{x^2 y}{2zw} = \frac{4xy^2}{3z^3 w}$?

   A. $y = \frac{3xz^2}{8}$

   B. $x = \frac{3yz^2}{8}$

   C. $z = \frac{3xy^2}{8}$

   D. $w = \frac{3xz^2}{8}$

HINT: For Q8, do you have part:part or part:whole ratios?
What actual numbers are you given?
What are you trying to find?

---

8. The ratio of students to faculty on the First Year College Experience Committee at a certain university is 1.2:1. If there are 22 people on the committee, how many faculty are on the committee?

   F. 7

   G. 10

   H. 15

   J. 19

9. The school newspaper staff is selling cookies to raise money for the next school year. The first student who sells 252 boxes earns a laptop. Eva sells on average 7 boxes per hour, while Sylvia sells on average 3 boxes every 30 minutes. How much time, in hours, will pass until at least one of the students sells enough boxes to earn a laptop?

   A. 15
   B. 23
   C. 36
   D. 42

10. Carmen and Eduardo are building a tree house. Their mother constructs a drawing to scale that uses only two different lengths of wood pieces. The ratio, in inches, of the wood pieces is 2:3. If the longer wood piece is 5.5 feet, then how long is the shorter wood piece? (12 inches = 1 foot)

    F. 3 feet, 8 inches
    G. 3 feet, 10 inches
    H. 4 feet, 2 inches
    J. 8 feet, 3 inches

PERCENTS

LEARNING OBJECTIVES

After this lesson, you will be able to:

- Calculate percents
- Calculate percent change

To answer a question like this

In 1960, scientists estimated a certain animal population in a particular geographical area to be 6,400. In 2000, the population had risen to 7,200. If this animal population experiences the same percent increase over the next 40 years, what will the approximate population be in 2040?

A. 8,000
B. 8,100
C. 8,500
D. 9,000

You need to know this

To calculate percents, use this basic equation:

$$\text{percent} = \frac{\text{part}}{\text{whole}} \times 100\%$$

Alternatively, use this statement: [blank] percent of [blank] is [blank]. Translating from English into math, you get [blank]% × [blank] = [blank].

Chapter 9
Rates, Ratios, Proportions, and Percents

You may sometimes need to calculate percent change on the ACT. You can determine the percent change in a given situation by applying this formula:

$$\text{percent charge} = \frac{\text{amount of charge}}{\text{original amount}} \times 100\%$$

If the change is an increase, the amount of change will be positive. If the change is a decrease, the amount of change will be negative. So, a change in population might be a 3% change, while the change in a sales price might be −40%.

Sometimes, more than one change will occur. Be careful here, as it can be tempting to take a "shortcut" by just adding two percent changes together (which will almost always lead to an incorrect answer). Instead, you'll need to find the total amount of the increase or decrease and then apply the formula.

You need to do this

To use the basic percents equation:

- Plug in the values for any two parts of the formula and solve for the third.
- In some calculations, it may be more convenient to express percents as decimals. To do this, use the formula above, but stop before you multiply by 100% at the end.

To calculate a percent change:

- Calculate the actual increase or decrease.
- Divide by the original amount (not the new amount!).
- Multiply by 100%.

Explanation

Use the percent change formula to find the percent change from 1960 to 2000.

$$\text{percent charge} = \frac{\text{amount of charge}}{\text{original amount}} \times 100\%$$

Plug in the values given in the question stem.

$$\frac{7,200 - 6,400}{6,400} = \frac{800}{6,400} = 0.125 \times 100\% = 12.5\%$$

Finally, apply this same percent increase to the population in the year 2000. Remember that 12.5% = 0.125. $7,200 + 7,200(0.125) = 8,100$. Hence, (B) is correct.

Drills

If percents give you trouble, study the information above and try out these drill questions before completing the Try on Your Own questions below. Drill answers can be found in Answers and Explanations.

a. Calculate 25% of 200.

b. Calculate $1.8 \times 75\%$.

c. Express $\frac{11}{15}$ as a percent.

d. Express 1.3×0.4 as a percent.

e. Express 150% of 60% as a percent.

Try on Your Own

Directions: Take as much time as you need on these questions. Work carefully and methodically. There will be an opportunity for timed practice at the end of the chapter.

1. A certain doctoral program requires two qualifying papers to graduate. The program's records show that 70% of students present a successful first qualifying paper. Of those students who pass, 40% fail their second qualifying paper. If the program accepted 500 doctoral candidates into the program over the past 10 years, how many graduated by passing both qualifying papers?

   A. 140
   B. 210
   C. 350
   D. 455

2. The managers of a restaurant calculated their business expenditures for the previous month. Overhead cost was $4,800, food cost was $8,000, and wages paid to employees were $6,500. What percent of the total expenditures did the greatest expense comprise? Round your answer to the nearest whole percent.

   F. 25%
   G. 29%
   H. 35%
   J. 41%

3. 12% of 50 is $\frac{3}{5}$ of what number?

   A. 8
   B. 9
   C. 10
   D. 11

4. What number is 16% of 25?

   F. 4
   G. 5
   H. 6
   J. 7

HINT: Questions like Q5 can be quick and easy to solve if you translate carefully from English to math.

---

5. 40% of 24 is $\frac{5}{2}$ of what number?

   A. 2.76
   B. 3.84
   C. 4.52
   D. 5.12

Chapter 9
Rates, Ratios, Proportions, and Percents

On Test Day

When a question features multiple percentages, you have to make a key strategic decision: Can you do the arithmetic on the percentages themselves and get the answer right away, or do you have to calculate each percentage individually and do the arithmetic on the actual values?

For example, suppose a car traveling 50 miles per hour increases its speed by 20 percent and then decreases its speed by 20 percent. Can you just say that its final speed is 50 miles per hour since $+20\% - 20\% = 0$? No, because after a 20% increase, the car's speed becomes 120% of the original: $1.2(50) = 60$. When the car "decreases its speed by 20 percent," that 20 percent is calculated based on the new speed, 60, not the original speed, and 20 percent of 60 is greater than 20 percent of 50. Thus, the car's final speed is lower than its starting speed: $50(1.2)(0.8) = 48$ miles per hour.

By contrast, suppose you have to find how many more pet owners than non–pet owners live in a certain region where there are 13,450 residents, 32 percent of whom don't own a pet and 68 percent of whom do. It may be tempting to find 32 percent of 13,450 ($0.32 \times 13,450 = 4,304$), then find 68 percent of 13,450 ($0.68 \times 13,450 = 9,146$), and finally subtract those two numbers to get the answer ($9,146 - 4,304 = 4,842$). This is a waste of time, even though it will give you the correct answer. Instead, you can quickly find the difference between the two percentages ($68 - 32 = 36$) and take 36 percent of the total to get the answer in one step: $13,450 \times 0.36 = 4,842$, which is the same answer because the totals are the same.

If you can do arithmetic using the percentages but choose to do arithmetic on the raw numbers instead, you'll waste time doing unnecessary work. However, if you can't do arithmetic on the percentages (as in the first example) but try anyway, you'll get an incorrect answer. Being able to tell whether you can or can't do the arithmetic on the percentages is a useful skill.

Luckily, the fundamental principle is simple: you can do arithmetic on the percentages as long as the percentages are out of the same total. If the totals are different, then you must convert the percentages into actual values. Focus on this principle as you practice with a question similar to one you've seen earlier:

1. A school admits applicants only if they are able to pass a written and an oral exam. Past records have shown that 60% of the applicants pass the written exam, and 80% of the applicants who pass the written exam go on to pass the oral exam. If there are 1,500 applicants, how many students will be admitted?

    A. 720
    B. 900
    C. 1,050
    D. 1,200

The answer and explanation can be found at the end of this chapter.

How Much Have You Learned?

Directions: For test-like practice, give yourself 10 minutes to complete this question set. Be sure to study the explanations, even for questions you got correct. They can be found at the end of this chapter.

1. Which of the following will result in an odd integer for any integer n?

   A. $3n^2$
   B. $4n^2$
   C. $3n^2 + 1$
   D. $4n^2 + 1$

2. Yeong-Ho owns two dogs. Each day, one dog eats $1\frac{1}{2}$ scoops of dog food, and the other eats $2\frac{3}{4}$ scoops of the same dog food. If one bag of this dog food contains about 340 scoops, how many days should it last for the two dogs?

   F. 80
   G. 85
   H. 92
   J. 100

3. If $a:b = 2:5$ and $b:c = 4:3$, what is the ratio of $a:c$?

   A. 2:3
   B. 5:3
   C. 8:15
   D. 15:8

4. If 12 inches equal 30.48 centimeters, how many centimeters are in 36 inches?

   F. 91.44
   G. 92.33
   H. 93.48
   J. 94.52

5. A construction company is building a group of houses that all have the same ratio of length to width. If one house has a ratio of 10:3 and another house has a ratio of 5:a, then what is the value of $2a + 4$?

   A. $\frac{3}{2}$
   B. 7
   C. 8
   D. 12

6. At a factory, Taj produces 23 toys per hour and Rosa produces 47 toys per hour. How many hours will it take for Taj and Rosa to produce 490 toys?

   F. 4
   G. 5
   H. 6
   J. 7

7. Ernesto is shopping at a store that is having a clearance sale. The price of everything in the store is discounted by 25%. If Ernesto buys a shirt originally priced at $22.00 and a 6% sales tax is added, what will be the total price of the shirt?

   A. $23.10
   B. $18.66
   C. $17.49
   D. $16.50

8. Atiya bought pants that were on clearance for 40% off the original price. She paid the cashier a total of $29.70 after sales tax. If sales tax is 10%, what was the original price of the pants?

   F. $39.52
   G. $45
   H. $48
   J. $52.18

9. Ryan and Kamini can make 30 gallons of chocolate milk in 5 hours. Ryan can make 2 gallons of chocolate milk every hour. How many gallons of chocolate milk can Kamini make every hour?

   A. 2
   B. 3
   C. 4
   D. 5

10. A 12-foot metal alloy bar weighs 114 pounds. What is the weight in pounds of a bar made out of the same alloy, with the same width and height, that is 3 feet 8 inches long?

    F. $27\frac{1}{2}$
    G. $34\frac{5}{6}$
    H. $41\frac{2}{3}$
    J. $49\frac{1}{6}$

Part 3
ACT MATH

Reflect

Directions: Take a few minutes to recall what you've learned and what you've been practicing in this chapter. Consider the following questions, jot down your best answer for each one, and then compare your reflections to the expert responses on the following page. Use your level of confidence to determine what to do next.

1. What is a ratio, and how is it different from a proportion?

   _____
   _____
   _____

2. If you're given a ratio of one quantity to another, what can you say about the total number of quantities?

   _____
   _____
   _____

3. Suppose the value of something increases by 20 percent. How can you calculate the final value in the fewest number of steps? What if the value decreases by 20 percent?

   _____
   _____
   _____

4. What is the percent change formula, and what is the biggest pitfall to avoid when using it?

   _____
   _____
   _____

Chapter 9
Rates, Ratios, Proportions, and Percents

Responses

1. What is a ratio, and how is it different from a proportion?

A ratio is the relative comparison of one quantity to another. For example, if the ratio of dogs to cats in an animal shelter is 3 to 5, then there are 3 dogs for every 5 cats. A proportion is two ratios set equal to each other.

2. If you're given a ratio of one quantity to another, what can you say about the total number of quantities?

Given a ratio, you know that the total must be a multiple of the sum of the ratio's parts. For example, if the ratio of dogs to cats is 3 to 5, then the total number of dogs and cats must be a multiple of 3 + 5, or 8. This means that when the ACT gives you one ratio, it's actually giving you several. If you're told that dogs:cats = 3:5, then you also know that dogs:total = 3:8 and cats:total = 5:8. You can use this "hidden" knowledge to your advantage.

3. Suppose the value of something increases by 20 percent. How can you calculate the final value in the fewest number of steps? What if the value decreases by 20 percent?

The fastest way to increase a value by 20 percent is to multiply it by 1.2, which is 100% + 20% = 120%. Similarly, to decrease something by 20 percent, you multiply it by 0.8, as that is 100% − 20% = 80%.

4. What is the percent change formula, and what is the biggest pitfall to avoid when using it?

The percent change formula is:

$$\text{percent change} = \frac{\text{amount of change}}{\text{original amount}} \times 100\%$$

A common mistake is to put the new amount on the bottom of the fraction rather than the original amount.

Next Steps

If you answered most questions correctly in the "How Much Have You Learned?" section, and if your responses to the Reflect questions were similar to those of the ACT expert, then consider ratios and the related topics in this chapter areas of strength and move on to the next chapter. Come back to this topic periodically to prevent yourself from getting rusty.

If you don't yet feel confident, review those parts of this chapter that you have not yet mastered, and try the questions you missed again. As always, be sure to review the explanations closely. Then go online (**kaptest.com/login**) for more practice. If you haven't already registered your book, do so at **kaptest.com/moreonline**.

GO ONLINE

kaptest.com/login

Answers and Explanations

Rates, Ratios, and Proportions

Drill Answers

a. 3
b. 2
c. 9
d. 5
e. 2

1. D
Difficulty: Medium
Category: Number and Quantity
Getting to the Answer: The question asks for the value of x and provides a proportion in which one term is x. Cross-multiply and simplify to solve for x:

$$\frac{5(x-2)}{9} = \frac{4}{3}$$
$$15(x-2) = 36$$
$$x - 2 = \frac{36}{15}$$
$$x = \frac{36}{15} + 2$$
$$x = \frac{36}{15} + \frac{30}{15}$$
$$x = \frac{66}{15}$$

Choice (D) is correct.

2. G
Difficulty: High
Category: Number and Quantity
Getting to the Answer: The question asks for the value of $x - y$. The value of y is provided, and x is part of a proportion with stacked fractions. Fractions inside of fractions can look confusing, but the cross-multiplication still works the same way:

$$\frac{\frac{3}{5}}{\frac{1}{2}} = \frac{x}{10}$$
$$\frac{3}{5}(10) = \frac{1}{2}x$$
$$6 = \frac{1}{2}x$$
$$12 = x$$

Remember that you need to find $x - y$. Since $x = 12$ and $y = 4$, $x - y = 8$; choice (G) is the correct answer.

3. A
Difficulty: Low
Category: Number and Quantity
Getting to the Answer: The question gives you a team's win-loss ratio and asks for the percentage of games that the team won. Since there were no ties, you can convert the given part-to-part ratio of 3:5 to the part-to-whole ratio of 3:8. (Note that the 8 comes from the fact that $3 + 5 = 8$.) To find the percentage of games won, convert that ratio to a percentage: $\frac{3}{8} \times 100\% = 37.5\%$.

This is the percentage of games won, so (A) is correct. Be careful; C is the percentage of games *lost* and is therefore incorrect.

4. H
Difficulty: Low
Category: Number and Quantity
Getting to the Answer: The question asks how many liters of water should be mixed with the juice from 10 lemons to create lemonade with the same concentration as mixing 4 liters of water with the juice from 6 lemons. Set up a proportion using the given information and designate the number of liters of water as w. Cross-multiply and solve for w:

$$\frac{w \text{ liters of water}}{10 \text{ lemons}} = \frac{4 \text{ liters of water}}{6 \text{ lemons}}$$
$$6w = 40$$
$$w = \frac{40}{6}$$
$$w = \frac{20}{3} = 6\frac{2}{3}$$

The question asks for w, so (H) is correct.

5. B
Difficulty: Medium
Category: Number and Quantity
Getting to the Answer: The question asks how much faster one train is than another. The choices are stated in terms of mph. You are given the distance of a certain trip and the time it takes each train to complete the

journey. Calculate each rate separately by plugging the given distance and time into the $d = rt$ formula.

$$d_1 = r_1 t_1 \qquad d_2 = r_2 t_2$$
$$228 = r_1(3) \qquad 228 = r_2(2.5)$$
$$76 = r_1 \qquad 91.2 = r_2$$

The question asks for the difference between the rates, which is $91.2 - 76 = 15.2$ mph, (B).

6. G
Difficulty: Low
Category: Number and Quantity
Getting to the Answer: The question asks how many packages of strawberries can be bought for $25 and gives the price for 2 packages of strawberries. Set up a proportion using the given information. Cross-multiply and solve for p.

$$\frac{2 \text{ packages}}{10 \text{ dollars}} = \frac{p \text{ packages}}{25 \text{ dollars}}$$
$$10p = 50$$
$$p = 5$$

This is the number of packages that you could buy with $25, so (G) is correct.

7. A
Difficulty: High
Category: Number and Quantity
Getting to the Answer: The question asks which choice is equivalent to the given proportion. Since the choices are stated in terms of different variables, your strategy is to cross-multiply and isolate for one variable at a time, then compare your results to the corresponding choice. You may have to do this multiple times until you find something that matches an answer choice.

$$\frac{x^2 y}{2zw} = \frac{4xy^2}{3z^3 w}$$
$$3x^2 y z^3 w = 8xy^2 zw$$
$$3xz^2 = 8y$$
$$\frac{3xz^2}{8} = y$$

This question relies on trial and error, so you may not arrive at this answer immediately. When you isolate y, the resulting expression matches choice (A), so that is the correct answer.

8. G
Difficulty: High
Category: Number and Quantity
Getting to the Answer: The question asks how many faculty are on a committee. You are given the total number of committee members and the ratio of students to faculty, which is 1.2:1.

Convert the part-to-part ratio to a part-to-whole ratio and use this ratio to solve for the number of faculty.

$$\frac{1 \text{ faculty}}{1 + 1.2 \text{ total}} = \frac{f \text{ faculty}}{22 \text{ total}}$$
$$(22)(1) = 2.2f$$
$$22 = 2.2f$$
$$10 = f$$

There are 10 faculty on the committee. Hence, (G) is correct.

9. C
Difficulty: Medium
Category: Number and Quantity
Getting to the Answer: The question asks how long it will take the more efficient of the two students selling cookies to reach a specific sales goal. You are given the rates at which both students are selling, but these rates are in different units. First, check to see which student is selling boxes at a faster rate. Sylvia sells 3 boxes every 30 minutes, or 6 boxes every hour. Eva sells 7 boxes per hour, so she will reach the goal first.

Now use the $d = rt$ formula to solve for t to determine how long it will take Eva to sell 252 boxes:

$$d = rt$$
$$352 = 7t$$
$$36 = t$$

This is how long it will take the faster student to sell the cookies, so (C) is correct. Note that D is how many hours it would take Sylvia, the student who sells at a slower rate, to sell the 252 boxes.

10. F

Difficulty: Medium
Category: Number and Quantity
Getting to the Answer: The question gives you the ratio of the lengths of two pieces of wood and asks for the length of the shorter piece. Set up a proportion and cross-multiply to solve.

$$\frac{2 \text{ in.}}{3 \text{ in.}} = \frac{x \text{ ft}}{5.5 \text{ ft}}$$
$$2(5.5) = 3x$$
$$\frac{11}{3} = x$$

Finally, convert $\frac{11}{3}$ into a mixed number of feet and inches.

$$\frac{11}{3} \text{ ft} = 3\frac{2}{3} \text{ ft}$$
$$\frac{2}{3} \text{ ft} \times \frac{12 \text{ in.}}{\text{ft}} = 8 \text{ in.}$$

This is the length of the shorter piece, so (F) is correct. Choice J is a strong distractor that you would choose if you reversed the ratio.

Percents

Drill Answers

a. 50
b. 1.35
c. 73.33%
d. 52%
e. 90%

1. B

Difficulty: Medium
Category: Number and Quantity
Getting to the Answer: The doctoral program admits a total of 500 students. Of these, 70% presented a passing first qualifying paper. Since 70% = 0.70 and "of" means "multiply," the number of students who passed their first qualifying paper is 500(0.70) = 350. Read the next part carefully. If 40% of students failed their second qualifying paper, then 60% of students passed. This means that the number of students who passed both papers is 350(0.60) = 210. Choice (B) is correct.

2. J

Difficulty: Low
Category: Number and Quantity
Getting to the Answer: The question asks you to find the greatest expenditure and calculate what percent of the total it was. Recall that percent = $\frac{\text{part}}{\text{whole}} \times 100\%$. The question asks about the highest expenditure, which is food cost. The total of the expenditures is $4,800 + $8,000 + $6,500 = $19,300. Plug these numbers into the percent formula.

$$\text{percent} = \frac{8,000}{19,300} \times 100\%$$
$$= 0.41451 \times 100\%$$
$$= 41.451\%$$

Round to the nearest whole number to get 41%, choice (J).

3. C

Difficulty: Medium
Category: Number and Quantity
Getting to the Answer: To understand what the question asks, carefully translate from English into math. Recall that "of" means multiply, "is" means equals, and "what number" means x. First convert 12% to 0.12.

$$0.12(50) = \frac{3}{5}x$$
$$6 = \frac{3}{5}x$$
$$6\left(\frac{5}{3}\right) = x$$
$$10 = x$$

You chose x to represent the number the question asked for, so (C) is correct.

4. F

Difficulty: Low
Category: Number and Quantity
Getting to the Answer: To understand what the question asks, carefully translate from English into math. Recall that "what number" means x, "is" means equals, and "of" means multiply. Convert 16% to 0.16.

$$x = (0.16)(25)$$
$$x = 4$$

This is the number that was asked for, so (F) is correct.

5. B

Difficulty: Medium
Category: Number and Quantity
Getting to the Answer: To understand what the question asks, carefully translate from English into math. Recall that "of" means multiply, "is" means equals, and "what number" means x.

$$0.40 \times 24 = \frac{5}{2}x$$
$$9.6 = \frac{5}{2}x$$
$$9.6\left(\frac{2}{5}\right) = x$$
$$3.84 = x$$

This is the value you need, so (B) is correct.

On Test Day

1. A

Difficulty: Medium
Category: Number and Quantity
Getting to the Answer: The question asks how many students will be admitted to a certain school. You're given the total number of applicants, the percent who pass the written exam, and the percent (of those who pass the written exam) who pass the oral exam. Start by multiplying the total number of applicants by the percent of applicants who pass the written exam:

$$1{,}500(0.60) = 900$$

Then multiply by the percent of applicants who pass the oral exam:

$$900(0.80) = 720$$

This gives the number of admitted applicants, so (A) is correct.

The students who pass the written exam and the students who pass the oral exam are separate groups, but the number of students who pass the oral exam is a subset of the number of students who pass the written exam. This means that the totals are different, and thus, you must calculate each percent independently. Someone who chooses to average the percents will end up with $1{,}500(0.7) = 1{,}050$, C, which is incorrect. Skipping the first percent and directly finding 80% of the original total (instead of 80% of those who pass the written exam) will also yield an incorrect answer, D: $1{,}500(0.8) = 1{,}200$.

How Much Have You Learned?

1. D

Difficulty: High
Category: Number and Quantity
Getting to the Answer: You need to find the expression that will always yield an odd integer. The question states that n is an integer, but it could be positive or negative or zero, and it could be even or odd. The answers contain variables, so Picking Numbers is an option.

Each choice contains an n^2, so start with A. Remember, n can be any integer, so you may as well pick an easy number to start with.

If $n = 2$, then:

$3n^2 = 3(4) = 12$, even. Eliminate A.

$4n^2 = 4(4) = 16$, even. Eliminate B.

$3n^2 + 1 = 12 + 1 = 13$, odd. Keep C.

$4n^2 + 1 = 16 + 1 = 17$, odd. Keep D.

To decide between C and D, pick another value for n. This time, try an odd value. (You can then try negative numbers if using an odd number doesn't help you narrow it down to the correct answer.)

If $n = 3$, then:

$3n^2 + 1 = 3(9) + 1 = 28$, even. Eliminate C.

Choice (D) is correct.

2. F

Difficulty: Medium
Category: Number and Quantity
Getting to the Answer: The question asks how many days it will take two dogs to consume a dog food bag of a certain size. You are told how much food each dog eats every day and how much food is in the bag. Since the dogs are eating from the same bag of food, add the number of scoops each dog eats per day to find how many total scoops per day are being eaten.

$$1\tfrac{1}{2} + 2\tfrac{3}{4}$$
$$\tfrac{3}{2} + \tfrac{11}{4}$$
$$\tfrac{6}{4} + \tfrac{11}{4}$$
$$\tfrac{17}{4}$$

Since you are given a rate and asked to solve for time, use the $d = rt$ formula.

$$340 = \frac{17}{4}t$$

$$340\left(\frac{4}{17}\right) = t$$

$$80 = t$$

Because t represents the number of days the food will last, (F) is correct.

3. C
Difficulty: Medium
Category: Number and Quantity
Getting to the Answer: The question asks for the ratio of a to c and provides the ratios of a to b and b to c. Notice that $\left(\frac{a}{b}\right)\left(\frac{b}{c}\right) = \frac{a}{c}$. To find $\frac{a}{c}$, simply multiply the two given ratios together.

$$\left(\frac{2}{5}\right)\left(\frac{4}{3}\right) = \frac{8}{15}$$

This is the ratio of a to c, so (C) is correct. Be certain that you answered the question that was asked. Choice D is the ratio of c to a.

4. F
Difficulty: Low
Category: Number and Quantity
Getting to the Answer: The question asks how many centimeters are equivalent to 36 inches. You are given the number of centimeters in 12 inches. Set up a proportion and cross-multiply to solve for c, the number of centimeters in 36 inches.

$$\frac{12 \text{ inches}}{30.48 \text{ centimeters}} = \frac{36 \text{ inches}}{c \text{ centimeters}}$$

$$12c = (30.48)36$$

$$12c = 1{,}097.28$$

$$c = 91.44$$

Because c is the variable you chose to represent the answer, (F) is correct.

5. B
Difficulty: Medium
Category: Number and Quantity
Getting to the Answer: The question asks for the value of $2a + 4$ and provides two equivalent ratios, one of which contains a. Begin by solving for a. Set up a proportion and cross-multiply:

$$\frac{10}{3} = \frac{5}{a}$$

$$10a = 15$$

$$a = \frac{3}{2}$$

You're not done yet, though. The question asks for $2a + 4$, so plug in $a = \frac{3}{2}$ to find the value of this expression.

$$2a + 4 = 2\left(\frac{3}{2}\right) + 4$$

$$= 3 + 4$$

$$= 7$$

This is the final answer, so (B) is correct. Be certain that you answered the question that was asked; choice A is the value of a.

6. J
Difficulty: Medium
Category: Number and Quantity
Getting to the Answer: The question asks how long, in hours, it will take for two workers to produce 490 toys. You are given the rates at which each worker produces toys. Since both workers' rates are given in toys per hour, you can add the two rates together to find how many toys both workers make per hour: $23 + 47 = 70$. Plug this rate and the total number of toys needed into the $d = rt$ formula.

$$490 = 70t$$

$$7 = t$$

This is the time it will take the workers to produce 490 toys, so (J) is correct.

Chapter 9
Rates, Ratios, Proportions, and Percents

7. C
Difficulty: Medium
Category: Number and Quantity
Getting to the Answer: The question asks what price Ernesto paid for a shirt. You are given the original price, a discount percentage, and a sales tax percentage. First determine the price of the shirt after the 25% discount. Recall that $22 - 22(0.25) = 22(0.75)$.

$$22(0.75) = 16.50$$

Now add the 6% sales tax by multiplying the price of the shirt by 1.06 (again, note that $100\% + 6\% = 106\% = 1.06$):

$$16.50(1.06) = 17.49$$

This is the final price of the shirt, so (C) is correct. Be certain that you considered everything stated in the question; D is the price without the sales tax added.

8. G
Difficulty: High
Category: Number and Quantity
Getting to the Answer: The question asks for the original price of a pair of pants for which Atiya paid $29.70. You are given the discount rate and the sales tax rate in percents. If Atiya bought her pants at a 40% discount, then she must have paid 60% of what the original price was. Call the original price p:

$$0.60p$$

Additionally, Atiya was taxed 10% on this purchase. Recall that $0.60p + 0.60p(0.10) = 1.10(0.60p)$:

$$1.10(0.60p)$$

Finally, you are told that she paid the cashier $29.70. Create an equation and solve for p:

$$1.10(0.60p) = 29.70$$
$$0.66p = 29.70$$
$$p = 45$$

The original price of the pants was $45, so (G) is correct.

Alternatively, you could use Backsolving to find the answer. Select either (G) or H as the value of p.

Using H, 48, results in an amount higher than that of the given sale price ($48(0.6)(1.1) = 31.68$). The correct answer must be either F or (G). Plugging 45 in as the value of p gives $45(0.6)(1.1) = 29.70$. Choice (G) is correct.

9. C
Difficulty: Medium
Category: Number and Quantity
Getting to the Answer: The question asks how much chocolate milk Kamini can make per hour. You are given the rate at which Ryan makes chocolate milk and told that Ryan and Kamini working together can make 30 gallons in 5 hours. Since both rates are given as gallons per hour, the rates can be added. Kamini's rate is not known, so call it k. Plug the given information into to the $d = rt$ formula. Simplify and solve for k.

$$30 = (2 + k)5$$
$$6 = 2 + k$$
$$4 = k$$

This is Kamini's rate, so (C) is correct.

10. G
Difficulty: Medium
Category: Number and Quantity
Getting to the Answer: The question asks for the weight of a metal bar that is 3 feet 8 inches long. You are given the weight of the same type of bar that is 12 feet long. Before setting up a proportion, convert the 8 inches of the 3 feet 8 inch bar into feet.

$$8 \text{ inches} \left(\frac{1 \text{ foot}}{12 \text{ inches}} \right)$$
$$\frac{8}{12} \text{ foot}$$
$$\frac{2}{3} \text{ foot}$$

Thus, 3 feet + 8 inches = 3 feet + $\frac{2}{3}$ feet = $3\frac{2}{3}$ feet = $\frac{11}{3}$ feet. Now, set up the proportion and cross-multiply to solve for the weight of the bar.

$$\frac{12 \text{ feet}}{114 \text{ lbs}} = \frac{\frac{11}{3} \text{ feet}}{w \text{ lbs}}$$
$$12w = 114 \left(\frac{11}{3} \right)$$
$$12w = 38(11)$$
$$w = \frac{38(11)}{12}$$
$$w = \frac{209}{6}$$

This is the final answer, but unfortunately, none of the answer choices are improper fractions. Convert it into a mixed number to match the format of the choices: $\frac{209}{6} = 34\frac{5}{6}$. The answer is (G).

[CHAPTER 10]

ALGEBRA

LEARNING OBJECTIVES

After completing this chapter, you will be able to:

- Add, subtract, multiply, and factor polynomials
- Isolate a variable
- Calculate the slope or midpoint of a line given two points
- Write the equation of a line in slope-intercept form
- Solve an inequality for a range of values
- Identify the graph of an inequality
- Determine the inequality given a graph
- Identify solutions to quadratic equations
- Solve systems of equations
- Translate word problems into equations and/or inequalities and solve

Part 3
ACT MATH

How Much Do You Know?

Directions: Try out the questions below. Show your work so that you can compare your solutions to the ones found on the next page. The "Category" heading in the explanation for each question gives the title of the lesson that covers how to solve it. If you answered the question(s) for a given lesson correctly, and if your scratchwork looks like ours, you may be able to move quickly through that lesson. If you answered incorrectly or used a different approach, you may want to take your time on that lesson.

1. What is the slope of the line given by the equation $-12x - 2y = 14$?

   A. -6
   B. $-\frac{1}{6}$
   C. $\frac{1}{6}$
   D. 6

2. At a certain toy store, tiny stuffed zebras cost $3 and giant stuffed zebras cost $14. The store doesn't sell any other sizes of stuffed zebras. If the store sold 29 stuffed zebras and made $208 in revenue in one week, how many tiny stuffed zebras were sold?

   F. 11
   G. 14
   H. 18
   J. 21

3. Which of the following expressions is equivalent to $\frac{2}{3}a(12a - 6b - 6a + 9b)$?

   A. $6a^2 b$
   B. $9ab$
   C. $2a^2 + ab$
   D. $4a^2 + 2ab$

4. What is the midpoint of a line segment with endpoints $(4, -4)$ and $(-2, 6)$?

   F. $(-1, 5)$
   G. $(0, 4)$
   H. $(1, 1)$
   J. $(\sqrt{5}, \sqrt{13})$

5. Brandy has a collection of comic books. If she adds 15 to the number of comic books in her collection and multiplies the sum by 3, the result will be 65 less than 4 times the number of comic books in her collection. How many comic books are in her collection?

   A. 85
   B. 100
   C. 110
   D. 145

Chapter 10
Algebra

6. Which of the following graphs represents the solution set for $5x - 10y > 6$?

   F.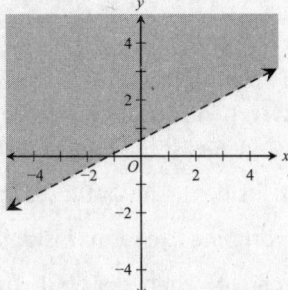

   G.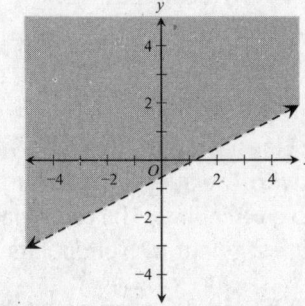

   H.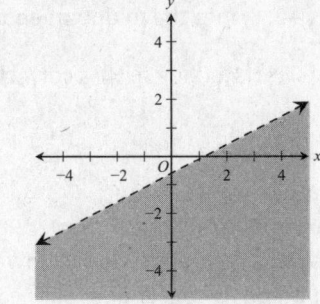

   J.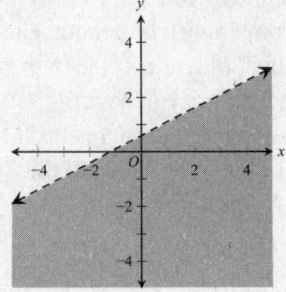

7. What is the solution for x in the system of equations below?
$$\begin{cases} 3x + 4y = 31 \\ 3x - 4y = -1 \end{cases}$$

   A. 4
   B. 5
   C. 6
   D. 9

8. Which of the following are solutions to the quadratic equation $(x + 1)^2 = \frac{1}{25}$?

   F. $x = -6, x = 4$
   G. $x = -\frac{6}{5}, x = -\frac{4}{5}$
   H. $x = -\frac{4}{5}, x = \frac{6}{5}$
   J. $x = \frac{4}{5}, x = \frac{6}{5}$

9. Which of the following inequalities is equivalent to $-2 - 4x \leq -6x$?

   A. $x \geq -2$
   B. $x \geq 2$
   C. $x \leq -1$
   D. $x \leq 1$

10. Which value(s) of x satisfies the equation $5|2x - 6| + 3 = 13$?

    F. 2
    G. 4
    H. -2 and 4
    J. 2 and 4

251

Answers and Explanations

How Much Do You Know?

1. A
Difficulty: Low
Category: Algebra: Linear Graphs
Getting to the Answer: To find the slope of a line given by an equation in standard form, rewrite the equation in slope-intercept form: $y = mx + b$. In this form, the coefficient of x gives you the slope, so manipulate the equation in the question to put it in slope-intercept form:

$$-12x - 2y = 14$$
$$-2y = 12x + 14$$
$$y = \frac{12x}{-2} + \frac{14}{-2}$$
$$y = -6x - 7$$

The slope of the equation is -6, which is (A).

2. H
Difficulty: Medium
Category: Algebra: Systems of Equations
Getting to the Answer: The question asks how many tiny stuffed zebras were sold. Carefully translate from English into math. Because both toys are zebras, z is likely to be a confusing choice for a variable. Instead, use t for tiny and g for giant.

$$t + g = 29$$
$$3t + 14g = 208$$

You now have a system of equations. You want to find t, so use combination to eliminate g. Multiply the first equation by -14 and add the result to the second equation. Then solve for t.

$$-14t - 14g = -406$$
$$+\ 3t + 14g = \ \ \ \ 208$$
$$\overline{\ \ \ \ \ \ \ \ \ \ -11t = -198}$$
$$t = \ \ \ 18$$

Don't waste time finding the value of g. The question asks only for the number of tiny stuffed zebras, so you're done. Choice (H) is correct.

3. D
Difficulty: Low
Category: Algebra: Polynomials
Getting to the Answer: The question asks you to simplify the expression. Resist the urge to distribute the $\frac{2}{3}a$ to each term inside the parentheses immediately; instead, first combine like terms inside the parentheses: $\frac{2}{3}a(6a + 3b)$. Then, distribute the $\frac{2}{3}a$: $4a^2 + 2ab$. Choice (D) is correct.

4. H
Difficulty: Low
Category: Algebra: Linear Graphs
Getting to the Answer: The question asks for the midpoint of the two given points. The coordinates of the midpoint of a line segment with endpoints (x_1, y_1) and (x_2, y_2) are $\left(\frac{x_1 + x_2}{2}, \frac{y_1 + y_2}{2}\right)$. Plug the points $(4, -4)$ and $(-2, 6)$ into the midpoint equation: $\left(\frac{4 + -2}{2}, \frac{-4 + 6}{2}\right) = (1, 1)$. Choice (H) is correct.

5. C
Difficulty: Medium
Category: Algebra: Word Problems
Getting to the Answer: The question asks how many comic books are in Brandy's collection. Call the number of comic books in Brandy's collection c. Then, translate methodically from English into math. First, "she adds 15 to the number" means $c + 15$. Then, she "multiplies the sum by 3," so you have $3(c + 15)$. "The result will be" indicates an equal sign, and "65 less than 4 times the number" is $4c - 65$. So this scenario can be modeled by the equation $3(c + 15) = 4c - 65$. Now solve for c:

$$3(c + 15) = 4c - 65$$
$$3c + 45 = 4c - 65$$
$$45 = c - 65$$
$$110 = c$$

Brandy has 110 comic books in her collection. Choice (C) is correct.

6. H

Difficulty: Medium
Category: Algebra: Graphing Inequalities
Getting to the Answer: The question asks you to match the given inequality to the correct graph. Start with straightforward math by rewriting the inequality in slope-intercept form. Remember that the inequality symbol flips when you divide by a negative:

$$5x - 10y > 6$$
$$-10y > -5x + 6$$
$$\frac{-10y}{-10} < \frac{-5x}{-10} + \frac{6}{-10}$$
$$y < \frac{1}{2}x - \frac{3}{5}$$

The y-intercept is $-\frac{3}{5}$, so you can eliminate F and J immediately. The "less than" symbol indicates that the shading should be below the dashed line (use the y-axis values to determine what's "less than" as needed), so (H) must be correct.

7. B

Difficulty: Low
Category: Algebra: Systems of Equations
Getting to the Answer: The question asks you to solve for the x-value in the system of equations. Any system of equations with the same number of equations as variables can be solved with either combination or substitution, but one approach will often be easier than the other. Because this system already has $+4y$ and $-4y$, combination is the better choice here:

$$3x + 4y = 31$$
$$+\ 3x - 4y = -1$$
$$6x = 30$$
$$x = 5$$

The question asks for the value of x, so (B) is correct. There is no need to find the value of y.

8. G

Difficulty: Medium
Category: Algebra: Quadratics
Getting to the Answer: The question asks you to solve for the solutions of the given quadratic. Both sides of this equation are already perfect squares, so take the square roots of both sides instead of FOILing the left side. Then, solve the resulting equations. Remember that there will be two equations to solve as a result of the square root step, both a positive case and a negative case:

$$(x + 1)^2 = \frac{1}{25}$$
$$\sqrt{(x+1)^2} = \sqrt{\frac{1}{25}}$$
$$x + 1 = \pm\frac{1}{5}$$

Now simplify each equation:

$$x = -1 + \frac{1}{5} = -\frac{5}{5} + \frac{1}{5} = -\frac{4}{5}$$

and

$$x = -1 - \frac{1}{5} = -\frac{5}{5} - \frac{1}{5} = -\frac{6}{5}$$

The solutions are $x = -\frac{6}{5}$ and $-\frac{4}{5}$. Choice (G) is correct.

Part 3
ACT MATH

9. D

Difficulty: Low
Category: Algebra: Solving Inequalities
Getting to the Answer: The question asks you to solve for the given inequality. You solve an inequality the same way you solve an equation, but with one difference: if you multiply or divide by a negative number, you must reverse the direction of the inequality symbol. To keep things simple, try to move the terms in such a way that you don't end up with negatives:

$$-2 - 4x \leq -6x$$
$$-2 + 2x \leq 0$$
$$2x \leq 2$$
$$x \leq 1$$

The values of x are less than or equal to 1. Choice (D) is correct.

10. J

Difficulty: Medium
Category: Algebra: Solving Equations
Getting to the Answer: The question asks you to solve for the values of x. Isolate x by first subtracting 3 from both sides and then dividing by 5:

$$5|2x - 6| + 3 = 13$$
$$5|2x - 6| = 10$$
$$|2x - 6| = \frac{10}{5}$$
$$|2x - 6| = 2$$

Recall that if $|x| = a$, then $x = a$ and $x = -a$. Therefore, you must split the absolute value equation into two separate equations and solve for x:

$$2x - 6 = 2$$
$$2x = 8$$
$$x = 4$$

and

$$2x - 6 = -2$$
$$2x = 4$$
$$x = 2$$

Therefore, $x = 2$ and $x = 4$. Choice (J) is correct.

POLYNOMIALS

LEARNING OBJECTIVE

After this lesson, you will be able to:

- Add, subtract, multiply, and factor polynomials

To answer a question like this

Which of the following expressions is equivalent to $x(x - 6) - 8(2 - x)$?

A. $3x - 16$
B. $6x - 16$
C. $x^2 - 14x - 16$
D. $x^2 + 2x - 16$

You need to know this

A **polynomial** is an expression composed of variables, exponents, and coefficients. By definition, a polynomial cannot have a variable in a denominator, and all exponents must be integers. Here are some examples of polynomial and non-polynomial expressions:

Polynomials	Non-polynomials
$23x^2$	$\frac{10}{z} + 13$
$\frac{x}{5} - 6$	$x^3 y^{-6}$
$y^{11} - 2y^6 + \frac{2}{3}xy^3 - 4x^2$	$x^{\frac{1}{2}}$
$z + 6$	$\frac{4}{y - 3}$

You need to do this

To add and subtract polynomials, start by identifying like terms—that is, terms in which both the types of variables and their exponents match. For example, x^2 and $3x^2$ are like terms; adding them would give $4x^2$ and subtracting them would give $x^2 - 3x^2 = -2x^2$. Note that you cannot add or subtract unlike terms. For example, there is no way to simplify $x^2 + y$. You can, however, multiply unlike terms: $x^2 \cdot y = x^2 y$.

To multiply two polynomials, multiply each term in the first factor by each term in the second factor, then combine like terms.

To factor a polynomial, find a value or variable that divides evenly into each term. For example: $2x^3 + 2x^2 + 2x = 2x(x^2 + x + 1)$.

Explanation

The question asks you to simplify the given expression. First, distribute the x and -8: $x^2 - 6x - 16 + 8x$. Then, combine like terms: $x^2 + 2x - 16$. Choice (D) is correct.

Try on Your Own

Directions: Take as much time as you need on these questions. Work carefully and methodically. There will be an opportunity for timed practice at the end of the chapter.

1. The expression $3(x + 4) - 7(2x - 5)$ is equivalent to:

    A. $-6x + 19$.
    B. $-6x - 23$.
    C. $-11x - 23$.
    D. $-11x + 47$.

2. Which of the following expressions is equivalent to $\frac{1}{4}x(-8x - 12y + 4x + 4y)$?

    F. $-x + 2xy$
    G. $-4x - 8xy$
    H. $-x^2 - 2y$
    J. $-x^2 - 2xy$

3. $(x^2 - 3x + 2) - (3x^2 - 3x - 2)$ is equivalent to:

    A. $-2x^2 - 6$.
    B. $-2x^2 + 4$.
    C. $-2x^2 - 6x + 4$.
    D. $-2x^2 + 6x - 4$.

HINT: For Q4, is there anything you can factor out to make the algebra easier?

4. For $x \neq 0$, $\frac{8x^6 - 16x^2}{2x^2} = ?$

    F. $4x^3 - 8$
    G. $4x^3 - 16x^2$
    H. $4x^4 - 8$
    J. $4x^4 - 8x$

HINT: For Q5, what is the most efficient way to approach this question?

5. If $a = 4$, what is the value of $\frac{4a^4 + 64b}{16}$?

    A. $4 + 16b$
    B. $64 + 4b$
    C. $32 + 16b$
    D. $16 + 64ba$

Chapter 10
Algebra

SOLVING EQUATIONS

LEARNING OBJECTIVE

After this lesson, you will be able to:
- Isolate a variable

To answer a question like this

If $5x = -17(3 - x)$, then $x = ?$

A. $-4\frac{1}{4}$

B. $-4\frac{1}{12}$

C. $4\frac{1}{3}$

D. $4\frac{1}{4}$

You need to know this

Isolating a variable means getting that variable by itself on one side of the equation. To do this, use inverse operations to manipulate the equation, remembering that whatever you do to one side of the equation, you must do to *both* sides.

If needed, review the order of operations information in chapter 7 before continuing on with this lesson.

You need to do this

It usually makes sense to proceed in this order:

- Eliminate any fractions.
- Collect and combine like terms.
- Divide to leave the desired variable by itself.

Explanation

The question asks you to solve for the given equation. First, distribute the -17 to each term inside the parentheses: $-51 + 17x$. Then, solve for x:

$$5x = -51 + 17x$$
$$-12x = -51$$
$$x = \frac{51}{12}$$

Convert the improper fraction to a mixed fraction: $\frac{51}{12} = 4\frac{3}{12}$, which reduces to $4\frac{1}{4}$. Choice (D) is correct.

Part 3
ACT MATH

Drills

If you find isolating a variable to be challenging, try out these drills before proceeding to the Try on Your Own set. Isolate the variable in each equation. Drill answers can be found in Answers and Explanations.

a. $2(a + 5) = 11 - (3 - 6a)$

b. $4(3 - r) = 2r + 18$

c. $\dfrac{2t}{3} - \dfrac{5t}{2} = \dfrac{5}{6}$

d. Isolate F: $C = \dfrac{5}{9}(F - 32)$

e. Isolate b: $A = \dfrac{1}{2}bh$

Try on Your Own

Directions: Take as much time as you need on these questions. Work carefully and methodically. There will be an opportunity for timed practice at the end of the chapter.

1. What is the value of x that satisfies the equation $15(x + 9) = -21$?

   A. $-\dfrac{52}{5}$
   B. -2
   C. 2
   D. $\dfrac{52}{5}$

2. If $9(a - 3) = 15a$, then $a = ?$

   F. $-4\dfrac{1}{2}$
   G. $-1\dfrac{1}{8}$
   H. $-\dfrac{2}{9}$
   J. $6\dfrac{3}{4}$

3. The two solutions to $|7x - 1| + 2 = 4$ are equal to which of the following pairs of equations?

   A. $7x + 1 = 4$
      $7x + 1 = -4$
   B. $7x - 1 = 2$
      $-(7x - 1) = 2$
   C. $7x - 1 = 6$
      $-(7x - 1) = 6$
   D. $7x - 1 = 2$
      $-(7x - 1) = 6$

HINT: For Q4, when absolute value is involved, what must be true?

4. Which of the following values of *x* satisfy the equation $|-x + 3| = -2$?

   F. 1
   G. 5
   H. 1 and 5
   J. There are no values of *x* for which the equation is true.

5. If $8(x - 2y) = 16x$, then what is *x* in terms of *y*?

   A. $-8y$
   B. $-2y$
   C. $2y$
   D. $4y$

LINEAR GRAPHS

LEARNING OBJECTIVES

After this lesson, you will be able to:
- Calculate the slope or midpoint of a line given two points
- Write the equation of a line in slope-intercept form

To answer a question like this

Which of the following is an equation of the line that crosses through $(-3, 4)$ and $(3, 6)$?

   A. $x + 3y = -15$
   B. $x - 3y = -15$
   C. $\frac{1}{3}x - y = 5$
   D. $3x + y = 5$

You need to know this

The answer choices in this question are written in standard form and need to be written in slope-intercept form: $y = mx + b$. In this form of a linear equation, *m* represents the slope of the line and *b* represents the y-intercept. You can think of the slope of a line as how steep it is. The y-intercept is the point at which the line crosses the y-axis and can be written as the ordered pair (0, *y*).

You can calculate the slope of a line if you know any two points on the line. The formula is $m = \frac{y_2 - y_1}{x_2 - x_1}$, where (x_1, y_1) and (x_2, y_2) are the coordinates of the two points on the line.

A line that moves from the bottom left to the top right has a positive slope. A line that moves from the top left to the bottom right has a negative slope. A horizontal line has a slope of zero, and a vertical line has an undefined slope.

Some ACT questions ask about parallel or perpendicular lines. Parallel lines have the same slope, while perpendicular lines have negative reciprocal slopes.

You need to do this

- Find the slope of the line.
- Write the equation in slope-intercept form, substituting the value of the slope you found and one of the known points for *x* and *y*.
- Solve for the *y*-intercept.

Explanation

The question asks you to solve for the given equation. The equation of a line is given by $y = mx + b$, where m is the slope of the line and b is the *y*-intercept. First, use the two points to find the slope:

$$m = \frac{y_2 - y_1}{x_2 - x_1}$$
$$= \frac{6 - 4}{3 - (-3)}$$
$$= \frac{2}{6} = \frac{1}{3}$$

Then, use the slope to find the *y*-intercept. Plug in $m = \frac{1}{3}$ and either of the given points for *x* and *y*:

$$y = mx + b$$
$$4 = \frac{1}{3}(-3) + b$$
$$4 = -1 + b$$
$$5 = b$$

The slope-intercept form of the line is $y = \frac{1}{3}x + 5$. The answer choices are written in standard form, so rewrite the equation:

$$y = \frac{1}{3}x + 5$$
$$3(y) = 3\left(\frac{1}{3}x + 5\right)$$
$$3y = x + 15$$
$$-x + 3y = 15$$
$$x - 3y = -15$$

The line that goes through the given points is $x - 3y = -15$. This matches (B).

Try on Your Own

Directions: Take as much time as you need on these questions. Work carefully and methodically. There will be an opportunity for timed practice at the end of the chapter.

1. If the equation of a line is $4x - 7y = 14$, what is the slope of the line?

   A. $-\frac{4}{7}$
   B. $\frac{4}{7}$
   C. $\frac{7}{4}$
   D. 7

HINT: For Q2, what equation can you create that will help you easily identify the y-intercept?
---

2. What is the y-intercept of the line that passes through the points $(1, -13)$ and $(-10, 31)$?

   F. -9
   G. -4
   H. 4
   J. 9

3. Given point $A(-3, -8)$, if the midpoint of segment AB is $(1, -5)$, what are the coordinates of point B?

   A. $(5, -2)$
   B. $(4, -2)$
   C. $(-1, -6.5)$
   D. $(-1, -1.5)$

4. The following graph represents which of the following equations?

   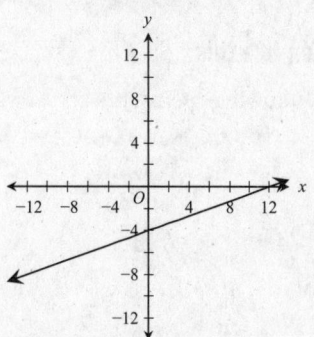

   F. $y = -3x + 4$
   G. $y = -\frac{1}{3}x + 4$
   H. $y = \frac{1}{3}x - 4$
   J. $y = 3x - 4$

HINT: For Q5, how can the format of the answer choices help you decide how to answer this question?
---

5. Which of the following equations best describes the linear relationship shown in the table below, where r represents the number of pounds of rice sold and d represents the price in dollars of one pound of rice?

Price of one pound	Projected number of pounds sold
$1.20	15,000
$1.40	12,500
$1.60	10,000
$1.80	7,500
$2.00	5,000
$2.20	2,500

   A. $r = 12,500d + 15,000$
   B. $r = -12,500d + 17,500$
   C. $r = 12,500d + 30,000$
   D. $r = -12,500d + 30,000$

Part 3
ACT MATH

SOLVING INEQUALITIES

LEARNING OBJECTIVE

After this lesson, you will be able to:

- Solve an inequality for a range of values

To answer a question like this

Which of the following represents all the values of x that satisfy the inequality $2 \leq 3 - \frac{x}{4} \leq 4$?

A. $x \geq 4$

B. $x \geq 16$

C. $-4 \leq x \leq 4$

D. $x \leq -4$ or $x \geq 4$

You need to know this

Linear inequalities are similar to linear equations but have two differences:

- You are solving for a **range of values** rather than a single value.
- If you multiply or divide both sides of the inequality by a negative, you must **reverse the inequality sign**.

You need to do this

- Eliminate any fractions.
- Collect and combine like terms.
- Divide to leave the desired variable by itself.
    - If you multiply or divide both sides of the inequality by a negative, reverse the inequality sign.
    - If possible, avoid moving the variable terms in such a way that the coefficients become negative.

Explanation

The question asks you to solve for the given inequality. This is a compound inequality, so whatever you do to one piece, you must do to all three pieces. First subtract 3, and then multiply all three parts by -4.

$$2 \leq 3 - \frac{x}{4} \leq 4$$
$$-1 \leq -\frac{x}{4} \leq 1$$
$$-4(-1) \geq -4\left(-\frac{x}{4}\right) \geq -4(1)$$
$$4 \geq x \geq -4$$

Flipping the entire inequality will more easily match it with the correct answer: $-4 \leq x \leq 4$. Choice (C) is correct.

Chapter 10
Algebra

Try on Your Own

Directions: Take as much time as you need on these questions. Work carefully and methodically. There will be an opportunity for timed practice at the end of the chapter.

1. Which of the following is equivalent to the inequality $-8x + 2y \leq 14$?

   A. $y \geq -4x - 7$
   B. $y \leq -4x + 7$
   C. $y \geq 4x - 7$
   D. $y \leq 4x + 7$

2. Which of the following represents the solution set for $-15 \leq 2x - 13 < 3$?

   F. $-1 \leq x < 8$
   G. $-2 \leq x < 16$
   H. $-5 \leq x < -1$
   J. $-14 \leq x < 8$

3. If $-3x + 7y \leq 4y + 6$ and x is an integer, which of the following statements must be true?

   A. $x \geq -y - 2$
   B. $x \geq -y + 2$
   C. $x \geq y - 2$
   D. $x \leq y + 2$

HINT: For Q4, if $|x| = a$, then what are the possible values for x?

4. Which of the following values of x satisfies the inequality $|2x + 5| < 11$?

   F. $-8 < x < 3$
   G. $-8 > x > 3$
   H. $-3 < x < -8$
   J. $-3 > x > 8$

5. Which of the following is the set of x such that $x + 2 > x + 1$?

   A. The empty set
   B. The set containing all real numbers
   C. The set containing all negative real numbers
   D. The set containing all positive real numbers

GRAPHING INEQUALITIES

LEARNING OBJECTIVES

After this lesson, you will be able to:
- Identify the graph of an inequality
- Determine the inequality given a graph

To answer a question like this

The solution to which inequality is represented in the graph shown?

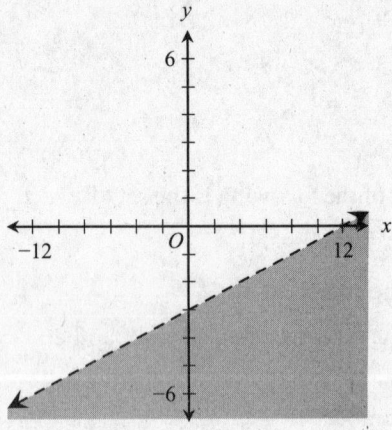

A. $x + 4y < -12$
B. $x + 4y > -12$
C. $x - 4y < 12$
D. $x - 4y > 12$

You need to know this

Linear inequalities in one variable are graphed on a number line as a point that is or is not filled in ("closed" or "open," respectively), with an arrow representing the location of the solutions as either less than or greater than the point.

- Use a closed circle (●) for inequalities with ≤ or ≥ signs because the point itself is included in the solution set.
- Use an open circle (○) for inequalities with < or > signs because the point itself is not included in the solution set.

While linear equations in two variables graph as simple lines, inequalities in two variables are graphed as shaded regions.

- Use solid lines for inequalities with ≤ or ≥ signs because the line itself is included in the solution set.
- Use dashed lines for inequalities with < or > signs because, in these cases, the line itself is not included in the solution set.
- The shaded region represents all points that make up the solution set for the inequality.

You need to do this

To graph a linear inequality in one variable, start by isolating the variable.

- For $x \leq a$ and $x \geq a$, use a closed circle (●).
- For $x < a$ and $x > a$, use an open circle (○).
- For $x < a$ and $x \leq a$, draw an arrow pointing to the left of the circle.
- For $x > a$ and $x \geq a$, draw an arrow pointing to the right of the circle.

To graph an inequality in two variables, start by writing the inequality in slope-intercept form, then graph the solid or dashed line.

- For $y > mx + b$ and $y \geq mx + b$, shade the region above the line.
- For $y < mx + b$ and $y \leq mx + b$, shade the region below the line.

If it's hard to tell which region is above/below the line (which can happen when the line is steep), compare the y-values on both sides of the line.

Explanation

The question asks you to match the correct inequality with the given graph. Don't answer this question too quickly! The shading is below the line, but that does not necessarily mean that the symbol in the equation will be the less than symbol ($<$). Start by writing the equation of the dashed line shown in the graph in slope-intercept form. Then use the shading to determine the correct inequality symbol.

The slope of the line shown in the graph is $\frac{1}{4}$ and the y-intercept is -3, so the equation of the dashed line is $y = \frac{1}{4}x - 3$. The graph is shaded below the boundary line, so use the $<$ symbol. When written in slope-intercept form, the inequality is $y < \frac{1}{4}x - 3$. The inequalities in the answer choices are written in standard form ($Ax + By = C$), so rewrite your answer in this form.

$$y < \tfrac{1}{4}x - 3$$
$$-\tfrac{1}{4}x + y < -3$$

Multiply everything by -4 to get integer coefficients, and don't forget to reverse the inequality symbol: $x - 4y > 12$. Choice (D) is correct.

Drills

If graphing inequalities gives you trouble, study the information above and try out these drill questions before completing the Try on Your Own questions below. Drill answers can be found in Answers and Explanations.

Graph the following inequalities.

a. $-1 < x \leq 3$

b. $|x + 1| \leq 3$

c. $y > 2x$

d. $y + 2 \leq x$

e. $x - 1 < y \leq x + 1$

Part 3
ACT MATH

Try on Your Own

Directions: Take as much time as you need on these questions. Work carefully and methodically. There will be an opportunity for timed practice at the end of the chapter.

HINT: For Q1, how do you solve an inequality that includes absolute value?

1. Which of the following represents the solution to the inequality $|2x - 5| > 11$?

    A.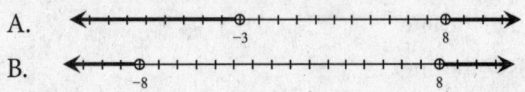
    B.
    C.
    D.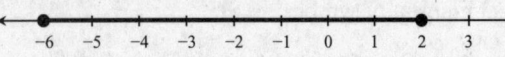

2. For the number line shown, which of the following inequalities describes the range of possible values for some number w?

    F. $|w - 2| \leq 2$
    G. $|w - 2| \leq 4$
    H. $|w + 2| \leq 2$
    J. $|w + 2| \leq 4$

3. Which of the following systems of inequalities includes the shaded region in the graph below?

    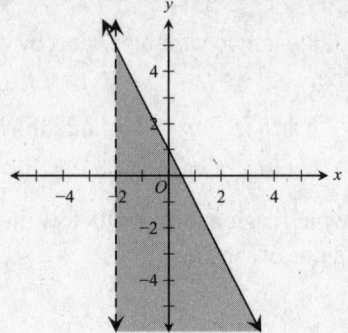

    A. $\begin{cases} x > -2 \\ y \leq -2x + 1 \end{cases}$

    B. $\begin{cases} x > -2 \\ y \leq -\frac{1}{2}x + 1 \end{cases}$

    C. $\begin{cases} y > -2 \\ y \leq -2x + 1 \end{cases}$

    D. $\begin{cases} y > -2 \\ y \geq -2x + 1 \end{cases}$

4. Which of the following graphs represents the region $2 < y - x < 3$ in the standard (x, y) coordinate plane?

F.
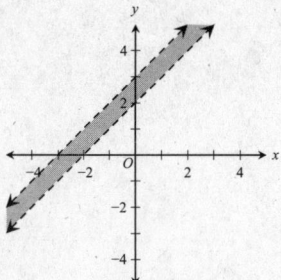

G.
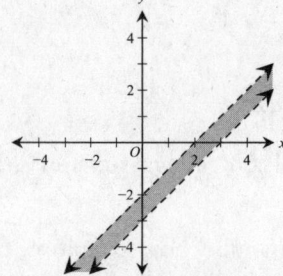

H.
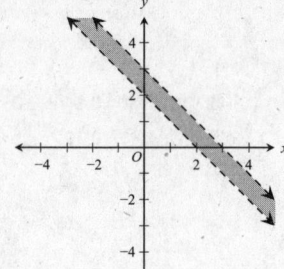

J.
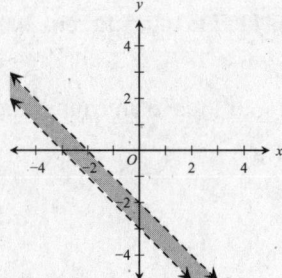

HINT: For Q5, how can thinking about absolute value as a distance help you approach this question more efficiently?

5. If the following number line below shows the range of possible values for some number b, which of the following inequalities shows the same possible values for b?

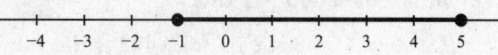

A. $|b - 5| \leq 1$
B. $|b - 5| \leq 2$
C. $|b - 2| \leq 5$
D. $|b - 2| \leq 3$

Part 3
ACT MATH

QUADRATICS

> **LEARNING OBJECTIVE**
>
> After this lesson, you will be able to:
>
> - Identify solutions to quadratic equations

To answer a question like this

If $x^2 + 8x = 48$ and $x > 0$, what is the value of $x - 5$?

A. -9
B. -1
C. 4
D. 9

You need to know this

A **quadratic** expression is a second-degree polynomial—that is, a polynomial containing a squared variable. You can write a quadratic expression as $ax^2 + bx + c$.

The **FOIL** acronym (which stands for First, Outer, Inner, Last) will help you remember how to multiply two binomials to create a quadratic expression: multiply the first terms together (ac), then the outer terms (ad), then the inner terms (bc), and finally the last terms (bd):

$$(a + b)(c + d) = ac + ad + bc + bd$$

FOIL can also be done in reverse if you need to go from a quadratic expression to its factors. To solve a quadratic equation by factoring, the quadratic expression must be set equal to zero. For example:

$$x^2 + x - 56 = 0$$
$$(x + 8)(x - 7) = 0$$

From the binomial factors, you can find the solutions, also called roots or zeros, of the equation. For two factors to be multiplied together and produce zero as the result, one or both of those factors must be zero. In the example above, either $x + 8 = 0$ or $x - 7 = 0$, which means that $x = -8$ or $x = 7$.

The quadratic formula can be used to solve any quadratic equation. It yields solutions to any quadratic equation that is written in standard form, $ax^2 + bx + c = 0$:

$$x = \frac{-b \pm \sqrt{b^2 - 4ac}}{2a}$$

The term under the square root, $b^2 - 4ac$, can help you determine how many real solutions there are. When the term is negative, there are no real solutions for x because negative numbers have no real square roots. When the term is 0, then the value of x will be $\frac{-b}{2a}$, which yields only one solution. Finally, when the term is positive, x will have two solutions because of the $\pm$ symbol.

Memorizing the following classic quadratic equations may save you time on test day:

- $x^2 - y^2 = (x + y)(x - y)$
- $x^2 + 2xy + y^2 = (x + y)^2$
- $x^2 - 2xy + y^2 = (x - y)^2$

You need to do this

Here are the steps for solving a quadratic equation by factoring:

- Set the quadratic expression equal to zero.
- Factor the squared term. For factoring, it's easiest when a, the coefficient in front of x^2, is equal to 1.
- Make a list of the factors of c. Remember to include negatives.
- Find the factor pair that, when added, equals b, the coefficient in front of x.
- Write the quadratic as the product of two binomials.
- Set each binomial equal to zero and solve.

To solve a quadratic using the quadratic formula, start by getting the quadratic equation into the form $ax^2 + bx + c = 0$. Then substitute a, b, and c into the quadratic formula and simplify.

When you see a pattern that matches the left or the right side of a classic quadratic equation, simplify by substituting its equivalent form. For example, say you need to simplify the following:

$$\frac{a^2 - 2ab + b^2}{a - b}$$

You would substitute $(a - b)(a - b)$ for the numerator and cancel to find that the expression simplifies to $a - b$:

$$\frac{a^2 - 2ab + b^2}{a - b} = \frac{(a - b)(a - b)}{a - b} = \frac{a - b}{1} = a - b$$

Explanation

The question asks you to first solve for x and then evaluate $x - 5$. When solving a quadratic equation, always start by rewriting the equation to make it equal to 0 (unless both sides of the equation are already perfect squares). Then, take a peek at the choices. If they are all integers, then factoring is probably the quickest method for solving the equation. If the answers include messy fractions or square roots, then the quadratic formula may be a better choice.

To make the original equation equal to 0, subtract 48 from both sides to get $x^2 + 8x - 48 = 0$. The choices are all integers, so try to factor the equation. Look for two numbers whose product is -48 and whose sum is 8: -4 and 12. This means the factors are $(x - 4)$ and $(x + 12)$.

Now, set each factor equal to 0 and solve to obtain $x = 4$ and $x = -12$. The question states that $x > 0$, so x must equal 4. Before selecting an answer, check that you answered the right question! The question asks for the value of $x - 5$, not just x, so the correct answer is $4 - 5 = -1$. (B) is correct.

Try on Your Own

Directions: Take as much time as you need on these questions. Work carefully and methodically. There will be an opportunity for timed practice at the end of the chapter.

1. If $x^2 - 4x - 6 = 6$, what are the possible values for x?

    A. -6 and -2
    B. -6 and 2
    C. 6 and -2
    D. 6 and 2

2. For all a and b, what is the product of $(b - a)$ and $(a + b)$?

    F. $-a^2 + b^2$
    G. $a^2 - b^2$
    H. $a^2 - 2ab + b^2$
    J. $-a^2 - 2ab + b^2$

Part 3
ACT MATH

HINT: For Q3, how are the answer choices formatted?

3. Which of the following are the roots of the equation $x^2 + 8x - 3 = 0$?

   A. $-8 \pm \sqrt{19}$
   B. $-4 \pm \sqrt{19}$
   C. $4 \pm \sqrt{19}$
   D. $8 \pm \sqrt{19}$

4. Which of the following is the simplified form of $\dfrac{x^2 - 4x + 4}{2x^2 + 4x - 16}$?

   F. $\dfrac{x}{x+4}$
   G. $\dfrac{x-2}{2(x+4)}$
   H. $\dfrac{x+2}{2(x-8)}$
   J. $\dfrac{x^2 - 4x + 1}{x^2 + 2x - 4}$

HINT: For Q5, what does "how long will it take the projectile to hit the ground" mean in terms of h and t?

5. A projectile is launched from a cannon on top of a building. The height of the projectile in feet can be modeled using the quadratic equation $h = -16t^2 + 128t + 320$, where h represents the height and t represents the number of seconds after the projectile was launched. After it is launched, how long will it take the projectile to hit the ground?

   A. 2 seconds
   B. 8 seconds
   C. 10 seconds
   D. 12 seconds

SYSTEMS OF EQUATIONS

LEARNING OBJECTIVE

After this lesson, you will be able to:

- Solve systems of equations

To answer a question like this

Which of the following pairs is a solution to the following system of equations:

$$\begin{cases} -x + 3y = 9 \\ 2x + 5y = 4 \end{cases}$$

A. $(-15, -2)$

B. $(-15, 2)$

C. $(-3, 2)$

D. $(3, -2)$

You need to know this

A **system** of two linear equations is the set of equations for two lines. "Solving" a system of two linear equations usually means finding the point where the two lines intersect.

- A system of linear equations may have no solution, one solution, or infinitely many solutions.
- If a system of equations has no solution, the lines are parallel: there is no point of intersection.
- If a system of equations represents two lines that intersect, then the system will have exactly one solution (for which the x- and y-values correspond to the point of intersection).
- If a system of equations has infinitely many solutions, the two equations actually represent the same line. For example, $2x + y = 15$ and $4x + 2y = 30$ represent the same line. If you divide the second equation by 2, you arrive at the first equation. Every point along this line is a solution.

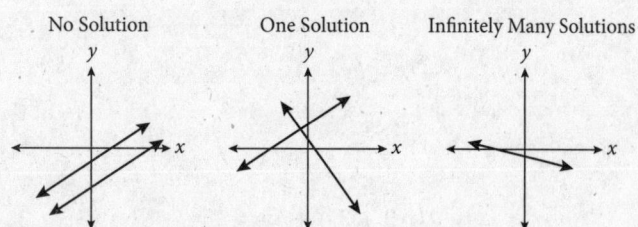

There are two algebraic ways to solve a system of linear equations: combination, a strategy that is also known as elimination, and substitution. For some ACT questions, substitution is faster; for others, combination is faster.

Substitution involves substituting the value of one variable into that variable's location in a second equation. Combining two equations means adding or subtracting them, usually with the goal of either eliminating one of the variables or solving for a combination of variables, e.g., $5n + 5m$.

You need to do this

To solve a system of two linear equations by substitution:

- Isolate a variable (ideally, one whose coefficient is 1) in one of the equations.
- Substitute the result into the other equation.

To solve a system of two linear equations by combination:

- Make sure that the coefficients for one variable have the same absolute value. (If they don't, multiply one equation by an appropriate constant. Sometimes, you'll have to multiply both equations by constants.)
- Either add or subtract the equations to eliminate one variable.
- Solve for the remaining variable, then substitute its value into either equation to solve for the other variable.

Explanation

The question asks you to solve for the given system of equations. You can solve this system by either substitution or combination. To use combination, multiply the first equation by 2 and then add it to the second equation to cancel out the x terms:

$$-2x + 6y = 18$$
$$+\quad 2x + 5y = 4$$
$$11y = 22$$
$$y = 2$$

Then, substitute $y = 2$ into one of the original equations to solve for x:

$$-x + 3(2) = 9$$
$$-x = 9 - 6$$
$$-x = 3$$
$$x = -3$$

Therefore, $(-3, 2)$ is a solution to the system of equations. Choice (C) is correct.

To use substitution, solve the first equation for x in terms of y and then plug that expression into the second equation:

$$-x + 3y = 9$$
$$-x = 9 - 3y$$
$$x = -9 + 3y$$

$$2(-9 + 3y) + 5y = 4$$
$$-18 + 6y + 5y = 4$$
$$11y = 22$$
$$y = 2$$

Finally, substitute $y = 2$ into one of the original equations to get $x = -3$.

Chapter 10
Algebra

Try on Your Own

Directions: Take as much time as you need on these questions. Work carefully and methodically. There will be an opportunity for timed practice at the end of the chapter.

1. What is the sum of the solutions for the system of equations below?

   $$\begin{cases} 6x = 20 \\ 3y + 7 = 14 \end{cases}$$

   A. $2\frac{5}{6}$
   B. 3
   C. $5\frac{2}{3}$
   D. $7\frac{7}{9}$

2. If A and B are polynomial expressions such that $A = 24xy + 13$ and $B = 8xy + 1$, how much greater is A than B?

   F. $32xy - 14$
   G. $16xy - 14$
   H. $16xy + 12$
   J. $32xy + 12$

3. If $2x + 5y = 49$ and $5x + 3y = 94$, then what is the value of the product of x and y?

   A. 17
   B. 34
   C. 48
   D. 51

HINT: For Q4, which is likely to be more efficient: substitution or combination? Why?

---

4. You are given the following system of equations:

   $$\begin{cases} x + 9y = 11 \\ 2x - 7y = -3 \end{cases}$$

   What is the value of $4x - 5y$?

   F. -6
   G. 1
   H. 2
   J. 3

HINT: For Q5, what part of the quadratic formula provides information about the number of roots for a quadratic equation or function?

---

5. You are given the following system of equations:

   $$\begin{cases} y = x \\ -py + qx^2 = r \end{cases}$$

   where p, q, and r are integers. For which of the following expressions will there be more than one real solution?

   A. $p^2 - 4qr < 0$
   B. $p^2 + 4qr < 0$
   C. $p^2 + 4qr > 0$
   D. $q^2 - 4pr > 0$

Part 3
ACT MATH

WORD PROBLEMS

LEARNING OBJECTIVE

After this lesson, you will be able to:
- Translate word problems into equations and/or inequalities and solve

To answer a question like this

At a school trivia competition, contestants can answer two kinds of questions: easy questions and hard questions. Easy questions are worth 3 points, and hard questions are worth 5 points. Chantrea knows that she correctly answered 21 questions and that she had a total of 79 points. How many hard questions did she answer correctly?

A.   7
B.   8
C.   12
D.   13

You need to know this

The ACT likes to test your understanding of how to describe real-world situations using math equations. For some questions, it will be up to you to extract and solve an equation; for others, you'll have to interpret an equation in a real-life context. The following table shows some of the most common phrases and mathematical equivalents you're likely to see on the ACT.

Word Problems Translation Table	
English	**Math**
equals, is, equivalent to, was, will be, has, costs, adds up to, the same as, as much as	=
times, of, multiplied by, product of, twice, double	×
divided by, out of, ratio	÷
plus, added to, sum, combined, increased by	+
minus, subtracted from, smaller than, less than, fewer, decreased by, difference between	−
a number, how much, how many, what	x, n, etc.

You need to do this

When translating from English to math, start by *defining the variables*, choosing letters that make sense. Then, *break the question down into small pieces*, writing down the translation for one phrase at a time.

Explanation

The question asks you to solve for how many hard questions Chantrea answered correctly. Both Backsolving and straightforward algebra work well here.

To solve algebraically, set up a system of equations with one equation that represents the number of questions of each type (e for easy and h for hard) and another that represents the number of points that Chantrea earned. Because she correctly answered 21 questions, $e + h = 21$. The number of points that she earned is $3e + 5h = 79$. Substitute $e = 21 - h$ into the second equation and solve for h:

$$3(21 - h) + 5h = 79$$
$$63 - 3h + 5h = 79$$
$$2h = 16$$
$$h = 8$$

To Backsolve, start with C. Remember that the choices represent the number of *hard* questions, not the number of *easy* questions. If Chantrea got 12 hard questions right, then she got $21 - 12 = 9$ easy questions right for a total of $9(3) + 12(5) = 27 + 60 = 87$ points. This is too many points, so she must have gotten fewer hard questions right.

Try (B). If she got 8 hard questions right, then she got $21 - 8 = 13$ easy questions right. This would give her a total of $13(3) + 8(5) = 39 + 40 = 79$ points, so (B) is correct.

Drills

If word problems give you trouble, study the information above and try out these drill questions before completing the Try on Your Own questions below. Drill answers can be found in Answers and Explanations.

Translate the following into math.

a. If n is greater than m, the positive difference between twice n and m.

b. A quarter of the sum of a and b is 4 less than a.

c. The product of y and 9 decreased by the sum of x and 7 is the same as dividing x decreased by z by 7 decreased by x.

d. The ratio of $4q$ to $7p$ is 5 to 2.

e. If $500 is taken from F's salary, then the combined salaries of F and G will be double what F's salary would be if it were increased by 50%.

Try on Your Own

Directions: Take as much time as you need on these questions. Work carefully and methodically. There will be an opportunity for timed practice at the end of the chapter.

1. An aquarium contains dolphins, sharks, and whales. There are twice as many dolphins as whales and 8 fewer sharks than dolphins and whales combined. If there are w whales, which of the following represents the number of sharks?

   A. $5w$
   B. $3w - 8$
   C. $10 + w$
   D. $3\sqrt{2w - 8}$

2. If paintbrushes cost $1.50 each and canvases cost 6 times that much, which of the following represents the cost, in dollars, of p paintbrushes and c canvases?

   F. $7.5pc$
   G. $10.5pc$
   H. $9c + 1.5p$
   J. $10.5(p + c)$

3. The toll for driving a segment of a certain freeway is $1.50 plus 25 cents for each mile traveled. Joy paid a $25.00 toll for driving a segment of the freeway. How many miles did she travel?

   A. 75
   B. 94
   C. 96
   D. 106

4. At a local theater, adult tickets cost $8 and student tickets cost $5. At a recent show, 500 tickets were sold for a total of $3,475. How many adult tickets were sold?

   F. 125
   G. 200
   H. 325
   J. 400

HINT: For Q5, what do the 20 pints of glaze represent in relation to v?

---

5. A ceramist uses $(v^2 + v)$ pints of glaze for v porcelain vases. What is the maximum number of vases the ceramist can glaze with 20 pints of glaze?

   A. 2
   B. 4
   C. 10
   D. 20

On Test Day

Remember that the ACT doesn't ask you to show your work; if you find the algebra in a question challenging, there is often another way to get to the answer.

There are multiple ways to approach this new question. First, use algebra; next use strategic guessing; and then use the Backsolving strategy you learned earlier. (You may see an even faster approach.) Time yourself for each approach. Which approach do you find easier? Which one was faster? Did you get the correct answer each time? Remember your preferred approach and try it first if you see a question like this on test day.

1. Which of the following values of x satisfies the equation $|2x - 6| = -4$?

    A. -1
    B. 1
    C. 1 and 5
    D. There are no values of x for which the equation is true.

The correct answer and multiple possible ways of solving the question can be found at the end of this chapter.

Part 3
ACT MATH

How Much Have You Learned?

Directions: For test-like practice, give yourself 10 minutes to complete this question set. Be sure to study the explanations, even for questions you got correct. They can be found at the end of this chapter.

1. How many distinct real roots does the equation $3x^3 + 30x^2 + 75x = 0$ have?

   A. 0
   B. 1
   C. 2
   D. 3

2. Point $P(-3, 5)$ and point $Q(0, 1)$ are points on the (x, y) coordinate plane. What is the midpoint between points P and Q?

   F. $\left(-\frac{3}{2}, 1\right)$
   G. $\left(-\frac{3}{2}, 3\right)$
   H. $(1, 3)$
   J. $\left(1, \frac{1}{2}\right)$

3. What is the y-intercept of the line that passes through the points $(1, 21)$ and $(4, 42)$?

   A. 7
   B. 9
   C. 14
   D. 19

4. What is the solution set for the equation $|2x - 3| = 13$?

   F. $\{-8, 8\}$
   G. $\{-5\}$
   H. $\{-5, 8\}$
   J. $\{5, -8\}$

5. Bye Bye Bugs charges a $275 annual fee for quarterly service plus $20 per additional visit. Pest Be Gone charges a $200 annual fee for quarterly service plus $25 per additional visit. For how many additional visits per year would the total charges from each exterminator be equal?

   A. 2
   B. 5
   C. 15
   D. 50

6. Which of the following systems of inequalities includes the shaded region in the graph shown?

   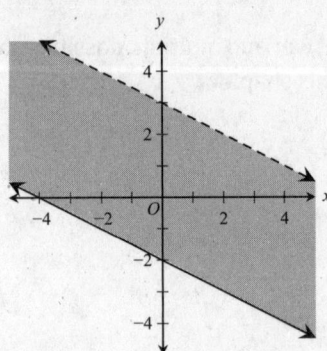

   F. $-\frac{1}{2}x - 2 \leq y < -\frac{1}{2}x + 3$
   G. $-\frac{1}{2}x - 2 < y \leq -\frac{1}{2}x + 3$
   H. $-2x - 2 \leq y < -2x + 3$
   J. $-2x - 2 < y \leq -2x + 3$

7. Which of the following expressions is equivalent to $\frac{1}{5}p(7q - p + 8q + 11p)$?

   A. $5p^2q$
   B. $25pq$
   C. $3pq + 2p^2$
   D. $15pq + 10p$

8. For the system of equations below, which of the following gives the solutions for x?

$$\begin{cases} y = x^2 \\ 24 + y = 10x \end{cases}$$

F. −6 and −4
G. −2 and 12
H. 3 and 8
J. 4 and 6

9. The two solutions to $|4x + 3| - 1 < 8$ are equal to which of the following pairs of inequalities?

A. $4x + 3 < 7$
   $4x + 3 > -7$
B. $4x + 3 < 7$
   $4x + 3 < -9$
C. $4x + 3 < 9$
   $4x + 3 < -9$
D. $4x + 3 < 9$
   $4x + 3 > -9$

10. Rasheed is contemplating whether to buy a membership for a trampoline park, which is $50 a year. As a member, Rasheed receives a 15% discount on jump tickets. If the non-membership price for a jump ticket is $12 per hour, for how many hours does Rasheed need to jump in order for the cost of the membership to be less than the total cost of buying jump tickets at the non-membership price?

F. 23
G. 25
H. 27
J. 28

Part 3
ACT MATH

Reflect

Directions: Take a few minutes to recall what you've learned and what you've been practicing in this chapter. Consider the following questions, jot down your best answer for each one, and then compare your reflections to the expert responses on the following page. Don't be intimidated by the number of reflection questions here. Answer them at your own pace, then use your level of confidence to determine what to do next.

1. How do you multiply two polynomials?
   _____
   _____
   _____

2. What should you do to isolate a particular variable in an equation?
   _____
   _____
   _____

3. What is the most useful equation for a line in the coordinate plane? Why?
   _____
   _____
   _____

4. When the ACT gives you two points on a line, what can you figure out?
   _____
   _____
   _____

5. How are parallel and perpendicular lines related to each other?
   _____
   _____
   _____

6. What types of keywords should you look for when translating English into math?
   _____
   _____
   _____

7. What is the difference between a linear inequality and a linear equation?
   _____
   _____
   _____

8. The rules for manipulating an inequality are very similar to those for manipulating an equation. What is the major difference?
   _____
   _____
   _____

9. When is substitution a good choice for solving a system of equations?
   _____
   _____
   _____

10. When is combination a good choice for solving a system of equations?
    _____
    _____
    _____

11. What does it mean if a system of equations has no solution? Infinitely many solutions?
    _____
    _____
    _____

12. How do you solve a system of one linear equation and one quadratic equation?
    _____
    _____
    _____

Responses

1. How do you multiply two polynomials?

Distribute each term in the first set of parentheses to each term in the second set, then combine like terms.

2. What should you do to isolate a particular variable in an equation?

Perform inverse operations until the variable is by itself on one side of the equal sign. If the equation has fractions, make them disappear by multiplying both sides of the equation by the denominator(s). If like terms appear on different sides of the equation, collect them on the same side so that you can combine them.

3. What is the most useful equation for a line in the coordinate plane? Why?

The best equation is slope-intercept form, $y = mx + b$, because it tells you the slope (m) and the y-intercept (b). Conversely, if you need to derive an equation yourself, you can plug the slope and y-intercept into slope-intercept form and you're done.

4. When the ACT gives you two points on a line, what can you figure out?

If you know two points, you can figure out the slope of the line with the equation $m = \frac{y_2 - y_1}{x_2 - x_1}$. From there, you can plug one of the points and the slope into slope-intercept form and find the y-intercept.

5. How are parallel and perpendicular lines related to each other?

Parallel lines never intersect, and they have equal slopes. Perpendicular lines intersect at a 90° angle, and they have negative reciprocal slopes.

6. What types of keywords should you look for when translating English into math?

Look for keywords that signal equality ("is," "has," "was"), variable names ("Marina's age," "the cost of one bathtub"), or one of the four arithmetic operations (addition, subtraction, multiplication, and division).

7. What is the difference between a linear inequality and a linear equation?

A linear equation is solved for a single value, whereas a linear inequality is solved for a range of values.

8. The rules for manipulating an inequality are very similar to those for manipulating an equation. What is the major difference?

When solving an inequality, you can do the same thing to both sides, just as you can for an equation. The big difference is that if you divide or multiply both sides of an inequality by a negative number, you have to flip the inequality sign.

9. When is substitution a good choice for solving a system of equations?

Substitution works best when at least one of the variables has a coefficient of 1, making the variable easy to isolate. This system, for example, is well suited for substitution:

$$a + 3b = 5$$
$$4a - 6b = 21$$

That's because in the first equation, you can easily isolate the a as $a = 5 - 3b$ and plug that result in for a in the other equation. By contrast, substitution would not be a great choice for solving this system:

$$2a + 3b = 5$$
$$4a - 6b = 21$$

If you used substitution now, you'd have to work with fractions, which is messy.

10. When is combination a good choice for solving a system of equations?

Combination is often a good choice. It is at its worst in systems such as this one:

$$2a + 3b = 5$$
$$3a + 5b = 7$$

Neither a-coefficient is a multiple of the other, and neither b-coefficient is a multiple of the other, so to solve this system with combination, you'd have to multiply both equations by a constant (for example, multiplying the first equation by 3 and the second equation by 2 to create a 6a term in both equations). But substitution wouldn't be stellar in this situation, either.

Note that combination may be particularly effective when the ACT asks for a combination of variables. For example, if a question based on the previous system of equations asked for the value of $5a + 8b$, then you could find the answer instantly by adding the equations together because $2a + 3a = 5a$ and $3b + 5b = 8b$.

11. What does it mean if a system of equations has no solution? Infinitely many solutions?

A system of equations with no solution represents two parallel lines, which never cross. The coefficient of a variable in one equation will match the coefficient of the same variable in the other equation, but the constants will be different. For example, this system has no solution:

$$2x + 3y = 4$$
$$2x + 3y = 5$$

Subtracting one equation from the other yields the equation $0 = -1$, which makes no sense.

If a system of equations has infinitely many solutions, then the two equations represent the same line. For example, this system has infinitely many solutions:

$$2x + 3y = 4$$
$$4x + 6y = 8$$

Dividing the second equation by 2 yields $2x + 3y = 4$, so while the two equations look different, they are actually the same.

12. How do you solve a system of one linear equation and one quadratic equation?

Put the linear equation in the form $y = mx + b$ and the quadratic equation in the form $y = ax^2 + bx + c$. Set the right side of each equation equal to one another, and solve.

Next Steps

If you answered most questions correctly in the "How Much Have You Learned?" section, and if your responses to the Reflect questions were similar to those of the ACT expert, then consider algebra an area of strength and move on to the next chapter. Come back to this topic periodically to prevent yourself from getting rusty.

If you don't yet feel confident, review those parts of this chapter that you have not yet mastered. Then, try the questions you missed again. As always, be sure to review the explanations closely. Then go online (**kaptest.com/login**) for more practice. If you haven't already registered your book, do so at **kaptest.com/moreonline**.

kaptest.com/login

Answers and Explanations

Polynomials

1. D
Difficulty: Low
Category: Algebra
Getting to the Answer: The question asks you to simplify the given expression. First, distribute the 3 and -7: $3x + 12 - 14x + 35$. Then, combine the like terms: $-11x + 47$. Choice (D) is correct.

2. J
Difficulty: Low
Category: Algebra
Getting to the Answer: The question asks you to simplify the given expression. Before distributing $\frac{1}{4}x$ to each term inside the parentheses, combine like terms inside the parentheses: $\frac{1}{4}x(-4x - 8y)$. Then, distribute the $\frac{1}{4}x$: $-x^2 - 2xy$. Choice (J) is correct.

3. B
Difficulty: Low
Category: Algebra
Getting to the Answer: The question asks you to simplify the given expression. First, distribute the -1 to each of the terms in the second set of parentheses: $-3x^2 + 3x + 2$. Now, combine like terms: $x^2 - 3x + 2 - 3x^2 + 3x + 2 = -2x^2 + 4$. Choice (B) is correct.

4. H
Difficulty: Medium
Category: Algebra
Getting to the Answer: The question asks you to simplify the given expression. Notice that you can factor out a $2x^2$ from each term in the numerator:

$$\frac{2x^2(4x^4 - 8)}{2x^2}$$

Then, cancel the $2x^2$, since it appears in both the numerator and denominator:

$$\frac{\cancel{2x^2}(4x^4 - 8)}{\cancel{2x^2}}$$

$$4x^4 - 8$$

$4x^4 - 8$ is equivalent to the given expression; (H) is correct.

5. B
Difficulty: Medium
Category: Algebra
Getting to the Answer: The question asks you to simplify the given expression with the known value of a. Simplifying before plugging in $a = 4$ will save you valuable time on test day. Notice that you can factor out 4 from each term in the numerator:

$$\frac{4(a^4 + 16b)}{16}$$

Then, cancel the 4, since it appears in both the numerator and the denominator:

$$\frac{a^4 + 16b}{4}$$

Now, plug in $a = 4$ and simplify:

$$\frac{4^4 + 16b}{4} = \frac{256 + 16b}{4}$$

$$= \frac{256}{4} + \frac{16b}{4}$$

$$= 64 + 4b$$

Choice (B) is correct.

Solving Equations

Drill Answers

a. $2(a + 5) = 11 - (3 - 6a)$
    $2a + 10 = 11 - 3 + 6a$
    $2a + 10 = 8 + 6a$
    $\quad\quad\; 2 = 4a$
    $\quad\quad\; \frac{1}{2} = a$

b. $4(3 - r) = 2r + 18$
    $12 - 4r = 2r + 18$
    $\quad\; -6 = 6r$
    $\quad\; -1 = r$

Part 3
ACT MATH

c. $\left(\dfrac{2}{2}\right)\dfrac{2t}{3} - \left(\dfrac{3}{3}\right)\dfrac{5t}{2} = \dfrac{5}{6}$

$\dfrac{4t}{6} - \dfrac{15t}{6} = \dfrac{5}{6}$

$-\dfrac{11t}{6} = \dfrac{5}{6}$

$6\left(-\dfrac{11t}{6}\right) = 6\left(\dfrac{5}{6}\right)$

$-11t = 5$

$t = -\dfrac{5}{11}$

d. $\dfrac{9}{5} \times C = \dfrac{9}{5} \times \dfrac{5}{9}(F - 32)$

$\dfrac{9}{5}C = F - 32$

$\dfrac{9}{5}C + 32 = F$

e. $A = \dfrac{1}{2}bh$

$2(A) = 2\left(\dfrac{1}{2}bh\right)$

$2A = bh$

$\dfrac{2A}{h} = b$

1. A
Difficulty: Low
Category: Algebra
Getting to the Answer: The question asks you to solve the given equation. Distribute 15 to each term in the parentheses: $15x + 135$. Then, solve for x:

$15x + 135 = -21$

$15x = -156$

$x = -\dfrac{156}{15}$

Reduce $-\dfrac{156}{15}$ to $-\dfrac{52}{5}$. Choice (A) is correct.

2. F
Difficulty: Low
Category: Algebra
Getting to the Answer: The question asks you to solve the given equation. First, distribute 9 to the two terms inside the parentheses: $9a - 27$. Then, solve for a:

$9a - 27 = 15a$

$-27 = 6a$

$-\dfrac{27}{6} = a$

Since $-\dfrac{27}{6}$ is not an answer, reduce it to $-\dfrac{9}{2}$. Then, write it as a mixed number: $-\dfrac{9}{2} = -4\dfrac{1}{2}$. This matches (F).

3. B
Difficulty: Medium
Category: Algebra
Getting to the Answer: The question asks you to solve for the given equation. Recall that if $|x| = a$, $x = a$ and $-x = a$. In this question, $|7x - 1| + 2 = 4$ simplifies to $|7x - 1| = 2$. Therefore, $7x - 1 = 2$ and $-(7x - 1) = 2$. This matches (B).

4. J
Difficulty: Medium
Category: Algebra
Getting to the Answer: The question asks you to solve the given equation, but there is no math necessary here! If you remember that absolute value represents distance on a number line and therefore cannot be negative, you'll immediately see that there are no values of x for which the equation is true because the right-hand side is -2. Choice (J) is correct.

5. B
Difficulty: Low
Category: Algebra
Getting to the Answer: The question asks you to solve for x. First, distribute 8 to each of the terms in the parentheses: $8x - 16y$. Then, isolate x:

$8x - 16y = 16x$

$-16y = 8x$

$-2y = x$

x in terms of y is $x = -2y$. The correct answer is (B).

Linear Graphs

1. B
Difficulty: Low
Category: Algebra
Getting to the Answer: The question asks for the slope of the given line equation. The equation of a line is $y = mx + b$, where m is the slope and b is the y-intercept. Rewrite the given equation to get y in terms of x.

$$4x - 7y = 14$$
$$-7y = -4x + 14$$
$$y = \frac{4}{7}x - 2$$

The slope of the line given by this equation is the coefficient of x, which is $\frac{4}{7}$. Choice (B) is correct.

2. F
Difficulty: Medium
Category: Algebra
Getting to the Answer: The question asks for the y-intercept of the line that passes through the given points. Here is another type of question in which you need to use the slope-intercept form of a line, $y = mx + b$. First, use the two given points and the slope formula to find the slope of the line:

$$m = \frac{y_2 - y_1}{x_2 - x_1} = \frac{31 - (-13)}{-10 - 1} = \frac{44}{-11} = -4$$

Now, plug this slope and the values of either point into $y = mx + b$ to find b (the y-intercept). Using $(1, -13)$, the result is $-13 = -4(1) + b$. Simplify the equation to get $b = -9$, which is (F).

Notice that G is a distractor; it's the slope of the line, not the y-intercept. Double-check that you're answering the right question before you make your selection.

3. A
Difficulty: Low
Category: Algebra
Getting to the Answer: The question asks for the endpoint of the line with the given endpoint and midpoint. The coordinates of the midpoint of a line segment with endpoints (x_1, y_1) and (x_2, y_2) are $\left(\frac{x_1 + x_2}{2}, \frac{y_1 + y_2}{2}\right)$. Setting $x_1 = -3$ and $y_1 = -8$, solve for x_2 and y_2.

First, $1 = \frac{-3 + x_2}{2}$, or $2 = -3 + x_2$. Add 3 to both sides to get $x_2 = 5$. You can already select (A) based on this because none of the other x-coordinates are correct.

For the record, you can find y_2 using the same process: $-5 = \frac{-8 + y_2}{2}$, or $-10 = -8 + y_2$. Add 8 to both sides to get $y_2 = -2$. Choice (A) is correct.

4. H
Difficulty: Low
Category: Algebra
Getting to the Answer: The question asks you to match one of the given line equations with the given graph. Use the graph to determine the y-intercept and the slope of the line. Then write an equation in slope-intercept form: $y = mx + b$. Once you have your equation, look for the answer choice that matches. The line crosses the y-axis at $(0, -4)$, so the y-intercept (b) is -4. The line rises 1 unit for every 3 units that it runs to the right, so the slope (m) is $\frac{1}{3}$. The equation of the line is thus $y = \frac{1}{3}x - 4$, which matches (H).

5. D
Difficulty: High
Category: Algebra
Getting to the Answer: The question asks you to solve for the line equation that models the given table; start by looking at the answer choices. The equations are given in slope-intercept form, so start by finding the slope. Substitute two pairs of values from the table (pick small numbers if possible) into the slope formula, $m = \frac{y_2 - y_1}{x_2 - x_1}$.

Keep in mind that the projected number of pounds sold depends on the price, so the price is the independent variable (x) and the projected number of pounds is the dependent variable (y). Using the points (1.2, 15000) and (2, 5000), the slope is calculated as follows:

$$m = \frac{5,000 - 15,000}{2 - 1.20}$$
$$= \frac{-10,000}{0.8}$$
$$= -12,500$$

Eliminate A and C because the slope is not correct. To choose between B and (D), you could find the y-intercept of the line, but this is a fairly time-consuming process. Instead, choose the simplest pair of values from the table, (2, 5000), and substitute them into both B and (D). Choice (D) is correct because the equation $5{,}000 = -12{,}500(2) + 30{,}000$ is true.

Solving Inequalities

1. D
Difficulty: Low
Category: Algebra
Getting to the Answer: The question asks you to solve for the given inequality. Since all of the choices are y in terms of x, solve for y:

$$-8x + 2y \leq 14$$
$$2y \leq 14 + 8x$$
$$y \leq 7 + 4x$$

The inequality is equivalent to $y \leq 4x + 7$. Choice (D) is correct.

2. F
Difficulty: Medium
Category: Algebra
Getting to the Answer: The question asks you to solve for the solution set of the given inequality. Straightforward algebra is the best approach here. Don't forget—whatever you do to one piece, you must do to all three pieces:

$$-15 \leq 2x - 13 < 3$$
$$-2 \leq 2x < 16$$
$$\frac{-2}{2} \leq \frac{2x}{2} < \frac{16}{2}$$
$$-1 \leq x < 8$$

The solution set is numbers greater than or equal to -1 but less than 8. Choice (F) is correct.

3. C
Difficulty: Medium
Category: Algebra
Getting to the Answer: The question asks you to solve for the given inequality. Since all of the choices are x in terms of y, solve for x. Remember that you need to flip the inequality when multiplying or dividing by a negative number:

$$-3x + 7y \leq 4y + 6$$
$$-3x \leq -3y + 6$$
$$x \geq y - 2$$

The inequality solved for x in terms of y is $x \geq y - 2$. Choice (C) is correct.

4. F
Difficulty: High
Category: Algebra
Getting to the Answer: The question asks you to solve for the given inequality. If $|x| = a$, then $x = a$ and $x = -a$. Accordingly, if $|x| < a$, $x < a$ and $x > -a$ because the direction of the inequality flips when multiplying or dividing by a negative. Therefore, $|2x + 5| < 11$ can be written as $2x + 5 < 11$ and $2x + 5 > -11$. Solve each inequality for x:

$$2x + 5 < 11$$
$$2x < 6$$
$$x < 3$$
$$2x + 5 > -11$$
$$2x > -16$$
$$x > -8$$

Thus, $-8 < x < 3$. Choice (F) is correct.

5. B
Difficulty: Medium
Category: Algebra
Getting to the Answer: The question asks you to solve for the given inequality. To find x such that $x + 2 > x + 1$, subtract x from both sides to obtain $2 > 1$. This inequality is true for any value of x, so the set of x is the set of all real numbers. Choice (B) is correct.

Graphing Inequalities

Drill Answers

a.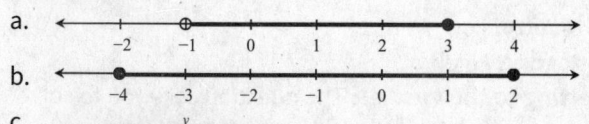

b.

c.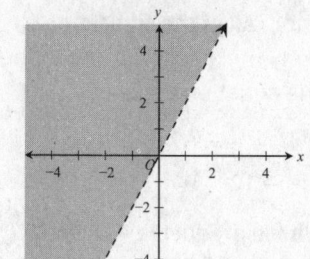

d.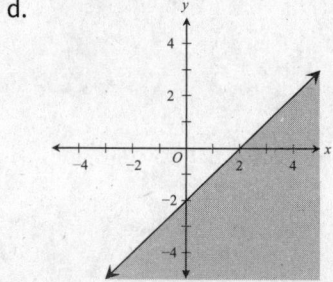

e.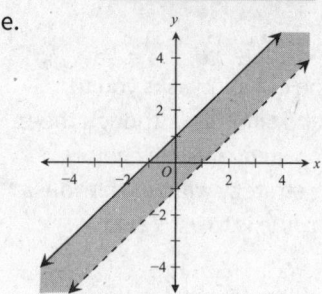

1. A
Difficulty: High
Category: Algebra
Getting to the Answer: The question asks you to solve for the given inequality. Whenever you encounter an absolute value inequality, you must rewrite it without the absolute value signs. The symbol here is $>$, so this will become two inequalities separated by an "or." Split $|2x - 5| > 11$ into $2x - 5 < 11$ or $2x - 5 < -11$ and solve each inequality separately.

$$2x - 5 > 11$$
$$2x > 16$$
$$x > 8$$

or

$$2x - 5 < -11$$
$$2x < -6$$
$$x < -3$$

Find the number line that matches. Choice (A) is correct.

2. J
Difficulty: Medium
Category: Algebra
Getting to the Answer: The question asks you to choose the correct inequality that matches the given number line. The shaded region in the number line shows a range from -6 to 2. The center is $\frac{-6 + 2}{2} = -2$, with -6 and 2 each 4 units away from the center. Recall that $|x - b| \leq a$ represents all numbers up to and including those that are a units away from the center b. Thus, the absolute value inequality is $|w - (-2)| \leq 4$ or $|w + 2| \leq 4$. This matches choice (J).

You can check your choice by solving for w algebraically:

$$w + 2 \leq 4$$
$$w \leq 2$$
$$w + 2 \geq -4$$
$$w \geq -6$$

The range of w is $-6 \leq w \leq 2$, which exactly matches the number line.

3. A
Difficulty: Medium
Category: Algebra
Getting to the Answer: The question asks you to match the correct system of inequalities with the given graph. First, determine the equation for each line in the graph. Then, determine the signs of the inequalities. The vertical line is dashed and passes through $x = -2$. The area to the right of the line is shaded, so the inequality is $x > -2$. Eliminate C and D. The other line is solid and has a slope of -2 (it moves down 2 units for every increase of 1 unit to the right) and a y-intercept of 1. The area below the line is shaded, so the inequality is $y \leq -2x + 1$. Choice (A) is correct.

Part 3
ACT MATH

4. F

Difficulty: Medium
Category: Algebra
Getting to the Answer: The question asks you to match the correct graph with the given inequality. Start by rewriting the compound inequality as two separate inequalities. Then write the inequalities in slope-intercept form, $y = mx + b$, where m is the slope and b is the y-intercept. Solving each one for y yields:

$$2 < y - x$$
$$y > x + 2$$
$$y - x < 3$$
$$y < x + 3$$

The two lines are parallel lines with a positive slope of 1. Thus, the lines must be increasing (going up) from left to right. Eliminate H and J. To decide between the two remaining choices, consider the y-intercepts of the lines. One line has a y-intercept of 2, and the other has a y-intercept of 3. This matches (F).

5. D

Difficulty: High
Category: Algebra
Getting to the Answer: The question asks you to solve for the possible values of b. One approach to this question is to solve each of the answer choices algebraically to get a range of values for b and then see which one gives you the same range as that shown in the figure. However, a faster method is to think of absolute value as a distance. The center of the shaded region is $\frac{-1+5}{2} = 2$, with -1 and 5 each 3 units away from the center. Therefore, the distance between b and 2 must be less than or equal to 3, so $|b - 2| \leq 3$. Choice (D) is correct.

You can confirm your choice by rewriting the absolute value inequality as a compound inequality and solving for b:

$$|b - 2| \leq 3$$
$$-3 \leq b - 2 \leq 3$$
$$-1 \leq b \leq 5$$

This inequality matches the number line exactly.

Quadratics

1. C

Difficulty: Low
Category: Algebra
Getting to the Answer: The question asks you to solve the given quadratic equation. All of the choices are integers, so factoring is likely the quickest route to the answer. Start by setting the equation equal to 0.

$$x^2 - 4x - 6 = 6$$
$$x^2 - 4x - 12 = 0$$

Now, find two numbers whose product is -12 and whose sum is -4. That's -6 and 2: $(x-6)(x+2) = 0$. Solving for x yields:

$$(x - 6) = 0 \rightarrow x = 6$$
$$(x + 2) = 0 \rightarrow x = -2$$

The possible values of x are -2 and 6. Choice (C) is correct.

2. F

Difficulty: Low
Category: Algebra
Getting to the Answer: The question asks you to multiply two expressions and simplify. Although there are variables in the question stem and the choices, using the Picking Numbers strategy will be laborious. The more straightforward route is to use FOIL:

$$(b - a)(a + b) = ba + b^2 - a^2 - ab$$
$$= b^2 - a^2$$

Note that the ab terms cancel out. Rearranging $b^2 - a^2$ gives you $-a^2 + b^2$, which is (F).

3. B

Difficulty: High
Category: Algebra
Getting to the Answer: The question asks you to solve for the given quadratic equation. The choices contain radicals, so use the quadratic formula. First, jot down the values for a, b, and c. You should also write down the formula itself so you're not trying to remember it and plug in values at the same time.

$$x = \frac{-b \pm \sqrt{b^2 - 4ac}}{2a}$$
$$a = 1, b = 8, c = -3$$

Carefully substitute the values into the formula and simplify.

$$x = \frac{-(8) \pm \sqrt{(8)^2 - 4(1)(-3)}}{2(1)}$$
$$= \frac{-8 \pm \sqrt{64 + 12}}{2}$$
$$= \frac{-8 \pm \sqrt{76}}{2}$$

This is not one of the choices, which tells you that you need to simplify the radical. To simplify the radical, look for a perfect square that divides evenly into 76.

$$x = \frac{-8 \pm \sqrt{4}\sqrt{19}}{2}$$
$$= \frac{-8 \pm 2\sqrt{19}}{2}$$
$$= -4 \pm \sqrt{19}$$

The roots of the given quadratic are $-4 \pm \sqrt{19}$, so (B) is correct.

4. G
Difficulty: Medium
Category: Algebra
Getting to the Answer: The question asks you to simplify the given expression. Factor the numerator and denominator. For the denominator, first factor out a 2 to get 1 for the x^2 coefficient. Then factor the quadratic as usual. If the numerator and denominator have any factors in common, cancel those factors.

$$\frac{x^2 - 4x + 4}{2x^2 + 4x - 16} = \frac{(x-2)(x-2)}{2(x^2 + 2x - 8)}$$
$$= \frac{(x-2)(x-2)}{2(x+4)(x-2)}$$
$$= \frac{x-2}{2(x+4)}$$

This is the most simplified form of the given expression; (G) is correct.

5. C
Difficulty: High
Category: Algebra
Getting to the Answer: The question asks how long it will take for the projectile to hit the ground after launch. To find the amount of time it takes for the projectile to hit the ground, find the value of t for which $h = 0$. The fact that 16 divides evenly into 32 (and therefore into 320) is a big hint that you'll be able to factor.

$$0 = -16t^2 + 128t + 320$$
$$0 = -16(t^2 - 8t - 20)$$
$$0 = t^2 - 8t - 20$$
$$0 = (t - 10)(t + 2)$$

Setting each factor equal to 0 gives $t = 10$ or $t = -2$. However, because time cannot be negative, the answer is $t = 10$ seconds. Choice (C) is correct.

Systems of Equations

1. C
Difficulty: Low
Category: Algebra
Getting to the Answer: The question asks you to solve for the sum of the given system of equations. Solve for x and y individually, and then add them together to find the final answer.

$$6x = 20$$
$$x = \frac{20}{6}$$
$$x = \frac{10}{3}$$
$$3y + 7 = 14$$
$$3y = 7$$
$$y = \frac{7}{3}$$

The sum is $x + y = \frac{10}{3} + \frac{7}{3} = \frac{17}{3}$. Writing $\frac{17}{3}$ as a mixed number yields $5\frac{2}{3}$, which matches (C).

2. H
Difficulty: Low
Category: Algebra
Getting to the Answer: The question asks how much greater A is than B. Determining how much greater A is than B means finding the difference between the two, $A - B$:

$$(24xy + 13) - (8xy + 1)$$
$$24xy + 13 - 8xy - 1$$
$$16xy + 12$$

A is $16xy + 12$ greater than B. Choice (H) is correct.

Part 3
ACT MATH

3. D

Difficulty: Medium
Category: Algebra
Getting to the Answer: The question asks you to solve for the product of x and y. First, solve for x and y individually. Then, multiply them together to find their product.

To solve using combination, you will need to multiply each equation by a constant. Suppose you want to eliminate x. The coefficients of the x terms are 2 and 5, so you need to multiply the equations by numbers that will give you -10 and 10 as your new x term coefficients. To do this, multiply the first equation by -5 and the second equation by 2:

$$-5(2x + 5y = 49)$$
$$2(5x + 3y = 94)$$

Now, add the resulting equations:

$$-10x - 25y = -245$$
$$+10x + 6y = 188$$
$$\overline{- 19y = -57}$$
$$y = 3$$

Next, plug $y = 3$ back into either equation and solve for x. This yields $x = 17$. Finally, multiply x and y together to obtain 51, which is (D).

4. J

Difficulty: High
Category: Algebra
Getting to the Answer: The question asks you to solve for the value of $4x - 5y$. To determine the value of $4x - 5y$, first find the solution to the system of equations. You can solve by either substitution or combination/elimination. However, since it is easy to isolate x in the first equation, substitution is preferred. Solve the first equation for x and then substitute it into the second equation to solve for y:

$$x = 11 - 9y$$
$$2(11 - 9y) - 7y = -3$$
$$22 - 18y - 7y = -3$$
$$-25y = -25$$
$$y = 1$$

Then, plug $y = 1$ into $x = 11 - 9y$ to find x: $x = 11 - 9(1) = 2$. Thus, $4x - 5y = 4(2) - 5(1) = 8 - 5 = 3$. Choice (J) is correct.

5. C

Difficulty: High
Category: Algebra
Getting to the Answer: The question asks you to choose the inequality that will have more than one real solution. Substitute $y = x$ into the second equation and set the equation equal to 0:

$$-py + qx^2 = r$$
$$-px + qx^2 - r = 0$$
$$qx^2 - px - r = 0$$

Recall that the quadratic formula for a quadratic equation in the form $ax^2 + bx + c = 0$ is $x = \frac{-b \pm \sqrt{b^2 - 4ac}}{2a}$. The term under the square root, $b^2 - 4ac$, determines how many real solutions there are. When the term is negative, there are no real solutions for x because negative numbers have no real square roots. When the term is 0, then the value of x will be $\frac{-b}{2a}$, which yields only one solution. Finally, when the term is positive, x will have two solutions because of the $\pm$ symbol.

Thus, there will be more than one solution if the term under the square root is greater than 0. Here $a = q$, $b = -p$, and $c = -r$. Substitute accordingly and solve:

$$b^2 - 4ac > 0$$
$$(-p)^2 - 4q(-r) > 0$$
$$p^2 + 4qr > 0$$

$p^2 + 4qr$ will produce more than one real solution. Choice (C) is correct.

Word Problems

Drill Answers

a. $2n - m$
b. $\frac{1}{4}(a + b) = a - 4$
c. $9y - (x + 7) = \frac{(x - z)}{7 - x}$
d. $\frac{4q}{7p} = \frac{5}{2}$
e. $F - 500 + G = 2(F + 0.50F)$

Chapter 10
Algebra

1. B
Difficulty: Medium
Category: Algebra
Getting to the Answer: The question asks for the correct expression of the number of sharks in terms of whales and dolphins. If w represents the number of whales, then the phrase "twice as many dolphins as whales" means that there are $2w$ dolphins. Therefore, "dolphins and whales combined" is $2w + w$, or $3w$. Because there are 8 fewer sharks than dolphins and whales combined, you need to subtract 8 from $3w$, which makes (B) correct.

You can also answer this question by using the Picking Numbers strategy. Pick a small, positive number, like 5, for the number of whales. If there are 5 whales and "twice as many dolphins as whales," then there must be 10 dolphins. Combine the number of whales and dolphins and subtract 8 from that sum to find the number of sharks: $(5 + 10) - 8 = 15 - 8 = 7$. Plug in $w = 5$ to determine which answer choice gives you a value of 7:

Choice A: $5(5) = 25$ Eliminate.

Choice (B): $3(5) - 8 = 15 - 8 = 7$ Keep.

Choice C: $10 + 5 = 15$ Eliminate.

Choice D: $3\sqrt{2(5) - 8} = 3\sqrt{2} \neq 7$ Eliminate.

Choice (B) is the only answer that works.

2. H
Difficulty: Low
Category: Algebra
Getting to the Answer: The question asks for the expression that represents the cost, in dollars, of p paintbrushes and c canvases. The total cost of the two kinds of items is the cost of one paintbrush multiplied by the number of paintbrushes purchased plus the cost of one canvas multiplied by the number of canvases purchased. Because a canvas costs "6 times" the cost of a paintbrush, a canvas costs $6(\$1.50) = \$9$.

Total cost of paintbrushes: $1.50 \times p = 1.5p$

Total cost of canvases: $9 \times c = 9c$

Sum of both: $9c + 1.5p$

$9c + 1.5p$ represents the expression for costs in dollars. Therefore, (H) is correct.

3. B
Difficulty: Medium
Category: Algebra
Getting to the Answer: The question asks you to determine how many miles Joy traveled. Backsolving works well on many word problems with integers in the choices. Start with the middle choice, C. If Joy drove 96 miles, she would have paid $\$1.50 + \$0.25(96) = \$25.50$. This is too much, so try (B). If she drove 94 miles, she would have paid $\$1.50 + \$0.25(94) = \$25.00$. Choice (B) is correct.

You could also set up an equation and solve algebraically. If m is the number of miles traveled, then the toll is $\$1.50 + \$0.25m$. Joy paid a total of $\$25.00$, so solve this equation:

$$\$1.50 + \$0.25m = \$25.00$$
$$\$0.25m = \$23.50$$
$$m = 94$$

This confirms that (B) is correct.

4. H
Difficulty: Medium
Category: Algebra
Getting to the Answer: The question asks how many adult tickets were sold. Algebra and Backsolving both work well on word problems like this one. Use the method that is more comfortable for you.

To solve this question algebraically, first translate it into a system of equations. At $8 per adult ticket and $5 per student ticket, the total amount of money collected can be written as $8a + 5s = 3,475$. Because there were 500 tickets total, $a + s = 500$. Plug $s = 500 - a$ into the first equation and solve for a:

$$8a + 5(500 - a) = 3,475$$
$$8a + 2,500 - 5a = 3,475$$
$$3a = 975$$
$$a = 325$$

Choice (H) is correct.

To Backsolve, start with (H). If there are 325 adult tickets, then there are $500 - 325 = 175$ student tickets. The total amount of money collected would be $\$325(8) + \$175(5)$, or $\$2,600 + \$875 = \$3,475$. Because this is the total given in the question, (H) is correct.

5. B

Difficulty: High
Category: Algebra
Getting to the Answer: The question asks for the maximum number of vases the ceramist can glaze with 20 pints of glaze. Because you want to know the value of v when the given expression is at most 20, set up an inequality and solve for v:

$$v^2 + v \leq 20$$
$$v^2 + v - 20 \leq 0$$
$$(v + 5)(v - 4) \leq 0$$
$$v \leq -5 \text{ and } 4$$

Thus, the maximum number of vases the ceramist can glaze is 4. (B) is correct.

On Test Day

1. D

Difficulty: Medium
Category: Algebra
Getting to the Answer: A strategic "guess" may be an efficient approach for this question; the question asks you to solve for the given equation, so there is no math actually necessary here. If you remember that absolute value represents distance on a number line and therefore cannot be negative, you'll immediately see that there are no values of x for which the equation is true because the right-hand side is -4. Choice (D) is correct.

However, you might not spot this shortcut, or the question might not provide such an easy way to eliminate 3 out of 4 choices. In that case, you'll want to consider algebra or Backsolving as alternative approaches.

To solve this equation algebraically, follow the order of operations, making sure you create two equations when you account for the absolute value symbols:

$$|2x - 6| = -4$$

$$2x - 6 = +(-4) \quad \text{or} \quad 2x - 6 = -(-4)$$
$$2x = 6 + (-4) \qquad\qquad 2x = 6 + 4$$
$$2x = 2 \qquad\qquad\qquad 2x = 10$$
$$x = 1 \qquad\qquad\qquad\; x = 5$$

Be careful! Plug these values back into the equation to ensure success. At this point, you'll notice that neither value works:

$$|2x - 6| = -4$$

$$|2(1) - 6| = -4 \quad \text{or} \quad |2(5) - 6| = -4$$
$$|3 - 6| = -4 \qquad\qquad |10 - 6| = -4$$
$$|-3| = -4 \qquad\qquad\quad |4| = -4$$
$$3 \neq -4 \qquad\qquad\qquad 4 \neq -4$$

If you choose to solve this question by Backsolving, consider the answer choices carefully. If you start with B and prove that $x \neq 1$, then you can eliminate both B and C:

$$|2(1) - 6| = -4$$
$$|3 - 6| = -4$$
$$|-3| = -4$$
$$3 \neq -4$$

Then, plug in A:

$$|2(-1) - 6| = -4$$
$$|-2 - 6| = -4$$
$$|-8| = -4$$
$$8 \neq -4$$

Since -1 is not a solution, (D) must be correct.

How Much Have You Learned?

1. C

Difficulty: High
Category: Algebra
Getting to the Answer: The question asks how many distinct roots the given equation has. The equation is a polynomial in one variable, so the greatest number of roots (solutions) it can have is equal to the highest power of the variable, which is 3. That doesn't mean the answer is 3, however, because you are counting the number of *distinct* real solutions. To solve the equation, start by factoring out the GCF (Greatest Common Factor), which is $3x$. Then factor:

$$3x^3 + 30x^2 + 75x = 0$$
$$3x(x^2 + 10x + 25) = 0$$
$$3x(x + 5)(x + 5) = 0$$

Setting each factor equal to 0 and solving for x yields $x = 0$, $x = -5$, and $x = -5$. There are only two distinct real solutions, 0 and -5, so (C) is correct.

2. G
Difficulty: Low
Category: Algebra
Getting to the Answer: The question asks for the coordinates of the midpoint between the two points given. The coordinates of the midpoint of a line segment with endpoints (x_1, y_1) and (x_2, y_2) are $\left(\frac{x_1 + x_2}{2}, \frac{y_1 + y_2}{2}\right)$. Plug the points $(-3, 5)$ and $(0, 1)$ into the formula: $\left(\frac{-3 + 0}{2}, \frac{5 + 1}{2}\right) = \left(-\frac{3}{2}, 3\right)$. Choice (G) is correct.

3. C
Difficulty: Low
Category: Algebra
Getting to the Answer: The question asks for the y-intercept of the line that passes through the given points. You are looking for the y-intercept, so use the slope-intercept form, $y = mx + b$. Unfortunately, you must find m before you can find b.

$$m = \frac{y_2 - y_1}{x_2 - x_1} = \frac{42 - 21}{4 - 1} = \frac{21}{3} = 7$$

Plug in $m = 7$ and the (x, y)-values for either point to find b. It's typically easier to work with smaller numbers, so use $(1, 21)$.

$$y = mx + b$$
$$21 = 7(1) + b$$
$$21 = 7 + b$$
$$14 = b$$

You don't need to write out the full equation of the line, since you only need to find b. Choice (C) is correct.

4. H
Difficulty: Medium
Category: Algebra
Getting to the Answer: The question asks for the solution set for the given equation. To solve an absolute value equation, you must always consider two possibilities: if $|2x - 3| = 13$, then the expression inside the absolute value signs could equal either 13 or -13:

$$2x - 3 = 13$$
$$2x = 16$$
$$x = 8$$

and

$$2x - 3 = -13$$
$$2x = -10$$
$$x = -5$$

Together, the two solutions form the solution set $\{-5, 8\}$, which is (H).

5. C
Difficulty: Medium
Category: Algebra
Getting to the Answer: The question asks for the number of additional visits in a year that would yield the same cost for both exterminators. Carefully translate from English into math.

Bye Bye Bugs: $\$275 + \$20 \times$ number of additional visits

Pest Be Gone: $\$200 + \$25 \times$ number of additional visits

Call v the number of additional visits and set the two equations equal to each other:

$$275 + 20v = 200 + 25v$$
$$75 = 5v$$
$$15 = v$$

It will take 15 additional visits for the cost of both exterminators to be equal. Choice (C) is correct.

6. F
Difficulty: Medium
Category: Algebra
Getting to the Answer: The question asks you to choose the inequality that matches the given graph. First, determine the equation for each line in the graph. Then, determine the sign of the inequality. The dashed line has a slope of $-\frac{1}{2}$ and a y-intercept of 3. The area below the dashed line is shaded, so $y < -\frac{1}{2}x + 3$. The solid line also has a slope of $-\frac{1}{2}$ and a y-intercept of -2. The area above the solid line is shaded, so $y \geq -\frac{1}{2}x - 2$. Thus, $-\frac{1}{2}x - 2 \leq y < -\frac{1}{2}x + 3$. Choice (F) is correct.

Part 3
ACT MATH

7. C
Difficulty: Low
Category: Algebra
Getting to the Answer: The question asks you to simplify the given expression. Before distributing the $\frac{1}{5}p$, combine like terms inside the parentheses: $\frac{1}{5}p(15q + 10p)$. Then distribute the $\frac{1}{5}p$: $3pq + 2p^2$. Choice (C) is correct.

8. J
Difficulty: High
Category: Algebra
Getting to the Answer: The question asks for the solutions of x. First, substitute $y = x^2$ into the second equation.

$$24 + x^2 = 10x$$

You now have a quadratic equation. Set it equal to 0, factor, and solve for x.

$$24 + x^2 = 10x$$
$$x^2 - 10x + 24 = 0$$
$$(x - 4)(x - 6) = 0$$

Thus, $x = 4$ and $x = 6$. Choice (J) is correct.

9. D
Difficulty: Medium
Category: Algebra
Getting to the Answer: The question asks for the two solutions to the given inequality. If $|x| = a$, then $x = a$ and $x = -a$. Similarly, for $|x| < a$, $x < a$ and $x > -a$. Recall that the direction of the inequality sign flips when you multiply or divide by a negative. Therefore, $|4x + 3| - 1 < 8$ can be written as $4x + 3 < 9$ and $4x + 3 > -9$. This matches (D).

10. J
Difficulty: High
Category: Algebra
Getting to the Answer: The question asks you to determine how many hours Rasheed needs to jump in order for the cost of the membership to be less than the total cost of buying jump tickets at the non-membership price. An individual non-membership ticket costs $12, so if Rasheed jumps for h hours, the total cost will be $12h$.

If Rasheed buys the membership, then the total cost will be the membership fee plus the discounted rate of the jump ticket per hour. The discounted ticket is $12 - (0.15 \times 12)$, or $12 \times 0.85 = 10.2$.

Set up an inequality to solve for the minimum number of hours, h, Rasheed needs to jump in order for the cost of the membership to be less than the total cost of buying jump tickets at the non-membership price.

$$50 + 10.2h < 12h$$
$$50 < 1.8h$$
$$27.8 < h$$

The smallest whole number greater than 27.8 is 28, so the answer is (J).

[CHAPTER 11]

TABLES, GRAPHS, STATISTICS, AND PROBABILITY

LEARNING OBJECTIVES

After completing this chapter, you will be able to:

- Draw inferences about data presented in a variety of graphical formats
- Calculate mean, median, mode, range, and expected value
- Calculate probabilities based on data sets

Part 3
ACT MATH

How Much Do You Know?

Directions: Try out the questions below. Show your work so that you can compare your solutions to the ones found on the next page. The "Category" heading in the explanation for each question gives the title of the lesson that covers how to solve it. If you answered the question(s) for a given lesson correctly, and if your scratchwork looks like the explanations, you may be able to move quickly through that lesson. If you answered incorrectly or used a different approach, you may want to take your time on that lesson.

1. Jamal has a suitcase that contains 2 white socks (and no other socks). He wants to add enough black socks so that the probability of randomly selecting a white sock is $\frac{1}{5}$. How many black socks should Jamal add to the suitcase?

   A. 6
   B. 7
   C. 8
   D. 9

2. What is the distance, on a number line, between the median and the range of the set $\{-9, -6, -2, 0, 4, 9\}$?

   F. -1
   G. 0
   H. 18
   J. 19

3. Jasmin's goal is to collect 200 cans of food during a food drive. During her first 4 days, she averages 10 cans per day. With 10 days remaining, Jasmin must average how many cans per day to meet her goal?

   A. 12
   B. 14
   C. 16
   D. 19

4. The following frequency chart shows the number of Ms. Kirkham's English students whose test scores fell within certain score ranges. All test scores are whole numbers. How many students have a test score in the interval 71–75?

Score range	Cumulative number of students
60–65	1
60–70	3
60–75	8
60–85	9
60–100	12

   F. 3
   G. 4
   H. 5
   J. 8

5. A certain baseball stadium has 12,000 seats. Based on several previous years' attendance rates, the owners of the stadium constructed the following table showing the daily attendance rates, expressed as decimals, and their probabilities of occurring for the coming baseball season. Based on the probability distribution in the following table, what is the expected number of seats that will be occupied on any given day during the coming baseball season?

Attendance rate	Probability
0.40	0.15
0.50	0.25
0.60	0.35
0.70	0.15
0.80	0.10

A. 5,400
B. 6,240
C. 6,960
D. 7,080

6. The data set {1, 3, −8, x, 10} has a mean of 7. What is the median of this data set?

F. −8
G. 3
H. 10
J. 29

7. Zaina's bookshelf contains 10 horror novels, 10 romance novels, 10 true crime books, and no other books. If Zaina chooses 2 books from the shelf at random to take with her on vacation, what is the probability that the two books she chooses will belong to the same genre?

A. $\frac{9}{87}$
B. $\frac{9}{29}$
C. $\frac{56}{87}$
D. $\frac{2}{3}$

8. The average of a list of 4 numbers is 100. If the first number is increased by 4, the second number decreased by 5, the third number increased by 6, and the fourth number increased by 1, what will the average be?

F. 97.5
G. 100
H. 101.5
J. 102

9. Janelle is planning to go out of town for 2 consecutive days and needs to create a watering schedule for her garden. During her time out of town, there is a 50% chance of rain each day. Assuming that the chance of rain is independent of the day, what is the probability that it will rain both days that she is gone?

   A. 0.25
   B. 0.50
   C. 0.75
   D. 1.00

10. A researcher is looking to evaluate the impact on blood pressure levels of stroking various types of pets. Her 120 research participants were grouped by the one type of pet they would be interacting with during the study.

    If 1 person from this research group is randomly selected, what is the probability that this person will interact with a dog or a cat?

    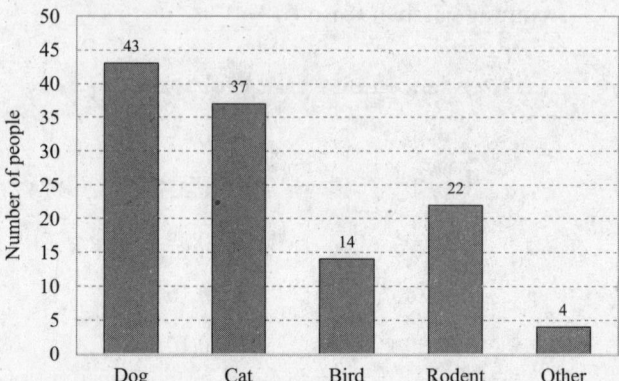

    F. $\dfrac{37}{120}$

    G. $\dfrac{43}{120}$

    H. $\dfrac{37}{43}$

    J. $\dfrac{80}{120}$

Chapter 11
Tables, Graphs, Statistics, and Probability

Answers and Explanations

How Much Do You Know?

1. C
Difficulty: Low
Category: Statistics and Probability: Probability
Getting to the Answer: The question asks how many black socks Jamal should add to a suitcase so that the probability of randomly selecting a white sock is $\frac{1}{5}$. In order for the probability of selecting one of the 2 white socks to be $\frac{1}{5}$, there must be 10 total socks in the suitcase, since $\frac{1}{5} = \frac{2}{10}$. Currently, the only socks in the suitcase are the 2 white socks, so Jamal must add $10 - 2 = 8$ black socks to the suitcase to bring the total to 10. Choice (C) is correct.

2. J
Difficulty: Medium
Category: Statistics and Probability: Statistics
Getting to the Answer: The question asks for the distance between the median and the range of the given set. In a set with an even number of values, the median is the average of the two middle numbers. The values are already in ascending order, so the two middle numbers are -2 and 0. The median is thus -1. This is not the answer to the question, though.

The range of a set of numbers is the biggest number minus the smallest number. The range is thus $9 - (-9) = 9 + 9 = 18$. This still is not the answer to the question; keep going.

The distance between -1 and 18 on a number line is $18 - (-1)$, or $18 + 1 = 19$. Choice (J) is correct.

3. C
Difficulty: Medium
Category: Statistics and Probability: Statistics
Getting to the Answer: The question asks how many cans per day Jasmin must collect in her remaining 10 days to meet her goal. Use the average formula:

$$\text{average} = \frac{\text{sum of terms}}{\text{number of terms}}$$

You are told that the average for the first 4 days is 10. Plug these values into the formula:

$$10 = \frac{\text{sum of terms}}{4}$$

The total number of cans that Jasmin collected in the first 4 days is therefore $10 \times 4 = 40$. Jasmin wants to collect 200 cans in all, so she needs to collect another $200 - 40 = 160$ cans. There are 10 days left, so use the average formula a second time:

$$\text{average} = \frac{160}{10}$$

Jasmin needs to average $\frac{160}{10} = 16$ cans per day to reach her goal. Choice (C) is correct.

4. H
Difficulty: Medium
Category: Statistics and Probability: Tables and Graphs
Getting to the Answer: The question asks how many students have a test score in the interval 71–75, but the interval 71–75 does not appear in the frequency chart. However, you can deduce the number of students in this interval by comparing the number of students in the 60–70 and 60–75 intervals.

According to the chart, there are 3 students in the 60–70 interval, and there are 8 students in the 60–75 interval. Since both intervals have the 60–70 range in common, the 5 additional students must have come from the 71–75 range.

Choice (H) is correct.

5. C
Difficulty: High
Category: Statistics and Probability: Probability
Getting to the Answer: The question asks for the expected number of seats that will be occupied on any given day during the coming baseball season. To calculate the expected value, multiply each value by its probability and add up the results:

$$
\begin{array}{rl}
(0.40 \times 0.15) & 0.060 \\
(0.50 \times 0.25) & 0.125 \\
(0.60 \times 0.35) \rightarrow & 0.210 \\
(0.70 \times 0.15) & 0.105 \\
+(0.80 \times 0.10) & +0.080 \\
\hline
& 0.580
\end{array}
$$

Be careful! This value represents the expected *attendance rate*, but the question asks for the expected number of *seats*. To find the expected number of seats, multiply the expected attendance rate by the total number of seats in the stadium, 12,000:

$$12{,}000(0.58) = 6{,}960$$

Choice (C) is correct.

6. G
Difficulty: Low
Category: Statistics and Probability: Statistics
Getting to the Answer: The question asks for the median of the given data set. To find the median, you must first find *x*. Apply the average formula to solve for *x*.

$$\text{average} = \frac{\text{sum of terms}}{\text{number of terms}}$$

$$7 = \frac{1 + 3 - 8 + x + 10}{5}$$

$$7 = \frac{6 + x}{5}$$

$$35 = 6 + x$$

$$29 = x$$

The median is the middle number when the data set is arranged in increasing order:

$$\{-8, 1, 3, 10, 29\}$$

3 is the median, and (G) is correct.

7. B
Difficulty: High
Category: Statistics and Probability: Probability
Getting to the Answer: The question asks for the probability that Zaina picks two books of the same genre. Use the probability formula:

$$\text{probability} = \frac{\text{\# of desired outcomes}}{\text{\# of possible outcomes}}$$

After Zaina chooses her first book, there will be $10 - 1 = 9$ books of that type left. Thus, the "desired" number of books is 9. There are $10 + 10 + 10 = 30$ total books to start with. After Zaina takes one, 29 books remain. Thus, the total number of possibilities is 29. Plugging these values into the probability formula yields $\frac{9}{29}$. Answer choice (B) is correct.

8. H
Difficulty: Medium
Category: Statistics and Probability: Statistics
Getting to the Answer: The question asks for the average of a list of 4 numbers after some changes are made. This scenario may look intimidating, but start with what you know: "the average of a list of 4 numbers is 100" can be written mathematically as:

$$\frac{a + b + c + d}{4} = 100$$

You don't know the individual variables' values, but that information is not necessary to answer this question. If you multiply both sides of the equation by 4, you can determine the sum of the four variables: $a + b + c + d = 400$. Then, use the numbers in the question stem to calculate the new sum: $400 + 4 - 5 + 6 + 1 = 406$. The new average, then, will be this new sum divided by the number of values: $406 \div 4 = 101.5$. Choice (H) is correct.

9. A
Difficulty: Medium
Category: Statistics and Probability: Probability
Getting to the Answer: Your task is to calculate the probability that it will rain two days in a row. The probability that multiple independent events will all occur is the product of their individual probabilities. The probability of rain each day is 50%, or 0.5. The probability of getting rain on both days is therefore $0.5 \times 0.5 = 0.25$, choice (A).

10. J
Difficulty: Low
Category: Statistics and Probability: Probability
Getting to the Answer: Probability is the ratio of the number of desired outcomes to the number of possible outcomes. Here, the desired outcome is that a participant has a dog or a cat. According to the graph, this is $43 + 37 = 80$ participants. The question states that there are 120 participants, which is the number of possible outcomes. So the probability that one randomly selected person will have either a dog or a cat is 80 out of 120, or $\frac{80}{120}$, which is (J).

Chapter 11
Tables, Graphs, Statistics, and Probability

TABLES AND GRAPHS

LEARNING OBJECTIVES

After this lesson, you will be able to:

- Solve math questions with real-world scenarios using one or more rates
- Create a ratio to represent the relationship between two numbers
- Set up a proportion and solve to find a missing value

To answer a question like this

Callum is playing a game in which he draws cards out of a standard 52-card deck. If he draws an odd number, he awards himself 2 points. If he draws an even number, he awards himself 3 points. If he draws a face card (jack, queen, king, or ace), he awards himself 4 points. Let the random variable x represent the total number of points awarded on any draw from the deck. What is the expected value of x? (Note: A standard deck of cards contains four copies of the numbers 2 through 10 and four copies of each of the face cards.)

A. 2
B. 2.85
C. 3
D. 3.57

You need to know this

The ACT uses some straightforward methods of representing data sets that you are probably already familiar with, such as **tables** and **bar graphs**. There are, however, some less common types of tables or graphs that show up from time to time that can be confusing at first glance.

Histograms, piecewise graphs, and circle graphs could all show up on the Math Test. They shouldn't be difficult to interpret, but it's helpful to keep in mind that the test maker often includes more information than you actually need. It's important to consider what the question asks for so that you find only the information that you need.

- **Histograms** look a lot like bar charts and can be read in the same way, but they show how many times a certain value shows up in a number range (as opposed to showing counts of various groups).
  - The numbers on the x-axis provide the boundaries for each bar's range.

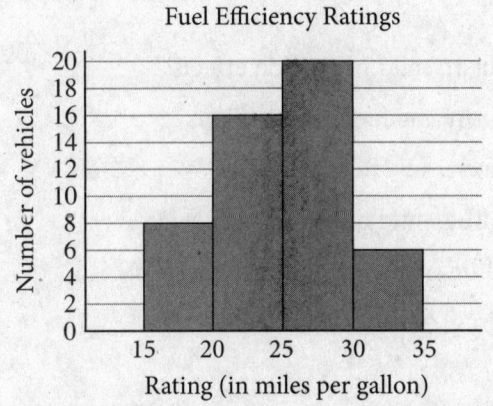

- **Piecewise graphs** are graphs created from functions that are defined, literally, by multiple pieces.
  - The domain, the set of x-values, is what determines the breaks between pieces.
  - The pieces can be similar or vastly different. All of the pieces could be horizontal segments of the same length that "jump" y-coordinates at designated x-values. Alternatively, one piece could be part of a linear function, one piece could be part of a quadratic function, one piece could be a single y-value, etc.

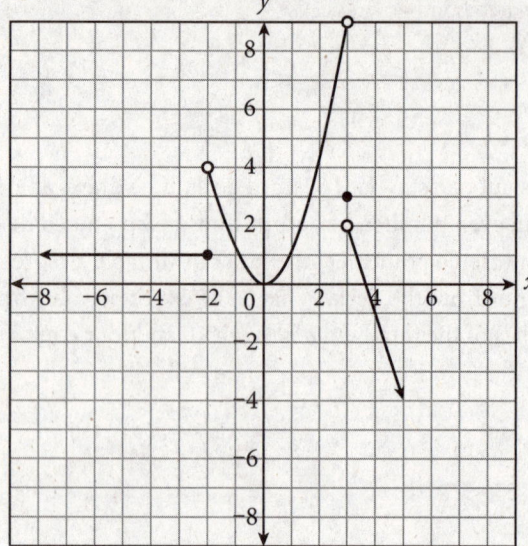

$$f(x) = \begin{cases} 1, & \text{if } x \leq -2 \\ x^2, & \text{if } -2 < x < 3 \\ 3, & \text{if } x = 3 \\ -3x + 11 & \text{if } x > 3 \end{cases}$$

- **Circle graphs** (also called **pie graphs**) represent data as parts of a circle where relative percentages dictate the portions of the circle.
  - When displaying data in a circle graph, find the measures of the central angles for each sector of the circle. To do this, multiply each percent by 360°.
  - For example, a sector that represents 35% of the data should have a central angle that measures approximately $0.35(360°) = 126°$.
  - When you're done, the percentages should sum to 100%, and the angle measures should sum to 360°.

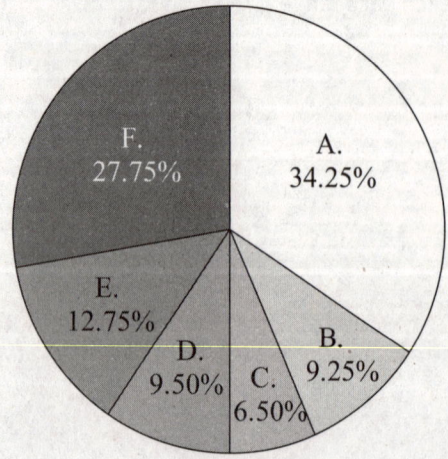

A. inert, mild or no side effects

B. inert, moderate side effects

C. inert, severe side effects

D. drug, mild or no side effects

E. drug, moderate side effects

F. drug, severe side effects

Chapter 11
Tables, Graphs, Statistics, and Probability

You need to do this

When presented with a question that uses a graph or table to present information, first inspect the format of the graph or table. What kind of graph or table is it? What information is presented on each axis? What information do you need to find in order to answer the question?

Find the information you need from the table or graph, and then use the information for any calculation the question might require, such as taking the average, finding the median, or determining the expected value.

Explanation

The question asks for the expected value of x. There is a lot of information in this question, so make a table to organize it:

Draw	Points
Odd	2
Even	3
Face	4

Next, determine the probability of drawing an odd, an even, or a face card. Remember that there are 4 odd numbers and 5 even numbers in each of the 4 suits:

Draw	Probability
Odd	$\frac{16}{52}$
Even	$\frac{20}{52}$
Face	$\frac{16}{52}$

Next, update the first table with the probabilities you found in the second table:

Draw	Probability	Points
Odd	$\frac{16}{52}$	2
Even	$\frac{20}{52}$	3
Face	$\frac{16}{52}$	4

Finally, calculate the expected value. Think of expected value as a weighted average: multiply the number of points Callum earns by the probability of getting these points and then adding those products together. Expected value is designed to give an idea of the "long-term" behavior of the probability distribution: how many points Callum would expect to earn per card if he kept drawing cards for years and years.

$$\frac{16}{52}(2) + \frac{20}{52}(3) + \frac{16}{52}(4)$$

$$\frac{32}{52} + \frac{60}{52} + \frac{64}{52}$$

$$\frac{156}{52}$$

$$3$$

The expected value of x is 3, so (C) is correct. This makes intuitive sense, since 3 points is the midpoint between 2 and 4.

Try on Your Own

Directions: Take as much time as you need on these questions. Work carefully and methodically. There will be an opportunity for timed practice at the end of the chapter.

HINT: Expected value is really just a weighted average. Review the first question and associated explanation from earlier in this lesson if needed to answer Q1.

1. Dr. Li has taught 1,520 university students over the past 10 years. The grade points (0–4) earned by past students and their corresponding probabilities are recorded in the table shown. Based on this probability distribution, what is the expected number of grade points that a randomly selected student in her class this semester can expect to earn?

Grade points	Probability
4	0.20
3	0.35
2	0.30
1	0.10
0	0.05

A. 2.0
B. 2.25
C. 2.55
D. 3

2. The following table shows the number of infants born in a certain hospital in August 2016. The table categorizes the births by gender and whether the infant was below, above, or within the healthy weight range, as defined by the World Health Organization. Approximately what percent of the infants born at this hospital in August 2016 were below the healthy weight range?

	Below range	Within range	Above range	Total
Male	1	56	10	67
Female	8	48	5	61
Total	9	104	15	128

F. 7%
G. 9%
H. 12%
J. 15%

Chapter 11
Tables, Graphs, Statistics, and Probability

3. The table shows the current inventory of Ariat's Boot Store. The table categorizes the boots by type and price range. Each week, Mr. Yin, the owner of Ariat's Boot Store, randomly selects one pair of cowboy boots and one pair of hiking boots to put in the store window display. What is the probability that this week's display includes a pair of hiking boots costing between $20 and $99?

	$20–59	$60–99	$100+	Total
Cowboy	56	88	23	167
Hiking	72	78	14	164
Total	128	166	37	331

A. $\frac{150}{331}$

B. $\frac{164}{331}$

C. $\frac{37}{82}$

D. $\frac{75}{82}$

4. Phase I clinical trials are run to determine the safety of an investigational drug. Dr. Gibbons is overseeing a treatment-resistant influence Phase I trial with 400 healthy participants. Half are given the drug, and half are given an inert pill. The circle graph below shows a distribution of the severity of common side effects. What percent of the participants experienced severe side effects?

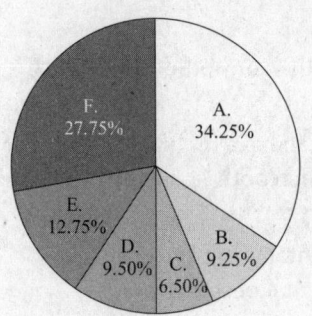

A. inert, mild or no side effects
B. inert, moderate side effects
C. inert, severe side effects
D. drug, mild or no side effects
E. drug, moderate side effects
F. drug, severe side effects

F. 6.50%

G. 21.25%

H. 27.75%

J. 34.25%

5. The following table shows the sales of all six items offered by Poppin Food Truck during the first day of the Allen Springs' Founder's Carnival. A total of 500 items were sold. How many more meals or appetizers costing more than $8.00 were sold than other items?

Item	Type	Cost	% of Total Sales
Poppin's Combo	Meal	$13.50	23%
Salad Combo	Meal	$10.50	17%
Child's Meal	Meal	$8.00	5%
Potato Skins	Appetizer	$8.50	27%
Onion Rings	Appetizer	$6.75	9%
Pretzel Waffle	Dessert	$9.00	19%

A. 125

B. 170

C. 225

D. 335

Part 3
ACT MATH

STATISTICS

LEARNING OBJECTIVE

After this lesson, you will be able to:

- Calculate mean, median, mode, range, and expected value

To answer a question like this

The average of a list of 3 distinct numbers is 20. A new list of 3 distinct numbers has the same median as the original list and the same largest number as the original list. The range of the new list is 3 greater than the range of the original list. What is the average of this new list of numbers?

A. 19
B. 20
C. 22
D. 23

You need to know this

Suppose a nurse took a patient's pulse at different times of day and found it to be 75, 78, 71, 71, and 68. Here are four fundamental statistics figures you can determine for this data set:

- **Mean** (also called arithmetic mean or average): The sum of the values divided by the number of values. For this data set, the mean pulse is $\frac{75 + 78 + 71 + 71 + 68}{5} = \frac{363}{5} = 72.6$.
  - When a question involves the mean, or average, it is often helpful to write out the average formula and use it to determine the missing piece(s):

  $$\text{average} = \frac{\text{sum of values}}{\text{\# of values}}$$

- **Median:** The value that is in the middle of the set when the values are arranged in ascending order. The pulse values in ascending order are 68, 71, 71, 75, and 78. The middle term is the third term, making the median 71. (If the list consists of an even number of values, the median is the average of the middle two values.)

- **Mode:** The value that occurs most frequently. The value that appears more than any other is 71, which appears twice (while all other numbers appear only once), so it is the mode.
  - If more than one value appears the most often, that's okay; a set of data can have multiple modes. For example, if the nurse took the patient's pulse a sixth time and it was 68, then both 71 and 68 would be modes for this data set.
  - A set of data can also have no mode. For example, if the nurse had accidentally written down the 71 twice and removed one, the new data set would not have any number that occurs the most frequently, and therefore, there would not be a mode.

- **Range:** The difference between the highest and lowest values. In this data set, the lowest and highest values are 68 and 78, respectively; so the range is $78 - 68 = 10$.

Chapter 11
Tables, Graphs, Statistics, and Probability

You need to do this

When a question involves averages or modes, the order of the values does not matter. To determine a missing value, write out the sum in the average formula as shown below:

$$\text{average} = \frac{\text{value 1} + \text{value 2} + \text{value 3} + \text{value 4}}{4}$$

Then, fill in the information given in the question stem and use algebra to solve.

To find the median, arrange all values in order. In a histogram, that means finding the group with the middle value.

Explanation

The question asks for the average of the new list after changes are made to the original list of numbers. Recall that $\text{average} = \frac{\text{sum of terms}}{\text{number of terms}}$. "The average of a list of 3 numbers is 20" can therefore be written as:

$$\frac{a+b+c}{3} = 20$$
$$a+b+c = 60$$

The new list contains the same median and the same largest number as the original list, so it also contains b and c. However, you are told that the range of the new list is 3 greater than the original list. This means that the smallest element of the new list is 3 smaller than a:

$$x = a - 3$$

Plug these numbers into the average formula and simplify. Remember that $a + b + c = 60$:

$$\begin{aligned}\text{average} &= \frac{x+b+c}{3}\\ &= \frac{(a-3)+b+c}{3}\\ &= \frac{(a+b+c)-3}{3}\\ &= \frac{60-3}{3}\\ &= \frac{57}{3}\\ &= 19\end{aligned}$$

The average of the new list is 19, so choice (A) is correct.

Part 3
ACT MATH

Try on Your Own

Directions: Take as much time as you need on these questions. Work carefully and methodically. There will be an opportunity for timed practice at the end of the chapter.

1. What is the average of the expressions $2x + 5$, $5x - 6$, and $-4x + 2$?

    A. $x - \frac{1}{3}$
    B. $x + \frac{1}{3}$
    C. $3x + 3$
    D. $3x - 3$

HINT: For Q2, what information do you need to determine the range of a data set?

---

2. The list of numbers 21, 31, 5, x, y, 12 has a median of 14. What is the range of the list?

    F. 26
    G. 27.25
    H. 31
    J. Cannot be determined from the given information

3. The following table gives the frequency of grades in certain grade intervals for 25 test grades in an AP Statistics class. Which interval contains the median of the grades?

Grade interval	Frequency
A (91–100)	5
B (81–90)	7
C (71–80)	7
D (61–70)	4
F (60 and below)	2

    A. A (91–100)
    B. B (81–90)
    C. C (71–80)
    D. D (61–70)

4. Lunenburg County has 4 public parks. The following pictograph shows the number of trees in each park. What is the average number of trees per park in Lunenburg County?

    Number of Trees in Public Parks in Lunenburg County

    East Side 🌳🌳🌳
    West Side 🌳🌳🌳🌳
    Town Center 🌳🌳
    Court House 🌳

    🌳 = 50 trees

    F. 75
    G. 125
    H. 150
    J. 200

5. The list of numbers 3, 6, 7, $2x + 1$, $x - 12$ has an arithmetic mean of 1.6. What is the mode of this list of numbers?

    A. 1
    B. 3
    C. 4
    D. 7

Chapter 11
Tables, Graphs, Statistics, and Probability

PROBABILITY

> **LEARNING OBJECTIVE**
>
> After this lesson, you will be able to:
> - Calculate probabilities based on data sets

To answer a question like this

Alicia is playing a game in which she draws marbles from a box. There are fifty marbles, numbered 1 through 50. Alicia draws one marble from the box and sets it aside, then draws a second marble. If both marbles have the same units digit, then Alicia wins. If the first marble she draws is numbered 25, what is the probability that Alicia will win on her next draw?

A. $\frac{1}{49}$

B. $\frac{2}{25}$

C. $\frac{4}{49}$

D. $\frac{9}{49}$

You need to know this

Probability is a fraction or decimal between 0 and 1 comparing the number of desired outcomes to the number of total possible outcomes.

- The formula is:

$$\text{probability} = \frac{\text{number of desired outcomes}}{\text{number of total possible outcomes}}$$

- A probability of 0 means that an event will not occur; a probability of 1 means that it definitely will occur.
  - For instance, if you roll a six-sided die, each side showing a different number from 1 to 6, the probability of rolling a number higher than 4 is $\frac{2}{6} = \frac{1}{3}$ because there are two numbers higher than 4 (5 and 6) and six numbers total (1, 2, 3, 4, 5, and 6).
  - To find the probability that an event will not happen, subtract the probability that the event will happen from 1.
  - Continuing the previous example, the probability of not rolling a number higher than 4 would be $1 - \frac{1}{3} = \frac{2}{3}$.
- The ACT tests probability in the context of data tables. Using a table, you can find the probability that a randomly selected data value (be it a person, an object, etc.) will fit a certain profile.
- Expected value is the weighted average of all possible values that the variable can take on; for the ACT, you will need to have a basic understanding of what expected value is and a strong understanding of how to calculate it based on a probability distribution table.
  - Calculating expected value from a probability distribution table is very straightforward: simply multiply each outcome by its corresponding probability and add the results.
  - Word problems that involve expected value will often call it something different, so look out for questions involving weighted averages and follow this process when needed.

Part 3
ACT MATH

You need to do this

- Determine the number of desired **and total** possible outcomes by looking at the table.
- Read the question carefully when **determining** the number of possible outcomes: do you need the entire set or a subset?
- Calculate probabilities and expected values based on the data in the table(s).

Explanation

The question outlines a game scenario **and asks** for the probability that Alicia wins on her next draw. Recall that probability = $\frac{\text{desired}}{\text{total}}$. Since Alicia has already drawn a 25, there are 49 marbles left in the box. She needs a 5, 15, 35, or 45 to match the units digit of 5 and win, so there are 4 desired numbers.

$$\text{probability} = \frac{\text{desired}}{\text{total}} = \frac{4}{49}$$

Choice (C) is correct.

Try on Your Own

Directions: Take as much time as you need on these questions. Work carefully and methodically. There will be an opportunity for timed practice at the end of the chapter.

HINT: For Q1, are the probabilities dependent or independent? What does that mean for your calculations?
---

1. In 3 fair coin tosses, what is the probability of obtaining at least 2 heads? (Note: In a fair coin toss, the 2 outcomes of heads and tails are equally likely.)

   A. $\frac{1}{8}$
   B. $\frac{1}{2}$
   C. $\frac{2}{3}$
   D. $\frac{7}{8}$

2. Two events are *dependent* if the outcome of one event affects the outcome of the other event. One of the following statements describes dependent events. Which one? (Note: The standard 52-card deck comprises 13 ranks in each of the 4 distinct card categories.)

   F. A coin lands heads up. Then an ace is drawn from a deck of cards.
   G. A coin lands tails up. Then a 6-sided die lies with a 5 face up.
   H. A 6-sided die lies with a 3 face up. Then a queen is drawn from a deck of cards.
   J. A king is drawn from a deck of cards and set aside. Then a queen is drawn from the same deck.

Chapter 11
Tables, Graphs, Statistics, and Probability

3. The following figure shows the number of people enrolled in different divisions in a local power-lifting meet. If 1 person is randomly selected out of the 150 total lifters, what is the probability that this person is a member of either the Class I or the Elite division?

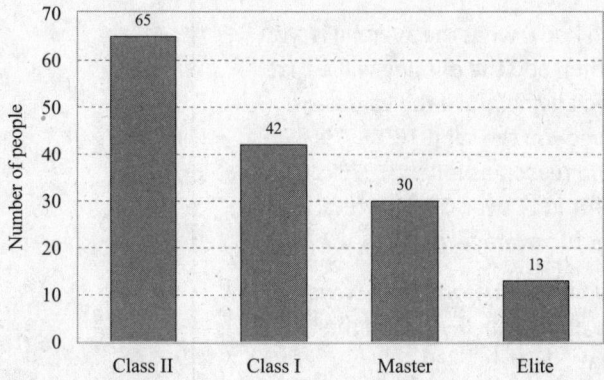

   A. $\dfrac{13}{150}$

   B. $\dfrac{42}{150}$

   C. $\dfrac{55}{150}$

   D. $\dfrac{95}{150}$

4. To be admitted into the Springfield Technological Academy, applicants must pass both a written and an oral test. Academy records show that 50% of applicants pass the written test, and 20% of the applicants who pass the written test pass the oral test. Based on these figures, how many persons in a random group of 800 applicants would you expect to be admitted to Springfield Technological Academy?

   F. 80
   G. 160
   H. 400
   J. 560

HINT: For Q5, don't stop too soon. Completing all of the steps for this question will take some time and careful calculator use.

5. In a darts tournament, Lorena and her friends use a scoring system that awards points only when the player hits the same number that is announced before throwing. Landing a dart anywhere within a number's "wedge" counts as a hit and earns a score of that number. No points are awarded for hitting a different number. The following table shows the probability of hitting the announced number and how many throws Lorena attempted. What is Lorena's expected total score from the tournament?

Number, n, announced	Probability of hitting n in a throw	Number of throws Lorena attempted
15	0.25	12
16	0.70	20
17	0.80	15
18	0.75	24
19	0.80	30
20	0.85	60

   A. 161
   B. 1,020
   C. 2,273
   D. 2,983

On Test Day

The average formula will serve you well on questions that ask about a sum of values or the average of a set of values, but for questions that give you the average and ask for a missing value in the data set, there is an alternative that can be faster: the balance approach.

The balance approach is based on the idea that if you know what the average is, you can find the totals on both sides of the average and then add the missing value that makes both sides balance out. This approach is especially helpful if the values are large and closely spaced. Imagine that a question gives you the set {976, 980, 964, 987, x} and tells you that the average is 970. You would reason as follows: 976 is 6 over the average, 980 is 10 over, 964 is 6 under, and 987 is 17 over. That's a total of $6 + 10 - 6 + 17 = 27$ over, so x needs to be 27 under the average, or $970 - 27 = 943$.

Try solving this question, which is similar to one you've seen before, both ways, using first the average formula and then the balance approach. If you find the latter to be fast and intuitive, add it to your test day arsenal.

1. Deepa scored 150, 195, and 160 in 3 bowling games. What should she score on her next bowling game if she wants to have an average score of exactly 175 for the 4 games?

    A. 205
    B. 195
    C. 185
    D. 175

The correct answer and both ways of solving can be found at the end of the chapter.

Chapter 11
Tables, Graphs, Statistics, and Probability

How Much Have You Learned?

Directions: For test-like practice, give yourself 10 minutes to complete this question set. Be sure to study the explanations, even for questions you got correct. They can be found at the end of this chapter.

1. The following table shows the number of students in Jordan High School. The table categorizes students by grade level and whether or not they are taking Driver's Education. Approximately what percent of juniors are NOT enrolled in Driver's Ed?

	Freshman	Sophomore	Junior	Senior	Total
Enrolled in Driver's Ed	98	381	200	85	764
Not enrolled in Driver's Ed	491	118	251	355	1,215
Total	589	499	451	440	1,979

   A. 13%
   B. 26%
   C. 44%
   D. 56%

2. A local company has 460 employees. Of these employees, 20% have a Master of Business Administration (MBA). Suppose two employees are randomly selected one at a time from the company's employees. What is the approximate probability that the first employee will have an MBA and the second will not?

   F. 0.20
   G. 0.16
   H. 0.46
   J. 0.80

3. Laisha works as a software salesperson. The following graph shows Laisha's sales for the year 2023. What is her median number of sales per month?

   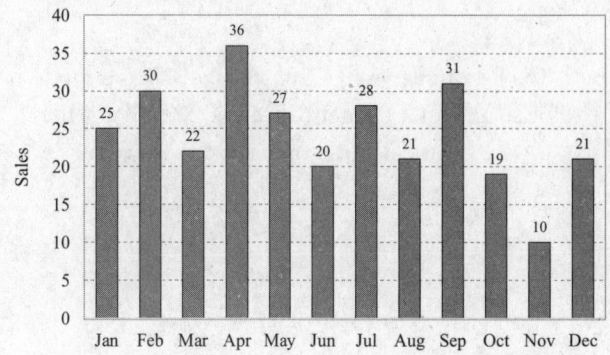

   A. 22
   B. 23.5
   C. 24.5
   D. 25

4. The average of a list of 5 numbers is 110. A new list of 5 numbers has the same first 3 numbers as the original list. The average of the last two numbers in the original list is 70, and the average of the last two numbers in the new list is 75. What is the average of this new list of numbers?

   F. 110
   G. 112
   H. 113.5
   J. 115

Part 3
ACT MATH

5. If you randomly pick an integer between 1 and 25, inclusive, what is the probability that it is both odd and prime?

   A. $\frac{7}{25}$
   B. $\frac{8}{25}$
   C. $\frac{9}{25}$
   D. $\frac{17}{25}$

6. The list of integers 15, 20, 26, x, y, 32 has a mode of 26 and an arithmetic mean of 27. What is the median of the list of numbers?

   F. 23
   G. 23.5
   H. 26
   J. 32

7. Roman is playing a game in which he draws cards from a standard 52-card deck. Roman draws one card from the deck, sets it aside, then draws a second card. Roman wins if the color of the first card is the same as the color of the second card. If the first card that Roman draws is red, what is the probability that he will win on his next draw? (Note: A standard deck of cards contains 26 red cards and 26 black cards.)

   A. $\frac{25}{104}$
   B. $\frac{25}{52}$
   C. $\frac{25}{51}$
   D. $\frac{1}{2}$

8. At the state fair, Mai plays a game in which she rolls a pair of fair 6-sided dice. She is awarded 10 points if the sum of the numbers on the dice is either 2 or 12. She is awarded 5 points if the sum of the numbers on the dice is between 3 and 5, inclusive, or 9 and 11, inclusive. Finally, she is awarded 3 points if the sum of the numbers on the dice is between 6 and 8, inclusive. Let the random variable x represent the total number of points awarded on any given roll of the dice. What is the approximate expected value of x? (Note: A fair 6-sided die has six sides numbered 1 through 6. When a fair die is rolled, each of the six outcomes is equally likely.)

   F. 3.55
   G. 4.39
   H. 5
   J. 6.79

9. Jin's Xtreme Xscape Rooms includes 3 keys to the doors out of the room. To make the puzzle more challenging, Jin adds 5 other keys that do not open any door. Jin puts all of the keys together in a bag. If you walk into the escape room and select a key at random, what is the probability that it will NOT open any door?

   A. $\frac{3}{8}$
   B. $\frac{3}{5}$
   C. $\frac{5}{8}$
   D. $\frac{7}{8}$

10. Consider the data set {1, 6, −1, 9, −5}. What is the positive difference between its range and its median?

    F. 1
    G. 5
    H. 13
    J. 15

Chapter 11
Tables, Graphs, Statistics, and Probability

Reflect

Directions: Take a few minutes to recall what you've learned and what you've been practicing in this chapter. Consider the following questions, jot down your best answer for each one, and then compare your reflections to the expert responses on the following page. Use your level of confidence to determine what to do next.

1. What are some common ways the ACT may present data?
   _____
   _____
   _____

2. What is the difference between median, mode, and range?
   _____
   _____
   _____

3. What is expected value?
   _____
   _____
   _____

4. What are two ways to calculate the probability of a single event?
   _____
   _____
   _____

Responses

1. What are some common ways the ACT may present data?

The ACT may present data in tables, bar graphs, histograms, pie graphs, and piecewise graphs.

2. What is the difference between median, mode, and range?

The median of a set is the middle value, whereas the mode is the most common value. The range of a set is the distance between the smallest value and the largest one.

3. What is expected value?

Expected value is the weighted average of all possible values that the variable can take on.

4. What are two ways to calculate the probability of a single event?

The fundamental probability formula is:

$$\text{probability} = \frac{\text{number of desired outcomes}}{\text{number of total possible outcomes}}$$

Alternatively, the probability that an event happens is 1 minus the probability that it doesn't happen.

Next Steps

If you answered most questions correctly in the "How Much Have You Learned?" section, and if your responses to the Reflect questions were similar to those of the ACT expert, then consider tables and graphs, statistics, and probability areas of strength and move on to the next chapter. Come back to this topic periodically to prevent yourself from getting rusty.

If you don't yet feel confident, review those parts of this chapter that you have not yet mastered, then try the questions you missed again. As always, be sure to review the explanations closely. Then go online (**kaptest.com/login**) for more practice. If you haven't already registered your book, do so at **kaptest.com/moreonline**.

GO ONLINE
kaptest.com/login

Answers and Explanations

Tables and Graphs

1. C
Difficulty: High
Category: Statistics and Probability
Getting to the Answer: The question asks for the expected number of grade points that a random student in Dr. Li's class will earn. Recall from the first question in this lesson that expected value is really a weighted average: calculate it by multiplying the grade points by the probability of getting these points and then adding everything together at the end.

$$4(0.20) + 3(0.35) + 2(0.30) + 1(0.10)$$
$$= 0.80 + 1.05 + 0.60 + 0.10$$
$$= 2.55$$

Choice (C) is correct.

2. F
Difficulty: Low
Category: Statistics and Probability
Getting to the Answer: The question asks for the percent of infants who were born below the healthy weight range. According to the table, 9 infants were born below the healthy weight range in August 2016. The table also shows that a total of 128 infants were born in August 2016. Plug these two numbers into the percent formula.

$$\text{percent} = \frac{\text{part}}{\text{whole}} \times 100\%$$
$$= \frac{9}{128} \times 100\%$$
$$\approx 0.07 \times 100\%$$
$$\approx 7\%$$

Choice (F) is correct.

3. D
Difficulty: Medium
Category: Statistics and Probability
Getting to the Answer: Read the question carefully! A pair of hiking boots is being randomly selected, not from the *total* number of boots, but from the *hiking boots* only. This means that you should look only at the second row of the table and ignore everything else.

According to the table, 72 hiking boots are in the $20–$59 range and 78 are in the $60–$99 range. Quickly find how many hiking boots are in the $20–$99 range by adding the two: $72 + 78 = 150$. There is a total of 164 hiking boots. Plug these numbers into the probability formula and simplify.

$$\text{probability} = \frac{\text{desired \#}}{\text{total \#}}$$
$$= \frac{150}{164}$$
$$= \frac{75}{82}$$

Choice (D) is correct.

4. J
Difficulty: Low
Category: Statistics and Probability
Getting to the Answer: Look carefully at the graph's legend. Categories C and F are both marked as severe side effects. Add these two percents together to get the total percentage of participants with severe side effects: $6.5\% + 27.75\% = 34.25\%$.

Choice (J) is correct.

5. B
Difficulty: Medium
Category: Statistics and Probability
Getting to the Answer: The question asks how many more items sold were either meals or appetizers costing more than $8.00. These items include Poppin's Combo, the Salad Combo, and the Potato Skins. (Be careful not to include the Child's Meal: it costs $8.00, which is not *more* than $8.00). According to the table, these make up 23%, 17%, and 27% of the sales. So $23\% + 17\% + 27\% = 67\%$ of the total sales. Since 500 total items were sold, $500(0.67) = 335$ items sold were either meals or appetizers costing more than $8.00.

To find the total number of other items sold, subtract the amount you found above from the 500 total items sold: $500 - 335 = 165$.

The question asks how many more items sold by Poppin Food Truck are meals or appetizers costing more than $8.00 than other items, so subtract these two numbers:
$335 - 165 = 170$.

Choice (B) is correct.

Statistics

1. B
Difficulty: Medium
Category: Statistics and Probability
Getting to the Answer: The question asks for the average of the given expressions, and all of the choices contain the variable x. Don't let this intimidate you, though. Just apply the average formula, combine like terms, and simplify:

$$\text{average} = \frac{\text{sum of terms}}{\text{number of terms}}$$
$$= \frac{(2x+5) + (5x-6) + (-4x+2)}{3}$$
$$= \frac{3x+1}{3}$$
$$= \frac{3x}{3} + \frac{1}{3}$$
$$= x + \frac{1}{3}$$

Choice (B) is correct.

2. J
Difficulty: High
Category: Statistics and Probability
Getting to the Answer: The question asks you to calculate the range of the given list, which includes two variables. Recall that the range is the biggest number in the list minus the smallest number in the list. The median is the middle number when the data set is arranged in increasing order. Since there are an even number of terms, the median is the average of the two middle terms.

In a question like this that allows for many possibilities for x and y, try Picking Numbers to see if you can find values that yield a median of 14.

One way is to let $x = 7$ and $y = 16$. This gives a median of 14 because $\frac{12+16}{2} = 14$. When the data set is arranged in increasing order, it looks like:

5, 7, 12, 16, 21, 31

The range of this data set is $31 - 5 = 26$.

Notice that letting $y = 16$ gives you considerable freedom for what you can pick for x. As long as x is less than 12, the median will still be 14. There is thus the possibility of obtaining a different value for the range. With this in mind, let $x = 3$ and $y = 16$. When the data set is arranged in increasing order, it looks like:

3, 7, 12, 16, 21, 31

The range of this data set is $31 - 3 = 28$.

Since there are at least two possibilities for the range, it cannot be determined from the information given. Choice (J) is correct.

3. C
Difficulty: Medium
Category: Statistics and Probability
Getting to the Answer: The question asks which interval contains the median of the grades. Recall that the median is the middle number when the data set is arranged in increasing order. Since there are 25 total terms, the median is the 13th term. Working upward from the lowest grades, there are 2 F's, 4 D's, and 7 C's, so the 13th term is in the C grade interval.

Choice (C) is correct.

4. G
Difficulty: Low
Category: Statistics and Probability
Getting to the Answer: The question asks for the average number of trees in the parks based on the pictograph. Since each tree in the pictograph represents 50 real trees, East Side contains 150 trees, West Side 200 trees, Town Center 100 trees, and Court House 50 trees. Plug these numbers into the average formula:

$$\text{average} = \frac{150 + 200 + 100 + 50}{4}$$
$$= \frac{500}{4}$$
$$= 125$$

Choice (G) is correct.

5. B
Difficulty: Medium
Category: Statistics and Probability
Getting to the Answer: The question asks for the mode of the given list of numbers. Don't let the variables intimidate you; just apply the average formula and solve for x:

$$\frac{3 + 6 + 7 + (2x+1) + (x-12)}{5} = 1.6$$
$$3 + 6 + 7 + 2x + 1 + x - 12 = 8$$
$$5 + 3x = 8$$
$$3x = 3$$
$$x = 1$$

Next, plug $x = 1$ back in to see what the data set looks like.

$$3, 6, 7, 3, -11$$

Finally, recall that the mode is the most frequently occurring number in the data set. The mode is thus 3; therefore, (B) is correct.

Probability

1. B
Difficulty: High
Category: Statistics and Probability
Getting to the Answer: The question asks for the probability of obtaining at least 2 heads when a coin is flipped 3 times. Since the coin is being flipped 3 times, the phrase "at least 2 heads" means either 2 heads *or* 3 heads. Consider each situation separately:

First, think about the different ways in which you could get 2 heads. It is helpful to write down the different possibilities for each coin:

$$\text{HHT}$$
$$\text{HTH}$$
$$\text{THH}$$

Now think about the ways in which you could get 3 heads. This is much simpler:

$$\text{HHH}$$

All together, there are $3 + 1 = 4$ different ways to obtain at least 2 heads.

Next, calculate the total number of possible outcomes of flipping a coin 3 times. Since each flip has exactly 2 possibilities (heads or tails), there are $(2)(2)(2) = 8$ possible outcomes.

Finally, plug these numbers into the probability formula:

$$\text{probability} = \frac{\text{\# of desired outcomes}}{\text{\# of total possible outcomes}}$$
$$= \frac{1+3}{8}$$
$$= \frac{4}{8}$$
$$= \frac{1}{2}$$

Choice (B) is correct.

2. J
Difficulty: Low
Category: Statistics and Probability
Getting to the Answer: The question defines dependent events and then asks you to find an example. Work through each answer choice systematically.

Flipping a coin and drawing a card are two completely separate processes and do not affect each other in any way. Therefore, F is incorrect.

Similarly, flipping a coin and rolling a die are independent events. Eliminate G.

Finally, rolling a die and drawing a card are also independent. Choice H is incorrect.

By process of elimination, (J) must be correct.

3. C
Difficulty: Low
Category: Statistics and Probability
Getting to the Answer: The question asks for the probability of randomly selecting a person who is competing in either the Class I or the Elite division. Recall that $\text{probability} = \frac{\text{\# of desired outcomes}}{\text{\# of total possible outcomes}}$. Since there are 150 lifters in the competition, the total is 150. There are 42 lifters in the Class I division and 13 lifters in the Elite division, so the number of desired lifters is $42 + 13 = 55$. Plug these numbers into the probability formula.

$$\text{probability} = \frac{\text{desired}}{\text{total}} = \frac{55}{150}$$

Choice (C) is correct.

Be certain that you answered the question that was asked. For example, choice D is the probability that the selected contestant is in the Class II or Master division.

4. F
Difficulty: Low
Category: Statistics and Probability
Getting to the Answer: You are being asked for the total number of students who will be admitted from a group of 800 applicants. First, calculate the number who pass the written test. Then, determine the number who pass the oral test as well.

The number of applicants who pass the written test is $800(0.50) = 400$. Out of these 400, only 20% pass the oral test. Thus, $400(0.20) = 80$ pass both the written and oral tests. Choice (F) is correct.

Be certain that you correctly interpreted the question. If you added the percentages to get a 70% pass rate, you would have incorrectly chosen J.

5. C
Difficulty: High
Category: Statistics and Probability
Getting to the Answer: Lorena's expected total score can be calculated by multiplying the number, n, by the probability of hitting n by the number of attempted throws:

- $0.25 \times 12 \times 15 = 45$
- $0.70 \times 20 \times 16 = 224$
- $0.80 \times 15 \times 17 = 204$
- $0.75 \times 24 \times 18 = 324$
- $0.80 \times 30 \times 19 = 456$
- $0.85 \times 60 \times 20 = 1,020$

These values represent Lorena's expected score based on the number announced. Lorena's expected total score, then, is the sum of these values: $45 + 224 + 204 + 324 + 456 + 1,020 = 2,273$ points, (C).

On Test Day

1. B
Difficulty: Medium
Category: Statistics and Probability
Getting to the Answer: The question asks what score a bowler must get for her next game to attain an average score of 175 for 4 games and gives the scores of her first 3 games. The average of a group of numbers is the sum of the values divided by the number of values. You can either set up and solve an equation involving the missing score or use the balance approach.

To answer the question algebraically, call the missing score x and set up the average equation:

$$\frac{150 + 195 + 160 + x}{4} = 175$$

$$505 + x = 700$$

$$x = 195$$

Choice (B) is correct.

Using the balance approach for averages, look at how far away each score in the question is from the desired average score. You could determine that the 150 score was 25 less than the desired average, the 195 score was 20 greater, and the 160 score was 15 less: $(-25) + 20 + (-15) = -20$. This is a total of 20 less than the desired average. Thus, the fourth score would need to be 20 more than the desired average to raise the average to 175: $175 + 20 = 195$. This approach also shows that (B) is correct.

How Much Have You Learned?

1. D
Difficulty: Low
Category: Statistics and Probability
Getting to the Answer: The question asks what percent of juniors are not enrolled in Driver's Ed. Recall that percent $= \dfrac{\text{part}}{\text{whole}} \times 100\%$. Since the question asks "what percent of juniors," the total number of juniors, 451, is the needed whole. According to the table, 251 juniors are not enrolled in Driver's Ed. Plug these numbers into the percent formula and simplify.

$$\text{percent} = \frac{\text{part}}{\text{whole}} \times 100\%$$

$$= \frac{251}{451} \times 100\%$$

$$\approx 0.556 \times 100\%$$

$$\approx 55.6\%$$

Choice (D) is correct.

Be certain that you answered the question that was asked! Choice C is the percentage of juniors that *are* enrolled in Driver's Ed.

2. G
Difficulty: Medium
Category: Statistics and Probability
Getting to the Answer: The question asks for the probability of selecting an employee with an MBA and then one without. First, find the probability of selecting an employee with a MBA degree.

$$0.20 \times 460 = 92 \text{ MBAs}$$

$$\text{probability} = \frac{\text{desired}}{\text{total}} = \frac{92}{460} = 0.20$$

Now, find the probability that the second employee selected will not have an MBA. Since you already picked out one employee, you must reduce the denominator by 1.

$$460 - 92 = 368$$

$$\text{probability} = \frac{\text{desired}}{\text{total}} = \frac{368}{459} \approx 0.8$$

In probability questions involving multiple events, the word "and" means to multiply. To find the probability of the first employee being an MBA *and* the second employee not, multiply the two individual probabilities together.

$$(0.2)(0.8) = 0.16$$

Since the question asks for the approximate probability, (G) is correct.

3. B
Difficulty: Low
Category: Statistics and Probability
Getting to the Answer: The question asks for the median of Laisha's sales in 2023. Recall that the median is the middle number when the data are arranged in increasing order. Since this data set is not in order, put it in order:

$$10, 19, 20, 21, 21, 22, 25, 27, 28, 30, 31, 36$$

This data set contains an even number of terms, so there are actually two middle numbers: 22 and 25. The median is the average of these two numbers.

$$\frac{22 + 25}{2} = \frac{47}{2} = 23.5$$

The median of Laisha's sales from 2023 is 23.5. Choice (B) is correct.

4. G
Difficulty: High
Category: Statistics and Probability
Getting to the Answer: The question asks for the average of the new list after changes are made to the original list. At its heart, this question is nothing more than a repeated application of the average formula:

$$\text{average} = \frac{\text{sum of terms}}{\text{number of terms}}$$

Methodically translate from English into math. "The average of a list of 5 numbers is 110" can be written as:

$$\frac{a + b + c + d + e}{5} = 110$$

This statement allows you to conclude that the sum of the variables $a + b + c + d + e$ is 550.

"A new list of 5 numbers has the same first 3 numbers as the original list" means that the new list includes a, b, and c. To avoid confusion, call the fourth and fifth numbers in the new list x and y.

Now, compare the averages of the last two numbers in each list. In the original list, the average of these two numbers is 70; this can be translated from English to math:

$$\frac{d + e}{2} = 70$$

This means the sum of $d + e = 140$, so the sum of $a + b + c = 550 - 140 = 410$.

Next, calculate the sum of the last two numbers in the new list. Fill in the average formula:

$$\frac{x + y}{2} = 75$$

This means that $x + y = 150$. Finally, "What is the average of this new list of numbers?" tells you what the question is asking for:

$$\frac{a + b + c + x + y}{5} = \text{average}$$

Since you determined that $a + b + c = 410$ and $x + y = 150$, you can plug these values into the formula:

$$\frac{410 + 150}{5} = \frac{560}{5} = 112$$

The average of the new list is 112. Choice (G) is correct.

5. B
Difficulty: Medium
Category: Statistics and Probability
Getting to the Answer: The question asks for the probability that a randomly selected integer between 1 to 25 inclusive will be both prime and odd. Recall that probability = $\frac{\text{desired}}{\text{total}}$. You are choosing out of a group of 25 numbers, so "total" is 25. To find "desired," simply write down all of the odd numbers between 1 and 25 and cross out the ones that are not prime, which leaves: 3, 5, 7, 11, 13, 17, 19, and 23. "Desired" is thus 8. Finally, plug these numbers into the probability formula.

$$\text{probability} = \frac{\text{desired}}{\text{total}} = \frac{8}{25}$$

Choice (B) is correct.

Be sure that you answered the correct question! You are asked about the numbers that are both **odd and prime**. You would arrive at C if you simply counted the number of primes between 1 and 25, not specifically the odd primes.

6. H
Difficulty: High
Category: Statistics and Probability
Getting to the Answer: The question asks for the median of the list of numbers. Recall that the mode of a data set is the number that occurs the most frequently. Thus, either $x = 26$, $y = 26$, or $x = y = 26$. At this point, you cannot tell.

Fortunately, you are also given that the arithmetic mean is 27. Set up an equation to obtain more information about x and y.

$$\frac{15 + 20 + 26 + x + y + 32}{6} = 27$$
$$15 + 20 + 26 + x + y + 32 = 162$$
$$93 + x + y = 162$$
$$x + y = 69$$

Since $26 + 26 = 52$, there is no way that x and y could both be 26. If $x = 26$, then $y = 69 - 26 = 43$. Thus, the list looks like:

$$15, 20, 26, 26, 32, 43$$

Recall that the median is the middle number when the data are arranged in increasing order. This data set contains an even number of terms, so there are actually two middle numbers: 26 and 26. The median is the average of these two numbers, which is just 26.

Thus, (H) is correct.

7. C
Difficulty: Medium
Category: Statistics and Probability
Getting to the Answer: The question asks for the probability that Roman will draw another red card, assuming that his first draw was also a red card. Recall that probability = $\frac{\text{desired}}{\text{total}}$. Since Roman has already picked out one card, there are 51 cards left in the deck. Similarly, since he has already set aside a red card,

there are 25 red cards left. Plug these two numbers into the probability formula.

$$\text{probability} = \frac{\text{desired}}{\text{total}} = \frac{25}{51}$$

Choice (C) is correct.

Be sure to read the question carefully! If you didn't remember that the first card drawn was not replaced in the deck, you would have picked B.

8. G
Difficulty: High
Category: Statistics and Probability
Getting to the Answer: This question outlines a game scenario and asks for the expected value. There is a lot of information here, so make a table to organize it:

Roll Total	Points
2 or 12	10
3, 4, 5, 9, 10, or 11	5
6, 7, or 8	3

Next, determine the probability of actually getting these rolls. Since there are two dice to keep track of, this is also best visualized with a table:

Roll Total	(Die 1, Die 2)	Probability
2	(1, 1)	$\frac{1}{36}$
3	(1, 2) (2, 1)	$\frac{2}{36}$
4	(1, 3) (2, 2) (3, 1)	$\frac{3}{36}$
5	(1, 4) (2, 3) (3, 2) (4, 1)	$\frac{4}{36}$

Chapter 11
Tables, Graphs, Statistics, and Probability

Roll Total	(Die 1, Die 2)	Probability
6	(1, 5) (2, 4) (3, 3) (4, 2) (5, 1)	$\frac{5}{36}$
7	(1, 6) (2, 5) (3, 4) (4, 3) (5, 2) (6, 1)	$\frac{6}{36}$
8	(2, 6) (3, 5) (4, 4) (5, 3) (6, 2)	$\frac{5}{36}$
9	(3, 6) (4, 5) (5, 4) (6, 3)	$\frac{4}{36}$
10	(4, 6) (5, 5) (6, 4)	$\frac{3}{36}$
11	(5, 6) (6, 5)	$\frac{2}{36}$
12	(6, 6)	$\frac{1}{36}$

Next, update the first table with the probabilities you found in the second table. Remember that if you want to find the probability of rolling a 3, 4, or 5, you must add these individual probabilities together:

Roll Total	Probability	Points
2 or 12	$\frac{2}{36}$	10
3, 4, 5, 9, 10, or 11	$\frac{18}{36}$	5
6, 7, or 8	$\frac{16}{36}$	3

Finally, calculate the expected value. Think of this as a weighted average: multiply the number of points Mai earns by the probability of getting these points and then add those products together.

$$10\left(\frac{2}{36}\right) + 5\left(\frac{18}{36}\right) + 3\left(\frac{16}{36}\right)$$

$$\frac{20}{36} + \frac{90}{36} + \frac{48}{36}$$

$$\frac{158}{36}$$

$$4.388$$

The expected value of x is 4.388, so (G) is correct. This makes sense since half of the results are 5 points, but there are more 3-point outcomes than 10-point outcomes. You would thus expect the result to be less than 5.

9. C
Difficulty: Low
Category: Statistics and Probability
Getting to the Answer: The question asks for the probability that a randomly selected key will not open any door. Recall that probability = $\frac{\text{desired}}{\text{total}}$. Since there were 3 keys originally and Jin added another 5, there are now 8 total. You are asked for the probability that a key does *not* open a door, so the desired number of keys is 5. Plug these numbers into the probability formula.

$$\text{probability} = \frac{\text{desired}}{\text{total}} = \frac{5}{8}$$

Choice (C) is correct.

Double-check that you answered the question that was asked. Choice A is the probability that the key *will* open a door.

10. H

Difficulty: Medium

Category: Statistics and Probability

Getting to the Answer: The question asks for the difference between the range and median of the given data set. The range is the difference between the highest and lowest values of the data set.

$$\text{range} = 9 - (-5) = 14$$

The median is the middle number when the numbers are arranged in increasing order.

$$\{-5, -1, 1, 6, 9\}$$

The median is 1.

The question asks for the difference between the range and the median, so subtract the two: $14 - 1 = 13$. Choice (H) is correct.

Be sure that you subtract the two values when finding the range. If you added 14 and 1, you would have picked J.

[CHAPTER 12]

FUNCTIONS

LEARNING OBJECTIVES

After completing this chapter, you will be able to:

- Apply function notation
- Define the domain and range of a function
- Evaluate the output of a function for a given input
- Interpret the graph of a function
- Write a function to describe a rule or data set
- Find coordinates of a point that is translated, reflected over an axis, or rotated about the origin
- Match graphs of basic trigonometric functions with their equations
- Use trigonometric concepts and basic identities to solve questions
- Given an equation or function, find an equation or function whose graph is a translation

Part 3
ACT MATH

How Much Do You Know?

Directions: Try out the questions below. Show your work so that you can compare your solutions to the ones found on the next page. The "Category" heading in the explanation for each question gives the title of the lesson that covers how to solve it. If you answered the question(s) for a given lesson correctly, and if your scratchwork looks like ours, you may be able to move quickly through that lesson. If you answered incorrectly or used a different approach, you may want to take your time on that lesson.

1. In the figure shown, what is the approximate value of $f(0) + g\left(\frac{1}{2}\right)$?

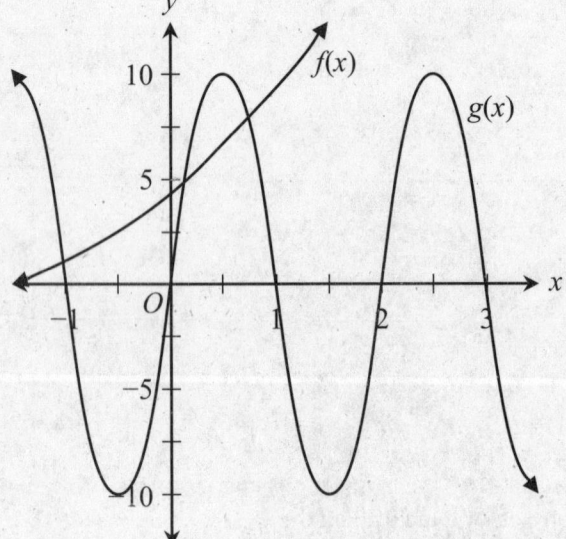

   A. 4
   B. 6
   C. 10
   D. 14

2. The following graph shows a transformation of the absolute value function, $f(x) = |x|$. Which equation best describes the transformation?

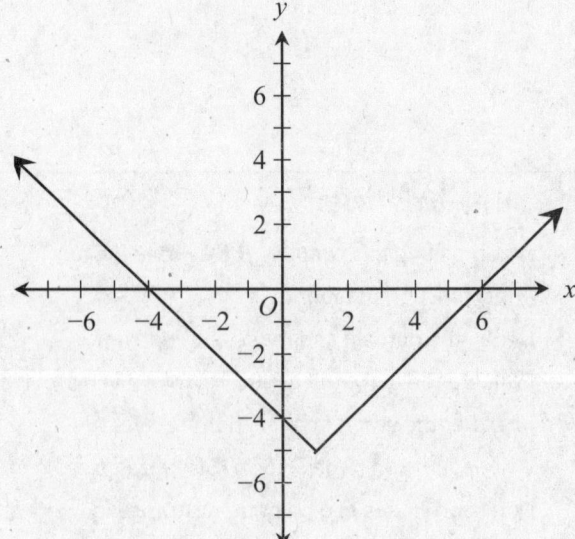

   F. $y = f(x + 1) - 5$
   G. $y = f(x - 1) - 5$
   H. $y = f(x - 1) + 5$
   I. $y = -f(x - 1) - 5$

3. If $a(x) = \sqrt{x^2 + 7}$ and $b(x) = x^3 - 7$, then what is the value of $\frac{a(3)}{b(2)}$?

   A. $\frac{\sqrt{11}}{20}$
   B. $\frac{1}{4}$
   C. $\sqrt{11}$
   D. 4

4. The following graph of f(x) is a quadratic equation. Which of the following represents the domain and range of the function?

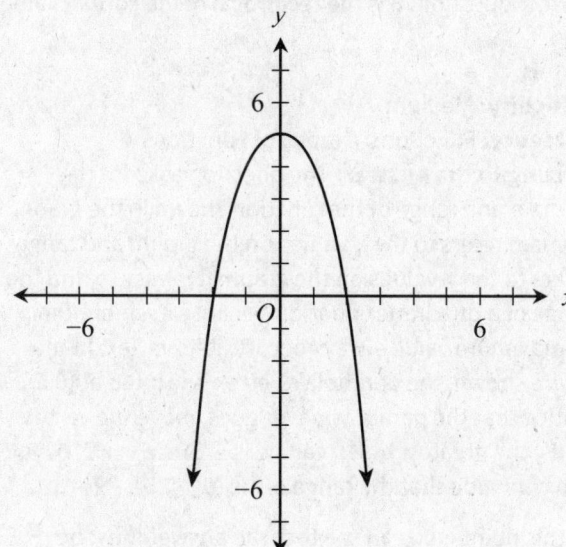

F. Domain: $f(x) \geq 5$; range: all real numbers
G. Domain: $f(x) \leq 5$; range: all real numbers
H. Domain: all real numbers; range: $f(x) \leq 5$
J. Domain: all real numbers; range: all real numbers

5. Which of the following correctly describes the range of the function $h(x) = 4x^2 - 9$?

A. All real numbers
B. All real numbers greater than or equal to -9
C. All real numbers between $-3/2$ and $3/2$
D. All real numbers between and including -9 and 9

6. If $p(x) = x^2 - 4x + 8$ and $q(x) = x - 3$, what is the value of $\dfrac{q(p(5))}{p(q(5))}$?

F. 0.4
G. 1
H. 2.5
J. 10

7. What is the amplitude of the function $f(x) = 4\sin(2x + \pi)$?

A. $\dfrac{1}{4}$
B. 2
C. π
D. 4

8. If $-2 \leq x \leq 2$, the maximum value of $f(x) = 1 - x^2$ is which of the following?

F. 2
G. 1
H. 0
J. -2

9. For the function $g(x) = 3x^2 - 5x - 7$, what is the value of $g(-2)$?

A. -29
B. -9
C. -5
D. 15

10. Suppose a polynomial function $p(x)$ has roots of -4 and 7. If $q(x)$ is a translation of $p(x)$ such that $q(x) = p(x - 2)$, through which two points must the graph of $q(x)$ pass?

F. $(-4, 0)$ and $(7, 0)$
G. $(-4, -2)$ and $(7, -2)$
H. $(-2, 0)$ and $(9, 0)$
J. $(-6, 0)$ and $(5, 0)$

Answers and Explanations

How Much Do You Know?

1. D
Difficulty: Low
Category: Functions: Graphs of Functions
Getting to the Answer: The question asks for the approximate sum of the values of the two functions on the graph at two specified points. Use the graph to find the y-values for the given x-values. For the graph f, when $x = 0$, $y = 4$. For the graph g, when $x = \frac{1}{2}$, $y = 10$. So, $f(0) + g\left(\frac{1}{2}\right) = 4 + 10 = 14$.

Thus, (D) is correct. Be certain that you answered the question that was asked. Choice B is what you would get if you evaluated $f\left(\frac{1}{2}\right) + g(0)$.

2. G
Difficulty: Medium
Category: Functions: Transformations
Getting to the Answer: The question asks for the choice that represents the transformation shown in the graph. Adding or subtracting inside of the function parentheses moves the function left or right. If you subtract 1 from x, the function shifts 1 to the right. The way the function moves is actually opposite of the sign; eliminate F.

Moving the function up or down is much more straightforward. The addition or subtraction *outside* of the parentheses moves the function vertically in the direction of the sign. In the above example, the function shifts down by 5, so the function should have −5 in the equation. Eliminate H.

The last difference is the positive or negative sign in front of the f(x − 1). A negative sign reflects, or flips, the function around the x-axis. Since the absolute value graph is opening upward, the sign should be positive. Eliminate J.

Therefore, (G) is correct.

3. D
Difficulty: Low
Category: Functions: Function Notation
Getting to the Answer: This question asks for the value of the function a(3) divided by the function b(2). The question defines the two functions, so just plug in the values:

$$\frac{a(3)}{b(2)} = \frac{\sqrt{(3)^2 + 7}}{(2)^3 - 7} = \frac{\sqrt{16}}{1} = \frac{4}{1} = 4$$

Hence, (D) is correct. Be certain that you answered the correct question; B is the reciprocal of the correct value.

4. H
Difficulty: Medium
Category: Functions: Graphs of Functions
Getting to the Answer: The question asks for the domain and range of the function shown in the graph. Domain refers to the x-values on the graph, and range refers to the y-values on the graph. It is easy to find the range of a quadratic equation because its minimum or maximum value always occurs at its vertex. In the figure shown, the parabola's vertex is located at (0,5). Notice that the parabola never goes above the vertex. Thus, the greatest that y can be is 5. Since $y = f(x)$, you can conclude that the range of f is $f(x) \leq 5$.

At this point, you can see that the answer must be (H). But, just to confirm, the domain is all real numbers because of the arrows on the parabola. These lines extend infinitely and thus will eventually pass through every x-value. Be certain that you correctly used domain and range since G reverses these.

5. B
Difficulty: Medium
Category: Functions: Function Notation
Getting to the Answer: The question asks which choice correctly describes the range of a given function. Range refers to the y-values on the graph (the "output" of the function). The function $4x^2 - 9$ is simply a transformed version of the more basic function x^2, an upward-opening parabola whose vertex is (0,0). Thinking about this more elementary function can help you understand the graph of $4x^2 - 9$.

Since the parabola x^2 opens upward, its minimum value is $y = 0$. Multiplying the x^2 by 4 makes the parabola "skinnier," but it will not affect its range. The −9 represents a downward shift. Thus, the minimum value is no longer 0, but −9. This means that the range is greater than or equal to −9.

Choice (B) is correct. Since you didn't have to do much calculating, be certain that your logic is correct.

6. H
Difficulty: Medium
Category: Functions: Function Notation
Getting to the Answer: The question asks for the value of dividing one nested combination of two functions

by another and provides the equations for the functions. When evaluating nested functions, start with the innermost parentheses and work your way out. First, find $p(5)$ and $q(5)$.

$$p(5) = (5)^2 - 4(5) + 8 \qquad q(5) = (5) - 3$$
$$p(5) = 25 - 20 + 8 \qquad q(5) = 2$$
$$p(5) = 13$$

Now, plug these values into the given expression and simplify.

$$\frac{q(p(5))}{p(q(5))} = \frac{q(13)}{p(2)} = \frac{(13) - 3}{(2)^2 - 4(2) + 8}$$
$$= \frac{10}{4 - 8 + 8}$$
$$= \frac{10}{4}$$
$$= 2.5$$

Choice (H) is correct. Be certain that you answered the exact question that was asked; F is the reciprocal of the correct value.

7. D
Difficulty: Medium
Category: Functions: Trigonometry on the Coordinate Plane
Getting to the Answer: The question asks for the amplitude of a given sine function. Think of the amplitude as the "height" of the sine function—the maximum difference from 0. The maximum value of $\sin(x)$ is 1, so its amplitude is 1. However, this question asks you to consider $4\sin(2x + \pi)$.

Think about the rules of translation: expressions inside the function parentheses affect horizontal shifts, while expressions outside the function parentheses affect vertical shifts. Since you are interested in the height of the sine function, the terms inside the function parentheses are irrelevant. The 4 on the outside vertically stretches the sine function by a factor of 4. Thus, the amplitude is $4(1) = 4$.

Choice (D) is correct.

8. G
Difficulty: Medium
Category: Functions: Function Notation
Getting to the Answer: The question asks for the maximum value of $f(x) = 1 - x^2$. You are given the allowable domain of x. The function $1 - x^2$ is simply a transformed version of the more basic function x^2, an upward-opening parabola whose vertex is (0,0). Thinking about this more elementary function can help you understand the graph of $1 - x^2$.

The negative sign in front of the x^2 term means that the parabola opens downward. Since the parabola x^2 opens downward, its maximum value is $y = 0$. The $+1$ shifts the function up by 1. Thus, the vertex is now at (0,1), and the maximum value is 1.

Choice (G) is correct.

9. D
Difficulty: Low
Category: Functions: Function Notation
Getting to the Answer: The question asks for the value of $g(x)$ when $x = 2$ and provides the equation for the function. Plug in $x = -2$ and simplify.

$$g(-2) = 3(-2)^2 - 5(-2) - 7$$
$$g(-2) = 3(4) - (-10) - 7$$
$$g(-2) = 12 + 10 - 7$$
$$g(-2) = 15$$

Hence, (D) is correct. Be certain that you used the correct value for x. Using $x = 2$ rather than $x = -2$ would result in choosing C.

10. H
Difficulty: High
Category: Functions: Transformations
Getting to the Answer: The question asks through which two points in the choices the graph of $q(x)$ passes. You are given that $q(x) = p(x - 2)$ and that $p(x)$ has roots of -4 and 7. Thus, the points $(-4, 0)$ and $(7, 0)$ lie on its graph.

Adding or subtracting inside of the function parentheses moves the function left or right. If you subtract 2 from x, the function shifts 2 to the right. Moving 2 to the right corresponds to *adding* 2 to the x-coordinate of every point on the graph of $p(x)$.

$$(-4 + 2, 0) = (-2, 0)$$
$$(7 + 2, 0) = (9, 0)$$

Thus, (H) is correct. J is a distractor as these points would result from shifting the graph 2 units to the left instead of 2 units to the right.

FUNCTION NOTATION

LEARNING OBJECTIVES

After this lesson, you will be able to:
- Apply function notation
- Define the domain and range of a function
- Evaluate the output of a function for a given input

To answer a question like this

If $f(x) = x^2 + \frac{x}{2}$, then $f(a + 2) =$

A. $a^2 + \frac{5a}{2} + 2$.

B. $a^2 + \frac{5a}{2} + 5$.

C. $a^2 + \frac{9a}{2} + 2$.

D. $a^2 + \frac{9a}{2} + 5$.

You need to know this

A **function** is a rule that generates one unique output for a given input. In function notation, the x-value is the input and the y-value, designated by $f(x)$, is the output. Be sure to note that other letters besides x and f may be used.

A linear function has the same form as the slope-intercept form of a line; just think of $f(x)$ as y:

$$f(x) = mx + b$$

In questions that describe real-life situations, the y-intercept will often be the starting point for the function. You can think of it as $f(0)$, or the value of the function where $x = 0$.

The set of all possible x-values is called the **domain** of the function, while the set of all possible y-values is called the **range**.

You need to do this

- To find $f(x)$ for some value of x, substitute the concrete value in for the variable and do the arithmetic.
- For questions that ask about the domain of a function, check whether any inputs are not allowed, such as those that would cause division by zero.
- For questions that ask about a function of a function, e.g., $g(f(x))$, start on the inside and work your way out.

Chapter 12
Functions

Explanation

The notation $f(a + 2)$ means that you should plug in $a + 2$ everywhere you see an x in the expression $x^2 + \frac{x}{2}$.

$$f(a + 2) = (a + 2)^2 + \frac{(a + 2)}{2}$$

Simplify and collect like terms.

$$(a + 2)(a + 2) + \frac{(a + 2)}{2} = a^2 + 4a + 4 + \frac{(a + 2)}{2}$$

$$= a^2 + 4a + 4 + \frac{a}{2} + \frac{2}{2}$$

$$= a^2 + 4a + 4 + \frac{a}{2} + 1$$

$$= a^2 + \frac{8a}{2} + 4 + \frac{a}{2} + 1$$

$$= a^2 + \frac{9a}{2} + 5$$

Choice (D) is correct.

Try on Your Own

Directions: Take as much time as you need on these questions. Work carefully and methodically. There will be an opportunity for timed practice at the end of the chapter.

1. What is $f(g(x + 2))$ if $f(x) = x^2 - 4x + 7$ and $g(x) = 7x - 3$?

   A. $49x^2 + 126x + 84$
   B. $63x^2 - 80x + 52$
   C. $25x^2 + 75x - 33$
   D. $-16x^2 - 22x + 5$

2. The approximate price of Stock X can be modeled by the given function, where t represents the number of minutes after 12 noon on a certain day. If $0 \leq t \leq 20$, approximately how much more, in dollars, was the price 5 minutes after 12 noon than 10 minutes after 12 noon?

   $$p(t) = -0.01t^2 - 0.08t + 10$$

   F. 1
   G. 8
   H. 9
   J. 17

HINT: For Q3, what do the numbers in the answer choices represent? What could cause you to stop too soon or go too far when calculating the answer to this question?

3. A company uses the function below to determine how much profit the company will make when it sells 150 units of a certain product that sells for x dollars per unit. How much more profit per unit will the company make if it charges $25 for the product than if it charges $20?

   $$p(x) = 150x - x^2$$

   A. $3.50
   B. $52.50
   C. $350
   D. $525

4. If $h(x) = 3x - 1$, what is the value of $h(5) - h(2)$?

F. 5
G. 9
H. 12
J. 14

5. If $f(x) = 3\sqrt{x^2 + 3x + 4}$, what is the value of $f(4)$?

A. $3\sqrt{2}$
B. $4\sqrt{2}$
C. 12
D. $12\sqrt{2}$

GRAPHS OF FUNCTIONS

LEARNING OBJECTIVES

After this lesson, you will be able to:
- Interpret the graph of a function
- Write a function to describe a rule or data set

To answer a question like this

A pep club is keeping track of how many students show up to home football games wearing their school colors. To encourage participation, there is a prize giveaway at each game. As the season continues, the prizes get more exciting and participation begins to increase.

If x represents the game number and $f(x)$ represents the number of students wearing school colors at game x, which of the following functions best models the information in the table?

Game	1	2	3	4	5	6	7	8
Number of students	5	11	21	35	53	75	101	131

A. $f(x) = x + 4$
B. $f(x) = 6x - 1$
C. $f(x) = x^2 + 4$
D. $f(x) = 2x^2 + 3$

Chapter 12
Functions

You need to know this

Interpreting graphs of functions is similar to interpreting graphs of equations. For example:

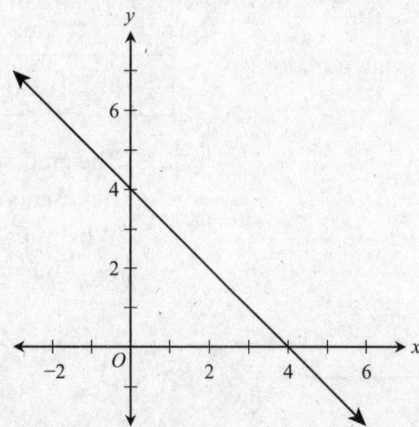

Say the graph shown represents the function $f(x)$, and you're asked to find the value of x for which $f(x) = 6$. Because $f(x)$ represents the output value, or range, you can translate this to, "When does the y-value equal 6?" To answer the question, find 6 on the y-axis, then trace over to the function (the line). Read the corresponding x-value: It's -2, so when $f(x) = 6$, x must be -2.

The ACT may sometimes ask about a function's **maximum** or **minimum**. These terms mean the greatest value and least value of the function, respectively. This graph of $f(x)$ does not have a maximum or minimum, as the arrows on the line indicate that it continues infinitely in both directions.

Modeling real-life situations using functions is the same as modeling them using equations; the only difference is the function notation and the rule that each input has only one output.

You need to do this

- Treat $f(x)$ as the y-coordinate on a graph.
- The maximum and minimum refer to a function's greatest and least y-coordinates, respectively.
- In word problems involving function notation, translate the math equations exactly as you learned in chapter 10 in the Word Problems lesson, but substitute $f(x)$ for y.

Explanation

This is not a linear expression because the y-values, or number of students, do not increase by the same number for each individual game. Eliminate A and B. Since only two answer choices are left, start plugging in x-values and eliminate the equation that is not true. When $x = 1$, both equations equal 5. However, when $x = 2$, C equals 8 and (D) equals 11. Since 11 matches the data in the table, (D) is correct.

Part 3
ACT MATH

Try on Your Own

Directions: Take as much time as you need on these questions. Work carefully and methodically. There will be an opportunity for timed practice at the end of the chapter.

1. What is the domain of the following function?

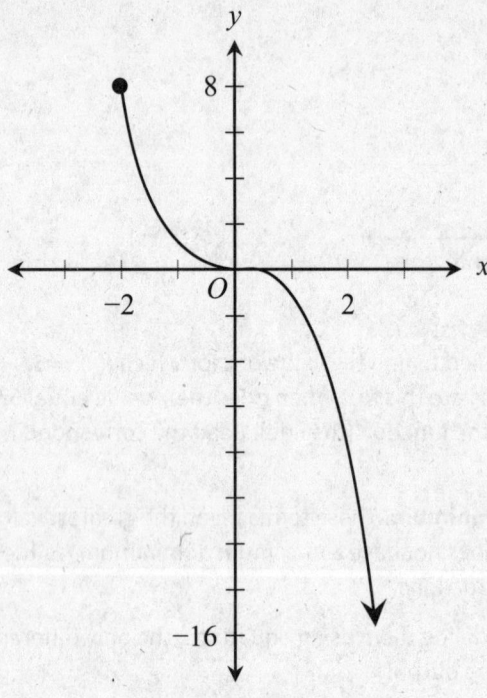

A. All real numbers
B. All real numbers less than or equal to 8
C. All real numbers greater than or equal to −2
D. All real numbers between −2 and 2

Use the graph for questions 2−3.

2. The graph that follows shows $h(x)$, which represents a portion of a polynomial function. What is the range of $h(x)$?

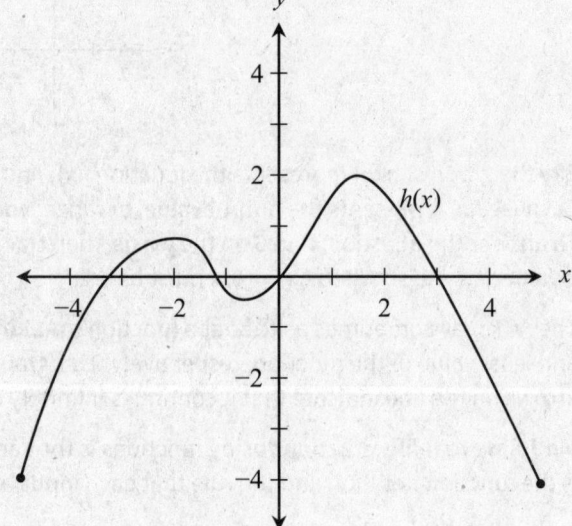

F. All real numbers greater than or equal to −5
G. All real numbers greater than or equal to −4
H. All real numbers between and including −5 and 5
J. All real numbers between and including −4 and 2

HINT: For Q3, what does g(x) = 0 mean in terms of the graph?

3. The graph that follows shows g(x), which represents a portion of a polynomial function. Given that $-5 \leq x \leq 5$, for how many values of x does g(x) = 0?

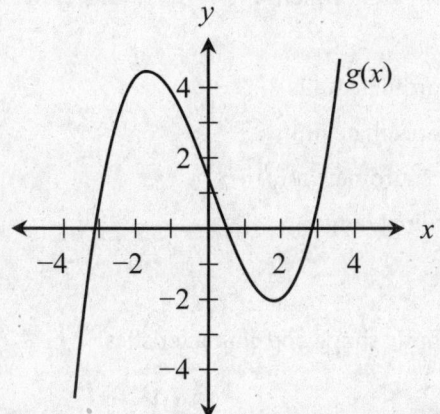

A. 1
B. 2
C. 3
D. 4

4. The following graph shows two functions, f(x) and g(x). Which of the following statements is true?

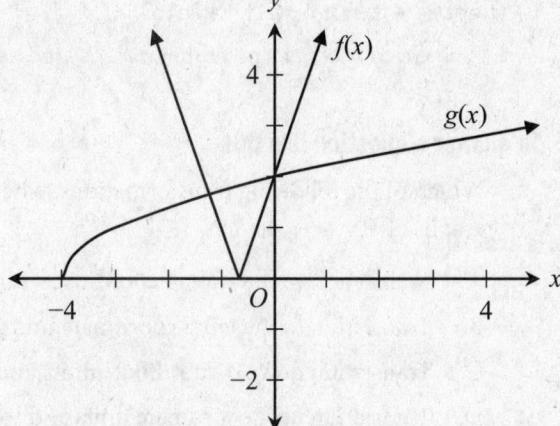

F. g(2) = 0.
G. f(x) > g(x) for all values of x.
H. (0, 2) is a solution for f(x) = g(x).
J. f(x) = 0 has exactly two solutions.

5. Which of the following is the equation that represents the data given in the table shown here?

x	−3	−2	−1	0	1	2	3	4
f(x)	−11	−7	−3	1	5	9	13	17

A. $y = -2x - 11$
B. $y = 4x + 1$
C. $y = 2x^2 + 9$
D. $y = 3x^2 - 7$

Part 3
ACT MATH

TRANSFORMATIONS

LEARNING OBJECTIVE

After this lesson, you will be able to:
- Find coordinates of a point that is translated, reflected over an axis, or rotated about the origin

To answer a question like this

Which of the following transformations, when applied to the parent function $y = |x|$, results in the graphs of $y = |x + 4| - 2$?

A. Translation to the right 4 coordinate units and up 2 coordinate units
B. Translation to the left 4 coordinate units and down 2 coordinate units
C. Translation down 4 coordinate units and to the right 2 coordinate units
D. Translation up 4 coordinate units and to the left 2 coordinate units

You need to know this

A **family of functions** is a group of functions that have the same basic shape and characteristics.

- The simplest function in a family is called the parent function.
- Learning the basic shapes of these parent functions can help you to recognize or write equations for more complex functions in the same family.

Equation family	Graph	Equation family	Graph
linear: $f(x) = x$	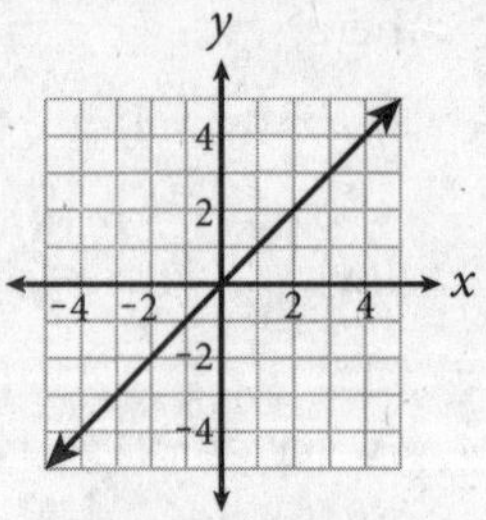	absolute value: $f(x) = |x|$	
quadratic: $f(x) = x^2$	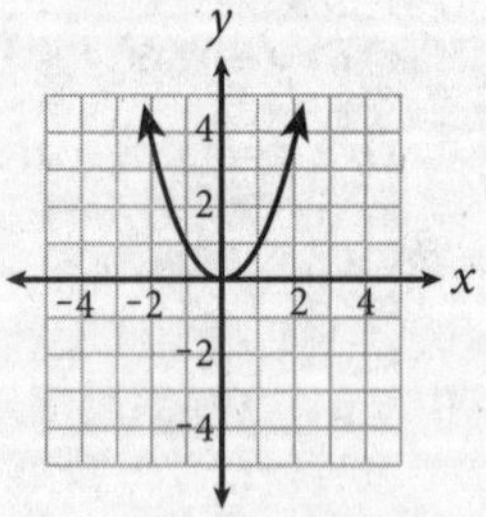	square root: $f(x) = \sqrt{x}$	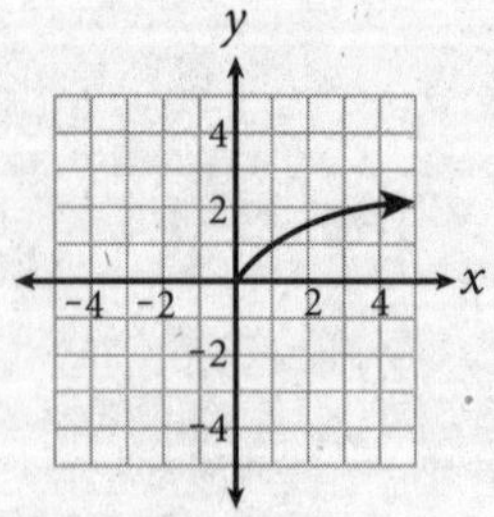
cubic: $f(x) = x^3$	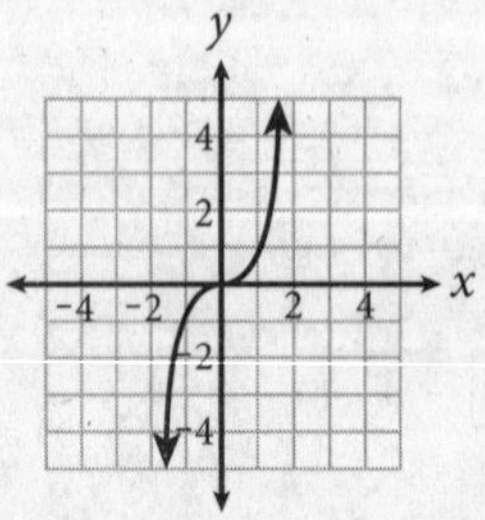	cube root: $f(x) = \sqrt[3]{x}$	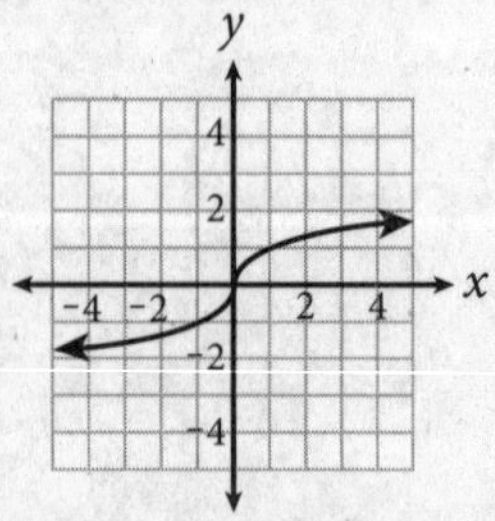

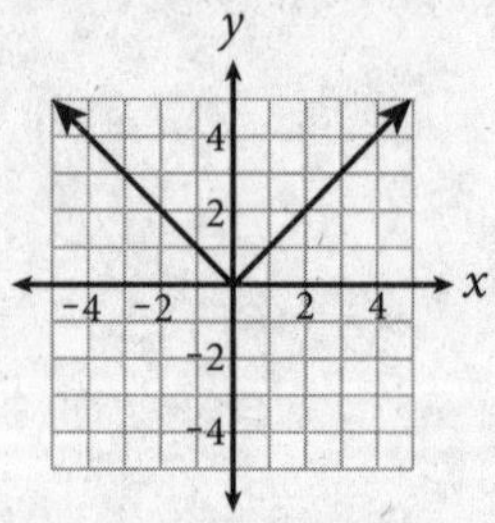

Equation family	Graph	Equation family	Graph
exponential: $f(x) = b^x$		logarithmic: $f(x) = \log_b x$	

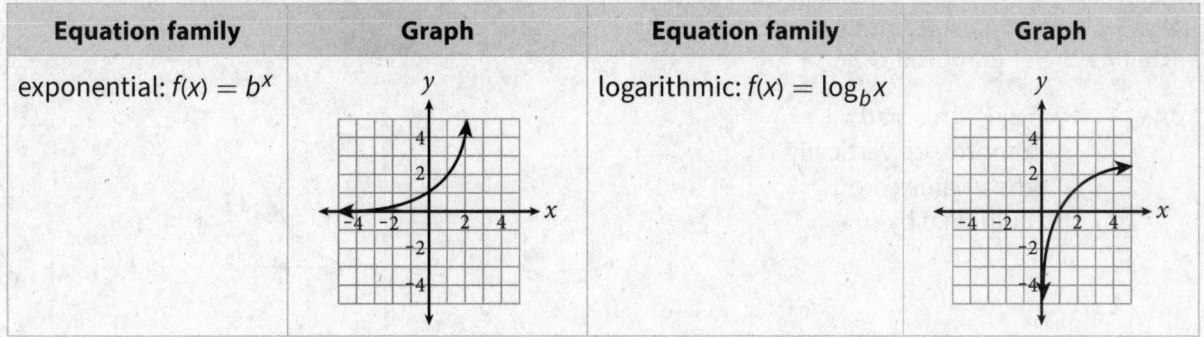

A **transformation** occurs when a change is made to the function's equation or graph. The most commonly tested transformations are translations (moving a graph up/down or left/right) and reflections (flips about an axis or other line). How do you know which is occurring? The following table provides some rules for altering the cubic function $f(x) = x^3$.

Algebraic change	Corresponding graphical change	Graph	
$f(x + a)$	$f(x)$ moves left a units		
$f(x - a)$	$f(x)$ moves right a units		
$f(x) + a$	$f(x)$ moves up a units		
$f(x) - a$	$f(x)$ moves down a units		
$f(-x)$	$f(x)$ is reflected over the y-axis (left to right)		
$-f(x)$	$f(x)$ is reflected over the x-axis (top to bottom)		

Part 3
ACT MATH

Algebraic change	Corresponding graphical change	Graph
$af(x)$	$f(x)$ is stretched or compressed vertically (the y-values are multiplied by a)	*(graph showing x^3 as solid line and $5x^3$ as dashed line, with y-axis marked at 100, 200, -100, -200 and x-axis from -4 to 4)*

- Adding or subtracting inside the parentheses of a function results in a horizontal translation. If the alteration is outside the parentheses, the result is a vertical translation.
- The same is true for reflections. When the negative is inside the parentheses (with the x), the reflection is horizontal; when the negative is outside the parentheses (away from the x), the reflection is vertical.
- Pay careful attention to horizontal translations—they are opposite of what they look like: $+a$ shifts to the left, while $-a$ shifts to the right.
- If you forget what a particular transformation looks like, you can always plug in a few values for x and plot the points to determine the effect on the function's graph.

You need to do this

Evaluate the function to be transformed:

- Is there addition or subtraction within grouping symbols (parentheses, absolute value, etc.)? If so, move horizontally the opposite way of the sign/operator.
- Is there addition or subtraction outside of grouping symbols? If so, move vertically the same way as the sign/operator.
- Is there a negative inside of the grouping symbols? If so, reflect horizontally.
- Is there a negative outside of the grouping symbols? If so, reflect vertically.
- Are the y-values being multiplied by another number? If so, the function is either being stretched or compressed.

Perform the transformations needed, choosing one point to follow at a time instead of trying to focus on the entire function.

Explanation

Look at the horizontal and vertical translations separately. Addition or subtraction inside of the absolute value sign will shift the graph horizontally in the *opposite* direction of the sign. Thus, $|x+4|$ shifts the graph 4 units to the left. Addition or subtraction outside the absolute value sign will shift the graph vertically in the same direction as the sign. So $|x+4|-2$ shifts the graph 2 units down.

Hence, (B) is correct.

Chapter 12
Functions

Try on Your Own

Directions: Take as much time as you need on these questions. Work carefully and methodically. There will be an opportunity for timed practice at the end of the chapter.

1. The vertex of an upward-facing parabola is at $(-3, 4)$. Which of the following represents the coordinates of the vertex after the parabola has been reflected about the x-axis?

   A. $(-3, -4)$
   B. $(-3, 4)$
   C. $(3, -4)$
   D. $(3, 4)$

2. The graph of $f(x) = 2x^3$ is translated 3 units to the right and 2 units down. Which of the following represents the equation of the graph after this translation?

   F. $(x-3)^3 - 2$
   G. $2(x+3)^3 + 2$
   H. $(x+3)^3 - 2$
   J. $2(x-3)^3 - 2$

3. The function $f(x)$ passes through the point (x, y). The function $g(x)$ is obtained by translating $f(x)$ 3 units to the left and 4 units up. Through which one of the following points must $g(x)$ pass?

   A. $(x-4, y+3)$
   B. $(x-3, y-4)$
   C. $(x-3, y+4)$
   D. $(x+3, y-4)$

4. The function $g(x)$ is translated 4 units to the right and 1 unit down to form $f(x)$. If $g(x) = \sqrt{x-5} + 3$, which of the following represents $f(x)$?

   F. $f(x) = \sqrt{x-6} + 7$
   G. $f(x) = \sqrt{x-1} + 4$
   H. $f(x) = \sqrt{x-4} - 1$
   J. $f(x) = \sqrt{x-9} + 2$

   HINT: For Q5, the functions may look more complicated than usual, but the standard transformation rules apply.
   ---

5. If $f(x) = e^x$ and $g(x) = e^{(x+3)} - 2$, which of the following describes the translation from $f(x)$ to $g(x)$?

   A. Translation to the left 3 coordinate units and down 2 coordinate units
   B. Translation to the left 2 coordinate units and down 3 coordinate units
   C. Translation to the left 3 coordinate units and up 2 coordinate units
   D. Translation to the right 3 coordinate units and up 2 coordinate units

Part 3
ACT MATH

TRIGONOMETRY ON THE COORDINATE PLANE

LEARNING OBJECTIVES

After this lesson, you will be able to:
- Match graphs of basic trigonometric functions with their equations
- Use trigonometric concepts and basic identities to solve questions
- Given an equation or function, find an equation or function whose graph is a translation

To answer a question like this

The graph of $g(x) = \cos(3x)$ is shown below. Which of the following lists represents the values of x for which $g(x) = 0$?

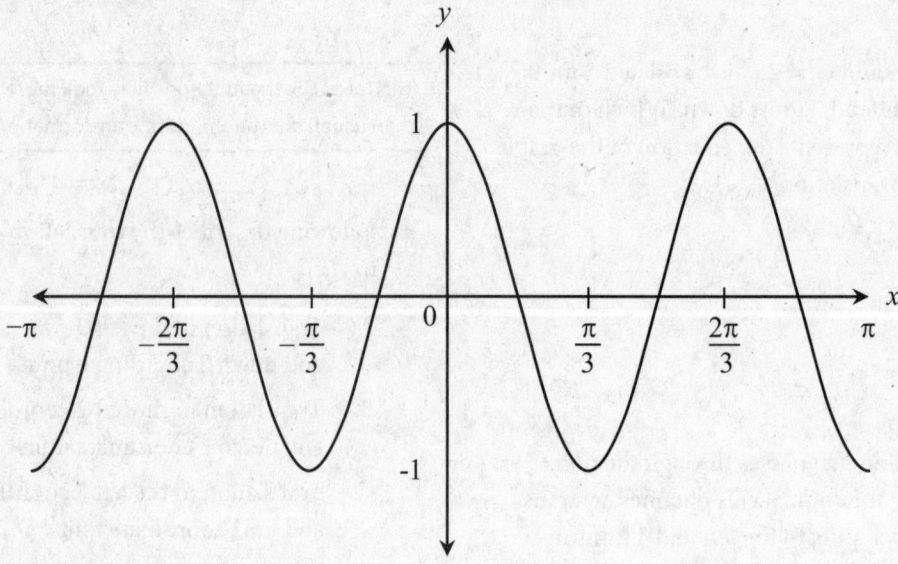

A. $-180°, -120°, -60°, 60°, 120°, 180°$
B. $-165°, -105°, -45°, 45°, 105°, 165°$
C. $-150°, -90°, -30°, 30°, 90°, 150°$
D. $-120°, -80°, -40°, 40°, 80°, 120°$

You need to know this

The ACT may ask you to recognize the graphs of the **sine**, **cosine**, and **tangent functions**, which are presented in the table below. You may also be asked to apply transformations to these graphs.

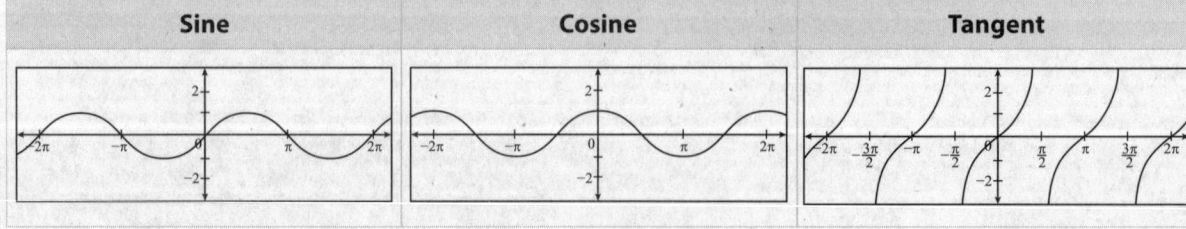

The domain of the sine and cosine functions is all real numbers, but notice that their graphs oscillate (bounce back and forth) between $y = -1$ and 1.

- This means the range of $y = \sin x$, and also $y = \cos x$ is $-1 \leq y \leq 1$.
- This is not true for tangent, which has a range of all real numbers.
- In other words, the maximum value of a standard sine or cosine function is 1 and the minimum value is -1, while the tangent function has no maximum or minimum.

When trigonometric functions are graphed, the horizontal axis is almost always measured in **radians**.

- The conversion rate is simple: $180° = \pi$ radians.
- Use this relationship as a conversion factor to convert degrees into radians: $90° \times \frac{\pi \text{ radians}}{180°} = \frac{\pi}{2}$ radians.
- You can also use this relationship to convert radians into degrees: $\frac{\pi}{2} \times \frac{180°}{\pi \text{ radians}} = 90°$.

You are also likely to see words such as **amplitude** and **period** in questions about trig functions.

- The amplitude of a wave function (such as sine or cosine) is the vertical distance from the center line (the horizontal at rest line) to the maximum or minimum value.
- For the standard sine and cosine functions, the amplitude is 1.
- The period of the standard sine and cosine functions is 2π because their graphs repeat every 2π units.
- The period of the standard tangent function is π.

There are three reciprocal trig functions: secant (sec), cosecant (csc), and cotangent (cot). Their values are the reciprocals of the sine, cosine, and tangent functions:

$$\csc x = \frac{1}{\sin x}$$

$$\sec x = \frac{1}{\cos x}$$

$$\cot x = \frac{1}{\tan x}$$

To find the value of one of these functions, flip the relationships given by SOHCAHTOA (which are covered in the Geometry chapter):

$$\csc x = \frac{\text{hypotenuse}}{\text{opposite}}$$

$$\sec x = \frac{\text{hypotenuse}}{\text{adjacent}}$$

$$\cot x = \frac{\text{adjacent}}{\text{opposite}}$$

Two other particularly useful trigonometric relationships include $\tan x = \frac{\sin x}{\cos x}$ and the Pythagorean identity: $\sin^2 x + \cos^2 x = 1$ (notice that it resembles the Pythagorean theorem).

You need to do this

- Identify the trigonometric information needed to answer the question.
- Use transformation rules or trig properties and relationships to determine unknown values.
- Use the x- and y-intercepts strategically to help eliminate choices or determine the correct answer.

Explanation

The question asks you to find the x-intercepts of the graph. Cosine functions are periodic in nature, with this curve crossing the x-axis halfway in between every maximum and minimum point. For instance, this function has a maximum at $x = 0$ and a minimum at $x = \frac{\pi}{3}$, resulting in an x-intercept at

$$\frac{1}{2}\left(0 + \frac{\pi}{3}\right) = \frac{\pi}{6}$$

The graph is in radians while the answer choices are in degrees, so you must convert from radians to degrees. Begin with the smallest, or leftmost, x-intercept in between the minimum at $-\pi$ and maximum at $-\frac{2\pi}{3}$.

$$\frac{1}{2}\left(-\pi - \frac{2\pi}{3}\right) = \frac{1}{2}\left(-\frac{3\pi}{3} - \frac{2\pi}{3}\right) = \frac{1}{2}\left(-\frac{5\pi}{3}\right) = -\frac{5\pi}{6}$$

Next, convert this value to degrees.

$$\frac{-5\pi \text{ radians}}{6}\left(\frac{180 \text{ degrees}}{\pi \text{ radians}}\right) = \frac{-900 \text{ degrees}}{6} = -150 \text{ degrees}$$

Answer choice (C) is the only that begins with a value of $-150°$ and therefore must be correct.

Try on Your Own

Directions: Take as much time as you need on these questions. Work carefully and methodically. There will be an opportunity for timed practice at the end of the chapter.

1. What is the period of the function $f(x) = 2 \sin\left(\frac{x}{4} - \pi\right) + 3$?

   A. $\frac{\pi}{4}$
   B. $\frac{\pi}{2}$
   C. 4π
   D. 8π

2. The functions $f(x) = \cos(x)$ and $g(x) = a \cos(x + b)$ have the same minimum value and are graphed in the standard (x, y) coordinate plane as shown. Which one of the following statements could be true?

   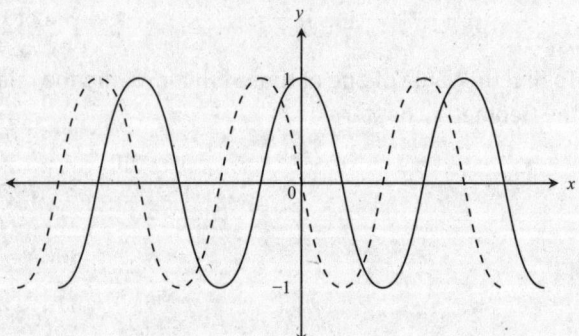

   F. $a = 1$ and $b = 0$
   G. $a < 1$ and $b > 0$
   H. $a = 1$ and $b > 0$
   J. $a < 1$ and $b = 0$

Chapter 12
Functions

> HINT: Some trigonometry on the coordinate plane questions can be answered using basic function transformation rules. Use what you know about translations, reflections, and scaling on the coordinate plane to answer a question like Q3.

3. One of the following graphs is the graph of $y = \frac{1}{2}\sin(2x) + 4$. Which one?

   A.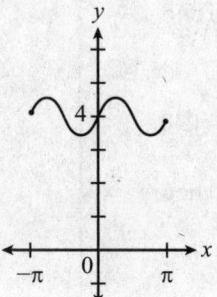

   B.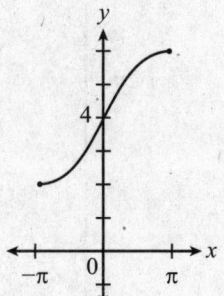

   C.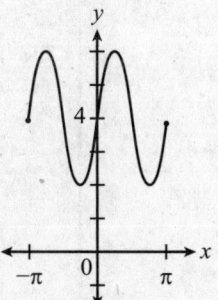

   D.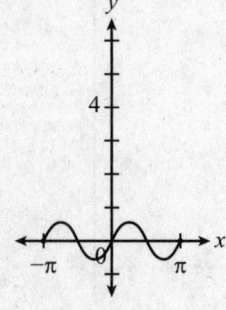

4. What is the amplitude of the function $f(x) = 2\cos(4x - \pi)$?

   F. 1
   G. $\frac{\pi}{2}$
   H. 2
   J. π

5. The graph of $y = a\cos(bx)$ is shown. One of the following values is equal to b. Which one?

   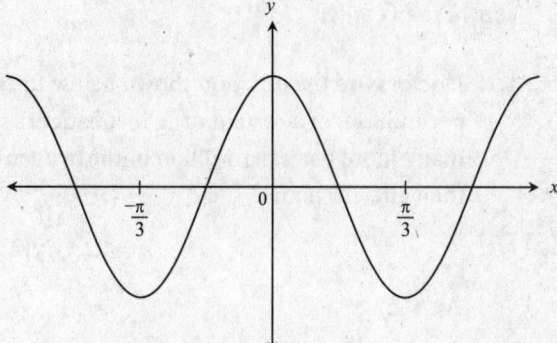

   A. $\frac{1}{3}$
   B. 1
   C. 3
   D. 6

Part 3
ACT MATH

On Test Day

The ACT likes to test the modeling of real-life situations. Get comfortable with function notation in these questions. Remember that you can write the equation of a line as $y = mx + b$ or as $f(x) = mx + b$, where m is the slope and b is the y-intercept. Both mean the same thing.

In a formula using function notation, the slope indicates rate of change. Often, in questions asking about real-life situations, the x-variable indicates time. In that case, the y-intercept (that is, the value of the function at $x = 0$, or $f(0)$) indicates the starting point. Practice this principle using the following question that is similar to one you've seen earlier:

1. Doctors use the function shown below to calculate the concentration, in parts per million, of a certain drug in a patient's bloodstream after t hours. How many more parts per million of the drug are in the bloodstream after 20 hours than after 10 hours?

$$c(t) = -0.05t^2 + 2t + 2$$

   A. 5
   B. 7
   C. 17
   D. 22

The correct answer and an explanation can be found at the end of this chapter.

Chapter 12
Functions

How Much Have You Learned?

Directions: For test-like practice, give yourself 10 minutes to complete this question set. Be sure to study the explanations, even for questions you got correct. They can be found at the end of this chapter.

1. Which of the following functions represents the data given below?

x	0	1	2	3	4	5	6	7
$f(x)$	-19	-11	-3	5	13	21	29	37

    A. $f(x) = 8x - 19$
    B. $f(x) = x^2 - 4$
    C. $f(x) = -8x + 19$
    D. $f(x) = (x-4)^2 - 19$

2. The graph of a function $h(x)$ is found by translating the graph of the function $g(x)$ up 4 units and left 3 units. If $g(x) = (x-1)^2$, then $h(x) = $?

    F. $(x-3)^2 + 4$
    G. $(x+2)^2 + 4$
    H. $(x+3)^2 + 4$
    J. $(x+4)^2 - 3$

3. Several values for the functions $g(x)$ and $h(x)$ are shown in the following table. What is the value of $g(h(3))$?

x	$g(x)$	x	$h(x)$
-6	-3	0	6
-3	-2	1	-4
0	-1	2	2
3	0	3	0
6	1	4	-2

    A. -1
    B. 0
    C. 1
    D. 6

4. If $f(x) = x^2 + 1$ and $g(x) = 3x + 1$, which of the following expressions represents $f(g(x))$?

    F. $3x^2 + 2$
    G. $3x^2 + 4$
    H. $9x^2 + 3x + 4$
    J. $9x^2 + 6x + 2$

5. If $f(x) = x^2 + 3x - 5$, what is the value of $f(x+h)$?

    A. $x^2 + 3x - 5 - h$
    B. $x^2 + 3x - 5 + 2h$
    C. $x^2h^2 + 2xh + 3x + 3h - 5$
    D. $x^2 + 2xh + 3x + h^2 + 3h - 5$

6. The rule of translation from $f(x)$ to $g(x)$ is $(x,y) \rightarrow (x - 1.5, y + 2.8)$. If $f(x)$ passes through $(-2.3, -1.2)$, which coordinate pair must $g(x)$ pass through?

    F. $(-0.8, -3.8)$
    G. $(0.8, 1.6)$
    H. $(2.7, -3.8)$
    J. $(-3.8, 1.6)$

7. If $x > 0$, $a = x \cos \theta$, and $b = x \sin \theta$, then which of the following is equivalent to $\sqrt{a^2 + b^2}$?

    A. 1
    B. x
    C. $2x$
    D. $x(\cos \theta + \sin \theta)$

Part 3
ACT MATH

8. If $f(x) = -4x + 1$ and $g(x) = \sqrt{x} + 2.5$, what is the value of $f\left(g\left(\frac{1}{4}\right)\right)$?

   F. -11
   G. 0
   H. 2.5
   J. 3

9. What is the range of the function shown here?

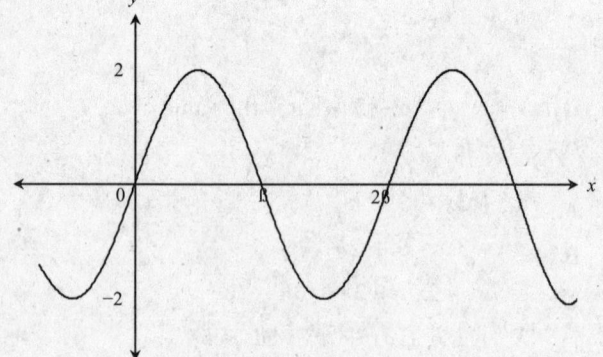

   A. All real numbers between and including -2 and 2
   B. All real numbers less than or equal to 2
   C. All real numbers between 0 and 2π
   D. All real numbers

10. Which trigonometric function could be represented by the following graph?

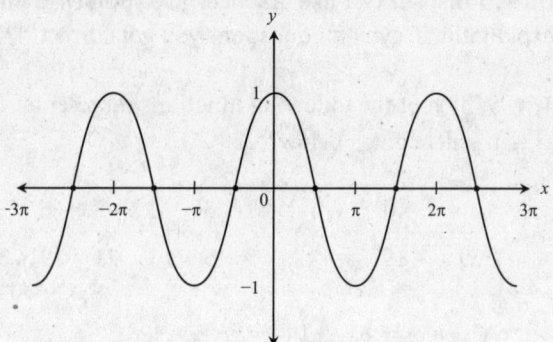

   F. $g(x) = \sin(x - \pi)$
   G. $g(x) = \sin(x + \pi)$
   H. $g(x) = \sin\left(x - \frac{\pi}{2}\right)$
   J. $g(x) = \sin\left(x + \frac{\pi}{2}\right)$

Chapter 12
Functions

Reflect

Directions: Take a few minutes to recall what you've learned and what you've been practicing in this chapter. Consider the following questions, jot down your best answer for each one, and then compare your reflections to the expert responses on the following page. Use your level of confidence to determine what to do next.

1. What are the domain and range of a function?

   _____
   _____
   _____

2. What is another way to write the function $f(x) = x + 4$?

   _____
   _____
   _____

3. In the function above, what does x represent? What does $f(x)$ represent?

   _____
   _____
   _____

4. What will the above function look like when graphed?

   _____
   _____
   _____

5. In a function whose x-value represents time, what does the y-intercept represent?

   _____
   _____
   _____

Responses

1. What are the domain and range of a function?

The domain of a function indicates the possible x-values, and the range of a function indicates the possible y-values. For example, in the function $f(x) = x^2$, the domain is all real numbers because any number can be squared, and the range is any number greater than or equal to 0, because x^2 can't be negative.

2. What is another way to write the function $f(x) = x + 4$?

When you graph the function on the xy-coordinate plane, you can replace $f(x)$ with y. This function is equivalent to $y = x + 4$.

3. In the function above, what does *x* represent? What does *f(x)* represent?

In this function, x is the input and $f(x)$ is the output.

4. What will the above function look like when graphed?

The slope of the line is 1 and its y-intercept is 4, so it will move from the lower left to the upper right and cross the y-axis at $y = 4$.

5. In a function whose *x*-value represents time, what does the *y*-intercept represent?

The y-intercept represents the initial quantity when $t = 0$. Say a function represents the progress of a machine manufacturing widgets at a rate of 6 widgets per hour. The machine adds the widgets it makes to a growing pile that consisted of 12 widgets when the machine started working. If this function were graphed as a function of time, the y-intercept would be 12—the pile of 12 widgets that was there when the machine started its task.

Next Steps

If you answered most questions correctly in the "How Much Have You Learned?" section, and if your responses to the Reflect questions were similar to those of the ACT expert, then consider functions an area of strength and move on to the next chapter. Come back to this topic periodically to prevent yourself from getting rusty.

If you don't yet feel confident, review those parts of this chapter that you have not yet mastered. All four lessons in this chapter cover question types that are fairly common on the ACT, and it is to your advantage to have a firm grasp on this material, so go back over it until you feel more confident. Then, try the questions you missed again. As always, be sure to review the explanations closely. Then go online (**kaptest.com/login**) for more practice. If you haven't already registered your book, do so at **kaptest.com/moreonline**.

GO ONLINE

kaptest.com/login

Answers and Explanations

Function Notation

1. A
Difficulty: Medium
Category: Functions
Getting to the Answer: The question asks for the value of two nested functions in terms of the variable x. Calculate this from the inside out, just like you would for any set of nested parentheses. First, calculate $g(x+2)$ by substituting $x+2$ wherever you see an x in the g function:

$$g(x+2) = 7(x+2) - 3$$
$$g(x+2) = 7x + 14 - 3$$
$$g(x+2) = 7x + 11$$

Then, plug this value of $g(x+2)$ into the f function, $f(x) = x^2 - 4x + 7$:

$$f(g(x+2)) = f(7x+11)$$
$$= (7x+11)^2 - 4(7x+11) + 7$$
$$= (7x+11)(7x+11) - 28x - 44 + 7$$
$$= 49x^2 + 77x + 77x + 121 - 28x - 37$$
$$= 49x^2 + 126x + 84$$

Thus, (A) is correct.

2. F
Difficulty: Medium
Category: Functions
Getting to the Answer: The phrase "how many more" indicates subtraction. The function p gives the price at different times after 12 noon. You must determine the price when $t = 5$ and $t = 10$ and then subtract these two quantities. Begin with $p(5)$:

$$p(5) = -0.01(5)^2 - 0.08(5) + 10$$
$$= -0.01(25) - 0.40 + 10$$
$$= -0.25 - 0.40 + 10$$
$$= 9.35$$

Then move on to $p(10)$:

$$p(10) = -0.01(10)^2 - 0.08(10) + 10$$
$$= -0.01(100) - 0.8 + 10$$
$$= -1 - 0.8 + 10$$
$$= 8.2$$

Subtracting yields $9.35 - 8.2 = 1.15$, which is approximately 1. Choice (F) is correct. Be sure that you answered the right question. Choice G is approximately $p(10)$, choice H is approximately $p(5)$, and choice J is a tempting incorrect answer if $p(10)$ and $p(5)$ are mistakenly added instead of subtracted.

3. A
Difficulty: High
Category: Functions
Getting to the Answer: Pay careful attention to the wording of this question. You are being asked NOT for the difference in profit but for the difference in profit *per unit*.

Begin by calculating $p(25)$ and $p(20)$ individually.

$$p(25) = 150(25) - (25)^2$$
$$= 3{,}750 - 625$$
$$= 3{,}125$$

$$p(20) = 150(20) - (20)^2$$
$$= 3{,}000 - 400$$
$$= 2{,}600$$

Since $p(25) - p(20) = 3{,}125 - 2{,}600 = 525$, it may be tempting to select D. However, the question is asking for the difference in profit *per unit,* so you must divide 525 by 150:

$$\frac{525}{150} = 3.5$$

Choice (A) is correct.

4. G
Difficulty: Low
Category: Functions
Getting to the Answer: The question asks for the difference between the two outputs of the function $h(x)$ when the given values of x are used as inputs. First, calculate $h(5)$ and $h(2)$ individually:

$$h(5) = 3(5) - 1$$
$$= 15 - 1$$
$$= 14$$

$$h(2) = 3(2) - 1$$
$$= 6 - 1$$
$$= 5$$

Since $h(5) - h(2) = 14 - 5 = 9$, (G) is correct. Confirm that you answered the question that was asked; F and J are the individual values of the function.

5. D
Difficulty: Low
Category: Functions
Getting to the Answer: The question asks for the value of $f(4)$ given that $f(x) = 3\sqrt{x^2 + 3x + 4}$. The notation $f(4)$ means that you should plug in a 4 everywhere there is an x in the equation $3\sqrt{x^2 + 3x + 4}$.

$$f(4) = 3\sqrt{(4)^2 + 3(4) + 4}$$
$$= 3\sqrt{16 + 12 + 4}$$
$$= 3\sqrt{32}$$
$$= 3\sqrt{16}\sqrt{2}$$
$$= 3(4)\sqrt{2}$$
$$= 12\sqrt{2}$$

Choice (D) is correct. Confirm that you used the correct values given in the question.

Graphs of Functions

1. C
Difficulty: Low
Category: Functions
Getting to the Answer: The question asks for the values of the domain of the function shown on the graph. Remember that *domain* is another word for x-values, which are shown on the horizontal axis of the graph. The leftmost point on the graph is the minimum value of the domain. This occurs at $x = -2$. Eliminate choices A and B.

Now find the maximum value of the domain by looking for the rightmost point. The arrow on the point $(2,-8)$ indicates that the graph keeps going toward infinity. Eliminate D.

Thus, choice (C) is correct.

2. J
Difficulty: Medium
Category: Functions
Getting to the Answer: The question asks for the range of the function shown on the graph. Remember that *range* is another word for y-values, which are shown on the vertical axis of the graph. The lowest y-value occurs at $y = -4$ because the dots indicate that the curve terminates at those points. The highest y-value is 2. Thus, the range of $h(x)$ is from -4 to 2.

Choice (J) is correct. Be certain that you determined the range; the domain is H.

3. C
Difficulty: Low
Category: Functions
Getting to the Answer: The question asks for the number of points on the graph at which the function equals 0. Remember that $y = g(x)$. Thus, the question is asking how many times $y = 0$. Look at the graph and see that this occurs 3 times. Therefore, (C) is correct. Be certain that you answered the question that was asked. Choice A is the number of points where $x = 0$.

4. H
Difficulty: Medium
Category: Functions
Getting to the Answer: The question asks which of the choices is true based on the graph of the two functions. Work through each choice systematically.

Eliminate F, since $g(2) \approx 2.5$.

Eliminate G, since $g(x) > f(x)$ between roughly $x = -1.2$ and $x = 0$.

Recall that a solution for $f(x) = g(x)$ occurs when the graphs of the functions touch or cross each other. Since one of the points where the two functions cross is at $(0, 2)$, (H) is correct.

For the record, J is incorrect because $f(x)$ has only one solution, at approximately $(-0.75, 0)$. Confirm that you answered the question that was asked.

5. B
Difficulty: Medium
Category: Functions
Getting to the Answer: The question asks which of the choices is the equation for the data given in the table. First, determine whether the data are in a linear or non-linear relationship. Since all the x-values increase by 1, the y-values should increase or decrease proportionally. Notice that the y-values always increase by 4 throughout the table, so this is indeed a linear relationship. Eliminate C and D.

The slope of the line is the coefficient of x in the linear equation. Since y increases by 4 for every 1 unit increase in x, that value is 4, and (B) is correct. You can confirm this by plugging 4 into the equation to obtain the y-value of 17.

Transformations

1. A
Difficulty: Medium
Category: Functions
Getting to the Answer: The question asks for the coordinates of the vertex of the given parabola after it is reflected about the x-axis. Reflecting about the x-axis will not change the x-coordinate but will reverse the sign of the y-coordinate. So, $(-3, 4)$ becomes $(-3, -4)$. Therefore, (A) is correct.

2. J
Difficulty: Low
Category: Functions
Getting to the Answer: The question asks which of the choices is the expression for $f(x)$ after performing the given horizontal and vertical translation. Addition or subtraction inside of the function parentheses will shift the graph horizontally in the *opposite* direction of the sign. Thus, a translation of 3 units to the right is obtained by subtracting 3 from inside the function parentheses so the function becomes $2(x-3)^3$.

Addition or subtraction outside of the function parentheses will shift the graph vertically in the same direction of the sign. Thus, a translation of 2 units down is obtained by subtracting 2 from outside the function parentheses: $2(x-3)^3 - 2$.

Choice (J) is correct. Be certain that you followed the correct procedures for translation; G and H shift the function 3 units to the left.

3. C
Difficulty: Medium
Category: Functions
Getting to the Answer: The question asks which of the choices is a point through which $g(x)$ passes given that $f(x)$ passes through (x, y). Since $g(x)$ is the result of performing the given horizontal and vertical translation on $f(x)$, you can perform the same translation on (x, y) to find a point through which $g(x)$ must pass. Translating 3 units to the left means subtracting 3 from the x-coordinate: $x - 3$. Translating 4 units up means adding 4 to the y-coordinate: $y + 4$. Thus, (C) is correct. You can readily verify this because it is the only choice with the term $y + 4$.

4. J
Difficulty: Medium
Category: Functions
Getting to the Answer: The question asks which of the choices is the given function translated 4 units to the right and 1 unit down. Translate the square root sign to the $\frac{1}{2}$ power. Addition or subtraction inside of the function parentheses will shift the graph horizontally in the *opposite* direction of the sign. Thus, a translation of 4 units to the right is obtained by subtracting 4 inside the parentheses. Translating 1 unit down subtracts 1 from the constant outside the radical.

So, $\sqrt{x-5} + 3 = (x-5)^{\frac{1}{2}} + 3$. After translation, this becomes $(x-5-4)^{\frac{1}{2}} + 3 - 1 = (x-9)^{\frac{1}{2}} + 2$. When returned to radical format, this matches (J). Ensure that you translated in the correct direction; G is a translation 4 units right and 1 unit up.

5. A
Difficulty: Medium
Category: Functions
Getting to the Answer: The question asks which of the choices describes the transformation of $f(x)$ to $g(x)$ and provides the exponential expressions for each function. Do not be intimidated by the exponential function! The same translation rules still apply.

Addition or subtraction inside of the function parentheses will shift the graph horizontally in the *opposite* direction of the sign. Here, the exponential function e acts like function parentheses. Thus, $e^{(x+3)}$ represents a translation of 3 units to the left. Eliminate B and D.

Addition or subtraction outside of the function parentheses will shift the graph vertically in the same direction of the sign. Thus, $e^{(x+3)} - 2$ represents a translation of 2 units down. Eliminate C.

Thus, (A) is correct. Be certain that you correctly applied the translation rules and used the proper signs.

Part 3
ACT MATH

Trigonometry on the Coordinate Plane

1. D
Difficulty: Medium
Category: Functions
Getting to the Answer: To answer this question, use function transformation rules. The period of a sine function is determined by the coefficient of x, so you can ignore the 2, π, and 3 values. When the coefficient of x is 1, the period of a sine function is 2π. When the coefficient of x is larger than 1, the graph is horizontally compressed, so the period of a sine function gets smaller. When the coefficient is smaller than 1, the graph is horizontally expanded, so the period of a sine function gets larger. In this function, the coefficient of x is $\frac{1}{4}$, so the period will be 4 times as big: $2\pi \times 4 = 8\pi$. Choice (D) is correct.

You could also use a trigonometry rule to answer this question. When a sine function has the setup $a \sin(bx)$, the period is $\frac{2\pi}{b}$. In this equation, $b = \frac{1}{4}$, so the period of the function is $\frac{2\pi}{\frac{1}{4}} = 8\pi$.

2. H
Difficulty: Medium
Category: Functions
Getting to the Answer: The question asks which of the choices could be true and refers to the given graph of two functions of $\cos(x)$, one of which appears to be the other shifted horizontally. The most basic form of the cosine function is $f(x) = \cos(x)$. Since the minimum and maximum values of both functions are the same, there is no scaling from $f(x)$ to $g(x)$. You can therefore deduce that $a = 1$. Since the graph does shift horizontally, $b \neq 0$. With the given information, b could be either positive or negative, but not 0. Hence, (H) is correct.

3. A
Difficulty: High
Category: Functions
Getting to the Answer: Use function transformation rules to answer this question. The graph of a basic sine function crosses both the x- and y-axes at (0,0) and has a period of 2π and an amplitude of 1. The sine function in the question has a vertical compression (from the $\frac{1}{2}$), a horizontal compression (from the 2), and a vertical shift (from the 4).

Eliminate D because it does not include a vertical shift. Eliminate B and C because they involve a vertical expansion (the amplitude is bigger than 1) instead of a vertical compression (the amplitude is smaller than 1). Choice (A) is correct because it has a horizontal compression (the period is smaller than 2π).

4. H
Difficulty: Medium
Category: Functions
Getting to the Answer: The question asks for the amplitude of the given function. Think of the amplitude as the "height" of the cosine function. The maximum value of $\cos(x)$ is 1, so its amplitude is 1. However, this question asks for the value of $2\cos(4x - \pi)$.

Think back to the rules of translation. Expressions inside the function parentheses affect horizontal shifts, while expressions outside the function parentheses affect vertical shifts. Since you are interested in the height of the cosine function, the terms inside the function parentheses are irrelevant. The 2 on the outside vertically stretches the cosine function by a factor of 2. Thus, the amplitude is $2(1) = 2$.

Choice (H) is correct. Since the question asks for amplitude, be certain that you considered only the y-value of the function.

5. C
Difficulty: Medium
Category: Functions
Getting to the Answer: The question asks about the value of b in the graph $y = a\cos(bx)$ based on the graph. The coefficient in front of x indicates a horizontal compression or expansion. The graph of a basic cosine function crosses the y-axis at (0,1) and has a period of 2π and an amplitude of 1. The period of this graph is $\frac{\pi}{3} - \left(-\frac{\pi}{3}\right) = \frac{2\pi}{3}$, which means that this graph has undergone a horizontal compression, as the period is smaller than 2π. Thus, b is greater than 1. Eliminate A and B.

As b is the coefficient in front of x, the period of the function can be calculated as $\frac{2\pi}{b}$. Set up the equation $\frac{2\pi}{3} = \frac{2\pi}{b}$, and recognize that $b = 3$. Choice (C) is correct.

On Test Day

1. A
Difficulty: Medium
Category: Functions
Getting to the Answer: The question is asking you to calculate $c(20) - c(10)$ for the given function since, in word problems, the phrase "how many more" indicates subtraction. Calculate $c(20)$ and $c(10)$ individually and then subtract:

$$c(20) = -0.05(20^2) + 2(20) + 2$$
$$= -0.05(400) + 40 + 2$$
$$= -20 + 40 + 2$$
$$= 22$$

$$c(10) = -0.05(10^2) + 2(10) + 2$$
$$= -0.05(100) + 20 + 2$$
$$= -5 + 20 + 2$$
$$= 17$$

Since $c(20) - c(10) = 22 - 17 = 5$, (A) is correct. Be certain that you answered the question that was asked since D and C are the individual values for $c(20)$ and $c(10)$.

So what does $c(0)$ represent? Since $c(t)$ represents the amount of the drug in parts per million present in the bloodstream after t hours, $c(0)$ represents the amount of the drug in parts per million present in the bloodstream after 0 hours—at the beginning of the treatment.

How Much Have You Learned?

1. A
Difficulty: Medium
Category: Functions
Getting to the Answer: The question asks for the function that creates the values shown in the table. First, determine whether the data are in a linear or a non-linear relationship. Since all the x-values increase by 1, the changes in the y-values will be consistent if it is a linear relationship. Notice that the y-values always increase by 8 throughout the table, so this is indeed a linear relationship. Eliminate B and D.

Since the y-values increase by 8 and the x-values increase by 1 at every point, the slope is 8. This is the value of the x-coefficient, so you can eliminate C. Thus, (A) is correct. You can plug any of the x-values into that equation to get the matching y-value in order to verify that it is the correct choice.

2. G
Difficulty: Medium
Category: Functions
Getting to the Answer: The question asks for the translation of $g(x)$ 4 units upward and 3 units to the left. Addition or subtraction inside of the function parentheses will shift the graph horizontally in the *opposite* direction of the sign. Thus, a translation of 3 units to the left is obtained by adding 3 inside the function parentheses. This means $(x - 1)^2$ becomes $(x + 2)^2$.

On test day, you could stop here since only (G) has the correct expression inside the parentheses. However, for the sake of completeness, recall that addition or subtraction outside of the function parentheses will shift the graph vertically in the same direction of the sign. Thus, a translation of 4 units up is obtained by adding 4 outside the parentheses.

Therefore, (G) is correct. Be certain that you used the correct values for the original function; using x rather than $x - 1$ would result in the expression in H.

3. A
Difficulty: Low
Category: Functions
Getting to the Answer: The question asks for the value of nested functions for $x = 3$, and you are given tables showing various x- and y-values for the two functions. Work from the inside out. Before trying to determine the equations for the functions, see if the tables already contain the values that you require. Find the y-value of the h function when $x = 3$. The table indicates that $h(3) = 0$.

Now evaluate $g(0)$ in the same way. The y-value when $x = 0$ is -1.

Choice (A) is correct. Be certain that you answered the question that was asked; reversing the functions would result in the value in D.

4. J

Difficulty: Medium
Category: Functions
Getting to the Answer: The question asks for the value of $f(g(x))$ in terms of x and provides both expressions. Calculate $f(g(x))$ by plugging $g(x) = 3x + 1$ into the f function.

$$f(g(x)) = (3x+1)^2 + 1$$
$$= (3x+1)(3x+1) + 1$$
$$= 9x^2 + 3x + 3x + 1 + 1$$
$$= 9x^2 + 6x + 2$$

Therefore, (J) is correct. Be certain that you evaluated the correct expression; $g(f(x))$ is G.

5. D

Difficulty: Medium
Category: Functions
Getting to the Answer: The question asks for the value of $f(x+h)$ given that $f(x) = x^2 + 3x - 5$. Calculate $f(x+h)$ by plugging in $x+h$ everywhere you see an x in the f function.

$$f(x+h) = (x+h)^2 + 3(x+h) - 5$$
$$= (x+h)(x+h) + 3x + 3h - 5$$
$$= x^2 + xh + xh + h^2 + 3x + 3h - 5$$
$$= x^2 + 2xh + 3x + h^2 + 3h - 5$$

Thus, (D) is correct.

6. J

Difficulty: Medium
Category: Functions
Getting to the Answer: The question asks which of the coordinate pairs is a valid value of $g(x)$. You are given the translation operations from $f(x)$ to $g(x)$ in terms of x- and y-coordinates, and the coordinates of a point through which $f(x)$ passes. Take the given point, subtract 1.5 from the x-coordinate, and add 2.8 to the y-coordinate:

$$(-2.3, -1.2)$$
$$(-2.3 - 1.5, -1.2 + 2.8)$$
$$(-3.8, 1.6)$$

Choice (J) is correct. Be certain that you used the correct values given in the question.

7. B

Difficulty: Medium
Category: Functions
Getting to the Answer: The question asks which of the choices is equivalent to $\sqrt{a^2 + b^2}$ and gives you the equations for a and b. Plug in the given values and simplify. Remember the Pythagorean identity: $\cos^2 \theta + \sin^2 \theta = 1$.

$$\sqrt{a^2 + b^2} = \sqrt{(x\cos\theta)^2 + (x\sin\theta)^2}$$
$$= \sqrt{x^2 \cos^2\theta + x^2 \sin^2\theta}$$
$$= \sqrt{x^2(\cos^2\theta + \sin^2\theta)}$$
$$= \sqrt{x^2(1)}$$
$$= x$$

Choice (B) is correct. Be certain that you used all the given values; omitting the x terms results in choice A.

8. F

Difficulty: Medium
Category: Functions
Getting to the Answer: The question asks for the value of nested functions when $x = \frac{1}{4}$ and provides the equations for both functions. Start by evaluating $g\left(\frac{1}{4}\right)$:

$$g\left(\frac{1}{4}\right) = \sqrt{\frac{1}{4}} + 2.5$$
$$= \frac{1}{2} + 2.5$$
$$= 3$$

Now evaluate $f(3)$:

$$f(3) = -4(3) + 1$$
$$= -12 + 1$$
$$= -11$$

Thus, (F) is correct. Be certain that you answered the question that was asked. Determining $g\left(f\left(\frac{1}{4}\right)\right)$ results in the value in H.

9. A
Difficulty: Medium
Category: Functions
Getting to the Answer: The question asks for the range of the function shown in the graph. Range refers to the maximum and minimum of the *y*-values of a function. Notice that the function never goes above 2 or below −2. Since the minimum value is −2 and the maximum value is 2, the range is all real numbers between −2 and 2, including those endpoints. Choice (A) is correct. Be certain that you found the range rather than the domain.

10. J
Difficulty: Medium
Category: Functions
Getting to the Answer: The question asks which trigonometric function could be shown on the graph. Notice that all the answer choices are of the form $\sin(x + k)$. Compare the parent function, $\sin(x)$, to the given graph and solve for the horizontal shift k.

Observe that the *y*-intercept of the graph is 1. Since the *y*-intercept occurs when $x = 0$, plug $x = 0$ into the equation $\sin(x + k) = 1$ and solve for k.

$$\sin(x + k) = 1$$
$$\sin(0 + k) = 1$$
$$\sin(k) = 1$$

Since $\sin\left(\frac{\pi}{2}\right) = 1$, you can conclude that $k = \frac{\pi}{2}$.

Therefore, (J) is correct.

[CHAPTER 13]

GEOMETRY

LEARNING OBJECTIVES

After completing this chapter, you will be able to:

- Identify equal angles when two parallel lines are crossed by a transversal
- Identify supplementary and vertical angles and determine missing angle measures
- Determine an unknown angle measure in a polygon using line and angle properties
- Calculate the value of the third angle in a triangle given the other two angle measures
- Identify similar triangles and apply their properties
- Apply relationships between side lengths and angle measures in a triangle
- Calculate the length of the third side of a right triangle given the other two side lengths
- Given one side length of a 45-45-90 or 30-60-90 triangle, calculate the other two
- Calculate the area or perimeter of a polygon or complex figure
- Perform unit conversions
- Answer math questions about circles using relationships among angles, arcs, distances, and area
- Relate properties of a quadratic function to its graph and vice versa
- Identify and calculate measurements within a complex figure
- Transfer information among multiple figures
- Calculate the volume and surface area of common three-dimensional (3D) figures
- Apply basic trigonometric ratios and formulas to answer questions involving right triangles

Part 3
ACT MATH

How Much Do You Know?

Directions: Try out the questions below. Show your work so that you can compare your solutions to the ones found on the next page. The "Category" heading in the explanation for each question gives the title of the lesson that covers how to solve it. If you answered the question(s) for a given lesson correctly, and if your scratchwork looks like the explanations, you may be able to move quickly through that lesson. If you answered incorrectly or used a different approach, you may want to take your time on that lesson.

1. In the figures shown, $\triangle ABC$ is similar to $\triangle DEF$. $\angle A$ corresponds to $\angle D$, $\angle B$ corresponds to $\angle E$, and $\angle C$ corresponds to $\angle F$. If the given lengths are of the same unit of measure, what is the value of x?

   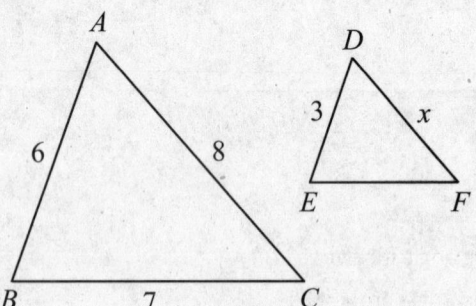

   A. 3
   B. 4
   C. 5
   D. 6

3. In the following figure, O is the center of the circle, and the ratio of the area of sector $OABC$ to the area of sector $OCDA$ is 3 to 5. What is the value of x?

   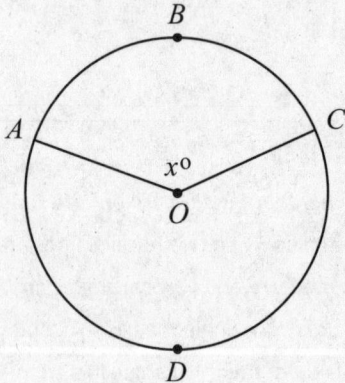

   A. 120
   B. 135
   C. 150
   D. 216

2. What is the area, in square centimeters, of the polygon in the figure shown here?

   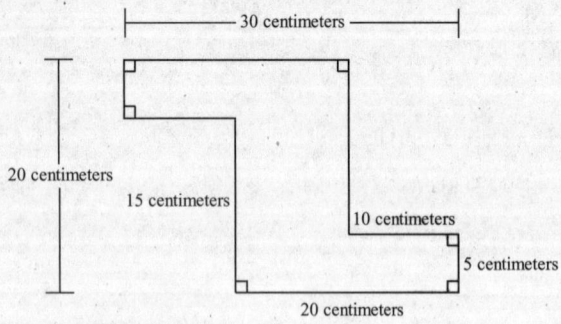

   F. 100
   G. 225
   H. 300
   J. 550

4. In the following figure, line t crosses parallel lines m and n. What is the degree measure of $\angle x$?

   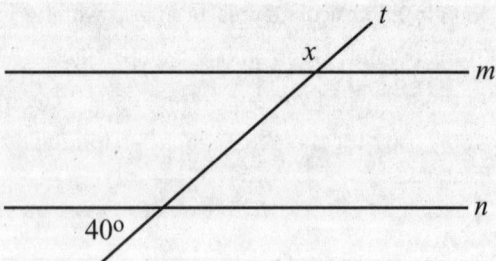

   F. 40°
   G. 60°
   H. 130°
   J. 140°

5. In the figure shown, $ABCD$ is a square, and $\overline{AB}$ is a diameter of the circle centered at O. If $\overline{AD}$ is 10 units long, what is the area, in square units, of the shaded region?

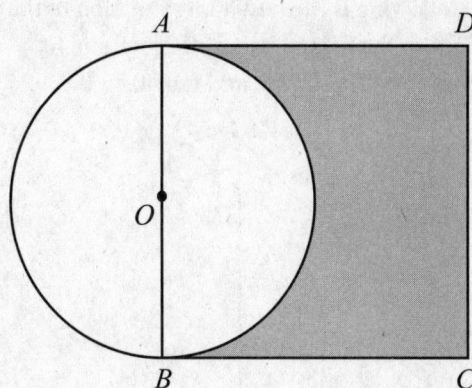

A. $100 - 25\pi$
B. $100 - \dfrac{25}{2}\pi$
C. $100 - 10\pi$
D. $100 - \dfrac{5}{2}\pi$

6. If an isosceles right triangle has a hypotenuse of 4 inches, what is the perimeter, in inches, of the triangle?

F. $4\sqrt{2}$
G. $4 + 4\sqrt{2}$
H. $4 + 8\sqrt{2}$
J. $8 + 4\sqrt{2}$

7. A certain rectangle is $(x + 3)$ units long and $(x + 7)$ units wide. If a square with sides of length x is removed from the interior of the rectangle, which of the following is an expression for the remaining area?

A. 21
B. $2x + 10$
C. $10x + 21$
D. $x^2 + 10x + 21$

8. A rectangular prism has three faces with areas of 28, 20, and 35 square centimeters. What is the volume of this solid in cubic centimeters?

F. 83
G. 140
H. 166
J. 196

9. Elizabeth plans to install artificial grass around the patio and fountain in her backyard as shown in the following figure. How many square feet of artificial grass does she need?

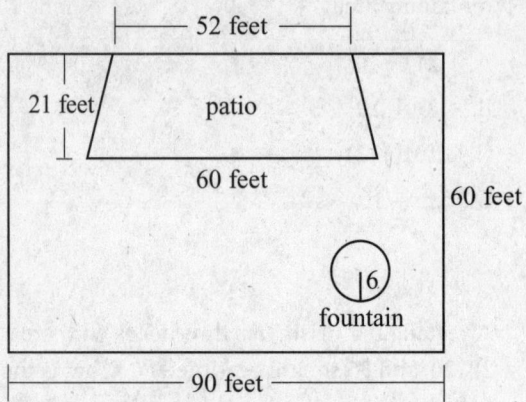

A. $4{,}140 - 12\pi$
B. $4{,}140 - 36\pi$
C. $4{,}224 - 12\pi$
D. $4{,}224 - 36\pi$

10. Armando wants to determine the height of a flagpole. He stands 100 feet from the base of the flagpole and measures the angle of elevation to be 40°, as shown in the following figure. Which of the following is the best approximation of the height of the flagpole, in feet? Note: sin 40° = 0.643, cos 40° = 0.766, and tan 40° = 0.839.

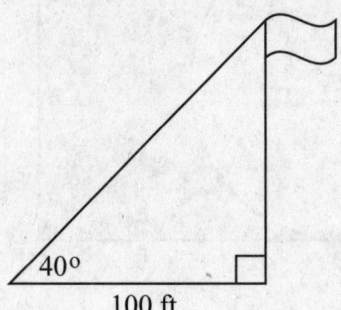

F. 50
G. 64
H. 77
J. 84

Chapter 13
Geometry

Answers and Explanations

How Much Do You Know?

1. B
Difficulty: Low
Category: Geometry: Triangle Properties
Getting to the Answer: You need to find the value of x. You are told that the triangles are similar and are given a figure with labeled side lengths. In similar triangles, corresponding sides are proportional. $\overline{DE}$ corresponds to $\overline{AB}$, and $\overline{DF}$ corresponds to $\overline{AC}$. Use this relationship to set up a proportion. Cross-multiply to solve for x.

$$\frac{\overline{AB}}{\overline{DE}} = \frac{\overline{AC}}{\overline{DF}}$$
$$\frac{6}{3} = \frac{8}{x}$$
$$6x = 3(8)$$
$$6x = 24$$
$$x = 4$$

You found the value of x, so you are done. Choice (B) is correct.

2. H
Difficulty: Medium
Category: Geometry: Complex Two-Dimensional Figures
Getting to the Answer: The area of the polygon can be found by dividing the polygon into two 5 cm × 20 cm rectangles and one 10 cm × 10 cm square. The area of the polygon is thus the sum of the areas of the rectangles and square: $2(5 \times 20) + (10 \times 10) = 300$ square centimeters. Choice (H) is correct.

Alternatively, the area of the polygon can be found by subtracting the two 10 cm × 15 cm rectangles from the larger 30 cm × 20 cm rectangle: $20 \times 30 - 2(10 \times 15) = 300$ square centimeters.

3. B
Difficulty: Medium
Category: Geometry: Circles and Parabolas
Getting to the Answer: You need to find the value of x. You are given a circle that is divided into two sectors. You are also given the ratio of the areas of the sectors: $\frac{OABC}{OCDA} = \frac{3}{5}$. Because the only angle measure you know is the whole circle (360°), you need to rewrite the given part-to-part ratio as a part-to-whole ratio:
$$\frac{OABC}{OABC + OCDA} = \frac{3}{3+5} = \frac{3}{8}.$$

Now use what you know about the parts of a circle: the ratio between the interior angle of a sector and 360° is the same as the ratio between the area of a sector and the area of the whole circle. This means that you can use the part-to-whole ratio from the areas to find the missing angle measure by setting up a proportion.

$$\frac{\text{area of sector}}{\text{area of circle}} = \frac{\text{central angle}}{360°}$$
$$\frac{3}{8} = \frac{x}{360°}$$
$$360(3) = 8x$$
$$1{,}080 = 8x$$
$$135 = x$$

You found the value of x. Choice (B) is correct.

4. J
Difficulty: Low
Category: Geometry: Lines and Angles
Getting to the Answer: When a transversal crosses parallel lines, the four acute angles formed are all equal, the four obtuse angles formed are all equal, and any angles that are not equal are supplementary. The angle marked x is obtuse, so it is supplementary to the given 40° angle. Since $180 - 40 = 140$, the answer is (J).

5. B
Difficulty: Medium
Category: Geometry: Complex Two-Dimensional Figures
Getting to the Answer: You are looking for the area of the shaded region. You are given a figure and told that $\overline{AB}$ is a diameter of the circle and that $\overline{AD}$ (one side of the square) is 10 units long.

First, determine which area you are actually looking for. Describe it in words first, and then apply the correct formulas. Finally, fill in the dimensions given in the question stem. The side of the square is 10 units. The radius of the circle is half the diameter, or 5.

$$\text{shaded region} = \text{square} - \text{semicircle}$$
$$A_{shaded} = s^2 - \frac{1}{2}\pi r^2$$
$$A_{shaded} = 10^2 - \frac{1}{2}\pi(5)^2$$
$$= 100 - \frac{1}{2}(25\pi)$$
$$= 100 - \frac{25}{2}\pi$$

Stop! Look back at the answer choices before you waste time trying to simplify. You already have a match. Choice (B) is correct.

6. G
Difficulty: Medium
Category: Geometry: Right Triangles
Getting to the Answer: An isosceles right triangle is a 45-45-90 triangle, which has sides in the ratio $x:x:x\sqrt{2}$. If the hypotenuse has a length of 4 inches, then the sides are each $\frac{4}{\sqrt{2}}$ or $2\sqrt{2}$ inches long. This means that the perimeter of the triangle is $2\sqrt{2} + 2\sqrt{2} + 4 = 4 + 4\sqrt{2}$, which is (G).

7. C
Difficulty: Medium
Category: Geometry: Polygons
Getting to the Answer: If you have trouble keeping track of the variables, you can Pick Numbers. However, many students find it slightly faster to work with variables in a question like this.

Use FOIL to find that the rectangle has an area of $(x + 3)(x + 7) = x^2 + 10x + 21$. The square that is being removed has an area of x^2, so the area after removing the square is $x^2 + 10x + 21 - x^2 = 10x + 21$, which is (C).

8. G
Difficulty: High
Category: Geometry: Three-Dimensional Figures
Getting to the Answer: To answer this question, sketch an "unfolded" drawing of the solid and add dimensions to your sketch as you reason through the information provided in the question:

```
              7
         ┌────────┐
       5 │   35   │
  ┌──────┼────────┼──────┐
  │  20  │   28   │  20  │ 4
  └──────┼────────┼──────┘
         │   35   │ 5
         ├────────┤
         │   28   │ 4
         └────────┘
              7
```

Opposite faces of a rectangular solid are congruent, so there are six faces with the corresponding areas shown above. Look for factors that will produce the given areas. These factors are the dimensions of the solid. Since $7 \times 4 = 28$, $7 \times 5 = 35$, and $4 \times 5 = 20$, the dimensions are 7 cm, 4 cm, and 5 cm. Finally, use the volume formula to arrive at the correct answer: $V = lwh = 7 \times 5 \times 4 = 140$ cubic centimeters, which is (G).

9. D
Difficulty: High
Category: Geometry: Complex Two-Dimensional Figures
Getting to the Answer: To determine the amount of artificial grass Elizabeth needs, subtract the area of the patio and the area of the fountain from the total area of the backyard. The total area of the backyard is 60 ft × 90 ft = 5,400 ft². The patio is in the shape of a trapezoid, so its area is $\frac{1}{2}(b_1 + b_2)h = \frac{1}{2}(52 + 60)21 = 1,176$ square feet. The area of the fountain represented by a circle is $\pi r^2 = \pi 6^2 = 36\pi$ square feet. Thus, the amount of artificial grass Elizabeth needs is $5,400 - 1,176 - 36\pi = 4,224 - 36\pi$ square feet. Choice (D) is correct.

10. J
Difficulty: High
Category: Geometry: Triangles and Trigonometry
Getting to the Answer: Don't try to do questions like these in your head. Set up an equation that relates the thing you're looking for to the things that you know and then solve.

You know the angle of elevation and the distance from the base of the flagpole, and you're looking for the height of the flagpole. In other words, you know one angle and the length of the side adjacent to it, and you're looking for the length of the side opposite it. Which trig function describes the relationship between an angle and the opposite and adjacent sides? Tangent does: $\tan 40° = \frac{h}{100}$, where h is the height of the flagpole.

Therefore, $100 \tan 40° = h$. The question tells you that $\tan 40°$ is approximately 0.839, so h is approximately $100(0.839) = 83.9$. The best approximation of this is (J).

Chapter 13
Geometry

LINES AND ANGLES

LEARNING OBJECTIVES

After this lesson, you will be able to:

- Identify equal angles when two parallel lines are crossed by a transversal
- Identify supplementary and vertical angles and determine missing angle measures
- Determine an unknown angle measure in a polygon using line and angle properties

To answer a question like this

Lines E, F, and G are parallel lines cut by transversal H as shown. What is the value of $a + b + c + d$?

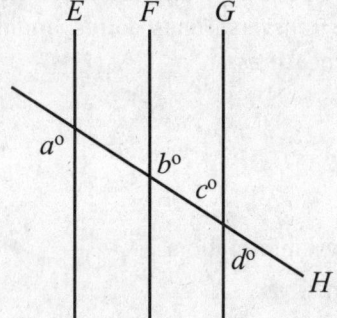

A. 270°
B. 360°
C. 540°
D. Cannot be determined from the given information

You need to know this

Adjacent angles can be added to find the measure of a larger angle. The following diagram demonstrates this.

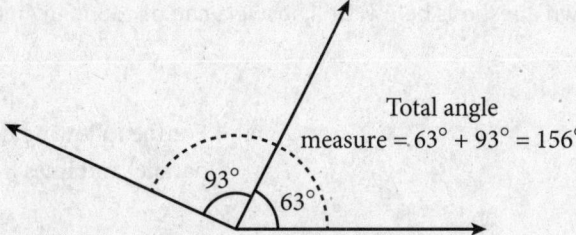

Two angles that sum to 90° are called **complementary angles**. Two angles that sum to 180° are called **supplementary angles**.

365

Part 3
ACT MATH

Two distinct lines in a plane will either intersect at one point or extend indefinitely without intersecting. If two lines intersect at a right angle (90°), they are **perpendicular** and are denoted with ⊥. If the lines never intersect, they are **parallel** and are denoted with ||.

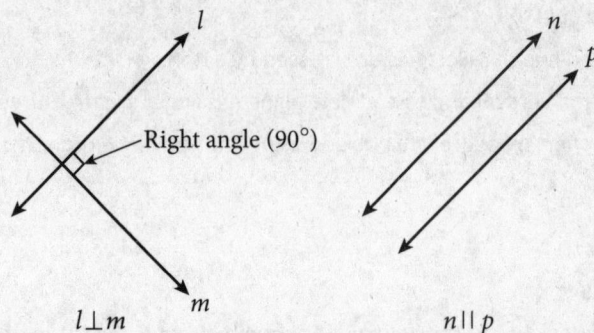

When a third line crosses two parallel lines, it creates two points of intersection and eight angles. This line is called a transversal. When a question involves parallel lines and one or more transversal lines, corresponding and supplementary angle relationships will help you identify missing angle measures.

You need to do this

- If the question does not include an image, draw one.
- Label the figure.
- Look for line and angle relationships that will allow you to determine new information.
- Add more information to the figure(s) as needed to answer the question.

Explanation

The question asks for the value of $a + b + c + d$. You are told that line H is a transversal through the parallel lines E, F, and G. There are no angle measures given, so you need to think about properties of parallel lines. The angles labeled a and b are obtuse angles; the angles labeled c and d are acute angles. Thus, angle a must be supplementary to angle d, and angle b must be supplementary to angle c. In other words, $a + d = 180$ and $b + c = 180$. Thus, $a + b + c + d = 180 + 180 = 360$. You found the sum of the four angle measures, so you are done. Choice (B) is correct.

Drills

If lines and angles give you trouble, study the information above and try out these drill questions before completing the Try on Your Own questions below. Drill answers can be found in Answers and Explanations.

Solve for the variable.

a.

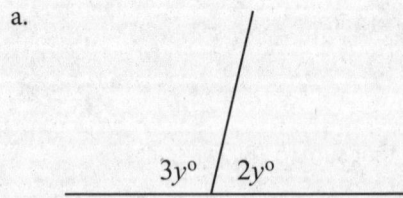

b. For the following figure, lines l and m are parallel and lines n and o are parallel.

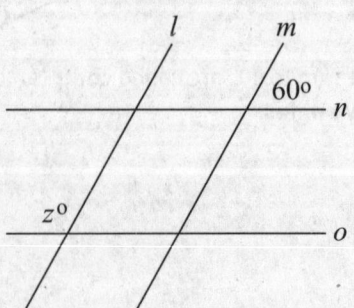

c.
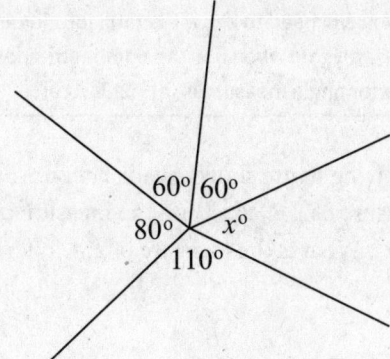

e.
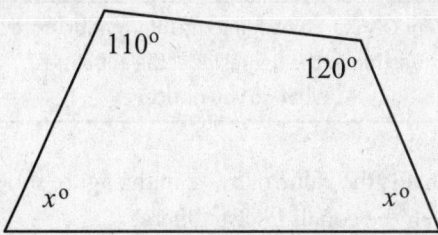

d.
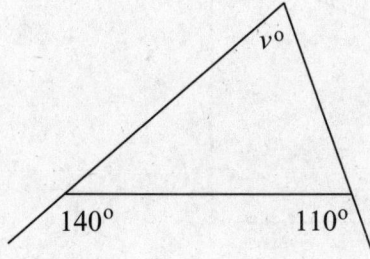

Try on Your Own

Directions: Take as much time as you need on these questions. Work carefully and methodically. There will be an opportunity for timed practice at the end of the chapter.

1. In the following figure, $\overline{CD}$ is parallel to $\overline{AB}$, and $\overline{PQ}$ intersects $\overline{CD}$ at R and $\overline{AB}$ at T. If the measure of $\angle CRP$ is 110°, what is the measure of $\angle ATQ$?

   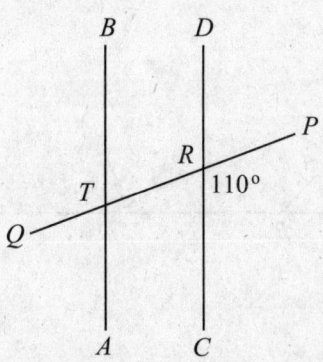

   A. 50°
   B. 70°
   C. 90°
   D. 110°

2. In the following figure, lines a and b are perpendicular, and line c passes through their point of intersection. What is the measure of y in terms of x?

   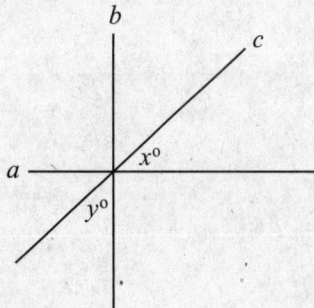

   F. $(45 + x)°$
   G. $(90 - x)°$
   H. $(90 + x)°$
   J. $(180 - x)°$

> HINT: For Q3, start by adding the information from the question to the figure: label the equalities. What do you notice?

> HINT: For Q4, you will need to know the total interior angle measure of a polygon: when n = the number of sides, the interior angle measure is $(n-2) \times 180°$.

3. What is the value of $b - c$ in the figure shown given the equalities listed here?

   $\overline{LM} = \overline{MN} = \overline{NO} = \overline{OL} = \overline{LN}$

   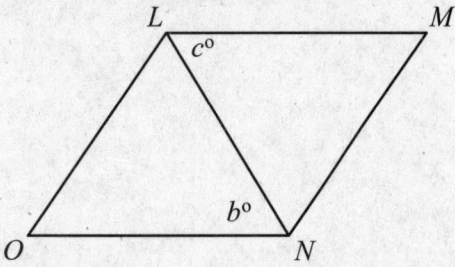

   A. -10
   B. 0
   C. 10
   D. 30

4. The following figure shows quadrilateral $ABCD$. The measure of $\angle B$ is $2x°$ and the measure of $\angle D$ is $3x°$. What is the measure of $\angle A$ in terms of x?

   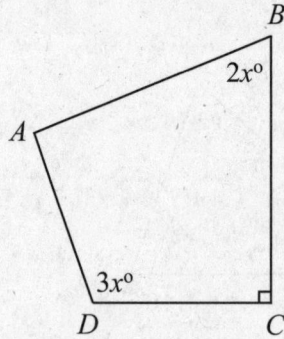

   F. $(90 + 5x)°$
   G. $(180 - 5x)°$
   H. $(180 + 5x)°$
   J. $(270 - 5x)°$

5. In the following figure, $\angle ABC = 45°$ and $\angle CDE = 155°$. What is $\angle BCD$?

   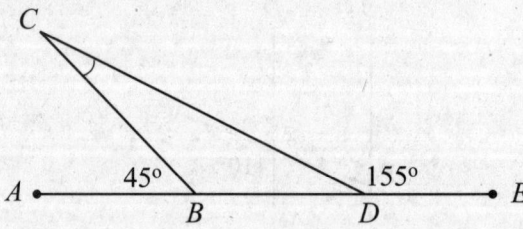

   A. $15°$
   B. $20°$
   C. $25°$
   D. $35°$

Chapter 13
Geometry

TRIANGLE PROPERTIES

LEARNING OBJECTIVES

After this lesson, you will be able to:

- Calculate the value of the third angle in a triangle given the other two angle measures
- Identify similar triangles and apply their properties
- Apply relationships between side lengths and angle measures in a triangle

To answer a question like this

In the following figure, K, L, N, and O lie on the same line. If $\overline{LM} = \overline{MN}$ and ∠NOP and ∠OPN are as marked, what is the measure of ∠KLM?

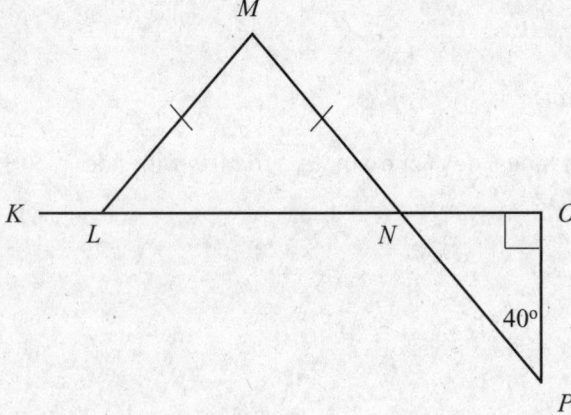

A. 125°
B. 130°
C. 135°
D. 140°

You need to know this

The **interior angles** of a triangle sum to 180°. If you know any two interior angles, you can calculate the third.

The corresponding angles and side lengths of **congruent triangles** are equal. **Similar triangles** have the same angle measurements and proportional sides. In the figure below, △ABC and △DEF have the same angle measurements, so the side lengths can be set up as the following proportion: $\frac{A}{D} = \frac{B}{E} = \frac{C}{F}$.

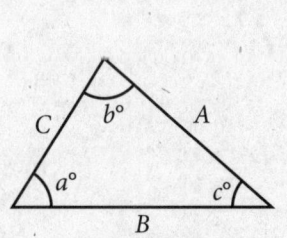
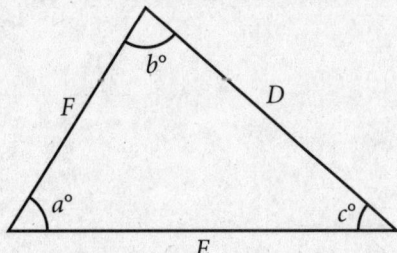

Part 3
ACT MATH

Two triangles are similar if three specific conditions are met:

- Two of their three angles are congruent (angle-angle). For example, two triangles that each have one 40° and one 55° angle are similar.

- Two of their three sides are in the same proportion and the intervening angle is congruent (side-angle-side). For example, a triangle with sides of 10 and 12 and an intervening angle of 40° and another triangle with sides of 20 and 24 and an intervening angle of 40° are similar.

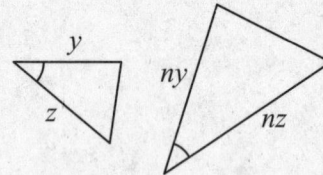

- Their three sides are in the same proportion (side-side-side). For example, a triangle with sides of 5, 6, and 8 and a triangle with sides 15, 18, and 24 are similar.

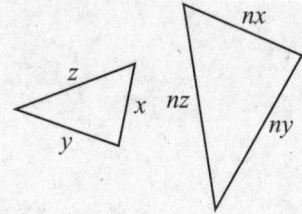

You need to do this

- Use line and angle properties to determine missing triangle angle measures.
- Determine whether two triangles are similar by checking for angle-angle, side-angle-side, or side-side-side relationships.
- Find a missing side length by setting up a proportion.

Explanation

You are trying to find $\angle KLM$, but you have very little information about this part of the figure. However, you do have a lot of information about $\triangle NOP$, so start there. Since there are 180 degrees in a triangle, $\angle ONP$ is $180° - 40° - 90° = 50°$. Angles ONP and MNL are vertical, so they are equal. Recall that angles that are opposite equal sides in a triangle are equal. Thus, $\angle MLN$ is also 50°. Finally, since $\angle MLN$ and $\angle KLM$ lie on a straight line, they are supplementary. Thus, $\angle KLM = 180° - 50° = 130°$ and (B) is correct.

Chapter 13
Geometry

Try on Your Own

Directions: Take as much time as you need on these questions. Work carefully and methodically. There will be an opportunity for timed practice at the end of the chapter.

1. In the following figure, $\overline{DE}$ is parallel to $\overline{AC}$. If $\overline{DF} = \overline{DE} = \overline{FE}$, then what is the measure of $\angle DAB$?

   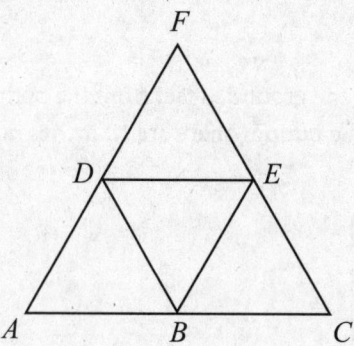

   A. 30°
   B. 45°
   C. 60°
   D. 70°

2. In isosceles triangle ABC, $\overline{AB}$ and $\overline{BC}$ are congruent. If $m\angle CAB = 27°$, what is the measure of $\angle ABC$?

   F. 27°
   G. 54°
   H. 126°
   J. 153°

3. If the measures of the angles of a triangle are in the ratio 2:3:7, what is the measure of the largest angle?

   A. 15°
   B. 30°
   C. 45°
   D. 105°

4. In the figure shown, what is the length of the altitude that passes through vertex X in $\triangle YXZ$?

   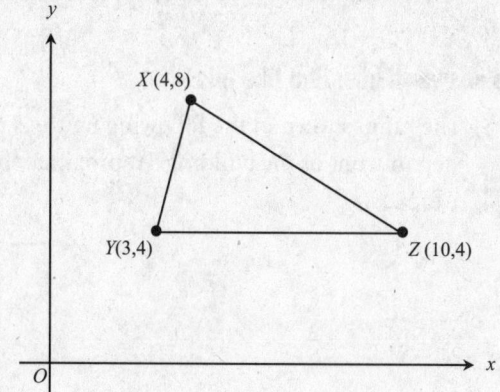

   F. $\sqrt{5}$
   G. 4
   H. $2\sqrt{5}$
   J. $2\sqrt{13}$

   HINT: For Q5, how does the dashed line segment help you answer this question?

5. $\triangle PQR$ has side lengths a, b, and c, as shown in the following figure. A dashed line segment, d, originates at point P and is perpendicular to $\overline{QR}$. What is the ratio of the length of d to the length of $\overline{PQ}$?

   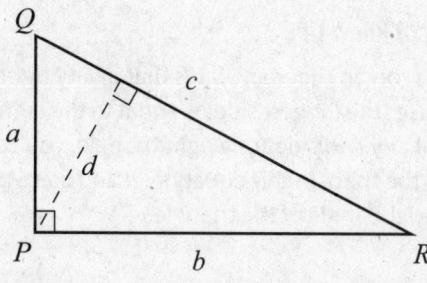

   A. $\dfrac{a}{c}$
   B. $\dfrac{b}{c}$
   C. $\dfrac{a}{b}$
   D. $\dfrac{b}{a}$

Part 3
ACT MATH

RIGHT TRIANGLES

LEARNING OBJECTIVES

After this lesson, you will be able to:

- Calculate the length of the third side of a right triangle given the other two side lengths
- Given one side length of a 45-45-90 or 30-60-90 triangle, calculate the other two

To answer a question like this

The ramp shown in the following figure is placed at a 30° angle with the ground, 8 feet from the bottom step in front of the building. Approximately how long, in inches, is the ramp? (There are 12 inches in 1 foot.)

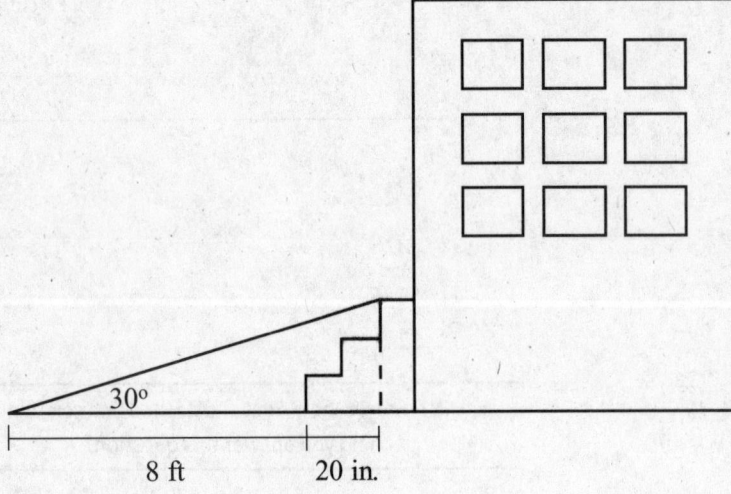

A. 84
B. 116
C. 128
D. 134

You need to know this

The Pythagorean theorem states that in any right triangle (and only in right triangles), the square of the hypotenuse (the longest side) is equal to the sum of the squares of the legs (the shorter sides). If you know the lengths of any two sides of a right triangle, you can use the Pythagorean equation, $a^2 + b^2 = c^2$, to find the length of the third. In this equation, a and b are the legs of the triangle and c is the hypotenuse, the side across from the right angle of the triangle.

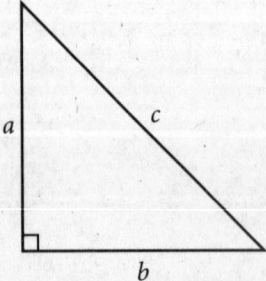

Consider an example: A right triangle has a leg of length 9 and a hypotenuse of length 14. To find the missing leg, plug the known values into the Pythagorean equation: $9^2 + b^2 = 14^2$. This simplifies to $81 + b^2 = 196$, which becomes $b^2 = 115$. Take the square root of both sides to find that $b \cong 10.7$.

Some right triangles have side lengths that are all integers. These sets of integer side lengths are called Pythagorean triples. The two most common Pythagorean triples on the ACT are 3-4-5 and 5-12-13. Look for multiples of these (for example, 6-8-10 and 10-24-26) as well. Memorizing these triples now can save you valuable calculation time on test day.

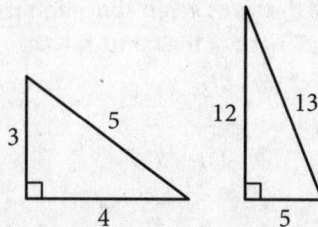

Special right triangles are defined by their angles. As a result, the ratios of their side lengths are always the same.

- If you know the length of any one of the three sides of a special right triangle, you can find the lengths of the other two.
- The ratio of the sides of a 45-45-90 triangle is $x:x:x\sqrt{2}$, where x is the length of each leg and $x\sqrt{2}$ is the length of the hypotenuse.
- The ratio of the sides of a 30-60-90 triangle is $x:x\sqrt{3}:2x$, where x is the shorter leg, $x\sqrt{3}$ is the longer leg, and $2x$ is the hypotenuse.
- These side length ratios are not provided to you on the ACT, so you should memorize them, especially if you are working to earn a top score.

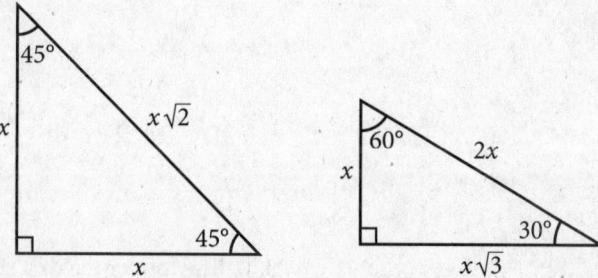

You need to do this

- Keep in mind that the Pythagorean theorem applies only to right triangles.
- When you need to find a side length of a right triangle, look first for the common Pythagorean triples or their multiples.
- If you cannot identify any Pythagorean triples, substitute any two known side lengths into the equation $a^2 + b^2 = c^2$, where c represents the hypotenuse, to find the third.
- Look for hidden special right triangles within other shapes. For example, an equilateral triangle can be bisected (cut in half) to form two congruent 30-60-90 triangles, and a square can be divided with a diagonal into two congruent 45-45-90 triangles.
- Use one known side length to deduce the other two in a special right triangle. For example, if the shorter leg of a 30-60-90 triangle has a length of 5, then the longer leg has a length of $5\sqrt{3}$, and the hypotenuse has a length of $5(2) = 10$.

Explanation

Two of the angles in the triangle have degree measures of 30 and 90, which means that the third angle must measure 60 degrees. Thus, you can use the properties of 30-60-90 triangles to help you. In a 30-60-90 triangle, the sides are always in the ratio $x : x\sqrt{3} : 2x$ (short leg:long leg:hypotenuse). The only length that you know is the long leg, the side represented by the ground and the width of the bottom two steps. Convert feet into inches so that the units are the same. The ramp is to be placed 8 feet $\times \dfrac{12 \text{ inches}}{1 \text{ foot}} = 96$ inches from the bottom step, and the steps themselves account for an additional 20 inches. This means that this leg of the triangle is $96 + 20 = 116$ inches long. Use the ratio of the sides given above to set up a proportion to find the length of the hypotenuse, which corresponds to the length of the ramp, r.

$$\frac{\sqrt{3}}{2} = \frac{116}{r}$$

$$\sqrt{3}\,r = 232$$

$$r \cong 133.95$$

The result is approximately 134 inches, which matches (D).

Try on Your Own

Directions: Take as much time as you need on these questions. Work carefully and methodically. There will be an opportunity for timed practice at the end of the chapter.

1. The hypotenuse of $\triangle ABC$ is 20 meters and $\angle ABC$ is 30°. What is the length, in meters, of AB?

   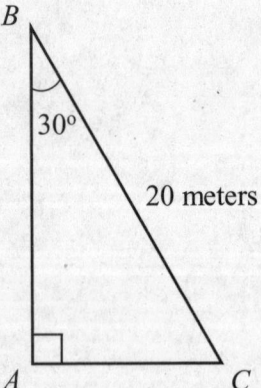

   A. 10
   B. $10\sqrt{2}$
   C. $10\sqrt{3}$
   D. $20\sqrt{3}$

2. The diagonal measure of a square tile is 18 inches. What is the side length, in inches, of the tile?

   F. 9
   G. $9\sqrt{2}$
   H. $9\sqrt{3}$
   J. $18\sqrt{2}$

3. The longer leg of a right triangle is twice the length of the shorter leg. If the length of the shorter leg is 6 inches, what is the length, in inches, of the hypotenuse?

   A. $3\sqrt{5}$
   B. $6\sqrt{5}$
   C. $9\sqrt{2}$
   D. 18

4. A playground slide is 10 feet long, and the base of the slide is 8 feet from the base of a ladder, as shown in the following figure. If the ladder is perpendicular to the ground, what is the height, in feet, of the ladder?

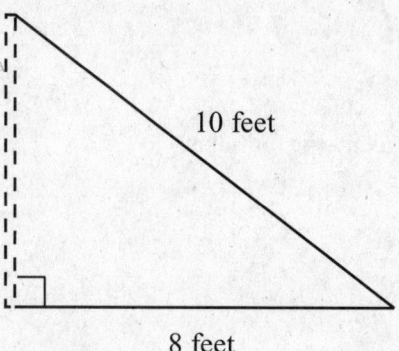

F. 3
G. 4
H. 5
J. 6

HINT: There are two approaches you can take to answer Q5. Which one is more efficient for you?

5. What is the length, in units, of side AB in the following diagram?

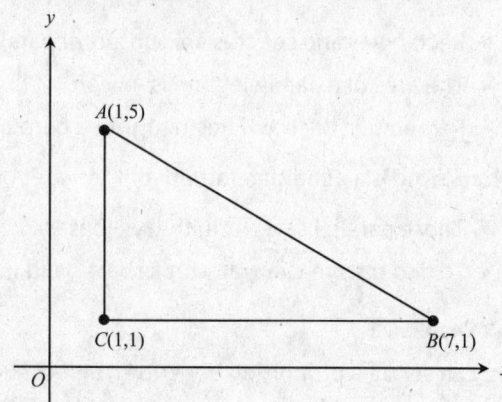

A. $\sqrt{13}$
B. 4
C. 6
D. $2\sqrt{13}$

POLYGONS

LEARNING OBJECTIVES

After this lesson, you will be able to:

- Calculate the area or perimeter of a polygon or complex figure
- Perform unit conversions

To answer a question like this

Jayden plans to order a rectangular rug for his dorm room. His roommate wants a rug that has a perimeter of 14 yards and covers an area of 12 square yards. What are the dimensions of the rug, in feet? (Note: 1 yard = 3 feet)

A. 4 by 27
B. 6 by 18
C. 7 by 14
D. 9 by 12

You need to know this

Perimeter and area are basic properties that all two-dimensional shapes have.

- The **perimeter** of a polygon can easily be calculated by adding the lengths of all its sides.
- **Area** is the amount of two-dimensional space a shape occupies.

Parallelograms are quadrilaterals with two pairs of parallel sides.

- Rectangles and squares are subsets of parallelograms.
- The area of a parallelogram is $A = bh$.
- Remember, base and height must be perpendicular when using geometric formulas.

A **trapezoid** is a quadrilateral with only one set of parallel sides.

- Those parallel sides form the two bases.
- To find the area, average those bases and multiply by the height.

Unit Conversion

You can set up a proportion to perform unit conversions. This is especially useful when there are multiple conversions or when the units are unfamiliar. On the ACT, you may see unit conversion involve scale factors related to maps or blueprints.

For example, though these units of measurement are no longer commonly used, there are 8 furlongs in a mile and 3 miles in a league. Say you're asked to convert 4 leagues to furlongs. A convenient way to do this is to set up a proportion so that equivalent units cancel:

$$4 \text{ leagues} \times \frac{3 \text{ miles}}{1 \text{ league}} \times \frac{8 \text{ furlongs}}{1 \text{ mile}} = 4 \times 3 \times 8 = 96 \text{ furlongs}$$

Notice that all the units cancel out except the furlongs, which is the unit you want.

You need to do this

- If a figure is not provided as part of the question, draw one.
- Label the figure with the given information.
- Use angle and line properties to determine missing values, such as base or height.
- Double-check the units in the question and the units in the choices to plan for any necessary unit conversion.
  - When unit conversion is necessary, set up a proportion to make equivalent units cancel. Keep track of the units by writing them down next to the numbers in the proportion.
  - You should be left with the units you're converting into.

Explanation

You can approach this question by setting up a system of equations using the formulas for the area and perimeter of a rectangle. The area is $l \times w$, and the perimeter is $l + l + w + w$ or $2l + 2w$.

$$l \times w = 12$$
$$2l + 2w = 14$$

Solve the second equation for l: $l = 7 - w$. Then substitute it into the first equation to solve for w:

$$(7 - w)w = 12$$
$$7w - w^2 = 12$$
$$0 = w^2 - 7w + 12$$
$$0 = (w - 3)(w - 4)$$
$$3 \text{ and } 4 = w$$

Thus, $l = 4$ and $w = 3$, respectively. Finally, use the 1 yard = 3 feet conversion factor to convert 3 and 4 yards into feet:

$$3 \text{ yards} \times \frac{3 \text{ feet}}{1 \text{ yard}} = 9 \text{ feet}$$

and

$$4 \text{ yards} \times \frac{3 \text{ feet}}{1 \text{ yard}} = 12 \text{ feet}$$

Choice (D) is correct.

Alternatively, you could Backsolve. All of the choices except C yield an area of length (feet) × width (feet) = area (square feet) = 108 ft², and $108 \text{ ft}^2 \times \frac{1 \text{ yd}}{3 \text{ ft}} \times \frac{1 \text{ yd}}{3 \text{ ft}} = 12 \text{ yd}^2$, so C is incorrect. The perimeters in choices A and B are larger than $14 \text{ yards} \times \frac{3 \text{ feet}}{1 \text{ yard}} = 42 \text{ feet}$. Only (D) works.

Drills

If polygons and unit conversions give you trouble, study the information above and try out these drill questions before completing the Try on Your Own questions below. Drill answers can be found in Answers and Explanations.

Solve the following.

a. What is the perimeter?

b. If perimeter is 48, $x = ?$

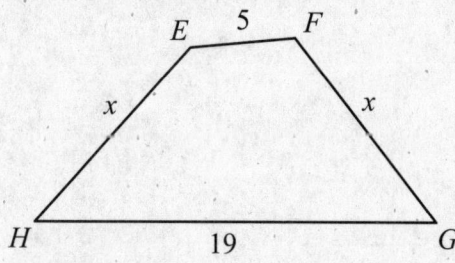

c. What is the area?

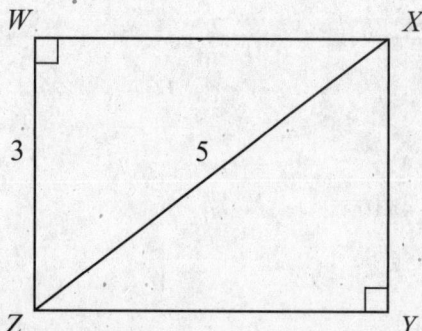

d. What is the area?

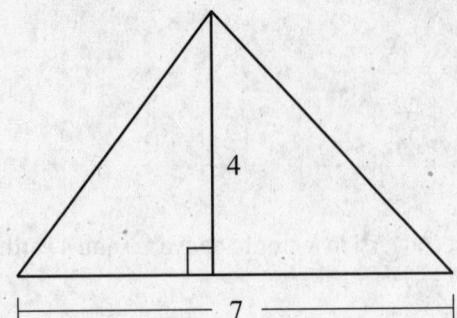

e. What is the area?

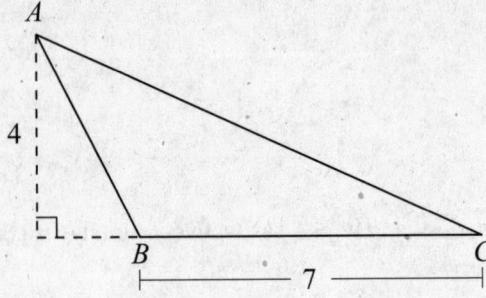

Try on Your Own

Directions: Take as much time as you need on these questions. Work carefully and methodically. There will be an opportunity for timed practice at the end of the chapter.

1. Triangle PQR has a base of 16 centimeters and an altitude of 10 centimeters. If the area of square ABCD is twice the area of $\triangle PQR$, what is the length, in centimeters, of a side of the square ABCD?

   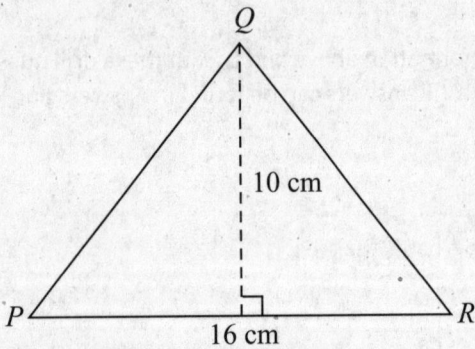

   A. 4
   B. $4\sqrt{5}$
   C. $4\sqrt{10}$
   D. $8\sqrt{5}$

2. As shown in the following figure, points $(-2, 2)$, $(4, 2)$, $(0, 5)$, and $(6, 5)$ are the vertices of a parallelogram. What is the area, in square units, of the parallelogram?

   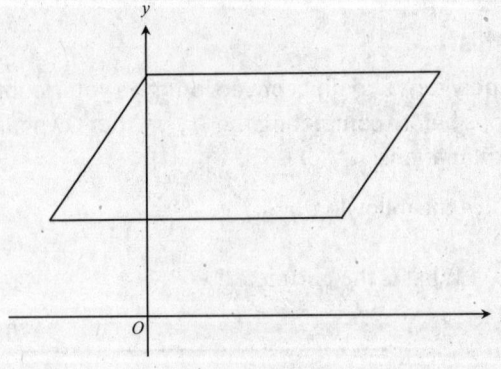

   F. 12
   G. 18
   H. 24
   J. 30

Chapter 13
Geometry

HINT: For Q3, how can you calculate the missing side lengths?

3. In the polygon shown below, all line segments join at right angles. What is the perimeter, in centimeters?

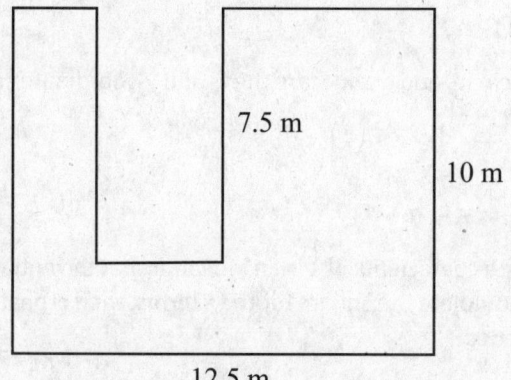

A. 4,500
B. 6,000
C. 9,700
D. 12,500

4. In the figure shown, $\overline{BE}$ is perpendicular to $\overline{AD}$, and the lengths of $\overline{AB}$, $\overline{BC}$, $\overline{CD}$, and $\overline{BE}$ are given in inches. What is the area, in square inches, of trapezoid ABCD?

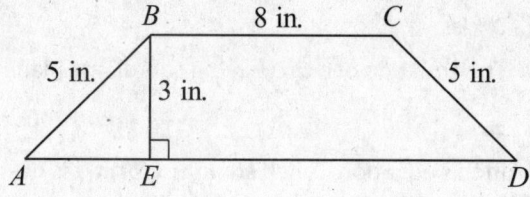

F. 24
G. 30
H. 34
J. 36

5. For the area of a square to triple, the new side lengths must be the old side lengths multiplied by which of the following?

A. $\sqrt{3}$
B. 3
C. 9
D. $\sqrt{27}$

CIRCLES AND PARABOLAS

LEARNING OBJECTIVES

After this lesson, you will be able to:

- Answer math questions about circles using relationships among angles, arcs, distances, and area
- Relate properties of a quadratic function to its graph and vice versa

To answer a question like this

A circle centered at (2, 2) has a radius of 5. A parabola on the same coordinate plane has a vertex at (0, 3) and passes through (−2, 7). At how many points do the circle and parabola intersect?

A. 0
B. 1
C. 2
D. 4

Part 3
ACT MATH

You need to know this

On the ACT, you might see a question with a system of equations that involves one parabola and one circle. This system is usually solved using a coordinate plane. Use the information in the following sections to graph and interpret circles and parabolas.

Circles

The equation of a circle in the coordinate plane is as follows:

$$(x - h)^2 + (y - k)^2 = r^2$$

In this equation, called **standard form**, r is the radius of the circle, and h and k are the x- and y-coordinates of the circle's center, respectively: (h, k).

You might also see what is referred to as **general for**:

$$x^2 + y^2 + Cx + Dy + E = 0$$

In the general form, the fact that there are x^2 and y^2 terms with coefficients of 1 is an indicator that the equation does indeed graph as a circle. To convert to standard form, complete the square for the x terms, then repeat for the y terms. Refer to chapter 10 for a quadratics review if needed.

The ACT may also ask you about the following parts of circles: arcs, central angles, and sectors. The ability to set up ratios and proportions correctly is essential for these questions. Review chapter 9 for more information on rates, ratios, proportions, and percents.

- An **arc** is part of a circle's circumference. If the circumference is divided into exactly two arcs, the smaller one is called the minor arc, and the larger one is called the major arc. If a diameter cuts the circle in half, the two arcs formed are called semicircles. An arc length can never be greater than the circle's circumference.
- An angle formed by two radii is called a **central angle**. Because a full circle contains 360°, a central angle measure cannot be greater than this.
- The part of a circle's area defined by a central angle is called a **sector**. The area of a sector cannot be greater than the circle's total area.

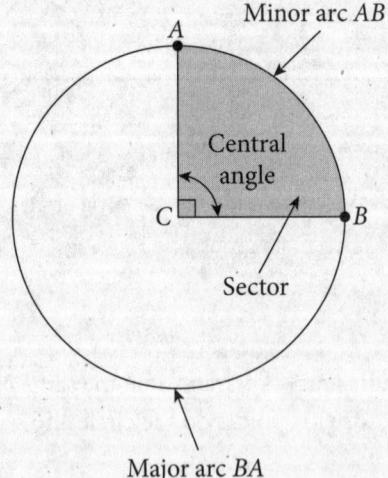

Here's a summary of the ratios formed by these three parts and their whole counterparts:

$$\frac{\text{central angle}}{360°} = \frac{\text{arc length}}{\text{circumference}} = \frac{\text{sector area}}{\text{circle area}}$$

Notice that all of these ratios are equal. Intuitively, this should make sense: when you slice a pizza into four equal slices, each piece should have $\frac{1}{4}$ of the cheese, crust, and sauce. If you slice a circle into four equal pieces, the same principle applies: each piece should have $\frac{1}{4}$ of the degrees, circumference, and area.

Parabolas

As defined in the Functions chapter, a quadratic function is a quadratic equation set equal to y or $f(x)$ instead of 0.

- Remember that the solutions (also called "roots" or "zeros") of any polynomial function are the same as the x-intercepts.
- To solve a quadratic function, substitute 0 for y, or $f(x)$, then solve algebraically.
- Alternatively, you can plug the equation into your graphing calculator and read the x-intercepts from the graph.

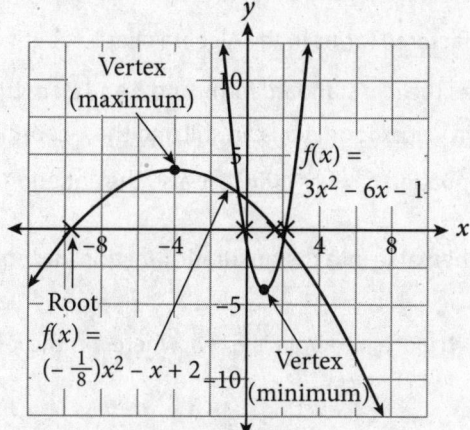

The graph of every quadratic equation (or function) is a **parabola**, which is a symmetric U-shaped graph that opens either upward or downward.

- To determine which way a parabola will open, examine the value of a in the equation.
- If a is positive, the parabola will open upward.
- If a is negative, it will open downward.
- Take a look at the examples above to see this graphically.

Like quadratic equations, quadratic functions will have zero, one, or two real solutions, corresponding to the number of times the parabola crosses the x-axis. Graphing is a powerful way to determine the number of solutions a quadratic function has:

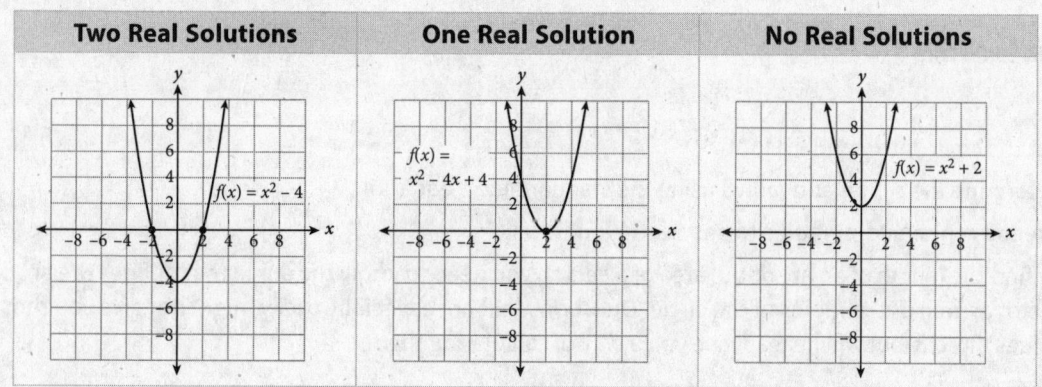

There are three algebraic forms that a quadratic equation can take: standard, factored, and vertex. Each is provided in the following table along with the graphical features that are revealed by writing the equation in that particular form:

Standard	Factored	Vertex
$y = ax^2 + bx + c$	$y = a(x - m)(x - n)$	$y = a(x - h)^2 + k$
y-intercept is c	Solutions are m and n	Vertex is (h, k)
In real-world contexts, starting quantity is c	x-intercepts are m and n	Minimum/maximum of function is k
Format needed to solve via quadratic formula	Vertex is halfway between m and n	Axis of symmetry is given by $x = h$

You've already seen standard and factored forms in the Algebra chapter, but vertex form might be new to you.

- In vertex form, a is the same as the a in standard form, and h and k are the coordinates of the **vertex** (h,k).
- If a quadratic function is not in vertex form, you can still find the x-coordinate of the vertex by plugging the appropriate values into the equation $h = \frac{-b}{2a}$, which is also the equation for the axis of symmetry (see graph that follows).
- Once you determine h, plug this value into the quadratic function and solve for y to determine k, the y-coordinate of the vertex.

The equation of the **axis of symmetry** of a parabola is $x = h$, where h is the x-coordinate of the vertex.

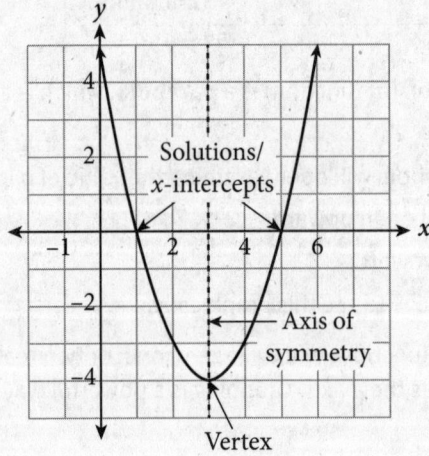

You need to do this

Circles

- Get the circle into standard form.
- Determine the center and radius using the standard form equation.
- Use the center and/or radius to answer the question.
- To find the length of an arc or the area of a sector, you need to know the angle that defines the arc or sector as well as the radius of the circle. Questions that are especially tricky might not give you those values directly but will instead give you a way of calculating them.

Parabolas

- To find the vertex of a parabola, get the function into vertex form: $y = a(x-h)^2 + k$, or use the formula $h = \frac{-b}{2a}$.
- To find the *y*-intercept of a quadratic function, plug in 0 for *x*.
  - To determine whether a parabola opens upward or downward, look at the coefficient of *a*.
  - If *a* is positive, it opens upward.
  - If *a* is negative, it opens downward.
- To determine the number of *x*-intercepts, set the quadratic function equal to 0 and solve or examine its graph.

To answer a question involving a system of equations with a parabola and a circle, take it one figure at a time until you find the point(s) of intersection and/or gather the information you need to answer the question.

Explanation

Sketch the circle and parabola to visualize the situation and make the question easier to answer. Since the circle is centered at (2, 2) and has a radius of 5, the vertex of the parabola (0, 3) lies within the circle. Since the parabola passes through (−2, 7), it opens upward and intersects the circle at two distinct points:

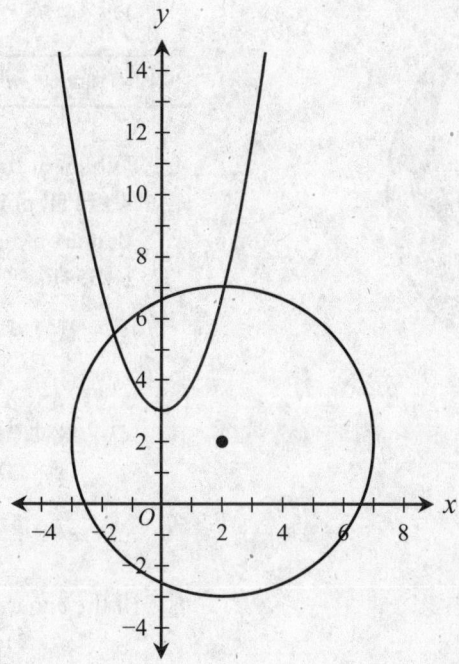

Choice (C) is correct.

Part 3
ACT MATH

Try on Your Own

Directions: Take as much time as you need on these questions. Work carefully and methodically. There will be an opportunity for timed practice at the end of the chapter.

1. What is the area, in square inches, of a circle that has a circumference of 8π inches?

   A. 8π
   B. 16π
   C. 32π
   D. 64π

2. The two circles shown below are tangent to each other. The radius of the larger circle is 75% greater than that of the smaller circle. What is the area, in square feet, of the shaded region?

   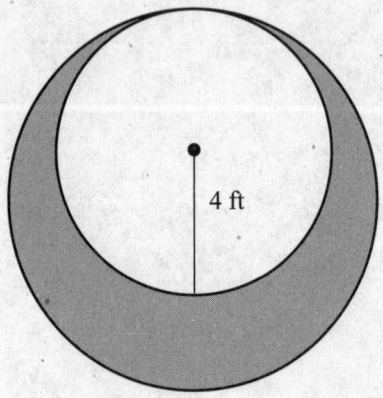

   F. 9π
   G. 10π
   H. 16π
   J. 33π

   HINT: What information in the question stem for Q3 is useful in determining the correct answer?

3. Earth makes one complete rotation about its axis every 24 hours, at a fairly constant rate. Assuming the Earth is a perfect sphere, through how many degrees would Quito, Ecuador, which lies on the Earth's equator, rotate from 12:00 noon on January 1 to 3:00 p.m. on January 2?

   A. 370°
   B. 385°
   C. 405°
   D. 415°

   HINT: For Q4, what does the distance of 5 represent?

4. Which of the following equations describes the set of all points (x, y) in the coordinate plane that are a distance of 5 units from the point $(-3, 4)$?

   F. $(x - 3) + (y + 4) = 5$
   G. $(x + 3)^2 + (y - 4)^2 = 5$
   H. $(x + 3)^2 + (y - 4)^2 = 25$
   J. $(x - 3)^2 + (y + 4)^2 = 25$

5. If the equation for a parabola is $y = (x + 3)^2 - 1$, which of the following best describes the solutions for x?

   A. 2 distinct negative real solutions
   B. 2 distinct positive real solutions
   C. 1 positive real solution and 1 negative real solution
   D. 2 real solutions that are not distinct

Chapter 13
Geometry

COMPLEX TWO-DIMENSIONAL FIGURES

LEARNING OBJECTIVES

After this lesson, you will be able to:
- Identify and calculate measurements within a complex figure
- Transfer information among multiple figures

To answer a question like this

The figure below shows a rectangular basketball court that is symmetric about the mid-court line (the vertical line with a shaded circle located in the middle of the figure). The shaded area is approximately what percent of the full court?

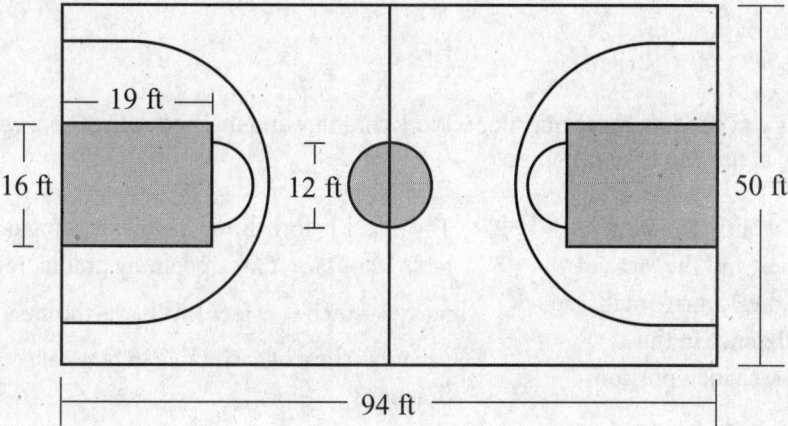

- A. 13.7%
- B. 15.3%
- C. 22.6%
- D. 37.4%

You need to know this

Some ACT math questions will combine multiple 2D figures, especially quadrilaterals, circles, and triangles.

- These questions can involve multiple formulas or steps.
- They can require other math skills, such as percent calculations.

You need to do this

- If a figure is not provided as part of the question, draw one.
- Label the figure with the given information.
- Use angle and line properties to determine missing values, such as base or height.
- Share information among figures when permissible.
- Double-check the units in the question and the units in the choices to plan for any necessary unit conversion.
- When unit conversion is necessary, set up a proportion to make equivalent units cancel.
- Pause for an extra moment before selecting your answer to confirm you really did answer the right question.
- Look out for other math skills needed to answer these questions.

Part 3
ACT MATH

Explanation

You are asked to find approximately what percent of the full court is constituted by the shaded regions. To do so, you need to use the percent formula, percent $= \frac{\text{part}}{\text{whole}} \times 100\%$. First, determine the area of the shaded regions. Next, find the area of the full basketball court. Finally, plug these numbers into the formula.

The shaded areas include the two equal rectangles that are 16 by 19 feet and the center circle that has a diameter of 12 feet. Use $2 \times l \times w$ to calculate the area of the 2 rectangles: $2 \times 16 \times 19 = 608$ square feet. Use $A = \pi r^2$ to calculate the area of the center circle: $\pi(6)^2 \approx 113$ square feet. The sum of the areas is thus approximately $608 + 113 = 721$ feet. The total area of the rectangular basketball court is $50 \times 94 = 4{,}700$ square feet. Now plug these numbers into the percent $= \frac{\text{part}}{\text{whole}} \times 100\%$ formula to calculate approximately what percent the shaded region is of the full court: $\frac{721}{4{,}700} \times 100\% = 15.3\%$. Choice (B) is correct.

Try On Your Own

Directions: Take as much time as you need on these questions. Work carefully and methodically. There will be an opportunity for timed practice at the end of the chapter.

1. The figure shows two flyer layouts. The area of the header is 17 square inches, and the areas of the logo and image are π and 9.5 square inches, respectively. What is the difference in the areas, in square inches, of the shaded portion between the two layouts?

   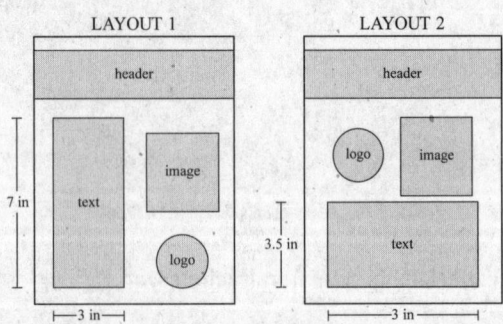

   A. 0
   B. 0.25
   C. 1.25
   D. 1.75

2. The figure below shows a scale drawing of the table layout for Yan's upcoming graduation party $\left(\frac{3}{4}\text{inch} = 9 \text{ feet}\right)$. What is the area, in square inches, of each table in the scale drawing?

   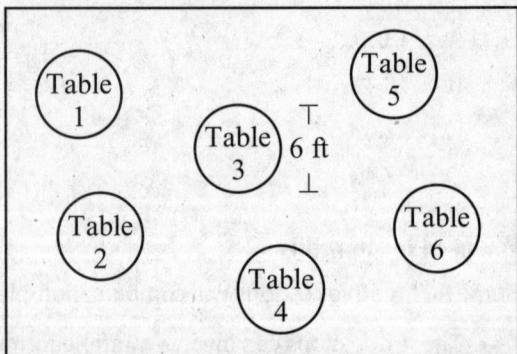

   F. $\frac{1}{16}\pi$
   G. $\frac{1}{4}\pi$
   H. $\frac{4}{9}\pi$
   J. $\frac{1}{2}\pi$

3. A circle with radius 5 is inscribed in a square. What is the difference between the area of the square and the area of the circle?

   A. 25π
   B. 50π
   C. $50 - 25\pi$
   D. $100 - 25\pi$

4. In the figure shown, the shaded region is a square with an area of 12 square units, inscribed inside equilateral triangle ABC. What is the perimeter of $\triangle ABC$?

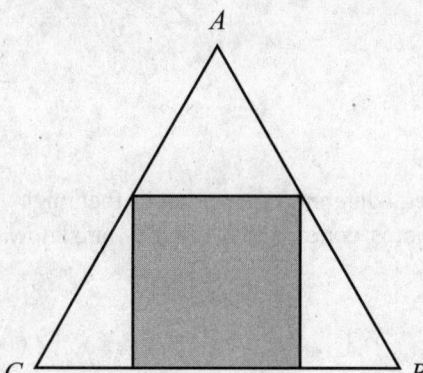

   F. $4 + \sqrt{3}$
   G. $4 + 6\sqrt{3}$
   H. $8 + 6\sqrt{3}$
   J. $12 + 6\sqrt{3}$

HINT: For Q5, what additional line segments can you add to the figure to help you get closer to determining the distance between $\overline{YZ}$ and $\overline{WX}$?

5. The semicircle below has a radius of r inches, and chord $\overline{YZ}$ is parallel to diameter $\overline{WX}$. If the length of $\overline{YZ}$ is 25% shorter than the length of $\overline{WX}$, what is the shortest distance between $\overline{YZ}$ and $\overline{WX}$ in terms of r?

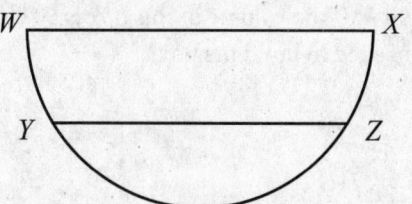

Note: Figure not drawn to scale

   A. $\dfrac{3}{4}\pi r$
   B. $\dfrac{5}{4}\pi r$
   C. $\dfrac{\sqrt{2}}{4}r$
   D. $\dfrac{\sqrt{7}}{4}r$

THREE-DIMENSIONAL FIGURES

> **LEARNING OBJECTIVE**
>
> After this lesson, you will be able to:
> - Calculate the volume and surface area of common three-dimensional (3D) figures

To answer a question like this

A rectangular box with an open top is constructed from cardboard to have a square base of area x^2 and height h. If the volume of this box is 50 cubic units, how many square units of cardboard, in terms of x, are needed to build the box?

A. $5x^2$

B. $6x^2$

C. $\frac{200}{x} + x^2$

D. $\frac{200}{x} + 2x^2$

You need to know this

Three-dimensional (3D) shapes are also called solids. There are several different types of solids that might appear on the ACT—rectangular solids, cubes, cylinders, prisms, spheres, cones, and pyramids—and knowing their structures will help you on test day.

The following diagram shows the basic anatomy of a 3D shape:

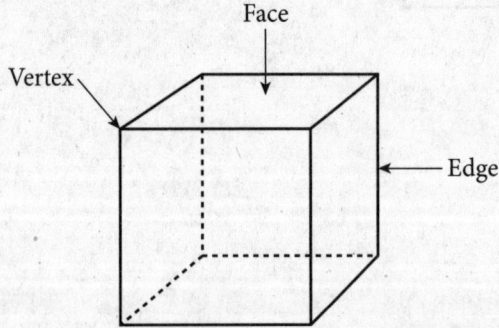

A **face** (or **surface**) is a two-dimensional (2D) shape that acts as one of the sides of the solid. Two faces meet at a line segment called an **edge**, and three faces meet at a single point called a **vertex**.

Volume

Volume is the amount of 3D space occupied by a solid. Volume is analogous to the area of a 2D shape. You can find the volume of many 3D shapes by finding the area of the base and multiplying it by the height: $(V = A_{base} \times h)$. In the table of formulas, the pieces that represent the areas of the bases are enclosed in parentheses.

Rectangular Solid	Cube	Right Cylinder
(figure with l, w, h)	(figure with s, s, s)	(figure with r, h)
$V = (l \times w) \times h$	$V = (s \times s) \times s = s^3$	$V = (\pi \times r^2) \times h$

These three 3D shapes are **prisms**. Almost all prisms on the ACT are right prisms; that is, all faces are perpendicular to those with which they share edges. You might see less common prisms, such as a triangular or a hexagonal prism, but don't worry: the volume of any right prism can be calculated by finding the area of the base and multiplying it by the height.

When you are not explicitly given the area of the base of a prism, you'll need to rely on your two-dimensional geometry knowledge to find it before calculating the volume of the prism.

More complicated 3D shapes include the right pyramid, right cone, and sphere. The vertex of a right pyramid or right cone will always be centered above the middle of the base. Their volume formulas are similar to those of prisms, albeit with different coefficients.

Some of these next formulas might look daunting, but you won't have to memorize them for test day; they'll be provided in the question stem if they are needed.

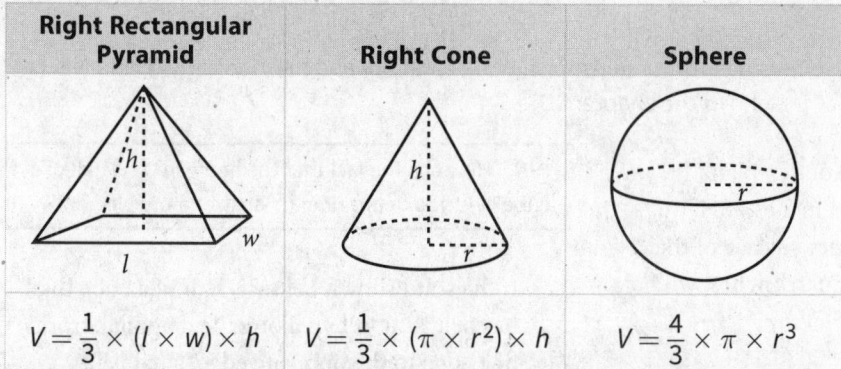

Right Rectangular Pyramid	Right Cone	Sphere
$V = \frac{1}{3} \times (l \times w) \times h$	$V = \frac{1}{3} \times (\pi \times r^2) \times h$	$V = \frac{4}{3} \times \pi \times r^3$

A right pyramid can have any polygon as its base, but the square variety is the one you're most likely to see on the ACT. Also note that the vertex above the base of a right pyramid or cone is not necessarily formed by an intersection of exactly three faces, as in prisms, but it is still a single point and is still called a vertex.

Surface Area

Surface area is the sum of the areas of all faces of a solid. To calculate the surface area of a solid, simply find the area of each face using your 2D geometry skills, then add them all together.

You won't be expected to know the surface area formulas for right pyramids, right cones, and spheres. On test day, they'll be provided for each question where they are needed. However, you could be asked to find the surface area of a prism, in which case you'll be given enough information to find the area of each surface of the solid.

You might think that finding the surface area of a solid with many sides, such as a right hexagonal prism, is a tall order. However, you can save time by noticing a vital trait: this prism has two identical hexagonal faces and six identical rectangular faces. Don't waste time finding the area of each of the eight surfaces. Find the area of one hexagonal face and one rectangular face only. Then multiply the area of the hexagonal face by 2 and the area of the rectangular face by 6, add the products together, and you're done. The same is true for other 3D shapes such as rectangular solids (including cubes), other right prisms, and certain pyramids.

Part 3
ACT MATH

You need to do this
- To answer questions that involve regular solids, look for ways to find the area of the base and the height.
- To answer questions that involve solids that are not regular, apply the appropriate formula.
- To answer questions that involve surface area, look for surfaces that are the same. Calculate the area of each kind of surface once, and then multiply by the number of identical surfaces in the solid.

Explanation
Use the given volume, 50, to get h in terms of x:

$$\text{volume} = \text{length} \times \text{width} \times \text{height}$$
$$50 = x^2 h$$
$$\frac{50}{x^2} = h$$

Since the box has an open top, the area you're looking for is equal to four lateral faces and one bottom face. Each lateral face has area $xh = x\left(\frac{50}{x^2}\right) = \frac{50}{x}$ square units, and the base has area x^2 square units. Thus, the total area you're looking for is:

$$4\left(\frac{50}{x}\right) + x^2 = \frac{200}{x} + x^2$$

Choice (C) is correct.

Try on Your Own
Directions: Take as much time as you need on these questions. Work carefully and methodically. There will be an opportunity for timed practice at the end of the chapter.

1. In the figure that follows, a wooden plank is shown with its dimensions in inches. If Hawanatu wants to spray-paint every surface of the plank, how much paint, in square inches, will Hawanatu need?

   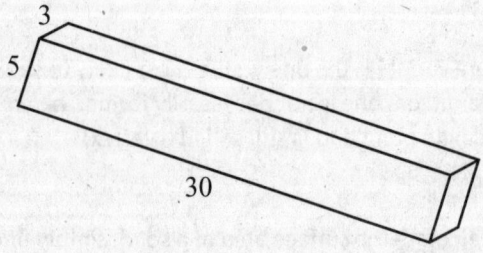

   A. 38
   B. 76
   C. 450
   D. 510

   HINT: How can the fact that the figure in Q2 is half of a cube help you determine the answer more efficiently?

2. If the solid shown below is half of a cube that has been cut in half along the diagonal, from one edge to the opposite edge, what is its volume?

   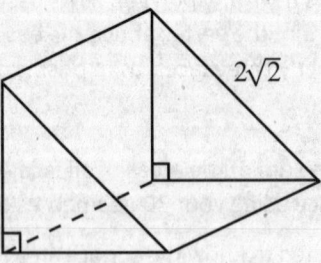

   F. 4
   G. $4\sqrt{2}$
   H. 8
   J. $8\sqrt{2}$

3. What is the volume, in cubic inches, of the cylinder shown below?

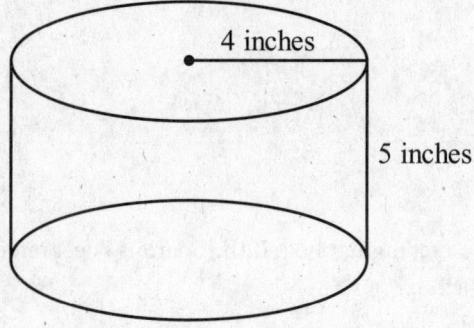

A. 20π
B. 40π
C. 60π
D. 80π

HINT: For Q4, which surfaces will you actually be covering with wrapping paper?

4. Mali bought several right cylindrical candles as party favors and plans to wrap them such that the gift paper wraps around the candle exactly once with no overlap. She wants to leave an extra 3 inches of wrapping paper past each end of the candles so she can tie both ends with a bit of ribbon. If each candle has a diameter of 4 inches and is 8 inches tall, how many square inches of wrapping paper will Mali need to wrap one candle?

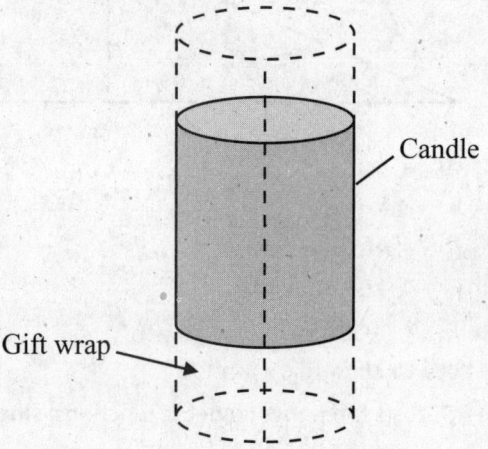

F. 40π
G. 44π
H. 56π
J. 64π

5. Noelle submerges a figurine into a tank of water to determine the volume of the figurine. The tank is 10 inches by 13 inches, and the water is filled to a depth of 5 inches. If the water level rises 0.4 inches when the figurine is submerged, what is the volume, in cubic inches, of the object?

A. 52
B. 130
C. 650
D. 702

Part 3
ACT MATH

TRIANGLES AND TRIGONOMETRY

LEARNING OBJECTIVE

After this lesson, you will be able to:

- Apply basic trigonometric ratios and formulas to answer questions involving right triangles

To answer a question like this

In the following figure, a surfboard is propped up against a rectangular box. If the board is 7 feet long, which of the following is closest to the height, in feet, of the box?

(Note: $\sin 23° \approx 0.3907$, $\cos 23° \approx 0.9205$, $\tan 23° \approx 0.4245$)

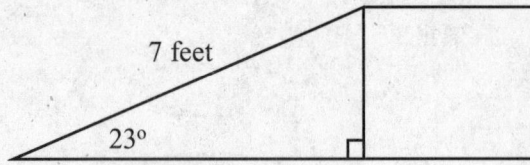

A. 2.7
B. 4.3
C. 5.6
D. 6.4

You need to know this

The ACT tests three trigonometric functions: **sine**, **cosine**, and **tangent**.

- All three are simply the ratios of side lengths within a right triangle.
- The notation for sine, cosine, and tangent functions always includes a reference angle—for example, $\cos x$ or $\cos \theta$. That's because you'll need to refer to the given angle within a right triangle to determine the appropriate side ratios.

There is a common mnemonic device for the sine, cosine, and tangent ratios: SOHCAHTOA (commonly pronounced: sew-kuh-TOE-uh). Here's what it represents:

- **S**ine is **O**pposite over **H**ypotenuse
- **C**osine is **A**djacent over **H**ypotenuse
- **T**angent is **O**pposite over **A**djacent

See the triangle and the table below for a summary of the ratios and what each equals for ∠A in △CAB:

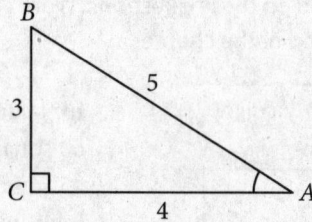

Sine (sin)	Cosine (cos)	Tangent (tan)
$\dfrac{\text{opposite}}{\text{hypotenuse}}$	$\dfrac{\text{adjacent}}{\text{hypotenuse}}$	$\dfrac{\text{opposite}}{\text{adjacent}}$
$\dfrac{3}{5}$	$\dfrac{4}{5}$	$\dfrac{3}{4}$

Complementary angles have a special relationship relative to sine and cosine:

- $\sin x° = \cos(90° - x°)$
- $\cos x° = \sin(90° - x°)$
- In other words, the sine of an acute angle is equal to the cosine of the angle's complement and vice versa. For example, $\cos 30° = \sin 60°$, $\cos 45° = \sin 45°$, and $\cos 60° = \sin 30°$.

You need to do this

Apply the appropriate trigonometric ratio to a right triangle, or use the relationship between the sine and cosine of complementary angles.

Explanation

You need to find the height of the box. You are given a figure that includes a right triangle and an angle measure, as well as the length of the surfboard. You are also given three trig values, which you may or may not need. Let x equal the height of the triangle (which is also the height of the box). Now, look at the triangle. You know the length of the hypotenuse, and you're looking for the side opposite the given angle. This tells you which trig function to use: $\sin x = \dfrac{\text{opp}}{\text{hyp}}$. The question states that $\sin 23° \approx 0.3907$. Use this information to solve for x:

$$\sin 23° = \dfrac{x}{7}$$
$$0.3907 = \dfrac{x}{7}$$
$$0.3907 \times 7 = x$$
$$2.7349 = x$$

The height of the box is approximately 2.7 feet, so choice (A) is correct.

Part 3
ACT MATH

Try on Your Own

Directions: Take as much time as you need on these questions. Work carefully and methodically. There will be an opportunity for timed practice at the end of the chapter.

HINT: The unit circle will help you answer Q1, a High difficulty question, more confidently.

---

1. If $0 \leq \theta \leq \pi$, what are the values of θ when $\sin \theta = \frac{1}{2}$?

   A. $\frac{\pi}{6}$ and $\frac{2\pi}{3}$

   B. $\frac{\pi}{6}$ and $\frac{5\pi}{6}$

   C. $\frac{\pi}{4}$ and $\frac{3\pi}{4}$

   D. $\frac{\pi}{3}$ and $\frac{4\pi}{3}$

2. In a right triangle with angle measure β, $\cos \beta = \frac{36}{39}$ and $\sin \beta = \frac{15}{39}$. What is the value of $\tan \beta$?

   F. $\frac{15}{36}$

   G. $\frac{36}{15}$

   H. $\frac{39}{36}$

   J. $\frac{39}{15}$

3. In the following figure, $\triangle ABC$ has an area of 60 square centimeters. If $\angle ABC$ is reduced to 45° and the length of $\overline{AC}$ is shortened accordingly, what is the new area, in square centimeters, of $\triangle ABC$? (Note: The area of a triangle is $\frac{1}{2}ab \sin x$, where a and b are the lengths of the sides and x is the angle between them.)

   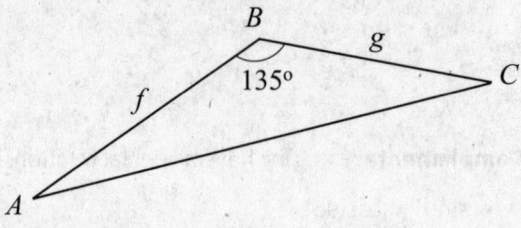

   A. 30
   B. 40
   C. 50
   D. 60

4. Eric is a glass collector. The figure below is one of the triangular glass fragments that Eric collected. Which of the following expressions is the value of z ? (Note: The law of sines states that for a triangle with sides of lengths a, b, and c and opposite angles of measure A, B, and C, respectively, $\frac{\sin A}{a} = \frac{\sin B}{b} = \frac{\sin C}{c}$.)

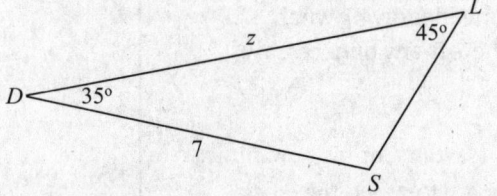

F. $\dfrac{7 \sin 35°}{\sin 45°}$

G. $\dfrac{7 \sin 35°}{\sin 100°}$

H. $\dfrac{7 \sin 100°}{\sin 35°}$

J. $\dfrac{7 \sin 100°}{\sin 45°}$

HINT: Q5 looks complicated, but the question stem gives you the formulas you need to answer the question correctly.

5. Triangle EFG is shown in the following figure. What is the length, in inches, of $\overline{EG}$? (Note: For a triangle with side lengths a, b, and c and opposite angles A, B and C, respectively, $\frac{\sin A}{a} = \frac{\sin B}{b} = \frac{\sin C}{c}$, and $c^2 = a^2 + b^2 - 2ab \cos C$.)

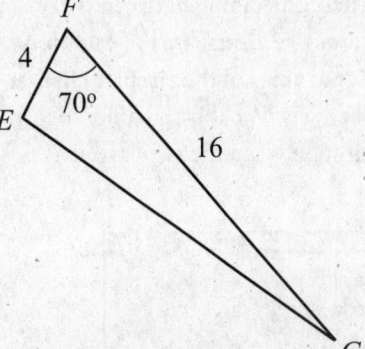

A. $4 \sin 70°$

B. $16 \sin 70°$

C. $\sqrt{16^2 + 4^2 - 2(16)(4) \cos 70°}$

D. $\sqrt{16^2 + 4^2 + 2(16)(4) \cos 70°}$

On Test Day

Occasionally, a question will give you more information than you need to determine the correct answer. Think about what information you really need to arrive at the answer before you begin your calculations so that you don't get sidetracked and spend time doing unnecessary work.

As you read through this question that is similar to an earlier one in the chapter, focus on planning your strategy to get the correct value and identifying what information you need to carry out that strategy. Note if there is any unnecessary information that you can ignore.

1. Lorenzo is deciding between two examination room layouts for his new clinic. The cross-sectional area of each square chair is 2 square feet, and the cross-sectional areas of the circular chair and exam table are π and 4.9 square feet, respectively. What is the difference in the areas, in square feet, of the shaded portion between the two layouts?

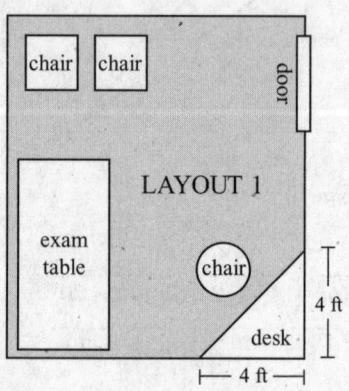
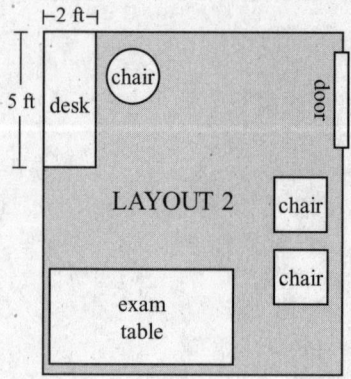

   A. 2
   B. 4
   C. 8
   D. 10

The explanation appears at the end of this chapter.

Chapter 13
Geometry

How Much Have You Learned?

Directions: For test-like practice, give yourself 10 minutes to complete this question set. Be sure to study the explanations, even for questions you got correct. They can be found at the end of this chapter. Note that this question set includes foundational topics in geometry covered in Math Fundamentals in chapter 6.

1. In the following figure, N is the intersection of segments $\overline{MO}$ and $\overline{LP}$. If $\overline{LM} = \overline{MN} = \overline{NL}$, what is the measure of $\angle NPO$?

    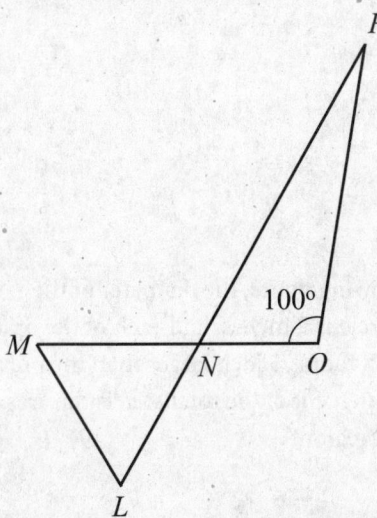

    A. 10°
    B. 15°
    C. 20°
    D. 25°

2. The ratio of the perimeters of two similar triangles is 4:7. The sides of the larger triangle are 10, 12, and 13 cm, respectively. What is the perimeter, in centimeters, of the smaller triangle?

    F. 11
    G. 12
    H. 20
    J. 26

3. During a hiking trip, Keesha and Dwayne decide to climb a mountain using two different routes to the top. Keesha takes the hiking route that travels 5 miles south, 6 miles east, 7 miles south, and 2 miles west to the summit; Dwayne uses the climbing route that starts at the same point as the hiking route but goes directly from there to the summit. Approximately how many miles in all will the two hike on the way to the summit?

    A. 29.42
    B. 32.65
    C. 33.42
    D. 34.00

4. The figure below shows $\triangle WXY$ in which Z is the midpoint of $\overline{WY}$ and $\overline{WX}$ is perpendicular to $\overline{YX}$. What is the length, in inches, of $\overline{WZ}$?

    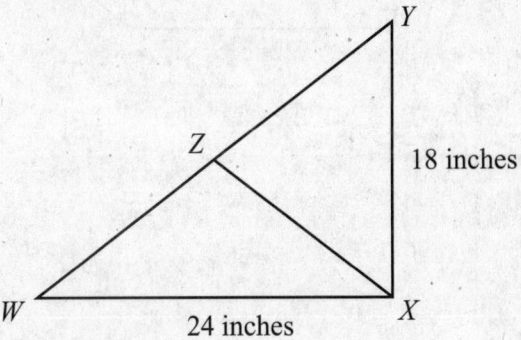

    F. 13
    G. 15
    H. 30
    J. 32

5. In the following figure, $\overline{CD} = \overline{BD}$ and $\angle BED$ is 17°. What is the measure, in degrees, of $\angle ABC$?

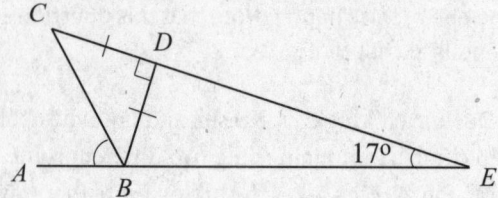

A. 30
B. 45
C. 54
D. 62

6. The figure below shows the floor dimensions of Akanksha's living room. She wants to install floor molding along the perimeter of the floor. How many feet of molding does she need?

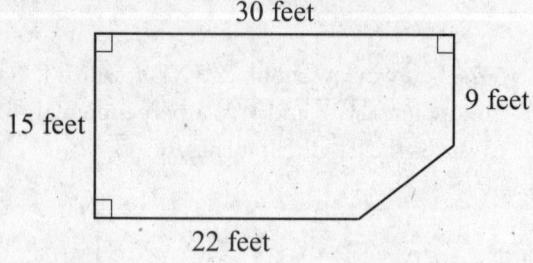

F. 76
G. 86
H. 90
J. 96

7. Yesenia has a rectangular orchard that she would like to divide into two triangular fields—one for planting orange trees and one for planting grapefruit trees—by building a fence from one corner of the field to the opposite corner. If the area of the field is 540 square feet and the length of the field is 36 feet, how many feet of fence will Yesenia need to create the divider?

A. 39
B. 51
C. 60
D. 81

8. In the following figure, the diameter of the smallest circle is 2 inches, and each of the other circles has a radius 1 inch larger than the previous. What percent of the total area is the area of the shaded region?

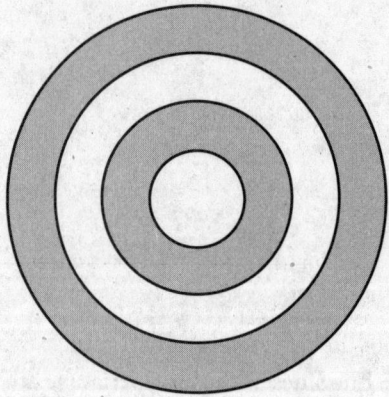

F. 37.5
G. 50
H. 62.5
J. 75

9. The opening of a perfectly cylindrical sewer tunnel has a circumference of 8π. The tunnel has a volume of 2,048π cubic feet. How many feet long is the tunnel?

   A. 62
   B. 84
   C. 128
   D. 156

10. In the following figure, point C is the center of the circle, and the measure of angle D is 37°. Which of the following expresses the length of the radius?

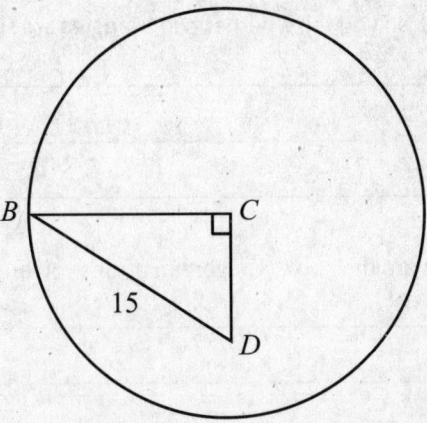

   F. 15 sin 53°
   G. 15 sin 37°
   H. 15 tan 53°
   J. 15 tan 37°

Part 3
ACT MATH

Reflect

Directions: Take a few minutes to recall what you've learned and what you've been practicing in this chapter. Consider the following questions, jot down your best answer for each one, and then compare your reflections to the expert responses on the following page. Use your level of confidence to determine what to do next.

1. How can you tell whether two triangles are similar?
   _____
   _____
   _____

2. What are the two Pythagorean triples you are most likely to see on test day?
   _____
   _____
   _____

3. What are the ratios of the side lengths of a 45-45-90 triangle? Of a 30-60-90 triangle?
   _____
   _____
   _____

4. When doing unit conversions, how can you make sure you're doing them correctly?
   _____
   _____
   _____

5. What is the standard form for the equation of a circle?
   _____
   _____
   _____

6. What is the relationship of a circle's central angle to the arc and sector the angle defines?
   _____
   _____
   _____

7. Which form of a quadratic equation gives its *y*-intercept? Which one gives its vertex?

___

8. How would you find the surface area of a right triangular prism with equilateral triangles as its bases?

___

Responses

1. How can you tell whether two triangles are similar?

There are three ways to tell:

- *Two of their three angles are congruent (angle-angle).*
- *Two of their three sides are in the same proportion and the intervening angle is congruent (side-angle-side).*
- *Their three sides are in the same proportion (side-side-side).*

2. What are the two Pythagorean triples you are most likely to see on test day?

The two most common Pythagorean triples on the ACT are 3:4:5 and 5:12:13. You may also see multiples of these, e.g., 6:8:10 or 10:24:26.

3. What are the ratios of the side lengths of a 45-45-90 triangle? Of a 30-60-90 triangle?

The side lengths of a 45-45-90 triangle are always in the ratio of $x:x:x\sqrt{2}$. The side lengths of a 30-60-90 triangle are always in the ratio of $x:x\sqrt{3}:2x$. Remember that the shortest side of any triangle is across from the smallest angle, and the longest side is across from the greatest angle.

4. When doing unit conversions, how can you make sure you're doing them correctly?

To do unit conversions correctly, set up the conversion in whichever way makes units cancel. For example, to convert 3 feet into inches, you multiply 3 feet by 12 inches per foot, because it cancels out the feet unit. If instead you multiplied 3 feet by 1 foot per 12 inches, then the resulting units would be "feet squared per inch," which makes no sense.

5. What is the standard form for the equation of a circle?

The equation of a circle in the coordinate plane is $(x - h)^2 + (y - k)^2 = r^2$, where r is the radius of the circle, and (h, k) is the ordered pair representing its center.

6. What is the relationship of a circle's central angle to the arc and sector the angle defines?

The central angle, the arc, and the sector are all in proportion to the full circle:

$$\text{central angle} = \frac{\text{arc length}}{\text{circumference}} = \frac{\text{sector area}}{\text{circle area}}$$

7. Which form of a quadratic equation **gives** its *y*-intercept? Which one gives its vertex?

The standard form is $y = ax^2 + bx + c$. *The constant c is the y-intercept. The vertex form is* $y = a(x-h)^2 + k$. *The constants* (h, k) *are the x- and y-values of the vertex.*

8. How would you find the surface area of a right triangular prism with equilateral triangles as its bases?

Calculate the area of one of the equilateral triangles and multiply by 2. Calculate the area of one of the rectangular faces and multiply by 3. Then add the results.

Next Steps

If you answered most questions correctly in the "How Much Have You Learned?" section, and if your responses to the Reflect questions were similar to those of the ACT expert, then consider geometry an area of strength and move on to the next chapter. Come back to this topic periodically to prevent yourself from getting rusty.

If you don't yet feel confident, review those parts of this chapter that you have not yet mastered. In particular, review the lessons on triangles, as these are important shapes on the ACT. Then, try the questions you missed again. As always, be sure to review the explanations closely. Then go online (**kaptest.com/login**) for more practice. If you haven't already registered your book, do so at **kaptest.com/moreonline**.

GO ONLINE

kaptest.com/login

Chapter 13
Geometry

Answers and Explanations

Lines and Angles

Drill Answers

a. 36°

b. 120°

c. 50°

d. 70°

e. 65°

1. B
Difficulty: Low
Category: Geometry
Getting to the Answer: To answer questions about angles formed when a transversal cuts parallel lines, figure out which angles are equal and which are supplementary. Remember that when a transversal crosses two parallel lines, all the acute angles are equal and all the obtuse angles are equal. Here, $\angle CRP = \angle ATR$ because $\overline{CD}$ and $\overline{AB}$ are parallel. $\angle ATR$ and $\angle ATQ$ are supplementary, so the measure of $\angle ATQ = 180° - 110° = 70°$. Choice (B) is correct.

2. G
Difficulty: Low
Category: Geometry
Getting to the Answer: Because lines a and b are perpendicular, the lines form four 90° angles. Line c, which passes through the intersection of lines a and b, creates two sets of vertical angles. The angle across from the angle that is $y°$ also equals $y°$, and the angle across from the angle that is $x°$ equals $x°$. Thus, $x° + y° = 90°$. Solving for y in terms of x gives $y = (90 - x)°$. Choice (G) is correct.

3. B
Difficulty: Medium
Category: Geometry
Getting to the Answer: Because $\overline{OL} = \overline{NM}$ and $\overline{LM} = \overline{ON}$, $\overline{LM}$ and $\overline{ON}$ must be parallel lines, making LN a transversal. Angles b and c are opposite interior angles, which means that they have congruent angle measures. Although you can calculate the actual values of b and c, the fact that $b = c$ means that $b - c$ will always equal 0, regardless of the actual angle measures. Choice (B) is correct.

4. J
Difficulty: Low
Category: Geometry
Getting to the Answer: In a quadrilateral, the sum of the interior angles is 360°. Thus, $\angle A + 2x° + 90° + 3x° = 360°$. Solving for $\angle A$ in terms of x gives $\angle A = 360° - 90° - 2x° - 3x°$. Thus, $\angle A = 270° - 5x°$, and (J) is correct.

5. B
Difficulty: Low
Category: Geometry
Getting to the Answer: Use the properties of supplementary angles to find the measures of $\angle DBC$ and $\angle BDC$: $\angle DBC = 180° - 45° = 135°$ and $\angle BDC = 180° - 155° = 25°$. The sum of the interior angles in a triangle equals 180°, so $\angle BCD = 180° - (135° + 25°) = 20°$. Choice (B) is correct.

Triangle Properties

1. C
Difficulty: Medium
Category: Geometry
Getting to the Answer: Since $\overline{DF} = \overline{DE} = \overline{FE}$, $\triangle DFE$ is an equilateral triangle and all the interior angles are 60°. $\overline{DE}$ is parallel to $\overline{AC}$, so $\angle FDE$ and $\angle DAB$ are corresponding angles. Thus, $\angle DAB$ is also 60°. Choice (C) is correct.

2. H
Difficulty: Low
Category: Geometry
Getting to the Answer: The question asks for the measure of $\angle ABC$. You know that $\overline{AB}$ and $\overline{BC}$ are congruent sides of $\triangle ABC$ and that $m\angle CAB = 27°$. Sketch out $\triangle ABC$ to visualize this information.

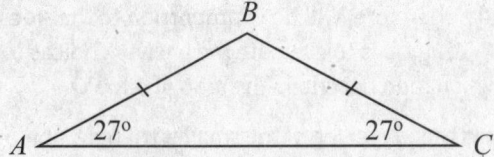

Because $\overline{AB}$ and $\overline{BC}$ are congruent, $m\angle ACB$ must also equal 27°. The sum of the measures of the interior angles of a triangle is 180°. Therefore, find $m\angle ABC$ by subtracting $2 \times 27°$ from 180°: $m\angle ABC = 180° - 54° = 126°$. You found the measure of $\angle ABC$, so you are done. Choice (H) is correct.

3. D
Difficulty: Medium
Category: Geometry
Getting to the Answer: The measures of the angles of a triangle sum to 180°. You can use the given ratio to represent the relative sizes of the angles. For example, if x equals one "part," the measures of the angles can be represented by 2x, 3x, and 7x. To find the size of one part, solve the equation $2x + 3x + 7x = 180°$. This simplifies to $12x = 180°$, or $x = 15°$. Be careful; this is not the answer. The question asks for the measure of the largest angle, which is $7x = 7(15) = 105°$. Choice (D) is correct.

4. G
Difficulty: Low
Category: Geometry
Getting to the Answer: The altitude is the perpendicular line from a vertex to the opposite side of the triangle. To find the altitude that passes through vertex X, look at the y-coordinates of X and the other side of the triangle. Vertex X has the y-coordinate 8, and both vertex Y and vertex Z have the y-coordinates 4. To find the altitude, simply use the y-coordinates by finding the difference between them: $8 - 4 = 4$. Thus, the length of the altitude from X to $\overline{YZ}$ is 4. Choice (G) is correct.

5. B
Difficulty: High
Category: Geometry
Getting to the Answer: When two triangles have two equal angles, they are similar triangles. When you notice a triangle within a triangle, like the one in this figure, pay special attention to the angles that are shared by both triangles.

The triangle with hypotenuse PQ, which is also length a, that is formed by the dashed line is similar to $\triangle PQR$. This is because they both contain a right angle and both have angle Q in common. The sides of this smaller triangle, therefore, will be in proportion to the sides of $\triangle PQR$. Your job is to evaluate the answer choices to find which ratio describes the ratio of d to PQ.

Side d is the longer leg of the smaller triangle, and b is the longer leg of $\triangle PQR$. Also, PQ(a) is the hypotenuse of the smaller triangle and c is the hypotenuse of $\triangle PQR$. Set up a proportion in order to solve for the ratio for d to PQ(a). Therefore, the ratio between the two pairs of sides is the same, and $\frac{d}{PQ} = \frac{d}{a} = \frac{b}{c}$. Choice (B) is correct.

Right Triangles

1. C
Difficulty: Medium
Category: Geometry
Getting to the Answer: Triangle ABC is a 30-60-90 triangle, and side AB is across from the 60° angle. Set up a proportion using the ratio of the sides in a 30-60-90 triangle, $x:x\sqrt{3}:2x$, to find the length of AB:

$$\frac{\sqrt{3}}{2} = \frac{AB}{20}$$
$$20\sqrt{3} = 2AB$$
$$10\sqrt{3} = AB$$

Choice (C) is correct.

2. G
Difficulty: Medium
Category: Geometry
Getting to the Answer: The diagonal of the square tile is also the hypotenuse of two 45-45-90 triangles.

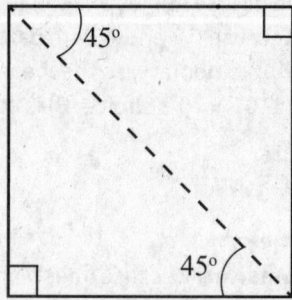

Use the ratio of the sides in a 45-45-90 triangle, $x:x:x\sqrt{2}$, to set up a proportion to determine the side length of the square. Let s be the side of the square:

$$\frac{s}{18} = \frac{1}{\sqrt{2}}$$
$$\sqrt{2}s = 18$$
$$s = \frac{18}{\sqrt{2}}$$

Rationalize this expression by multiplying the numerator and denominator by $\sqrt{2}$: $\frac{18}{\sqrt{2}} \times \frac{\sqrt{2}}{\sqrt{2}} = \frac{18\sqrt{2}}{2} = 9\sqrt{2}$. Choice (G) is correct.

3. B
Difficulty: Low
Category: Geometry
Getting to the Answer: Since the length of the shorter leg is 6 inches and the length of the longer leg is twice the length of the shorter leg, the length of the longer leg is $2 \times 6 = 12$. Use the Pythagorean theorem, $a^2 + b^2 = c^2$, to find the hypotenuse c:
$c = \sqrt{6^2 + 12^2} = \sqrt{36 + 144} = \sqrt{180} = 6\sqrt{5}$. Choice (B) is correct.

4. J
Difficulty: Low
Category: Geometry
Getting to the Answer: The figure shown is a right triangle. The length of the hypotenuse equals the length of the slide, which is 10 feet, and the length of the long leg equals the distance between the base of the slide and the ladder, which is 8 feet. Since you are given two of the sides, you can use the Pythagorean theorem, $a^2 + b^2 = c^2$, to determine the third side. Let a equal the height of the ladder:

$$a = \sqrt{c^2 - b^2}$$
$$= \sqrt{10^2 - 8^2}$$
$$= \sqrt{36}$$
$$= 6$$

Choice (J) is correct.

If you recognized that the sides were a multiple of the Pythagorean triple 3:4:5, then you could avoid using the Pythagorean theorem and quickly see that the third side must be $3 \times 2 = 6$.

5. D
Difficulty: Medium
Category: Geometry
Getting to the Answer: In the figure above, $\overline{AB}$ is the hypotenuse of a right triangle. $\overline{AC}$ is 4 units and $\overline{CB}$ is 6 units, so use the Pythagorean theorem, $a^2 + b^2 = c^2$, to find the length of $\overline{AB}$:

$$c = \sqrt{a^2 + b^2}$$
$$= \sqrt{4^2 + 6^2}$$
$$= \sqrt{52}$$
$$= \sqrt{4}\sqrt{13}$$
$$= 2\sqrt{13}$$

Choice (D) is correct.

Alternatively, you could use the distance formula, which is derived from the Pythagorean theorem: $d = \sqrt{(y_2 - y_1)^2 + (x_2 - x_1)^2}$. The distance between points A and B is therefore $d = \sqrt{(1 - 5)^2 + (7 - 1)^2} = 2\sqrt{13}$.

Polygons

Drill Answers

a. 14
b. 12
c. 12
d. 14
e. 14

1. C
Difficulty: Medium
Category: Geometry
Getting to the Answer: First, use $A_{triangle} = \frac{1}{2}bh$ to calculate the area of $\triangle PQR$: $A_{PQR} = \frac{1}{2}(16)(10) = 80$.
Then, determine the area of the square. Since the area of square $ABCD$ is twice the area of $\triangle PQR$, the area of square $ABCD$ is $2 \times 80 = 160$. Use $A_{square} = s^2$ to determine the length of a side: $s = \sqrt{160} = \sqrt{16}\sqrt{10} = 4\sqrt{10}$, which is (C).

2. G
Difficulty: Low
Category: Geometry
Getting to the Answer: Use the formula $A = bh$ to determine the area of the parallelogram. The length of the base, b, is the distance between -2 and 4, which is 6. The height, h, is the perpendicular distance from the base to the top of the parallelogram, which is the change in the y-coordinate values: $5 - 2 = 3$. Thus, the area is $6 \times 3 = 18$ square units, which matches (G).

3. B
Difficulty: Low
Category: Geometry
Getting to the Answer: Imagine moving the short horizontal side to the top of the polygon to form a rectangle that is 10 meters by 12.5 meters. Then, add the perimeter of that rectangle to the two sides that are 7.5 meters to get the perimeter of the polygon: $2(10) + 2(12.5) + 2(7.5) = 60$ meters. Finally, use

Part 3
ACT MATH

1 meter = 100 centimeters to convert 60 m to centimeters: 60 m × $\frac{100 \text{ cm}}{1 \text{ m}}$ = 6,000 cm. Choice (B) is correct.

4. J
Difficulty: Medium
Category: Geometry
Getting to the Answer: The formula for the area of a trapezoid is $A = \left(\frac{b_1 + b_2}{2}\right)h$, where b_1 and b_2 are the lengths of the parallel sides. You could also think of this formula as the height times the average of the bases.

You are given the height (3 inches), one base (8 inches), and enough information to determine the other base. Notice that $\triangle ABE$ is a 3-4-5 triangle, so $AE = 4$ inches. And if you were to drop an altitude down from point C, you'd get another 3-4-5 triangle on the right:

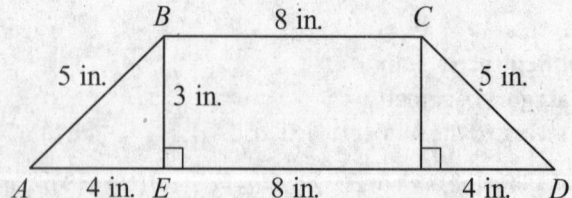

Now you can see that the bottom base is 16 inches. Plug these numbers into the area formula:

$$A = \left(\frac{b_1 + b_2}{2}\right)h$$
$$= \left(\frac{8 + 16}{2}\right) \times 3$$
$$= 12 \times 3$$
$$= 36$$

The answer is (J).

If you don't remember the area formula of a trapezoid on test day, you can also just find the areas of the two side triangles and the rectangle in the middle and add them all up.

5. A
Difficulty: Medium
Category: Geometry
Getting to the Answer: Picking Numbers can make a theoretical question like this much more concrete. If you are not sure which answer choice makes the most sense, assume that each side starts with length 1 and try each answer choice out. The area starts as $1 \times 1 = 1$, so triple the area is 3. Begin testing with the middle answer choice:

C: area = $(1 \times 9)(1 \times 9) = 81$. This is too big, so try a smaller choice.

B: area = $(1 \times 3)(1 \times 3) = 9$. Still too big.

(A): area = $(1 \times \sqrt{3})(1 \times \sqrt{3}) = \sqrt{3} \times \sqrt{3} = 3$.

Choice (A) is correct.

Circles and Parabolas

1. B
Difficulty: Medium
Category: Geometry
Getting to the Answer: You need to find the area of the circle, and you are given the circumference of the circle. As with most circle questions, the first thing you need to do is find the radius. Use the given circumference and the circumference formula to find r.

$$C = 2\pi r$$
$$8\pi = 2\pi r$$
$$4 = r$$

Now you can use the radius to find the area:
$A = \pi r^2 = \pi(4)^2 = 16\pi$. You found the area, 16π, so you are done. Choice (B) is correct.

2. J
Difficulty: Medium
Category: Geometry
Getting to the Answer: The area of the shaded region can be determined by subtracting the area of the smaller circle from the area of the larger circle. First, find the radius of the larger circle. Then, use $A = 2\pi r^2$ to calculate the area of each circle. Finally, find the difference in areas.

Since the radius of the larger circle is 75% greater than that of the smaller circle, the radius of the larger circle is $4 + 4 \times 0.75 = 7$. The area of the smaller circle is $\pi(4)^2 = 16\pi$, and the area of the larger circle is $\pi(7)^2 = 49\pi$. This means the area of the shaded region is $49\pi - 16\pi = 33\pi$ square feet. Choice (J) is correct.

3. C
Difficulty: High
Category: Geometry
Getting to the Answer: Think logically to answer this question. Because Earth makes a complete rotation about its axis in 24 hours, any point on the equator must rotate through 360° during that time.

Quito rotates 360° in the 24 hours from noon on January 1 to noon on January 2. There are 3 hours between noon on January 2 and 3:00 p.m. on January 2, so it rotates an additional $\frac{3}{24} \times 360° = 45°$, for a total of $360° + 45° = 405°$. Choice (C) is correct.

4. H
Difficulty: High
Category: Geometry
Getting to the Answer: The set of points described in the question stem form a circle centered at $(-3, 4)$. The distance of 5 represents the length of its radius. This means that you have everything you need to use the standard equation for a circle with center (h,k) and radius r. The equation is:

$$(x - h)^2 + (y - k)^2 = r^2$$
$$(x - (-3))^2 + (y - 4)^2 = 5^2$$
$$(x + 3)^2 + (y - 4)^2 = 25$$

The answer is (H).

5. A
Difficulty: Medium
Category: Geometry
Getting to the Answer: To find the solutions for x, set the equation equal to 0 and solve for x.

$$0 = (x + 3)^2 - 1$$
$$1 = (x + 3)^2$$
$$\sqrt{1} = x + 3$$
$$\pm 1 = x + 3$$
$$-4 \text{ and } -2 = x$$

Both values of x are negative, so (A) is correct.

Alternatively, you could graph the equation. The solutions for x are the x-intercepts of the graph. In this graph, the parabola intersects the x-axis in two places, both to the left of the origin. This means that the equation has two different negative real solutions:

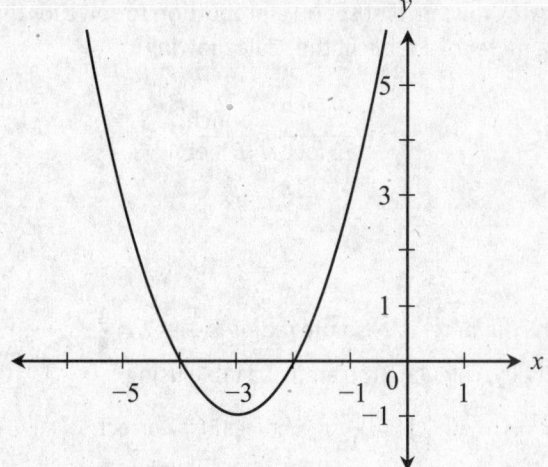

Choice (A) is correct.

Complex Two-Dimensional Figures

1. D
Difficulty: High
Category: Geometry
Getting to the Answer: The difference in the areas of the shaded portion between the two layouts arises solely from the different sizes of the text boxes. Thus, you need to calculate the difference in the areas of the text boxes only. The rectangular text box in Layout 1 has an area of $l \times w = 7 \times 3 = 21$ square inches. The rectangular text box in Layout 2 has an area of $l \times w = 6.5 \times 3.5 = 22.75$ square inches. The difference in the areas of the text boxes, and therefore of the shaded portions between the layouts, is $22.75 - 21 = 1.75$ square inches, which matches (D).

2. F
Difficulty: Medium
Category: Geometry
Getting to the Answer: A scale can be written in the form of a fraction. The question states that the scale here is $\frac{3}{4}$ inches to 9 feet, which can be written as $\frac{\frac{3}{4}}{9}$. To find the area, in square inches, of each table in the

scale drawing, first set up a proportion to solve for the diameter of a table in the scale drawing.

$$\frac{\frac{3}{4} \text{ inch}}{9 \text{ feet}} = \frac{x \text{ inch}}{6 \text{ feet}}$$

$$\frac{18}{4} = 9x$$

$$\frac{1}{2} = x$$

The diameter is $\frac{1}{2}$, so the radius is $\frac{1}{2} \div 2 = \frac{1}{4}$. Finally, calculate the area of a table using πr^2: $A = \pi \left(\frac{1}{4}\right)^2 = \frac{1}{16}\pi$. Choice (F) is correct.

3. **D**
Difficulty: Medium
Category: Geometry
Getting to the Answer: Because the question does not provide you with a figure, draw one to visualize what you are being asked.

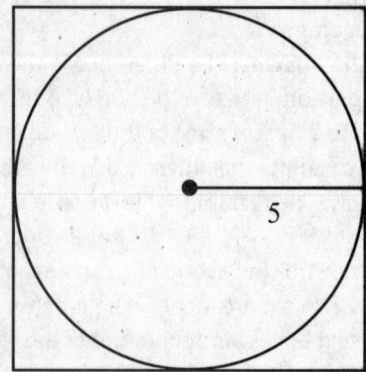

The circle is inscribed within the square, so its radius is half the side of the square. The circle has a radius of 5, so the square has a side of $2 \times 5 = 10$. Therefore, the area of the circle is $5^2\pi = 25\pi$, and the area of the square is $10^2 = 100$. The difference between the area of the square and the area of the circle is thus $100 - 25\pi$, which is (D).

4. **J**
Difficulty: High
Category: Geometry
Getting to the Answer: You want to find the perimeter of the triangle. Unfortunately, you do not have much concrete information about it yet. Instead, start with what you know about the shaded square. Because its area is 12, each side must be $\sqrt{12} = \sqrt{4}\sqrt{3} = 2\sqrt{3}$. Jot this down because you'll need it later.

Triangle *ABC* is an equilateral triangle, so each of its interior angles measures 60°. This means that the two vertical sides of the square each represent the longer leg of a 30-60-90 triangle (the small white triangles on the sides).

Use the ratio of the sides, $x:x\sqrt{3}:2x$, to determine the length of the short leg. Since the length of the long leg is $2\sqrt{3}$, the short legs are each 2. You now have the length of the base of the large equilateral triangle: $2 + 2\sqrt{3} + 2 = 4 + 2\sqrt{3}$.

Because the triangle is equilateral, each side of the triangle has length $4 + 2\sqrt{3}$. The perimeter is the sum of all three sides, so multiply the side length by 3 to get $12 + 6\sqrt{3}$. Choice (J) is correct.

5. **D**
Difficulty: High
Category: Geometry
Getting to the Answer: You need to determine the shortest distance between the two chords in terms of *r*. You are told that $\overline{WX}$ is the diameter and that $\overline{YZ}$ is 25% smaller than $\overline{WX}$. One of the simplest ways to discover new information in tough geometry questions is to draw additional lines. Start with an additional radius (call it *r*) that extends from the center of the diameter of the semicircle to $\overline{YZ}$. Then add a line that represents the shortest distance between the two chords. This creates a right triangle.

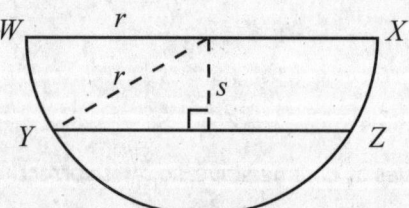

You know that $\overline{YZ}$ is 25% shorter than $\overline{WX}$, so $\overline{YZ} = \frac{3}{4}\overline{WX}$. Since $\overline{WX}$ is the diameter of the circle, $\overline{WX} = 2r$. Combine these two equations to determine the other side of the right triangle, $\frac{1}{2}\overline{YZ}$:

$$\overline{YZ} = \frac{3}{4}\overline{WZ}$$

$$\overline{YZ} = \frac{3}{4}(2r)$$

$$\overline{YZ} = \frac{3}{2}r$$

$$\frac{1}{2}\overline{YZ} = \frac{3}{4}r$$

You now have two of the three sides of the right triangle and can solve for the third using the Pythagorean theorem.

$$\left(\frac{3}{4}r\right)^2 + s^2 = r^2$$
$$\frac{9}{16}r^2 + s^2 = r^2$$
$$s^2 = \frac{16}{16}r^2 - \frac{9}{16}r^2$$
$$s^2 = \frac{7}{16}r^2$$
$$s = \pm\frac{\sqrt{7}}{4}r$$

Distance can't be negative, so (D) is the correct answer.

Three-Dimensional Figures

1. D
Difficulty: Medium
Category: Geometry
Getting to the Answer: You need to determine the amount of paint that Hawanatu needs in square inches. You are given a rectangular prism with several dimensions. Jot these down: $l = 30$, $w = 3$, $h = 5$. The amount of paint needed to cover the surface is the same as the total surface area of the solid. Use $SA = 2(wl + hl + hw)$ to find the amount of paint needed: $2[3(30) + 5(30) + 5(3)] = 2(90 + 150 + 15) = 510$ square inches. Choice (D) is correct.

2. F
Difficulty: High
Category: Geometry
Getting to the Answer: You need to find the volume of the solid. You are told that the solid is half a cube, and you are given the length of one part. Since the shape is half a cube, the perpendicular edges are equal and form the legs of a 45-45-90 triangle. Use the ratio of the sides, $x:x:x\sqrt{2}$, to determine the length of the legs (and the edges of the half cube). Since the hypotenuse is $2\sqrt{2}$, the length of the leg is 2.

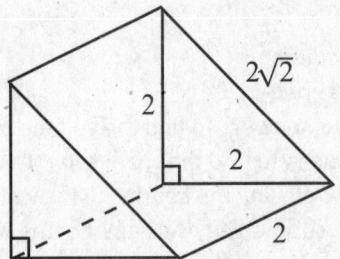

The volume of the whole cube is $V_{cube} = s^3 = (2)^3 = 8$. Thus, the volume of the half-cube figure is 4. Choice (F) is correct.

3. D
Difficulty: Medium
Category: Geometry
Getting to the Answer: Your task is straightforward: find the volume of the cylinder. You are given a figure that includes the dimensions $r = 4$ and $h = 5$. The volume of a cylinder is the area of its base (a circle) times its height. Jot down the formula and fill in the given dimensions: $V = \pi r^2 h = \pi(4)^2 (5)$. This expression simplifies to $V = 80\pi$ cubic inches. Choice (D) is correct.

4. H
Difficulty: High
Category: Geometry
Getting to the Answer: You need to find the amount of wrapping paper required to wrap one candle. You are given a figure and the dimensions of the candle. You are also told that there will be extra paper on each end. Covering a 3D shape with gift wrap means that you are working with surface area.

Recall that the formula for the surface area of a cylinder is $2\pi r^2 + 2\pi rh$, but be careful. The circular top and bottom of the candle will not be covered, so the surface area of the gift wrap is just $2\pi rh$. You are given that the diameter of the candle is 4 inches, so assuming the thickness of the gift wrap is negligible, $r = 2$ inches. Since Mali wants the gift wrap to be 3 inches past the top and bottom of the candle, the height of the gift wrap is $h = 3 + 8 + 3 = 14$ inches. Plug these numbers into $2\pi rh$ and simplify: $2\pi(2)(14) = 56\pi$ square inches. Check that your answer is in the correct units. Choice (H) is correct.

Part 3
ACT MATH

5. A
Difficulty: Medium
Category: Geometry
Getting to the Answer: To find the volume of the figurine, you need to find the change in the volume of the water after placing the figurine in the water. After the figurine is submerged, the height of the water rises 0.4 inches, but the length and width do not change. You can multiply these dimensions by a height of 0.4 to find the volume of the figurine: $10 \times 13 \times 0.4 = 52$ cubic inches. Choice (A) is correct.

Alternatively, you could determine the volume before and after the figurine is submerged and then calculate the difference:

$$V_{before} = 10(13)(5)$$
$$= 650$$
$$V_{after} = 10(13)(5.4)$$
$$= 702$$
$$V_{after} - V_{before} = 702 - 650$$
$$= 52$$

As expected, this matches (A).

Triangles and Trigonometry

1. B
Difficulty: High
Category: Geometry
Getting to the Answer: The question asks you to find the values of θ when $\sin \theta = \frac{1}{2}$. Use the unit circle to determine that for θ between 0 and π, $\sin \theta = \frac{1}{2}$ occurs when $\theta = \frac{\pi}{6}$ and $\frac{5\pi}{6}$. This matches (B).

If you do not know the unit circle by memory, draw a sketch. Since θ is between 0 and π, draw θ in Quadrants I and II.

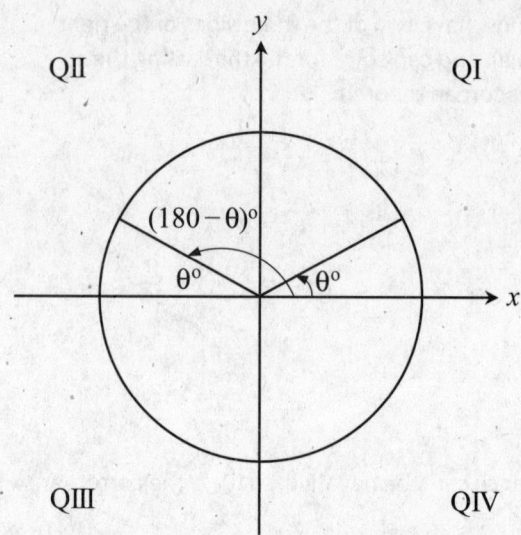

Recall that the definition of sine is $\frac{opposite}{hypotenuse}$. Form a right triangle using θ and label the opposite side 1 and the hypotenuse 2. Note that these sides correspond to those of a 30-60-90 triangle. Use the ratio of the sides, $x : x\sqrt{3} : 2x$, to determine θ. The angle opposite 1 is 30°. Thus, $\theta = 30°$ and $180° - 30° = 150°$.

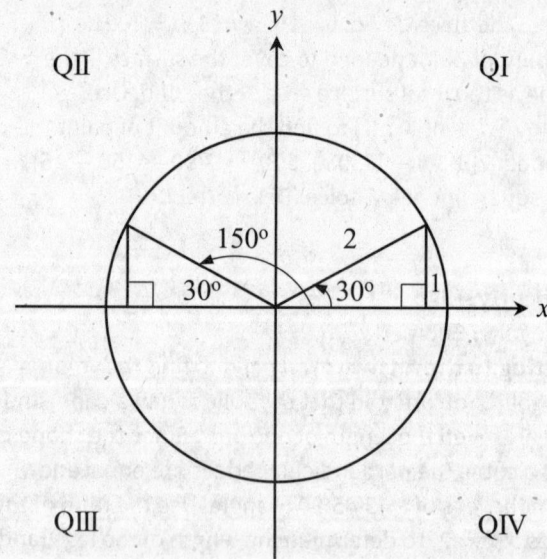

Convert your answer into radians using the conversion factor $180° = \pi$ radians: $30° = \frac{\pi}{6}$ and $150° = \frac{5\pi}{6}$. Finally, double-check that you used the correct interval for θ. Choice (B) is correct.

2. F
Difficulty: Medium
Category: Geometry
Getting to the Answer: Since $\cos = \frac{\text{adj}}{\text{hyp}}$ and $\sin = \frac{\text{opp}}{\text{hyp}}$, the side adjacent to β is 36 units long, the hypotenuse is 39 units long, and the side opposite is 15 units long. To determine the value of $\tan β$, use the relationship $\tan = \frac{\text{opp}}{\text{adj}}$: $\tan β = \frac{15}{36}$, so choice (F) is correct.

3. D
Difficulty: High
Category: Geometry
Getting to the Answer: Use $\frac{1}{2}ab \sin x$ to compare the areas of the original and new triangles. The area of the original triangle is $\frac{1}{2}fg \sin 135°$, and the area of the new triangle is $\frac{1}{2}fg \sin 45°$. The only difference is the angle.

On the unit circle, 45°, which is between 0° and 90°, is in Quadrant I, and 135°, which is between 90° and 180°, is in Quadrant II. Note that $180° − 135° = 45°$.

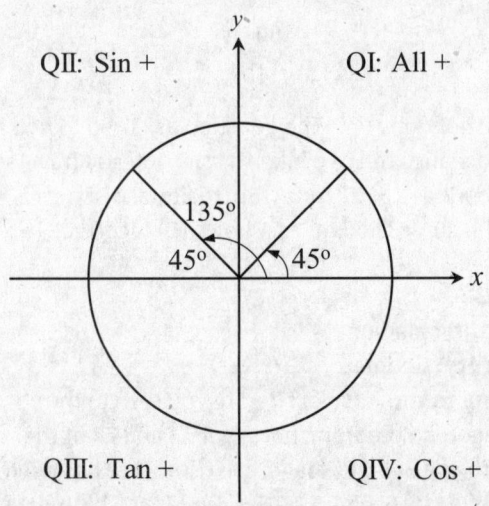

You might have heard of the mnemonic *All Students Take Calculus* to remember the order *All, Sin, Tan, Cos* as you move counter-clockwise around the unit circle; like PEMDAS, there are multiple mnemonics that can be used to remember this information. In Quadrants I and II, sin is positive. Therefore, $\sin 135° = \sin 45°$, and the areas are equal. The new area is also 60 square centimeters, so (D) is correct.

4. J
Difficulty: High
Category: Geometry
Getting to the Answer: On test day, be on the lookout for questions that simply ask you to plug values into a given formula. They may look tough, but they don't require you to do much thinking.

Here, the question is asking for the expression that represents the value of *z*. Since you know the values of two of the three angles in the triangle, you can deduce that the unmarked angle has a measure of $180° − 35° − 45° = 100°$. You are given the length of $\overline{DS}$ along with its opposite angle, so plug that information into the law of sines to solve for *z*:

$$\frac{\sin 45°}{7} = \frac{\sin 100°}{z}$$
$$z \sin 45° = 7 \sin 100°$$
$$z = \frac{7 \sin 100°}{\sin 45°}$$

Choice (J) is correct.

5. C
Difficulty: High
Category: Geometry
Getting to the Answer: For $\triangle EFG$, $\overline{FG} = 16$, $\overline{EF} = 4$, and $\angle F = 70°$. Use the second formula, $c^2 = a^2 + b^2 − 2ab \cos C$, to find $\overline{EG}$:

$$\overline{EG} = \sqrt{e^2 + g^2 − 2eg \cos F}$$
$$= \sqrt{16^2 + 4^2 − 2(16)(4) \cos 70°}$$

This matches (C).

On Test Day

1. A
Difficulty: High
Category: Geometry
Getting to the Answer: The difference in the areas of the shaded portion between the two layouts arises solely from the different desk shapes. Thus, you need to calculate the difference in the cross-sectional area of the desks only; ignore the other furniture. The triangular desk in Layout 1 has an area of $\frac{1}{2}bh = \frac{1}{2}(4)(4) = 8$ square feet. The rectangular desk in Layout 2 has an area of $l \times w = 5 \times 2 = 10$ square feet. The difference in the areas of the desks, and therefore of the shaded portions between the layouts, is $10 − 8 = 2$ square feet, which matches (A).

How Much Have You Learned?

1. C
Difficulty: Medium
Category: Geometry
Getting to the Answer: Since $\overline{LM} = \overline{MN} = \overline{NL}$, $\triangle MNL$ is an equilateral. Thus, each interior angle is 60°. Vertical angles are congruent, so $\angle PNO$, which is opposite $\angle MNL$, also has a measure of 60°. The sum of the measures of the interior angles of a triangle is always 180°. Therefore, $\angle NOP = 180° - 60° - 100° = 20°$, which is (C).

2. H
Difficulty: Low
Category: Geometry
Getting to the Answer: The corresponding sides in similar triangles are proportional. Since the perimeter is the sum of all the sides, the perimeters are proportional as well. Set up the following equation to solve for the perimeter of the smaller triangle, denoted by x:

$$\frac{\text{perimeter smaller}}{\text{perimeter larger}} = \frac{4}{7} = \frac{x}{10 + 12 + 13}.$$

$$\frac{4}{7} = \frac{x}{35}$$
$$140 = 7x$$
$$20 = x$$

The correct answer is (H).

3. B
Difficulty: Medium
Category: Geometry
Getting to the Answer: You are asked to find the number of miles that Keesha and Dwayne will hike on their way to the summit. You are given verbal descriptions of the hikers' paths to the summit, but it is much easier to understand the situation if you draw a diagram of Keesha and Dwayne's routes. After drawing and labeling the diagram with the information given, look for a way to create a right triangle by drawing in additional lines. Then, fill in the lengths of any new segments that you draw.

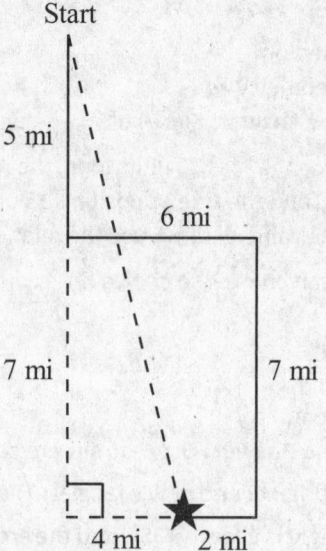

Use the Pythagorean theorem to calculate the distance that Dwayne hikes.

$$c^2 = (5 + 7)^2 + 4^2$$
$$c^2 = 144 + 16$$
$$c^2 = 160$$
$$c = \sqrt{160}$$

You're not done yet! The question asks you to find the total distance the two hikers travel. Keesha traveled $5 + 6 + 7 + 2 = 20$ miles. So, the total distance is $\sqrt{160} + 20 = 32.65$ miles. Choice (B) is correct.

4. G
Difficulty: Medium
Category: Geometry
Getting to the Answer: Before you rush to the Pythagorean theorem, note that 18 and 24 fit the pattern of a 3-4-5 Pythagorean triple that has been multiplied by 6: $(3:4:5) \times 6 = 18:24:30$. This means that $\overline{WY}$ is 30, but the question asks for the length of $\overline{WZ}$. Since Z is the midpoint of $\overline{WY}$, $\overline{WZ}$ is half of 30, or 15. Choice (G) is correct.

5. D
Difficulty: Medium
Category: Geometry
Getting to the Answer: Since $\angle CDB$ and $\angle BDE$ are on a straight line, they are supplementary. Because $\angle CDB$ is 90°, $\angle BDE$ is also 90°. The sum of the interior angles of a triangle equals 180°, so $\angle EBD$ is $180° - 90° - 17° = 73°$. Because $\overline{CD} = \overline{BD}$, $\triangle CDB$ is a 45-45-90 triangle. Thus, $\angle DBC = 45°$. Angles ABC, DBC, and EBD are supplementary, so $\angle ABC = 180° - 73° - 45° = 62°$. This matches (D).

6. G
Difficulty: Low
Category: Geometry
Getting to the Answer: To determine the total amount of molding needed, find the perimeter of the floor. Notice that the diagonal is the hypotenuse of a triangle that has a height of $15 - 9 = 6$ feet and a base of $30 - 22 = 8$ feet.

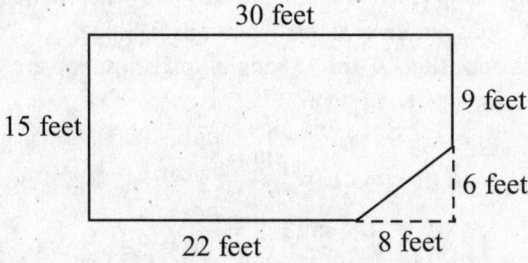

If you do not recognize the Pythagorean triple $(3:4:5) \times 2 = 6:8:10$, use the Pythagorean theorem $(a^2 + b^2 = c^2)$ to calculate the hypotenuse.

$$c^2 = 8^2 + 6^2$$
$$c^2 = 100$$
$$c = 10$$

Add up all the sides to calculate the total length of molding Akanksha needs: $15 + 9 + 30 + 22 + 10 = 86$ feet. Choice (G) is correct.

7. A
Difficulty: Low
Category: Geometry
Getting to the Answer: You need to find the length of the fence. You are told that the orchard is rectangular and that Yesenia will split it diagonally into two triangles. You're also given some dimensions: $A = 540$ square feet and $l = 36$ feet.

Draw and label a figure to visualize the situation.

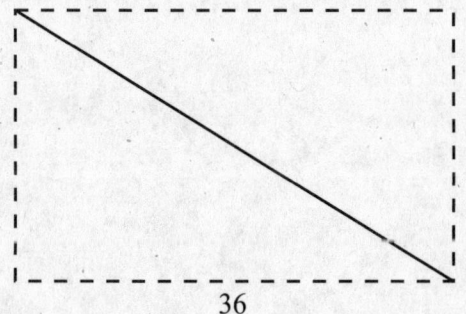

The area of a rectangle is the product of its length and width. Because you know the length and the area, you can find the width:

$$A = lw$$
$$540 = 36w$$
$$15 = w$$

Add the width to the diagram. Now you know that the fence is the hypotenuse of a right triangle with legs of lengths 15 and 36. Before turning to the Pythagorean theorem, look for a Pythagorean triplet to save time. Indeed, this is a 5-12-13 triangle multiplied by 3. Therefore, the hypotenuse—and the amount of fence needed—is $13 \times 3 = 39$ feet, which is (A).

If you didn't recognize this fact, you could also have plugged these numbers into the Pythagorean theorem, $a^2 + b^2 = c^2$.

$$c^2 = 15^2 + 36^2$$
$$c^2 = 225 + 1{,}296$$
$$c = \sqrt{1{,}521}$$
$$= 39$$

8. H
Difficulty: High
Category: Geometry
Getting to the Answer: First, determine the radius of each circle. Starting from the innermost circle, the radii for the circles are 1, 2, 3, and 4 inches, respectively.

The area of the smaller shaded ring is the area of the small shaded circle minus the small white circle: $4\pi - \pi = 3\pi$ square inches. The area of the larger shaded ring is the area of the larger shaded circle minus the larger white circle: $16\pi - 9\pi = 7\pi$ square inches.

The total area of the shaded region is therefore the sum of the shaded areas: $3\pi + 7\pi = 10\pi$ square inches.

Finally, calculate the percent of the total area the shaded area represents using the formula $\frac{\text{part}}{\text{whole}} \times 100\%$. Thus, the percent is $\frac{10\pi}{16\pi} \times 100\% = \frac{5}{8} \times 100\% = 62.5\%$. Choice (H) is correct.

9. C
Difficulty: Medium
Category: Geometry
Getting to the Answer: The question tells you that the circumference of the opening (which is a circle) is 8π, so substitute this value into the formula for circumference and solve for r:

$$C = 2\pi r$$
$$8\pi = 2\pi r$$
$$4 = r$$

You can now find h, which represents the length of the tunnel. Use the formula $V = \pi r^2 h$:

$$2{,}048\pi = \pi(4)^2(h)$$
$$2{,}048 = 16h$$
$$128 = h$$

The tunnel is 128 feet long, which is (C).

10. G
Difficulty: High
Category: Geometry
Getting to the Answer: Remembering the acronym SOHCAHTOA can get you through a lot of trig questions. This question is asking for the length of $\overline{BC}$. The only length you are given is that of the hypotenuse of the triangle, so start by checking for either a cosine or sine relationship (since the tangent part of the acronym, TOA, does not involve the hypotenuse). Since $\overline{BC}$ is opposite $\angle D$, the 37° angle, you can set up an equation involving sin 37°:

$$\sin = \frac{\text{opp}}{\text{hyp}}$$
$$\sin(37°) = \frac{BC}{15}$$
$$15\sin(37°) = BC$$

Choice (G) is correct.

[CHAPTER 14]

ACT MATH: TIMING AND SECTION MANAGEMENT STRATEGIES

> **LEARNING OBJECTIVE**
>
> After this lesson, you will be able to:
>
> - Triage the ACT Math section by making quick decisions about which questions to do and which to skip

ACT Math: Timing and Section Management Strategies

The Math Test has 45 questions to be completed in 50 minutes, which means you'll have a little more than one minute per question. This is an average, though. Some questions will be straightforward, meaning that you can get the correct answer in 30 seconds or less. Others will be more difficult and time-consuming. Test takers who start at the beginning of the section, answering the questions in order and only moving on to the next question when the previous one is complete, may find that they get bogged down. They may not make it to the end of the section, potentially missing questions that they could have answered correctly.

An alternative approach allows you to be flexible as you move through the section. Flexibility earns more points because you will be able to choose which questions you will answer. As you read a new question, take a moment to gauge your gut reaction:

- Does this question seem quick and easy? Do it immediately.
- Does this question seem time-consuming but manageable? Skip it for now. Put a circle around it on the paper test or flag the question with the tool on the digital test. Try any of these flagged questions on a second pass through the section.
- Does this question look confusing or difficult? Skip it. Don't be concerned about flagging questions like this. You'll approach them only after you have worked on the other questions in the section, and only if you have time.

Try to make this decision quickly. The more you practice, the easier it will be to recognize which questions are easier and which are more challenging for you.

When you approach a test section this way, you'll end up taking two or three passes through it. This technique ensures that you'll get all the easy points first, and if you run out of time, you'll know that the questions you didn't attempt were the hardest in the section and would have been tougher to answer correctly anyway.

Before the end of the section, make sure you have answered every question since there is no penalty for guessing. Also, be very careful when marking your answers on the paper test. It's easy to skip a question but then forget to skip a line on your answer grid. This can result in placing answers incorrectly on your paper answer sheet. The digital test will allow you to see which ones have been answered, flagged, or unanswered.

If you tend to finish the Math sections early but find that you are making mistakes, you may consider briefly pausing at the final step of the Kaplan Method to check your logic and calculations before choosing your response to each question.

Chapter 14
ACT Math: Timing and Section Management Strategies

How Much Have You Learned?

Directions: Use this question set to practice effective question triage. Skip those questions that you feel will take too long; come back to them if you have time. Try to get as many questions correct as you can in 16 minutes. As always, be sure to study the explanations, even for questions you got correct. They can be found at the end of this chapter.

1. What are the roots of $3x^2 + 5x - 3$?

   A. $\dfrac{5 \pm \sqrt{51}}{3}$

   B. $\dfrac{5 \pm \sqrt{61}}{6}$

   C. $\dfrac{-5 \pm \sqrt{51}}{3}$

   D. $\dfrac{-5 \pm \sqrt{61}}{6}$

2. $\triangle XYZ$ is similar to $\triangle UVW$. If $\overline{XY} = 10$, $\overline{YZ} = 6$, and $\overline{UV} = 15$, then what is the length of $\overline{VW}$?

   F. 4
   G. 9
   H. 11
   J. 25

3. Which of the following is equivalent to $(3 - 8i)(5 + 3i)$?

   A. $39 - 31i$
   B. $-9 - 31i$
   C. $39 + 49i$
   D. $-9 + 49i$

4. A customer of a retail store purchases an item for $23.10 after a 10% tax. If the item was discounted by 30%, what was the original price of the item in dollars?

   F. 24
   G. 27
   H. 30
   J. 33

5. Which of the following is equivalent to tan E?

   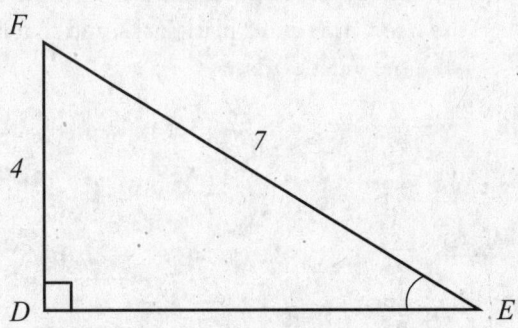

   A. $\dfrac{4}{7}$

   B. $\dfrac{4}{\sqrt{33}}$

   C. $\dfrac{7}{\sqrt{33}}$

   D. $\dfrac{\sqrt{33}}{4}$

6. If the first term of an arithmetic sequence is 3 and the 32nd term is 127, what is the 17th term?

   F. 75
   G. 71
   H. 67
   J. 63

7. A circle has a diameter of 8 feet. If the circle's area were tripled, what would its new radius be in feet?

   A. $4\sqrt{3}$
   B. $8\sqrt{3}$
   C. 12
   D. 24

Part 3
ACT MATH

8. Kareem has a standard deck of 52 cards. What is the likelihood that he will pick a red face card after one red face card has already been picked and removed from the deck? (For this question, a face card is classified as a Jack, Queen, King, or Ace. There are four of each face card in a standard deck: two black and two red. For example, there are 2 red Jacks and 2 black Jacks, and so forth with the other cards...)

   F. $\dfrac{7}{51}$
   G. $\dfrac{7}{52}$
   H. $\dfrac{8}{51}$
   J. $\dfrac{25}{51}$

9. If $a:b = 3:7$ and $c:b = 4:5$, what is the ratio of a to c?

   A. 3:4
   B. 4:3
   C. 15:28
   D. 28:15

10. Which of the following equations describes $f(x)$?

x	-2	-1	0	1	2
f(x)	-6	-2	2	6	10

    F. $f(x) = 2x^2 + 5x + 2$
    G. $f(x) = 2x^2 + 5x - 2$
    H. $f(x) = 4x + 2$
    J. $f(x) = 4x - 2$

11. Let $f(x) = -3x + 3$ and $g(x) = -5x + 8$. What is the value of $f(g(1))$?

    A. −6
    B. 0
    C. 8
    D. 12

12. Let $f(x) = -4x - 2$ and $g(x) = 2x$. What is the solution that satisfies both $f(x)$ and $g(x)$?

    F. $\left(-\dfrac{2}{3}, -\dfrac{1}{3}\right)$
    G. $\left(-\dfrac{1}{3}, -\dfrac{2}{3}\right)$
    H. $\left(\dfrac{1}{3}, \dfrac{2}{3}\right)$
    J. $\left(\dfrac{2}{3}, \dfrac{1}{3}\right)$

13. Suppose $f(x) = x^2$ and $g(x) = (x+4)^2 - 2$. Which of the following points lies on $g(x)$ if $(-2, 4)$ lies on $f(x)$?

    A. $(-6, -2)$
    B. $(-6, 2)$
    C. $(2, 2)$
    D. $(2, 6)$

14. Given the data set $\{-5, 8, 6, -3, -1\}$, what is the positive difference between the arithmetic mean and median?

    F. 1
    G. 2
    H. 4
    J. 5

15. If the base of a scale model is 12 inches by 18 inches and the shorter side of the real object is 14 feet, then how long in feet is the longer side of the real object?

   A. 9
   B. 15
   C. 20
   D. 21

Answers and Explanations

How Much Have You Learned?

1. D
Difficulty: Medium
Category: Algebra
Getting to the Answer: The question asks you to find the roots, or solutions, of the given quadratic equation. Because all the answer choices contain square roots, the best strategy is to use the quadratic formula: $x = \frac{-b \pm \sqrt{b^2 - 4ac}}{2a}$. Write down that $a = 3$, $b = 5$, and $c = -3$, and plug the values into the quadratic formula.

$$x = \frac{-(5) \pm \sqrt{(5)^2 - 4(3)(-3)}}{2(3)}$$
$$= \frac{-5 \pm \sqrt{25 + 36}}{6}$$
$$= \frac{-5 \pm \sqrt{61}}{6}$$

Hence, (D) is correct. Be careful to keep track of all negative signs when plugging in: the incorrect choices result from one or more misplaced negatives.

2. G
Difficulty: Medium
Category: Geometry
Getting to the Answer: This question asks for the length of the segment $\overline{VW}$ in the second triangle given certain lengths of two similar triangles. Look carefully at the order in which the vertices of the similar triangles are stated, as that will tell you which segments correspond to each other. With the given segments, $\overline{XY}$ corresponds to $\overline{UV}$, while $\overline{YZ}$ corresponds to $\overline{VW}$. Let x represent $\overline{VW}$, and create an equation with proportions to solve for x.

$$\frac{6}{10} = \frac{x}{15}$$
$$10x = 90$$
$$x = 9$$

$\overline{VW} = 9$, so (G) is correct. Choice J results from setting up the proportion incorrectly.

3. A
Difficulty: Medium
Category: Number and Quantity
Getting to the Answer: This question asks you to evaluate an expression that contains imaginary numbers. Use FOIL and keep careful track of the negative signs while multiplying. Plug in the value $i^2 = -1$ when appropriate.

$$(3 - 8i)(5 + 3i) = 15 + 9i - 40i - 24i^2$$
$$= 15 - 31i - 24i^2$$
$$= 15 - 31i - 24(-1)$$
$$= 15 - 31i + 24$$
$$= 39 - 31i$$

Choice (A) is correct. Notice that B is the answer you would get if you plugged in 1 instead of -1 for i^2.

4. H
Difficulty: High
Category: Number and Quantity
Getting to the Answer: The question asks for the original price of an item before a 30% discount and a 10% tax. First, calculate the discounted price before the tax by using the equation $x + 0.1x = 23.10 \rightarrow 1.1x = 23.10 \rightarrow x = 21$. Set up another equation that shows that when the original price is reduced by 30%, it equals $21. Since reducing the original 100% by 30% yields 70%, you get $0.7x = 21 \rightarrow x = 30$. The original price of the item is $30, which matches (H).

Alternatively, you can Backsolve, starting with (H). If the discount is 30% and the tax is 10%, then $30(0.7)(1.1) = \$23.10$, which matches the purchase price.

5. B
Difficulty: Medium
Category: Geometry
Getting to the Answer: The question asks you to solve for tan E. Because $\tan = \frac{\text{opposite}}{\text{adjacent}}$, use the Pythagorean theorem to solve for the adjacent side:
$a^2 + (4)^2 = (7)^2 \rightarrow a^2 + 16 = 49 \rightarrow a^2 = 33 \rightarrow a = \sqrt{33}$.
The side opposite angle E is 4, so $\tan E = \frac{4}{\sqrt{33}}$ and (B) is correct.

Another way to find the answer is to use Elimination. The side opposite angle E is 4, so 4, or one of its factors, should be in the numerator of the answer. This eliminates C and D. The adjacent side can't be 7, because that's the hypotenuse. Thus, A is incorrect. Only (B) is left, so it must be correct.

6. H
Difficulty: High
Category: Number and Quantity
Getting to the Answer: The question asks you to solve for a_{17}, given that the first term of the arithmetic sequence is 3 and the 32nd term is 127. Use the arithmetic sequence equation $a_n = a_1 + (n-1)d$ and plug in all the given information to first solve for d, the common difference between each term:

$$a_{32} = a_1 + (32-1)d$$
$$127 = 3 + 31d$$
$$124 = 31d$$
$$4 = d$$

Now use the same equation to solve for a_{17}:

$$a_{17} = 3 + (17-1)(4)$$
$$= 3 + (16)(4)$$
$$= 3 + 64$$
$$= 67$$

The 17th term in the arithmetic sequence is 67. Thus, (H) is correct. Be certain that you used $n-1$ rather than n in your calculations.

7. A
Difficulty: Medium
Category: Geometry
Getting to the Answer: The question asks what the radius of a circle with an 8-foot diameter would become if its area were tripled. First, use the diameter given to calculate the radius of the circle: $d = 2r \rightarrow 8 = 2r \rightarrow 4 = r$. Next, use the area formula for a circle, $A = \pi r^2$, to find the area: $A = \pi(4)^2 = 16\pi$. The question states that the circle's area is tripled, so its new area is $3 \times 16\pi = 48\pi$. Use the area of the larger circle to calculate the radius: $(48\pi) = \pi r^2 \rightarrow 48 = r^2 \rightarrow \sqrt{48} = \sqrt{16}\sqrt{3} = 4\sqrt{3} = r$. Therefore, (A) is correct. Choice B may be tempting, but this is the diameter, not the radius.

8. F
Difficulty: High
Category: Statistics and Probability
Getting to the Answer: The question asks how likely it is to pick a red face card after one has already been picked with no replacement. Use the probability formula: Probability $= \frac{\text{desired}}{\text{total}}$. There are $4(2) = 8$ red face cards in a standard deck of 52 cards. After one is picked and removed, only 7 red face cards and 51 total cards remain, so the probability is $\frac{7}{51}$. Hence, (F) is correct. If you did not remember to decrease the denominator by the card that was already drawn, you would have arrived at G.

9. C
Difficulty: High
Category: Number and Quantity
Getting to the Answer: You are given two ratios with three variables. If you have two ratios, $a:b$ and $c:b$, you can derive $a:c$ by making the b term the same in each ratio. Since $5(7) = 35$, multiply each ratio by the factor that will get you to $b = 35$. Use 5 for $a:b$ and 7 for $c:b$. The result is $5(3:7) = 15:35$ and $7(4:5) = 28:35$. Now that the b terms are the same, $a:b = 15:35$ and $c:b = 28:35$, you can rewrite the ratio $a:b:c$ as $15:35:28$. This means that the ratio of $a:c$ is $15:28$, which is (C).

Alternatively, you can recognize that $\frac{a}{b} \times \frac{b}{c} = \frac{a}{c}$ and plug in the given values (inverting $c:b$ to get $b:c$) to determine that $\frac{a}{c} = \frac{3}{7} \times \frac{5}{4} = \frac{15}{28}$.

10. H
Difficulty: Medium
Category: Functions
Getting to the Answer: This question asks for the definition of $f(x)$ that is consistent with the data in the table. Notice that all the choices are either quadratic or linear, so check the table to see which relationship fits $f(x)$. All the x-values increase by one, while all the y-values increase by 4. This means that the table represents a linear equation with a slope of 4, so eliminate the quadratic choices F and G. Determine the y-intercept to further eliminate choices: the table shows the point $(0, 2)$ is the y-intercept, which eliminates choice J. Thus, (H) is correct.

Alternatively, you could plug a point from the table to determine the equation for f(x). The table says that plugging $x = 1$ into f(x) should yield 6. Plugging $x = 1$ into (H) gives $f(1) = 4(1) + 2 = 6$. None of the other choices yield 6, so (H) is correct.

11. A
Difficulty: Low
Category: Functions
Getting to the Answer: This question asks you to solve for the composite function f(g(1)). Start with solving for g(1): $g(1) = -5(1) + 8 = 3$. Now you can solve for f(g(1)) or f(3): $f(x) = -3(3) + 3 = -6$. Therefore, (A) is correct. Note that if you had incorrectly found g(f(1)), you would have selected C.

12. G
Difficulty: Low
Category: Functions
Getting to the Answer: This question asks for the solution to the system of equations f(x) and g(x). Set equations for f(x) and g(x) equal to each other and solve for x.

$$2x = -4x - 2$$
$$6x = -2$$
$$x = -\frac{1}{3}$$

This means that $x = -\frac{1}{3}$ satisfies both functions. Note that (G) is correct since it is the only choice with that x-value. If you needed to calculate the y-value, you could plug in $x = -\frac{1}{3}$ to either function and simplify.

13. B
Difficulty: Medium
Category: Functions
Getting to the Answer: The question asks which of the choices lies on the graph g(x). You could plug the x-coordinate of each choice into g(x) and see which one produces the matching y-coordinate, but you will find the answer more quickly if you apply the properties of function transformations. Notice that, compared to f(x), g(x) translates 4 units to the left and 2 units down. You can confirm this by setting the inside of what is being squared equal to zero and solving: $x + 4 = 0 \rightarrow x = -4$. This is the reason for the horizontal shift of 4 units to the left. The term on the outside of the square is the vertical shift, which is more straightforward: the function shifts 2 units down because of the subtraction of 2. Take the given point on f, subtract 4 from the x-coordinate, and subtract 2 from the y-coordinate: $(-2 - (4), 4 - (2)) = (-6, 2)$. Thus, (B) is correct.

14. G
Difficulty: Medium
Category: Statistics and Probability
Getting to the Answer: The question asks for the positive difference between the arithmetic mean and median of the given data set. First, calculate the mean by adding all the given numbers and dividing by the total amount of numbers.

$$\frac{-5 + 8 + 6 - 3 - 1}{5} = \frac{5}{5} = 1$$

Next, find the median by arranging the list in ascending order and locating the middle number. $\{-5, 8, 6, -3, -1\} \rightarrow \{-5, -3, -1, 6, 8\}$, so -1 is the median. Remember that the question asks for the positive difference between the two values, which is $1 - (-1) = 1 + 1 = 2$. Thus, (G) is correct.

15. D
Difficulty: Medium
Category: Number and Quantity
Getting to the Answer: The question asks for the length of the longer side of the real object given information about the scale model. Notice that the scale model is given in inches, while the choices are given in feet. However, because the units will cancel when you set up a proportion, don't waste time converting everything into feet. Set up a proportion and solve:

$$\frac{12}{18} = \frac{14}{x}$$
$$12x = 252$$
$$x = 21$$

The longer side of the real object is 21 feet. Therefore, (D) is correct. Choice A results from setting up the proportion incorrectly.

TEST YOURSELF: ACT MATH

Directions: For test-like timing, give yourself 50 minutes to complete the following 45 questions.

1. Which of the following is the value for the given expression?

   $||4 - 7| - |-10 + 2||$

   A. -11
   B. -5
   C. 5
   D. 11

2. What is the slope of the line that corresponds to the equation $6x - 5y = 4$ in the standard (x, y) coordinate plane?

   F. $-\dfrac{6}{5}$
   G. $-\dfrac{5}{6}$
   H. $\dfrac{5}{6}$
   J. $\dfrac{6}{5}$

3. In the given figure, $\triangle ABC$ and $\triangle DEF$ are similar triangles with the given side lengths in meters. What is the perimeter of $\triangle DEF$, in meters?

   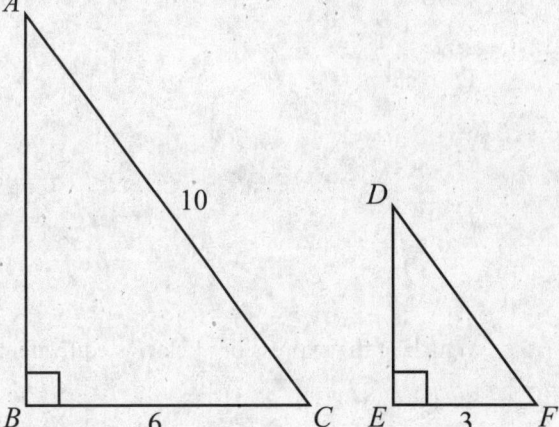

   A. 8
   B. 12
   C. 16
   D. 24

4. Over the course of 8 days, Marie counted the number of toys she put away each day after babysitting. The given table shows the data recorded for each day. What is the median?

Number of Toys Put Away	
Day 1	10
Day 2	8
Day 3	12
Day 4	7
Day 5	5
Day 6	12
Day 7	5
Day 8	9

F. 7.5
G. 8
H. 8.5
J. 9

5. Which of the expressions below is equivalent to $9x^2\left(-\frac{1}{3}y + 3x - 21x\right)$?

A. $8x^3$
B. $18y^2$
C. $6x^2y - 8x^3$
D. $-3x^2y - 162x^3$

6. For the polygon shown in the given figure, all adjacent line segments are perpendicular to one another. The dimensions given are in feet. What is the perimeter of the object, in feet?

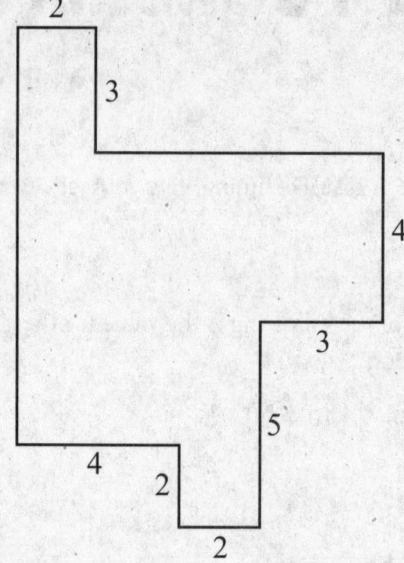

F. 36
G. 39
H. 40
J. 42

7. A wooden rod length of $12\frac{2}{3}$ feet is cut into 3 pieces, with nothing left over and with no loss of wood in the cuts themselves. If the lengths of two of the pieces are $6\frac{5}{9}$ feet and $3\frac{13}{18}$ feet, what is the length of the third piece, in feet?

A. $2\frac{7}{18}$
B. $2\frac{11}{18}$
C. $3\frac{7}{18}$
D. $4\frac{11}{50}$

8. A linear relationship is drawn in the standard (x, y) coordinate graph given. Which of the following equations correctly reflects the relationship?

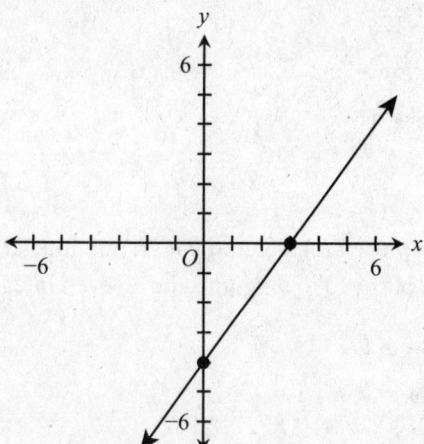

F. $y = -\frac{3}{4}x - 4$
G. $y = -\frac{3}{4}x + 4$
H. $y = \frac{4}{3}x - 4$
J. $y = \frac{4}{3}x + 4$

9. $\frac{6.4 \times 10^{-3}}{2.0 \times 10^4}$ is equal to which of the following?

A. 3.4×10^{-12}
B. 3.2×10^{-7}
C. 3.2×10^{-1}
D. 3.1×10^1

10. What is the value of $f(-3)$ for the given equation?

$$f(x) = 7x - (3x^2 - 2)$$

F. -46
G. -4
H. 4
J. 46

11. At 12:00 p.m., Ming sat down on a merry-go-round that was facing due west. By 12:30 p.m., heavy winds had rotated the merry-go-round 270° clockwise. If the rate of rotation was kept constant, how many degrees clockwise would the merry-go-round rotate in 45 minutes?

A. 305°
B. 335°
C. 360°
D. 405°

12. What is the midpoint of the line segment in the (x, y) coordinate plane that begins at $(-2, -4)$ and ends at $(1, 2)$?

F. $\left(-\frac{1}{2}, -1\right)$
G. $\left(-\frac{1}{2}, 1\right)$
H. $\left(\frac{1}{2}, -1\right)$
J. $\left(\frac{1}{2}, 1\right)$

13. A math teacher owns 10 pairs of pants, 2 pairs of shoes, and 6 shirts. Each outfit the teacher wears includes a combination of 1 shirt, 1 pair of shoes, and 1 pair of pants. How many possible outfits could the math teacher wear?

A. 120
B. 62
C. 26
D. 18

Part 3
ACT MATH

14. If $9 - 3(y - 3) \leq 0$, which of the following correctly characterizes the range of possible values for y?

   F. $y \leq -6$
   G. $y \leq 3$
   H. $y \geq -6$
   J. $y \geq 6$

15. If 1,024 is the first term, what is the eighth term in the geometric sequence 1,024, 512, 256, 128, ...?

   A. 8
   B. 16
   C. 32
   D. 64

16. What is the y-intercept of the line in the standard (x, y) coordinate plane that goes through the points $(-1, 2)$ and $(5, -2)$?

   F. $-\frac{2}{3}$
   G. 1
   H. $\frac{4}{3}$
   J. 2

17. In the given figure, point F is on EG, and points B and C are on AD. AD is parallel to EB. What is the measure of $\angle ABF$?

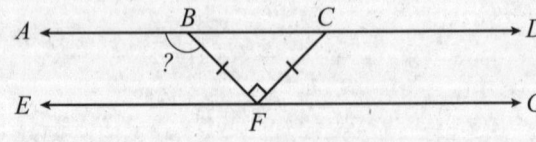

   A. 45°
   B. 90°
   C. 120°
   D. 135°

18. In the standard (x, y) coordinate plane, what is the distance, in coordinate units, between $(7, -3)$ and $(-2, 5)$?

   F. 17
   G. $\sqrt{17}$
   H. $\sqrt{85}$
   J. $\sqrt{145}$

19. If a is an even integer and b is an odd integer, which of the following must be an even integer?

   A. $2a + b$
   B. $4a - b$
   C. $a^2 b$
   D. $\frac{7b}{a}$

20. What is the value of $q(p(-3))$ given that $p(x) = 7 - x^2$ and $q(x) = 4 - x$?

   F. -42
   G. -12
   H. 6
   J. 20

21. The time it takes to complete a certain job is directly proportional to the number of units produced. If it takes 22 minutes to produce 18 units, how many units are produced in 33 minutes?

   A. 12
   B. 27
   C. 40
   D. 54

22. Deja is playing with building blocks and has a landscape that is 2 feet by 1.5 feet where the blocks snap in. Each building block is 2 inches by 1 inch by 0.5 inches. What is the minimum number of building blocks Deja needs to cover the entire landscape, in a single layer, if the building blocks are all oriented in the same direction?

   F. 108
   G. 216
   H. 432
   J. 864

23. Fifty students went on a camping trip: 14 are freshman, 14 are sophomores, 24% are juniors, and the rest are seniors. If one of the students is chosen at random, what is the probability that the person chosen will NOT be a senior?

   A. $\frac{1}{5}$
   B. $\frac{7}{25}$
   C. $\frac{7}{10}$
   D. $\frac{4}{5}$

24. A business made a pie chart, by category, for its total expenditures for the previous month. Based on the given pie chart, what percent of the total expenditures came from the category with the least amount spent, rounded to the nearest percent?

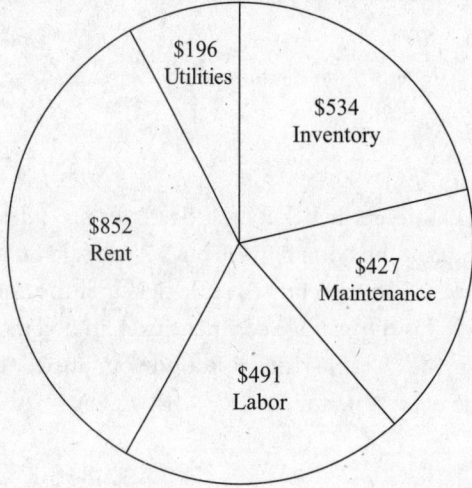

   F. 8%
   G. 17%
   H. 20%
   J. 34%

25. The given figure shows that points F and G are on the segment $\overline{EH}$, where $\overline{EH}$ is 35 units long. How many units long, if it can be determined, is $\overline{FG}$, given that $\overline{EG}$ is 15 units long and $\overline{FH}$ is 25 units long?

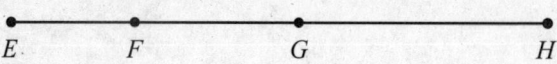

   A. 5
   B. 10
   C. 15
   D. Cannot be determined from the given information

26. The price of a stock increased by 40 percent in Year 1, and then increased by an additional 30 percent in Year 2. By what percent did the price of the stock increase over the 2-year period?

   F. 93%
   G. 82%
   H. 70%
   J. 35%

27. A charity raffle ticket costs $4.00 for pre-sales and $5.00 at the door. Amelie buys 7 pre-sale raffle tickets and then buys 2 raffle tickets at the door. What is the average cost per ticket, in dollars, for Amelie's 9 raffle tickets? Round your answer to the nearest penny.

   A. $3.11
   B. $4.22
   C. $4.50
   D. $5.43

28. In the given diagram, which of the following expressions gives the correct length of $\overline{AC}$ in $\triangle ABC$?

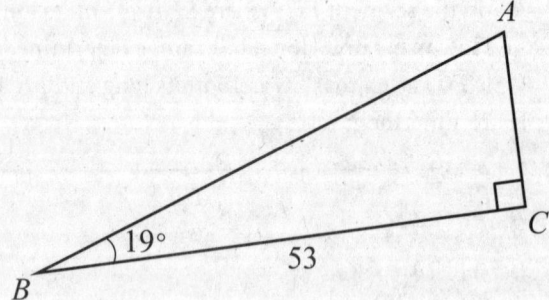

   F. $\dfrac{53}{\cos 19°}$
   G. $\dfrac{53}{\tan 71°}$
   H. $53 \tan 19°$
   J. $53 \cos 71°$

29. Which of the following expressions is equivalent to $x^4 \sqrt[5]{x^2} \cdot y^3 \sqrt{y^7}$?

   A. $x^2 y^3 \sqrt[6]{x^3 y^2}$
   B. $x^3 y^4 \sqrt{xy}$
   C. $x^4 y^6 \sqrt[10]{x^4 y^5}$
   D. $x^6 y^6$

30. A department store's sales are shown in the table. Approximately what percentage of the department store's sales in the month of January did Accessories account for? (Assume that the department store only generates sales in the 3 departments listed.)

Department	Month			
	Jan	Feb	Mar	Apr
Clothing	$1,150	$1,220	$1,080	$1,240
Shoes	$1,000	$1,050	$1,350	$830
Accessories	$750	$720	$950	$810

   F. 23%
   G. 26%
   H. 29%
   J. 33%

31. A solvent manufacturing company is producing toluene and storing it in two different vats with 10,000 gallons of capacity each. Vat A currently contains 450 gallons of toluene, and its contents are increasing at a rate of 40 gallons per minute. Vat B currently contains 1,250 gallons of toluene, and its contents are increasing at a rate of 15 gallons per minute. In how many minutes will the two vats contain equal amounts of toluene?

   A. 30
   B. 32
   C. 48
   D. 60

32. The coach of a basketball team documented the number of free throws that his team of 19 players made during their final game of the season. The bar graph shows the results. What fraction of the players made fewer than 2 free throws?

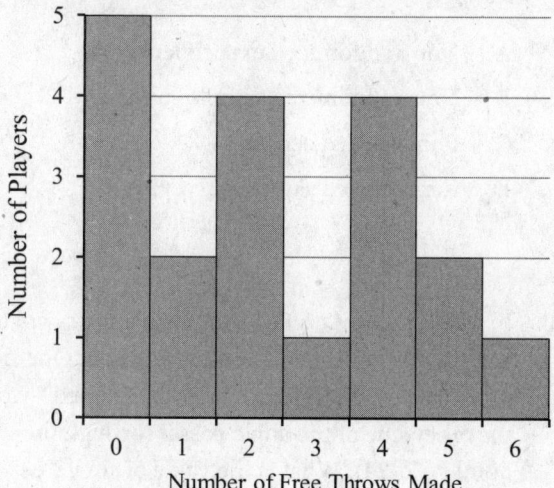

F. $\dfrac{1}{5}$

G. $\dfrac{7}{19}$

H. $\dfrac{11}{19}$

J. $\dfrac{4}{5}$

33. A group of unrelated high school students were surveyed and each was asked how many siblings they have. Their responses are reported in the table shown. Based on the survey responses, what is the average (mean) number of siblings for the students in this group?

Number of Siblings	Number of Students
0	3
1	7
2	5
3	4
4	2
5	1

A. 1.7

B. 1.9

C. 2.1

D. 2.3

34. If $\log_2 16^2 = x$, what is the value of x?

F. -8

G. -6

H. 8

J. 16

35. A circle in the standard (x, y) coordinate plane is tangent to both the x-axis and the line $y = 6$. Which of the following could be the equation of the circle?

A. $x^2 + (y - 3)^2 = 36$

B. $(x - 3)^2 + y^2 = 36$

C. $(x - 3)^2 + (y + 3)^2 = 9$

D. $(x + 3)^2 + (y - 3)^2 = 9$

Part 3
ACT MATH

36. Which of the following expressions is equal to $\frac{i}{3-i}$?

   F. $3i$

   G. $-\frac{1}{8} + \frac{3i}{10}$

   H. $\frac{1}{10} - \frac{3i}{10}$

   J. $-\frac{1}{10} + \frac{3i}{10}$

37. The number of trees in a certain park can be shown in the given matrix:

   $\begin{matrix} \text{Oak} & \text{Elm} & \text{Pine} & \text{Birch} \\ [70 & 30 & 40 & 50] \end{matrix}$

   A park ranger estimates the ratios of the number of healthy trees to the total number of trees for each kind of tree and constructs the following matrix using the ratios:

   $\begin{matrix} \text{Oak} \\ \text{Elm} \\ \text{Pine} \\ \text{Birch} \end{matrix} \begin{bmatrix} 0.4 \\ 0.6 \\ 0.8 \\ 0.7 \end{bmatrix}$

   Given these matrices, what is the park ranger's estimate for the number of healthy trees in the park?

   A. 113
   B. 115
   C. 117
   D. 118

38. The height of a right circular cylinder is 10 inches with a radius of 9 inches. What is the volume, in cubic inches, of this cylinder?

   F. 405π
   G. 480π
   H. 640π
   J. 810π

39. A company wants to get feedback from its employees about their experience working for the company. Out of 1,000 employees, 200 are selected at random to take the survey. Which of the following best describes the company's testing?

   A. Non-randomized experiment
   B. Non-randomized sample survey
   C. Randomized census
   D. Randomized sample survey

40. In the standard (x, y) coordinate plane drawn, the angle ψ is shown; its vertex is the origin. One side of the angle is located on the positive x-axis, while the other side of the angle passes through the point $(-7, 24)$. What is the value of $\sin \psi$?

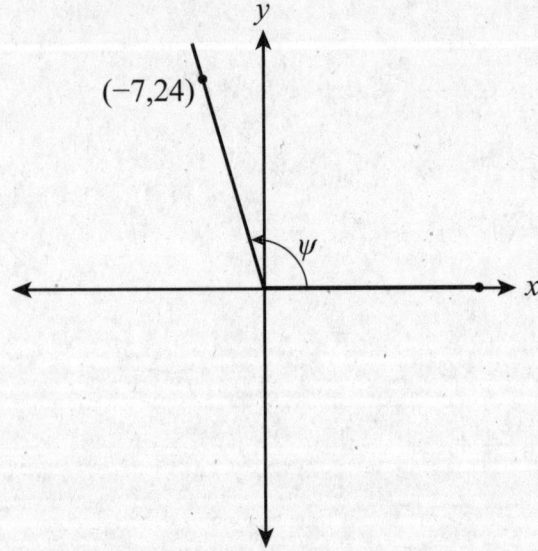

   F. $-\frac{7}{24}$

   G. $-\frac{24}{25}$

   H. $\frac{7}{25}$

   J. $\frac{24}{25}$

41. The growth of a particular bacterial colony, P, in a Petri dish can be modeled by the equation $P = \dfrac{3^{2t-1}}{h} + 200$, where t is time measured in days, such that $t > 0$. The variable h represents a growth coefficient, such that $0 < h \leq 10$. In ideal heat and moisture conditions, $h = 0.5$. Which of the following values represents the population of the bacterial colony after 5 days of growth under ideal heat and moisture conditions?

   A.   10,041.5
   B.   39,566
   C.   354,494
   D.   10,077,896

42. If $f(x) = \dfrac{3}{4}\sin(2x - \pi)$, what is the amplitude of the function $f(x)$?

   F. $\dfrac{1}{2}$
   G. $\dfrac{3}{4}$
   H. $\dfrac{4}{3}$
   J.   2

43. The given graph in the standard (x, y) coordinate plane shows parabolas from a shared family. What is the general equation that describes this family of parabolas for all $n \geq 1$?

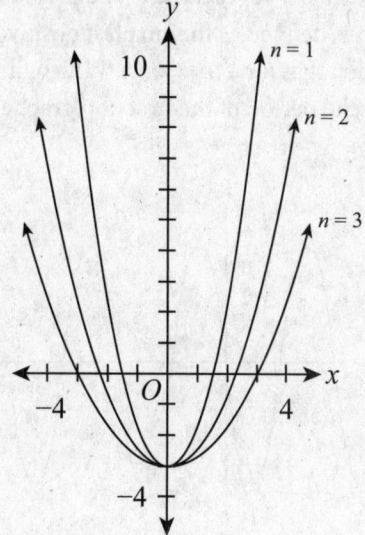

   A. $y = -\dfrac{1}{n}x^2 - 3$
   B. $y = -nx^2 - 3$
   C. $y = \dfrac{1}{n}x^2 - 3$
   D. $y = nx^2 - 3$

Part 3
ACT MATH

44. The trigonometric function shown is graphed in the standard (x,y) coordinate plane. The equation of the function is of the form $f(x) = y = a\cos(bx + c)$, where a, b, and c are constants. The graph regularly repeats itself. The period of the function is defined as the smallest positive number r such that $f(x + r) = f(x)$. Which of the following is the period of the function graphed above?

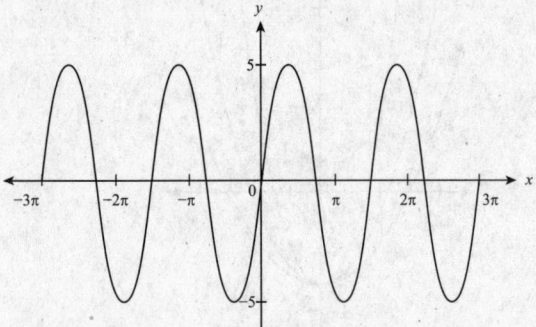

F. $\dfrac{3\pi}{4}$

G. $\dfrac{3\pi}{2}$

H. $\dfrac{\pi}{2}$

J. 3π

45. What is the expected value of X, a discrete random variable, based on the given probability distribution table?

x	Probability $P(X = x)$
0	$\dfrac{1}{3}$
1	$\dfrac{1}{12}$
2	$\dfrac{1}{24}$
3	0
4	0
5	$\dfrac{7}{24}$
6	$\dfrac{1}{4}$

A. $\dfrac{1}{12}$

B. $\dfrac{1}{4}$

C. $\dfrac{19}{8}$

D. $\dfrac{25}{8}$

Answers and Explanations

1. C
Difficulty: Low
Category: Number and Quantity
Getting to the Answer: The question asks for the value of the expression, so follow the order of operations to simplify. Solve the arithmetic, taking care not to make careless mistakes with the absolute value bars or negative signs:

$$||4 - 7| - |-10 + 2||$$
$$= ||-3| - |-8||$$
$$= |3 - 8|$$
$$= |-5|$$
$$= 5$$

The expression simplifies to 5, so (C) is correct.

2. J
Difficulty: Low
Category: Algebra
Getting to the Answer: The question asks for the slope of the given line, so convert the equation into slope-intercept form ($y = mx + b$) by solving for y. First, subtract $6x$ from both sides and then divide by -5. Make sure to change the signs when dividing or multiplying by a negative.

$$6x - 5y = 4$$
$$-5y = -6x + 4$$
$$\frac{-5}{-5}y = \frac{-6}{-5}x + \frac{4}{-5}$$
$$y = \frac{6}{5}x - \frac{4}{5}$$

In slope-intercept form, m represents the slope of the line. Therefore, the slope of this line is $\frac{6}{5}$, and (J) is correct.

3. B
Difficulty: Medium
Category: Geometry
Getting to the Answer: The question asks for the perimeter of $\triangle DEF$, but you are only given the length of one side, so you need to solve for the remaining side lengths. Because $\triangle ABC$ and $\triangle DEF$ are similar triangles, the corresponding sides between the two triangles will have the same ratio. Set up a proportion and solve for side $\overline{DF}$:

$$\frac{\overline{BC}}{\overline{EF}} = \frac{\overline{AC}}{\overline{DF}}$$
$$\frac{6}{3} = \frac{10}{\overline{DF}}$$
$$6\overline{DF} = 3 \times 10$$
$$\overline{DF} = \frac{3 \times 10}{6} = 5$$

Now two sides of $\triangle DEF$ are known.

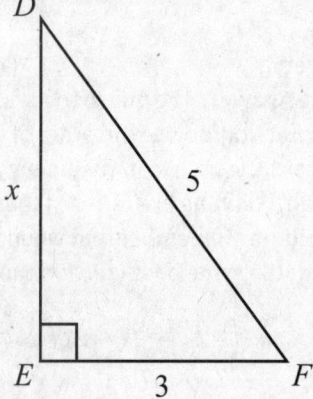

Because two sides are known and it is a right triangle, use the Pythagorean theorem, $a^2 + b^2 = c^2$, to solve for the unknown side:

$$3^2 + x^2 = 5^2$$
$$9 + x^2 = 25$$
$$x^2 = 25 - 9 = 16$$

Take the square root of both sides to find x:

$$x^2 = 16$$
$$\sqrt{x^2} = \sqrt{16}$$
$$x = 4$$

Alternatively, you might have recognized that this triangle was a 3:4:5 right triangle. Perimeter is the sum of all the side lengths, so the perimeter of $\triangle DEF$ is $3 + 4 + 5 = 12$. Hence, (B) is correct.

Another way to solve this is to first use the Pythagorean theorem to show that side $\overline{AB} = 8$, which makes the perimeter of $\triangle ABC = 24$. The ratio of the similar triangles is 2:1, so the perimeter of $\triangle DEF$ is half of that of $\triangle ABC$ or $24 \div 2 = 12$. This matches (B).

Part 3
ACT MATH

4. H
Difficulty: Low
Category: Statistics and Probability
Getting to the Answer: The question asks for the median of the given data set. The median of a data set is the middle value when the values are arranged in ascending order. If the data set contains an even number of values, as is the case here, then the median can be found by averaging the middle two numbers in the data set. Start by rearranging the values in order: 5, 5, 7, 8, 9, 10, 12, 12. Now select the two middle values and average them: $\frac{8+9}{2} = 8.5$. Choice (H) is correct.

5. D
Difficulty: Low
Category: Algebra
Getting to the Answer: The question asks for an equivalent expression, so use the order of operations to simplify. Resist the urge to immediately distribute the $9x^2$. Instead, combine like terms in the parentheses and then distribute. Remember that when you multiply exponents with the same base you add the exponents.

$$9x^2\left(-\frac{1}{3}y + 3x - 21x\right)$$
$$= 9x^2\left(-\frac{1}{3}y - 18x\right)$$
$$= -3x^2y - 162x^3$$

The expression simplifies to $-3x^2y - 162x^3$, so (D) is correct.

6. J
Difficulty: Medium
Category: Geometry
Getting to the Answer: The question asks you to determine the perimeter based on an incomplete listing of the lengths of all the sides of the 10-sided polygon. The line segments are all perpendicular to one another, so all of the line segments are either horizontal or vertical. This means that the sum of the horizontal line segments at the top must equal the sum of the horizontal line segments at the bottom. Likewise, the sum of the vertical line segments on the left must equal the sum of the vertical line segments on the right. This can be thought of as a rectangle. The perimeter is then $2w + 2l$ or $2(w + l)$, where w is the width and l is the length.

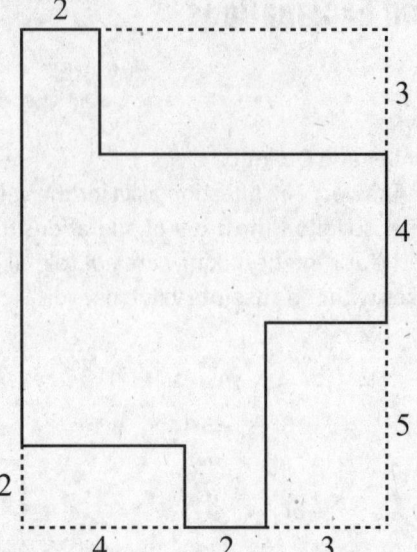

In this case, the bottom base (w) is $4 + 2 + 3 = 9$ and the right side (l) is $3 + 4 + 5 = 12$. Plugging these values into the perimeter formula, $2(w + l)$, gives $2(9 + 12) = 2(21) = 42$. Since 42 is the perimeter, (J) is correct.

7. A
Difficulty: Medium
Category: Number and Quantity
Getting to the Answer: The question asks for the length of the third wooden piece, so set up an equation to represent the situation. Let the length of the unknown piece be x. Because the lengths of the three pieces of wood must equal the length of the original wooden rod, set up the following equation:
$6\frac{5}{9} + 3\frac{13}{18} + x = 12\frac{2}{3}$.

Now solve for x by converting the mixed fractions to improper fractions and finding a common denominator to combine the terms. Then express your answer as a mixed fraction to match the form of the answer choices.

$$\frac{59}{9} + \frac{67}{18} + x = \frac{38}{3}$$
$$x = \frac{38}{3} - \frac{59}{9} - \frac{67}{18}$$
$$x = \frac{228}{18} - \frac{118}{18} - \frac{67}{18}$$
$$x = \frac{43}{18}$$
$$x = 2\frac{7}{18}$$

Since x is the length of the third wood piece, (A) is correct.

8. H

Difficulty: Medium
Category: Algebra
Getting to the Answer: The question asks for the linear equation that represents the given graph. Notice that the line passes through the points (3, 0) and (0, −4). Recall that a line in slope-intercept form is defined by $y = mx + b$, where m is the slope and b is the y-intercept. Use the slope formula, $\frac{y_2 - y_1}{x_2 - x_1}$, to solve for m:

$$m = \frac{(-4) - (0)}{(0) - (3)} = \frac{-4}{-3} = \frac{4}{3}$$

You could also determine the slope by examining the graph. To go from (0, −4) to (3, 0), you must rise by 4 units and move to the right by 3 units. This also yields a slope of $\frac{4}{3}$. Eliminate F and G.

To determine b, look at the graph. The line crosses the y-axis at −4, so the y-intercept b is −4. Therefore, the equation is $y = \frac{4}{3}x - 4$, and (H) is correct.

9. B

Difficulty: Low
Category: Number and Quantity
Getting to the Answer: The question asks you to determine which of the given choices are equivalent to the given expressions. When dealing with scientific notation, it is important to separate the digit terms (in this case, 6.4 and 2.0) from the exponential terms. Work on each piece separately and bring the results together at the end. Remember that when you divide exponents with the same base, you subtract the exponents:

$$\frac{6.4 \times 10^{-3}}{2.0 \times 10^{4}} = \frac{6.4}{2.0} \times \frac{10^{-3}}{10^{4}}$$
$$= 3.2 \times 10^{-3-4}$$
$$= 3.2 \times 10^{-7}$$

Choice (B) is correct.

10. F

Difficulty: Medium
Category: Functions
Getting to the Answer: The question asks you to find $f(-3)$ for the given function. For every instance of x, substitute −3 and evaluate:

$$f(x) = 7x - (3x^2 - 2)$$
$$f(-3) = 7(-3) - (3(-3)^2 - 2)$$
$$f(-3) = -21 - (27 - 2)$$
$$f(-3) = -21 - 25$$
$$f(-3) = -46$$

Choice (F) is correct.

11. D

Difficulty: Medium
Category: Number and Quantity
Getting to the Answer: The merry-go-round rotates 270° in 30 minutes. That is 9° per minute. So, 9° × 45 minutes = 405°. Thus, (D) is correct. Alternatively, if you prefer an algebraic approach, set up a proportion and solve:

$$\frac{270}{30} = \frac{x}{45}$$
$$12,150 = 30x$$
$$405 = x$$

$x = 405°$, which confirms that (D) is correct.

12. F
Difficulty: Medium
Category: Algebra
Getting to the Answer: The question asks for the midpoint of the two given points. Draw a sketch to visualize the situation:

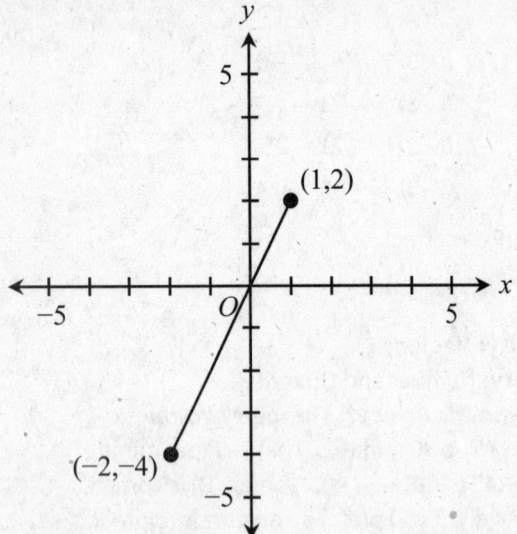

By drawing the diagram, you can see that the solution should be in the third quadrant, where both coordinates will be negative. This means (F) is correct.

The algebraic approach is to use the midpoint formula, $\left(\frac{x_1 + x_2}{2}, \frac{y_1 + y_2}{2}\right)$, which is the average of the x- and y-coordinates of the endpoints of the line segment.

$$\left(\frac{x_1 + x_2}{2}, \frac{y_1 + y_2}{2}\right)$$
$$\left(\frac{-2 + 1}{2}, \frac{-4 + 2}{2}\right)$$
$$\left(-\frac{1}{2}, -1\right)$$

Again, (F) is correct.

13. A
Difficulty: Low
Category: Number and Quantity
Getting to the Answer: The question asks you to determine how many possible outfits the math teacher can wear with the given numbers of pants, shoes, and shirts. For each of the 10 pairs of pants, the teacher can wear either of 2 pairs of shoes. The number of combinations of pants and shoes is represented by $2 \times 10 = 20$. For each of these 20 combinations of pants and shoes, the teacher can wear any of the 6 shirts. The number of combinations of pants and shoes together with shirts is therefore represented by $20 \times 6 = 120$. The number of unique combinations of all three items is 120, so (A) is correct.

14. J
Difficulty: Medium
Category: Algebra
Getting to the Answer: The question asks for the range of possible values for y, given the inequality. Solve the inequality for y as you would an equation, but make sure that you flip the inequality sign any time you multiply or divide both sides of the inequality by a negative number.

$$9 - 3(y - 3) \leq 0$$
$$-3(y - 3) \leq -9$$
$$y - 3 \geq 3$$
$$y \geq 6$$

Choice (J) is correct.

15. A
Difficulty: Low
Category: Number and Quantity
Getting to the Answer: The question asks for the eighth term in the given geometric sequence. In a geometric sequence, each term is multiplied by the same number, called the common ratio, to get to the next term. In this sequence, each term is multiplied by $\frac{1}{2}$ to get the next one. Use the geometric sequence formula, $a_n = a_1 r^{n-1}$, where a_1 is the first number of the sequence, r is the common ratio, and a_n is the nth term of the sequence, to solve for a_8:

$$a_n = a_1 r^{n-1}$$
$$a_8 = 1{,}024 \left(\frac{1}{2}\right)^{8-1}$$
$$a_8 = 1{,}024 \left(\frac{1}{128}\right)$$
$$a_8 = 8$$

Another way to solve is to divide by 2 until you get to the 8th term:

$$\frac{128}{2} = 64$$
$$\frac{64}{2} = 32$$
$$\frac{32}{2} = 16$$
$$\frac{16}{2} = 8$$

Either way, (A) is correct.

16. H
Difficulty: Medium
Category: Algebra
Getting to the Answer: The question asks for the y-intercept of a line that passes through the two given points. The slope-intercept equation is $y = mx + b$, where m is the slope and b is the y-intercept. First, solve for m using the slope formula, $\frac{y_2 - y_1}{x_2 - x_1}$:

$$\frac{-2-2}{5-(-1)} = \frac{-4}{6} = -\frac{2}{3}$$

Then, solve for b by plugging the slope and one of the points into the slope-intercept equation. The point $(-1, 2)$ is shown here:

$$y = mx + b$$
$$y = -\frac{2}{3}x + b$$
$$2 = -\frac{2}{3}(-1) + b$$
$$2 = \frac{2}{3} + b$$
$$2 - \frac{2}{3} = b$$
$$\frac{6}{3} - \frac{2}{3} = b$$
$$\frac{4}{3} = b$$

The y-intercept of the line is $\frac{4}{3}$, and (H) is correct.

17. D
Difficulty: Medium
Category: Geometry
Getting to the Answer: The question asks for the measure of $\angle ABF$ in the given diagram. Note that $\angle ABF$ and $\angle CBF$ are supplementary angles (they make a straight line), so $\angle ABF = 180° - \angle CBF$.

Since two sides of $\triangle BCF$ are congruent, this triangle is isosceles. Because $\angle BFC$ is 90°, the other two angles must be 45° ($180° = 90° + 45° + 45°$). Thus, $\angle CBF = \angle BCF = 45°$, and $\angle ABF = 180° - \angle CBF = 180° - 45° = 135°$. Thus, (D) is correct.

18. J
Difficulty: Medium
Category: Geometry
Getting to the Answer: The question asks for the distance between two given points, so use the distance formula $d = \sqrt{(x_2 - x_1)^2 + (y_2 - y_1)^2}$, which employs the Pythagorean theorem to find the length of the hypotenuse if you were to draw a triangle:

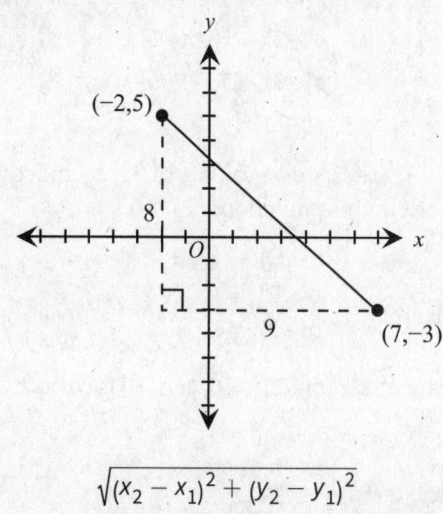

$$\sqrt{(x_2 - x_1)^2 + (y_2 - y_1)^2}$$
$$= \sqrt{(-2 - 7)^2 + (5 - (-3))^2}$$
$$= \sqrt{(-9)^2 + (8)^2}$$
$$= \sqrt{81 + 64}$$
$$= \sqrt{145}$$

The distance between the given points is $\sqrt{145}$, so (J) is correct.

19. C
Difficulty: Medium
Category: Number and Quantity
Getting to the Answer: The question asks for the choice that is always even. Pick Numbers for a and b to eliminate incorrect choices.

Let $a = 2$ and $b = 3$:
Choice A: $2(2) + 3 = 7 =$ odd, eliminate.
Choice B: $4(2) - 3 = 5 =$ odd, eliminate.
Choice (C): $(2)^2(3) = 12 =$ even, keep.
Choice D: $\frac{7(3)}{2}$ — not an integer, eliminate.

With all other answers eliminated, the correct answer is (C). Alternatively, you may have recognized the number properties even × even = even and even × odd = even and selected (C) without having to Pick Numbers.

20. H
Difficulty: Medium
Category: Functions
Getting to the Answer: The question asks for the value of $q(p(-3))$. For nested functions, evaluate the inside function first and then work your way out. Start by substituting -3 for x in the p function:

$$p(x) = 7 - x^2$$
$$p(-3) = 7 - (-3)^2$$
$$p(-3) = 7 - 9$$
$$p(-3) = -2$$

Since $p(-3) = -2$, now evaluate $q(-2)$ by substituting -2 for x in the q function:

$$q(x) = 4 - x$$
$$q(-2) = 4 - (-2)$$
$$q(-2) = 6$$

This means that $q(p(-3)) = 6$, and (H) is correct.

21. B
Difficulty: Low
Category: Number and Quantity
Getting to the Answer: The question asks how many units are produced in 33 minutes. The statement that "the time it takes to complete a certain job is directly proportional to the number of units produced" implies that the ratio $\dfrac{\text{time to complete the job, in minutes}}{\text{units produced}}$ must be equal for all instances of the job. Therefore, you can set up a proportion and solve (let u be the unknown number of units produced):

$$\frac{22}{18} = \frac{33}{u}$$
$$22u = 18(33)$$
$$u = \frac{594}{22}$$
$$u = 27$$

In 33 minutes, 27 units can be produced and (B) is correct.

22. G
Difficulty: Medium
Category: Geometry
Getting to the Answer: The question asks for the minimum number of building blocks needed to cover the entire landscape. To determine the minimum number, you need to calculate the area of the largest face of one block and the area of the landscape. The largest face of one block has a length of 2 inches and a width of 1 inch, which yields an area of $2 \times 1 = 2$ square inches. Note that the height (0.5 in.) is irrelevant.

Since the dimensions of the block are in inches, first convert the units of the landscape from feet to inches. There are 12 inches in a foot, so 2 feet is $2(12) = 24$ inches and 1.5 feet is $1.5(12) = 18$ inches. The total area is thus $24 \times 18 = 432$ square inches. Therefore, the minimum number of building blocks needed to fill up the entire landscape is the total area of the landscape divided by the area of the largest face of one block: $432 \div 2 = 216$. Choice (G) is correct.

23. D
Difficulty: Medium
Category: Statistics and Probability
Getting to the Answer: The question asks for the probability that a student selected at random will *not* be a senior. The probability of not selecting a senior is the total number of non-seniors (freshman + sophomores + juniors) divided by the total number of students (50). Since the number of juniors is given as a percent, calculate the number of juniors: $50 \times 0.24 = 12$. Thus, the number of non-seniors is 14 freshman + 14 sophomores + 12 juniors = 40. So, the probability of choosing a non-senior is $\dfrac{40}{50} = \dfrac{4}{5}$, and (D) is correct.

Remember that the probability of something not happening equals 1 minus the probability of it actually happening. Therefore, alternatively, you could subtract the probability of selecting a senior from 1 to determine the probability of not selecting a senior: $1 - \dfrac{10}{50} = \dfrac{40}{50} = \dfrac{4}{5}$. This matches (D).

24. F
Difficulty: Low
Category: Statistics and Probability
Getting to the Answer: Start by identifying the category of the smallest slice of the pie chart, since the question asks for the percent of the total from the least expenditure category. The utilities category is the smallest at $196, and the total spent is $196 + $427 + $491 + $534 + $852 = $2,500. Use the percent formula, percent $= \dfrac{\text{part}}{\text{whole}} \times 100\%$, where $196 is the part and $2,500 is the whole. Don't forget to multiply by 100 to convert your answer into a percent.

$\frac{196}{2,500} = 0.0784 \times 100\% = 7.84\%$

Rounded to the nearest percent, 7.84% is 8%. Thus, the business's utilities expenditure was 8% of the previous month's total expenditures. (F) is correct.

25. A
Difficulty: Medium
Category: Number and Quantity
Getting to the Answer: The question asks for the length of segment $\overline{FG}$. Notice that from the segment lengths given, $\overline{FG}$ is the intersection because $\overline{FG}$ is in both $\overline{EFG}$ and $\overline{FGH}$.

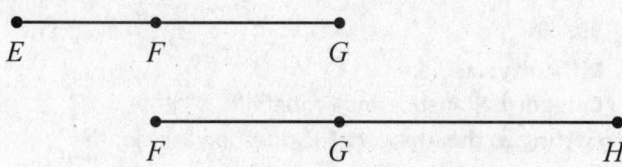

This means that you can find $\overline{FG}$ by subtracting the length of $\overline{EH}$ (35) from the sum of $\overline{EG}$ (15) and $\overline{FH}$ (25), which is 40. So, $40 - 35 = 5$. Hence, (A) is correct.

To solve this algebraically, let x be the length of $\overline{FG}$. Thus, $\overline{EF} = 15 - x$ and $\overline{GH} = 25 - x$. Create an equation for the total length of $\overline{EH}$ and solve for x.

$$(15 - x) + x + (25 - x) = 35$$
$$40 - x = 35$$
$$5 = x$$

26. G
Difficulty: Medium
Category: Number and Quantity
Getting to the Answer: The question asks for the percent increase of the stock over a 2-year period. Since the original price of the stock is not given, picking a number will be helpful. Usually, the easiest number to work with when dealing with percent change is 100. Let the price of the stock be $100 at the beginning of Year 1. In Year 1, it increased by $40\% \times \$100 = \$40$ to $140. In Year 2, it increased another 30%, or $30\% \times 140 = \$42$, to $\$140 + \$42 = \$182$. Plugging these values into the percent change formula,
$\frac{\text{final amount} - \text{initial amount}}{\text{initial amount}} \times 100\%$, gives:

$$\frac{\$182 - \$100}{\$100} \times 100\% = \frac{\$82}{\$100} \times 100\% = 82\%$$

Therefore, the price of the stock increased by 82%. Choice (G) is correct.

27. B
Difficulty: Medium
Category: Statistics and Probability
Getting to the Answer: The question asks for the average cost per ticket for the 9 raffle tickets. First, calculate the total cost of the 9 tickets Amelie bought. Since Amelie bought 7 pre-sale tickets and 2 tickets at the door, she paid a total of $7 \times \$4.00 + 2 \times \$5.00 = \$28 + \$10 = \$38$. Therefore, the average cost per ticket is given by:

$$\text{average} = \frac{\text{sum of items}}{\text{number of items}} = \frac{\$38.00}{9} \approx \$4.22$$

Thus, (B) is correct.

28. H
Difficulty: Medium
Category: Geometry
Getting to the Answer: The question asks for the length of $\overline{AC}$. Since the answer choices are trigonometric expressions, use SOHCAHTOA to relate each side of the triangle to the angle measuring 19°, which is $\angle ABC$. $\overline{AC}$ is the opposite side and $\overline{BC}$ is the adjacent side of this angle; thus, they can be related using the tangent function.

$$\tan x° = \frac{\text{opposite}}{\text{adjacent}}$$
$$\tan 19° = \frac{\overline{AC}}{53}$$
$$53 \tan 19° = \overline{AC}$$

(H) is correct.

29. C
Difficulty: High
Category: Number and Quantity
Getting to the Answer: Convert from radical form to exponential form and combine like terms:

$$x^4 \sqrt[5]{x^2} \cdot y^3 \sqrt{y^7} = x^{\frac{4}{1}} x^{\frac{2}{5}} \cdot y^{\frac{3}{1}} y^{\frac{7}{2}}$$
$$= x^{\frac{20}{5}} x^{\frac{2}{5}} \cdot y^{\frac{6}{2}} y^{\frac{7}{2}}$$
$$= x^{\frac{20}{5} + \frac{2}{5}} \cdot y^{\frac{6}{2} + \frac{7}{2}}$$
$$= x^{\frac{22}{5}} \cdot y^{\frac{13}{2}}$$

Note that the answer choices are in radical form, so now reverse this process by converting the improper fractions into mixed fractions. The leftover fractions will require a common denominator when they are converted back into radical form.

$$x^{\frac{22}{5}}y^{\frac{13}{2}} = x^{4\frac{2}{5}}y^{6\frac{1}{2}}$$
$$= x^4 x^{\frac{2}{5}} y^6 y^{\frac{1}{2}}$$
$$= x^4 y^6 x^{\frac{4}{10}} y^{\frac{5}{10}}$$
$$= x^4 y^6 \sqrt[10]{x^4 y^5}$$

The given expression is equivalent to $x^4 y^6 \sqrt[10]{x^4 y^5}$. (C) is correct.

30. G
Difficulty: Medium
Category: Statistics and Probability
Getting to the Answer: The question asks for the approximate percentage of sales in January that were from Accessories. This is equal to January Accessories sales ($750), divided by the total sales in January for all 3 departments ($1,150 + $1,000 + $750):

$$\frac{\$750}{\$1,150 + \$1,000 + \$750} = \frac{\$750}{\$2,900} = \frac{\$15}{\$58}$$

Therefore, $\frac{15}{58} \approx 0.2586$ and $0.2586 \times 100 = 25.86\%$. This means that Accessories sales is approximately 26% of the January sales, so (G) is correct.

31. B
Difficulty: High
Category: Number and Quantity
Getting to the Answer: Write an equation that sets the volume of Vat A equal to the volume of Vat B after x minutes. Since the volume of Vat A, which initially was 450 gallons, is increasing at a rate of 40 gallons per minute, the volume of Vat A after x minutes equals $450 + 40x$. Similarly, since the volume of Vat B, which initially was 1,250 gallons, is increasing at a rate of 15 gallons per minute, the volume of Vat B after x minutes is $1,250 + 15x$. Set the two equal to each other and solve for x:

$$450 + 40x = 1,250 + 15x$$
$$40x = 800 + 15x$$
$$25x = 800$$
$$x = 32$$

Therefore, it will take 32 minutes before the vats contain equal amounts of toluene. (B) is correct.

32. G
Difficulty: Medium
Category: Statistics and Probability
Getting to the Answer: The question asks what fraction of players made fewer than 2 free throws. The total number of players was given as 19, so use the bar graph to find how many players made fewer than 2 free throws. The bar graph shows that 5 players scored 0 free throws and that 2 players scored 1 free throw. This means that 7 players scored fewer than 2 free throws. The fraction of players that scored fewer than 2 free throws is therefore $\frac{7}{19}$, and (G) is correct.

33. B
Difficulty: Medium
Category: Statistics and Probability
Getting to the Answer: The question asks for the average number of siblings within a particular group of students. To find the average, divide the total number siblings by the total number of students. For efficiency, calculate the total number of siblings by multiplying each number of siblings by the number of students who has that number of siblings, and then add these values together. For example, there are 3 students who have no siblings, which is a total of $3(0) = 0$. There are 7 students who have exactly 1 sibling, which is $7(1) = 7$, and so on.

$$\text{average} = \frac{\text{sum of terms}}{\text{number of terms}}$$

$$\text{average} = \frac{3(0) + 7(1) + 5(2) + 4(3) + 2(4) + 1(5)}{3 + 7 + 5 + 4 + 2 + 1}$$

$$= \frac{42}{22}$$

$$\approx 1.9$$

Since the average number of siblings is about 1.9, (B) is correct.

34. H
Difficulty: High
Category: Number and Quantity
Getting to the Answer: The question asks for the value of x in the given logarithmic equation. Convert the equation into exponential form using the fact that $\log_b a = x$ is the same as $b^x = a$ (which you might remember by thinking that *the base is the base* and *the edge is the exponent*):

$$\log_2 16^2 = x$$
$$2^x = 16^2$$

When the variable that you are solving for is in an exponent, try to make both bases equal. Rewrite 16^2 as $(2^4)^2 = 2^8$. Now that both bases are the same, set the exponents equal to each other and solve:

$$2^x = 2^8$$
$$x = 8$$

Thus, the value of x equals 8, and (H) is correct.

35. D
Difficulty: High
Category: Geometry
Getting to the Answer: The question asks for the equation of the circle described. Recall that the standard equation for a circle is $(x - h)^2 + (y - k)^2 = r^2$, where (h, k) is the center of the circle and r is its radius. To find the equation, start by drawing a rough sketch of the circle in relation to the xy-plane and then work by the process of elimination. Since the circle is tangent to both the x-axis and the horizontal line $y = 6$, the circle must lie above the x-axis. This means that the y-coordinate of its center must be positive. Eliminate B, which has its center at (3, 0), and C, which has its center at (3, -3). Finally, note from your sketch that the diameter of the circle must extend from a point on the line $y = 6$ to a point on the x-axis, so the diameter is 6 and the radius is 3. Since $r^2 = 3^2 = 9$, (D) is correct.

36. J
Difficulty: High
Category: Number and Quantity
Getting to the Answer: The question asks for an equivalent expression. When imaginary numbers are in the denominator of a fraction, the denominator must be rationalized by multiplying by its conjugate, remembering that $i^2 = -1$.

$$\frac{i}{(3-i)} \times \frac{(3+i)}{(3+i)} = \frac{3i + i^2}{9 - i^2}$$
$$= \frac{3i - 1}{9 - (-1)}$$
$$= \frac{-1 + 3i}{10}$$
$$= -\frac{1}{10} + \frac{3i}{10}$$

Choice (J) is correct.

37. A
Difficulty: Medium
Category: Number and Quantity
Getting to the Answer: The question asks for the park ranger's estimate for the number of healthy trees in the park. The second matrix indicates the percentage of each type of tree that is healthy (represented as decimals). Multiply the number of each type of tree by its corresponding decimal and add all of these values together to get the total number of healthy trees: $70(0.4) + 30(0.6) + 40(0.8) + 50(0.7) = 28 + 18 + 32 + 35 = 113$. Thus, (A) is correct.

38. J
Difficulty: Medium
Category: Geometry
Getting to the Answer: The question asks for the volume of the described cylinder. Use the volume formula $V = \pi r^2 h$:

$$V = \pi r^2 h$$
$$= \pi(9^2)(10)$$
$$= \pi(81)(10)$$
$$= 810\pi$$

Choice (J) is correct.

39. D
Difficulty: Low
Category: Statistics and Probability
Getting to the Answer: The question asks for the method that describes the company's testing. First, check whether the testing is non-randomized or randomized. The question states that the employees selected to take the survey were chosen at random, so eliminate A and B. Next, use process of elimination on the remaining choices. A census is a survey conducted on the entire population, so eliminate C. Choice (D) must be correct because a smaller group, or sample, of all the employees was chosen to complete the survey.

40. J
Difficulty: Medium
Category: Geometry
Getting to the Answer: The question asks for sin ψ—and it's okay if you aren't familiar with the ψ symbol, which represents the Greek letter *psi*. If it makes this question easier to think through, you can always substitute a θ or even just an x. To remember which quadrants are positive, you might recall a mnemonic,

such as *All Students Take Calculus*, which signifies which trigonometric functions are positive in the order of the quadrants, starting in Quadrant 1 (top right) and moving counterclockwise: All, Sine, Tangent, Cosine. Sine is always positive in the first two quadrants, so eliminate F and G. Draw a right triangle from the given coordinate to the *x*-axis and label the known lengths.

Note the trigonometric identity $\sin(x) = \sin(180° - x)$, and then use the Pythagorean theorem to solve for the hypotenuse of the right triangle.

$$a^2 + b^2 = c^2$$
$$(7)^2 + (24)^2 = c^2$$
$$625 = c^2$$
$$25 = c$$

Recall that $\sin = \dfrac{\text{opposite}}{\text{hypotenuse}}$. The opposite side is 24 and the hypotenuse is 25, so $\sin \psi = \dfrac{24}{25}$. Choice (J) is correct.

41. B
Difficulty: Medium
Category: Algebra
Getting to the Answer: The question asks for the value of the bacteria population after 5 days under ideal heat and moisture conditions. Plug the given values, $h = 0.5$ and $t = 5$, into the given formula.

$$P = \dfrac{3^{2t-1}}{h} + 200$$
$$P = \dfrac{3^{2(5)-1}}{(0.5)} + 200$$
$$P = 39{,}566$$

The population of the bacteria colony is 39,566 after 5 days in ideal heat and moisture conditions, so (B) is correct.

42. G
Difficulty: High
Category: Functions
Getting to the Answer: The question asks for the amplitude of the given function. Recall that the amplitude of a function in the form $f(x) = A\sin(Bx + C)$ is $|A|$. This means that $\dfrac{3}{4}$ is the amplitude, and (G) is correct.

43. C
Difficulty: High
Category: Functions
Getting to the Answer: The question asks for the general equation that describes the family of parabolas graphed. All of the parabolas open upward, so the coefficient of the x^2 term must be positive; eliminate A and B. The only difference between the remaining choices is the coefficient of the x^2 term. The larger the coefficient is, the slimmer the parabola will be. The smaller the coefficient is, the wider the parabola becomes. The graph indicates that as *n* gets larger, the parabola widens, meaning the coefficient of the x^2 term becomes smaller. In other words, $\dfrac{1}{1} > \dfrac{1}{2} > \dfrac{1}{3}$. Therefore, (C) is correct.

44. G
Difficulty: High
Category: Functions
Getting to the Answer: The question asks for the period of the graphed function. The period is the distance that passes along the *x*-axis until the graph repeats itself. At the origin, the graph is heading upward; the next time that the graph crosses the *x*-axis and is heading upward is in between π and 2π at $\dfrac{3\pi}{2}$. Choice (G) is correct.

45. D
Difficulty: High
Category: Statistics and Probability
Getting to the Answer: The question asks for the expected value from the given probability distribution table. Use the formula $E(X) = x_1p_1 + x_2p_2 + \ldots + x_ip_i$.

$$E(X) = 0\left(\dfrac{1}{3}\right) + 1\left(\dfrac{1}{12}\right) + 2\left(\dfrac{1}{24}\right) + 3(0) + 4(0)$$
$$+ 5\left(\dfrac{7}{24}\right) + 6\left(\dfrac{1}{4}\right)$$
$$E(X) = \dfrac{1}{12} + \dfrac{2}{24} + \dfrac{35}{24} + \dfrac{6}{4}$$
$$E(X) = \dfrac{2}{24} + \dfrac{2}{24} + \dfrac{35}{24} + \dfrac{36}{24}$$
$$E(X) = \dfrac{75}{24}$$

Because $\dfrac{75}{24}$ is not a choice, simplify the fraction: $\dfrac{75}{24} = \dfrac{25}{8}$. Hence, (D) is correct.

[PART 4]

ACT READING

[CHAPTER 15]

THE METHOD FOR ACT READING

> **LEARNING OBJECTIVES**
>
> After completing this chapter, you will be able to:
> - Read passages strategically by applying the ACT Reading Passage Strategy
> - Effectively and efficiently apply the Method for ACT Reading Questions

How to Do ACT Reading

The ACT Reading Test is usually made up of three independent passages and one set of paired passages, each approximately 650–900 words long and accompanied by 9 questions, for a total of 36 questions in the section. To tackle all of this effectively in 40 minutes, the most successful test takers:

- Read the passages strategically to zero in on the text that leads to points.
- Approach the questions with a method that minimizes rereading and leads directly to correct answers.

The key to maximizing correct answers on the ACT Reading Test is learning in advance the kinds of questions that the test asks. ACT Reading questions focus more on the author's purpose (*why* the author wrote the passage) and the passage's structure (*how* the author makes and supports their points) than on the details or facts of the subject matter (*what* the passage is about). You can answer these predictable questions confidently by reading more effectively, and paying attention to *how* and *why* the author wrote the passage or chose to include certain words or examples.

In this chapter, we'll give you an overview of how to tackle Reading passages and questions. The other chapters in this unit will help you become a stronger reader and present the five ACT Reading question types, as well as provide you with tips for improving your approach to literature and paired passages.

Part 4
ACT READING

Try the passage and questions that follow on your own. Then, keep reading to compare your approach to our recommendations for how to approach ACT Reading.

INFORMATIONAL: The following passage is adapted from an article in a travel journal on tourism in Mexico.

Before tourism became a mainstay of the economy, the value of terrain in Mexico was defined by the arability of the land. To many Americans, tropical tourist-oriented beach towns
[5] such as Acapulco and Puerto Vallarta characterize Mexico. These may be the most common sorts of destinations for foreign travelers, but they certainly are not the most representative areas of the country itself. These cities, and others
[10] like them, are set up to be attractive to the tourist trade, for better or worse. But the land and culture are vastly different from those of the *altiplano*, or high plain. The function and appearance of each type of terrain dictate this
[15] divergence.

A tropical beach is a specialized area, not only because it cannot be found outside of specific latitude measurements; any living thing must be highly specialized to survive there or else must
[20] acclimate quickly. This is a hard area to live in: the closer a land dweller moves to the ocean, the fewer there are of the resources necessary to sustain life. Specialized areas in nature are analogous to remote settlements of people in
[25] forbidding environments, untouched by the outside world. Surroundings dictate the life of a consumer—human or otherwise—and, through adaptation, one is nearly defined by the other. In sharp contrast is the tourist in the tropics,
[30] who has likely settled upon a destination by how different it looks from home. In order to appeal to such tourists, the beach towns often contain deliberate marks of earlier civilizations, but these contrivances do not characterize the history or
[35] culture of the portions of the country inhabited for function rather than beauty.

Mexico's beach towns import resources to accommodate a great number of people, but the terrain itself generally lacks certain basic human
[40] necessities: soil suitable for plant cultivation and sufficient reserves of drinking water, both of which occur naturally in the temperate and fertile *altiplano* region. A traveler in Acapulco would learn no more about the foundations of
[45] Mexican agriculture than a visitor to Yellowstone Park would learn about New York City. While the tourist often delights in the year-round heat and humidity of the coast, the Mayan people, the first known to flourish in coastal Mexico,
[50] are considered to have been brilliant in their eschewing of the natural hazards and barrenness of tropical beaches rather than reveling in this environment. The Mayans relied on the discovery and utilization of *cenotes*, natural springs that
[55] provided fresh water. Without a *cenote* nearby, the Mayans would not settle in a locale, no matter how picturesque.

The tropical coast is uniformly regulated by the ocean, but the *altiplano* is a tapestry of
[60] microclimates that vary from one mile to the next. The coast extends laterally, breaking only for the mouth of a river or the edge of a mountain range, where cliffs are slowly eroding into future beaches. The *altiplano*, on the other hand,
[65] expands in all directions and gradually fades into the mountains. The coast presents a border; the *altiplano* is expansive and indefinite. The difference is akin to that between a gymnasium and an open market. A gymnasium is set up to
[70] provide a basic range of functions, and because of this, a person familiar with one gymnasium will find similar equipment and be able to obtain a similar experience at another. The gymnasium is equipped to sustain its patrons for a short
[75] period of time. It presents a widely understood and repeatable experience to visitors. Any great variance would do customers a disservice. The market, conversely, represents the surroundings through products and vendors. When there
[80] are avocados at a market, there are avocados in fields nearby. If one product is found in a disproportionately large number of vendors' stands, it is likely well suited for cultivation or popular with local consumers. The local

85 residents set the tone for both what is available and what is popular. A different market keeps only the conventions of the seller and buyer; the local residents and agricultural terrain dictate price, product, and appearance. The traveler's
90 preferences are not addressed. An unseasoned cut of meat may not be available, and its replacement may include an array of flavors completely new to a foreign palate. A desired apple could be a rare and exotic indulgence and may give way to the
95 ubiquitous guava.

The best way to experience foreign lands, therefore, is a less conventional way: through areas defined by local culture rather than by tourists, avoiding both the prepared environments
100 and the artificial familiarity that defines them.

1. The main purpose of the passage is to:

    A. argue that more people ought to visit the tropical beaches of Mexico instead of its *altiplano* regions.

    B. assert that without the contributions of the *altiplano*, Mexico's beach resort towns would not be able to sustain themselves or their visitors.

    C. state that the *altiplano* is more diverse and rich in life than tropical beaches.

    D. contend that travel to foreign countries is best experienced in places that reflect the local culture instead of places that reflect the tourist industry.

2. According to the passage, what makes a tropical beach a specialized area?

    F. It cannot exist outside of particular longitudes.

    G. It resembles a gymnasium.

    H. Land-based life has difficulty finding the resources to survive there.

    J. One tropical beach is much like any other tropical beach.

3. As it is used in line 26, the word *dictate* most nearly means:

    A. command action.

    B. speak for recording.

    C. forbid response.

    D. shape development.

4. The passage most strongly suggests that the Mayan people were the first to flourish in coastal Mexico because they:

    F. adapted to thrive in the year-round heat and humidity.

    G. successfully discovered enough *cenotes* to support the population.

    H. conveniently avoided the risks of living on the coastline.

    J. avoided confrontations with others by using the coast as a border.

5. The comparison between a gymnasium and an open market in paragraph four is meant to:

    A. contrast tourists who visit the coast with those who visit the *altiplano*.

    B. show that inland areas are better equipped than beach towns to accommodate the needs of visitors.

    C. emphasize that beach resorts are set up to cater to visitors in a way that the *altiplano* is not.

    D. indicate that consumer goods are less available on the coast than inland.

Part 4
ACT READING

Strategic Reading

The ACT Reading Test is an open-book test: the passage is right there for you to reference. Because of the way the test is constructed, it is in your best interest to read fairly quickly, noting the outline of the passage as you go and writing notes in the margins or on scratch paper as you read. Your goal is to get a solid understanding of the main idea without wasting time memorizing details. You can think of this process of outlining the passage as **mapping** it: you are taking note of its major features but letting go of the minor details.

Be sure to read the pre-passage blurb, the short introduction that comes before the passage. Identify any information that helps you to understand the topic of the passage or to anticipate what the author will discuss. For the passage above, the blurb states the topic (tourism) and announces that the passage is an excerpt from "a travel journal on tourism in Mexico." That's an invitation to keep your eye out for a perspective on tourism in Mexico as you read.

You'll learn all the skills you need to **read strategically** in chapter 16, but for now, here's an example of an expert's strategic thinking and passage map notes. Don't worry if your notes don't look exactly like this (or even anything like this, yet). Follow the expert's thought process in the discussion that follows the passage to see what the expert was thinking and asking as they read the passage.

INFORMATIONAL: The following passage is adapted from an article in a travel journal on tourism in Mexico.

Before tourism became a mainstay of the economy, the value of terrain in Mexico was defined by the arability of the land. To many Americans, tropical tourist-oriented beach towns
5 such as Acapulco and Puerto Vallarta characterize Mexico. These may be the most common sorts of destinations for foreign travelers, but they certainly are not the most representative areas of the country itself. These cities, and others
10 like them, are set up to be attractive to the tourist trade, for better or worse. But the land and culture are vastly different from those of the *altiplano*, or high plain. The function and appearance of each type of terrain dictate this
15 divergence.

beach towns vs. altiplano; beaches = tourism

ANALYSIS

Pre-passage blurb: The passage will address tourism in Mexico.

¶1 This paragraph introduces a contrast in how land in Mexico is valued, based on tourism or arability. The author connects tourism with tropical beach cities but says these areas are not "representative" of Mexico. The author then contrasts this with the *altiplano* (note the "But" at the beginning of the sentence in line 11). It seems like coming paragraphs will discuss how "function and appearance" lead to this contrast.

A tropical beach is a specialized area, not only because it cannot be found outside of specific latitude measurements; any living thing must be highly specialized to survive there or else must
20 acclimate quickly. This is a hard area to live in: the closer a land dweller moves to the ocean, the fewer there are of the resources necessary to sustain life. Specialized areas in nature are analogous to remote settlements of people
25 in forbidding environments, untouched by the outside world. Surroundings dictate the life of a consumer—human or otherwise—and, through adaptation, one is nearly defined by the other. In sharp contrast is the tourist in the tropics,
30 who has likely settled upon a destination by how different it looks from home. In order to appeal to such tourists, the beach towns often contain deliberate marks of earlier civilizations, but these contrivances do not characterize the history or
35 culture of the portions of the country inhabited for function rather than beauty.

Mexico's beach towns import resources to accommodate a great number of people, but the terrain itself generally lacks certain basic human
40 necessities: soil suitable for plant cultivation and sufficient reserves of drinking water, both of which occur naturally in the temperate and fertile *altiplano* region. A traveler in Acapulco would learn no more about the foundations of
45 Mexican agriculture than a visitor to Yellowstone Park would learn about New York City. While the tourist often delights in the year-round heat and humidity of the coast, the Mayan people, the first known to flourish in coastal Mexico,
50 are considered to have been brilliant in their eschewing of the natural hazards and barrenness of tropical beaches rather than reveling in this environment. The Mayans relied on the discovery and utilization of *cenotes*, natural springs that
55 provided fresh water. Without a *cenote* nearby, the Mayans would not settle in a locale, no matter how picturesque.

---

beaches require adaptation; tourists just want good looks

altiplano has better resources than beach; Maya smart for avoiding beach

---

¶2 The author discusses the function and appearance of tropical beaches. They are "specialized" environments; organisms must adapt to survive. "In sharp contrast"—the author wants to make a point—tourists are attracted by appearance, not function.

¶3 This paragraph emphasizes the necessity of basic resources. The author again contrasts beaches and *altiplano*, saying that the beach lacks resources available in the "temperate and fertile" *altiplano*. The author clearly favors the *altiplano*. The second part of the paragraph contains another contrast ("While," line 46), this time between the tourists and the Maya, "brilliant" for settling only where they could find resources.

The tropical coast is uniformly regulated by the ocean, but the *altiplano* is a tapestry of
60 microclimates that vary from one mile to the next. The coast extends laterally, breaking only for the mouth of a river or the edge of a mountain range, where cliffs are slowly eroding into future beaches. The *altiplano*, on the other hand,
65 expands in all directions and gradually fades into the mountains. The coast presents a border; the *altiplano* is expansive and indefinite. The difference is akin to that between a gymnasium and an open market. A gymnasium is set up to
70 provide a basic range of functions, and because of this, a person familiar with one gymnasium will find similar equipment and be able to obtain a similar experience at another. The gymnasium is equipped to sustain its patrons for a short
75 period of time. It presents a widely understood and repeatable experience to visitors. Any great variance would do customers a disservice. The market, conversely, represents the surroundings through products and vendors. When there
80 are avocados at a market, there are avocados in fields nearby. If one product is found in a disproportionately large number of vendors' stands, it is likely well suited for cultivation or popular with local consumers. The local
85 residents set the tone for both what is available and what is popular. A different market keeps only the conventions of the seller and buyer; the local residents and agricultural terrain dictate price, product, and appearance. The traveler's
90 preferences are not addressed. An unseasoned cut of meat may not be available, and its replacement may include an array of flavors completely new to a foreign palate. A desired apple could be a rare and exotic indulgence and may give way to the
95 ubiquitous guava.

The best way to experience foreign lands, therefore, is a less conventional way: through areas defined by local culture rather than by tourists, avoiding both the prepared environments and the
100 artificial familiarity that defines them.

altiplano is varied and extensive; gym/market analogy

author: *altiplano* better to visit; not artificial

¶4 This paragraph expands on the contrast between the beach and *altiplano*. There's more information about the *altiplano*, shown as a series of contrasts with the beach. Again, the author's language choices favor the *altiplano*, describing it as a "tapestry" that "expands in all directions." Then, the author presents an extended analogy comparing the beach to a gym—limited and uniform, catering to its customers—and the *altiplano* to a market—varied and expansive, a product of many local factors.

¶5 The last paragraph states the author's opinion: that foreign visitors should seek out local culture, not artificial sculpted environments.

Chapter 15
The Method for ACT Reading

To sum up **the big picture**, pause for a moment after reading to consider the passage's main idea and the author's purpose for writing it.

BIG PICTURE SUMMARY

Main idea: Although most tourists opt to visit Mexico's resort towns, the author argues that these towns are not representative of the country as a whole.

Author's purpose: To argue that tourists should visit popular areas like the Mexican coast less often and should instead visit areas that cater more to locals, like the *altiplano*.

Notice that the ACT expert reads actively, consistently paraphrasing what the author has said, identifying the author's viewpoint, asking what must come next, and never getting too caught up in details.

Think about how the ACT expert used the ACT Reading Passage Strategy to read this passage strategically:

- Extract everything you can from the pre-passage blurb
- Read each paragraph actively
- Summarize the passage's big picture

Don't worry if your notes don't look exactly like the ones in this book. When you review a set of strategic thinking notes, focus on comparing your overall thought process and main takeaways to those of a strategic test taker and determine at least one way you can read more effectively and efficiently next time. When you take the time to read strategically first, you are more likely to answer questions both efficiently and correctly.

The Method for ACT Reading Questions

Once you've read the passage strategically, you're ready for the questions. ACT experts use a simple four-step method to tackle each question quickly and confidently.

> **ACT READING QUESTION METHOD**
>
> Step 1. Unpack the question stem
>
> Step 2. Research the answer
>
> Step 3. Predict the answer
>
> Step 4. Find the one correct answer

Because different question types require different strategies, start by **unpacking the information in the question stem** and identifying the question type while ignoring the answer choices. There are only five types of questions in the Reading Test, so knowing what type of question you're answering will help you decide where to look for your answer. You'll learn how to do this important step in chapter 17.

Next, based on the type of question, **research the passage** or your passage map to get the information you need. The incorrect answer choices on a multiple-choice test actually have a name: distractors. Distractors are carefully crafted to sound correct and take your attention away from the correct choice, so if you read all of the answer choices as soon as you finish examining the question stem, you risk getting distracted from what's actually supported by the passage. With the relevant part of the passage in mind, **predict** what the correct answer will say before you look at the answer choices.

Part 4
ACT READING

Finally, check your prediction against the choices and **find the one correct answer** that matches. Because ACT experts arm themselves with strong predictions in step 3, they can often zero in on the correct response without wasting time by rereading or hunting around in the passage to check each answer. You'll go over the strategies and tactics that experts use for steps 2–4 in chapter 18.

Take a look at our expert's application of the Method for ACT Reading Questions to the questions from the Mexico tourism passage.

Question	Explanation
1. The main purpose of the passage is to: A. argue that more people ought to visit the tropical beaches of Mexico instead of its *altiplano* regions. B. assert that without the contributions of the *altiplano*, Mexico's beach resort towns would not be able to sustain themselves or their visitors. C. state that the *altiplano* is more diverse and rich in life than tropical beaches. D. contend that travel to foreign countries is best experienced in places that reflect the local culture instead of places that reflect the tourist industry.	**Step 1: Unpack the question stem.** The question stem includes the phrase "main purpose," which indicates that it is a Global question. **Step 2: Research the answer.** To answer this type of question, you should review the main idea summary in your notes. **Step 3: Predict the answer.** Predict that the correct answer will describe the author's preference for areas like the *altiplano*, which display the diversity of the local population, over places like tropical beaches, which are specialized to cater to tourism. **Step 4: Find the one correct answer.** Choice (D) matches this prediction and is correct. Choices B and C, while factually accurate, do not fully capture the main idea of the whole passage. Choice A is the opposite of the point the author is making.

Chapter 15
The Method for ACT Reading

Question	Explanation
2. According to the passage, what makes a tropical beach a specialized area? F. It cannot exist outside of particular longitudes. G. It resembles a gymnasium. H. Land-based life has difficulty finding the resources to survive there. J. One tropical beach is much like any other tropical beach.	**Step 1: Unpack the question stem.** The question stem includes the phrase "According to the passage," which indicates that it is a Detail question. **Step 2: Research the answer.** The tropical beach as a specialized area is discussed in the second paragraph, which describes the beach as "the least livable area: the closer a land dweller moves to the ocean, the fewer there are of the resources necessary to sustain life." **Step 3: Predict the answer.** Predict that these regions are specialized because it is hard to live there due to the lack of resources. **Step 4: Find the one correct answer.** Choice (H) matches the prediction and is correct. Choice F is a distortion; the passage states that tropical beaches cannot exist outside of certain *latitudes*, not *longitudes*. Choice G is a misused detail; while the author does compare tropical beach towns to gymnasiums, the resemblance is not the reason why such locations are specialized. Finally, choice J does not address what makes these areas specialized.
3. As it is used in line 26, the word *dictate* most nearly means: A. command action. B. speak for recording. C. forbid response. D. shape development.	**Step 1: Unpack the question stem.** The question stem includes the clues "As used in line" and "the word . . . most nearly means," which indicate that it is a Vocab-in-Context question. **Step 2: Research the answer.** To answer a question like this, read a little bit above and below line 26 and think about what the word *dictate* means here. **Step 3: Predict the answer.** Predict that the environment *impacts* or *molds* the living things that dwell there. **Step 4: Find the one correct answer.** Choice (D) matches the prediction and is correct. Choices A and B are other meanings of *dictate* that do not fit the context of the sentence: surroundings cannot *command*, or *speak*. Choice C is incorrect because *dictate* does not specifically mean *forbid*.

Question	Explanation
4. The passage most strongly suggests that the Mayan people were the first to flourish in coastal Mexico because they: F. adapted to thrive in the year-round heat and humidity. G. successfully discovered enough *cenotes* to support the population. H. conveniently avoided the risks of living on the coastline. J. avoided confrontations with others by using the coast as a border.	**Step 1: Unpack the question stem.** The question stem includes the phrase "most strongly suggests," indicating that it is an Inference question. Use the strong keyword clue "Mayan" and your passage map to lead you to paragraph three. **Step 2: Research the answer.** Tropical beaches' inhospitable nature is discussed in paragraph three, which states that tropical beaches usually lack basic necessities like drinking water. Lines 48–49 mention the Maya as the "first known to flourish," so read around those lines for the reason. The rest of the paragraph discusses the brilliance of the Maya in avoiding barren tropical coasts in favor of *cenotes*, which provided the fresh water they needed. **Step 3: Predict the answer.** Predict that the *cenotes* were likely the reason why the Maya flourished in coastal regions where others had not. **Step 4: Find the one correct answer.** Choice (G) matches the prediction and is correct. Choice F is a distortion; the passage says that tourists enjoy the heat and humidity in order to contrast them with the Maya. Choice H contradicts the passage, which says that Mayans thrived in certain coastal regions. Finally, choice J is out of scope; the passage does not mention any potential conflicts with others.

Question	Explanation
5. The comparison between a gymnasium and an open market in paragraph four is meant to: A. contrast tourists who visit the coast with those who visit the *altiplano*. B. show that inland areas are better equipped than beach towns to accommodate the needs of visitors. C. emphasize that beach resorts are set up to cater to visitors in a way that the *altiplano* is not. D. indicate that consumer goods are less available on the coast than inland.	**Step 1: Unpack the question stem.** The question stem includes the clue "is meant to," indicating that it is a Function question. **Step 2: Research the answer.** Use your passage map to predict how the comparison contributes to the main idea of the passage. The fourth paragraph compares beach areas to the *altiplano*. The comparison between a predictable gymnasium experience and the unique experience of an open-air market is used as an analogy for the tourist-centered beach compared to the local-focused *altiplano*. **Step 3: Predict the answer.** Predict that the reference is meant to show that the beach resort towns are set up more specifically for the needs of visitors than the *altiplano* is. **Step 4: Find the one correct answer.** Choice (C) matches the prediction and is correct. Choice A is out of scope; there is no comparison between different types of tourists. Choice B is opposite; the author says that the beach towns, not the *altiplano*, are set up for tourists. Finally, choice D is out of scope; the passage never compares the quantities of consumer goods in the different areas.

Putting It All Together

To recap, to efficiently tackle the ACT Reading Test, make sure you:

- Never skip the pre-passage blurb. Quickly assess it to gather any information that provides context for the passage or that helps you anticipate what the author will cover.
- Read *actively*, asking what the author's purpose is in writing each paragraph. Anticipate where the passage will go. "Map" the passage by jotting down a short summary of each paragraph. On a paper-based test, you might also circle or underline keywords that indicate the author's opinion, details the author emphasized, and comparisons and contrasts made in the text. On a computer-based test, use the highlighting tool for the same purpose.
- Pause for a moment after reading the passage to summarize the big picture: quickly note the main idea and the author's purpose for writing the passage.
- Once you have strategically read the passage, use the Method for ACT Reading Questions to attack the question set.

Part 4
ACT READING

> **ACT READING QUESTION METHOD**
>
> Step 1. Unpack the question stem
>
> Step 2. Research the answer
>
> Step 3. Predict the answer
>
> Step 4. Find the one correct answer

By reading strategically and using the Method for ACT Reading Questions every time you practice, you'll internalize the steps. By test day, you'll be attacking this section efficiently and accurately without even thinking about it.

In the next section, you'll see another ACT Reading passage, this time with 9 questions. Try to apply the ACT Reading Passage Strategy and the ACT Reading Question Method presented in this lesson to read and answer the questions as quickly and confidently as possible.

Chapter 15
The Method for ACT Reading

How Much Have You Learned?

Directions: Take as much time as you need on these questions. Assess your work by comparing it to the expert responses at the end of the chapter.

INFORMATIONAL: This passage is adapted from a 2018 article.

The history of the New York City subway system, quickly told: the first stations opened in 1904, and over the next century, it expanded to 472 stations, more than any other subway system
5 in the world, with 850 miles of track. Operating 24 hours a day, seven days a week, with an average weekday ridership of approximately 5.7 million, it is the planet's 7th-busiest rapid transit system. While the system is, on many levels, an amazing
10 achievement, it is also beset by a problem that harms both quality of life and economic activity. Such a large system must inevitably suffer from service interruptions and delays; normal wear and tear combined with the sheer age of the system
15 necessitates regular maintenance. However, there is no consensus as to the best way to accomplish the required repairs.

The current maintenance scheme is designed to minimize service interruptions. A subway line in
20 need of repair will be taken out of service during a comparatively less busy time, such as nights or weekends, while another line is re-routed to cover as many as possible of the missing line's stops. The main advantage to this approach is that trains
25 are not taken out of service during rush hour, when most subway trips occur; subway service generally remains predictable, and commuters are, for the most part, able to use the system to get to their destinations on time.

30 But critics are quick to point out the disadvantages to this approach. Perhaps most obvious is the confusion caused by trains switching lines. The labyrinthine system is hard enough to navigate at the best of times, especially
35 for tourists. A subway rider on the A train naturally expects the train to make stops on the A line. If, instead, it is diverted temporarily to the F line, the rider may find herself miles from her intended destination.

40 While annoying, the confusion arising from route switching is hardly the most serious problem with the current approach to repairs. Because the system runs 24 hours a day, routine maintenance can generally be done only during
45 the temporary closures on nights and weekends. This means that more serious repair and crucial preventative maintenance are often neglected. Problems that could have been fixed or prevented reasonably expeditiously given a slightly longer
50 closure wind up leading to major breakdowns and service interruptions later on.

On rare occasions, such breakdowns have resulted in entire subway lines being shut down for months or even a year. Beginning in 2019, for
55 example, the L train connecting lower Manhattan to parts of Brooklyn is scheduled to close for as much as 15 months for long overdue service and upgrades. In a city fewer than half of whose households own a car, this can have serious
60 economic impacts. Residents of the affected area may face a much longer commute via an alternate subway line if one is available; or, if there is no alternate subway service, they may need to take other, potentially more expensive, modes of
65 transportation, such as taxis or ferries. Moreover, studies indicate that increased stress from the commute to work can lead to lower productivity, and that businesses near the impacted lines may see decreased revenue as potential customers have
70 a harder time getting to them.

One controversial proposal for reducing breakdowns and the resulting transit interruptions is to end the subway's 24-hour service and to shut down for several hours each night. Proponents
75 of this plan argue that this would allow time, on a regular rather than sporadic basis, for more preventative maintenance. This, they claim, would ultimately lead to more consistent service; rather than shutting down entire lines for long periods
80 of time, there would merely be shorter service

outages overnight, when fewer people use the subway system. While this may seem a preferable outcome to the economic consequences of a total shutdown resulting from a breakdown, it has its
85 liabilities as well. While most subway trips may occur during rush hour, not everyone works during the daytime. New York is famously known as the "the city that never sleeps." Doctors, nurses, bartenders, police officers, and firefighters are
90 just a few examples of occupations whose workers need transportation at all hours of the day and night. Rather than be subjected to a relatively short period of inconvenience, these workers would find their commutes irrevocably altered.
95 One thing, at least, is clear: the city must carefully consider many economic and social factors in designing a subway maintenance plan.

1. The main purpose of the passage is to:

   A. argue that the New York City subway system maintenance plan should be altered.

   B. explain the effects of the current New York City subway system maintenance plan and a proposed alternative.

   C. discuss the economic and social importance of the New York City subway system.

   D. show how the history of the New York City subway system has resulted in the current maintenance crisis.

2. Based on the passage, advocates of the current New York City subway maintenance plan would most likely agree that:

   F. given its size, the city's subway system is one of the most well maintained in the world.

   G. avoiding service interruptions during rush hour is a paramount consideration when designing a maintenance schedule.

   H. confusion caused by route switching is a minor inconvenience for commuters and tourists.

   J. operating the subway system 24 hours a day, seven days a week is untenable given the wear and tear it causes.

3. Based on the passage, which statement best describes a claim that critics of the current subway maintenance plan would likely make?

   A. The negative impacts that arise from neglecting preventative maintenance outweigh the benefits of minimizing subway service interruptions.

   B. When devising a subway maintenance plan, no factor is more important than avoiding rush hour service interruptions.

   C. The negative impact from subway line closures is greater on commuters than it is on businesses near the affected lines.

   D. Slightly longer periods of scheduled maintenance would help the subway system minimize rush hour service interruptions.

4. As it is used in line 33, the word *labyrinthine* most nearly means:

   F. subterranean.

   G. mythological.

   H. meandering.

   J. complicated.

5. In the third paragraph, the discussion of two specific subway lines (lines 35–39) primarily serves to:

   A. support the contention that line switching has a negative impact on tourism.

   B. illustrate one problem created by the current subway maintenance plan.

   C. underline the importance of minimizing subway service interruptions.

   D. quantify the social costs that arise from extended subway repair schedules.

6. The primary purpose of the fifth paragraph (lines 52–70) is to:

   F. illustrate the impact of the current maintenance plan on one subway line.
   G. advocate for increased funding for subway repair and maintenance.
   H. provide support for a proposal to curtail 24-hour subway service.
   J. outline the negative impacts of extended subway line outages.

7. The passage indicates that non–rush hour commuters:

   A. would risk losing public transportation options if 24-hour subway service were suspended.
   B. would face only minor inconveniences if 24-hour subway service were suspended.
   C. work primarily in health care and its related fields.
   D. are among the strongest advocates for a change to the current subway maintenance plan.

8. The author most likely refers to New York City as "the city that never sleeps" (lines 87–88) to:

   F. highlight an example of one of the ways in which the city is depicted in popular culture.
   G. provide support to a counterargument to the proposal to close the subway for a portion of the night.
   H. identify the anticipated economic and social benefits of nightly subway shutdowns for maintenance.
   J. advocate for the importance of residents in noisy urban environments being able to get an adequate amount of rest.

9. Based on the passage, with which of the following statements would the author most likely agree?

   A. The controversy surrounding New York City's subway system reflects similar issues for mass transit in many American cities.
   B. Without major changes to its subway maintenance plan, New York City will be unable to provide regular service to its 5.7 million weekly riders.
   C. Any plan for maintaining New York City's subway system will entail advantages and disadvantages for commuters.
   D. The social and economic costs resulting from New York City's current subway maintenance schedule justify an end to 24-hour, seven-day subway service.

Part 4
ACT READING

Reflect

Directions: Take a few minutes to recall what you've learned and what you've been practicing in this chapter. Consider the following questions, jot down your best answer for each one, and then compare your reflections to the expert responses on the following page. Use your level of confidence to determine what to do next.

1. Describe active, or strategic, reading on ACT passages:

2. What do ACT experts mean by summarizing the big picture of a passage?

3. How can writing brief "passage notes" help you answer ACT Reading questions more effectively?

4. What does an ACT expert look for in the question stem of an ACT Reading question?

5. Why do expert test takers predict or characterize the correct answer to each ACT Reading question before assessing the answer choices?

6. What will you do differently on future passages and their questions?

Chapter 15
The Method for ACT Reading

Responses

1. Describe active, or strategic, reading on ACT passages.

Because the ACT asks many questions about why an author has written the passage or about how the author makes a point, expert test takers read for the author's purpose and main idea. Noting keywords that indicate a shift or contrast in points of view or that indicate opinions and emphases helps keep ACT experts on point as they anticipate where the passage will go.

2. What do ACT experts mean by summarizing the big picture of a passage?

To read for the big picture means to be able to accurately summarize the main idea of a passage and note the author's purpose for writing it. The big picture summary helps you answer Global questions and questions that ask about the author's opinion or point of view.

3. How can writing brief "passage notes" help you answer ACT Reading questions more effectively?

Jotting down passage notes provides a reference "map" to the subject or purpose of each paragraph in the passage. It helps you locate specific subjects or opinions expressed in the passage when they are called out in the questions.

4. What does an ACT expert look for in the question stem of an ACT Reading question?

Each question stem indicates the type of question and contains clues as to whether the answer will come from researching the passage text or from the big picture summary. Many question stems have specific clues (for example, line numbers or references to details from the passage) that tell you precisely where to research.

5. Why do expert test takers predict or characterize the correct answer to each ACT Reading question before assessing the answer choices?

Predicting or characterizing the correct answer allows you to evaluate each answer choice one time and avoid rereading for every answer choice. Incorrect answers often distort what the passage said or misuse details from the passage, so it's best to research the passage once to know what the correct answer must say before diving into the choices.

6. What will you do differently on future passages and their questions?

There is no one-size-fits-all answer to this question. Each student has individual initial strengths and opportunities in the Reading section. What's important here is that you're honestly self-reflective. Take what you need from the expert's examples and strive to apply it to your own performance. Many test takers convince themselves that they'll never get faster or more confident in ACT Reading, but the truth is, many test takers who now routinely ace the Reading section were much slower and more hesitant before they learned to approach this section systematically and strategically.

Next Steps

If you answered most questions correctly in the "How Much Have You Learned?" section, and if your responses to the Reflect questions were similar to those of the ACT expert, then consider the ACT Reading Question Method an area of strength and move on to the next chapter. Come back to this topic periodically to prevent yourself from getting rusty.

If you don't yet feel confident, review those parts of this chapter that you have not yet mastered. Then, try the questions you missed again. As always, be sure to review the explanations closely. Then go online (**kaptest.com/login**) for more practice. If you haven't already registered your book, do so at **kaptest.com/moreonline**.

Answers and Explanations

How Much Have You Learned?

INFORMATIONAL: This passage is adapted from a 2018 article.

　　The history of the New York City subway system, quickly told: the first stations opened in 1904, and over the next century, it expanded to 472 stations, more than any other subway system
(5) in the world, with 850 miles of track. Operating 24 hours a day, seven days a week, with an average weekday ridership of approximately 5.7 million, it is the planet's 7th-busiest rapid transit system. While the system is, on many levels, an amazing
(10) achievement, it is also beset by a problem that harms both quality of life and economic activity. Such a large system must inevitably suffer from service interruptions and delays; normal wear and tear combined with the sheer age of the system
(15) necessitates regular maintenance. However, there is no consensus as to the best way to accomplish the required repairs.

　　The current maintenance scheme is designed to minimize service interruptions. A subway line in
(20) need of repair will be taken out of service during a comparatively less busy time, such as nights or weekends, while another line is re-routed to cover as many as possible of the missing line's stops. The main advantage to this approach is that trains
(25) are not taken out of service during rush hour, when most subway trips occur; subway service generally remains predictable, and commuters are, for the most part, able to use the system to get to their destinations on time.

(30)　　But critics are quick to point out the disadvantages to this approach. Perhaps most obvious is the confusion caused by trains switching lines. The labyrinthine system is hard enough to navigate at the best of times, especially
(35) for tourists. A subway rider on the A train naturally expects the train to make stops on the A line. If, instead, it is diverted temporarily to the F line, the rider may find herself miles from her intended destination.

NYC subway: how to repair? diff. views

Current approach: night and weekend repairs

Critics: line switch confusion

ANALYSIS

Pre-passage blurb: Though the passage blurb does not give many details, it does identify that the passage is from an "article"; expect an academic tone.

¶1 The first few sentences introduce the New York subway system with its history and various facts. The contrast word "While" signals a transition to a discussion of problems with maintenance and service interruptions. The author previews that the article will discuss the lack of "consensus" about addressing these issues.

¶2 The first sentence indicates that this paragraph discusses the current maintenance plan. Its goal is to "minimize service interruptions." The author describes this plan and its "main advantage."

¶3 The contrast keyword "But" shows the transition to a discussion of the "disadvantages" pointed out by "critics" of the current plan.

Chapter 15
The Method for ACT Reading

      While annoying, the confusion arising from
route switching is hardly the most serious
problem with the current approach to repairs.
Because the system runs 24 hours a day, routine
maintenance can generally be done only during
45 the temporary closures on nights and weekends.
This means that more serious repair and crucial
preventative maintenance are often neglected.
Problems that could have been fixed or prevented
reasonably expeditiously given a slightly longer
50 closure wind up leading to major breakdowns
and service interruptions later on.

      On rare occasions, such breakdowns have
resulted in entire subway lines being shut down
for months or even a year. Beginning in 2019, for
55 example, the L train connecting lower Manhattan
to parts of Brooklyn is scheduled to close for
as much as 15 months for long overdue service
and upgrades. In a city fewer than half of whose
households own a car, this can have serious
60 economic impacts. Residents of the affected area
may face a much longer commute via an alternate
subway line if one is available; or, if there is no
alternate subway service, they may need to take
other, potentially more expensive, modes of
65 transportation, such as taxis or ferries. Moreover,
studies indicate that increased stress from the
commute to work can lead to lower productivity,
and that businesses near the impacted lines may
see decreased revenue as potential customers have
70 a harder time getting to them.

      One controversial proposal for reducing
breakdowns and the resulting transit interruptions
is to end the subway's 24-hour service and to shut
down for several hours each night. Proponents
75 of this plan argue that this would allow time, on
a regular rather than sporadic basis, for more
preventative maintenance. This, they claim, would
ultimately lead to more consistent service; rather
than shutting down entire lines for long periods
80 of time, there would merely be shorter service
outages overnight, when fewer people use the
subway system. While this may seem a preferable
outcome to the economic consequences of a total
shutdown resulting from a breakdown, it has its

Even worse: major breakdowns

¶4 This paragraph discusses an even more "serious problem" with the current plan: required maintenance may not be done and breakdowns may occur.

Eco. & soc. harms of shutdowns

¶5 This paragraph provides more details about the problems caused by the "major breakdowns" mentioned in the previous paragraph. The phrase "for example" indicates a specific instance of a major breakdown, and the keyword "Moreover" introduces another problem.

Alt. proposal: stop 24-hour service Pros Cons

¶6 The final paragraph discusses an alternate, "controversial proposal" for maintaining the subways. The author includes arguments from both "Proponents" and critics (signaled by the contrast word "While") of the plan. The author doesn't pick a side but concludes with the neutral viewpoint that any plan must be carefully considered.

463

85 liabilities as well. While most subway trips may occur during rush hour, not everyone works during the daytime. New York is famously known as the "the city that never sleeps." Doctors, nurses, bartenders, police officers, and firefighters are
90 just a few examples of occupations whose workers need transportation at all hours of the day and night. Rather than be subjected to a relatively short period of inconvenience, these workers would find their commutes irrevocably altered.
95 One thing, at least, is clear: the city must carefully consider many economic and social factors in designing a subway maintenance plan.

BIG PICTURE SUMMARY

Main idea: There are different views about the best way to perform repairs and maintenance on the extensive New York subway system.

Author's purpose: To objectively describe the pros and cons of various approaches to maintaining the New York subway system.

1. B
Difficulty: Medium
Category: Global
Getting to the Answer: Consult your big picture summary and find the one answer that matches the passage's scope and the author's purpose. Here, the author does not take a side but lays out advantages and disadvantages to both the current maintenance plan and one proposal offered by critics of the current plan. That matches (B).

Choice A distorts the author's position. He doesn't advocate for the critics of the current plan. Choice C is too broad. It misses the key subject of subway maintenance. Choice D is too narrow. This answer describes only the first paragraph.

2. G
Difficulty: High
Category: Inference
Getting to the Answer: The phrases "Based on the passage" and "most likely agree" in the question stem indicate that this is an Inference question, since what it asks for is implied but not directly stated in the passage. The current maintenance plan is outlined in paragraph two. You're told that its goal is to "minimize service interruptions" and that its main advantage is that trains operate during rush hour. Combining those statements leads to the correct answer, (G).

Choice F is out of scope. New York's subway maintenance is not compared to subway systems. Choice H misuses a detail from the passage. The author says critics think route switching is a problem, but he says nothing about how serious a problem those who support the current plan consider route switching to be. They might understand that it causes a major inconvenience but still be willing to reroute trains in order to keep the subway open during rush hour. Choice J states a position taken by critics, not advocates, of the current plan.

3. A
Difficulty: High
Category: Inference
Getting to the Answer: The phrases "Based on the passage" and "would likely" indicate an Inference question. Note that this question asks specifically for the position of the *critics* of the current plan. The correct answer will be implied but not directly

stated by the passage text. The critics' objections to the current plan are laid out primarily in paragraphs three and four. They make two arguments. First, line switching for routine maintenance can be confusing and frustrating for riders (paragraph three). Second, and worse, the limited time allowed for routine maintenance prevents important preventative maintenance from taking place (paragraph four). That leads to severe service outages that can last for weeks or months. This second criticism accords with the correct answer, (A).

Choice B is something that advocates, not opponents, of the current plan might say. See paragraph two for this argument. Choice C is an irrelevant comparison. Paragraph five lays out the social and economic impacts of extended subway line closures to both riders and businesses, but it doesn't assert that the impacts are worse for one group or the other. Choice D distorts the critics' argument. They contend that slightly longer periods of scheduled maintenance would allow time for preventative maintenance, not that it would reduce rush hour interruptions.

4. J
Difficulty: Easy
Category: Vocab-in-Context
Getting to the Answer: Check the sentence in which the word was used to determine the author's intended meaning. The correct answer can be substituted for the word without changing the meaning of the sentence. Here, the author uses *labyrinthine* to describe the New York subway system's complexity, given the "confusion" that could be caused by line switching and the assertion that the system is "hard enough to navigate at the best of times." Choice (J) fits perfectly.

Choice F means *underground*. That is true of the subway system, of course, but it would be redundant for the author to use *labyrinthine* in this way. Choice G plays off the famous labyrinth from Greek mythology, but this definition does not fit the word *labyrinthine* or the context of the sentence. Choice H suggests that the subway system is random or wandering. While the huge system may be difficult to navigate at times, it isn't random.

5. B
Difficulty: High
Category: Function
Getting to the Answer: The phrase "serves to" tags this as a Function question, asking for the role a specific detail plays in the passage. Research the lines cited in the question stem to see why the author has included this example. The third paragraph introduces the first disadvantage cited by critics of the current subway maintenance schedule. The detail referenced in the question stem provides an example. That purpose is accurately described in the correct answer, (B).

Choice A misuses a detail from the passage. You're told that line switching—the problem being discussed—is particularly difficult for tourists, but referring to tourists only is too narrow and is not the reason the author included this example. Choice C refers to the rationale provided by supporters of the current maintenance plan in paragraph two. In D, the word "quantify" suggests that the example provides numbers to show the impact of the current maintenance plan. That's something the author never does in this passage.

6. J
Difficulty: Low
Category: Function
Getting to the Answer: On this Function question, you're asked for the author's purpose for including an entire paragraph. Consult your passage notes to see the role of paragraph five in the passage. Paragraph five details some of the social and economic harms caused by shutting down subway lines. That matches (J).

Choice F distorts the purpose of the paragraph. The specific line—the L train—is given as an example of an extended shutdown, but the harms described in the paragraph apply to all similar extended service outages. Choice G is outside the scope of the passage. The author does not discuss the need for increased funding. Choice H refers to a proposal from paragraph six. The author never endorses that proposal and does not use paragraph five to support it.

7. A
Difficulty: Medium
Category: Detail
Getting to the Answer: The phrase "[t]he passage indicates" shows this to be a Detail question. The correct answer will paraphrase a statement made explicitly in the text. The author discusses non–rush hour commuters in paragraph six. He lists some examples of these commuters—"doctors, nurses, bartenders, police officers, and firefighters"—and explains that a cessation of 24-hour subway service could permanently alter their commutes. That matches choice (A).

Choice B is the opposite of what the passage says. The current system creates minor inconveniences for these workers when their subway lines are rerouted or closed for repair, but a suspension of 24-hour service would entail a permanent disruption. Choice C distorts the paragraph. Doctors and nurses are among the non–rush hour commuters, but that doesn't mean they are the majority of them. Choice D is outside the scope of the passage. The author does not discuss which occupations show the strongest support for a change in subway maintenance.

8. G
Difficulty: Medium
Category: Function
Getting to the Answer: The phrase "most likely . . . to" signals that this is a Function question, so examine the context of the cited lines and ask yourself why the author chose to mention that New York is called "the city that never sleeps." The phrase appears in a paragraph about a "controversial proposal" for closing the subway for a few hours at night to do maintenance. The author provides the reasoning of the "Proponents" of this proposal, and the word "While" in line 82 transitions to a discussion of reasons why the proposal might be a bad idea: people who work at night would be negatively impacted. The phrase supports this counterargument by emphasizing that New York is known for its high level of activity at night; this matches (G).

Choices F and J are incorrect because the author's focus is on subway maintenance plans, not on depictions of New York City or getting enough sleep. Choice H is opposite; the phrase is used in the argument *against* nightly shutdowns.

9. C
Difficulty: High
Category: Inference
Getting to the Answer: For an open-ended Inference question like this one, predict the correct answer based on your big picture summary. Consider also any thesis statement or conclusion that sums up the author's point of view. This author outlines both sides of a debate and discusses the advantages and disadvantages to both the current subway maintenance plan and proposed alternatives. The author's conclusion at the end of the passage is neutral, encouraging the city to carefully consider all factors without advocating for a specific outcome. This matches up with the correct answer, (C).

Choice A strays beyond the scope of the passage. Be careful not to bring in bigger issues if the author has not discussed them in the passage. Choice B is too extreme. To be sure, the author considers subway maintenance a major issue but stops short of dire predictions like the one stated in this answer choice. Choice D matches the position of one side in the debate, but not that of the author, who remains neutral throughout.

[CHAPTER 16]

ACT READING PASSAGE STRATEGIES

LEARNING OBJECTIVES

After completing this chapter, you will be able to:

- Identify keywords that promote active reading and relate the passage text to the questions
- Create short, accurate passage notes that help you research the text efficiently
- Summarize the big picture of the passage

Part 4
ACT READING

How Much Do You Know?

Directions: In this chapter, you'll learn how ACT experts actively read the passage, take notes, and summarize the main idea to prepare themselves to answer all of the passage's questions quickly and confidently. You saw this kind of reading modeled in the previous chapter. To get ready for the current chapter, take five minutes to actively read the following passage by:

1. noting the keywords that indicate the author's point of view and the passage's structure
2. jotting down a quick summary of each paragraph
3. summarizing the big picture (the passage's main idea and the author's purpose for writing it)

When you're done, compare your work to the passage notes that follow.

INFORMATIONAL: This passage explores the relationship between the immigrant experience and one person's career choice.

My grandfather was born in a turbulent time in Russia. His non-communist lineage made him unwelcome before he had left the womb. His father, an officer in the Russian army, was
5 considered an enemy of the communist Bolsheviks, so my grandfather lived less than a year in what was his native Moscow and spent most of his younger years moving across Asia. Despite this, he had pride in being Russian, associated with
10 Russians throughout his life, and would frequently quiz me on Russian history. This all in tribute to a country that ended up under hostile rule during the time his mother was pregnant with him.

As a child, exiled to Siberia, my grandfather
15 heard his father tell of the greatness that existed within the country that had forced the family into exile. It was known that, first with his parents, and later as an adult, my grandfather was going to have to seek a new place to call home.
20 Despite this foregone conclusion, Russia was still romanticized, and my grandfather learned to treat the country with reverence. This was in contrast to the sentiments found in other recently exiled Russians, who would not simply lament the actions
25 taken by the country but disparage all eight million square miles. In my family's search for a place to settle, attempting to forge a consistent identity was nearly impossible, as no one knew whether the next location would hold for a month, let alone a year.
30 All hoped for an unattainable "new Moscow."

The first long-term refuge was found, ironically, in China, which would have its own communist revolution. After several years of relative stability, this revolution precipitated the move to the
35 United States. Upon arrival in San Francisco, my grandfather, along with my grandmother and their young son, my father, found other Russian immigrants who were also new to the country. "*Ya amerikanets,*" people would say, and despite the fact
40 that they were recent immigrants who associated primarily with those of shared ethnicity and circumstance, they would play the role they desired and repeat "*ya amerikanets*"—"I am American." They would share many stories about their native
45 land, but did not repeat "*ya russkiy,*" because being Russian went without saying. While it was clear that this would be the last country my grandfather would reside in and that he wished to become more American, it was perhaps the most confusing
50 of times. It was less a problem of acclimating to an adopted setting and more of dealing with a permanent setting at all. The only consistency throughout the first thirty years of my grandfather's life was the knowledge that every "home" was
55 temporary, and now this was no longer the case. I often wonder if his successful career in the real estate business had anything to do with what must have been a rare transformation of circumstance.

Not only was my grandfather interested in
60 real estate, but he was also keen on the importance of ownership, a naturally discordant view to that of the then Soviet Union. Thus, selling homes became a purpose in addition to an occupation.

Part of his success in real estate was owed to strategic compromise. Considering American sentiments regarding Russia during the Cold War, there were times that he was sure he lost certain house sales due to his last name and accent. However, to those willing to listen, he found advantages to informing people that he was an exiled Russian who ardently disagreed with the communist government. He would also point out his pride in being a new American and allow a potential buyer to degrade Russia without blinking.

Fortunately, the 1950s were a time of settling across the country, and this made real estate a very lucrative profession. It wasn't just this that attracted my grandfather, though; he also saw it as an opportunity to give tiny parts of the country to other people—returning the favor, in a way.

Yet, it always seemed that something vital still rested in the opposite hemisphere. Once communism fell, he began returning to Russia yearly. He and my grandmother never showed the family pictures from Russia the way they would from the various cruise ships they traveled on; it could be deduced that returning to Russia was a journey of personal necessity for him rather than pleasure, and the encounter elucidated his existence in a way that being solely American could not. In selling real estate, my grandfather had worked to make this unnecessary. I believe that he wished for people to keep those houses and pass them down to later generations, giving the space a sort of familial permanence rather than a fleeting stay.

For most, the thought of real estate agents conjures up images of smiling advertisements on benches and buses and the skill of selling something so important. Many are wary of salespeople in general, questioning the practice of convincing people something is in their best interest when the salesperson stands to personally benefit. My grandfather did financially benefit from sales, but there was more to it: his realization of the American dream only made him want to be a part of others reaching for the same thing, whether their native home was around the block or thousands of miles away.

Part 4
ACT READING

Answers and Explanations

How Much Do You Know?

INFORMATIONAL: This passage explores the relationship between the immigrant experience and one person's career choice.

My grandfather was born in a turbulent time in Russia. His non-communist lineage made him unwelcome before he had left the womb. His father, an officer in the Russian army, was
5   considered an enemy of the communist Bolsheviks, so my grandfather lived less than a year in what was his native Moscow and spent most of his younger years moving across Asia. Despite this, he had pride in being Russian, associated with
10 Russians throughout his life, and would frequently quiz me on Russian history. This all in tribute to a country that ended up under hostile rule during the time his mother was pregnant with him.

   As a child, exiled to Siberia, my grandfather
15 heard his father tell of the greatness that existed within the country that had forced the family into exile. It was known that, first with his parents, and later as an adult, my grandfather was going to have to seek a new place to call home.
20 Despite this foregone conclusion, Russia was still romanticized, and my grandfather learned to treat the country with reverence. This was in contrast to the sentiments found in other recently exiled Russians, who would not simply lament the actions
25 taken by the country but disparage all eight million square miles. In my family's search for a place to settle, attempting to forge a consistent identity was nearly impossible, as no one knew whether the next location would hold for a month, let alone a year.
30 All hoped for an unattainable "new Moscow."

   The first long-term refuge was found, ironically, in China, which would have its own communist revolution. After several years of relative stability, this revolution precipitated the move to the
35 United States. Upon arrival in San Francisco, my grandfather, along with my grandmother and their young son, my father, found other Russian immigrants who were also new to the country. "*Ya amerikanets*," people would say, and despite the fact
40 that they were recent immigrants who associated

ANALYSIS

Pre-passage blurb: From this blurb, you learn that the passage will focus on one person's career choice and, in particular, how that person's career choice is impacted by being an immigrant.

grandfather, chaotic childhood

¶1 The author introduces his grandfather and gives some background, focusing in particular on his grandfather's chaotic and unstable childhood.

still loves Russia

¶2 This paragraph provides additional context about why the author's grandfather still feels positively toward Russia, despite his unstable, chaotic childhood.

primarily with those of shared ethnicity and circumstance, they would play the role they desired and repeat "*ya amerikanets*"—"I am American." They would share many stories about their native
45 land, but did not repeat "*ya russkiy*," because being Russian went without saying. While it was clear that this would be the last country my grandfather would reside in and that he wished to become more American, it was perhaps the most confusing
50 of times. It was less a problem of acclimating to an adopted setting and more of dealing with a permanent setting at all. The only consistency throughout the first thirty years of my grandfather's life was the knowledge that every "home" was
55 temporary, and now this was no longer the case. I often wonder if his successful career in the real estate business had anything to do with what must have been a rare transformation of circumstance.

Not only was my grandfather interested in
60 real estate, but he was also keen on the importance of ownership, a naturally discordant view to that of the then Soviet Union. Thus, selling homes became a purpose in addition to an occupation.

Part of his success in real estate was owed to
65 strategic compromise. Considering American sentiments regarding Russia during the Cold War, there were times that he was sure he lost certain house sales due to his last name and accent. However, to those willing to listen, he found
70 advantages to informing people that he was an exiled Russian who ardently disagreed with the communist government. He would also point out his pride in being a new American and allow a potential buyer to degrade Russia without blinking.

75 Fortunately, the 1950s were a time of settling across the country, and this made real estate a very lucrative profession. It wasn't just this that attracted my grandfather, though; he also saw it as an opportunity to give tiny parts of the country to
80 other people—returning the favor, in a way.

Yet, it always seemed that something vital still rested in the opposite hemisphere. Once communism fell, he began returning to Russia yearly. He and my grandmother never showed the
85 family pictures from Russia the way they would

moves to US, becomes real estate agent

¶3 In this paragraph, the author's grandfather starts to find stability: first in China, then in the United States. There, the author's grandfather finds a group of immigrants like him, and the author reflects on his grandfather's journey. At the end of this paragraph, it's revealed that his grandfather is a real estate agent.

real estate is his vocation

¶4 The author expands on his grandfather's career choice, adding a deeper meaning behind the choice.

allows people to insult Russia

¶5 The author opens by discussing his grandfather's willingness to strategically compromise, even if it meant degrading the home country he felt so positively about.

wants to give back

¶6 Selling homes was not just a career or a source of income for the author's grandfather; rather, it was a way for him to help others in the way he felt he had been helped.

from the various cruise ships they traveled on; it could be deduced that returning to Russia was a journey of personal necessity for him rather than pleasure, and the encounter elucidated his existence
(90) in a way that being solely American could not. In selling real estate, my grandfather had worked to make this unnecessary. I believe that he wished for people to keep those houses and pass them down to later generations, giving the space a sort of
(95) familial permanence rather than a fleeting stay.

For most, the thought of real estate agents conjures up images of smiling advertisements on benches and buses and the skill of selling something so important. Many are wary of
(100) salespeople in general, questioning the practice of convincing people something is in their best interest when the salesperson stands to personally benefit. My grandfather did financially benefit from sales, but there was more to it: his
(105) realization of the American dream only made him want to be a part of others reaching for the same thing, whether their native home was around the block or thousands of miles away.

visits Russia every year

¶7 Now that Russia is more open than it was in the author's grandfather's past, he makes a point to visit yearly but does not share these journeys with his family. The author has a sense that his grandfather uses this annual trip to remind himself of his motivations.

wants to give people a home

¶8 Real estate agent may not have seemed like an obvious career choice for the author's grandfather, but his motivation to help others find their own *native homes*, wherever that may be, resulted in both his own financial success and his success in an unexpected career.

BIG PICTURE SUMMARY

Main idea: A Russian immigrant attempts to make a life and find a purpose in his new homeland through selling real estate.

Author's purpose: To reminisce about his grandfather's life experiences, memories, and impact.

ACT READING STRATEGIES: KEYWORDS, PASSAGE NOTES, AND THE BIG PICTURE SUMMARY

> **LEARNING OBJECTIVES**
>
> After this lesson, you will be able to:
> - Identify keywords that promote active reading and relate the passage text to the questions
> - Create short, accurate passage notes that help you research the text efficiently
> - Summarize the big picture of the passage

To read and map a passage like this

INFORMATIONAL: This passage is adapted from a 2019 essay about astrobiology.

Astrobiology, also known as exobiology, is a complex, multidisciplinary science dedicated to studying the possibility of life outside the confines of Earth. Humanity has speculated for centuries
[5] about whether or not we are alone in the universe, but with the advent of space exploration in the 1950s and 1960s, for the first time in human history there was the possibility of actually exploring the surface of alien planets. Scientists
[10] and engineers worked together to build what they called landers, spacecraft capable not only of landing on other planets, but also of exploring and photographing them.

When the first of the two Viking landers touched
[15] down on Martian soil on July 20, 1976, and began to send camera images back to Earth, the scientists at the Jet Propulsion Laboratory could not suppress a certain nervous anticipation. Like people who hold a ticket to a lottery, they had a one-in-a-million
[20] chance of winning. The first photographs that arrived, however, did not contain any evidence of life. They revealed merely a barren landscape littered with rocks and boulders. The view resembled nothing so much as a flat section of desert. In
[25] fact, the winning entry in a contest at J.P.L. for the photograph most accurately predicting what Mars would look like was a snapshot taken from a particularly arid section of the Mojave Desert.

The scientists were soon ready to turn their
[30] attention from visible life to microorganisms. The twin Viking landers carried out experiments designed to detect organic compounds. Researchers thought it possible that life had developed on early Mars just as it is thought to have developed on
[35] Earth, through the gradual chemical evolution of complex organic molecules. To detect biological activity, Martian soil samples were treated with various nutrients that would produce characteristic by-products if life forms were active in the soil.
[40] The results from all three experiments were inconclusive. The fourth experiment heated a soil sample to look for signs of organic material but found none—an unexpected result because organic compounds were thought to have been present due
[45] to the steady bombardment of the Martian surface by meteorites.

The absence of organic materials, some scientists speculated, was the result of intense ultraviolet radiation penetrating the atmosphere
[50] of Mars and destroying organic compounds in the soil. Although Mars' atmosphere was at one time rich in carbon dioxide and thus thick enough to protect its surface from the harmful rays of the sun, the carbon dioxide had gradually left the
[55] atmosphere and been converted into rocks. This means that even if life had gotten a start on early Mars, it could not have survived the exposure to ultraviolet radiation that occurred when the atmosphere thinned. Mars never developed a
[60] protective layer of ozone as Earth did.

Despite the disappointing Viking results, there are those who still keep open the possibility of life on Mars. They point out that the Viking data cannot be considered the final word on
[65] Martian life because the two landers sampled only

limited—and uninteresting—sites. The Viking landing sites were not chosen for what they might tell of the planet's biology. They were chosen primarily because they appeared to be safe for
[70] landing a spacecraft. The landing sites were on parts of the Martian plains that appeared relatively featureless according to orbital photographs.

The type of terrain that these researchers suggest may be a possible hiding place for active
[75] life has an Earthly parallel: the ice-free region of southern Victoria Land, Antarctica, where the temperatures in some dry valleys average below zero. Organisms known as endoliths, a form of blue-green algae that has adapted to this harsh
[80] environment, were found living inside certain translucent, porous rocks in these Antarctic valleys. The argument based on this discovery is that if life did exist on early Mars, it is possible that it escaped worsening conditions by similarly seeking refuge
[85] in rocks. Skeptics object, however, that Mars in its present state is simply too dry, even compared with Antarctic valleys, to sustain any life whatsoever.

Should Mars eventually prove barren of life, as some suspect, then this finding would have
[90] a significant impact on the current view of the chemical origins of life. It could be much more difficult to get life started on a planet than scientists thought before the Viking landings.

The possibility exists, of course, that our
[95] definition of what constitutes life may not hold true throughout the universe. It has long been speculated that our current belief that all life must contain carbon, oxygen, calcium, chlorine, potassium, and phosphorous simply because this holds true on our
[100] planet might be too narrow a view. In 2010, NASA scientists believed they had discovered a bacterium that used arsenic in place of phosphorous, though these exciting findings later proved to be incorrect. The possibility remains, however, that future
[105] astrobiologists exploring the Martian surface from 140 million miles away might be able to make use of a more advanced definition of what we call "life."

You need to know this

- ACT Reading passages are preceded by short blurbs that tell you about the author and/or the source of the passage.
- There are three categories of keywords that reveal an author's purpose and point of view and that unlock the passage's structure:
    - **opinion and emphasis**—words that signal that the author finds a detail noteworthy (e.g., *especially, crucial, important, above all*) or has an opinion about it (e.g., *fortunately, disappointing, I suggest, it seems likely*)
    - **connection and contrast**—words that suggest that a subsequent detail continues the same point (e.g., *moreover, in addition, also, further*) or that indicate a change in direction or point of difference (e.g., *but, yet, despite, on the other hand*)
        - In some passages, connection keywords may show steps in a process or developments over time (e.g., *traditionally, in the past, recently, today, first, second, finally, earlier, since*)
    - **evidence and example**—words that indicate an argument (the use of evidence to support a conclusion), either the author's or someone else's (e.g., *thus, therefore, because*), or that introduce an example to clarify or support another point (e.g., *for example, this shows, to illustrate*)

You need to do this

Apply the ACT Reading Strategy to every Reading passage:

- Extract everything you can from the pre-passage blurb
- Read each paragraph actively
- Summarize the passage's big picture

Chapter 16
ACT Reading Passage Strategies

Extract everything you can from the pre-passage blurb

Quickly prepare for the passage by unpacking the pre-passage blurb.

- What do the title and date of the original book or article tell you about the author and her purpose for writing?
- What information can you glean from the source (nonfiction book, novel, academic journal, etc.)?
- Is there any other information that provides context for the passage?

Read each paragraph actively

Note keywords (marking them may help) and use them to focus your reading on:

- The author's purpose and point of view
- The relationships between ideas
- The examples or other support provided for passage claims

WHY PAY ATTENTION TO KEYWORDS?

Keywords indicate opinions and signal structure that make the difference between correct and incorrect answers on ACT questions. Consider this test-like question and two potential choices:

The passage author most clearly indicates that coffee beans that grow at high altitudes typically produce:

A. dark, mellow coffee when brewed.

B. light, acidic coffee when brewed.

To answer that based on an ACT passage, you will need to determine whether the author said:

Type X coffee beans grow at very high altitudes, so they produce a dark, mellow coffee when brewed.

That would make choice (A) correct. But if the author instead said:

Type X coffee beans grow at very high altitudes, *but* they produce a *surprisingly* dark, mellow coffee when brewed.

Then choice (B) would be correct. The facts in the statements did not change at all, but the correct answer to the ACT question would be different in each case because of the keywords the author chose to include.

As you read, jot down brief, accurate passage notes. These notes can be referred to as a **passage map** because they will guide you as you research your answers.

- Paraphrase the text (put it into your own words) as you go.
- Ask, "What's the author's point and purpose?" for each paragraph.

Summarize the passage's big picture

At the end of the passage, pause for a few seconds to summarize the passage's big picture. Doing so will help you understand the passage as a whole and prepare you to answer Global questions. Ask yourself:

- "What is the main idea of the entire passage?" (If the author had only a few seconds to state what she thinks is most important, what would she say?)
- "Why did the author write it?" (State the purpose as a verb, e.g., *to explain, to explore, to argue, to rebut,* etc.)

Explanation

INFORMATIONAL: This passage is adapted from an essay about astrobiology.

Astrobiology, also known as exobiology, is a complex, multidisciplinary science dedicated to studying the possibility of life outside the confines of Earth. Humanity has speculated for centuries
[5] about whether or not we are alone in the universe, but with the advent of space exploration in the 1950s and 1960s, for the first time in human history there was the possibility of actually exploring the surface of alien planets. Scientists
[10] and engineers worked together to build what they called landers, spacecraft capable not only of landing on other planets, but also of exploring and photographing them.

When the first of the two Viking landers touched
[15] down on Martian soil on July 20, 1976, and began to send camera images back to Earth, the scientists at the Jet Propulsion Laboratory could not suppress a certain nervous anticipation. Like people who hold a ticket to a lottery, they had a one-in-a-million
[20] chance of winning. The first photographs that arrived, however, did not contain any evidence of life. They revealed merely a barren landscape littered with rocks and boulders. The view resembled nothing so much as a flat section of desert. In
[25] fact, the winning entry in a contest at J.P.L. for the photograph most accurately predicting what Mars would look like was a snapshot taken from a particularly arid section of the Mojave Desert.

The scientists were soon ready to turn their
[30] attention from visible life to microorganisms. The twin Viking landers carried out experiments designed to detect organic compounds. Researchers thought it possible that life had developed on early Mars just as it is thought to have developed on
[35] Earth, through the gradual chemical evolution of complex organic molecules. To detect biological activity, Martian soil samples were treated with various nutrients that would produce characteristic by-products if life forms were active in the soil.
[40] The results from all three experiments were inconclusive. The fourth experiment heated a soil sample to look for signs of organic material but

ANALYSIS

Pre-passage blurb: In the pre-passage blurb, you learn the topic of the essay: astrobiology.

astrobiology: finding non-Earth life

¶1 The author defines astrobiology and provides a brief explanation for why it is a field of study.

Mars landing no signs of life

¶2 The author changes tone in the second paragraph, prompting excitement, only to shift back into a more neutral voice for the second half of the paragraph as she describes the disappointing results of the Viking landers in 1976.

inconclusive tests for microorganisms

¶3 This paragraph transitions from what was expected out of the initial landing to what happened next, describing the next set of efforts undertaken to better study life beyond Earth, this time with a focus on microorganisms. Unfortunately, the results from these experiments were inconclusive.

found none—an unexpected result because organic compounds were thought to have been present due to the steady bombardment of the Martian surface by meteorites.

The absence of organic materials, some scientists speculated, was the result of intense ultraviolet radiation penetrating the atmosphere of Mars and destroying organic compounds in the soil. Although Mars' atmosphere was at one time rich in carbon dioxide and thus thick enough to protect its surface from the harmful rays of the sun, the carbon dioxide had gradually left the atmosphere and been converted into rocks. This means that even if life had gotten a start on early Mars, it could not have survived the exposure to ultraviolet radiation that occurred when the atmosphere thinned. Mars never developed a protective layer of ozone as Earth did.

Despite the disappointing Viking results, there are those who still keep open the possibility of life on Mars. They point out that the Viking data cannot be considered the final word on Martian life because the two landers sampled only limited—and uninteresting—sites. The Viking landing sites were not chosen for what they might tell of the planet's biology. They were chosen primarily because they appeared to be safe for landing a spacecraft. The landing sites were on parts of the Martian plains that appeared relatively featureless according to orbital photographs.

The type of terrain that these researchers suggest may be a possible hiding place for active life has an Earthly parallel: the ice-free region of southern Victoria Land, Antarctica, where the temperatures in some dry valleys average below zero. Organisms known as endoliths, a form of blue-green algae that has adapted to this harsh environment, were found living inside certain translucent, porous rocks in these Antarctic valleys. The argument based on this discovery is that if life did exist on early Mars, it is possible that it escaped worsening conditions by similarly seeking refuge in rocks. Skeptics object, however, that Mars in its present state is simply too dry, even compared with Antarctic valleys, to sustain any life whatsoever.

no organic material b/c UV?

¶4 There is some speculation around why organic materials are absent; some scientists believe it was the result of intense UV light.

may be life elsewhere, testing locations limited

¶5 Scientists haven't given up; more research is needed, and they have suggestions about how this research can be better conducted.

how life could exist in rocks

¶6 Although Earth and Mars are very different planets, there is one place in Antarctica that might allow us to study the development of life in very dry places without leaving the planet; there are skeptics, though.

Should Mars eventually prove barren of life, as some suspect, then this finding would have
[90] a significant impact on the current view of the chemical origins of life. It could be much more difficult to get life started on a planet than scientists thought before the Viking landings.

impact if no life — ¶7 If Mars does prove to be completely free of life, this finding could still impact our collective scientific knowledge.

The possibility exists, of course, that our
[95] definition of what constitutes life may not hold true throughout the universe. It has long been speculated that our current belief that all life must contain carbon, oxygen, calcium, chlorine, potassium, and phosphorous simply because this holds true on our
[100] planet might be too narrow a view. In 2010, NASA scientists believed they had discovered a bacterium that used arsenic in place of phosphorous, though these exciting findings later proved to be incorrect. The possibility remains, however, that future
[105] astrobiologists exploring the Martian surface from 140 million miles away might be able to make use of a more advanced definition of what we call "life."

definition of life may change — ¶8 Our very definition of life may be incorrect. There is still much more to learn in the field of astrobiology!

BIG PICTURE SUMMARY

Main idea: Despite initial tests for Martian life yielding inconclusive results, the continued search for possible life-forms could yield valuable information.

Author's purpose: To inform the reader about both a brief history of and the predicted future of astrobiology discoveries.

Now, try another passage on your own. Use the ACT Reading strategies and tactics you've been learning to read and map this passage as quickly and accurately as you can.

Chapter 16
ACT Reading Passage Strategies

Try on Your Own

Directions: Actively read and map the following passage by:

1. mark keywords (opinion and emphasis, connection and contrast, or evidence and example)
2. jotting down brief, accurate passage notes that reflect good paraphrases of each paragraph
3. summarizing the big picture

When you're done, compare your work to that of an expert in the explanations found at the end of the chapter.

INFORMATIONAL: This passage is adapted from an article about modern architecture.

Fallingwater, a small country house constructed in 1936, stands as perhaps the greatest residential building achievement of the American architect Frank Lloyd Wright.
[5] In designing the dwelling for the Pittsburgh millionaire Edgar J. Kaufmann, Wright was confronted with an unusually challenging site beside a waterfall deep in a Pennsylvania ravine. However, Wright viewed this difficult location
[10] not as an obstacle but as a unique opportunity to put his architectural ideas into concrete form.

In the early 1930s, Edgar J. Kaufmann's son, Edgar J. Kaufmann Jr., studied with Wright as an apprentice at Wright's Taliesin Studio in Spring
[15] Green, Wisconsin. At the time, architecture critics deemed Wright's style anachronistic and assumed that his career was coming to an end. Kaufmann Jr., on the other hand, greatly admired Wright's work and was delighted to introduce his parents
[20] to the esteemed architect. Shortly thereafter, the Kaufmanns asked Wright to design Fallingwater.

The site Kaufmann chose for his country getaway was originally the location of a cabin in Mill Run, Pennsylvania, that he offered as a vacation
[25] retreat for the numerous employees he oversaw at Kaufmann's Department Store, located in downtown Pittsburgh. When the Great Depression struck, Kaufmann's employees could no longer afford the cost of traveling more than 60 miles to Mill Run,
[30] and Kaufmann decided that the land, a wooded area nestled along the banks of a mountain stream called Bear Run, was an ideal location for a vacation home. Kaufmann had assumed that the home would stand at the bottom of a nearby waterfall, where it would
[35] provide a perfect venue from which to appreciate the view. However, Wright had other ideas. When Wright showed Kaufmann his plans, Kaufmann initially balked, but Wright convinced him that incorporating the falls into the design of the house
[40] was far preferable. In the end, Wright was able to turn Fallingwater into an artistic link between untamed nature and domestic tranquility—and a masterpiece in his brilliant career.

Edgar J. Kaufmann's original plan to build
[45] his house on the ample flat land at the bottom of the waterfall would indisputably have proven less challenging. Wright's more daring response to the site required builders to construct the house on a small stone precipice atop the falls. Wright
[50] further proposed extending the living room of the house out over the rushing water and making use of modern building techniques so that no vertical supports would be needed to hold up the room. Wright brilliantly utilized the "cantilever"
[55] technique, in which steel rods are laid inside a shelf of concrete, eliminating the need for external supports. Unfortunately, however, the builders did not employ an adequate amount of reinforcing steel to support the first floor. Kaufmann had hired
[60] consulting engineers to review Wright's design prior to Fallingwater's construction, but Wright dismissed the engineers' claims that the main floor girders needed additional support. Over time, the first floor cantilever began to sag, and in 2002, a technique
[65] called post-tensioning was used to permanently repair the gradual collapse.

Despite Wright's miscalculation, Fallingwater, as a whole, is an impressive structure. Rather than allowing the environment to determine the placement and shape of the house, Wright sought to construct a home that intentionally confronted and interacted with the landscape. Each bedroom has its own terrace, and cornerless windows open outward so that window panes do not obstruct the spectacular view. In addition, Fallingwater contains a great many traditional and natural building materials. The home's 5,300-square foot expanse includes custom-designed black walnut wood furniture and walls and floors constructed of locally sourced sandstone. The boulders that provide the foundation for the house also extend up through the floor and form part of the fireplace. A staircase in the living room extends down to an enclosed bathing pool at the top of the waterfall. To Wright, the ideal dwelling in this spot was not simply a modern extravaganza or a direct extension of natural surroundings; rather, it was a little of both.

Architecture enthusiasts have taken a wide range of approaches to understanding this unique building. Some have asserted that the house exalts the artist's triumph over untamed nature. Others have compared Wright's building to a cave, providing a psychological and physical safe haven from a harsh, violent world. The members of the American Institute of Architects named Fallingwater the "best all-time work of American architecture," and the Western Pennsylvania Conservancy, which has owned and preserved Fallingwater since 1963, hails the building as an inspiration.

Edgar Kaufmann Jr. may have summed up the innovation and awe of Fallingwater best when he said, "Wright understood that people were creatures of nature; hence, an architecture which conformed to nature would conform to what was basic in people. . . . Sociability and privacy are both available, as are the comforts of home and the adventures of the seasons." This, then, is Frank Lloyd Wright's achievement in Fallingwater: a home that connects the human and the natural for the invigoration and exaltation of both.

Chapter 16
ACT Reading Passage Strategies

How Much Have You Learned?

Directions: Take five minutes to actively read the following passage by:

1. noting the keywords
2. jotting down passage notes next to each paragraph
3. summarizing the big picture

When you're done, compare your work to the explanations at the end of the chapter.

INFORMATIONAL: This passage is adapted from an article about how humans develop language.

  The influential theory of universal grammar (UG) postulates that all humans have an innate, genetic understanding of certain grammatical "rules," which are universal across all languages
[5] and absolutely not affected by environment. The idea of such a universal grammar has a long history, starting with Roger Bacon's thirteenth-century book *Overview of Grammar* and continuing through the Renaissance with attempts to construct
[10] an ideal language. In the eighteenth century, the first edition of the Encyclopedia Britannica included a section dedicated to universal grammar. In modern times, however, the linguistic theory of universal grammar is most closely associated
[15] with Noam Chomsky, who did much to codify and popularize it in the 1950s–1970s. According to Chomsky, we are all born with a knowledge of "deep structure," basic linguistic constructions that allow us, if not to understand all languages, at least
[20] to understand how they are put together. From there, we have only to learn how the parameters are set in our particular language in order to create an unlimited number of "correct" utterances.

  For example, he suggests that structure
[25] dependency—a rule that says that sentences are defined by phrase structure, not linear structure—is inherent to all languages, with minor variations. Thus, the meaning of a sentence is really dependent on the meaning of its phrases, rather than each
[30] individual word. In addition, the head parameter rule stipulates that each phrase contains a "head" (main) word, and all languages have the head word in essentially the same position within the phrase.

  Chomsky's famous sentence "Colorless green ideas
[35] sleep furiously" exemplifies this theory of universal grammar—while the sentence itself is meaningless, it is easily recognizable as a grammatical sentence that fits a basic but higher level of organization. "Furiously sleep ideas green colorless," on the other
[40] hand, is obviously not a grammatical sentence, and it is difficult to discern any kind of meaning in it. For other evidence to support this theory, Chomsky points to our relative ease in translating one language to another; again, while we may
[45] not necessarily recognize individual words in an unfamiliar language, we can certainly recognize and engage with sentences that are grammatical.

  This evidence is still fairly theoretical, receiving play mostly in the linguistic sphere rather than in
[50] the biological sciences. Most of those researching the theory seem more concerned with attempting to draw universal parallels across languages than with searching for biological evidence of such phenomena. We might ask: Where exactly are
[55] these universal grammar constraints located in our genetic code? How and when are they altered by natural evolutionary processes—or do they remain relatively unaltered and non-mutated from generation to generation? As both languages and
[60] human beings evolve over time, does UG also evolve or stay relatively stable?

  Even within the linguistic sphere, Chomsky's theory has drawn criticism. Some scientists suggest that by ignoring the role of environment
[65] in language development, Chomsky completely discredits the possibly important effect our surroundings could have on language development. Still other researchers say that universal grammar

is not nearly as ordered and absolute as Chomsky and other linguists make it out to be—that merely identifying similarities in different languages does not prove that a universal grammar underlies them. They suggest that since the universal grammar theory is not falsifiable, it is in fact pseudoscientific rather than scientific, the result of our flawed human tendency to impose order where there is none.

More recent researchers have begun to advocate that, rather than focusing on explaining linguistic similarities among various languages, we instead acknowledge the evolutionary roots of language and look specifically for neurobiological explanations. Claiming that the humanistic exploration of universal grammar is too abstract, they recommend that we instead view language (and grammar) as a function of the brain. Some progress has been made in studying the neurobiology of language; for instance, scientists have identified specific regions of the brain that handle language. However, these findings are simple and preliminary, offering little insight into the vast intricacy of human language use.

Neither linguistics nor biology alone is sufficient to understand the foundations of language. Language is unbelievably complex: even a single word can offer several definitions and associations. Thus, any single connection between, say, two languages causes those myriad associations to become oversimplified and sterile. For example, simply pointing out that the subject of a sentence is in the same position in Turkish and English as an illustration of UG merely acknowledges that single linguistic association, while failing to consider any social circumstances that may cause the mind to modify that grammar. In short, say scientists, not until we create a better marriage between biology and linguistics—and a better understanding of the human brain—can we even begin to address the complexities of human language development.

Chapter 16
ACT Reading Passage Strategies

Reflect

Directions: Take a few minutes to recall what you've learned and what you've been practicing in this chapter. Consider the following questions, jot down your best answer for each one, and then compare your reflections to the expert responses on the following page. Use your level of confidence to determine what to do next.

1. Why do ACT experts note keywords as they read?
   _____
   _____
   _____

2. What are the three categories of keywords? Provide some examples from each category.

   1. _____
      - Examples:
        - _____
        - _____
        - _____
   2. _____
      - Examples:
        - _____
        - _____
        - _____
   3. _____
      - Examples:
        - _____
        - _____
        - _____

3. Why do ACT experts jot down passage notes on their scratch paper or on their test booklet?
   _____
   _____
   _____

4. What are the elements of a strong big picture summary?
   _____
   _____
   _____

Responses

1. Why do ACT experts note keywords as they read?

Keywords indicate what the author finds important, express their point of view about the subject and details of the passage, and signal key points in the passage structure. Keywords are the pieces of text that help test takers see which parts of the passage are likely to be mentioned in questions and help the test taker to distinguish between correct and incorrect answer choices about those parts of the passage.

2. What are the three categories of keywords? Provide some examples from each category.

   1. *Opinion and emphasis*
      - Examples:
        - *indeed*
        - *quite*
        - *masterfully*
        - *inadequate*
   2. *Connection and contrast*
      - Examples:
        - *furthermore*
        - *plus*
        - *however*
        - *on the contrary*
   3. *Evidence and example*
      - Examples:
        - *according to*
        - *since*
        - *for instance*
        - *such as*

3. Why do ACT experts jot down passage notes on their scratch paper or on their test booklet?

Passage notes help the test taker research questions that ask about details, examples, and arguments mentioned in the passage by providing a "map" to their location in the text. Passage notes can also help students answer questions about the passage structure and the purpose of a specific paragraph.

4. What are the elements of a strong big picture summary?

A strong big picture summary prepares a test taker to answer any question about the main idea of the passage or the author's primary or overall purpose in writing it. After reading the passage, ACT experts pause to ask, "What is the main idea of the entire passage?" and "Why did the author write it?"

Chapter 16
ACT Reading Passage Strategies

Next Steps

If you answered most questions correctly in the "How Much Have You Learned?" section, and if your responses to the Reflect questions were similar to those of the ACT expert, then consider strategic reading and passage mapping areas of strength and move on to the next chapter. Come back to this topic periodically to prevent yourself from getting rusty.

If you don't yet feel confident, review those parts of this chapter that you have not yet mastered. Then, try the questions you missed again. As always, be sure to review the explanations closely. Then go online (**kaptest.com/login**) for more practice. If you haven't already registered your book, do so at **kaptest.com/moreonline**.

GO ONLINE

kaptest.com/login

Part 4
ACT READING

Answers and Explanations

Try on Your Own

INFORMATIONAL: This passage is adapted from an article about modern architecture.

Fallingwater, a small country house constructed in 1936, stands as perhaps the greatest residential building achievement of the American architect Frank Lloyd Wright.
5 In designing the dwelling for the Pittsburgh millionaire Edgar J. Kaufmann, Wright was confronted with an unusually challenging site beside a waterfall deep in a Pennsylvania ravine. However, Wright viewed this difficult location
10 not as an obstacle but as a unique opportunity to put his architectural ideas into concrete form.

In the early 1930s, Edgar J. Kaufmann's son, Edgar J. Kaufmann Jr., studied with Wright as an apprentice at Wright's Taliesin Studio in Spring
15 Green, Wisconsin. At the time, architecture critics deemed Wright's style anachronistic and assumed that his career was coming to an end. Kaufmann Jr., on the other hand, greatly admired Wright's work and was delighted to introduce his parents
20 to the esteemed architect. Shortly thereafter, the Kaufmanns asked Wright to design Fallingwater.

The site Kaufmann chose for his country getaway was originally the location of a cabin in Mill Run, Pennsylvania, that he offered as a vacation
25 retreat for the numerous employees he oversaw at Kaufmann's Department Store, located in downtown Pittsburgh. When the Great Depression struck, Kaufmann's employees could no longer afford the cost of traveling more than 60 miles to Mill Run,
30 and Kaufmann decided that the land, a wooded area nestled along the banks of a mountain stream called Bear Run, was an ideal location for a vacation home. Kaufmann had assumed that the home would stand at the bottom of a nearby waterfall, where it would
35 provide a perfect venue from which to appreciate the view. However, Wright had other ideas. When Wright showed Kaufmann his plans, Kaufmann initially balked, but Wright convinced him that incorporating the falls into the design of the house

Fallingwater: architectural achievement by FLW

how FLW came to design Fallingwater

location; below vs. on falls

ANALYSIS

Pre-passage blurb: The blurb tells you that the topic of this passage is modern architecture.

¶1 This paragraph introduces you to both Fallingwater and Frank Lloyd Wright. Fallingwater is significant not because of its difficult location but because of how Wright used the location as an opportunity to showcase his unique architectural ideas.

¶2 Despite the opinion of critics that his career was coming to an end, Wright was commissioned to build Fallingwater after the Kaufmann family was introduced to him by their son.

¶3 Kaufmann chose an ideal location for his vacation home: the bottom of a waterfall. Wright was able to convince him to build the home around the falls, which linked nature and domestic life.

was far preferable. In the end, Wright was able to turn Fallingwater into an artistic link between untamed nature and domestic tranquility—and a masterpiece in his brilliant career.

Edgar J. Kaufmann's original plan to build his house on the ample flat land at the bottom of the waterfall would indisputably have proven less challenging. Wright's more daring response to the site required builders to construct the house on a small stone precipice atop the falls. Wright further proposed extending the living room of the house out over the rushing water and making use of modern building techniques so that no vertical supports would be needed to hold up the room. Wright brilliantly utilized the "cantilever" technique, in which steel rods are laid inside a shelf of concrete, eliminating the need for external supports. Unfortunately, however, the builders did not employ an adequate amount of reinforcing steel to support the first floor. Kaufmann had hired consulting engineers to review Wright's design prior to Fallingwater's construction, but Wright dismissed the engineers' claims that the main floor girders needed additional support. Over time, the first floor cantilever began to sag, and in 2002, a technique called post-tensioning was used to permanently repair the gradual collapse.

Despite Wright's miscalculation, Fallingwater, as a whole, is an impressive structure. Rather than allowing the environment to determine the placement and shape of the house, Wright sought to construct a home that intentionally confronted and interacted with the landscape. Each bedroom has its own terrace, and cornerless windows open outward so that window panes do not obstruct the spectacular view. In addition, Fallingwater contains a great many traditional and natural building materials. The home's 5,300-square foot expanse includes custom-designed black walnut wood furniture and walls and floors constructed of locally sourced sandstone. The boulders that provide the foundation for the house also extend up through the floor and form part of the fireplace. A staircase in the living room extends down to an enclosed bathing pool at the top of

challenges

¶4 Kaufmann had a safer plan to build his home at the bottom of the falls, but Wright was more daring. He used a technique that allowed the living room to extend over the falls. Although this design was brilliant (even though it ignored the engineers' recommendation for more support), it did need repairs in 2002.

house interacts w/nature

¶5 This paragraph lists several examples of how Wright was able to turn Fallingwater into a masterpiece that combined modern design with nature.

85 the waterfall. To Wright, the ideal dwelling in this spot was not simply a modern extravaganza or a direct extension of natural surroundings; rather, it was a little of both.

Architecture enthusiasts have taken a wide
90 range of approaches to understanding this unique building. Some have asserted that the house exalts the artist's triumph over untamed nature. Others have compared Wright's building to a cave, providing a psychological and physical safe
95 haven from a harsh, violent world. The members of the American Institute of Architects named Fallingwater the "best all-time work of American architecture," and the Western Pennsylvania Conservancy, which has owned and preserved
100 Fallingwater since 1963, hails the building as an inspiration.

critical responses

¶6 Paragraph 6 gives you insight into the opinion of other architects, which was overwhelmingly positive.

Edgar Kaufmann Jr. may have summed up the innovation and awe of Fallingwater best when he said, "Wright understood that people were
105 creatures of nature; hence, an architecture which conformed to nature would conform to what was basic in people. . . . Sociability and privacy are both available, as are the comforts of home and the adventures of the seasons." This, then, is
110 Frank Lloyd Wright's achievement in Fallingwater: a home that connects the human and the natural for the invigoration and exaltation of both.

connects human and nature

¶7 The conclusion to the passage sums up by revealing Kaufmann's thoughts on Fallingwater: a home that connects humans with nature for the benefit of both.

BIG PICTURE SUMMARY

Main idea: Fallingwater, an unusual and impressive building, was an architectural achievement by Frank Lloyd Wright.

Author's purpose: To inform the reader about the history of a unique piece of architecture.

As with the other passages in this chapter, don't worry about whether you used the exact language found in the expert's passage map and big picture summary. Instead, focus on how the expert used the skills and strategies outlined here to prepare herself to tackle the question set with speed and confidence.

Chapter 16
ACT Reading Passage Strategies

How Much Have You Learned?

INFORMATIONAL: This passage is adapted from an article about how humans develop language.

The influential theory of universal grammar (UG) postulates that all humans have an innate, genetic understanding of certain grammatical "rules," which are universal across all languages
[5] and absolutely not affected by environment. The idea of such a universal grammar has a long history, starting with Roger Bacon's thirteenth-century book *Overview of Grammar* and continuing through the Renaissance with attempts to construct
[10] an ideal language. In the eighteenth century, the first edition of the Encyclopedia Britannica included a section dedicated to universal grammar. In modern times, however, the linguistic theory of universal grammar is most closely associated
[15] with Noam Chomsky, who did much to codify and popularize it in the 1950s–1970s. According to Chomsky, we are all born with a knowledge of "deep structure," basic linguistic constructions that allow us, if not to understand all languages, at least
[20] to understand how they are put together. From there, we have only to learn how the parameters are set in our particular language in order to create an unlimited number of "correct" utterances.

For example, he suggests that structure
[25] dependency—a rule that says that sentences are defined by phrase structure, not linear structure—is inherent to all languages, with minor variations. Thus, the meaning of a sentence is really dependent on the meaning of its phrases, rather than each
[30] individual word. In addition, the head parameter rule stipulates that each phrase contains a "head" (main) word, and all languages have the head word in essentially the same position within the phrase. Chomsky's famous sentence "Colorless green ideas
[35] sleep furiously" exemplifies this theory of universal grammar—while the sentence itself is meaningless, it is easily recognizable as a grammatical sentence that fits a basic but higher level of organization. "Furiously sleep ideas green colorless," on the other
[40] hand, is obviously not a grammatical sentence, and it is difficult to discern any kind of meaning in it. For other evidence to support this theory,

ANALYSIS

Pre-passage blurb: The blurb tells you that the article is about how humans develop language.

theory of UG through history

¶1 The theory of UG has been prevalent throughout history. It states that all humans have an innate understanding of universal grammar rules. These rules are not affected by environment and are universal across all languages.

ex. of rules that support UG

¶2 This paragraph gives two specific examples of rules that support Chomsky's theory of UG. The structure dependency rule says that sentences are defined by phrases, and the head parameter rule states that each phrase has a main word that is in the same position across languages. Chomsky also points to the ease by which we can translate from one language to another as further evidence to support his theory.

Chomsky points to our relative ease in translating one language to another; again, while we may
45 not necessarily recognize individual words in an unfamiliar language, we can certainly recognize and engage with sentences that are grammatical.

This evidence is still fairly theoretical, receiving play mostly in the linguistic sphere rather than in
50 the biological sciences. Most of those researching the theory seem more concerned with attempting to draw universal parallels across languages than with searching for biological evidence of such phenomena. We might ask: Where exactly are
55 these universal grammar constraints located in our genetic code? How and when are they altered by natural evolutionary processes—or do they remain relatively unaltered and non-mutated from generation to generation? As both languages and
60 human beings evolve over time, does UG also evolve or stay relatively stable?

ev. = theoretical, biological?

¶3 This paragraph tells you that the theory of UG is prominent mostly in the area of linguistics and not in biology. There are genetic questions relating to the theory: is UG evolving or stable over time?

Even within the linguistic sphere, Chomsky's theory has drawn criticism. Some scientists suggest that by ignoring the role of environment
65 in language development, Chomsky completely discredits the possibly important effect our surroundings could have on language development. Still other researchers say that universal grammar is not nearly as ordered and absolute as Chomsky
70 and other linguists make it out to be—that merely identifying similarities in different languages does not prove that a universal grammar underlies them. They suggest that since the universal grammar theory is not falsifiable, it is in fact
75 pseudoscientific rather than scientific, the result of our flawed human tendency to impose order where there is none.

criticism

¶4 Paragraph 4 gives you insight into what critics think. Some say Chomsky's theory ignores the influence environment could have on language. Others say that similarities and differences among languages do not mean that a universal theory ties them together. There is a question as to whether the theory is science at all.

More recent researchers have begun to advocate that, rather than focusing on explaining
80 linguistic similarities among various languages, we instead acknowledge the evolutionary roots of language and look specifically for neurobiological explanations. Claiming that the humanistic exploration of universal grammar is too abstract,
85 they recommend that we instead view language (and grammar) as a function of the brain. Some progress has been made in studying the

lang. and brain

¶5 Recently, researchers have looked for neurobiological explanations for language. So far, this brain research has offered little insight into the intricacies of human language.

neurobiology of language; for instance, scientists have identified specific regions of the brain that handle language. However, these findings are simple and preliminary, offering little insight into the vast intricacy of human language use.

Neither linguistics nor biology alone is sufficient to understand the foundations of language. Language is unbelievably complex: even a single word can offer several definitions and associations. Thus, any single connection between, say, two languages causes those myriad associations to become oversimplified and sterile. For example, simply pointing out that the subject of a sentence is in the same position in Turkish and English as an illustration of UG merely acknowledges that single linguistic association, while failing to consider any social circumstances that may cause the mind to modify that grammar. In short, say scientists, not until we create a better marriage between biology and linguistics—and a better understanding of the human brain—can we even begin to address the complexities of human language development.

biology & linguistics both needed

¶6 In this concluding paragraph, you learn that it is necessary to better merge biology and linguistics to understand the complexities of human language; anything less would be an oversimplification of a complex process.

BIG PICTURE SUMMARY

Main idea: Chomsky's theory of innate linguistic structure is popular among linguists but does not address biological influences on language development.

Author's purpose: To inform the reader about the limitations and possibilities of universal grammar.

[CHAPTER 17]

IDENTIFYING QUESTION TYPES

LEARNING OBJECTIVES

After completing this chapter, you will be able to:

- Unpack ACT Reading question stems by
  - distinguishing among the five ACT Reading question types
  - determining if the correct answer is best found by researching the passage text or by consulting your big picture summary

Part 4
ACT READING

How Much Do You Know?

Directions: In this chapter, you'll learn to unpack ACT Reading question stems (step 1 of the ACT Reading Question Method). Unpacking a question stem means pinpointing your task (as identified by the question type) and noting where the answer will be found (a specific reference within the passage text or in your big picture summary). For your reference as you complete this quiz, here are the ACT Reading question types:

- **Global**—asks about big picture ideas, including both main idea and tone
- **Detail**—asks about explicitly stated facts or details
- **Inference**—asks about points that are unstated but strongly suggested
- **Function**—asks why or how the author wrote specific parts of the text
- **Vocab-in-Context**—asks for the intended meaning of a word as it is used in the passage, or the best word to fit the meaning of a phrase in the passage.

For each of the following question stems, identify the question type, cite the language in the stem that helped you identify that type, and indicate where you would begin to research the question: either your big picture summary or a specific part of the text.

Example

The passage most strongly suggests that public transportation options in rural locations:

Question type: *Inference*

Identifying language: *"most strongly suggests"*

Research where? *passage, where author discusses public transportation in rural areas*

---

1. The main purpose of the passage is to:

    Question type:
    Identifying language:
    Research where?

2. In the context of the passage, the final sentence of the second paragraph mainly serves to:

    Question type:
    Identifying language:
    Research where?

3. According to the passage, why did the narrator's grandfather and other recent immigrants say "*ya amerikanets*"?

    Question type:
    Identifying language:
    Research where?

4. According to the passage, what made settling in America a difficult time for the narrator's grandfather?

    Question type:
    Identifying language:
    Research where?

5. The passage suggests that the "advantage" the narrator's grandfather found in telling people about his relationship with Russia was:

    Question type:
    Identifying language:
    Research where?

6. In the passage, the author's grandfather traveled to Russia because:

    Question type:
    Identifying language:
    Research where?

Chapter 17
Identifying Question Types

7. The passage author mentions the typical view people have of real estate agents to:

   Question type:
   Identifying language:
   Research where?

8. As it is used in line 105, the word *realization* most nearly means:

   Question type:
   Identifying language:
   Research where?

9. It can reasonably be inferred that author's grandfather was attracted to real estate as a profession because:

   Question type:
   Identifying language:
   Research where?

Part 4
ACT READING

Answers and Explanations

How Much Do You Know?

1. The main purpose of the passage is to:

   Question type: Global
   Identifying language: "main purpose"
   Research where? big picture summary

2. In the context of the passage, the final sentence of the second paragraph mainly serves to:

   Question type: Function
   Identifying language: "mainly serves to"
   Research where? passage map, second paragraph

3. According to the passage, why did the narrator's grandfather and other recent immigrants say "*ya amerikanets*"?

   Question type: Detail
   Identifying language: "According to the passage"
   Research where? passage map to find the paragraph where the narrator's grandfather and other immigrants say this

4. According to the passage, what made settling in America a difficult time for the narrator's grandfather?

   Question type: Detail
   Identifying language: "According to the passage"
   Research where? passage notes to find the paragraph where the grandfather's move to America is mentioned

5. The passage suggests that the "advantage" the narrator's grandfather found in telling people about his relationship with Russia was:

   Question type: Inference
   Identifying language: "The passage suggests"
   Research where? passage map to find the paragraph where the grandfather is telling people about his relationship with Russia

6. In the passage, the author's grandfather traveled to Russia because:

   Question type: Detail
   Identifying language: "in the passage"
   Research where? passage map to find where the grandfather's travel to Russia is discussed

7. The passage author mentions the typical view people have of real estate agents to:

   Question type: Function
   Identifying language: "the passage author mentions . . . to"
   Research where? passage map to locate the typical view about real estate agents

8. As it is used in line 105, the word *realization* most nearly means:

   Question type: Vocab-in-Context
   Identifying language: "the word . . . most nearly means"
   Research where? passage, line 105

9. It can reasonably be inferred that author's grandfather was attracted to real estate as a profession because:

   Question type: Inference
   Identifying language: "can reasonably be inferred"
   Research where? passage map to find where the author's grandfather discussed his work as a real estate agent

HOW TO UNPACK ACT READING QUESTION STEMS

LEARNING OBJECTIVES

After this lesson, you will be able to:

- Unpack ACT Reading question stems by
  - distinguishing among the five ACT Reading question types
  - determining if the correct answer is best found by researching the passage text or by consulting your big picture summary

To unpack question stems like these

1. The main purpose of the passage is to:
2. The passage most strongly suggests that an important difference between Mars and Earth is that, unlike Earth, Mars:
3. According to the passage, which of the following describes the atmosphere of Mars?
4. The passage suggests that Mars is void of organic compounds because:
5. As it is used in line 88, the word *barren* most nearly means:
6. In the context of the passage, how does the evolution of life on Earth relate to the possibility that life may exist in Martian rocks?
7. The author mentions blue-green algae in the sixth paragraph to:
8. It can reasonably be inferred from the passage that the possibility mentioned in line 94 refers to:
9. In the passage, which of the following is listed as a compound that is necessary for life?

You need to know this

There are five question types, each of which defines a specific task:

- **Global**—asks about big picture ideas, including both main idea and tone
  - The point of view from which the passage is told is best described as:
  - The main purpose of the passage is to:
  - The passage as a whole can best be described as:
- **Detail**—asks about explicitly stated facts or details
  - According to the passage, what makes a tropical beach a specialized area?
  - According to the passage, which of the following is true of the New York City subway system?
  - Which of the following details does the author emphasize about non–rush hour commuters?
- **Inference**—asks about points that are unstated but supported by the passage
  - The passage most strongly suggests that the Mayan people were the first to flourish in coastal Mexico because they:
  - Based on the passage, which choice best describes a claim that critics of the current subway maintenance plan would likely make?

Part 4
ACT READING

- **Function**—asks why or how the author wrote specific parts of the text
  - The comparison between a gymnasium and an open market in paragraph 4 is meant to:
  - In the third paragraph, the discussion of two specific subway lines (lines 35–39) primarily serves to:
  - The narrator describes what she is seeing as she travels in lines 54–60 to:
- **Vocab-in-Context**—asks for the intended meaning of a word as it is used in the passage
  - As it is used in line 26, the word *dictate* most nearly means:
  - As it is used in line 33, the word *labyrinthine* most nearly means:
  - As it is used in line 33, the phrase *lost in translation* refers to:

There are specific types of clues in ACT Reading question stems that can help you answer questions more accurately and efficiently:

- **Line numbers**—Mentions of "line 53" or "lines 37–40," often in parentheses, tend to stand out and give you a clear place to start your research.
- **Paragraph numbers**—A reference to "paragraph 5," "the third paragraph," or "the last two paragraphs" is not as precise as a line reference but will still give you an idea of where to look. Start with your passage notes for the paragraph.
- **Quoted text** (often accompanied by line numbers)—Check the context of the quoted term or phrase to see what the author meant by it in the passage.
- **Proper nouns**—Names like "Professor James," "World War II," and "Baltimore" will likely stand out in question stems due to the capitalization. If a particular proper noun is discussed in only part of the passage, it narrows the range of text you have to research.
- **Specific content clues**—Sometimes a question stem will repeat terminology used in part of the passage, like "federalism" or "action potentials." Use your passage map to direct your research to the right part of the passage.
- **Whole passage clues**—If a question lacks specific content clues but refers to the passage as a whole or to the author in general, you are likely dealing with a Global question or an open-ended Inference question, which should lead you to your big picture summary rather than to rereading parts of the text.

You need to do this

ACT READING QUESTION METHOD

Step 1. Unpack the question stem

Step 2. Research the answer

Step 3. Predict the answer

Step 4. Find the one correct answer

Step 1. Unpack the question stem

- Identify the question type and anticipate how it will need to be answered.
- Note research clues that indicate how best to research the correct answer.

You will complete Steps 2, 3, and 4 in Answering Reading Questions.

Chapter 17
Identifying Question Types

Why distinguish question types in ACT Reading?

Unpacking the question stem puts you in control. You'll know exactly what the question is asking, where to find the correct answer, and what form the correct answer will take.

- **Global:** The correct answer must take the entire passage into account. A choice that reflects only part of the passage is incorrect.
- **Detail:** The correct answer must be stated in the passage explicitly. A choice that is not directly stated in the passage is incorrect.
- **Inference:** The correct answer will be a conclusion that can be drawn from the passage. A choice that draws too strong of a conclusion from the evidence available in the passage is incorrect.
- **Function:** The correct answer will say *why* a certain detail is included. Look up the detail and then ask yourself what the author was trying to accomplish by putting it there.
- **Vocab-in-Context:** The correct answer will give the meaning of a word as it is used in the context of the passage, or the word that most nearly means a phrase from the passage. Choices that connect to the common meanings of the word are often incorrect.

Correct answers to Reading questions are never random or vague. They are tailored to the precise language of the stem, so being able to distinguish the question types will save you time and eliminate confusion during the test.

Explanations

1. This is a Global question. The identifying language in the question stem is "the main purpose." You can locate support for the correct answer in your big picture summary and passage map notes.

2. This is an Inference question. The identifying language in the question stem is "The passage most strongly suggests." You can locate support for the correct answer in the passage, using your passage map notes to help guide you to the answer more efficiently.

3. This is a Detail question. The identifying language in the question stem is "According to the passage." You can locate the correct answer in the passage, using your passage map notes to guide you to the correct paragraph more efficiently.

4. This is an Inference question. The identifying language in the question stem is "suggests." You can use your passage map to locate where organic compounds are discussed and learn why they are absent on Mars.

5. This is a Vocab-in-Context question. The identifying language in the question stem is "as it is used in line 88" and "most nearly means." You can locate support for the correct answer by reading the entire sentence that includes the word and more, if needed.

6. This is an Inference question. The identifying language in the question stem is not as clear, but the more open-ended phrasing is a clue that it might be Inference rather than Detail. You can locate support for the correct answer in the passage, using your passage map to figure out where the researchers talked about potential life in Martian rocks.

7. This is a Function question. The identifying language in the question stem is "The author mentions . . . to." You can locate support for the correct answer by going back to the cited example and rereading the entire paragraph.

8. This is an Inference question. The identifying language in the question stem is the word *inferred*. You can locate support for the correct answer in the passage by going to line 94, rereading the sentence, and reviewing your big picture summary for a reminder of the passage as a whole, if needed.

9. This is a Detail question. The identifying language in the question stem is that the question asks for something *listed* in the paragraph. You can locate the correct answer by going back to the final paragraph and researching what is stated as a necessary component for life.

Try on Your Own

Directions: Analyze each of the following question stems by:

1. naming the question type
2. identifying the word or phrase that describes your task
3. noting how best to research the correct answer (research the text or consult the big picture summary)

1. The passage as a whole can best be described as a:

   Question type:
   Identifying language:
   Research where?

2. According to the passage, architecture critics regarded Frank Lloyd Wright's career prior to Fallingwater's construction (lines 15–17) as:

   Question type:
   Identifying language:
   Research where?

3. It can be reasonably inferred that the site chosen for Fallingwater was:

   Question type:
   Identifying language:
   Research where?

4. The author mostly likely mentions the phrases "black walnut wood" and "locally sourced sandstone" (lines 78–80) to emphasize which of the following points?

   Question type:
   Identifying language:
   Research where?

5. Which of the following details explains the advantage of a cantilever design?

   Question type:
   Identifying language:
   Research where?

6. It can reasonably be inferred that the miscalculation the author mentions in line 67 refers to:

   Question type:
   Identifying language:
   Research where?

7. In the context of the passage, the information in lines 72–85 mainly serves to:

   Question type:
   Identifying language:
   Research where?

8. Architecture enthusiasts' comparisons of Fallingwater to a cave (lines 93–95) most strongly suggest that the house provides a sense of:

   Question type:
   Identifying language:
   Research where?

9. As it is used in line 112, the phrase *invigoration and exaltation* most nearly means:

   Question type:
   Identifying language:
   Research where?

For any question types that you misidentified, return to the definitions and question stem examples before you try the "How Much Have you Learned?" questions in this chapter.

Chapter 17
Identifying Question Types

How Much Have You Learned?

Directions: For practice identifying Reading question types, analyze each of the following question stems by:

1. naming the question type
2. identifying the word or phrase that describes your task
3. noting how best to research the correct answer (research the text or consult the big picture summary)

1. The point of view from which the passage is told is best described as:

   Question type:
   Identifying language:
   Research where?

2. Based on the passage, how do Renaissance efforts to design a language relate to Chomsky's theory of universal grammar?

   Question type:
   Identifying language:
   Research where?

3. As it is used in line 99, the word *sterile* most nearly means:

   Question type:
   Identifying language:
   Research where?

4. Which of the following statements best summarizes Chomsky's claims in the first paragraph?

   Question type:
   Identifying language:
   Research where?

5. According to the passage, universal grammar's structure dependency rule states that:

   Question type:
   Identifying language:
   Research where?

6. The author most likely uses the quotes "Colorless green ideas sleep furiously" and "Furiously sleep ideas green colorless" to:

   Question type:
   Identifying language:
   Research where?

7. The passage suggests that the researchers mentioned in line 68 believe which of the following?

   Question type:
   Identifying language:
   Research where?

8. One of the main purposes of the fifth paragraph is to:

   Question type:
   Identifying language:
   Research where?

9. As it is used in line 106, the phrase *a better marriage* most nearly means:

   Question type:
   Identifying language:
   Research where?

Part 4
ACT READING

Reflect

Directions: Take a few minutes to recall what you've learned and what you've been practicing in this chapter. Consider the following questions, jot down your best answer for each one, and then compare your reflections to the expert responses on the following page. Use your level of confidence to determine what to do next.

1. Why is it important to always unpack the question stem before proceeding?
   _____
   _____
   _____

2. Can you name five ACT Reading question types and cite words or phrases that identify each one?

   1. _____
      - Identifying language: _____
        _____

   2. _____
      - Identifying language: _____
        _____

   3. _____
      - Identifying language: _____
        _____

   4. _____
      - Identifying language: _____
        _____

   5. _____
      - Identifying language: _____
        _____

3. How will you approach ACT Reading question stems differently as you continue to practice and improve your performance in the Reading section? What are the main differences you see between ACT Reading questions and those you're used to from tests in school?
   _____
   _____
   _____

Responses

1. Why is it important to always unpack the question stem before proceeding?

Knowing the ACT Reading question types makes you a more strategic and efficient reader because the test maker uses the same question types on every test. Fully analyzing each question stem helps you research the text more effectively, predict the correct answer in a way that fits the question stem, and avoid incorrect answers made from misreading the question.

2. Can you name five ACT Reading question types and cite words or phrases that identify each one? (*answers in no particular order*)

   1. Global
      - Identifying language: *the passage as a whole, main purpose of the passage*
   2. Detail
      - Identifying language: *according to the passage, in the passage, which of the following details*
   3. Inference
      - Identifying language: *most strongly suggests, can reasonably be inferred*
   4. Function
      - Identifying language: *in the context of the passage, mainly serves to, the main point of the [second] paragraph*
   5. Vocab-in-Context
      - Identifying language: *as used in line [number], the word most nearly means*

3. How will you approach ACT Reading question stems differently as you continue to practice and improve your performance in the Reading section? What are the main differences you see between ACT Reading questions and those you're used to from tests in school?

There is no one-size-fits-all answer here. Reflect on your own strengths and areas for future growth as you consider how to best improve your performance in the ACT Reading section. Depending on the kinds of classes and teachers you've had in high school, the skills rewarded on ACT Reading questions may be more or less familiar, but test takers need to be aware of their own instincts as readers and break certain reading habits to master this section of the test. The more you give yourself an honest self-assessment, the better prepared you'll be to handle all of the ACT Reading question types confidently.

Next Steps

If you answered most questions correctly in the "How Much Have You Learned?" section, and if your responses to the Reflect questions were similar to those of the ACT expert, then consider identifying reading question types an area of strength and move on to the next chapter. Come back to this topic periodically to prevent yourself from getting rusty.

If you don't yet feel confident, review the material in this chapter, and then try the questions you missed again. As always, be sure to review the explanations closely. Then go online (**kaptest.com/login**) for more practice. If you haven't already registered your book, do so at **kaptest.com/moreonline**.

kaptest.com/login

Part 4
ACT READING

Answers and Explanations

Try on Your Own

1. The passage as a whole can best be described as a:

   Question type: Global
   Identifying language: "passage as a whole"
   Research where? passage map

2. According to the passage, architecture critics regarded Frank Lloyd Wright's career prior to Fallingwater's construction (lines 15–17) as:

   Question type: Detail
   Identifying language: "According to the passage"
   Research where? lines 15–17

3. It can be reasonably inferred that the site chosen for Fallingwater was:

   Question type: Inference
   Identifying language: "It can be reasonably inferred"
   Research where? the paragraph that talks about Fallingwater's location

4. The author mostly likely mentions the phrases "black walnut wood" and "locally sourced sandstone" (lines 78–80) to emphasize which of the following points?

   Question type: Function
   Identifying language: "author most likely mentions"
   Research where? around the cited lines

5. Which of the following details explains the advantage of a cantilever design?

   Question type: Detail
   Identifying language: "Which of the following details"
   Research where? the paragraph that discusses advantages of cantilever design

6. It can reasonably be inferred that the miscalculation the author mentions in line 67 refers to:

   Question type: Inference
   Identifying language: "It can reasonably be inferred"
   Research where? line 67 and the surrounding lines

7. In the context of the passage, the information in lines 72–85 mainly serves to:

   Question type: Function
   Identifying language: "serves to"
   Research where? the cited lines and the passage map to determine how the cited lines fit within the whole

8. Architecture enthusiasts' comparisons of Fallingwater to a cave (lines 93–95) most strongly suggest that the house provides a sense of:

   Question type: Inference
   Identifying language: "most strongly suggests"
   Research where? the cited lines

9. As it is used in line 112, the phrase *invigoration and exaltation* most nearly means:

   Question type: Vocab-in-Context
   Identifying language: "As it is used in line 112 . . . most nearly means"
   Research where? at least the entire sentence that includes the cited phrase

Chapter 17
Identifying Question Types

How Much Have You Learned?

1. The point of view from which the passage is told is best described as:

   Question type: Global
   Identifying language: "point of view from which the passage is told"
   Research where? big picture summary, passage map

2. Based on the passage, how do Renaissance efforts to design a language relate to Chomsky's theory of universal grammar?

   Question type: Inference
   Identifying language: "Based on the passage"
   Research where? passage, where author discusses Renaissance efforts to design a language

3. As it is used in line 99, the word *sterile* most nearly means:

   Question type: Vocab-in-Context
   Identifying language: "most nearly means"
   Research where? passage, line 99

4. Which of the following statements best summarizes Chomsky's claims in the first paragraph?

   Question type: Detail
   Identifying language: "summarizes"
   Research where? passage, the details of paragraph 1

5. According to the passage, universal grammar's structure dependency rule states that:

   Question type: Detail
   Identifying language: "According to the passage"
   Research where? passage, where author discusses structure dependency rule

6. The author most likely uses the quotes "Colorless green ideas sleep furiously" and "Furiously sleep ideas green colorless" to:

   Question type: Function
   Identifying language: "author most likely"
   Research where? passage, where author references the quotes "Colorless green ideas sleep furiously" and "Furiously sleep ideas green colorless," big picture summary, passage map

7. The passage suggests that the researchers mentioned in line 68 believe which of the following?

   Question type: Inference
   Identifying language: "passage suggests"
   Research where? passage, around line 68

8. One of the main purposes of the fifth paragraph is to:

   Question type: Function
   Identifying language: "main purposes of the . . . paragraph"
   Research where? passage, paragraph 5, big picture summary, passage map

9. As it is used in line 106, the phrase *a better marriage* most nearly means:

   Question type: Vocab-in-Context
   Identifying language: "most nearly means"
   Research where? passage, line 106

[CHAPTER 18]

ANSWERING READING QUESTIONS

LEARNING OBJECTIVES

After completing this chapter, you will be able to:
- Research the answer in the passage text or your big picture summary
- Predict the correct answer
- Identify the one correct answer choice

Part 4
ACT READING

How Much Do You Know?

Directions: In this chapter, you'll learn how best to research, predict, and find the correct answers to ACT Reading questions. For this quiz, first take a couple of minutes to refresh your memory of the passage, which you first saw in chapter 16. Then, for each question:

1. research the answer in the passage text or from your big picture summary
2. predict the correct answer in your own words
3. identify the one correct answer

INFORMATIONAL: This passage explores the relationship between the immigrant experience and one person's career choice.

My grandfather was born in a turbulent time in Russia. His non-communist lineage made him unwelcome before he had left the womb. His father, an officer in the Russian army, was
5 considered an enemy of the communist Bolsheviks, so my grandfather lived less than a year in what was his native Moscow and spent most of his younger years moving across Asia. Despite this, he had pride in being Russian, associated with
10 Russians throughout his life, and would frequently quiz me on Russian history. This all in tribute to a country that ended up under hostile rule during the time his mother was pregnant with him.

As a child, exiled to Siberia, my grandfather
15 heard his father tell of the greatness that existed within the country that had forced the family into exile. It was known that, first with his parents, and later as an adult, my grandfather was going to have to seek a new place to call home.
20 Despite this foregone conclusion, Russia was still romanticized, and my grandfather learned to treat the country with reverence. This was in contrast to the sentiments found in other recently exiled Russians, who would not simply lament the actions
25 taken by the country but disparage all eight million square miles. In my family's search for a place to settle, attempting to forge a consistent identity was nearly impossible, as no one knew whether the next location would hold for a month, let alone a year.
30 All hoped for an unattainable "new Moscow."

The first long-term refuge was found, ironically, in China, which would have its own communist revolution. After several years of relative stability, this revolution precipitated the move to the
35 United States. Upon arrival in San Francisco, my grandfather, along with my grandmother and their young son, my father, found other Russian immigrants who were also new to the country. "*Ya amerikanets*," people would say, and despite the fact
40 that they were recent immigrants who associated primarily with those of shared ethnicity and circumstance, they would play the role they desired and repeat "*ya amerikanets*"—"I am American." They would share many stories about their native
45 land, but did not repeat "*ya russkiy*," because being Russian went without saying. While it was clear that this would be the last country my grandfather would reside in and that he wished to become more American, it was perhaps the most confusing
50 of times. It was less a problem of acclimating to an adopted setting and more of dealing with a permanent setting at all. The only consistency throughout the first thirty years of my grandfather's life was the knowledge that every "home" was
55 temporary, and now this was no longer the case. I often wonder if his successful career in the real estate business had anything to do with what must have been a rare transformation of circumstance.

Not only was my grandfather interested in
60 real estate, but he was also keen on the importance of ownership, a naturally discordant view to that of the then Soviet Union. Thus, selling homes became a purpose in addition to an occupation.

Part of his success in real estate was owed to
65 strategic compromise. Considering American sentiments regarding Russia during the Cold War, there were times that he was sure he lost certain house sales due to his last name and accent.

However, to those willing to listen, he found advantages to informing people that he was an exiled Russian who ardently disagreed with the communist government. He would also point out his pride in being a new American and allow a potential buyer to degrade Russia without blinking.

Fortunately, the 1950s were a time of settling across the country, and this made real estate a very lucrative profession. It wasn't just this that attracted my grandfather, though; he also saw it as an opportunity to give tiny parts of the country to other people—returning the favor, in a way.

Yet, it always seemed that something vital still rested in the opposite hemisphere. Once communism fell, he began returning to Russia yearly. He and my grandmother never showed the family pictures from Russia the way they would from the various cruise ships they traveled on; it could be deduced that returning to Russia was a journey of personal necessity for him rather than pleasure, and the encounter elucidated his existence in a way that being solely American could not. In selling real estate, my grandfather had worked to make this unnecessary. I believe that he wished for people to keep those houses and pass them down to later generations, giving the space a sort of familial permanence rather than a fleeting stay.

For most, the thought of real estate agents conjures up images of smiling advertisements on benches and buses and the skill of selling something so important. Many are wary of salespeople in general, questioning the practice of convincing people something is in their best interest when the salesperson stands to personally benefit. My grandfather did financially benefit from sales, but there was more to it: his realization of the American dream only made him want to be a part of others reaching for the same thing, whether their native home was around the block or thousands of miles away.

1. Which of the following statements best expresses the main point of the passage as a whole?

   A. Immigrants would often rather live in their native land.
   B. American-born people tend not to understand how displacement affects immigrants.
   C. Immigrants who acclimate well to America may still have indelible ties to their native land.
   D. Immigrants are sometimes surprised by the stability offered to them in America.

2. According to the passage, the narrator's grandfather's birth happened:

   F. prior to communist rule.
   G. under communist rule.
   H. after the family had been exiled by the communist rulers.
   J. after the fall of communism.

3. Line 30 mainly serves to indicate the narrator's emphasis that the exiles:

   A. wished for a counter-revolution led by opponents to communism.
   B. yearned for a home that they had lost.
   C. longed to rebuild and revitalize Moscow.
   D. preferred to settle near other Russians.

4. Which of the following statements best explains why the narrator's grandfather and other recent immigrants say "*ya amerikanets*"?

   F. They wanted to become American.
   G. They were worried about anti-Russian sentiment.
   H. It reinforced the immigrant community.
   J. It distanced them from their origins.

5. According to the passage, settling in America was difficult for the narrator's grandfather because:

   A. San Francisco was different from any place he'd been before.
   B. he had to adjust to the idea of having a permanent home.
   C. he did not speak the language when he first arrived.
   D. he knew he would never be able to live in Russia again.

6. The passage most strongly suggests that the advantage that the narrator's grandfather found in telling real estate buyers about his relationship with Russia is that:

   F. it gave him an edge over competitors because it was a gimmick they could not match.
   G. it made potential customers more inclined to buy from him because they felt pity for him.
   H. it gave him an edge over competitors because customers viewed him as more honest.
   J. it made potential customers more inclined to buy from him because he catered to their worldview.

7. According to the passage, the speaker's grandfather traveled to Russia because:

   A. it was an enjoyable vacation.
   B. the communist government fell.
   C. he felt a personal need to go.
   D. the cruise ships stopped there.

8. The description of the typical view people have of real estate agents in lines 96–99 primarily functions to:

   F. express the narrator's discomfort with the profession.
   G. undermine the validity of this view.
   H. set up a contrast with the narrator's grandfather.
   J. help the narrator make a personal connection with readers.

9. As it is used in line 105, the word *realization* most nearly means:

   A. the fruition of a desire.
   B. full understanding of an idea.
   C. a sudden epiphany.
   D. profit from a transaction.

Chapter 18
Answering Reading Questions

Answers and Explanations

How Much Do You Know?

Suggested Passage Map Notes

¶1: grandfather, chaotic childhood

¶2: still loves Russia

¶3: moves to US, becomes real estate agent

¶4: real estate is his vocation

¶5: allows people to insult Russia

¶6: wants to give back

¶7: visits Russia every year

¶8: wants to give people a home

BIG PICTURE SUMMARY

Main idea: A Russian immigrant attempts to make a life and find a purpose in his new homeland through selling real estate.

Author's purpose: To reminisce about his grandfather's life experiences, memories, and impact.

---

1. C
Difficulty: High
Category: Global
Getting to the Answer: Since this question asks for the main point, it is a Global question. Refer to your passage notes in order to answer it. The passage makes it clear throughout that both Russia and America are extremely important to the identity of the narrator's grandfather. The correct answer is (C).

Choice A does not fit the passage, since the narrator's grandfather is clearly pleased to be American. The passage does not discuss how American-born people view displacement, so B is out of scope. Choice D, while discussed in the passage, is far too narrowly focused to be the main point.

2. G
Difficulty: Medium
Category: Detail
Getting to the Answer: The clue "According to the passage" shows that this is a Detail question, so refer to your notes to find out where to research. Information about the grandfather's early life is in the first paragraph. In lines 2–5, the author states that the grandfather's "non-communist lineage made him unwelcome before he had left the womb," and his father "was considered an enemy of the communist Bolsheviks." The last sentence in the first paragraph (lines 11–13) states that the country came under "hostile rule" while the grandfather's mother was pregnant with him. If his father was an enemy of communists, then the "hostile rule" would have been communist rule. Therefore, you can predict that the grandfather was born under communist rule. Choice (G) is correct. Choices F, H, and J contradict that statement.

3. B
Difficulty: Medium
Category: Function
Getting to the Answer: The phrase "mainly serves to" in the question stem identifies this as a Function question. For context, read the surrounding lines in addition to the one cited. The passage states that, in searching for a place to settle, the exiles hoped for a place like the one they left. However, the narrator calls this *unattainable*. Predict that this line emphasizes the exiles' homesickness and pain. Choice (B) is correct.

Choice A is out of scope; the passage never discusses a counter-revolution. Choice C contradicts the passage; the "new Moscow" that the narrator cites refers not to a new version of the old city but to a new city that is like the one they left. Finally, choice D is incorrect because settling near other Russians is not *unattainable*.

4. F
Difficulty: Medium
Category: Detail
Getting to the Answer: Sometimes you will see questions, like this one, for which the question type is difficult to determine based on the wording alone. Here, it might be either a Detail or an Inference question, depending on whether the passage directly tells you why the phrase was used. Either way, you will need to research in the passage. According to the passage, "*ya amerikahets*" means "I am American," and the immigrants said it in order to "play the role" they wanted. You can predict that they aspired to be American, which matches (F).

While the passage does state that the narrator's grandfather was the victim of some anti-Russian sentiments, this is not mentioned until the fifth paragraph. This makes choice G outside the scope of this question. The passage never mentions reinforcing the community, so H is incorrect. Finally, J contradicts the passage, which says that "being Russian went without saying."

5. B
Difficulty: Low
Category: Detail
Getting to the Answer: The clue "According to the passage" shows that this is a Detail question. Review your passage notes; the third paragraph discusses the grandfather's move to America. Go back to that paragraph and look for what made settling in America difficult for him. Lines 46–55 state that this period was confusing because the grandfather had never settled anywhere permanently. Predict that the narrator's grandfather had to accustom himself to staying in one place. Choice (B) is correct.

While A and D may be true, a new, non-Russian place was not what caused the difficulty, according to the passage. It is not clear in the passage whether the grandfather spoke English upon arrival, so C is incorrect.

6. J
Difficulty: Medium
Category: Inference
Getting to the Answer: The phrase "most strongly suggests" in this question stem is a clue that it is an Inference question. Since the stem does not provide a line or paragraph number, use your passage notes to locate the relevant text in paragraphs 5 and 6, which discuss the grandfather's real estate sales. Here, the passage states that the grandfather lost sales because of anti-Russian bias from some customers, but he gained standing with others by telling them that he was an anti-communist exile and allowing them to insult Russia. You can predict that indulging his customers' bias allowed him to make more sales. Choice (J) is correct.

The passage does not compare him with competitors in any way, so F and H are out of scope. There is no evidence in the passage that customers pitied him, so G is also incorrect.

7. C
Difficulty: Medium
Category: Detail
Getting to the Answer: The phrase "According to the passage" shows that this is a Detail question. Paragraph 7 calls the trip "a journey of personal necessity." Predict that the speaker's grandfather felt compelled to go. The correct answer is (C).

Choice A is the exact opposite of what the passage says in lines 86–89. The fall of communism in Russia may have allowed him to go, but it is not the reason that he decided to travel there, so B is also incorrect. Finally, choice D is a distortion; while the passage mentions trips on cruise ships, it suggests they were separate from the trips to Russia.

8. H
Difficulty: Medium
Category: Function
Getting to the Answer: The wording "primarily functions to" indicates that this is a Function question. After describing a typical view of real estate agents in the final paragraph, the speaker immediately goes on to say that the grandfather does not fit this depiction. You can predict that the description is necessary background information to show the contrast with the narrator's grandfather. This matches (H).

Choice F is a distortion; while the speaker acknowledges that some people feel discomfort with salespeople, that is not the purpose of the description. Choice G is extreme; the speaker merely wants to say that the grandfather is not like this. Choice J is incorrect because the speaker goes on to contradict the image described, so there is no personal connection with readers.

9. A
Difficulty: High
Category: Vocab-in-Context
Getting to the Answer: This question displays the wording characteristic of a Vocab-in-Context question: "the word . . . most nearly means." The sentence indicated discusses the "realization of the American dream" and the desire to help others trying to do the same, so you can predict that in this context *realization* means achievement or gain. Choice (A) is correct.

Choices B and C both describe the most common meanings of the word, which are rarely correct for this type of question. Choice D refers to a transaction, which does not fit with the discussion of the American dream.

HOW TO ANSWER ACT READING QUESTIONS

> **LEARNING OBJECTIVES**
>
> After this lesson, you will be able to:
> - Research the answer in the passage text or your big picture summary
> - Predict the correct answer
> - Identify the one correct answer choice

To answer questions like these

INFORMATIONAL: This passage is adapted from a 2019 essay about astrobiology.

Astrobiology, also known as exobiology, is a complex, multidisciplinary science dedicated to studying the possibility of life outside the confines of Earth. Humanity has speculated for centuries [5] about whether or not we are alone in the universe, but with the advent of space exploration in the 1950s and 1960s, for the first time in human history there was the possibility of actually exploring the surface of alien planets. Scientists [10] and engineers worked together to build what they called landers, spacecraft capable not only of landing on other planets, but also of exploring and photographing them.

When the first of the two Viking landers touched [15] down on Martian soil on July 20, 1976, and began to send camera images back to Earth, the scientists at the Jet Propulsion Laboratory could not suppress a certain nervous anticipation. Like people who hold a ticket to a lottery, they had a one-in-a-million [20] chance of winning. The first photographs that arrived, however, did not contain any evidence of life. They revealed merely a barren landscape littered with rocks and boulders. The view resembled nothing so much as a flat section of desert. In [25] fact, the winning entry in a contest at J.P.L. for the photograph most accurately predicting what Mars would look like was a snapshot taken from a particularly arid section of the Mojave Desert.

The scientists were soon ready to turn their [30] attention from visible life to microorganisms. The twin Viking landers carried out experiments designed to detect organic compounds. Researchers thought it possible that life had developed on early Mars just as it is thought to have developed on [35] Earth, through the gradual chemical evolution of complex organic molecules. To detect biological activity, Martian soil samples were treated with various nutrients that would produce characteristic by-products if life forms were active in the soil. [40] The results from all three experiments were inconclusive. The fourth experiment heated a soil sample to look for signs of organic material but found none—an unexpected result because organic compounds were thought to have been present due [45] to the steady bombardment of the Martian surface by meteorites.

The absence of organic materials, some scientists speculated, was the result of intense ultraviolet radiation penetrating the atmosphere [50] of Mars and destroying organic compounds in the soil. Although Mars' atmosphere was at one time rich in carbon dioxide and thus thick enough to protect its surface from the harmful rays of the sun, the carbon dioxide had gradually left the [55] atmosphere and been converted into rocks. This means that even if life had gotten a start on early Mars, it could not have survived the exposure to ultraviolet radiation that occurred when the atmosphere thinned. Mars never developed a [60] protective layer of ozone as Earth did.

Despite the disappointing Viking results, there are those who still keep open the possibility of life on Mars. They point out that the Viking data cannot be considered the final word on [65] Martian life because the two landers sampled only limited—and uninteresting—sites. The Viking landing sites were not chosen for what they might tell of the planet's biology. They were chosen primarily because they appeared to be safe for landing a spacecraft. The landing sites were on parts of the Martian plains that appeared relatively featureless according to orbital photographs.

The type of terrain that these researchers suggest may be a possible hiding place for active life has an Earthly parallel: the ice-free region of southern Victoria Land, Antarctica, where the temperatures in some dry valleys average below zero. Organisms known as endoliths, a form of blue-green algae that has adapted to this harsh environment, were found living inside certain translucent, porous rocks in these Antarctic valleys. The argument based on this discovery is that if life did exist on early Mars, it is possible that it escaped worsening conditions by similarly seeking refuge in rocks. Skeptics object, however, that Mars in its present state is simply too dry, even compared with Antarctic valleys, to sustain any life whatsoever.

Should Mars eventually prove barren of life, as some suspect, then this finding would have a significant impact on the current view of the chemical origins of life. It could be much more difficult to get life started on a planet than scientists thought before the Viking landings.

The possibility exists, of course, that our definition of what constitutes life may not hold true throughout the universe. It has long been speculated that our current belief that all life must contain carbon, oxygen, calcium, chlorine, potassium, and phosphorous simply because this holds true on our planet might be too narrow a view. In 2010, NASA scientists believed they had discovered a bacterium that used arsenic in place of phosphorous, though these exciting findings later proved to be incorrect. The possibility remains, however, that future astrobiologists exploring the Martian surface from 140 million miles away might be able to make use of a more advanced definition of what we call "life."

1. The primary purpose of the second paragraph (lines 14–28) is to convey that:
   A. scientists were disappointed by the inconclusive results of their experiments.
   B. theories about how life developed on Earth were shown to be flawed.
   C. there was no experimental confirmation that life existed on Mars.
   D. meteorite bombardment of the Martian surface is less constant than scientists predicted.

2. The passage suggests that an important difference between Mars and Earth is that, unlike Earth, Mars:
   F. accumulated organic compounds in its soil.
   G. lies in the path of harmful rays of ultraviolet radiation.
   H. once possessed an atmosphere rich in carbon dioxide.
   J. could not sustain any life that developed.

3. According to the passage, which of the following describes the atmosphere of Mars?
   A. Rich in carbon dioxide
   B. Lacks a protective ozone layer
   C. Contains rocks converted from organic compounds
   D. Not susceptible to ultraviolet radiation

4. The passage suggests that Mars is void of organic compounds because:
   F. the lack of an ozone layer did not allow life to proliferate on Mars.
   G. they were destroyed by constant meteorite bombardment.
   H. carbon dioxide left the atmosphere and was converted to rocks.
   J. endoliths were found living in hidden areas.

5. The passage states that the Viking landing sites were chosen because of their:

   A. scientific value.
   B. safety.
   C. biology.
   D. diversity.

6. As it is used in line 88, the word *barren* most nearly means:

   F. full of rocks.
   G. abundantly productive.
   H. with a reddish hue.
   J. void of life.

7. Based on the passage, the researchers' argument that life may exist in Martian rocks rests on the idea that:

   A. organisms usually adopt identical survival strategies in similar environments.
   B. life developed in the form of blue-green algae on Mars.
   C. life could have evolved in the same way on two different planets.
   D. organisms that survived in Antarctica could survive on Mars.

8. The author mentions blue-green algae in the sixth paragraph primarily to:

   F. give an example of a translucent organism that existed on Earth and Mars.
   G. draw a similarity between survival mechanisms of terrestrial and, potentially, Martian organisms.
   H. show how Martian organisms escaped harsh environments by seeking out shelter in rocks.
   J. draw a parallel between the harsh conditions in Martian valleys and Antarctic valleys.

9. In the final paragraph, which of the following is listed as a compound that is necessary for life?

   A. Arsenic
   B. Sodium
   C. Potassium
   D. Magnesium

You need to know this

Use clues to direct your research to a specific part of the passage or to your big picture summary.

- **Line numbers**—Reread the indicated text and possibly the lines before and after; look for keywords indicating why the referenced text has been included or how it's used.
- **Paragraph numbers**—Consult your passage notes to see the paragraph's purpose and scope before rereading the text. Sometimes your passage map alone is enough to find an answer.
- **Quoted text**—Go back to the passage to read the entire quote if the stem or answer choices use ellipses (. . .). Then check the surrounding context of the quoted term or phrase to see what the author meant by it in the passage.
- **Proper nouns**—Use your passage map or look for capital letters in the text to find the term, and then check the context to see why the author included it in the passage; note whether the author had a positive, negative, or neutral evaluation of it.
- **Specific content clues**—Use your passage notes to help you search the passage for terms or ideas mentioned in the question stem; these clues will usually refer to something the author offered an opinion about or emphasized.

- **Whole passage clues**—Begin by reviewing your big picture summary, and only go back to the passage if you can't find the information you need. If you do get stuck, the first and last paragraphs are typically the best places to go for global takeaways.

Predicting what you're looking for in the correct answer saves time and reduces confusion as you read each choice.

ACT Reading questions always have one correct answer and three incorrect choices.

- The correct answer will match what the passage says in a way that responds to the task set out in the question stem.
- Incorrect choices often fall into one of five categories. Not every incorrect choice matches one of these types exactly, but learning to spot them can help you eliminate some incorrect choices more quickly.
  - **Out of scope**—contains a statement that is too broad, too narrow, or beyond what the passage discusses
  - **Extreme**—contains language that is too strong (*all, never, every, none*) to be supported by the passage
  - **Distortion**—based on details or ideas from the passage, but distorts or misstates what the author says or implies
  - **Opposite**—directly contradicts what the correct answer must say
  - **Misused detail**—accurately states something from the passage, but in a manner that incorrectly answers the question

You need to do this

ACT READING QUESTION METHOD

Step 1. Unpack the question stem

Step 2. Research the answer

Step 3. Predict the answer

Step 4. Find the one correct answer

Step 1. Unpack the question stem

- This step is covered in chapter 17. Make sure you have completed that lesson before continuing through this one.

Step 2. Research the answer

- When clues point to a specific part of the passage (line or paragraph numbers, quotations, content discussed only in particular paragraphs), begin by rereading the specified text and immediate context.
  - If the immediate context does not provide enough information to answer the question, gradually expand outward, rereading sentences that come before and after.
- With whole passage clues or questions that seem to lack clear content clues, begin by reviewing your big picture summary.
- If you can't figure out where to research the question and your big picture summary doesn't help either, consider using process of elimination, skipping the question and coming back to it later, or just making a guess.

Step 3. Predict or characterize what the correct answer will say or suggest

- Don't worry about phrasing your prediction as a complete sentence or about repeating exactly the language used in the passage. Just try to answer the question in your own words based on your research.
- If you struggle to predict, use your active reading of the passage to characterize the correct answer, setting expectations about characteristics it must possess.
  - For example, if the author has a negative view of a topic in the question, expect a correct answer with negative language and eliminate choices that suggest a positive or neutral view.

Step 4. Find the one correct answer

- Identify the choice that matches your prediction, if possible.
  - Don't expect a word-for-word match, but look for a correspondence of ideas. For example, if you predict that the function of a detail is to "provide support for the main idea," an answer choice that says it "supplies evidence for the author's thesis" would likely be correct.
- If there is no clear match, use process of elimination.
  - Eliminate any choice that contradicts your prediction or that clearly falls into one of the five incorrect choice categories.
  - Choose the only answer remaining, or guess among those you were unable to eliminate.

Try on Your Own

Directions: Put the expert question strategies to work on the following passage. First, take a few minutes to refresh your memory of the passage below, which you first saw in chapter 16. Then, for each question:

1. identify the question type
2. note where/how you will research the answer
3. jot down your prediction of the correct answer
4. find the one correct answer

INFORMATIONAL: This passage is adapted from an article about modern architecture.

Fallingwater, a small country house constructed in 1936, stands as perhaps the greatest residential building achievement of the American architect Frank Lloyd Wright.
5   In designing the dwelling for the Pittsburgh millionaire Edgar J. Kaufmann, Wright was confronted with an unusually challenging site beside a waterfall deep in a Pennsylvania ravine. However, Wright viewed this difficult location
10 not as an obstacle but as a unique opportunity to put his architectural ideas into concrete form.

In the early 1930s, Edgar J. Kaufmann's son, Edgar J. Kaufmann Jr., studied with Wright as an apprentice at Wright's Taliesin Studio in Spring
15 Green, Wisconsin. At the time, architecture critics deemed Wright's style anachronistic and assumed that his career was coming to an end. Kaufmann Jr., on the other hand, greatly admired Wright's work and was delighted to introduce his parents
20 to the esteemed architect. Shortly thereafter, the Kaufmanns asked Wright to design Fallingwater.

The site Kaufmann chose for his country getaway was originally the location of a cabin in Mill Run, Pennsylvania, that he offered as a vacation
25 retreat for the numerous employees he oversaw at Kaufmann's Department Store, located in downtown Pittsburgh. When the Great Depression struck, Kaufmann's employees could no longer afford the cost of traveling more than 60 miles to Mill Run,
30 and Kaufmann decided that the land, a wooded area nestled along the banks of a mountain stream called Bear Run, was an ideal location for a vacation home.

Kaufmann had assumed that the home would stand at the bottom of a nearby waterfall, where it would provide a perfect venue from which to appreciate the view. However, Wright had other ideas. When Wright showed Kaufmann his plans, Kaufmann initially balked, but Wright convinced him that incorporating the falls into the design of the house was far preferable. In the end, Wright was able to turn Fallingwater into an artistic link between untamed nature and domestic tranquility—and a masterpiece in his brilliant career.

Edgar J. Kaufmann's original plan to build his house on the ample flat land at the bottom of the waterfall would indisputably have proven less challenging. Wright's more daring response to the site required builders to construct the house on a small stone precipice atop the falls. Wright further proposed extending the living room of the house out over the rushing water and making use of modern building techniques so that no vertical supports would be needed to hold up the room. Wright brilliantly utilized the "cantilever" technique, in which steel rods are laid inside a shelf of concrete, eliminating the need for external supports. Unfortunately, however, the builders did not employ an adequate amount of reinforcing steel to support the first floor. Kaufmann had hired consulting engineers to review Wright's design prior to Fallingwater's construction, but Wright dismissed the engineers' claims that the main floor girders needed additional support. Over time, the first floor cantilever began to sag, and in 2002, a technique called post-tensioning was used to permanently repair the gradual collapse.

Despite Wright's miscalculation, Fallingwater, as a whole, is an impressive structure. Rather than allowing the environment to determine the placement and shape of the house, Wright sought to construct a home that intentionally confronted and interacted with the landscape. Each bedroom has its own terrace, and cornerless windows open outward so that window panes do not obstruct the spectacular view. In addition, Fallingwater contains a great many traditional and natural building materials. The home's 5,300-square foot expanse includes custom-designed black walnut wood furniture and walls and floors constructed of locally sourced sandstone. The boulders that provide the foundation for the house also extend up through the floor and form part of the fireplace. A staircase in the living room extends down to an enclosed bathing pool at the top of the waterfall. To Wright, the ideal dwelling in this spot was not simply a modern extravaganza or a direct extension of natural surroundings; rather, it was a little of both.

Architecture enthusiasts have taken a wide range of approaches to understanding this unique building. Some have asserted that the house exalts the artist's triumph over untamed nature. Others have compared Wright's building to a cave, providing a psychological and physical safe haven from a harsh, violent world. The members of the American Institute of Architects named Fallingwater the "best all-time work of American architecture," and the Western Pennsylvania Conservancy, which has owned and preserved Fallingwater since 1963, hails the building as an inspiration.

Edgar Kaufmann Jr. may have summed up the innovation and awe of Fallingwater best when he said, "Wright understood that people were creatures of nature; hence, an architecture which conformed to nature would conform to what was basic in people. . . . Sociability and privacy are both available, as are the comforts of home and the adventures of the seasons." This, then, is Frank Lloyd Wright's achievement in Fallingwater: a home that connects the human and the natural for the invigoration and exaltation of both.

Chapter 18
Answering Reading Questions

BIG PICTURE SUMMARY

Main idea: Fallingwater, an unusual and impressive building, was an architectural achievement by Frank Lloyd Wright.

Author's purpose: To inform the reader about the history of a unique piece of architecture.

1. Which of the following statements best expresses the main idea of the passage?

    A. Fallingwater's designs were heavily influenced by its owner's wealth, social position, and political opinions.
    B. Fallingwater proved to be only as durable as construction techniques available at the time would allow.
    C. Wright designed Kaufmann's home to be both impressive and in harmony with its natural surroundings.
    D. Wright proved that humans can triumph over the natural, untamed landscape and claim it as their own.

2. In the passage, architecture critics regarded Frank Lloyd Wright's style and career prior to Fallingwater's construction as:

    F. antiquated but likely to rebound.
    G. out of date and declining.
    H. admirable and well-regarded.
    J. requiring additional support.

3. It can be reasonably inferred from the passage that the site chosen for Fallingwater was:

    A. the location of a cabin that Kaufmann banned his employees from using after they failed to properly care for the property.
    B. unlikely to have been selected if Kaufmann's employees had continued to use it as a refuge from the urban atmosphere of Pittsburgh.
    C. postponed for several years due to the difficulty of constructing a house on a small stone precipice atop the falls.
    D. strategically chosen based on the location of the waterfall in proximity to wildlife such as white-tailed deer.

4. The passage most strongly suggests that Edgar J. Kaufmann's original plans for the site were:

    F. straightforward and conventional.
    G. daring and bold.
    H. idealistic and whimsical.
    J. socially outlandish and culturally unorthodox.

5. The author most likely used the phrases "black walnut wood" and "locally sourced sandstone" (lines 78–80) to:

    A. emphasize that black walnut trees should be used sparingly to prevent deforestation.
    B. highlight that sandstone is a preferable building material because of its stability.
    C. emphasize that Fallingwater features multiple types of organic building materials.
    D. highlight that natural elements are essential to creating a cave-like environment.

6. As it is used in line 112, the phrase *invigoration and exaltation* most nearly means:

    F. robustness and jubilation.
    G. renewing and superiority.
    H. briskness and blessing.
    J. inspiration and glorification.

7. It can reasonably be inferred from the passage that the miscalculation the author mentions in line 67 refers to:

    A. an issue that might have been prevented if Wright had heeded engineers' warnings.
    B. a suboptimal structure plagued by gravitational forces that led to a complete collapse.
    C. cornerless windows that open outward to offer an unobstructed view of the landscape.
    D. a staircase that extends down to an enclosed bathing pool at the top of the waterfall.

8. In the context of the passage, the information in lines 72–85 mainly serves to:

    F. argue that Fallingwater would not have suffered from gradual collapse if it had been built during a time of advanced engineering.
    G. describe the intricacies of Wright's "cantilever" technique and its subsequent consequences.
    H. explain specific ways in which Fallingwater and the surrounding natural beauty enhance one another.
    J. show how architecture enthusiasts have generated a myriad of theories regarding the significance of Fallingwater.

9. Architecture enthusiasts' comparisons of Fallingwater to a cave (lines 93–95) most strongly suggest that the house provides a sense of:

    A. familial warmth accompanied by a sense of belonging.
    B. murkiness that is exacerbated by the dampness of the structure.
    C. inescapable claustrophobia that could lead one to panic.
    D. security and safety that is both literal and emotional.

Chapter 18
Answering Reading Questions

Answers and Explanations

Suggested Passage Map Notes:

¶1: astrobiology: finding non-Earth life

¶2: Mars landing no signs of life

¶3: inconclusive tests for microorganisms

¶4: no organic material b/c UV?

¶5: may be life elsewhere, testing locations limited

¶6: how life could exist in rocks

¶7: impact if no life

¶8: definition of life may change

BIG PICTURE SUMMARY

Main idea: Despite initial tests for Martian life yielding inconclusive results, the continued search for possible lifeforms could yield valuable information.

Author's purpose: To inform the reader about both a brief history of and the predicted future of astrobiology discoveries.

1. C
Difficulty: Medium
Category: Function
Getting to the Answer: A question asking for "the primary purpose" of a paragraph is a Function question. Use your passage notes to answer these questions. Your notes should indicate that paragraph 2 discusses four experiments carried out by the Viking landers. These experiments were designed to detect signs of life but were inconclusive. Look for a match for this general prediction. The correct answer is (C).

Choice A is a distortion; while it is reasonable to think that the scientists would be disappointed by the results, this is not mentioned in this paragraph. Choice B is out of scope; no such conclusions are suggested about Earth. Choice D both contradicts information in the passage—which describes the bombardment as steady—and isn't part of this paragraph, so it is also incorrect.

2. J
Difficulty: High
Category: Inference
Getting to the Answer: The clue "The passage suggests" indicates that this is an Inference question, but the question stem does not point to any one paragraph definitively. When you receive limited help from the question stem, use your passage notes to help you confirm or rule out choices. Eliminate F because, according to paragraph 2, no organic compounds were found in Martian soil. Choice G is incorrect because the question asks for a difference between Earth and Mars. Both Earth and Mars lie in the path of ultraviolet radiation; the crucial distinction is that Earth is shielded by ozone. Choice H is also a distortion because the passage does not mention the amount of carbon dioxide in Earth's atmosphere. In paragraph 4, the passage tells us that even if life had begun on Mars, it could not have survived. The correct answer, then, is (J).

3. B
Difficulty: Low
Category: Detail
Getting to the Answer: You can recognize this as a Detail question because of the phrase "According to the passage." Check your passage notes to find where the passage described Mars' atmosphere and then go to the fourth paragraph to form your prediction. Paragraph 4 says that the Martian atmosphere did not develop a protective ozone layer. Choice (B) is correct.

Choices A, C, and D all contradict information in paragraph 4.

4. F
Difficulty: Medium
Category: Inference
Getting to the Answer: You can tell this is an Inference question because of the phrase "the passage suggests." Paragraph 4 gives details about why Mars lacks organic compounds. Ultraviolet radiation penetrated the atmosphere and destroyed organic compounds in the soil; this occurred because Mars did not develop a protective ozone layer. Put these pieces together to get answer choice (F).

Choice G distorts what the passage says; meteorite bombardment was not mentioned in relation to the destruction of organic compounds. Choice H is another distortion because, while true, this is not why Mars is void of organic compounds. Choice J is a misused detail; endoliths are mentioned in reference to Antarctic valleys on Earth, not Mars.

5. B
Difficulty: Low
Category: Detail
Getting to the Answer: The wording "The passage states" identifies this as a Detail question. While the question stem does not contain a line reference, the answer to a Detail question will be stated directly in the passage. Your notes should help direct you to paragraph 5. In lines 68–70, the passage says, "They were chosen primarily because they appeared to be safe for landing a spacecraft." This matches (B) exactly. None of the other choices match this statement.

6. J
Difficulty: Medium
Category: Vocab-in-Context
Getting to the Answer: This question has the distinctive phrasing of a Vocab-in-Context question, including "As it is used" and "most nearly means." Use the context of the passage to help answer this question. Pretend that the word *barren* is a blank, read around the cited line for clues, and make a prediction. The clues from the passage include: "did not contain any evidence of life." A good prediction for this word is "empty." Choice (J) is correct.

Be careful with F! Even though the passage mentions that the area is littered with rocks, *barren* refers to the fact that there was no evidence of life. Choice G is opposite of what the passage suggests, and H references ideas from elsewhere in the passage.

7. C
Difficulty: High
Category: Inference
Getting to the Answer: With Inference questions skim your notes to help you find the location of the relevant details in the passage. Martian rocks are discussed in paragraph 6: the author states that some scientists hypothesize that life on Mars may have "escaped worsening conditions by . . . seeking refuge in rocks" (lines 83–85), as happened on Earth. Predict that a way in which organisms may adapt to harsh conditions is similar on Earth and on Mars. Choice (C) is correct.

Choice A is a distortion of the facts in the passage. This passage only discusses potential similarities between harsh environments on Earth and Mars, not in any other locations, and the author's statement that Mars is much drier than even the driest part of Antarctica proves that the two environments are not actually similar, only that they have some potential similarities. Additionally, the only organism discussed is blue-green algae. Choice B is incorrect because blue-green algae developed on Earth, not Mars. Choice D is incorrect because it suggests that the same organisms that survive in Antarctica could also survive on Mars, but there is no evidence to support that; the author uses the example of Antarctic life only to illustrate a theory of how Martian life might have adapted.

8. G
Difficulty: Medium
Category: Function
Getting to the Answer: "The author mentions . . . to" is a clue that this is a Function question. Paragraph 6 discusses a terrestrial organism that has adapted to harsh conditions: blue-green algae. The passage further states that this argument is based on the idea that an organism on Mars could have escaped harsh conditions by seeking refuge in rocks, like the blue-green algae have done on Earth. The author discusses how blue-green algae have survived and how it could be possible for Martian organisms to adapt and survive in a similar way. Choice (G) is correct.

Choice F is a distortion; the rocks were translucent, not the blue-green algae. Choice H also twists the facts in the passage, which merely suggests that this is a possibility, not a certainty. Finally, choice J is out of scope; Martian valleys are not mentioned.

9. C
Difficulty: Low
Category: Detail
Getting to the Answer: This question asks for something listed in the final paragraph, so it is a Detail question. When answering a question like this, take a moment to go back to the passage to research your answer. Here, you should eliminate all answer choices that are not listed as compounds that are necessary for life. The last paragraph does not mention B or C at all, so they are not correct. Choice A is incorrect because, while arsenic is mentioned in the final paragraph, it is not among the compounds that are believed to be necessary for life. Potassium, (C), is part of the list and is correct.

Try on Your Own

Suggested Passage Map Notes

¶1: Fallingwater: architectural achievement by FLW

¶2: how FLW came to design Fallingwater

¶3: location; below vs. on falls

¶4: challenges

¶5: house interacts w/nature

¶6: critical responses

¶7: connects human and nature

BIG PICTURE SUMMARY

Main idea: Fallingwater, an unusual and impressive building, was an architectural achievement by Frank Lloyd Wright.

Author's purpose: To inform the reader about the history of a unique piece of architecture.

1. C
Difficulty: Medium
Category: Global
Getting to the Answer: This is a Global question because it is asking for the main idea of the passage. Use your big picture summary and passage notes to answer this question. Paragraph 1 introduces Fallingwater as one of Wright's greatest achievements and paragraph 7 concludes that Fallingwater interconnects humans and nature. Predict that Fallingwater is amazing and reflects nature, which matches (C).

The passage offers no evidence that Kaufmann's money, social status, or political beliefs influenced Wright's designs; A is incorrect. Choice B is incorrect because durability refers to a specific aspect of Fallingwater's construction, but Global questions are concerned with the passage as a whole. In addition, it was Wright's dismissal of the engineers' recommendation to provide additional support for the main floor girders that led to durability issues, not the limitations of the available construction techniques. Choice D is a distortion; Wright wanted the house to be an "extension of natural surroundings," not a triumph over them.

2. G
Difficulty: Medium
Category: Detail
Getting to the Answer: The phrase "In the passage" is a clue that this is a Detail question. Paragraph 2 discusses Wright's career before Kaufmann asked him to design Fallingwater. Lines 15–17 state that "architecture critics deemed Wright's style anachronistic and assumed that his career was coming to an end." *Anachronistic* refers to something that is not in its correct time period, so predict that critics thought that Wright's designs were too old to be relevant and that his career was deteriorating. Choice (G) is correct.

The critics did think that Wright's technique was antiquated, but they did not think it was likely to rebound; F is incorrect. Choices H and J are misused details. Edgar J. Kaufmann Jr., not the critics, admired Wright and held him in high regard, and Fallingwater's main floor girders, not Wright, required additional support.

3. B
Difficulty: Medium
Category: Inference
Getting to the Answer: The clue "It can be reasonably inferred" shows that this is an Inference question. Review your notes; the location of Fallingwater is discussed in paragraph 3. Lines 23–27 state that the site was "originally the location of a cabin . . . that he offered as a vacation retreat for the numerous employees he oversaw at Kaufmann's Department Store, located in downtown Pittsburgh." However, "When the Great Depression struck, Kaufmann's employees could no longer afford the cost of traveling more than 60 miles to Mill Run" (lines 27–29). Since Kaufmann decided to build a new home on that site only after his employees ceased traveling to the cabin, it can be inferred that if his employees had not stopped using the cabin, Kaufmann may not have decided to build a new home there. Choice (B) is correct.

Choices A and D are out of scope; the passage does not mention how well (or poorly) Kaufmann's employees cared for the property or what type of wildlife existed near the waterfall. Choice C is a distortion; it took some convincing for Kaufmann to agree to build Fallingwater at the top of the waterfall, but the passage does not state that construction was postponed.

4. F
Difficulty: Medium
Category: Inference
Getting to the Answer: This is an Inference question because the question stem includes the word *suggests*. The correct answer to an Inference question will always be directly supported by the text. Your passage notes should point you to the fourth paragraph. The author writes that Kaufmann had originally planned to put the house on a flat site near the bottom of the waterfall, but Wright convinced him to accept a more daring location right over the waterfall. Predict that Kaufmann's original plans were not daring but traditional; the correct answer is (F).

Choices G and H are the opposite of the prediction; Wright's design, not Kaufmann's plan, was daring, bold, idealistic, and whimsical. Choice J is out of scope; the passage never indicates how the plans were considered within a social or cultural context.

5. C
Difficulty: Medium
Category: Function
Getting to the Answer: The phrase "most likely used . . . to" indicates that this is a Function question. For more context, read the surrounding lines in addition to the one cited. The passage states that "Fallingwater contains a great many traditional and natural building materials" (lines 75–77). Predict that the phrases emphasize the natural materials that Wright used. Choice (C) is correct.

Choices A and B are out of scope; the passage does not mention deforestation or the stability of sandstone. The author doesn't mention the idea of a cave until the next paragraph, so D is incorrect.

6. J
Difficulty: High
Category: Vocab-in-Context
Getting to the Answer: This question includes wording characteristic of a Vocab-in-Context question: "the phrase . . . most nearly means." The sentence indicated is the final sentence in a paragraph that begins with the statement "Edgar Kaufmann Jr. may have summed up the innovation and awe of Fallingwater best," so you can predict that in this context *invigoration and exaltation* means "innovation and awe." Choice (J) is correct.

Choice F includes definitions of *vigor* and *exultation*, which sound similar to *invigoration* and *exaltation* but have different meanings. Choices G and H are distortions; they represent other possible definitions of these words, but they do not make sense when plugged back into the sentence.

7. A
Difficulty: Medium
Category: Inference
Getting to the Answer: This is an Inference question because it asks for what "can reasonably be inferred." The line reference provided is at the very beginning of paragraph 5, and it refers to the miscalculation discussed in the previous paragraph. Your passage notes should indicate that paragraph 4 is about Wright's decision to use the "cantilever" technique. Lines 57–59 state that "the builders did not employ an adequate amount of reinforcing steel to support the first floor." Furthermore, "Wright dismissed the engineers' claims that the main floor girders needed additional support. Over time, the first floor cantilever began to sag, and in 2002, a technique called post-tensioning was used to permanently repair the gradual collapse" (lines 61–66). This information indicates that if Wright had listened to the engineers and included additional reinforcing steel, the cantilever may not have started to sag. Choice (A) is correct.

Choice B is extreme; the passage says that the collapse was gradual, not complete. Choices C and D are misused details; both answer choices are mentioned in the passage, but they are notable features that demonstrate how Fallingwater's design embraces nature, not examples of miscalculations.

8. H
Difficulty: Medium
Category: Function
Getting to the Answer: The phrase "serves to" shows that this is a Function question. Use your passage notes to review the main purpose of the paragraph that contains the sentences indicated by the question stem. Your notes should show that paragraph 5 discusses the ways in which Fallingwater intertwines impressive architecture with natural beauty. Predict that lines 72–85 provide details about this connection; (H) is correct.

Choice F is incorrect because the passage does not discuss whether Fallingwater would have proven more durable if it had been built during a period of more advanced engineering. Choices G and J are incorrect because they reflect the purposes of the fourth and sixth paragraphs, respectively, not the fifth paragraph.

9.   D
Difficulty: High
Category: Inference
Getting to the Answer: When an Inference question asks for a characterization of an opinion, be sure to keep in mind whose opinion it is. Here, it is the architecture enthusiasts' notions of a cave that are important. According to the cited sentence, architecture enthusiasts compared Fallingwater to a cave because the house provided "a psychological and physical safe haven from a harsh, violent world" (lines 94–95). The critics' use of cave imagery suggests a feeling of safety, which matches (D).

Choices A, B, and C are distortions of what the architecture enthusiasts alluded to in their characterization. Eliminate these choices because the passage does not provide support for a sense of familial warmth, murkiness, or claustrophobia.

Part 4
ACT READING

How Much Have You Learned?

Directions: Take a few minutes to refresh your memory of the passage below, which you first saw in chapter 16, and then answer the associated questions. Try to use the various ACT Reading question strategies you learned in this chapter. Be sure to study the explanations, even for questions you got correct. They can be found at the end of this chapter.

INFORMATIONAL: This passage is adapted from an article about how humans develop language.

The influential theory of universal grammar (UG) postulates that all humans have an innate, genetic understanding of certain grammatical "rules," which are universal across all languages
[5] and absolutely not affected by environment. The idea of such a universal grammar has a long history, starting with Roger Bacon's thirteenth-century book *Overview of Grammar* and continuing through the Renaissance with attempts to construct
[10] an ideal language. In the eighteenth century, the first edition of the Encyclopedia Britannica included a section dedicated to universal grammar. In modern times, however, the linguistic theory of universal grammar is most closely associated
[15] with Noam Chomsky, who did much to codify and popularize it in the 1950s–1970s. According to Chomsky, we are all born with a knowledge of "deep structure," basic linguistic constructions that allow us, if not to understand all languages, at least
[20] to understand how they are put together. From there, we have only to learn how the parameters are set in our particular language in order to create an unlimited number of "correct" utterances.

For example, he suggests that structure
[25] dependency—a rule that says that sentences are defined by phrase structure, not linear structure—is inherent to all languages, with minor variations. Thus, the meaning of a sentence is really dependent on the meaning of its phrases, rather than each
[30] individual word. In addition, the head parameter rule stipulates that each phrase contains a "head" (main) word, and all languages have the head word in essentially the same position within the phrase. Chomsky's famous sentence "Colorless green ideas
[35] sleep furiously" exemplifies this theory of universal grammar—while the sentence itself is meaningless, it is easily recognizable as a grammatical sentence that fits a basic but higher level of organization. "Furiously sleep ideas green colorless," on the other
[40] hand, is obviously not a grammatical sentence, and it is difficult to discern any kind of meaning in it. For other evidence to support this theory, Chomsky points to our relative ease in translating one language to another; again, while we may
[45] not necessarily recognize individual words in an unfamiliar language, we can certainly recognize and engage with sentences that are grammatical.

This evidence is still fairly theoretical, receiving play mostly in the linguistic sphere rather than in
[50] the biological sciences. Most of those researching the theory seem more concerned with attempting to draw universal parallels across languages than with searching for biological evidence of such phenomena. We might ask: Where exactly are
[55] these universal grammar constraints located in our genetic code? How and when are they altered by natural evolutionary processes—or do they remain relatively unaltered and non-mutated from generation to generation? As both languages and
[60] human beings evolve over time, does UG also evolve or stay relatively stable?

Even within the linguistic sphere, Chomsky's theory has drawn criticism. Some scientists suggest that by ignoring the role of environment
[65] in language development, Chomsky completely discredits the possibly important effect our surroundings could have on language development. Still other researchers say that universal grammar is not nearly as ordered and absolute as Chomsky
[70] and other linguists make it out to be—that merely identifying similarities in different languages does not prove that a universal grammar underlies them. They suggest that since the universal grammar theory is not falsifiable, it is in fact
[75] pseudoscientific rather than scientific, the result of our flawed human tendency to impose order where there is none.

More recent researchers have begun to
advocate that, rather than focusing on explaining
80 linguistic similarities among various languages,
we instead acknowledge the evolutionary roots of
language and look specifically for neurobiological
explanations. Claiming that the humanistic
exploration of universal grammar is too abstract,
85 they recommend that we instead view language
(and grammar) as a function of the brain.
Some progress has been made in studying the
neurobiology of language; for instance, scientists
have identified specific regions of the brain that
90 handle language. However, these findings are
simple and preliminary, offering little insight into
the vast intricacy of human language use.

    Neither linguistics nor biology alone is sufficient
to understand the foundations of language.
95 Language is unbelievably complex: even a single
word can offer several definitions and associations.
Thus, any single connection between, say, two
languages causes those myriad associations to
become oversimplified and sterile. For example,
100 simply pointing out that the subject of a sentence is
in the same position in Turkish and English as an
illustration of UG merely acknowledges that single
linguistic association, while failing to consider any
social circumstances that may cause the mind to
105 modify that grammar. In short, say scientists, not
until we create a better marriage between biology
and linguistics—and a better understanding of the
human brain—can we even begin to address the
complexities of human language development.

1. The passage as a whole can best be described as:

    A. an argument against the validity of an outdated theory.
    B. a description of how scientific understanding of a topic has evolved historically.
    C. an examination of a well-known theory and how it might be improved.
    D. a defense of the contributions of a theory in spite of its imperfections.

2. Based on the passage, which statement best describes how Renaissance efforts to design a language relate to Chomsky's theory of universal grammar?

    F. Renaissance linguists based their undertaking on Chomsky's theory.
    G. Both believed in the possibility of perfecting language.
    H. Chomsky's theory was inspired in part by that constructed language.
    J. They share underlying assumptions about human language.

3. According to the passage, Chomsky's claim that an "innate, genetic understanding":

    A. allows humans to understand all language.
    B. allows humans to understand all language structure.
    C. allows humans to easily speak in multiple languages.
    D. explains that grammar is a natural function of the human brain.

4. According to the passage, universal grammar's structure dependency rule states that:

   F. the linear arrangement of words defines the meaning of sentences.
   G. a sentence's grammatical structure is dependent upon its meaning.
   H. a sentence's meaning relies on the meaning of the phrases that comprise it.
   J. head words are the most critical to understanding the meaning of sentences.

5. The author includes the quotes "Colorless green ideas sleep furiously" and "Furiously sleep ideas green colorless" primarily to:

   A. support the idea that humans can recognize grammatical and ungrammatical structures regardless of content.
   B. show the importance of word order in determining whether a statement is grammatical or not.
   C. identify the correct position of the head word in two different phrase structures.
   D. demonstrate why it is easy to translate from one language to another even when dealing with unfamiliar vocabulary.

6. The questions in the third paragraph primarily serve to:

   F. demonstrate that biology is a better lens for examining language.
   G. suggest potential theoretical weaknesses of universal grammar.
   H. list topics universal grammar seeks to elucidate.
   J. dismiss the possibility of an evolutionary basis for language.

7. The passage suggests that the researchers mentioned in line 68 believe which of the following?

   A. Identifying similarities across all known languages is the only way to prove universal grammar correct.
   B. Universal grammar is not chaotic enough to be a scientific theory.
   C. For a theory to be truly scientific, it must be possible to prove it wrong.
   D. Pseudoscience is a major problem in the field of linguistics.

8. One of the main purposes of the fifth paragraph is to:

   F. introduce the idea of examining language through neurobiology.
   G. describe the evolutionary development of language.
   H. outline the strides made in studying how the brain produces language.
   J. identify criticisms of the theory of universal grammar.

9. As it is used in line 106, the phrase *a better marriage* most nearly means:

   A. a more equitable partnership.
   B. a more effective synthesis.
   C. stronger communication.
   D. a permanent relationship.

Chapter 18
Answering Reading Questions

Reflect

Directions: Take a few minutes to recall what you've learned and what you've been practicing in this chapter. Consider the following questions, jot down your best answer for each one, and then compare your reflections to the expert responses on the following page. Use your level of confidence to determine what to do next.

1. Why do ACT experts research and predict the correct answer to Reading questions before reading the answer choices?

    _____
    _____
    _____

2. What are the types of research clues contained in ACT Reading question stems?

    _____
    _____
    _____

3. What are the five common incorrect answer choice types associated with ACT Reading questions?

    - _____
    - _____
    - _____
    - _____
    - _____

4. How will you approach the process of answering ACT Reading questions more strategically going forward? Are there any specific habits you will practice to make your approach to ACT Reading more effective and efficient?

    _____
    _____
    _____

Responses

1. Why do ACT experts research and predict the correct answer to Reading questions before reading the answer choices?

Expert test takers know that the correct answer to each ACT Reading question is based on the text of the passage. They research to avoid answering based on memory or on a whim. Predicting the correct answer before reading the choices increases accuracy and speed by helping the test taker avoid rereading, confusion, and comparing answer choices to one another.

2. What are the types of research clues contained in ACT Reading question stems?

Line numbers, paragraph numbers, quoted text, proper nouns, specific content clues, and whole passage clues.

3. What are the five common incorrect answer choice types associated with ACT Reading questions?

   - *Out of scope*
   - *Extreme*
   - *Distortion*
   - *Opposite*
   - *Misused detail*

4. How will you approach the process of answering ACT Reading questions more strategically going forward? Are there any specific habits you will practice to make your approach to ACT Reading more effective and efficient?

There is no one-size-fits-all answer here. Reflect on your own habits in answering ACT Reading questions and give yourself an honest self-assessment. Consider the strategies you've seen experts use in this chapter, and put them to work in your own practice to increase your accuracy, speed, and confidence.

Next Steps

If you answered most questions correctly in the "How Much Have You Learned?" section, and if your responses to the Reflect questions were similar to those of the ACT expert, then consider answering reading questions an area of strength and move on to the next chapter. Come back to this topic periodically to prevent yourself from getting rusty.

If you don't yet feel confident, review the material in this chapter, and then try the questions you missed again. As always, be sure to review the explanations closely. Then go online (**kaptest.com/login**) for more practice. If you haven't already registered your book, do so at **kaptest.com/moreonline**.

GO ONLINE

kaptest.com/login

Answers and Explanations

How Much Have You Learned?

Suggested Passage Map Notes

¶1: theory of UG through history

¶2: ex. of rules that support UG

¶3: ev. = theoretical, biological?

¶4: criticism

¶5: lang. and brain

¶6: biology & linguistics both needed

BIG PICTURE SUMMARY

Main idea: Chomsky's theory of innate linguistic structure is popular among linguists but does not address biological influences on language development.

Author's purpose: To inform the reader about the limitations and possibilities of universal grammar.

---

1. C
Difficulty: Medium
Category: Global
Getting to the Answer: The phrasing "The passage as a whole" shows that this is a Global question. Consult your notes for an overview. The passage is fairly neutral; it describes universal grammar and then discusses criticisms of the theory and how to resolve them. The correct answer is (C).

Choice A is extreme; the passage does not argue that universal grammar is invalid or outdated, only that it has flaws. The passage is not focused on the history of universal grammar, despite a brief outline in the first paragraph, so B is incorrect as well. Choice D is a distortion; the passage does not defend universal grammar.

2. J
Difficulty: High
Category: Inference
Getting to the Answer: The clue words "Based on the passage" identify this as an Inference question. The first paragraph states that universal grammar proposes that all humans have an inherent understanding of universal language principles. It then goes on to say, "The idea of such a universal grammar has a long history," including Renaissance linguists attempting to design an ideal language. You can predict that universal grammar and Renaissance linguists had similar beliefs about humans' innate understanding of grammar. This matches (J).

Choice F is incorrect because Chomsky's work came after that of the Renaissance linguists. Choice G is a distortion; while the Renaissance linguists believed this, there is no evidence that Chomsky did. Choice H is out of scope; the passage gives no information about what inspired Chomsky's theory.

3. B
Difficulty: Medium
Category: Detail
Getting to the Answer: The clue words "According to the passage" and "Chomsky's claim" in the question stem show that the answer must have been directly stated in the passage. Thus, this is a Detail question. Go back to the first paragraph to find out what Chomsky said. According to Chomsky, we can innately perceive how languages "are put together." Predict that the correct answer should have something to do with how humans can intuitively understand the deep structure of languages. Answer choice (B) is correct.

Choices A and C are extreme; while humans can grasp the structure of all languages, they cannot necessarily understand or speak all languages. Choice D is mentioned in the passage, but it is given as a possible direction for future research. There is no evidence that Chomsky himself is concerned with human biology.

4. H
Difficulty: Low
Category: Detail
Getting to the Answer: This question stem includes the phrase "According to the passage," showing that it is a Detail question. The passage discusses the structure dependency rule in the second paragraph; predict that a sentence's structure and meaning depend on its phrases. Choice (H) is correct.

Choice F is the opposite of what's needed; the passage says that neither linear structure nor individual words define sentence meanings. Choice G is also opposite; meaning depends on structure, not vice versa. Finally, the passage does not discuss how head words relate to meaning, so J is incorrect.

5.   A
Difficulty: Medium
Category: Function
Getting to the Answer: The wording "the author includes ... to" marks this as a Function question. Research the context of these quotes to determine why the author included them. In the passage, they are offered as examples of unmistakably grammatical and ungrammatical sentences. Choice (A) is correct.

Choice B is a distortion; although the word order changes, the passage explicitly states that grammar is defined by phrases, not linear structure. Choice C is incorrect because the passage does not identify any head words. Choice D is incorrect because the example sentences are not translated.

6.   G
Difficulty: Medium
Category: Function
Getting to the Answer: The phrase "primarily serve to" indicates that this is a Function question. Go back to paragraph 3 to determine the purpose of the cited questions. The first part of the paragraph contrasts the purely linguistic investigations of universal grammar with its lack of biological inquiry. Since the cited questions all relate to the biological implications of the theory, you can predict that they are included to point out possible oversights in universal grammar. Choice (G) is correct.

Choice F is extreme; the author is merely suggesting that biology should be considered, not that it is better. Choice H is the opposite of the correct answer; the point of the questions is that universal grammar has not addressed these topics. Finally, the author is not dismissing any theory here, so J is incorrect.

7.   C
Difficulty: Medium
Category: Inference
Getting to the Answer: The clue word *suggests* indicates that this is an Inference question. The researchers from the cited line have multiple opinions listed in the passage, which makes a precise prediction difficult here. Instead, read lines 62–77 to get a general idea of what they think, and then go through the answer choices one by one, eliminating until you find a match.

Choice A is incorrect because the researchers do not offer a way to prove universal grammar correct. Choice B is a distortion; while the researchers do say

universal grammar is too ordered, they do not suggest that increased chaos would make it more scientific. However, they do say that being impossible to disprove makes universal grammar pseudoscientific; therefore, you can infer that they believe a legitimately scientific theory must be possible to disprove. Choice (C) is correct.

Once you have found an answer that fits the passage, you can move on without checking any remaining choices. However, if you are unsure, you can check all four. Choice D is out of scope; the passage does not discuss whether pseudoscience is a major problem in linguistic studies.

8.   F
Difficulty: Medium
Category: Function
Getting to the Answer: The phrase "One of the main purposes" shows that this is a Function question. Consult your notes to determine the function of the fifth paragraph and predict that it discusses neurobiological investigations of language. The correct answer is (F).

Choice G is out of scope; the passage does not explain how language evolved. Choices H and J are misused details; although the paragraph mentions some discoveries and one criticism, neither is one of its overall purposes.

9.   B
Difficulty: Medium
Category: Vocab-in-Context
Getting to the Answer: This question has the distinctive wording of a Vocab-in-Context question: "the phrase ... most nearly means." Read the sentence that includes the cited line to determine what this phrase means in context. The passage suggests that both linguistics and biology, working together, are needed to understand language. Predict that the phrase means "improved integration." The correct answer is (B).

Choice A is incorrect because the passage does not suggest that the current relationship between the disciplines is unfair. Choice C is incorrect because the disciplines need to integrate, not just communicate. Choice D is incorrect because the passage does not suggest a permanent relationship.

[CHAPTER 19]

LITERATURE PASSAGES

LEARNING OBJECTIVES

After completing this chapter, you will be able to:

- Draw inferences about characters' motivations and relationships
- Identify the tone of a literature passage

How Much Do You Know?

Directions: In this chapter, you'll learn to apply the ACT Reading strategies you've learned to literature passages. Take 10 minutes to actively read this passage and answer the 9 accompanying questions. Pay close attention to the relationships between characters as you read. When you're finished, compare your work to the explanations on the following pages.

LITERARY NARRATIVE: This passage is adapted from a short essay within a memoir.

The liminal state of being somewhere entirely new, entirely alien: is there any feeling like it? Heavy with potential, exciting, but always, just beneath the surface, there is the fluttery-
5 heart feeling of fear of the unknown. There was supposed to be a shopping center, and in it a department store, for all those things that somehow, between being taken from the cabinets and drawers of the past and arriving in cardboard
10 boxes to the present, managed to disappear. But how to find it?

Now, I suppose, it is as simple as plugging information into a phone, but this was before the days of such ubiquitous magic. Imagine, if you
15 can, not having satellites and geocached location data, the word "googol" still referring only to a number. There were maps, but I had no map. There were people, but they were strangers, all of them strangers, and the fluttery dread was enough to
20 prevent my asking them for help.

But there was also something quixotic about it all—a quest! An adventure! Standing on the front steps of this house where the bed was against the wrong wall, and the hot water took so much longer
25 to gush from the tap, and the backyard smelled of fresh-cut grass rather than the turned earth of my old garden. This had been the right decision. Surely, it must have been. The warm air, the breeze, the smell of fried food from the restaurant at the end
30 of the street, with its OPEN "24/7" sign and dirty windows. The restaurant owners, and all those who lived in the tall, narrow houses around me—they had made a home here. I could do the same.

So, shoulders set and deep breath taken, I set
35 off to see the unknown vanquished, turning right, reciting to myself the vague directions from the landlord: take a right, look for the bridge with the red railing, and then it's on the left, just past Crane Street, you can't miss it. (I probably could, I
40 remember thinking at the time. I was, and am, quite talented at missing things, to be completely honest.) My determination was a thin, delicate veneer that I pretended was armor-strong as my familiar old boots began their journey down a new sidewalk
45 (new to me only, though, judging by the cracks and the stubborn late blooms pushing through them; the tree roots forcing concrete into tiny, craggy mountains).

And there was something, too, to realizing that
50 one day, and probably sooner than now seemed possible, I would sigh to think of having to walk this way, bored of it all, wondering if I could get by without trash bags or coffee filters or lemon juice for one more day. I wouldn't even notice
55 anymore the blue mailbox of the house two doors down from mine, nor the crooked little pine tree across the street, nor the way the street sign at the intersection was bent in the middle. I wouldn't need to look at that sign anymore to know the road
60 that I was crossing. (That street was Hawthorn, by the way, and my own street was Oak, despite the aforementioned pine. There were oaks as well, as I recall, though they might have been something else; my knowledge of trees generally extends to
65 "conifer" versus "deciduous" and no further.)

I would walk one day, then, with my head down, but with much less hesitation, no more wondering if I'd gone too far without noticing the bridge with the red railing or Crane Street,
70 because I'd know where the bridge was, and Crane Street, and everything else in this sprawling maze of a city. I'd know which buses to take, which stores had better prices than the one where I was going, which restaurants had the best
75 desserts, which houses had a cat who liked to sit on the porch and watch me pass.

And how mundane it would all be! How easy, how *dull*. There was dread in that, too, when I realized. Because there was beauty in
80 the unfamiliar, though it was fragile, easy as an eggshell to shatter into a million pieces when one stopped noticing it and no longer felt the need to be so cautious. This quest of mine was one to savor for as long as it lasted.

85 And there, as promised, was the bridge with the red railing, and the creek beneath was rocky and quick, shimmering, and beyond it, the boxy-brick, pocked-and-pitted walls of what must be my destination. Just a generic shopping center,
90 like so many hundreds of others. But still, who knew what awaited me inside? More unknown magic: perhaps a book of spells, or a genie's lamp, or a gateway to a new world. There was only one way to find out. And I had made it this far—I
95 would make it to the end.

1. Based on the passage, the narrator's attitude can best be described as:

    A. desperate, but tentatively hopeful.
    B. uncertain, but ultimately upbeat.
    C. excited, but initially dour.
    D. cynical, but nonetheless determined.

2. The narrator describes what she is seeing as she travels in lines 54–60 in order to:

    F. share with the reader more information to help paint a mental picture of the new place in which the narrator lives.
    G. contrast these details with the place where the narrator lived before she moved and describe what is different about the two places.
    H. compare what she sees to what she remembers from several other places she has lived.
    J. give examples of things that the narrator will no longer notice when the same trip becomes tedious and dull.

3. As it is used in line 2, the word *alien* most nearly means something that is:

    A. sinister and threatening.
    B. unfamiliar and strange.
    C. out-of-place but exciting.
    D. unwelcoming but peaceful.

4. The phrase "I set off to see the unknown vanquished" in the fourth paragraph mainly serves to:

    F. continue the mental theme of seeing the trip to the store as a fantastical quest.
    G. show the difficulty of overcoming fear of the unknown when in a new place.
    H. describe the way in which the narrator chose to travel to her new home.
    J. convey to the reader the dangers of not knowing where you're going.

5. It can reasonably be inferred from the passage that the narrator is writing about a time period:

    A. in the present day.
    B. in the ancient past.
    C. in the near future.
    D. in the recent past.

6. In lines 79–83, the narrator's comparison of finding beauty in the unknown to an eggshell primarily serves to:

    F. emphasize how much stronger she will be when she knows her surroundings better.
    G. accentuate how difficult it is to know one's own strength when faced with being in a new place.
    H. highlight how delicate her current viewpoint is compared to how she will feel later.
    J. indicate how mentally fragile she is feeling after she has come to a new place to live.

7. According to the passage, the narrator was given directions to the shopping center by:

   A. her landlord.
   B. restaurant owners.
   C. her real estate agent.
   D. the neighbors.

8. In the context of the passage, the description of the new city as a "sprawling maze" serves to:

   F. point out the lack of planning that went into the city.
   G. spotlight the difference between her old home and her new one.
   H. underscore her own dislike of using a map to find the shopping center.
   J. emphasize her current lack of knowledge of the city.

9. What do the narrator's fanciful ideas regarding what she may find at the shopping center (lines 90–93) suggest about her?

   A. She truly believes she will find something magical inside the shopping center.
   B. She wants to prolong the sense of adventure after completing her initial "quest."
   C. She is not certain of what types of items the shopping center might sell.
   D. She is fighting the potential for shopping trips to become mundane and tedious.

Chapter 19
Literature Passages

Answers and Explanations

How Much Do You Know?

Suggested Passage Map Notes

¶1: narrator just moved, excited & nervous

¶2: needs store, lacks tools to find it

¶3–4: changing feelings about new home and "quest"—excitement, uncertainty, determination

¶5–6: narr. will be familiar and bored in future

¶7: narr. wants to keep sense of adventure

¶8: finds store, thinks about future adventures

BIG PICTURE SUMMARY

Main idea: The narrator is recounting how it feels to navigate a new location for the first time.

Author's purpose: To describe her current feelings and anticipate how those feelings might change in the future.

---

1. B
Difficulty: Medium
Category: Inference
Getting to the Answer: Consult your notes to refresh your memory and ask yourself how you might describe the narrator's attitude: while the narrator questions her decision to move to a new area, she ultimately chooses to try to see exploring her new environment as an enjoyable adventure. This matches (B).

The other answer choices all contain one part that is too extreme. While *tentatively hopeful* might accurately describe the narrator's attitude, *desperate* is too strong a word for how she feels, so A is incorrect. In C, while the narrator is indeed *excited*, there is nothing *dour*, or gloomy, about her attitude at the beginning of the passage. And finally, in D, the narrator could be said to be *nonetheless determined*, but her attitude is not *cynical*.

2. J
Difficulty: Low
Category: Function
Getting to the Answer: The phrase "in order to" in the question stem tells you this is a Function question. Review these lines in the passage. The narrator uses all the details of what she is seeing in her new neighborhood as a contrast to what will happen in the future, when she no longer notices those things because the familiar trip to the store will have lost its luster. This matches (J).

In F, while the narrator is in fact helping paint a mental picture of the new area, that is not why those details are included. Choice G might be a tempting choice if you did not refer back to the passage—the narrator does compare the house she lives in now to where she lived before, but that comparison was earlier in the passage. Multiple past residences are not discussed in the passage, making H incorrect.

3. B
Difficulty: Medium
Category: Vocab-in-Context
Getting to the Answer: The phrase "most nearly means" indicates this is a Vocab-in-Context question. Refer back to the first paragraph to see how the narrator uses the word *alien*. It appears in the second line, alongside her description of being in a place that is "entirely new." Predict that *alien* relates to that idea; it refers to a place in which the narrator is not yet entirely comfortable. This matches (B), which is the correct answer.

While the narrator is not yet comfortable with her new location, nothing implies that she finds it either sinister or threatening; A is too extreme and thus incorrect. Choice C might be tempting, but while it describes the narrator's overall feeling over the course of the passage, it isn't what is meant by the word *alien* specifically; C is incorrect. Choice D is out of scope; nothing is said about the narrator's new location being unwelcoming or peaceful.

4. F
Difficulty: Medium
Category: Function
Getting to the Answer: Since the question asks how a particular phrase is used, this is a Function question. Ask yourself how that particular phrase functions in relation to the rest of the passage. The narrator is trying to see her trip as "a quest! An adventure!" and you could predict that this phrase continues to use the kind of language you might associate with such a viewpoint. This matches (F), which is the correct answer.

While the narrator does discuss the fear of being in a new place, she is not referring to that fear when using the phrase quoted, making G incorrect. The narrator is describing going to the department store, not her home, which means H is out. Finally, the narrator does not discuss any true dangers at all (if anything, she seems to realize her fears are unfounded), which means you can eliminate J.

5.   D
Difficulty: Low
Category: Inference
Getting to the Answer: The question asks what "can reasonably be inferred," making this an Inference question. Look at your passage notes to get a feel for when the narrator might be writing, and eliminate answer choices as you go. In the second paragraph, the narrator discusses cell phones that can be used to look up where something is located not yet existing, which eliminates A. Throughout the passage, the narrator is looking for a shopping center, a relatively modern invention, which eliminates B. There is nothing at all in the passage implying it might be set in the near future, so C is out. This leaves (D); based on the passage, it does appear likely the narrator is writing of a time in the recent past, so (D) is correct.

6.   H
Difficulty: Medium
Category: Function
Getting to the Answer: Here, you are asked why the narrator makes a particular comparison, making this a Function question. Why does the narrator compare her current feeling to an eggshell? Review the lines in question. Predict that the narrator is emphasizing how easy that feeling would shatter with the passing of time. Now review the answer choices: (H) most closely matches the prediction.

Choices F, G, and J are all out of scope. They may or may not be true of the narrator, but none of them are why the narrator compared finding beauty in the unknown to an eggshell.

7.   A
Difficulty: Low
Category: Detail
Getting to the Answer: "According to the passage" indicates that this is a Detail question. Refer back to the paragraph in which the narrator discusses being given directions. The landlord gave her the directions—this matches (A). The narrator does not mention speaking to the restaurant owners, a real estate agent, or her neighbors, eliminating B, C, and D.

8.   J
Difficulty: Medium
Category: Function
Getting to the Answer: This is a Function question. It wants to know why the narrator describes the city the way she did. Refer back to the line as well as the lines immediately around it. Predict that the narrator is emphasizing how little she knows now about the city compared to what she will know once it has grown familiar to her. This matches (J)—she calls the city a "sprawling maze" because it is currently unfamiliar.

Nothing is said about whether or not the city was planned, so F is incorrect. While the narrator does discuss differences between her old home and her new home, this isn't why she called the city a "sprawling maze," making G incorrect. Finally, while the narrator mentions maps, all she says is that she has none, not that she dislikes using them, so H is incorrect.

9.   B
Difficulty: Medium
Category: Inference
Getting to the Answer: "Suggest" indicates that this is an Inference question. Refer back to the final paragraph, and predict that the narrator means that she will continue to imagine herself on an adventure despite having found what she was looking for originally (the shopping center). Choice (B) matches the prediction and is the correct answer.

There is nothing to indicate that the narrator truly believes she will find magical items in the shopping center, eliminating A. She may or may not be certain of what the shopping center sells, but this isn't why she mentions finding magical things inside, eliminating C. And while she does believe going shopping in this new place will eventually become boring, she does not reference magical items in relation to that, eliminating D.

Chapter 19
Literature Passages

HOW TO READ ACT LITERATURE PASSAGES

> **LEARNING OBJECTIVES**
>
> After this lesson, you will be able to:
> - Draw inferences about characters' motivations and relationships
> - Identify the tone of a literature passage

One passage in each ACT Reading section is a literature passage: an excerpt from a novel or short story. The ACT literature passage will be labeled **LITERARY NARRATIVE**. Some test takers may find fiction more engaging and feel comfortable reading dialogue and interpreting an author's descriptions of characters and settings. Others may find their strengths lie in more concrete, nonfiction passages on science and social studies. Don't make a snap judgment based on how you feel now, though. Practice all of the passage types to give yourself an honest, informed assessment. You'll find more tips and strategies on how best to approach the section in the chapter on ACT Reading section management.

To read passages and answer questions like these

LITERARY NARRATIVE: This passage is adapted from a collection of short stories in the 1980s.

She had a little ball she liked to bounce, until one day she didn't. One minute it was there, the next—it wasn't. Even at six years old, she knew bouncy balls didn't just . . . just *disappear*. But
5 it was only her, and the empty hallway, and no bouncy ball.

She crawled around looking for it, even though it hadn't fallen, because it had vanished in mid-air. But it was nowhere. It hadn't slipped into one of the
10 floor vents (it was too big, anyway), it hadn't rolled under a door. It was just gone.

She didn't tell anyone about it; she knew they wouldn't believe her. "You always lose things. Stop being so *careless*." The same things they said
15 when she really had misplaced one of her schoolbooks, or her hairbrush, or half of a pair of socks. But this was different.

And it wasn't the only time it happened.

Things around her had a perplexing, marvelous
20 habit of disappearing. Never when anyone was around, and never when she might have predicted it. Sometimes those mysteriously purloined items came back, though. Like the doorknob. It once vanished as she was turning it, only to
25 reappear as she backed away, startled, her hand still outstretched and curved around something that was no longer there. She remembered the feeling in the moment, a vertiginous swoop of discomfort. But a few seconds later, there it was
30 again. She wasn't just seeing things—she'd felt it go, the cold metal against her palm, and then nothing. Or there was the time she put her pencil down on her desk and when she reached for it again, it wasn't there. Instead, she found it later,
35 on the middle of her bed.

She grew up, as children will do, and got used to the experience. Nothing important ever disappeared permanently, thankfully—or at least, not in *that* way. She *wished* sometimes she could
40 blame her odd, thieving ghost for her missing homework.

And was it a ghost? Or something else? There was no way to know. It never bothered anyone else in the house—not her mother, or father, or
45 her little sister, or even the various pets they had over the years. As she grew older, she sometimes asked for things back, and usually, they would eventually show up, though in odd places. Once, she demanded her favorite hair clip back, and it
50 appeared on top of her head. "Oh, *very funny*."

But it was friendly, for the most part. It didn't pinch, or rattle the cupboards menacingly, or make things go bump in the night. It merely took things. Perhaps, she reasoned, it was the ghostly equivalent of a magpie. She read up about ghosts, and apparently, what hers did was not all that unusual. Sometimes, she read aloud, in case her ghost was also curious about others of its kind and what they did. "But no pulling the covers off my bed at night, ghost. That's just creepy."

She wondered if it had a name. She simply thought of it as her ghost, no greater eponymity required. It followed her away from home, to college, where it thieved the thumbtacks from her corkboard and pens from the cup on her desk. It followed her to her first apartment, taking spoons and refrigerator magnets and, once, the charger for her phone. She demanded that one back, too. She found it behind a bookcase in the spare bedroom, a room she did not use unless she had visitors. There were no visitors at the time.

It never left wherever she was living. She could go to work, and anything that disappeared was her own fault, or at best the fault of her coworker who seemed to believe the snacks and drinks in the fridge were intended to be shared by anyone too penny-pinching to bother to bring their own. She could go out with friends, and not have to worry about disappearing French fries. It was a home ghost.

Eventually, she married and had children, and they, like others, were not bothered by the ghost, though her children teased her about her inability to keep track of things; what had been exasperating to her parents was a joke to the kids. But she knew the ghost approved of them, because one day, her six-year-old daughter came running to find her, grinning with excitement and delight:

"Mommy, look! It just appeared out of nowhere! Like *magic*!"

A bouncy ball.

1. The point of view from which the passage is told is best described as that of:
   A. a first-person narrator who tells a story that continues throughout her life.
   B. a first-person narrator who offers insights into the thoughts of other characters as she chronicles the events in her life.
   C. a limited third-person narrator who relates events from the perspective of the main character.
   D. an omniscient third-person narrator who relates the thoughts and actions of the characters.

2. According to the passage, the first time an object disappeared, the girl:
   F. thought she had lost or misplaced it.
   G. found it later in an unexpected place.
   H. was afraid to tell her parents.
   J. saw it vanish before her eyes.

3. The narrator most likely mentions the episode with the doorknob to:
   A. illustrate that the girl is not hallucinating.
   B. support the idea that the ghost is friendly.
   C. demonstrate that any objects that disappear are later returned.
   D. question whether the objects are actually disappearing.

4. According to the passage, when the girl first starts to notice items disappearing, she feels:
   F. concerned.
   G. delighted.
   H. frightened.
   J. worried.

5. Which of the following statements best captures the reason that the girl reads aloud from books about ghosts?

   A. Reading aloud makes the girl more confident and calms her fears.
   B. The girl wants to help the ghost learn about other ghosts.
   C. The girl hopes her parents will overhear her and learn about the ghost.
   D. The girl is learning to read, and she is interested in ghosts.

6. According to the passage, the main character is responsible when objects disappear from:

   F. her childhood bedroom.
   G. her college apartment.
   H. her workplace.
   J. her home as an adult.

7. The statement "There were no visitors at the time" (line 71) primarily serves to suggest that:

   A. the ghost put the phone charger behind the bookcase.
   B. the phone charger had disappeared much earlier than the girl thought.
   C. earlier visitors may have borrowed the phone charger.
   D. the ghost would not return the charger.

8. According to the passage, the frequent disappearance of objects caused the girl's parents to:

   F. demand the objects be returned.
   G. scold her for carelessness.
   H. spend money to replace the missing objects.
   J. become annoyed.

9. It can reasonably be inferred from the passage that the girl believes that the ghost approves of her children because:

   A. the children were never bothered by the ghost.
   B. the ghost returned the first object taken from the girl.
   C. the children thought the ghost was a joke.
   D. objects stopped disappearing once the children were born.

Part 4
ACT READING

You need to know this

The ACT does not generally test symbolism, but it does test your ability to draw inferences about characters' relationships and attitudes and to recognize how the author creates a specific tone or effect.

Unpack the Pre-Passage "Blurb"

Be sure to read the little blurb that precedes an ACT Reading passage; this can be especially helpful on literature passages. The blurb may give you the author's name, the title of the book or short story from which the passage was adapted, and the original publication date. When necessary, it may provide information about the main characters and setting.

Author. If you happen to know the author, great, but don't expect to. If the name rings a bell that helps you identify the time frame or setting of the passage, take advantage of that, but otherwise, let it go. No questions will ask about the author's identity or biographical information.

Title. A book's title may help you identify its genre—tragedy, romance, coming-of-age stories, etc. It may also give you clues about the setting or theme of the passage.

Publication date. The ACT has used literature passages drawn from various time periods over the last 200 years or so. Obviously, language use and references will be different in passages from the 1850s than in those from the 1950s, and you can potentially use that information to gather context about social conditions and historical events, or even about unusual vocabulary.

Characters and setting. When the test adds any information beyond author, title, and date, pay close attention. The people writing the test questions felt this information was essential for test takers to know, and it will always give you a head start in interpreting the passage and anticipating where the story is likely to go. Knowing, for example, that the main character is an adolescent or a mother, or knowing that a story takes place in a coal-mining town or an aristocratic palace, will change your understanding of the passage from the outset.

Tune In to the Narrator's "Voice"

Within the first few lines, you will be able to distinguish a passage written in first person (the narrator is the main character, knowing only what that character knows) from one written in third person (the narrator is separate from the characters). Keeping this in mind as you read will help you spot the purpose of each paragraph and will help you later with Inference questions (e.g., "Based on the passage, with which of the following would the narrator/character most likely agree?").

In addition, take note of language that indicates the narrator's or a character's point of view. In a standard science or social studies passage, opinion and emphasis keywords help you keep track of an author's ideas about a topic. In literature passages, the author may put these ideas in the mind or the mouth of a character or in the way a scene or object is described. Take note of the passage's tone (e.g., joyful, nostalgic, anxious, angry, hopeful, ironic, satirical, etc.), especially if an event or conversation brings about a change in tone. Typically, one or more of the questions will reward your attention to the passage's tone and characters' points of view.

Track What Happens and the Main Character's Reaction or Response

In a standard ACT Reading passage such as natural science or social studies, you can use an author's purpose to anticipate where the passage will go. When the author says there is a debate over a recent theory, expect the next couple of paragraphs to lay out one side and then the other. If the author introduces a new idea, there will probably be an example to illustrate it. Literature passages unfold a little differently, but if you are reading actively, you can still anticipate and track the development of the story. Use what you know about a character to anticipate the action and to interpret the character's reactions. If an older worker who is concerned about having enough money for retirement has a conversation with their boss, you can understand what they're after, even if they are using language that talks around the subject. If a studious young man absorbed in a book is interrupted by a boisterous group of revelers, you can expect some annoyance or judgment in his reaction, even if he doesn't say anything to the newcomers. Keeping track of these things will help you jot down good paragraph summaries, just as you would in nonfiction passages.

When a character's reaction or response to an event surprises you, consider whether this signals a change in the tone of the passage or indicates that you've glossed over or misunderstood something about the character or situation. In either case, it's always valuable to track not only the plot but also the character's reactions to and interpretations of what is happening.

Use What You Already Know About ACT Reading Strategies and Question Types

While literature passages have a distinct look and feel, the questions that accompany them are of the same types as those that follow standard science and social studies passages. Thus, while the best test takers apply a few unique reading strategies tailored to literature, their overall approach remains similar to what they use for all passages. In every case, ACT experts read actively to prepare themselves for the question set. To do that, they read for the big picture, for the author's (or in this case, narrator's or characters') opinions and point of view, and for the passage's structure by noting the purpose and main idea of each paragraph.

For the most part, the questions that accompany literature passages are worded similarly to those for science or social studies passages. However, in literature passages, you may also see questions asking:

- for the passage's theme (which corresponds to its main idea)
- about a shift in the narrator's focus
- how the author creates a certain effect
- what is going on in a character's mind

As long as you read actively for tone and characters' motivations, you'll be ready for questions like these.

You need to do this

- Use the pre-passage blurb to identify all that you can about:
  - The author's identity
  - The time frame and location
  - The passage's main character or characters
- Quickly recognize whether the passage is in first person or third person.
- Focus on the main character's defining characteristics: mental traits (attitudes, opinions, desires, and conflicts), and demographics if they relate to the bigger story of the passage (such as age, social position, occupation, race, and gender).
- Anticipate the character's responses to events or interactions with other characters.
- Note the purpose of each paragraph as you read.

Part 4
ACT READING

Answers and Explanations

Suggested Passage Map Notes

¶1–2: girl, 6 yrs old, ball disappears

¶3: doesn't tell anyone

¶4–6: objects really disappear, not seeing things

¶7–9: ghost? description

¶10: "home" ghost

¶11–13: adult, ghost still with her

BIG PICTURE SUMMARY

Main idea: The author shares instances when a "home ghost" has taken and replaced items over the years.

Author's purpose: To describe the author's interactions with a ghost over time.

---

1. C
Difficulty: Medium
Category: Global
Getting to the Answer: There will be several types of questions on the ACT that will test your knowledge of basic literary concepts. This passage has a narrator who describes the events and tells the story from the point of view of the girl, so (C) is correct.

A good clue that the passage does not have a first-person narrator is the lack of the word "I" in the text. A first-person narrator tells the story from the narrator's own perspective. Eliminate A and B. An omniscient narrator knows everything, but this narrator wonders whether there is really a ghost; an omniscient narrator would know the answer to that question. Eliminate D as well.

2. J
Difficulty: Medium
Category: Detail
Getting to the Answer: The phrase "According to the passage" tells you that this is a Detail question. The first time an object disappears is mentioned in the first two paragraphs, so return there and read carefully. Line 8 states, "it had vanished in mid-air," which matches (J), the correct answer.

Choice F is a subtle distortion of information in the passage. Although the girl looked for the ball, she knew that it hadn't fallen and was too big to fall into a floor vent. At the end of the text, the girl's daughter finds the ball, so G is incorrect. Choice H is also incorrect. The girl chooses not to tell her parents, but she is never described as being afraid to do so.

3. A
Difficulty: High
Category: Function
Getting to the Answer: The phrase "most likely mentions . . . to" is a clue that this is a Function question. The doorknob anecdote appears in the fifth paragraph. The sample passage map notes tell you that this section is explaining that the girl is not just seeing things disappear, but that the objects actually do vanish. The doorknob story emphasizes that by noting that the girl was able to feel the object until it disappeared. This story brings in the sense of touch to show that the girl's eyes are not deceiving her. This matches (A).

Choices B is a misused detail; the ghost is friendly, but that is not why the author describes the incident with the doorknob. Choice C is extreme; the passage only says that some objects are returned, not all of them. Choice D is an opposite choice. The anecdote is supporting, not questioning, the fact that the objects are actually disappearing.

4. G
Difficulty: Medium
Category: Detail
Getting to the Answer: Because this question includes the phrase "According to the passage," you can identify it as a Detail question. Whenever you are asked about an emotion, there will be a keyword in the passage that will support the correct choice. The context clue in the question tells you to identify the girl's feelings when she first starts to notice objects disappearing, so return to the beginning of the passage and scan for a keyword. The first sentence of the fifth paragraph describes the disappearances as "perplexing and marvelous," so the girl may be confused by them, but she also enjoys them. Choice (G) is correct.

Choices F, H, and J all have negative connotations not supported by the passage.

544

5. B
Difficulty: Medium
Category: Detail
Getting to the Answer: This question includes few clues as to question type; it might be either a Detail or an Inference question, depending on whether the passage states the reason or if you need to infer it. Your first step to answering it, however, is the same: find the part of the passage that discusses the girl reading aloud and research there. The passage map directs you to the middle of the passage, paragraphs 7–9, for the description of the ghost. Reading aloud, the detail mentioned in the question, is found in the eighth paragraph, when the girl reads aloud "in case her ghost was also curious about others of its kind." This matches (B), the correct answer.

No other choice is mentioned in the passage, so they are all incorrect.

6. H
Difficulty: Medium
Category: Detail
Getting to the Answer: The phase "according to the passage" shows that this is a Detail question. The passage map indicates that the tenth paragraph describes the ghost as a "home" ghost. The second sentence of that paragraph states that when things go missing at the girl's workplace, it is either her fault or the fault of one of her coworkers. Choice (H) is correct.

The incorrect choices are all the opposite of what's in the passage. These are all places where objects have disappeared because of the ghost.

7. A
Difficulty: Medium
Category: Function
Getting to the Answer: The wording "The statement . . . serves to" marks this as a Function question. The lines cited in the question appear in the ninth paragraph, where the sample passage map indicates that there is a discussion of characteristics of the ghost. Review the paragraph. The anecdote about the missing phone charger is described, the girl requests the return of the charger, and she later finds it in the guest room. The narrator states "There were no visitors at the time" to emphasize that the disappearance and reappearance of the charger was due to the ghost, not anyone else. Choice (A) is correct.

Choices B and C are not mentioned in the text, and so are incorrect. Choice D contradicts the passage; the ghost did return the charger.

8. J
Difficulty: High
Category: Detail
Getting to the Answer: You can identify this as a Detail question because of the clue "According to the passage." The girl's parents are mentioned twice in the passage: once in the third paragraph and once in the last paragraph. In the third paragraph, her parents chide her for being careless, but the text states that they are doing so "when she really had misplaced" one of her things, not because the ghost had made some object disappear. Eliminate G. In the last paragraph, the girl's parents are described as "exasperated," and this matches (J), the correct answer. Choices F and H are not mentioned in the passage, so they are incorrect.

9. B
Difficulty: Medium
Category: Inference
Getting to the Answer: The girl's children are only mentioned in the final paragraphs, so review that section to identify why the girl believes her ghost approves of her children. That context clue is mentioned in line 86, followed by an anecdote of the girl's own six-year-old daughter "magically" finding the same ball that was the first object of the girl's to disappear. The implication is that the ghost showed its approval of the child by returning the ball. Choice (B) is correct.

Choice A is a misused detail; it accurately describes the relationship of the ghost and the children, but it is not mentioned as the sign of the ghost's approval and is thus incorrect. Choice C is a subtle distortion of information in the passage. The children thought the disappearing objects were lost by their mother; her "carelessness" was the joke, not the ghost. Choice D contradicts the passage; it is clear that disappearances continued after the narrator's children were born.

Try on Your Own

Directions: Actively read this literature passage and answer the questions that follow. Remember to note the tone of the story as you read and pay close attention to characters' attitudes and relationships.

LITERARY NARRATIVE: This passage is excerpted from a series of short biographical stories from the 1970s.

There was a smoothness to the rhythm of her days. She was an old, old woman, and her name was Betty, and each of her days was just like the last. First thing, the careful way she had to
5 move, when it was early and everything about her seemed to have turned stiff and cold in the night. Easing into it, sitting up, joints slowly remembering how to do their creaky old job, but not happy about it.

10 She made coffee with a percolator, filling it from the sink. Her son had gotten her one of those coffee machines with the little plastic cups the year before, for her birthday, but she just couldn't take to using it. It was alien. She no longer knew
15 how to deal with alien. So she put it away in the cabinet, where it wouldn't take up all her counter space, and got it out when her son visited, so he wouldn't know she didn't appreciate his thoughtfulness.

20 She drank her coffee slowly. Sometimes she sat on the porch, when the weather was nice, and watched the sun rise over the old crackerbox houses, houses older even than she was. But more often she sat at her worn kitchen table, still linoleum-surfaced,
25 aluminum-legged, perhaps not the style anyone would choose in the now, but things had been different in the then. She made breakfast with her second cup of coffee: a slice of toast, sometimes with jam, others with honey. She did have a sweet tooth.
30 And she knew her doctor wouldn't like that second cup of coffee (and probably not the first, either), but she had lived long enough for such indulgences. Besides, if she didn't tell him, who was going to? Nobody, that was who.

35 After breakfast, she dressed: another slow process. Rolling up her stockings, her fingers shaky as they buttoned up her dress. Then she saw to her hair, combing it, all that fluffy white where once there had been smooth chestnut
40 brown. Makeup, as her mother had taught her to do it, not too much, just enough to bring some color to her cheeks.

Most days, after she was dressed it was time for her stories on the TV. That was the rest of
45 her morning, one show giving way to the next, the usual commercials for Metamucil and heart medicine and walk-in bathtubs. They knew who was watching those shows. She supposed there were people who studied that kind of thing, who
50 was watching what and when. So it was this stuff during the weekdays, and ads for cars in the evenings, and sugary breakfast cereals and McDonalds toys on Saturday mornings. Although her granddaughter didn't watch much TV—she
55 was always on her phone, watching stuff that way.

(Betty also had a cell phone, and like the coffee machine it was a gift from her son, and like the coffee machine it mostly sat unused. She didn't see the point. She had a perfectly good phone on
60 the wall in the kitchen, and one by her recliner in the living room, and that was good enough.)

For lunch she might have a sandwich, sometimes a bowl of soup if the day was cold or rainy. And with her lunch a glass of milk, because
65 she had heard that it was good for older women to get plenty of calcium, it helped prevent that bone disease where they broke too easily. She read magazines with her lunch, or worked in her crossword puzzle book—she picked one up a few
70 times a month from the market. She was good at them, though by now, there were some clues she knew they used over and over, and she wished they'd come up with new ones instead.

After lunch, it was time for chores. She liked to
75 sweep; it reminded her of doing it in her father's store, hardly as tall then as the broom handle. He'd had a tobacco shop, back when everyone and

their dog seemed to smoke, and she remembered the lovely smell of it, all those jars of smoky-sweet
80 brown-and-red shreds of tobacco. She'd swept and danced and pretended she was a princess forced into penury, like in the movies.

In the evening, she watched the news while she ate dinner, though it sometimes made her sad to
85 see all the things people did to each other. It was all just so terrible; it hadn't been like that when she was a child. Sometimes, after, she watched a movie, if there was anything good on. If not, she might read a book; she did like those stories about
90 people living in villages in Ireland or Scotland. And then the day was over—just like the day before, and it was time to undo all that she had done, return to her nightgown and slip beneath her quilt, sleeping in the safe knowledge that
95 tomorrow would be just the same as today.

1. Betty's attitude toward technology throughout the entire passage could best be described as reluctance to:

   A. have any modern technology at all in her home.
   B. understand any modern technology purchased for her by others.
   C. use modern technology developed after she grew old.
   D. admit there is modern technology she doesn't understand.

2. It can most reasonably be inferred from lines 44–50 that Betty believes the products in the commercials shown during the day:

   F. are marketed to older people like herself.
   G. are marketed to those who are retired.
   H. are things she should consider purchasing.
   J. are things her granddaughter would not want.

3. In the first paragraph, the author describes the way Betty moves slowly when she wakes up in the morning in order to:

   A. contrast it with the way she later moves when she is getting dressed and brushing her hair.
   B. reinforce with supporting details the idea that Betty is elderly, as was stated at the very beginning.
   C. provide the reader with additional information about what waking up is like for all older people.
   D. set up a parallel with the later descriptions of how Betty goes to bed again at the end of the night.

4. Based on the passage, which of the following statements most accurately describes Betty's attitude toward her doctor and his opinion on her drinking coffee?

   F. She feels some guilt for having the second cup of coffee, but not about having the first, even though he would approve of neither.
   G. She chooses not to think about it because she knows she is not supposed to be drinking coffee at her age.
   H. She believes it is acceptable because her son bought her a coffee maker, even though she knows the doctor would not approve of it.
   J. Because he does not know she drinks it, she is dismissive of his potential disapproval of her drinking coffee.

5. One of the primary purposes of the sixth paragraph is to:

    A. emphasize the differences between Betty's life and her granddaughter's life.
    B. provide a factual example of why Betty would be better off without a cell phone.
    C. further reinforce Betty's dislike of technology she seems to consider superfluous.
    D. show that Betty believes technology should progress no further than it already has.

6. The author most likely uses the word *safe* in the final paragraph to:

    F. highlight that the area where Betty lives does not have crime problems.
    G. stress that Betty finds comfort in following the same routine each day.
    H. accentuate that Betty knows nothing bad will happen while she's asleep.
    J. emphasize that going to bed is easier for Betty than getting up in the morning.

7. Chronologically, which of the following events happened first?

    A. Betty receiving the coffee maker as a gift from her son
    B. Betty helping to sweep out her father's tobacco shop
    C. Betty putting her makeup on the way that her mother taught her
    D. Betty sitting outside on the porch on days when the weather is nice

8. Based on the information in lines 74–87, what can most reasonably be inferred about Betty's memories of childhood?

    F. She has fond memories of childhood, but she might view them with somewhat rose-colored glasses.
    G. She does not like to reflect on her childhood because she had to work too young and the world is even less kind now.
    H. She looks back on her childhood as a time when nothing ever went wrong and the world was a safer, better place.
    J. She does not remember her childhood well, but she believes the world is a better place now than then.

9. In the first paragraph, the word *rhythm* most nearly means:

    A. ups and downs.
    B. a series of sounds.
    C. a poetic feeling.
    D. recurring events.

How Much Have You Learned?

Directions: For test-like practice, give yourself 10 minutes to complete this question set. Be sure to study the explanations, even for questions you got correct. They can be found at the end of this chapter.

LITERARY NARRATIVE: This passage is adapted from an essay about family pets.

I knew a cat once named Reginald. (Reginald, of all things to name a cat!) Reginald had known the harshness of life. He should have been a mean old thing, with his torn-up ears, fur patchy and
[5] matted, scars on the pale skin beneath, his tail crooked from a break that had healed badly. Ugly as sin, was Reginald; big and orange-furred. And he would have had every right to trust no one and no thing, because just looking at him, you
[10] could tell that very few ones or things had ever treated him well until he found his way to our neighborhood.

But I've never met a sweeter cat. He would come looking for a little love, purring up
[15] a storm, and he'd happily take a bowl of food, though he never wanted to come inside. He was an outdoorsman; it was where he had always been. Everyone in the neighborhood knew Reginald. I don't know who named him, but we all knew
[20] that was his name. He was a collective cat. Where he came from, I don't know either, but he was already old when he showed up. A cat like Reginald seemed the type who was born old, old and weary, but happy for any taste of affection.

[25] I had three cats of my own at the time, and they were fat old things, spoiled rotten. They'd see Reginald out the window sometimes and hiss and spit and puff up, but Reginald paid them no mind. He knew his place in the world.
[30] And I guess he was smart enough to understand that glass stood between him and them, and there was nothing they could do about it, no matter how much they postured. He'd sit outside to wash his uneven orange fur, taking pride in what he
[35] had, keeping himself clean as well as he could.

Some of the children in the neighborhood liked to pretend he was as mean as he looked, and it almost seemed like he could understand them— they'd run and shriek and hide, and he'd come
[40] after them, not getting too close, just looking at them with his big golden eyes, and they'd run again, laughing and shouting at one another to *be careful, be careful, there he is!* He'd do it as long as they continued. They weren't really scared; the
[45] same children would be out the next day with a slice of ham or turkey, feeding it to him bit by bit as he purred and purred and purred.

In winter, I would leave my garage door cracked, so he had somewhere to go, and I wasn't
[50] the only one. As I said, he wasn't interested in coming inside, but a place out of the cold, with an old blanket or towels to lay on, seemed to be acceptable to him. On snowy days, I'd warm up a can of food for him, and he accepted that too.
[55] Meanwhile, my own pudgy beasts batted at the snow through the windows, and I wondered how quickly they'd retreat if they were to feel the actual bite of it.

Reginald disappeared late in the spring
[60] five or six years after he first appeared in our neighborhood. Someone said that cats went off by themselves to die. There was a field that disappeared into the woods, and people swore they had seen him heading that way, slow and
[65] arthritic by then. I don't know if that's true, but if there was any cat who would have wanted to die with dignity, on his own terms, it was Reginald. I hope that whatever happened to him, it was painless. He deserved at least that much blessing
[70] in his difficult life.

My own cats have vet care, howling through it, fighting me about going into their carriers. Reginald probably never saw a vet in his life. My cats have every amenity provided them and
[75] certainly expect to continue to be catered to. Reginald asked for nothing, but we gave him what we could.

But I sometimes find myself wondering how different my own cats would be, if they had been

80 through what Reginald did: would they still
know how to be affectionate? Would they be like
Reginald, purring and head-butting, appreciative
of every scrap? Do they understand that things
could be very different for them?

85 I suspect they don't, but I do. When I fill
their food bowls, or scoop out their litter box,
or wash their blankets, I think of Reginald,
even now, when many years have passed since
he disappeared. I make sure their every whim
90 is satisfied, because they might have been in
Reginald's place, and it breaks my heart to think
of them going through what he went through.
But I also like to think that, spoiled as they are in
their present life, they might, like Reginald, still
95 know how to appreciate a little human kindness.
They might play games with kids, unconcerned
about their status as the designated monster. They
might accept a place to sleep in the garage on cold
nights. I hope someone would give them those
100 things, if I could not.

And I also hope that wherever Reginald is now,
he's okay. I hope he's warm, and dry, and well-fed.
I hope his ears and his fur are whole. I hope there
are games to play.

105 I hope he is at peace.

1. The passage as a whole might best be characterized as the author's:

   A. attempt to come to terms with the hardship of life for stray animals.
   B. explanation of how and why her cats are different from Reginald.
   C. reminiscence about a friendly neighborhood stray and her own cats.
   D. exploration of human nature when a neighborhood cares for a cat.

2. It can be reasonably inferred that the author believes that Reginald viewed his place in the world:

   F. with affable acceptance; he took what was offered to him and appreciated it, but saw no need to ask for more.
   G. with begrudging amiability; he knew that what he needed was only offered as long as he acted in an expected way.
   H. with necessary wariness; he was aware that the people around him might turn on him as it seemed had happened in the past.
   J. with unnecessary greed; rather than choose to live with one person, he wanted to take from the whole neighborhood.

3. In the passage, the primary purpose of lines 25–29 is to:

   A. provide an explanation for why the author's cats are different from Reginald.
   B. juxtapose Reginald and the author's cats.
   C. explore the similarities between the author's cats and Reginald.
   D. attempt to explain why Reginald behaved as he did when he saw the author's cats.

4. In the ninth paragraph (lines 85–100), it is reasonable to conclude that one of the reasons the author cares for her cats as she does is because:

   F. she worries that she won't be able to take care of them in the future.
   G. she is required to take good care of them since she owns them.
   H. she feels some sense of guilt that she couldn't do more for Reginald.
   J. she thinks that they would not be able to care for themselves like Reginald.

5. As it is used in line 69, *blessing* most nearly means:

   A. a small gift.
   B. a source of protection.
   C. a peaceful prayer.
   D. an act of acceptance.

6. In the context of the passage, the statements about Reginald in lines 3–16 primarily function to:

   F. establish why Reginald behaved as he did.
   G. contrast Reginald's appearance with his demeanor.
   H. show that Reginald had lived a hard life.
   J. indicate that Reginald's appearance was deserved.

7. The author most likely calls Reginald an "outdoorsman" in line 17 to:

   A. reinforce his behavior outside as opposed to inside.
   B. anthropomorphize Reginald's choice to stay outside.
   C. identify why Reginald became a cat for the neighborhood.
   D. provide a reason why Reginald was not allowed inside the house.

8. The passage as a whole strongly suggests that Reginald:

   F. was able to appreciate whatever was offered to him.
   G. had often gotten into fights as a younger cat.
   H. was able to understand the rules of the games children played.
   J. had always understood he was not a house cat.

9. The passage suggests that Reginald's personality affected his later life in that:

   A. he was grudgingly cared for by people who felt sorry for him.
   B. he became reluctantly affectionate as he learned to trust people.
   C. he was readily helped out by people in the neighborhood.
   D. he was a favorite of neighborhood children but not adults.

Part 4
ACT READING

Reflect

Directions: Take a few minutes to recall what you've learned and what you've been practicing in this chapter. Consider the following questions, jot down your best answer for each one, and then compare your reflections to the expert responses on the following page. Use your level of confidence to determine what to do next.

1. What are ACT Reading literature passages? How do expert test takers adjust their active reading to tackle literature passages most effectively?

   _____
   _____
   _____

2. How are the questions that accompany literature passages different from those that accompany standard science and social studies passages?

   _____
   _____
   _____

3. How confident do you feel with literature passages? What can you do in practice to improve your performance and gain even more confidence with these types of passages?

   _____
   _____
   _____

Responses

1. What are ACT Reading literature passages? How do expert test takers adjust their active reading to tackle literature passages most effectively?

On each ACT test, one reading stimulus is taken from a work of fiction, such as a novel or short story. Expert test takers actively read literature passages by paying attention to what happens to the main character and how he or she responds to these events.

2. How are the questions that accompany literature passages different from those that accompany standard science and social studies passages?

For the most part, questions accompanying literature passages are similar to those from standard nonfiction passages, but in literature you may see:

- *Global questions that focus on a description of the point of view of the passage*
- *Inference questions that ask what the passage's narrator (as opposed to its author) would agree with*
- *Function questions that ask how or why a character (as opposed to the author) used a detail or reference from the text*

3. How confident do you feel with literature passages? What can you do in practice to improve your performance and gain even more confidence with these types of passages?

There is no one-size-fits-all answer for this question. Give yourself an honest self-assessment. If you feel that literature passages are a strength, that's great! Continue to practice them so that you'll be able to rack up the points associated with these passages on test day. If you feel less confident about literature passages, review the strategies in this chapter and try to consistently apply the expert approaches outlined here whenever you practice passages in this format.

Next Steps

If you answered most questions correctly in the "How Much Have You Learned?" section, and if your responses to the Reflect questions were similar to those of the ACT expert, then consider literature passages an area of strength and move on to the next chapter. Come back to this topic periodically to prevent yourself from getting rusty.

If you don't yet feel confident, review the material in this chapter, especially the sections on characters' responses and points of view. Then try the questions you missed again. As always, be sure to review the explanations closely. Then go online (**kaptest.com/login**) for more practice. If you haven't already registered your book, do so at **kaptest.com/moreonline**.

GO ONLINE

kaptest.com/login

Answers and Explanations

Try on Your Own

Suggested Passage Map Notes

¶1: Betty: old woman waking up

¶2: B prefers old coffee machine, not new; son wants to help

¶3–5: morning routine; B likes her way, but aware of others'

¶6: B sees no use for cell phone

¶7: lunch

¶8: cleaning, childhood memories

¶9: end of day, next day will be same

BIG PICTURE SUMMARY

Main idea: Betty is an older woman with a routine who generally feels times were better before technology and other "new" things took over.

Author's purpose: To recount a typical day in Betty's life.

1. C
Difficulty: Medium
Category: Global
Getting to the Answer: The phrase "throughout the passage" indicates that this is a Global question (albeit one that also asks you to infer something). Because it is difficult to make a prediction about the correct answer in broad cases like this one, review your passage notes before looking at the answer choices. Knock them out one by one.

Choice A is too extreme. The passage says Betty allows modern technology in her home, but she doesn't necessarily use all of it. Choice B is a distortion. While the passage says that Betty is reluctant to use the coffee maker and the cell phone her son purchased for her, it doesn't say she won't use them because they were purchased by him.

Now look at (C). In the second paragraph, it says, "She no longer knew how to deal with alien." However, she can turn on a TV, implying that she was able to learn how to use technology earlier in life. Choice (C) is a reasonable inference based on the passage as a whole and is correct. Choice D is incorrect because the passage does not include anything to support or refute Betty's willingness to admit when she's struggling to understand modern technology.

2. F
Difficulty: Low
Category: Inference
Getting to the Answer: The clue words "most reasonably be inferred" indicate that this is an Inference question. Review the referenced lines and those immediately around them. Based on the paragraph, you might predict that Betty believes the target market for those things shown on daytime TV commercials are older people who might be more likely to have health or mobility issues. This matches (F).

Choice G is not supported; there is nothing to indicate that Betty believes people who are retired are the marketing demographic of the commercials. Choices H and J are out of scope; there is no way to know whether Betty has considered buying any of the things advertised or whether her granddaughter would want them.

3. B
Difficulty: Medium
Category: Function
Getting to the Answer: "Describes . . . in order to" should stand out as a clue that this is a Function question. Review your passage notes. Predict that the correct answer will show that Betty's waking-up process is slow because she's so very old. Choice (B) is correct.

Choice A can be eliminated because the two situations are not set up in contrast to one another. Choice C is too extreme; while this is true of Betty, you can't say for sure that the same is true of all older people. Choice D has the same problem as A. While both waking up and returning to bed are described, they are not presented as parallels to one another.

Chapter 19
Literature Passages

4. J
Difficulty: Low
Category: Inference
Getting to the Answer: This is an Inference question. Your notes say that the doctor is mentioned in the third paragraph. Predict that the correct answer will indicate that Betty considered what the doctor might say, but then decided it didn't matter because she wasn't going to tell him and neither was anyone else. That matches (J).

Choice F might be tempting because she thinks about what her doctor would say at the same point in the passage where the second cup is mentioned, but there is no indication that the second cup is the actual cause of her guilt. Choice G is not supported by the passage, because clearly she is thinking of it. Finally, H is not supported because no link is made between the coffee maker her son got her and her attitude toward the doctor.

5. C
Difficulty: High
Category: Function
Getting to the Answer: The phrase "One of the primary purposes" should serve as a clue that this is a Function question. The question wants to know why a particular paragraph was included in the passage. Review your notes on the sixth paragraph and predict that the paragraph was included to show another example of something, like the coffee maker described earlier, that Betty considers unnecessary in her life because she already has something that serves the exact same purpose. Choice (C) is correct.

The paragraph does highlight a difference between Betty's life and that of her granddaughter: her granddaughter watches things on her phone. That's not the reason why the paragraph was included, however, so A is incorrect. For B, while Betty herself seems to believe there's no reason to have a cell phone, this would not be considered a factual reason—it's just her opinion. Finally, in D, while Betty doesn't see the need to change her own technology, there is nothing to indicate she opposes it progressing for the rest of the world.

6. G
Difficulty: Medium
Category: Function
Getting to the Answer: "The author . . . uses" indicates this is a Function question. Refer back to the final paragraph. The word *safe* comes before *knowledge*—the knowledge that tomorrow will be the same as the day Betty has just experienced. Predict that the word is used to emphasize that she likes each day to be the same. This matches (G).

Both F and H are out of scope; nothing is said in the passage about crime or about what Betty thinks will happen while she's asleep. And while J is implied to be true, that isn't the reason why the author uses the word *safe*.

7. B
Difficulty: Medium
Category: Detail
Getting to the Answer: Since this question asks about particular events, it is a Detail question. Review your notes to make sure you remember the order in which things occurred in Betty's life. There's no way to predict, so review the answer choices and figure out which came first.

Choice A happened while Betty was an adult, but we don't know exactly when. Choice (B) came before A (as it happened during Betty's childhood), so A must be incorrect. Choice C happened in the passage, so it came after both A and (B) and must therefore be incorrect. D does not happen at any particular time in the passage, but it definitely happened after the Betty's childhood, so (B) is the correct choice.

8. F
Difficulty: Medium
Category: Inference
Getting to the Answer: The clue words "what can reasonably be inferred" tell you this is an Inference question. Review the lines listed to make your prediction: Betty seems to have enjoyed helping out in her father's shop, and she believes, based on the news, that things are different now than they were when she was young. Choice (F) is correct.

There is nothing in the passage to support the idea that Betty feels she was forced to work too young; if anything, as mentioned above, she seems to have enjoyed the work. Choice G is incorrect. In H, while she does seem to believe the world was a safer and better place when she was young, there's nothing in the passage to indicate that nothing ever went wrong for her then. Finally, in J, nothing in the passage supports the idea that she doesn't remember her childhood well. If anything, the opposite is true.

9. D
Difficulty: Low
Category: Vocab-in-Context
Getting to the Answer: "Most nearly means" tells you this is a Vocab-in-Context question. How is the word *rhythm* used in this passage? In the first paragraph, the *rhythm* is each day being like the last. This matches (D). Choices A, B, and C don't match the way the word is used in the context of the passage.

How Much Have You Learned?

Suggested Passage Map Notes

¶1: Reginald: stray cat who had hard life

¶2: R sweet anyway, neighborhood cares for him

¶3: narr. cats vs. R

¶4: children play w/ R

¶5: winter care

¶6: R disappears; narr. hopes he had easy death

¶7–9: narr. compares own cats' lives to R's life, hopes they would still be happy

¶10–11: narr. hopes for happy afterlife for R

BIG PICTURE SUMMARY

Main idea: Reginald is a beloved neighborhood cat whose life is very different from the narrator's own pets.

Author's purpose: To compare the life experiences of a friendly neighborhood cat with the lives of the narrator's house cats.

1. C
Difficulty: Medium
Category: Global
Getting to the Answer: "The passage as a whole" indicates that this is a Global question. Review your notes and predict that the correct answer will be something that includes the author discussing both Reginald and the author's cats. That matches (C).

While the author does consider how hard it is for stray cats, as well as how her cats are different from Reginald, neither A nor B encompasses the passage as a whole. Finally, while the author does say that Reginald was cared for by the neighborhood, there is no exploration of human nature, knocking out D.

2. F
Difficulty: Medium
Category: Inference
Getting to the Answer: The clue words "reasonably inferred" signal that this is an Inference question. Review your notes: the author seems to believe Reginald was content with his way of life. Choice (F) is the best match for this.

There is nothing to indicate that Reginald was *begrudging*, or that he was acting as he did only in order to gain something for himself, which eliminates G. He seems to have been the opposite of wary, which eliminates H. And he wasn't greedy, he was just "an outdoorsman" who preferred not to choose one place to call home, which eliminates J.

3. B
Difficulty: Low
Category: Function
Getting to the Answer: "Primary purpose of lines . . ." serves as a clue that this is a Function question. Refer back to those lines in the passage. Predict that the author describes her own cats to show how different they were from Reginald. This matches (B).

While the author is writing about how different her cats are from Reginald, she doesn't explain why in the referenced lines, which eliminates A. The author is highlighting differences, not similarities, which eliminates C. Finally, you can eliminate D because while the author does go on to describe how Reginald behaved when her cats were posturing and offers a potential explanation why, she is not yet discussing that explanation in the referenced lines.

4. H
Difficulty: Medium
Category: Inference
Getting to the Answer: The words "reasonable to conclude" should clue you in that this is an Inference question. The author says that "it breaks my heart to think of them going through what he went through," so predict that the correct answer is related to that. The best match for the prediction is (H).

While the author does mention in that paragraph the possibility of not being able to care for her cats, she doesn't say that she expects this to happen, as in F. There is nothing in the passage to indicate she feels it is an obligation to care for them, as in G. Finally, while she worries that they would potentially struggle to care for themselves, this is not the reason why she cares for them, as in J.

5. A
Difficulty: Low
Category: Vocab-in-Context
Getting to the Answer: The phrase "most nearly means" indicates that this is a Vocab-in-Context question. Refer back to the line in question. The author is discussing a painless death for Reginald, so predict that *blessing* is used to mean something like "favor." This matches (A).

While B, C, and D are all acceptable definitions of *blessing*, none of them match the way in which the author of the passage uses the word.

6. G
Difficulty: Medium
Category: Function
Getting to the Answer: "In the context of the passage" and "functions to" indicate this is a Function question. Refer back to the referenced lines and those around them. Predict that the author contrasts Reginald's friendly personality with his appearance. This matches (G).

Choice F is a distortion; rather than his appearance matching his behavior, Reginald's appearance was in contrast to how he behaved. In H, while Reginald's appearance does indicate he had not lived an easy life, this isn't *why* the author described his appearance and personality. Choice J is not supported by the passage at all; the author, if anything, seems to believe that Reginald deserved better than what he had gotten from life.

7. B
Difficulty: Medium
Category: Function
Getting to the Answer: The phrase "author most likely" signals that this is a Function question. Why does the author describe Reginald as an *outdoorsman*? This is a word that would normally be used to describe a person, but it is in this case used to describe a cat. This matches (B).

Choice A is not supported because the passage says nothing about Reginald's behavior when inside as opposed to outside. While Reginald is described as a neighborhood cat, this is not why the author uses the term *outdoorsman*, eliminating choice C. And in choice D, the author never indicates that Reginald would not have been welcomed into the house, just that he chose to remain outdoors.

8. F
Difficulty: Medium
Category: Global
Getting to the Answer: The clue words "passage as a whole" indicate this is a Global question. It is often difficult to make specific predictions about Global questions, so go choice by choice, eliminating as you go.

Choice (F) is supported by the passage: the author mentions several times how much Reginald seemed to appreciate anything that was given to him. Choice G might or might not be true; though the author discusses Reginald having scars, she does not provide evidence that he got into fights. Choice H is too extreme. While the author says Reginald seemed to play monster for the children, there is nothing to indicate he understood the games they played generally. Choice J, like G, might or might not be true. The author says nothing about Reginald's ability to understand he was not a house cat.

9. C
Difficulty: Low
Category: Inference
Getting to the Answer: The word "suggests" indicates this is an Inference question. Refer to your notes to get an idea of how Reginald's personality impacted his life, and predict that his affectionate nature meant he became a cat everyone in the neighborhood helped care for. This matches (C), the correct answer.

There is nothing to indicate people "grudgingly" cared for him out of sympathy, which eliminates A. Similarly, nothing in the passage supports the idea that he became affectionate only reluctantly, eliminating B. Finally, while the passage supports that Reginald was popular with the neighborhood children, nothing indicates that he wasn't also popular with the adults (indeed, the passage author seems to be an adult), eliminating D.

[CHAPTER 20]

PAIRED PASSAGES

> **LEARNING OBJECTIVES**
>
> After completing this chapter, you will be able to:
> - Apply unique strategies to effectively read ACT Reading paired passages in preparation for their question sets
> - Identify the variations on common ACT Reading questions as they are used in paired passages

Part 4
ACT READING

How Much Do You Know?

Directions: In this chapter, you'll learn to apply the ACT Reading strategies you've learned to paired passages. Take 10 minutes to read the following paired passages and answer the 9 accompanying questions. When you're finished, compare your work to that of an ACT expert on the following pages. Identify ways in which the expert reads these paired passages differently than she would an independent passage.

INFORMATIONAL: Passage A is adapted from an online article about the difficulty women have historically had being successfully published using their own names. Passage B is adapted from an essay about the history of anonymous works.

Passage A

In 1913, modernist author Virginia Woolf wrote an essay for the *Times Literary Supplement*, originally published anonymously. In this essay, she discusses a particular phenomenon suffered by
5 female writers of the past: a lack of respect within their lifetimes for their talents. She frames this essay around Jane Austen, who was, during Woolf's lifetime, in the midst of a resurgence of popularity.

It is difficult to imagine two writers more
10 different from one another than Woolf, who lived from 1886 to 1941, and Austen, who died in 1817, more than half a century before Woolf was born; Woolf's labyrinthine, stream-of-consciousness style and arduous prose stand in sharp contrast
15 to Austen's witty social commentaries masked as lighthearted novels. In the essay, while Woolf clearly respects Austen as a writer, she does criticize what she perceives as timidity in Austen's writing. Woolf refers at one point to Austen removing a
20 hedge from one of her novels when she found out they didn't grow where the story is set, "rather than run the risk of inventing one which could not exist." Austen, Woolf believed, was too afraid to test boundaries.

25 But consider this belief in light of another essay by Woolf. In 1929's "A Room of One's Own," she discusses a proverbial sister of William Shakespeare, equal in genius and equal in desire to make her living as a playwright but prevented from doing
30 so because she is a woman. Until the nineteenth century, Woolf says, it was almost impossible for a woman to become a successful writer. This was because, "unless her parents were exceptionally rich or very noble" and gave their blessing, she was
35 unlikely to have the opportunities necessary to develop her craft.

This second essay potentially sheds light on Austen and her writing style. In "A Room of One's Own," Woolf discusses how limited life must have
40 been for women in the past. Jane Austen, who began her professional writing career in 1811 and died in 1817, never married, and while she was educated, it would have been a far more limited education than a wealthy man would have received
45 at the same time. She was forced to publish her works anonymously, even when they proved popular. As Woolf herself famously wrote, "I would venture to guess that Anon . . . was often a woman."

Should it come as a surprise, then, under the
50 conditions of Austen's upbringing and career, that she was rather rigid and conservative in the way she told her stories? It was hard enough for her to be published at all. She did not have the wealth or the increased freedoms of Woolf, writing a
55 century later. Whether Woolf is right or wrong in her criticism of Austen as a timid writer, it is surely easily understood why, based on Woolf's own 1929 essay, Austen chose to write as she did.

Passage B

In 1967, Roland Barthes, a French literary critic,
60 wrote an essay entitled "La mort de l'auteur," "The Death of the Author." In the essay, Barthes makes the argument that authors and their works should be considered entirely separately from one another: a text should be interpreted on its own terms, rather
65 than through a lens of biographical scrutiny.

But what of the other form of "death of the author": the infamous Anonymous, authors who published with no credit given to them for their craft? Books now considered to be classics that were
70 originally published anonymously include Mary Shelley's *Frankenstein* and the works of Jane Austen.

And who is Mary Ann Evans? Likely, few would immediately recognize her name, but many would be able to come up with at least one work written by George Eliot. This was Evans' pen name, employed because she wanted her works to be taken seriously rather than dismissed as the light romances that were then believed to be the sole purview of female writers. When the Brontë sisters sought publication, they too did so under anonymity; Charlotte, Emily, and Anne Brontë became in print the masculine-sounding Currer, Ellis, and Acton Bell.

Now certainly, authorial anonymity is not limited to women. While many women published anonymous works because use of their own names might result in dismissal of the seriousness of their work or even outright rejection from publishers, some men, including such well-known figures as Edgar Allan Poe, Thomas Paine, Alexander Hamilton, and James Madison, published anonymously at various points in their careers to avoid the risk of personal consequences or concerns. It is even true that women could, in rare, lucky circumstances, find success under their own names: Ann Radcliffe, for instance, was one of the most successful authors of the late 1700s, writing wildly popular Gothic fiction.

Regardless of Radcliffe's unusual success, however, it is clear that many women who sought a career in writing in the Georgian and Victorian eras felt the need to disguise who they truly were, or were compelled to do so by publishers afraid of public reception. "Death of the author," in these cases, often meant that women in writing only had their true identities, and the associated respect they might earn from their talent, revealed after their own quite literal deaths.

1. In Passage A, Woolf's choice to publish her 1913 essay anonymously while criticizing Austen as a timid writer could best be described as:

   A. hypocritical; Austen had a choice and still chose anonymity, while Woolf did not.
   B. ironic; Woolf was criticizing behavior that could be called very similar to her own.
   C. symbolic; Woolf likely chose anonymity as a point of solidarity with women in Austen's time.
   D. modernistic; Woolf used her own novel-writing techniques to showcase Austen's.

2. In the context of Passage A, the details of Austen's personal life and education provide support for the author's claim that:

   F. Austen had reasons to write in a manner that could be called "timid."
   G. Austen's work is superior to Woolf's work because Austen had greater obstacles to overcome.
   H. despite her "rigid and conservative" novels, Austen is a better writer than she might seem.
   J. Woolf's criticism of Austen's timidity is well-founded.

3. As it is used in line 14, the word *sharp* most nearly means:

   A. raised and pitchy.
   B. razor-like and dangerous.
   C. abrupt and unexpected.
   D. notable and different.

4. In the third paragraph (lines 83–97) of Passage B, the author mentions other reasons some authors have chosen to publish anonymously primarily in order to:

F. establish the notion that women have never chosen to publish anonymously, but some men have chosen to do so.
G. set up a contrast between the common reasons men and women published anonymously in the past.
H. entertain the idea that while both men and women have published anonymously, more men did it than women.
J. showcase the possibility that there are better reasons to choose to publish anonymously than public reaction.

5. In Passage B, it can most reasonably be inferred that Ann Radcliffe's success as an author might best be attributed to:

A. being a female author at a time when those were rare.
B. having her real name attached to her works.
C. writing in a genre that was then very popular.
D. publishing under a pen name everyone at the time recognized.

6. Based on the information in the first paragraph (lines 59–65) of Passage B, it can be most reasonably inferred that Roland Barthes believed:

F. women were not given enough credit for their writing talent in past centuries.
G. knowing the details of a writer's life is not necessary for literary criticism.
H. only after an author dies can someone truly criticize their written works.
J. men and women often published anonymously for different reasons.

7. In the context of Passage B, the statements in lines 72–82 serve to:

A. provide additional information on why women might be forced to publish anonymously.
B. offer a contrast between women who publish as Anonymous and those who use pen names.
C. set up a comparison between women and men who publish anonymously.
D. show that in some cases women adopted male pen names in order to be more commercially successful writers.

8. Compared to Passage B, Passage A is more directly focused on:

F. literary essays about an author who is discussed in the passage.
G. the similarities between the works of two anonymous authors.
H. an overarching theory that explains all anonymous texts.
J. the importance of considering authors apart from their life context.

9. Passage B expands upon which of the following details from Passage A?

A. men in the past might publish anonymously for the same reasons women often did.
B. women in the past sometimes published anonymously.
C. Jane Austen chose to remain an anonymous author during her lifetime.
D. women in the past often chose masculine-sounding pen names.

Answers and Explanations

How Much Do You Know?

Passage Map Notes

Passage A:

¶1: VW essay about disrespected female writers and JA

¶2: contrasts between VW & JA, VW criticism of JA

¶3: 2nd VW essay: hard for past female writers

¶4–5: 2nd essay relates to JA

Passage B:

¶1: RB: "death of the author"—separate writer & text

¶2: author: "death of the author"—female writers stuck w/ anonymity

¶3: men sometimes anon, but not b/c had to be

¶4: female writers only get credit after death

BIG PICTURE SUMMARY

Passage A:

Main idea: The limited social approval of female writers may explain why Jane Austen did not take many risks in her writing.

Author's purpose: To defend Jane Austen against Woolf's earlier criticism using Woolf's argument in "A Room of One's Own."

Passage B:

Main idea: Many female authors wrote under male pseudonyms because they would not have been taken seriously otherwise.

Author's purpose: To explain why some authors, especially female authors, published anonymously.

---

1. B
Difficulty: High
Category: Inference
Getting to the Answer: The phrase "could best be described as" gives you the clues necessary to identify this as an Inference question. Predict that the correct answer will recognize that Woolf could also be called a "timid" writer in choosing anonymity even as she criticized that characteristic in Austen's writing. This matches (B).

While Woolf's behavior might be called hypocritical, as in A, the second part flips the situation: it was Woolf who had a choice, not Austen. In C, there is no evidence given for symbolism in Woolf's essay or in her choice to remain anonymous when it was published. Finally, in D, while Woolf's novel-writing techniques are discussed, the passage does not say she used those particular techniques in showcasing Austen's.

2. F
Difficulty: Medium
Category: Function
Getting to the Answer: The phrase "supports the author's claim" indicates this is a Function question. Refer back to that part of the passage and identify the author's opinion. The details of Austen's life are found in lines 40–47, and the author's opinion is introduced in lines 49–52. Predict that the correct answer will show that these details were included to support the idea that it was very difficult for women who wrote in Austen's time, which might help explain the style that Woolf criticizes. This matches (F).

In G, while the conditions of Austen's life may have been more difficult than those of Woolf, the author is not trying to make one writer appear superior to the other. Nor does the author attempt to prove that Austen is a better writer than her novels make her appear, which eliminates H. Finally, in J, the author's claim is misstated. The author uses Woolf's own words to argue that Austen was not necessarily timid, but constrained by the circumstances of her time.

3. D
Difficulty: Low
Category: Vocab-in-Context
Getting to the Answer: "Most nearly means" tells you that this is a Vocab-in-Context question. Refer back to the line referenced. *Sharp* here refers to contrast—the author of the passage discusses how Woolf's and Austen's writing differ from each another. This matches (D), which is correct.

Note, however, that all the incorrect answer choices are acceptable definitions of *sharp*. Always make sure it is clear in your mind how the author is using a word with multiple definitions before you start looking at the answer choices!

4. G
Difficulty: Medium
Category: Function
Getting to the Answer: Use the clue words "primarily in order to" to establish that this is a Function question. Refer back to the paragraph referenced, and read it for additional context. Predict that the correct answer will show that the author of the passage was acknowledging that men were also published anonymously, but it was by choice, whereas women had to publish anonymously to get their work published or taken seriously. Choice (G) matches this prediction, and is correct.

Choice F contradicts the passage, which states that women did publish anonymously. Choice H is out of scope; the passage does not discuss whether more men or women publish anonymously. Finally, J is a distortion. The author's intent is to create a contrast between reasons to publish anonymously, not to prove that reasons other than public reaction are preferable.

5. C
Difficulty: Low
Category: Inference
Getting to the Answer: The phrase "most reasonably be inferred" indicates that this is an Inference question. Refer to the third paragraph of Passage B, where Radcliffe is discussed. Predict that the correct answer will show that Radcliffe's success can be attributed to her writing popular Gothic fiction. This matches (C), which is correct.

Choices A and B are both distortions; female authors *were* rare at the time, and Radcliffe's choice to have her real name attached to her works was unusual, but her success came despite those things, not because of them. Choice D is simply factually incorrect, based on the information in the passage: Radcliffe was the rare exception, a successful female writer in the 1700s despite not using a pen name or publishing anonymously.

6. G
Difficulty: Low
Category: Inference
Getting to the Answer: The phrase "most reasonably inferred" offers you clues to identify this as an Inference question. Refer back to the first paragraph to refresh your memory on Barthes's beliefs. Predict that the correct answer will show that Barthes believed an author's work and their biography should be kept separate. This matches (G).

While F is part of the passage, it is not something Barthes necessarily believed. For H, Barthes was referring to "death" in a metaphorical sense, not a literal one. And J, like F, is in the passage, but the information in the passage does not suggest that Barthes believed this.

7. D
Difficulty: Medium
Category: Function
Getting to the Answer: "[S]erve to" tells you that this is a Function question. The author initially discusses women who published anonymously, but in the lines referenced, goes on to list some who adopted masculine-sounding pen names instead. Predict the correct answer will reflect this. The correct answer, then, is (D).

Choice A is incorrect because the lines referenced do not discuss why women might be forced to publish anonymously. It specifically mentions that in these cases, women chose to use male-sounding pen names. Choice B is incorrect because no contrast was given between the two groups. Choice C is incorrect because the information was not given in order to set up a comparison.

8. F
Difficulty: High
Category: Global
Getting to the Answer: Since the question asks you to compare the focuses of the two passages, this is a Global question. Consult your big picture summaries of both passages, and think about how they compare. Passage A is concerned with responding to Woolf's literary criticism of Jane Austen using another of Woolf's own essays about the difficulty of being a woman writer in the past. Passage B discusses how common it was, especially for women authors, to write anonymously; the passage also explains various reasons for anonymity. Analyze the choices to find the one that reflects the focus of Passage A. Choice (F) is correct; Passage A uses Woolf's literary essays to discuss Austen.

Choice G is incorrect because it distorts the details in Passage A; although the passage identifies that both Woolf (at least for her essay in the *Times Literary Supplement*) and Austen wrote anonymously, the passage only emphasizes the differences between their works. Choices H and J are incorrect because they better reflect Passage B. For H, Passage B discusses anonymous writing, though not an overarching theory about the practice. Choice J refers to Barthes's "death of the author" argument that is mentioned in Passage B.

9. B
Difficulty: Medium
Category: Detail
Getting to the Answer: The phrase "which of the following details" signals that this is a Detail question. It is difficult to make a prediction based on such a broad question, so review each answer choice, knocking out incorrect answers as you go.

While Passage B does discuss men publishing anonymously, this is not discussed at all in Passage A. Choice A is incorrect. Choice (B) is supported by the passages: Passage A mentions that Woolf wrote an essay anonymously and that Austen was forced into anonymous publication. Passage B gives information on some of the potential reasons why women wrote anonymously. So (B) is correct. Choice C is not supported at all by Passage A, which specifically mentions that Austen was forced to publish anonymously, not that she chose to do so. Choice D, like A, is discussed in Passage B but is not mentioned at all in Passage A.

Part 4
ACT READING

HOW TO APPROACH ACT PAIRED PASSAGES

> **LEARNING OBJECTIVES**
>
> After this lesson, you will be able to:
>
> - Apply unique strategies to effectively read ACT Reading paired passages in preparation for their question sets
> - Identify the variations on common ACT Reading questions as they are used in paired passages

What are paired passages?

Typically, one pair of shorter passages take the place of a single longer passage in the ACT Reading section. Occasionally, all four passages on an ACT Reading Test will be independent passages, but you should be prepared to encounter a paired passage set on test day.

The two passages share the same topic (although each will usually have its own take on the subject matter). The combined length of the paired passages is approximately the length of most single passages, so you don't have much, if any, extra reading to do.

In this chapter, you'll learn how ACT experts actively read paired passages a little differently than they read single passages, and you'll see how the test uses variations of standard ACT Reading questions to test your comprehension of both passages.

To read passages and answer questions like these

INFORMATIONAL: Passage A is adapted from a magazine article about recent technological efforts in conservation. Passage B is adapted from an online article about the success of using artificial intelligence to stop poachers.

Passage A

Conservationists are struggling to address the decimation of a growing number of plant and animal species due to environmental and human-made circumstances. Protecting the Earth's
[5] biodiversity requires a better understanding of the behavior of animals in their natural habitats and the factors leading to their decline; this is one aspect of conservation where technology can lend a hand. Artificial intelligence, commonly referred
[10] to as AI, has proved to be an important resource in the fight to protect species that already are, or might soon qualify as, endangered. The ability of AI to rapidly process large quantities of data makes it ideal for analyzing the decades of extensive
[15] tracking information researchers have gathered. More importantly, AI may reveal patterns that might not be readily discernible solely through human analysis.

The cheetah population in sub-Saharan Africa
[20] is a specific example of a species that has faced severe threats on several fronts. From 1900 to 2015, cheetahs saw an estimated 93% decline in population. This same time period also saw a 76% reduction in land that was formerly classified
[25] as cheetah habitat. Additionally, smuggling and common misperceptions about the dangers of cheetahs to livestock exacerbated the population decline. Initially, as conservationists began to realize the need to protect cheetahs in their native
[30] habitat, they focused on centuries-old tracking techniques. More recently, however, researchers have recognized how effective AI can be in conservation efforts.

Starting in 2001, the WildTrack team of researchers worked with statistical analysis software development companies JMP and SAS to create the Footprint Identification Technique, or FIT. Conservationists collected several high-quality digital images—footprints in the sand, snow, mud, and other natural substrates—and uploaded these images into the JMP software. The researchers then selected landmark points to form a basic outline of each footprint. AI extrapolates more details from the footprint, which is then assigned as a unique identifier for that specific cheetah. This non-invasive "digital tag" is then used in combination with GPS to precisely track individual cheetahs in their natural habitat.

This same technology can be used to identify and track a variety of endangered or vulnerable species (the WildTrack team has developed algorithms for more than 15 species). Progressive learning algorithms, which allow the AI to use mathematical models to identify species, sex, and age-class, become more accurate as the amount of established data grows. Conservation experts can use the collected data to predict the movements of isolated populations, track births and deaths within the population, and determine the best locations for reintroducing species to their native habitat. With so much work still to be done to protect the Earth's endangered species, conservationists are embracing the power of AI and looking for even more sophisticated applications in the future.

Passage B

For years, wildlife reserves and the animals who live there have been under attack. Poaching, the illegal hunting and capturing of wild animals, is the leading human cause of the severe decline in numbers of certain species. Many poachers use technology to aid them in their illegal activity. For example, some poachers track elephants and rhinos using GPS and night-vision goggles and kill them for their tusks and horns. Conservation officials are working to counter these attacks by applying AI-modeling; the sheer size of most wildlife reserves requires a technologically advanced approach to most effectively protect the animals from poachers.

The Protection Assistant for Wildlife Security (PAWS) program employs machine learning and behavior modeling to aid wildlife reserve patrols. By combining data about previous poaching activity and patrol routes, the system can predict where future poaching will likely take place and design continuously changing patrol routes using game-theory modeling. The constant variations of the routes prevent poachers from picking up on patterns, which in turn increases the chance of catching poachers in the act. PAWS manages to seamlessly blend machine learning with human knowledge: the algorithm provides a few different routes, and patrollers can choose the best one based on their years of experience working to prevent poaching.

Another aspect of the patrols that benefits from technology is route optimization that accounts for the terrain. While a substantial quantity of data, gathered over years of conservation work, exists about the most trafficked routes of animals frequently targeted by poachers, past patrol routes often involved climbs or descents that greatly limited the amount of land secured by regular patrols. Now AI can calculate the best routes for both the human patrollers and the drones in order to maximize the patrolled area. During an eight-month trial of the program at Uganda's Queen Elizabeth National Park, rangers found approximately 10 times as many poachers in areas designated as high-probability versus low-probability by the algorithm.

Those taking the lead in the efforts to end poaching for good sincerely hope that the AI-enhanced patrol routes will serve as a significant deterrent for poachers. As AI systems continue to find more effective solutions through data analysis, conservation experts feel confident that, with the help of technology, they can win the battle against poachers.

Part 4
ACT READING

1. According to Passage A, AI is a valuable conservation resource because:

   A. it allows conservation officials to thwart attacks by poachers.
   B. it can allow researchers to uncover norms that human analysis might miss.
   C. it can calculate patrol routes for human and drone patrollers.
   D. it is the best way for researchers to protect endangered species.

2. The author of Passage A most likely mentions the statistics in lines 21–25 to show:

   F. how AI has helped the cheetah population recover.
   G. how soon cheetahs will become extinct.
   H. how AI has helped prevent cheetahs from being attacked by poachers.
   J. how serious the threat facing the cheetah population is.

3. Based on Passage A, it can most reasonably be inferred that the decline in cheetah populations is due largely to:

   A. poachers attacking the cheetahs at an unprecedented rate.
   B. loss of land in natural cheetah habitats.
   C. tracking cheetahs using the Footprint Identification Technique.
   D. famine and drought, resulting in a lack of food for cheetah populations.

4. As it is used in line 74, the word *counter* most nearly means:

   F. to oppose.
   G. to promote.
   H. to ignore.
   J. to tally.

5. According to Passage B, PAWS aids conservation officials in protecting animals from poachers by:

   A. using centuries-old tracking techniques to find poachers.
   B. using an algorithm to provide only the best route to track poachers.
   C. combining human knowledge with computer learning to give patrollers options.
   D. using a non-invasive digital tag to track animals.

6. It can most reasonably be inferred that the author of Passage B uses the phrase "win the battle" (line 116) to refer to the hope that wildlife reserves will eventually be:

   F. ignored by both poachers and conservation officials alike.
   G. emptied of wild animals after being overrun by poachers.
   H. completely protected with the help of AI.
   J. managed in a way that balances the needs of all groups.

7. Passage A and Passage B are similar in that they both support the use of AI to:

   A. limit the negative effect poachers are having on certain wildlife populations.
   B. preserve the natural habitats of species that are experiencing population decline.
   C. eliminate the need for human intervention in the protection of wildlife.
   D. protect wildlife species from the threats causing population decline.

8. Compared to Passage A, Passage B focuses more on:

   F. using AI to track species in their native habitats.
   G. using AI-enhanced technology against poachers.
   H. using machine learning to aid in conservation education.
   J. using AI to calculate large quantities of data.

568

9. It can be reasonably inferred that after learning about AI capabilities such as the Footprint Identification Technique, the conservationists described in Passage B would likely:

   A. utilize these capabilities to aid in catching poachers.
   B. dismiss these capabilities as unnecessary.
   C. praise these capabilities as revolutionary.
   D. question the ethical nature of these capabilities.

You need to know this

Paired passages always address the same topic but will likely have different purposes and may reflect different opinions. Common relationships between the passages include:

- (Passage A) An excerpt from a piece of literature, and (Passage B) a related essay by the same author
- (Passage A) A history of an issue and/or a person, and (Passage B) a commentary on or evaluation of the same issue or person
- (Passage A) A report on an event or a conflict, and (Passage B) a report on a different-but-related event or conflict
- (Passage A) Commentary on an issue as reflected through one context, and (Passage B) commentary on the same issue reflected through a different context

The authors of paired passages may disagree with each other but do not have to.

When paired passages refer to the same detail, each author may have a different reason for including the detail and a different point of view toward it.

The question set accompanying paired passages addresses the passages in order: roughly, the first third of the questions are about Passage A, the next third are about Passage B, and the final third are about the relationships between the two passages.

Some questions that address the relationships between the passages are variations on standard ACT Reading question types.

You need to do this

Unpack the blurb to discover all that you can about each passage and author; anticipate the possible relationships between the passages.

Manage your active reading and the question set strategically by completing the following steps:

- Actively read Passage A as you would a standard passage—note keywords, jot down the purpose of each paragraph, and summarize the big picture.
- Answer the questions associated exclusively with Passage A (roughly, the first third of the question set).
- Actively read Passage B as you would a standard passage—note keywords, jot down the purpose of each paragraph, and summarize the big picture.
- Answer the questions associated exclusively with Passage B (roughly, the next third of the question set).
- Answer the questions that ask about both passages in relationship to each other (the final third of the question set).

Part 4
ACT READING

Research, predict, and answer questions exclusively addressing one of the passages as you would any standard ACT Reading question.

When answering questions that address the relationships between the passages, keep the following strategies in mind:

- To predict and answer Global questions comparing or contrasting both passages, consider your big picture summaries.
- To research, predict, and answer Inference questions comparing or contrasting both passages:
  - Locate the piece of text at issue in the question stem.
  - Consider the other author's likely reaction to or opinion of that piece of text. Locate the piece of text that supplies the other author's likely response.

Answers and Explanations

Suggested Passage Map Notes

Passage A:

¶1: AI helpful for conservation

¶2: cheetah conservation situation

¶3: FIT: AI used to track cheetah footprints

¶4: FIT helpful for other species also

Passage B:

¶5: using AI to counter poachers

¶6: PAWS: AI helps suggest varied patrol routes

¶7: AI considers terrain, plans patrols for max effectiveness

¶8: conservationists hopeful

BIG PICTURE SUMMARY

Passage A:

Main idea: AI technology helps environmentalists preserve endangered animal species by gathering data about their movements.

Author's purpose: To describe how AI technology aids in tracking endangered animals.

Passage B:

Main idea: AI technology makes anti-poaching wildlife patrols more effective by generating unpredictable patrol routes using game theory and by optimizing patrol routes for the given terrain.

Author's purpose: To describe how AI technology can assist environmentalists in countering poachers.

---

1. B
Difficulty: Medium
Category: Detail
Getting to the Answer: The phrase "according to Passage A" shows that this is a Detail question, so it is important to check the passage for support. The end of the first paragraph tells us that AI can process large quantities of data, but, more importantly, it may reveal patterns that human analysis may miss. This matches (B) nicely.

Choices A and C reference information from Passage B. Choice D is extreme; beware of words like "best" or "worst." The passage talks about the benefits of AI but never states that it is the best way to protect endangered species.

2. J
Difficulty: Medium
Category: Function
Getting to the Answer: The wording "the author . . . to show" tells us that this is a Function question. Paragraph 2 begins by stating that the cheetah population has faced severe threats. It tells us that from 1900 to 2015, the cheetah population saw a 93% decline in population and a 76% reduction in habitat. These statistics, then, serve to demonstrate the severity of the threat to the cheetah population. Choice (J) is correct.

Choice F is the opposite of what the statistics show; the cheetah population is in decline, not recovery. Choice G is extreme, as the passage never states that the cheetah will become extinct. Choice H refers to information from Passage B.

3. B
Difficulty: Medium
Category: Inference
Getting to the Answer: "Based on" and "it can most reasonably be inferred" are phrases that indicate an Inference question. The correct answer will require you to link together facts in the passage to form a conclusion. The passage tells you that the cheetah population is in decline due to several factors, but, at the same time that the 93% population decline occurred, there was a 76% loss of cheetah habitat—a significant statistic. You can conclude, then, that the decline is largely due to the loss of land, which matches (B).

Choice A refers to information in Passage B. Choice C does as well, and it is a misused detail; the Footprint Identification Technique was used to help the cheetah population, not hurt it. Choice D is out of scope; drought and famine were not discussed in this passage.

Part 4
ACT READING

4. F
Difficulty: Medium
Category: Vocab-in-Context
Getting to the Answer: This question, like all Vocab-in-Context questions, asks you to identify what a word "most nearly means." Reread the sentence for context and predict a new word by pretending that "counter" is a blank in the sentence. A good prediction here would be something similar to "go against" the attacks by poachers. Choice (F) matches.

Choice G is the opposite of what the passage suggests. Choice H is incorrect because conservation officials do not want to ignore the attacks of poachers. Choice J refers to the action of counting, which also does not describe conservationists' intentions toward poachers.

5. C
Difficulty: Medium
Category: Detail
Getting to the Answer: This question begins with, "According to Passage B," which indicates that it is a Detail question. Your strategy here should be to go back to the passage where PAWS is mentioned to get the correct answer. Paragraph 2 states that the system blends machine learning with human knowledge that patrollers can use to track poachers. This matches (C).

Choices A and D are misused details; they refer to cheetah-tracking methods discussed in Passage A. Choice B is extreme, as the passage states that the algorithm provides patrollers with options, not just the best route.

6. H
Difficulty: Medium
Category: Inference
Getting to the Answer: Inference questions require you to use facts in the passage to determine something that is not stated directly. Here you are tasked with figuring out what the unstated hope is. Refer to the final paragraph of Passage B to help you predict that the hope is that AI will help conservationists win the fight against poachers. This matches (H).

Answer choice F is the opposite of what you are looking for, as it contradicts the information in the passage. Choice G also contradicts what the passage states—this passage is about preservation; it is not about poachers overrunning natural habitats. Choice J might be tempting, but it distorts the facts; conservationists are not interested in protecting the needs of poachers.

7. D
Difficulty: Medium
Category: Global
Getting to the Answer: This question is Global in nature because it asks about a similarity between the two passages in their entirety. Both passages deal with AI being used in wildlife conservation efforts. This matches (D).

Choice A refers to Passage B only. Choice B refers to Passage A. Answer choice C is out of scope; this passage does not discuss AI replacing humans.

8. G
Difficulty: Medium
Category: Global
Getting to the Answer: Read this question carefully. It asks what "Passage B focuses more on," making it an open-ended question involving both passages. Since an open-ended question like this is difficult to predict an answer for, use this approach: work through the choices one by one to find the correct answer. Note that the question is focused on Passage B, so you can immediately eliminate any choice not mentioned in Passage B. Choice F refers to the Footprint Identification Technique mentioned in Passage A; eliminate it. Choice (G) is correct; Passage A does not discuss poachers, whereas techniques to address poaching are the main idea of Passage B.

You can move on after finding the correct answer, but if you want to, check the others: neither passage discusses education, so H is incorrect. Choice J refers to information mentioned in Passage A, not Passage B.

9. A
Difficulty: Medium
Category: Inference
Getting to the Answer: This question uses the phrase "it can be reasonably inferred" to ask us what one group might do with new information. The facts presented in each passage will help. The conservationists described by the author of Passage B are focused on stopping poachers. The Footprint Identification Technique is currently used to track cheetahs, but it can be used to track other species. It is reasonable to conclude that the conservationists described in Passage B would use this technique to help track poachers, so (A) is correct.

Choice B is the opposite of the correct answer; both authors deem it necessary to help wildlife. Choice C is extreme; while the author of Passage B would likely see the positive side of using the Footprint Identification Technique, the words *praise* and *revolutionary* do not match the tone of the passage. Choice D is out of scope, as ethics are not mentioned.

Part 4
ACT READING

Try on Your Own

Directions: Actively read this paired passage set and answer its accompanying questions. Take note of any question stems that are specifically tailored to fit paired passages so that you can research, predict, and answer them strategically.

INFORMATIONAL: Passage A was adapted from a speech given by a prominent city planner. Passage B was adapted from a speech given by a community organizer promoting the inclusion of a new community center in a Chicago suburb.

Passage A

The North American suburb is an architectural and civic phenomenon that arose in response to the need to "get away" from the city and all the noise, pollution, and stress that went along with
5 it. Suburban communities, however, were not sufficient by themselves to support a full life. The people who lived in them needed to work, shop, and socialize, and most of the active part of their lives remained fixed in urban centers. Therefore,
10 suburbs were clustered around their parent cities, with all the suburban inhabitants commuting daily to the city center for work and play.

All of this seems perfectly logical and inevitable. The suburb should be the perfect
15 halfway point between city and country—away from the noise, congestion, and pollution, but not so far away that there's no access to culture, to income, to all the exciting benefits of urban life. In reality, though, few suburbs have actually
20 approached this ideal. Some critics have charged that, as suburbs have grown to the size of sprawling towns themselves, they are revealed as communities somehow devoid of community necessities. They lack local stores, community
25 centers, and places for kids to hang out; instead, they offer parking lots, chain stores, and strip malls.

The structure of the modern suburb, while offering a respite from city pollution, has created
30 health and environmental risks of its own. Because of the separation of living and commercial spaces imposed by many suburban zoning laws, nearly every activity, aside from visiting adjacent houses or the occasional neighborhood park, requires
35 an automobile trip. All of this driving creates pollution. Of course, America has had a long love affair with the car, and any city planner who thinks he can single-handedly change that is in for a rude surprise. Surely, though, we must begin
40 to balance the appeal and freedom of the car with ecological and civic responsibility.

This does not mean, however, that we need to abandon suburbs altogether, as some have suggested. Instead, we need to more knowingly
45 pursue that ideal of the best of city and country. Suburbs could be fascinating and beautiful places; we need only exercise our power to determine the nature of the places in which we live.

Passage B

"America doesn't need any more!" is a common
50 refrain for those who see suburbs merely as a means to line construction companies' pockets without contributing much to the value and diversity of American culture. I, however, see the problem of suburbs as one of degree rather than
55 kind. I haven't given up yet on the possibility of infusing the suburbs with public spaces that we can be proud of, that are rewarding to the human spirit. What can be done to bring diversity and character into these respites from the hustle and
60 bustle of the city?

A crucial starting point is reshaping the narrative of what the suburbs are intended to be a respite from. As young people form family units and those families grow, naturally they desire more
65 space. In most major cities the desire for more space comes at a significant premium, one which all too often middle-income families are unable to afford. The suburbs have the potential to serve as a happy medium: an affordable neighborhood with space for
70 families to grow, all of the more robust amenities of a major city in close proximity, and a pace of life less frenetic than traditionally expected in the city.

For these public spaces to truly be representative, more is needed. We need community engagement
75 that will help us explore our identity, discover

what we value, and determine what makes us different from the surrounding areas. In turn, this will allow us to celebrate the character of our unique community in our public spaces. I, for
80 one, do believe that the developers that we work with are invested in our community beyond just their financial bottom line. The proposed projects each reflect thoughtful attempts to appeal to our entire community; now, we have an opportunity to
85 determine which one resonates the most with us.

The suburbs still have the potential to deliver on the core principles that led to their development. Space to spread out need not mean distancing ourselves from our neighbors. The cities do not
90 hold a monopoly on character; we are the architects of the character of our community, and that is what America needs more of: community architects, ready to go to work.

1. In Passage A, the discussion in the final paragraph implies that the author:

   A. blames poor city planning for the existence of the suburb.
   B. thinks today's suburbs are actually fascinating and beautiful.
   C. believes most people take too little interest in their surroundings
   D. is optimistic about the possibilities of the American suburb.

2. According to the third paragraph of Passage A, city planners need to consider:

   F. accepting suburban residents' reluctance to give up driving.
   G. minimizing every boundary between residential and retail space.
   H. placing more local stores and kids' hangouts across the street from houses.
   J. moving the local parks to safer and more accessible neighborhoods.

3. The main purpose of Passage A is to:

   A. bemoan the detrimental effect suburbs have had on individual quality of life.
   B. discourage the suburb dweller's dependence on the automobile.
   C. encourage a different, more effective vision of the place of suburbs in communities.
   D. call for a return to the type of suburb that prevailed before World War II.

4. As used in line 66 in Passage B, the word *premium* most nearly refers to a living space that is:

   F. a prize that might be won.
   G. part of an insurance policy.
   H. a high price.
   J. higher quality.

5. In Passage B, lines 68–72 mainly function as examples of reasons why:

   A. suburbs have the potential to be comparable to or even better for families than city living.
   B. diversity might naturally come to suburban living spaces.
   C. suburban living is inherently superior to urban living in all situations.
   D. families usually choose to move from urban areas to suburban areas as they have children.

6. Based on the first paragraph of Passage B, it can reasonably be inferred that the author believes:

   F. more needs to be done to make urban living spaces affordable to families as they grow.
   G. construction companies charge too much for projects that do not serve communities.
   H. suburban communities are currently harmful to the spirits of people living there.
   J. many who decry suburbs are basing their beliefs on things that are possible to change.

7. The authors of both Passage A and Passage B would most likely agree with which of the following statements?

   A. Urban spaces should be seen as less desirable places to live for the majority of the population.
   B. While suburban spaces have not always lived up to their potential, there are ways to continue to improve them.
   C. Research would probably show that living in an urban area is more affordable for most families.
   D. Nobody who currently lives in a suburban area feels the sense of community that urban areas provide.

8. Compared to the author of Passage B, the author of Passage A discusses more:

   F. specific criticisms of suburban spaces.
   G. reasons why suburban living is more affordable.
   H. specific ways to improve suburban living.
   J. the need for more diversity in suburban spaces.

9. How would the author of Passage A likely respond to Passage B's assertion that "developers that we work with are invested in our community beyond just their financial bottom line"?

   A. The author of Passage A is likely to agree with it because suburban areas are designed to be affordable.
   B. The author of Passage A is likely to agree with it because developers are now supporting local stores and community centers.
   C. The author of Passage A is likely to disagree with it because suburbs currently seem to be designed without community in mind.
   D. The author of Passage A is likely to disagree with it because suburban areas are rarely profitable for anyone.

Chapter 20
Paired Passages

How Much Have You Learned?

Directions: For test-like practice, give yourself 10 minutes to complete this question set. Be sure to study the explanations, even for questions you got correct. They can be found at the end of this chapter.

LITERARY NARRATIVE: Passage A is adapted from the essay "The Language Barrier or Silence" by Joseph Fellows. Passage B is adapted from the essay "The First and Last Time" by Randy Benson.

Passage A by Joseph Fellows

I hadn't slept the night before I left, nor could I even doze on the plane. Piqued and red-eyed is not how I had envisioned my first day abroad. I had also hoped to have a little bit of the German
5 language under my belt before mingling with locals.

Unfortunately, the absurdly unpredictable nature of the *der/die/das* articles frustrated me so much that I never really got past the general salutations and simple, commonly used phrases. I was
10 therefore stubbornly determined to get as much mileage out of *danke* and *bitte* as I could. Every German person in Tegel Airport must have thought me incredibly gracious but dimwitted. I tried saying *freut mich, Sie kennenzulernen* (nice to meet you)
15 to the cab driver that I hailed, and after three tries, each receiving a quizzical stare in return, I gave up and simply told him my destination in English. I then squeezed myself into the tiny Peugeot; evidently, SUVs are not fashionable in Europe.

20 The bed-and-breakfast I had booked was nice—very quaint, but obviously a tourist spot. The owner was a scowling old woman who said little and waddled around, pointing and grunting, rightfully assuming I was linguistically stunted.
25 Thoroughly intimidated by the locals and their language, I decided to take a walk through historic Berlin in hopes of bonding with the nature and architecture, rather than the people. I was immediately glad that I did. Despite being
30 exhausted and surly, I found myself awestruck and humbled by the ubiquitous artistry of the city.

Despite knowing little about World War II and having been born forty years after, I was profoundly affected by my first view of the Kaiser
35 Wilhelm Gedächtniskirche (Memorial Church), with its crushed steeple and bomb-ravaged stone walls, existing in jarring juxtaposition to the surrounding modern architecture.

Further east near the Berlin Zoo, I found
40 a lovely park along the murky water of the Landwehrkanal, and eventually, I came to a massive traffic circle. In the midst of this automotive maelstrom of Berlin rush hour stood the magnificent Siegessäule (Victory Column).
45 The immaculate craftsmanship against the verdant horizon and cerulean sky—there are no words in any language to describe it. So I sat on a stone bench, smiled contentedly, and said nothing.

Passage B by Randy Benson

My room was gray and windowless, with a
50 cement floor painted blood-red. The mattress had no sheets, but I was too disoriented to care. Bad way to start the semester. Why had I decided to follow Greg here anyway?

After we stored our bags in a locker at Termini,
55 Greg marched me to a trattoria where we feasted on pasta, fish, veal, salad, cheese, and fruit. After the meal, Greg took me on a bistro-and-basilica tour. "C'mon, Paisan'. I'm gonna show you how to do Rome right."

60 After two churches and two restaurants, I said to Greg, "I understand loving the food here. But what's your thing with churches?"

Greg looked at me like I had a trinity of heads. "I know you're not really that clueless, Paisan'. Quit
65 being such a middle-class American sophomore and ask me a real question, like 'Gee, Greg, that bone church we just went through makes me wonder whatever would possess a herd of Capuchin monks to make artistic masterpieces out
70 of their own skeletal remains.'"

Actually, the thought of the bone church made the hunk of Fontinella cheese I'd just wolfed down twist in my stomach. "No. I don't wanna talk about the bones. I wanna know why you're
75 dragging me through churches. Is it just a scenic way to pace ourselves between bistros?"

"You mean to tell me, Paisan', that you really got nothing out of St. Peter's?"

I wasn't going to admit it to Greg, but St. Peter's
80 really was kind of awesome. Made my jaw drop, actually.

"Eh. It's a big church. Who cares?"

"You should, Paisan'. This is Rome, man. The Republic. The Empire. The Church. In a place
85 like this, I shouldn't have to agitate you into an outburst of culture. Up 'til now, everything about life has numbed you. This place is gonna wake up your soul." At this, he pushed another hunk of Fontinella at me, and I had no confidence that it
90 would sit any better than the last after one more church full of bones.

After seven more churches and three more bistros, we finally ground to a halt at the Cafe Montespiné. The locals gawked at the Americani
95 and engaged Greg in conversations that mixed French, Greek, Italian, and Martian. We dragged ourselves out of Montespiné at 4:30 in the morning, with half of our newfound friends still acting like the night was just starting.

100 Which is why I woke up this morning, bleary-eyed, in the previous night's clothes, my head heavy as a crushed Italian moon-rock breakfast roll. Maybe not the best way to start the semester. But I have to admit—it was quite a start.

1. The narrator of Passage A includes the interaction with the cab driver (lines 13–17) primarily in order to:

   A. explain how the narrator got from the airport to the bed-and-breakfast.
   B. provide an example of the narrator's inexperience with the German language.
   C. show the affinity that the narrator has for the German language.
   D. explain how to greet someone unfamiliar in German.

2. In the third paragraph of Passage A (lines 20–31), the narrator's decision to go for a walk is prompted by:

   F. his insecurity that had developed because of his frustration with the German language.
   G. his anger toward the owner of the bed-and-breakfast.
   H. his eagerness to sightsee and experience all the city had to offer.
   J. his stubborn determination to succeed at speaking the German language.

3. In Passage B, the narrator's descriptions of Greg suggest that the narrator sees Greg as:

   A. too daring and bold to be a traveling companion in the future.
   B. compelling enough to follow and see what happens next.
   C. too numb to experience any pleasure in Rome.
   D. a fanatic driven by a passion for churches.

4. In Passage B, the phrase "I wasn't going to admit it to Greg" (line 79) primarily serves to:

   F. illustrate the narrator's unwillingness to follow Greg's scheme.
   G. argue that admiration of Roman churches is a more private matter.
   H. call attention to the jaw-dropping nature of St. Peter's.
   J. suggest the favorable influence that Greg's tour is having on the narrator.

5. In the last paragraph of Passage B (lines 100–104), the narrator summarizes his:

   A. transition from sleep to regret for staying out the previous night.
   B. transition from sleep to a celebratory embrace of new life circumstances.
   C. recognition of the previous night as a unique way to begin his stay in Rome.
   D. return to a reality made much happier by the absence of Greg.

6. Compared to Passage B's narrator, Passage A's narrator spends more time discussing:

   F. the history of the city he is visiting.
   G. his interactions with the local people.
   H. the various religious landmarks he encounters.
   J. his inability to speak the local language fluently.

7. Which of the following statements best describes the tones of the two passages?

   A. Passage A is impersonal and historical, whereas Passage B is thoughtfully nostalgic.
   B. Passage A is animated and comical, whereas Passage B is serious and introspective.
   C. Both passages begin with a sense of trepidation but end with an air of equability and calm.
   D. Both passages begin humorously and end on a note of introspection.

8. Both Passage A and Passage B highlight the narrators':

   F. individual reactions to novel surroundings and non-native languages.
   G. emotional shortcomings in response to stressful stimuli.
   H. determination to impress others with recently honed language skills.
   J. decisions to return home after unsuccessful attempts to acclimate in unfamiliar countries.

9. Which of the following best describes the narrators' reactions to the architecture in the cities they visited?

   A. Passage A's narrator appreciates the architecture, whereas Passage B's narrator is indifferent.
   B. Passage A's narrator does not notice the architecture, whereas Passage B's narrator is wholly captivated by it.
   C. Passage A's narrator and Passage B's narrator both begin by appreciating the architecture and then grow tired of it.
   D. Passage A's narrator finds peace by looking at the architecture, whereas Passage B's narrator has a more complicated response to it.

Part 4
ACT READING

Reflect

Directions: Take a few minutes to recall what you've learned and what you've been practicing in this chapter. Consider the following questions, jot down your best answer for each one, and then compare your reflections to the expert responses on the following page. Use your level of confidence to determine what to do next.

1. What are ACT Reading paired passages? How do expert test takers adjust their active reading to tackle paired passages most effectively?

   _____
   _____
   _____

2. How are the question sets that accompany paired passages different from those accompanying standard independent passages?

   _____
   _____
   _____

3. How confident do you feel with paired passages? What can you do in practice to improve your performance and gain even more confidence with this type of passage?

   _____
   _____
   _____

Responses

1. What are ACT Reading paired passages? How do expert test takers adjust their active reading to tackle paired passages most effectively?

On most ACT tests, one Reading stimulus is a pair of shorter passages instead of a single, long passage. Expert test takers actively read each passage and answer the questions exclusively associated with each. Then, experts compare and contrast the passages' big pictures and details and answer questions associated with both.

2. How are the question sets that accompany paired passages different from those accompanying standard independent passages?

Usually, the first third of the question set exclusively addresses Passage A; the next third exclusively addresses Passage B; and the final third addresses comparisons and contrasts between the passages. The questions that address both passages reward students who accurately summarize the big picture of each passage and who can determine how one author would likely respond to something argued or proposed by the other author.

3. How confident do you feel with paired passages? What can you do in practice to improve your performance and gain even more confidence with this type of passage?

There is no one-size-fits-all answer for this question. Give yourself an honest self-assessment. If you feel that paired passages are a strength, congratulations! Continue to practice them so that you'll be able to rack up the points associated with these passages on test day. If you feel less confident about the paired passage format, review the strategies in this chapter and try to consistently apply the expert approaches outlined here whenever you practice passages in this format.

Next Steps

If you answered most questions correctly in the "How Much Have You Learned?" section, and if your responses to the Reflect questions were similar to those of the ACT expert, then consider paired passages an area of strength and move on to the next chapter. Come back to this topic periodically to prevent yourself from getting rusty.

If you don't yet feel confident, review the material in this chapter, and then try the questions you missed again. As always, be sure to review the explanations closely. Then go online (**kaptest.com/login**) to use your Qbank for more practice. If you haven't already registered your book, do so at **kaptest.com/moreonline**.

GO ONLINE
kaptest.com/login

Part 4
ACT READING

Answers and Explanations

Try on Your Own

Suggested Passage Map Notes

Passage A:

¶1: suburb origins

¶2: ideal vs. actual

¶3: necessity of cars leads to pollution

¶4: need to improve suburbs

Passage B:

¶1: we can & should improve suburbs

¶2: what suburbs ought to be

¶3: community engagement → uniqueness → improvement

¶4: author sees potential, calls on audience

BIG PICTURE SUMMARY

Passage A:

Main idea: Suburbs often lack the necessities of every-day life and their reliance upon cars creates pollution.

Author's purpose: To describe the ways in which suburbs are less than perfect and suggest that they could be improved.

Passage B:

Main idea: Suburbs can be made to have character with thoughtful planning.

Author's purpose: To argue that suburbs have the potential to allow residents more than they would have in cities without sacrificing community identity.

1. D
Difficulty: Low
Category: Inference
Getting to the Answer: The clue word *implies* shows that this is an Inference question. Do not rely on your memory; go back to the last paragraph of Passage A and research what was said. The author claims that we do not "need to abandon suburbs altogether" and that "suburbs could be fascinating and beautiful places." Choice (D) matches these sentiments and is thus correct.

Choice A is incorrect because the author never casts *blame*. Choice B may be tempting, but it goes beyond what is actually stated in the text. The author says that suburbs have the potential to be beautiful, not that they already are. Finally, choice C is incorrect because the passage never discusses people taking interest in their surroundings.

2. F
Difficulty: Low
Category: Detail
Getting to the Answer: The phrase "According to" is a clue that this is a Detail question. It directs you to the third paragraph, so go back and do some research. The author says that Americans love their cars and that "any city planner who thinks he can single-handedly change that is in for a rude surprise." Predict that the correct answer must therefore have something to do with how people love driving. Choice (F) is correct.

Choice G is extreme; the author does not advocate minimizing *every* boundary. Choice H is a misused detail; while the author suggests that more local stores and places for young people are needed, they are not the focus of this paragraph. Finally, J is incorrect because there is no mention of "safer and more accessible neighborhoods" in this paragraph.

3. C
Difficulty: Medium
Category: Global
Getting to the Answer: You can tell this is a Global question because it asks for "The main purpose" of the passage. When answering Global questions, look back at your notes for each paragraph, think of the big picture, and do not be distracted by details. The passage begins by explaining how suburbs naturally developed out of cities and then moves into a discussion of some of the negative aspects of suburban living. However, the passage ends on a note of optimism, with the author claiming that "we need to more knowingly pursue that ideal of the best of city and country."

Predict that the correct answer should say something about how the suburbs are by and large a sensible idea but could be better still. Choice (C) is correct.

Choice A is too extreme; since the author concludes optimistically, he is not *bemoaning* the effects of suburbs throughout the whole passage. Choice B is too narrow to be the answer to a Global question; automobiles are mentioned in the fourth paragraph only. Finally, choice D is out of scope; the passage never discusses suburbs before World War II.

4.   H
Difficulty: Low
Category: Vocab-in-Context
Getting to the Answer: "As it is used" should serve as a clue that this is a Vocab-in-Context question. Refer back to the second paragraph of Passage B, where a larger living space in the city is described as something many families will be "unable to afford." Predict that *premium* in this case means "expensive." This matches (H).

The other answer choices are all acceptable meanings for the word *premium*, but none of them matches the way that the word is used within the context of the passage.

5.   A
Difficulty: High
Category: Function
Getting to the Answer: The keyword *function* tells you that this is, yes, a Function question! Refer back to the lines in question, which are immediately preceded by "The suburbs have the potential to serve as a happy medium." Predict that the correct answer will reflect this. This matches (A), which is the correct answer.

While the author does encourage increased diversity in suburban areas, he is not specifically addressing this need in the lines referenced, eliminating B. Choice C is too extreme; while the author does encourage suburban living, he implies it could be roughly equal to living in an urban environment, not automatically better. Choice D is too extreme. The author is giving reasons why suburbs might be appealing to growing families, but does not say anything about whether or not families *usually* choose to move to suburbs as a result.

6.   J
Difficulty: Medium
Category: Inference
Getting to the Answer: The clue words "can reasonably be inferred" indicate this is an Inference question. The question asks for something the author might believe, so it is difficult to make a specific prediction. Instead, look at each answer choice, eliminating them one by one.

For F, while the author does discuss the higher cost of living in urban areas, that is not part of this paragraph; eliminate it. Choice G is a distortion; the passage suggests that other people believe this, not that the author does. Choice H is extreme; while the author does say that suburbs could be more rewarding, the paragraph does not imply that they are actively harmful. Finally, (J) is supported by the passage—the author discusses how some believe that suburban areas are just a way for construction companies to make money, but the author believes they do not have to be that way. (J) is correct.

7.   B
Difficulty: Medium
Category: Inference
Getting to the Answer: The keywords "most likely agree" signal that this is an Inference question. It asks for a statement with which both authors would most likely agree, so review your notes on both passages. This is too broad a question to make a prediction, so eliminate answer choices one by one until you find one that fits.

Choice A is too broad: both authors discuss some of the advantages that come from urban living. Choice (B) would be supported by both authors: they both discuss some of the problems in suburbs, but believe these can be fixed with better planning and effort. You can stop at this point, but if you did look at C or D: C is not supported by the author of Passage B, who specifically discusses the higher cost of living in urban areas for families needing more space. Choice D is too extreme to be supported by the author of Passage A, who does criticize the lack of community in suburban areas, but never says that absolutely nobody in a suburban area feels a sense of community.

Part 4
ACT READING

8. F
Difficulty: Low
Category: Global
Getting to the Answer: Because this stem asks us to compare one passage to another, this is a Global question. Review your notes on both passages. What does Passage A focus on that Passage B does not? Passage A focuses more on what people specifically complain about regarding suburbs, so predict that the correct answer will reflect this. And it does—choice (F) matches the prediction, and is correct.

Affordability, as in G, and a need for diversity, as in J, are actually things discussed in Passage B. Neither passage discusses specific ways to improve suburbs, though both say they believe it is possible, which means you can eliminate H.

9. C
Difficulty: High
Category: Inference
Getting to the Answer: Asking how the author would "likely respond" signals that this is an Inference question. Predict that while the two authors agree that suburban areas are a good idea theoretically, the author of Passage A would be unlikely to agree that current developers are invested in the community, as the author of Passage B suggests here, because all the evidence in suburbs as they currently exist points to the contrary. This matches (C).

The author of Passage A does not discuss affordability at all, so you have no frame of reference as to whether he would agree that current developers are designing affordable locations or not, which eliminates A. Though Passage A does cite lack of local stores and community centers as a criticism some have made of suburbs, there is nothing to support the idea that developers are focusing more on building them now, which eliminates B. Similarly, the author of Passage A does not discuss the profitability of suburbs, which eliminates D.

How Much Have You Learned?

Suggested Passage Map Notes
Passage A:

¶1: Sleepless flight; learned very limited German

¶2: More language trouble

¶3: Intimidated but goes for walk

¶4: Beautiful Berlin has impressive architecture

¶5: Content with trip in silence

Passage B:

¶1: Bare room, disoriented

¶2: Greg (G) takes lead, Paisan' = Narrator (N)

¶3: Why churches?

¶4: Bone churches

¶5: N doesn't understand

¶6–8: N impressed by St. Peter's, acts unimpressed

¶9: G excited about Rome

¶10: Late night with locals

¶11: N has rough morning, admits interesting start

BIG PICTURE SUMMARY
Passage A:

Main idea: The narrator is feeling frustrated with the language of a foreign country but finds pleasure in the aesthetics of his surroundings.

Author's purpose: To relate a story about feeling out of place in a foreign environment.

Passage B:

Main idea: Despite initial reservations, the narrator has an intense first day and night studying abroad after following Greg.

Author's purpose: To recount his first day and night in a new city while studying abroad.

1. B
Difficulty: Low
Category: Function
Getting to the Answer: The wording "The narrator ... includes ... in order to" identifies this as a Function question. Every part of a passage contributes to the purpose of the larger section. According to the sample passage map for Passage A, the interaction between the narrator and the cab driver shows the narrator having language troubles, which is a theme throughout the passage. Choice (B) is correct.

Although A and D describe features of paragraph 1, they do not reflect the reason the narrator included the interaction. It's clear that the narrator does NOT have an affinity, or natural talent, for the German language, so C is incorrect.

2. F
Difficulty: Medium
Category: Detail
Getting to the Answer: This question stem provides few clues as to question type; it might be either a Detail or an Inference question, depending on whether the passage states directly what prompted the narrator's walk. However, the first step to answering it will be the same regardless: find the appropriate section of the passage to research and determine the answer. In the third paragraph, the narrator mentions being "Thoroughly intimidated by the locals and their language" when describing his decision to go for a walk. Choice (F) is correct.

Although the narrator pointed out that the owner was "scowling," there is no evidence that he is actually angry with her, so G is incorrect. The narrator did express his desire to "bond with nature and architecture," but "all the city has to offer" would include the people in it as well, so H is incorrect. Choice J might be tempting because of the narrator's self-professed stubborn determination in line 10, but that detail is not connected to the narrator's reason for taking a walk.

3. B
Difficulty: Medium
Category: Inference
Getting to the Answer: The clue word "suggest" marks this as an Inference question. For an Inference question that asks about a relationship, use the information provided about that relationship to form a prediction. The narrator expresses mixed feelings about going along with Greg. In the first paragraph, the narrator conveys some ambivalence when he wonders, "Why had I decided to follow Greg here anyway?" (lines 52–53). However, the narrator follows Greg all day and half the night, and he admits to enjoying St. Peter's. Choice (B) is correct. The narrator is compelled by Greg's behavior and tour-guide tendencies, and he thereby remains curious enough to stay with Greg through the entire night's tour.

When a character has mixed feelings, watch out for answer choices that are too extreme, such as A. Choice C is the opposite of how the narrator sees Greg, who seems to enjoy Rome immensely. This more closely resembles how Greg describes the narrator. Choice D is not supported by the passage. Although Greg does want to tour historical churches, nothing about his stated reasons for doing so suggests fanaticism.

4. J
Difficulty: Medium
Category: Function
Getting to the Answer: The phrasing "the narrator uses . . . in order to" shows that this is a Function question. It asks about the purpose of a particular part of Passage B in relation to the whole. In short, why does the narrator reveal that he is unwilling to admit to Greg that he admires St. Peter's? The function of a part of a literary narrative passage often has to do with the characters' feelings, values, or relationships. The fact that the narrator isn't going to admit his enjoyment to Greg shows that the narrator is enjoying himself in spite of his protests, so (J) is correct.

When answering Function questions, watch out for answer choices that describe the passage without revealing the cited text's function within the passage. Because the narrator is willing to follow Greg all day, F is incorrect. While the narrator's attitude may call attention to St. Peter's, the point of the passage is not to praise St. Peter's; it is to describe two characters and their interaction. Thus, H is incorrect. Choice G is out of scope because nothing in the text indicates that the narrator sees admiration of churches as a private matter.

5. C
Difficulty: Medium
Category: Detail
Getting to the Answer: The words *author summarizes* show this question is asking about something the passage states directly, so it is a Detail question. Use your passage map notes for the final paragraph as a prediction. The sample passage map states that the narrator had a rough morning but viewed the previous day as an interesting experience. Only (C) accurately expresses that the previous night was an interesting experience without adding an extreme emotion.

Choices A, B, and D do not align with the narrator's tone: A is too negative, whereas B and D are too positive.

6. J
Difficulty: Medium
Category: Global
Getting to the Answer: When asked to compare two passages as a whole, use the main focus of each passage to form a prediction. Passage A focuses on the narrator's frustrations with the language barrier in Berlin, whereas Passage B describes a whirlwind tour through Rome. While the narrator of Passage B mentions "conversations that mixed French, Greek, Italian, and Martian" (lines 95–96), language is not a major theme in Passage B as it is in Passage A. The correct answer is (J).

Although both narrators mention some historical facts, interactions with locals, and the names of religious landmarks they've encountered, these topics are presented as supporting details in both texts rather than central points of each passage as a whole. Choices F, G, and H are incorrect.

7. C
Difficulty: High
Category: Global
Getting to the Answer: The tone of a passage includes the narrators' attitudes toward the subject matter. Pay attention to shifts in attitude. Both narrators are anxious at the start of their respective passages, but both come to appreciate their individual experiences in a foreign country. Thus, (C) is correct.

Choice A is a distortion; Passage A is a personal account of the narrator's interaction with people and emotional reaction to the environment, so it is not impersonal or historical. Nothing about Passage B makes it more nostalgic, or longing for the past, than Passage A. Choice B mixes up the passages: Passage A is more serious and introspective than Passage B, while Passage B is more animated and playful. Choice D is reversed: both narrators employ humor to highlight their dissatisfaction with the start of their travels.

8. F
Difficulty: Medium
Category: Global
Getting to the Answer: The question stem asks for what both passages prominently feature. Each passage describes the experience of visiting a foreign country from the personal perspective of the narrator, which matches (F).

Choice G is extreme; both narrators feel frustration, but the passages do not portray that emotion as a shortcoming. Passage A's narrator does discuss speaking a foreign language, but he admits that he was not fluent, and Passage B does not mention anything about the narrator's "determination" to impress by speaking another language, so H is incorrect. If H was tempting, note that Passage B's narrator includes the word *Martian* (line 96) to imply that the other actual languages were as alien to him as a language spoken on another planet. Lastly, since neither narrator mentions returning home, J is out of scope.

9. D
Difficulty: High
Category: Inference
Getting to the Answer: Since you are asked to describe feelings that are not directly stated, this is an Inference question. When asked to compare two passages in this way, use your passage maps to form a prediction. According to the map for Passage A, the narrator is impressed by Berlin's architecture and feels content. According to the map for Passage B, its narrator questions why he and his companion are visiting so many churches, and he hides his awestruck reaction to St. Peter's. Choice (D) is correct because it describes Narrator A's contentment and Narrator B's less clearly defined response. If additional support is need for you to confidently select choice (D), note that in the fifth paragraph (lines 71–76), the architecture upsets his stomach. The subsequent paragraphs reveal it also was jaw-dropping, and the narrator feels an inexplicable need to keep up the ruse of disinterest.

Choice A is incorrect because Narrator B is secretly in awe of St. Peter's, which shows that he is *not* "indifferent." Choice B is incorrect because Narrator A *does* notice the architecture and Narrator B is not *entirely* captivated by it. Choice C is incorrect because Narrator A does *not* grow tired of the architecture.

[CHAPTER 21]

ACT READING: TIMING AND SECTION MANAGEMENT STRATEGIES

> **LEARNING OBJECTIVE**
>
> After completing this chapter, you will be able to:
> - Recognize at a glance which passages in a section are likely to be easiest for you

Timing

You have 40 minutes to complete 4 passages with 9 questions each, so you need to complete each passage and its accompanying questions in an average of 10 minutes to finish on time. (Note that passages are not all the same length or difficulty, so some will take longer than others.) After 20 minutes, you should be about halfway done with the Reading questions. When the time reaches 5 minutes left, you should ideally be working on the fourth set of questions.

Note that this is a brisk pace. Reading strategically can help, as can triaging questions and skipping those that you can quickly determine will be time-consuming. Your real task is not actually to attempt all the questions in 40 minutes but to get as many points from the section as you can.

Section Management

You may want to triage entire passages on the Reading section, not just questions. Some test takers have a hard time with literature or natural science, while others struggle more with humanities or social science passages; if you have distinct preferences about subject matter, you might consider leaving a particular passage type for last. For example, the Reading section always opens with the literature passage. If that's the passage you feel least confident about, it makes sense to skip it and do it last. (Just be careful with your answer bubbling.)

Moving efficiently through this section is important, but that does not mean that you should skip over any text. Reading all of the text in the passage is essential to answering questions efficiently and accurately.

Remember that you probably won't spend the same amount of time on each question. Every question counts for the same number of points, so be sure to complete the questions you find easiest to answer first.

There is one exception to the "read the passage first" rule: when you have only five minutes remaining in the Reading section and at least one passage left to start. In this case, skip the passage and look for the questions that could be researched quickly. Vocab-in-Context questions, for example, can usually be answered using only the full sentence containing the word or phrase, and Detail questions might provide line references to tell you exactly where to look. Finally, remember not to leave anything blank; when you have one minute left, do a final answer check to confirm you didn't miss anything.

When considering the structure of the entire test, keep in mind that you will have a break before each section. If you start reading the same sentence over and over, put your pencil down, close your eyes, and take three slow, deep breaths. The more focused you can remain, the easier it will be for you to determine each correct answer.

There is an additional half-length Reading section in the "How Much Have You Learned?" section of this chapter. Use it to practice timing: skip questions you find too time-consuming, return to them if you have time, and keep an eye on the clock. When you are finished, check your work and reflect on how well you managed the pacing.

How Much Have You Learned?

Directions: Use this question set to practice effective question triage. Skip those questions that you feel will take too long; come back to them if you have time. Try to get as many questions correct as you can in 20 minutes. As always, be sure to study the explanations, even for questions you got correct. They can be found at the end of this chapter.

LITERARY NARRATIVE: This passage is adapted from a short story about summertime in the author's hometown.

Ivan Pavlov was a physiologist who researched learned behaviors and the ways in which repeat exposure to specific stimuli can result in behaviors that occur without intention.

At the sound of the whistle, Pavlovian, we'd all push up from the sides of the pool. (We never used the ladders or the steps in the shallow end. It was a point of pride to have the strength to
5 push up from the sides.) For the next 20 minutes, we had to be out, all the kids; let the adults have some time without us splashing and screaming and generally creating pandemonium. We all went to the same place, compelled, drawn like flies: the
10 snack bar. Jiang first, because he was the oldest, his legs were longer. He was bossy, sometimes. Aisha came next, pretending like she didn't even care anymore, even though we all knew she did, or she would have stayed by the side of the pool, on one
15 of those lounge chairs that had the long vinyl slats that always stuck to your skin. Then Faiyaz and Neerav, who only we could tell apart besides their parents. Wolf—he was Wolfgang, named for his grandfather, but he hated the name—was usually
20 last, because he was never in the same hurry the rest of us always seemed to be in. It didn't matter, because there were a thousand kids, all in clumps, pushing and shouting, as if the bored teenage girl doling out ice cream was going to suddenly decide
25 to close up shop.

We pushed and shouted, too. Pushing and shouting just seemed to be part of what you were supposed to do, and so we did it. Neerav sometimes seemed to be shouting just for the enjoyment of
30 adding his voice to the cacophonous mess. The bored teenage girl probably took a lot of aspirin. When we finally got our turn at the counter, we all got the same thing, ignoring the bags of chips and the M&Ms and the cans of soda. Each and every
35 time, all of us in it together: ice cream. We were there to buy ice cream.

It wasn't even *good* ice cream—the stuff we had in our freezers at home was better by far. But we were all dropped off at the pool to spend our
40 summer mornings, and ice cream was our shared snack of choice. Little bits of memory come back with the scent of chlorine or hot pavement, even now: Wolf counting quarters because he never remembered to bring much money; the rest of us
45 had crumpled dollar bills we kept rolled up in our towels. The way the paper peeled off the top of the ice cream, the little stick to push it up. The ice cream was usually on the stale side, freezer-burnt. But it was the best-tasting ice cream in all the
50 world, because we could buy it ourselves. Kids don't have a whole lot of power, but we bought ice cream from the bored teenage girl at the snack bar by our own choice.

We'd go back to the lounge chairs to eat, sitting
55 there watching the kids still waiting to get theirs, or the adults who swam laps, smooth and steady. Wolf would be covered in ice cream before the end of it, his face and arms sticky and streaked orange; for some reason he could never keep it from dripping.
60 We'd be back in the water soon enough anyway, and it would all wash away again. Aisha ate hers slowly, while Faiyaz and Neerav competed to see who could finish first. Jiang sat on the edge of one of the round metal tables, one long leg swinging,
65 staring off at nothing in particular.

Long, slow summer days. It was too hot to run except for ice cream, when we were out of the water. Sometimes, we played with the other kids at the pool—Marco Polo, the normal sort of thing—but
70 more often, it was just us. We were together, and that was enough.

At some point, we must have begun to outgrow it. Did Jiang give up ice cream at the pool first, or Aisha? Aisha seems more likely. There came a
75 day when we were too old to care. By then we had money, allowances we earned doing chores at home.

We saved up for less ephemeral things—books, or clothes, or Neerav's endless supply of comic books. But we couldn't say when, precisely, it happened, though we must have been aware of it at the time.

We all still talk on the phone now, and of course we can go out together anytime we like, but summer days at the neighborhood pool seem to have gone the same way as the sticky orange ice cream—just not around anymore. The world changed, it seems, between the time of our childhood summers and now, and the disappearance of those pools, of the snack bars and adult swim time, was part of that change. Or maybe we just no longer notice them, because there's no one to blow the whistle, nowhere to run for ice cream?

1. The passage as a whole is characterized by the author's sense of:

    A. cynicism, in light of her changed perception of the world as an adult.
    B. nostalgia, looking back on what seem to be fond memories of childhood.
    C. heartlessness, considering her jaded memories of the past.
    D. wonder, as seen in her knowledge that ice cream tasted better as a child.

2. Based on the final paragraph, it can be reasonably inferred that the author is:

    F. an adult.
    G. a child.
    H. an elderly person.
    J. a college student.

3. The author most likely uses the word *Pavlovian* in line 1 to describe:

    A. the way that the whistle sounded to the kids in the pool.
    B. the reaction of the kids to the whistle when pushing out of the pool.
    C. the pandemonium created by all the kids being in the pool together.
    D. the rush of the kids all running to the snack bar.

4. In the context of the passage, the primary function of lines 77–78 is to give an example of something that:

    F. stands in contrast to going to the pool.
    G. was a worse use of money than ice cream.
    H. stands in contrast to buying ice cream.
    J. was a better use of money than going to the pool.

5. According to the passage, the author describes the ice cream she bought as a child at the pool as:

    A. the best-tasting ice cream in the world, though old and covered with frost.
    B. a waste of everyone's money, which is why everyone quit buying ice cream.
    C. too expensive, as Wolf often did not have enough money to buy it.
    D. freezer-burnt and stale, which is why everyone chose M&Ms or bags of chips over ice cream.

6. The passage most strongly suggests in lines 10–14 that:

    F. the author remembered that Jiang always liked the ice cream more than Aisha did.
    G. ice cream consumption is only for kids who are spending the day at the pool.
    H. deciding not to go to the pool and eat ice cream is a normal part of growing up.
    J. Aisha wants to appear to be more mature than the other kids at the pool.

7. As it is used in line 30, *mess* most nearly means:

   A. a dirty area.
   B. a difficult situation.
   C. a disordered state.
   D. a place to eat.

8. Based on the final paragraph, it can be inferred that the author of the passage believes that:

   F. community pools were built for children, not adults.
   G. adults were not allowed at the snack bar at the pool.
   H. there are not as many community pools now.
   J. childhood friends should always keep in touch.

9. The author most likely mentions "the scent of chlorine or hot pavement" in the third paragraph to:

   A. indicate what stood out most strongly to her while at she and her friends were at the pool.
   B. show that pools smelled the same way in the past that they do in the present.
   C. imply that smells of chlorine and hot pavement are often associated with one another.
   D. share particular smells that still remind her of the times that she and her friends ate ice cream at the pool.

INFORMATIONAL: This passage was adapted from an article about land art in a small art newspaper.

Humans have always bent their imaginations to aesthetically reshape the world around them. However, a particular problem for early artists seems to have been finding ways to make artwork
[5] last. It was not an easy task to create artwork with natural and often perishable materials. Despite these difficulties, countless examples of ancient art fill museums throughout the world, from the cave drawings in Lascaux to Egyptian hieroglyphics to
[10] Greek sculpture. However, a modern movement called land art, which embraces this difficulty, has gained recognition around the world. Land art is defined as art that either naturally deteriorates or is deliberately dismantled after it is constructed.

[15] Land or earth art was first developed during the mid-1960s as a backlash in the art community against the increasing commercialization of art and seclusion of art from the natural world. Artists like Alan Sonfist sought to incorporate nature in
[20] their work as well as return to the fundamental principles upon which they believed art was based. The pioneers of land art rejected museums and art galleries as the rightful settings for creative work. They sought to remove the "plastic" influences and
[25] what they viewed as the corrosive influence on pure aesthetics. Thus, land art began with a mission to create three-dimensional works set in and wrought from the natural world.

The dawn of the movement coincided with
[30] an emerging ecological movement. Land artists typically prefer the rural to the urban, sometimes searching for a spiritual connection with the earth. Land artworks from the movement's inception recall much older land works like Stonehenge, the
[35] Nazca Lines of Peru, or the Great Pyramids of Giza. Constructed in remote locations such as the deserts of the American West, they experiment with perceptions of light, space, and even the passage of time. In so doing, they evoke the spirituality of far
[40] more ancient works.

Above all, land artists utilize simple materials. Unlike other minimalist artists, land artists use only natural media such as rocks, soil, sand, wood, water, and even plant matter in the creation of
[45] their masterpieces. Land art icon Robert Smithson constructed his work *Spiral Jetty* using nothing more than stones, mud, algae, and water. Created in the Great Salt Lake in 1970 during a severe drought, *Spiral Jetty* was a 1,500-meter spiral of
[50] rocks that projected from the lake shore and was allowed to deteriorate without intervention. The Jetty was covered by the lake within a few years and remained underwater until 2004 when, to the delight of contemporary artists, another drought
[55] revealed the 30-year-old sculpture.

Another feature of land art is its massive scale, which typically prevents it from being displayed in any museum or gallery. Since land art makes extensive use of landscape, entire vistas can be
[60] said to be part of a work. The sheer size of land art thus requires collaboration between artists and engineers, as well as the employment of laborers and volunteers, in order to complete a project. For example, Australian artist Andrew Rogers's piece
[65] *Rhythms of Life* was constructed in twelve different sites around the world, making the work the largest piece of aesthetic art to date—a feat reminiscent of Christo and Jeanne-Claude's 1991 *Umbrellas* project, which placed massive blue and yellow umbrellas in
[70] selected stretches of the Japanese countryside and the California mountains. Christo, however, denies the label of "land artist," claiming that his and his wife's work does not share the common principles of land art, since it neither rejects gallery art nor
[75] eschews the use of synthetic building materials.

Despite the artists' ideological differences, Christo and Jeanne-Claude's work does share other similarities to the work of land artists in that both are intentionally short-lived. Land art is extensively
[80] photographed during exhibition but afterward exists only on film or in memory. Some critics and art lovers decry limiting public access to a work of art by deliberately creating it to be temporary. Because creating land art often requires substantial
[85] funding, allowing the finished product to fall into ruin or even purposefully dismantling it is considered by critics of the movement to be a waste of resources. Land artists counter such indictments

by pointing out that they only borrow the elements of nature to produce their work, and once a piece has been exhibited, they feel justified in returning the materials to their rightful owner. Moreover, they assert that the very ephemeral nature of their works is an integral part of those works. Land artworks that capture the imagination can live on in memory and appear even greater to the public consciousness than they really were. As Christo once stated, "Do you know that I don't have any artworks that exist? They all go away when they're finished . . . giving my works an almost legendary character. I think it takes much greater courage to create things to be gone than to create things that will remain."

The same could be said of the land art movement itself. Because of their massive scale, land artworks are costly to produce. Land artists frequently rely on wealthy private patrons, foundations, or government grants in order to create their masterpieces. With economic downturns came a loss of funding, and in recent years the movement has faded. Or, perhaps, it has transformed—as all movements must once they have done their work to change and inspire others.

10. The author's attitude toward the passage's main topic can best be described as:

F. critical and dismissive.
G. skeptical and disappointed.
H. passionate and dedicated.
J. interested and supportive.

11. According to the passage, why did ancient artists have a difficult time creating lasting artworks?

A. Such works were not popular among land artists of the time.
B. The media available to ancient artists were prone to decay.
C. Patrons refused to pay the necessary expense for such work.
D. The elements of nature succumbed to human-made endeavors.

12. According to the passage, which of the following is true of the land art movement's inception?

F. The movement originated with the creation of *Spiral Jetty* by Robert Smithson.
G. The movement began as a backlash against the creation of permanent artworks.
H. The movement was primarily motivated by a desire to use natural materials in art.
J. The movement was a negative reaction to attributes of modern art during the 1960s.

13. The passage most strongly suggests that some ancient land works were concerned with:

A. the natural world.
B. the rural/urban divide.
C. time and space.
D. permanence.

14. It can be reasonably inferred from the fourth paragraph that one distinction between minimalist artists and land artists is that minimalist artists:

F. create works that are extremely small.
G. prefer exotic components over ordinary ones.
H. are uninterested in spiritual aspects of art.
J. make use of synthetic materials in their work.

15. As it is used in line 45, the word *icon* most nearly means:

A. religious idol.
B. small graphic symbol.
C. revered person.
D. representative image.

16. In the context of the passage, the quote in lines 98–102 mainly serves to:

　F. argue that none of the preeminent works of modern art still exist.

　G. demonstrate that when Christo and Jeanne-Claude dismantle their artwork, they exhibit a courage entirely lacking in land artists.

　H. show that the destruction of a piece of artwork can enhance that work's reputation in the minds of critics and admirers.

　J. provide information about how artists care very little about wasting natural resources when they allow their artwork to be destroyed.

17. The main purpose of the sixth paragraph (lines 76–102) is to:

　A. examine the implications of creating artworks that exist for a brief period of time.

　B. refute criticism of land art and the work of Christo and Jeanne-Claude.

　C. analyze the difference between land art and Christo and Jeanne-Claude's work.

　D. provide examples of legendary pieces of land art.

18. According to the passage, what happens to the building materials of land artwork after it is taken apart?

　F. They are recycled.

　G. They revert to nature.

　H. They pass to a new owner.

　J. They are used in future art.

Answers and Explanations

Suggested Passage Map Notes

¶1: kids at pool getting snacks, friends introduced

¶2: always rowdy, get the same thing: ice cream

¶3: narrator reflects on ice cream taste, appearance

¶4: how friends ate differently

¶5: how things used to be

¶6–7: narr. reflects: outgrew it, sense of loss

BIG PICTURE SUMMARY

Main idea: The narrator reminisces about her summer days at the pool and reflects on how life has changed since her childhood.

Author's purpose: To describe happy childhood memories.

---

1. B
Difficulty: Low
Category: Global
Getting to the Answer: "The passage as a whole" signals that this is a Global question. Review your notes and predict that the author is looking back on a happy time in her life. This matches (B).

A and C can be eliminated because there is no cynicism nor heartlessness displayed by the author. D is not supported by the passage; though the author says that the ice cream she bought at the pool tasted good, she never says that ice cream as a whole tasted better when she was a child.

2. F
Difficulty: Low
Category: Inference
Getting to the Answer: The phrase "reasonably inferred" tells you that this is an Inference question. In the final paragraph, the author mentions "between the time of our childhood summers and now"—predict that they have grown up since the time she is writing about. This matches (F).

This same phrase eliminates G because the author discusses childhood as being in the past. Choices H and J are not supported by the passage; the author may or may not be either elderly or a college student.

3. B
Difficulty: High
Category: Function
Getting to the Answer: The clue words "author most likely uses" indicate that this is a Function question. The blurb at the beginning of the passage describes Ivan Pavlov and his work: Pavlov studied how people learn to respond to repeated stimuli with automatic behavior. *Pavlovian* must relate to the context of the passage, so refer to the line in question, and predict that *Pavlovian* is used here to describe how the kids all seem to automatically leave the pool when the whistle sounds. That matches (B).

A is incorrect because it is the kids' reaction that is described as *Pavlovian*, not the sound of the whistle itself. Neither the pandemonium nor the snack bar are referenced as *Pavlovian*, eliminating C and D.

4. H
Difficulty: Medium
Category: Function
Getting to the Answer: The phrase "primary function" lets you identify this as a Function question. Review the cited lines and predict that the correct answer will identify that books, clothes, and comic books were bought instead of ice cream. This matches (H).

Choices F and J can be eliminated because the author is contrasting what she and the others bought later to ice cream; there is no indication in the passage of whether they had to pay to use the pool at all. Choice G may or may not be true; while the author says this is what everyone later chose to spend their money on, she doesn't say that those things are a worse use of money than ice cream. (If anything, she implies that they were a better use because they lasted longer!)

5. A
Difficulty: Low
Category: Detail
Getting to the Answer: The clue words "According to the passage" tell you that this is a Detail question. Review your notes and refer to the third paragraph, which describes the ice cream. Predict that the author describes the ice cream as "on the stale side, freezer-burnt" to show that it really wasn't all that good. Nonetheless, it was "the best-tasting ice cream in all the world" because the kids bought it themselves. This matches (A).

Choice B is out of scope; the passage does not support that the kids stopped buying ice cream because they considered it a waste of money. Choice C is incorrect because, while Wolf is mentioned as never remembering to bring much money, there is no support that the author believed it to be too expensive. Finally, D is a distortion; the low quality of the ice cream is described, but that did not deter the kids from considering it the snack of choice.

6. J
Difficulty: High
Category: Inference
Getting to the Answer: The phrase "most strongly suggests" indicates that this is an Inference question. Refer back to the lines in question and review what's stated: "Jiang... was the oldest... Aisha came next, pretending like she didn't even care anymore, even though we all knew she did, or she would have stayed by the side of the pool." The author's assertion that Aisha pretended not to care and was *more likely* to be the first one to outgrow it supports a prediction that Aisha tries to act older than her age. This matches (J).

Although the author describes the way the ice cream is consumed, there's nothing to support the statement that Jiang liked the ice cream *more* than Aisha, so F is incorrect. Choice G is extreme; although the ice cream seems like an essential part of the pool-day experience, the author explicitly states that not only was there ice cream at home, but also it was better than the ice cream at the pool. Although the author talks about outgrowing it, there is no evidence that the author believes one outgrows pools and ice cream entirely, especially given her observation of adults at the pool while she was there as a child.

7. C
Difficulty: Medium
Category: Vocab-in-Context
Getting to the Answer: The phrase "most nearly means" tells you that this is a Vocab-in-Context question. Refer back to the line in question, and predict that *mess* here means something like "unruly." The best match for this is (C).

While A, B, and D are all other definitions of *mess*, none of them matches the way the word is used within the passage.

8. H
Difficulty: Medium
Category: Inference
Getting to the Answer: "Based on the final paragraph" is an indication that this could an Inference question. Refer to your notes for the final paragraph, but realize it is hard to make a firm prediction from such a broad question. Instead, check each answer choice, eliminating them out one by one until you find the choice supported by the paragraph in question.

While the author does describe going to the community pool as a child, there is nothing to support the idea that she thinks such pools are just for children, which eliminates F. There is also nothing to support the idea that she thinks snack bars are just for children, which eliminates G. The author states that "The world changed, it seems, between the time of our childhood summers and now, and the disappearance of those pools, the snack bars and adult swim time, was part of that change." She does follow this by saying, "maybe we just no longer notice them," but this is presented as speculation, not counter-evidence, so (H) is correct. (If you're curious, note that J is too extreme—while the author says that she has kept up with the childhood friends from the passage, she never says that all childhood friends should stay in touch.)

9. D
Difficulty: Medium
Category: Function
Getting to the Answer: The phrase "most likely mentions... to" tells you that this is a Function question. Look back to the third paragraph to remind yourself why the author mentioned the chlorine and hot pavement. Predict that the correct answer will show that these smells bring up memories of eating ice cream at the pool. This matches (D).

Choice A may or may not be true; just because those particular smells bring back memories doesn't mean they stood out most strongly when she was a child. Nothing is said about how pools smell now versus then, nor about an association between chlorine and hot pavement, which eliminates B and C.

Chapter 21
ACT Reading: Timing and Section Management Strategies

Suggested Passage Map Notes

¶1: land art embraces impermanent art

¶2: reacted against contemporary art

¶3: connection to natural world

¶4: use natural materials

¶5: massive scale

¶6: impermanence; critics vs. artists

¶7: movement faded/changed

BIG PICTURE SUMMARY

Main idea: Land art is a modern art style and movement based on art that is designed to be impermanent and steeped in nature.

Author's purpose: To inform the reader about the land art movement.

---

10. J
Difficulty: Medium
Category: Global
Getting to the Answer: The clues "author's attitude" and "main topic" indicate this is a Global question; consult your notes to determine the author's view of land art. The passage is mostly descriptive in tone, but it does present land art as unusual and interesting. Moreover, the author's positive view of the movement comes through in some places: in the sixth paragraph, the author defends land art, and in the final paragraph, the author refers to land art inspiring others. Choice (J) is therefore correct.

Choice F is opposite; the passage does not dismiss land art but explores it thoroughly. While it mentions some criticisms of the movement, it immediately offers counters to these criticisms. Choice G is also opposite; the author is interested in and enthusiastic about land art, not skeptical or dismissive. Choice H is extreme; while the tone is generally positive, "passionate and dedicated" goes too far.

11. B
Difficulty: Low
Category: Detail
Getting to the Answer: The phrase "According to the passage" indicates that this is a Detail question. The first paragraph describes materials available to ancient artists as "perishable" (line 6). Choice (B) matches this prediction.

Choice A is a misused detail; the passage describes land art as a contemporary movement. Choice C is also a misused detail; there is no mention of patrons for ancient art, only modern works. Finally, choice D is a distortion; while the passage does describe ancient media as perishable, it does not suggest that "human-made endeavors" themselves caused the natural materials to deteriorate.

12. J
Difficulty: Medium
Category: Detail
Getting to the Answer: "According to the passage" is a clue that this is a Detail question. The second paragraph discusses the influences that led to the land art movement as a "backlash . . . against the increasing commercialization of art and seclusion of art from the natural world" (lines 16–18). Predict that land art opposed these trends. Choice (J) matches this prediction and is correct.

Choice F is a misused detail; the passage never states that *Spiral Jetty* was the first land artwork. Choice G is a distortion; the first paragraph discusses the impermanence of land art, but the author never suggests that land art was a direct reaction against permanent art. Choice H is extreme; the passage does discuss the use of natural materials in land art but never suggests that land art originated specifically from a desire to use such materials.

13. C
Difficulty: Medium
Category: Inference
Getting to the Answer: The phrase "most strongly suggests" shows that this is an Inference question. In paragraph 3, the passage states that land art recalls ancient land works through their interest in light, space, and time. Predict that ancient art will share these same concerns. This matches choice (C).

Choice A is a concern of land art, but not one that the passage connects to ancient land works. Choice B is out of scope; while the passage states that land artists prefer rural to urban, it does not mention the divide between them. Finally, choice D is a misused detail; the passage discusses the problem of permanence for ancient artists but not for ancient land works.

14. J
Difficulty: Medium
Category: Inference
Getting to the Answer: The phrase "reasonably inferred" shows that this is an Inference question. The fourth paragraph contrasts other minimalists with land artists by stating that land artists prefer to use natural materials. You can conclude that other minimalists at least sometimes use non-natural materials to create art. The correct answer is (J).

Choice F is out of scope; the passage does not discuss the typical size of minimalist works. Choice G is a distortion; although the passage states that land artists prefer simple materials, the phrasing "other minimalist artists" suggests that minimalists in general may prefer them as well. The contrast is between natural and synthetic, not simple and exotic. Similarly, while the passage states that some land artists were concerned with spiritual aspects of nature, the passage does not discuss this with regard to other minimalists, so H is incorrect.

15. C
Difficulty: Medium
Category: Vocab-in-Context
Getting to the Answer: This stem has the characteristic wording of a Vocab-in-Context question. Read the sentence to determine how the word is being used in the passage. Here, *icon* refers to a specific, important artist. Choice (C) matches this prediction.

Choices A, B, and D all represent other meanings of the word *icon*. The sentence uses the phrase "Land art icon" to describe a person (Robert Smithson), and it is not logical to describe a person as either a "land art small graphic symbol" or a "land art representative image," so B and D are incorrect. While a person can be described as a religious idol, the sentence and paragraph do not contain any support for the idea that Robert Smithson is a religious idol, so A is incorrect.

16. H
Difficulty: High
Category: Function
Getting to the Answer: The wording "serves to" identifies this as a Function question. Examine the context in the paragraph to determine the author's purpose. The author quotes Christo, who uses words like *legendary* and *courage*, to support the explanation of artists' reasons for allowing their work to be destroyed. You can predict that this quote reinforces the idea that impermanence can raise the stature of art. Choice (H) captures this sentiment.

Choice F is extreme; the passage never states that no successful artworks still exist. Choice G is opposite; the paragraph cites similarities between land artists and Christo and Jeanne-Claude, not differences. Choice J is a distortion of the information in the passage; critics say that land artists waste resources, but land artists argue that they only borrow materials. It's possible that some land artists do waste resources, but the cited Christo quote does not support the idea that artists in general care very little about waste.

17. A
Difficulty: Medium
Category: Function
Getting to the Answer: The phrase "main purpose" is a clue that this is a Function question. Review your notes to determine what the author wants to communicate in the sixth paragraph. This paragraph describes the consequences of creating short-lived artwork, so (A) is correct.

Choice B is out of scope; the author does address criticism, just not for the entire paragraph. Choice C is out of scope; this comparison is made, but that is not one of the primary purposes of the whole paragraph. Finally, choice D is out of scope; the author does not provide any examples in this paragraph.

18. G
Difficulty: Medium
Category: Detail
Getting to the Answer: The phrase "According to the passage" shows that this is a Detail question. Lines 88–92 state that the materials from land art are taken from nature and returned to nature. Choice (G) is correct.

Choice F is out of scope; the passage does not discuss recycling. Choice H is opposite; the passage describes nature as the rightful owner of the materials, so the materials are returned to a previous owner, not passed to a new one. Choice J is out of scope; the passage does not describe the reuse of land art materials.

TEST YOURSELF: ACT READING

Directions: For test-like timing, give yourself about 40 minutes to complete the following 36 questions.

Passage I

LITERARY NARRATIVE: This passage, which is set in the late 1990s, is adapted from a memoir by a Nicaraguan-American author.

My mother knew immediately what the old man was referring to when he told her to turn right *donde fue la farmacia Ixchen*—where the Ixchen pharmacy used to be. Directions in this
5 country are for those who knew all that had happened here, not for outsiders. Street addresses may exist on a government map, but no one uses them. Instead, everyone describes a path using landmarks, and you had better know that "toward
10 the lake" means north, and that the pharmacy used to be on that corner, where now only grass and trees grow amid the rubble.

We trudged forward under the blazing sun. "Mom, when was the last time it rained here?" I
15 asked. She made no response; her pace slowed, as she stared at a high concrete wall across the dirt road.

"Mom! Does it ever rain in Nicaragua?" I repeated insistently.

20 "Look," she said, pulling my hand. As we crossed over to the wall, I kicked pebbles, annoyed that she was ignoring my inquiries. She knelt down and traced her forefinger across the uneven concrete. "See these marks, Yesenia?" she
25 murmured. I remained silent, just as she had.

"These were made by bullets. There was a lot of fighting along this street. A lot of people..." Her voice trailed off, lost in mourning.

With that, it was as if someone else was
30 resentful, someone else was hot and tired and hungry. I tried to think of a man I had never met, who had died in this fighting just before I was born. My memories of him were not even my own; I could only picture a worn photograph that
35 my mother always carried, its edges tattered from being touched over and over. In it, my father smiles conspiratorially, as if he has just told a joke but is trying to look serious for the camera. Next to him, my mother's head is turned, both indignant and
40 amused. I had always wondered what joke he told at that moment but never dared to ask, sensing that the memory would be too private.

This was our first trip back to the country since we left just after the war. My father had
45 fought on the victorious side, so with speeches and ceremonies we were honored, alongside other bereft families, for our sacrifice, but the hole in my mother was too big to fill with speeches. Her brother, my uncle Carlos, was living in the United
50 States and invited her north to start over again.

I was too young to remember the journey, which was not in an air-conditioned plane but rather on the roof of a freight train chugging precariously up the map. I never learned the details of our crossing
55 or of the first several years after we arrived. What most evokes my early childhood is a smell: the scent of pine trees artificially replicated by air fresheners. My mother would religiously hang those dark green pine trees from the rear-view
60 mirror of the unpleasantly pungent station wagon we shared with Uncle Carlos. This all-American aroma surrounded us protectively at all times.

A decade, then almost another, passed. Now we were back to visit, and our first stop was to see Don
65 Lorenzo, my father's uncle and my oldest living relative, a modest, stately man who was very ill.

"You found this new house okay?" he asked in a light, raspy Spanish like fine sandpaper, as we sat on his porch.

"Yes, they told me to turn where the pharmacy used to be. What happened to it?" my mother replied.

They continued to talk. My Spanish was not quite good enough for me to participate fully. Lost in my own thoughts, I sipped my soda and watched the one-eyed cat skulk along the wall behind Don Lorenzo, stalking some kind of massive spindly bug. Meanwhile, Necio, the slavering pit bull, never took its menacing eyes off the cat.

Out of nowhere, a cottontail rabbit, all fluff and enormous ears, crossed nonchalantly in front of the pit bull. What is this, a zoo? Why isn't that thing being eaten? I snorted at the absurdity of the scene, only to suppress a laugh with a blush as Don Lorenzo and my mother turned.

"There it is," said Don Lorenzo, looking right at me. "The smile. The same as your father had." I froze. My childish reactions were suddenly infinitesimal compared to something enormous and foreign as a planet inside me. I watched my mother's hand slip into her purse unconsciously; I knew she was touching the photograph.

At that moment, I felt more connected to my father than ever before or since. I no longer needed to know the joke; in fact, I knew that I would probably not understand it. At the same time, I somehow knew the joke completely. It was not an arbitrary rabbit, but something else equally ridiculous and touching that had provoked my father's sense of humor—a sense likely amplified in "serious" situations, as I realized with another leap. Like me, he laughed inappropriately and was reprimanded frequently, or so I imagined.

Later, we visited the cemetery; there were plenty of carved letters in stone, but no picture, no new information about the man and his secret smile. Before long a rain shower burst from the sky, sending us running for cover and turning the dusty roads into streams of mud.

1. It can reasonably be inferred that the narrator's mother doesn't finish her sentence when they are at the concrete wall because:

   A. she forgets what she was going to say.
   B. she is overcome by her recollections.
   C. she changes her mind about sharing her thoughts.
   D. she is tired and hungry.

2. The narrator describes Don Lorenzo as a man who is:

   F. conspiratorial and silly.
   G. weathered and menacing.
   H. dignified, but unwell.
   J. quiet, but impatient.

3. According to the passage, the narrator moved to the United States to live with:

   A. her father's brother.
   B. her mother's brother.
   C. her father's uncle.
   D. her mother's uncle.

4. The author most likely uses of the words "worn" and "its edges tattered" (lines 34–35) to emphasize which of the following points?

   F. The photograph is very important to the narrator's mother and has been damaged by how frequently she touches it.
   G. The narrator's mother has not been careful with the photograph, leading to it being damaged.
   H. The narrator used to want to see the photograph frequently but was too young to be careful with it, damaging it.
   J. Despite it being damaged, the photograph is very important to Don Lorenzo, who has no photographs of his own of his late nephew.

5. Which of the following statements best describes the narrator's view of Nicaragua?

   A. It feels shockingly familiar to her, though she has no memories of having lived there as a young child.
   B. It feels alien and strange to her, and she feels more like a visitor than someone returning home.
   C. It feels overwhelming to her, as she wants desperately to get to know better who her father really was.
   D. It feels hot and uncomfortable, and she hopes that the weather will improve so she can enjoy it.

6. The passage most strongly suggests that the "hole" (line 47) the narrator describes as being left in her mother refers to:

   F. the physical injuries that her mother sustained during the war in Nicaragua.
   G. the difficulty her mother had in choosing to leave Nicaragua.
   H. the emotional injury caused by the death of the narrator's father.
   J. the marks in the high concrete wall that were made by bullets.

7. It can reasonably be inferred from the passage that the all-American aroma of the air fresheners referred to in lines 55–58 is mentioned to:

   A. emphasize that her early memories are not of the war-torn Nicaragua where she was born.
   B. contrast her early childhood memories with her mother's early childhood memories.
   C. juxtapose her vague memories of her father with a clear memory from childhood.
   D. compare what she wishes she could remember of childhood with what she actually remembers.

8. The passage as a whole can best be described as an exploration of:

   F. the history of the narrator's father's military service.
   G. how the narrator's parents met and fell in love.
   H. the contentious relationship between the narrator's mother and the narrator's father's family.
   J. what the narrator knew about the father who passed away before she was born and the country she left as a young child.

9. The narrator most likely uses the phrase "or so I imagined" (line 103) to convey how:

   A. the narrator and her father had a similar sense of humor.
   B. the narrator's father was often reprimanded for laughing inappropriately.
   C. the narrator felt, rather than knew, her father had certain traits.
   D. the narrator realized that the specific content of the joke was unimportant.

Passage II

INFORMATIONAL: This passage is adapted from an article about architecture and democracy.

The physical arrangement of the courtroom is a far cry from the apolitical, public-spirited space it was once idealized to be. Centuries ago, courtrooms were designed to welcome the public, who would
5 attend proceedings in droves, depending on the case. The layout did not give any one party, including the judge, a positional advantage, and security measures were nominal, if included at all.

Today, court officers flank the courtroom
10 entrance in the back and stand at the front as well, monitoring the room for rule violations, and invariably, the proceedings are separated from the viewing area by a low wall or divider. The topography of the space, which includes a raised
15 platform for the judge, allows the judge to observe the room's activity from an elevated position, clearly a calculated architectural choice. It often feels more like a theater than anything else—a performance rather than a truth-seeking enterprise.

20 Members of the public who choose to attend courtroom proceedings must submit to stringent security measures, and they are given intractable courtroom conduct rules. If audience members do not adhere to the rules, they can be charged with
25 contempt of court. If found guilty of being disobedient or disrespectful toward a court of law and its officers, a person can be fined, jailed, or both.

It's not just the security measures, architectural
30 features, and strict attendance policies that leave courtrooms feeling less than welcoming to the public. All these are coupled with the "legalese" used by lawyers—most of which many lay people have not heard, let alone fully understand—the
35 adversarial, sometimes hostile, nature of the litigation process; and the general attitude of resentment and reluctance that pervades juries.

In 2003, Bexar County, Texas took on the challenge of changing all this with an innovative,
40 pioneering project aimed at meeting the needs of children who are requested to testify in front of a judge: the county designed court accommodations that enable children to testify in the courtroom in a non-threatening and comforting environment. It
45 was a radical departure from the typical modern approach to courtroom design and renovation, and it sprang from consensus in the county that a special courtroom to accommodate the high number of children who are asked to testify was
50 critical.

A design team was formed that included architectural, electrical, and mechanical engineers; a child psychologist; and the local deputy director of court technology. The design team, working with
55 county officials, determined that two courtrooms were needed, along with two hearing rooms and two interview rooms.

The creation of dual rooms made clear the significant role that technology would play.
60 According to the Center for Legal and Court Technology, "Each courtroom would need all technological tools available to present a case. The extensive use of video would be expected to allow a participant in any location within the complex to
65 communicate with another participant anywhere else. For example, a judge might need to interview a child in chambers with other participants viewing from the hearing room or courtroom."

The design even included a special waiting
70 room, created for the protection and entertainment of children. In addition to adhering to strict security measures, the waiting room is replete with games and books for children of all ages. Staff members are accustomed to welcoming
75 children who are initially perplexed, if not anxious. The comfortable room and the assurances from those around them help to assuage children's apprehension.

Unfortunately, endeavors like this remain rare
80 and are, as in the case of Bexar County, typically restricted to individuals with specific needs, such as children, and it is unlikely that a redesign of standard courtrooms will follow suit. Law is a highly traditional profession that pays, by its nature,
85 great respect to authority. Statutes and sacred, guiding documents, such as both state and federal

constitutions, are given the utmost respect, and violations of them are taken seriously, involving law enforcement if necessary. Architecture has reflected
90 that somber, inherently hierarchical model.

    Perhaps the most striking example of hierarchical American courthouse architecture is the Supreme Court itself. Forty-four steps rise up to meet its ingress; massive red curtains hang
95 among intricate molding to adorn the front of the courtroom; the elevation of the justices is striking; and spectators are cabined by rank and admission standards. Considering the high-stakes decisions made in the walls of the building, one
100 might think these features are not only expected but also appropriate. Few would dispute the importance of the single branch of government that has the authority to strike down laws deemed unconstitutional.

105   Yet, law can be respected while still being made accessible, understandable and, in courtrooms, comfortable enough for witnesses to participate. If witnesses are too intimidated to testify, the courtroom fails to fulfill its fundamental purpose.

10. Which of the following statements best expresses the main purpose of the passage?

    F. Courtrooms should be centers of spirited debate.
    G. Courtroom architecture should reflect an appropriate respect for authority.
    H. It is important to examine how courtroom architecture reflects American values and facilitates justice.
    J. Prior to 2003, the discrepancy between American legal ideals and the realities of courtrooms had not been addressed.

11. The author likely mentions that a courtroom "often feels more like a theater" in lines 17–18 to:

    A. point out that legal proceedings are often scripted.
    B. provide an example of an alternative courtroom design.
    C. underscore how current courtrooms may not feel open and welcoming.
    D. emphasize how judges must consider viewers throughout legal proceedings.

12. It can reasonably be inferred that the "legalese" that the author mentions in line 32 refers to:

    F. authority and tradition in the courtroom.
    G. phrases that are often unfamiliar to the general public.
    H. incendiary language that provokes anger and resentment.
    J. architectural terms such as *ingress* and *molding*.

13. Based on the passage, which of the following statements best describes the author's attitude toward the specialized courtrooms in Bexar County, Texas?

    A. They are appropriate for children but may not be relevant to all standard courtrooms.
    B. They do not properly respect the authority of legal proceedings.
    C. They are an example of how innovations can create accessible and inviting courtrooms.
    D. The redesign may not be sufficiently public-spirited and apolitical.

14. In the passage, the author portrays the use of video in the Bexar County courtrooms as instrumental in:

    F. allowing participants to view proceedings and testify while in physically separate places.
    G. accommodating a special waiting room for children's ease, protection, and entertainment.
    H. preventing incarcerated defendants from traveling to the courthouse.
    J. assisting the judge in observing proceedings both during and after court sessions.

15. The author uses the phrase "within the complex" (line 64) in order to:

    A. examine the intricacies of designing buildings that successfully address legal and psychological needs.
    B. discuss the complications of communicating with people via video rather than in person.
    C. emphasize the ornate architecture features that reflect the staid model of courtrooms.
    D. indicate that multiple buildings comprise the Bexar County courtrooms.

16. The author uses the word "unlikely" (line 82) to refer to how it is unrealistic to expect:

    F. standard courtrooms to adopt a less hierarchical style in the near future.
    G. court officers to become even more authoritarian.
    H. the law to be considered a traditional profession.
    J. residents of Bexar County, Texas to utilize their specialized courtrooms.

17. The author's use of the words and phrases "striking," "Forty-four steps," and "massive" (lines 91–94) most nearly serves to emphasize which of the following points?

    A. The law, as well as courtroom proceedings, must be given the utmost respect.
    B. Stratified architecture in courtrooms is strongly ingrained in the United States.
    C. The Supreme Court is designed to look like the most prestigious court in the United States.
    D. The elevation of the Supreme Court Justices is extreme and striking, even by American standards.

18. According to the passage, most standard courtrooms today are characterized by:

    F. a raised platform for the judge and a waiting room for children.
    G. forty-four steps in front of the entrance and a considerable elevation of the justices.
    H. court officers at the entrance in the back and red curtains in the front.
    J. a raised platform for the judge and a divider separating the viewing area from the proceedings.

Passage III

INFORMATIONAL: This passage is adapted from an essay by a linguist on the power of words.

In 1940, Benjamin Lee Whorf wrote an article in *MIT Technology Review* called "Science and Linguistics," in which he argued, among other things, that people's native language constrains
5 their minds and prevents them from being able to understand certain concepts. Whorf believed that if a language is missing the word for a particular idea, then its speakers should not be able to understand that particular principle.

10 In particular, Whorf's article discusses the Hopi language and the way it assigns verbs such as *wari*, which means to run, to both present and past tense. In addition, rather than saying, "the rain lasted five days," a Hopi language speaker
15 would state the fact as "the rain stopped on the fifth day" because the language does not include plural nouns such as days.

Whorf concluded that without knowledge of a language that is temporal—such as English or
20 Spanish—a Hopi language speaker would be unable to understand scientific concepts such as velocity because it hinges on the ability to distinguish and quantify changes in time. Whorf does not dismiss the idea of being able to incorporate some type of
25 scientific understanding of physics, but he does state that an evaluation of the physical world would be vastly different within the Hopi language than within a temporal language and may even require different mathematics.

30 Whorf's contentions, while clearly stated and well reasoned, weren't fully embraced at the time. People throughout the world are quite capable of thinking about the future and past, even if they lack the terminology for it. Think, for instance,
35 about a young child telling a teacher that a toy fell off a shelf, but not yet aware of the past tense: "Toy fall down," the child says, clearly referring to a past event and with apparent full understanding that the event has already happened.

40 Twenty years after Whorf's claim was published, renowned linguist Roman Jakobson arrived at a related but more nuanced conclusion. "Languages," Jakobson argued, "differ essentially in what they must convey and not in what they may convey."
45 Therefore, if language shapes how we think, it does so by determining what we're obligated to think about rather than conveying all that it is possible to think about.

Consider this example offered by linguist
50 Guy Deutscher in *The New York Times* in 2010, reflecting on the difference between English and Mandarin: "If I want to tell you in English about a dinner with my neighbor, I have to tell you something about the timing of the event: I have
55 to decide whether we dined, have been dining, are dining, will be dining, and so on. Mandarin, on the other hand, does not oblige its speakers to specify the exact time of the action in this way because the same verb form can be used for past,
60 present or future actions." In other words, two languages may convey shared concepts such as time in vastly different ways.

Deutscher stressed that this does not mean that someone who speaks Mandarin exclusively would
65 be unable to understand the concept of time, rather that the person wouldn't have to articulate timing every time they wanted to tell a story about a meal. Could this mean Mandarin speakers think less about time than English speakers? Perhaps.

70 A very intriguing illustration of "linguistic obligation" is among speakers of the Australian Aboriginal language Guugu Yimithirr, which lacks coordinates related to the self, such as "in front of," "behind," "left of," "right of," and so on. The
75 language strictly uses geographical coordinates to describe directions—that is, north, south, east, and west. But what happens when they don't know where north is?

This is the fascinating part...because *it doesn't*
80 *happen*. Native Guugu Yimithirr speakers do not have that problem—they *always* know where north is, even without a compass, and accordingly, they know where the other cardinal directions are as well. While a native English speaker, reliant
85 on self-focused directional terminology, will most certainly not develop the same intuitive sense of

cardinal direction as one who was raised to rely solely on the geographical coordinates from birth, Guugu Yimithirr speakers are raised to be aware
90 of cardinal directions at all times. As a result, they're as aware of cardinal directions as English speakers might be that their toes are "in front" and their heels are "at the back" of their feet.

To an extent, then, Whorf was right. He may
95 have missed the mark in positing that we cannot imagine or feel what we cannot say, but clearly, what we must say can leave us with modes of thinking and seeing that are far more influenced by language than we realize. It is important to note
100 that Whorf concluded his article with the sentiment that there is a great deal of diversity among linguistic systems throughout the globe and no one language should be considered the pinnacle. Rather, Whorf called for further research to be conducted
105 in the spirit of both curiosity and humility.

19. As it is used in line 19, the word *temporal* most nearly means to be:

    A. concerned with nonreligious affairs.
    B. capable of acknowledging time.
    C. easier to understand.
    D. exhibiting secular attitudes.

20. In the context of the passage, the example of a child communicating with a teacher is included in lines 30–39 to:

    F. indicate that conceptual misunderstandings derive from poorly constructed phrases and sentences.
    G. show how a person may fully comprehend a concept without knowing how to properly convey it.
    H. illustrate the importance of early childhood education in developing effective language skills.
    J. make clear that the incorrect use of grammar may lead to confusion and frustration.

21. It can reasonably be inferred from the passage that the "nuanced conclusion" referred to in line 42 is:

    A. Whorf's clear but incomplete theory regarding the Hopi language.
    B. the deduction that cultural context is necessary when interpreting languages.
    C. an example Deutscher provides to support a new argument.
    D. the idea that language influences what speakers are obligated to consider.

22. The statement "two languages may convey shared concepts such as time in vastly different ways" in lines 60–62 primarily functions to:

    F. undermine Whorf's contentions.
    G. establish the principal foundation of linguistics.
    H. summarize one linguist's perspective.
    J. show how the concept of time affects understanding.

23. According to the passage, compared to English speakers, Mandarin speakers:

    A. spend fewer minutes each day thinking about time.
    B. dine with friends and neighbors more frequently.
    C. are less adept at event planning and scheduling.
    D. do not have to specify the exact time of an action.

24. According to the passage, which of the following statements best describes how linguist Roman Jakobson is generally regarded?

    F. Jakobson was originally criticized but is now revered.
    G. Current scholars feel largely indifferent toward Jakobson.
    H. Jakobson and his scholarship are regarded in high esteem.
    J. Jakobson's theories are well-respected but his character has been called into question.

25. In the passage, "linguistic obligation" (lines 70–71) describes as the way in which language:

    A. requires speakers to apply specific concepts that they presumably understand.
    B. forces non-native speakers to identify information gaps within their own vocabulary.
    C. urges scholars to conduct additional studies that focus solely on social constructs.
    D. engenders feelings of disorientation when fundamental terms are not clearly defined.

26. The passage author most likely asks, "But what happens when one doesn't know where north is?" (lines 77–78) to:

    F. raise a dilemma that current research is unable to solve.
    G. point out a difficulty that many people face.
    H. introduce an important attribute of a key example.
    J. propose a caveat to a theory.

27. In the context of the passage, the author revisits Whorf's thesis in the last paragraph to:

    A. acknowledge his contribution to linguistics.
    B. reveal that his original theory was actually correct.
    C. continue to point out the shortcomings in his findings.
    D. credit him with new discoveries.

Passage IV

INFORMATIONAL: This passage is adapted from an article about the magnetic field of the Earth.

The Earth's magnetic field is an invisible force that affects many aspects of the natural world. Migratory animals, such as birds, use the magnetic field to guide their trajectory—without it, they
[5] likely would be unable to return so precisely to the same area each season. Humans similarly benefit from the effects of the magnetic field. For example, the sun's radiation is severe enough to cause significant damage to humans, but the combination
[10] of the filtering effects of the atmosphere and the protective barrier from the magnetic field make it possible for humans to live on Earth's surface without suffering from immediate radiation damage when exposed to sunlight. This powerful
[15] natural force has gradually revealed a surprisingly complex history—with not entirely reassuring implications for the future.

How did this magnetic field originate? Its genesis is unclear, but the prominent theory is called the
[20] dynamo effect, which posits that the iron core in the center of the Earth generates the field. Heat from radioactive decay compels the outermost part of the Earth's iron core to move. Iron is a conductive material, and its movement engenders an
[25] electric current that interacts with magnetic forces, which creates a self-sustaining magnetic field.

Other forces also significantly influence the Earth's magnetic field. For example, Venus has an iron core similar to that of Earth. If the core
[30] were the sole source of the magnetic field, Venus should experience similar magnetic effects, but there is no magnetic field surrounding Venus. It is likely that the planet's rotation affects the field generation; Earth rotates on its axis once every
[35] 24 hours, while Venus completes a rotation every 116 Earth days.

If Earth's magnetic field were unvarying, it would be an interesting geological feature but would have relatively little immediate impact. Studies of
[40] iron deposits in rocks, however, indicate that the field has undergone both significant and ongoing changes. Iron is a magnetic substance, so it will align with nearby magnetic fields—this effect can be seen on a small scale by watching iron filings
[45] attracted to a simple magnet. On a larger scale, iron is present in volcanic lava. When the lava is liquefied, the iron is free to move and orient in a natural position. After the lava hardens, the iron particles are unable to move; a lava rock that
[50] solidified at a particular point in time will therefore have iron particles oriented in the direction of magnetic north at that time.

By studying lava rocks from various periods, scientists have determined that magnetic north
[55] has moved. Over the course of thousands of years, magnetic north shifted not only around the north pole, but also around the south pole: the field has been shown to completely reverse itself. Thus while today compass needles point toward
[60] the north pole, several thousand years ago, they would have been drawn south.

It was assumed that shifting the Earth's magnetic field from one pole to another took thousands of years. Since scientists have been observing the field,
[65] however, there has been substantial movement from the geographic North Pole. Magnetic north is slowly drifting toward Siberia at an increasingly rapid pace. Since 1831, magnetic north has moved 600 miles. Interestingly, the magnetic field is
[70] also significantly weakening. It is approximately 15% weaker than it was 200 years ago. This rapid movement combined with the reduced strength is prompting scientists to reevaluate their original timeline. Instead of several thousand years, it is
[75] entirely possible that magnetic north can switch poles after only a few hundred years. Some scientists believe that in the future, it could reverse in as few as 75 years.

If this is the case, magnetic north may move to
[80] the geographic south pole in the very near future. While the hypothesis is not wholly embraced by the scientific community, the effects of a reversed magnetic north are worth discussing, especially given that this switch could have profound effects
[85] on everyday life. Electrical grids use the Earth's magnetic field to function, and could become

inoperable as the field weakens. The field would be likely to continue to weaken until it reversed completely and remain weak for some time after.
90 Through this entire period, electrical systems would be at risk.

Another important point to consider is that people's health could be directly affected because the magnetic field protects us from radiation, so a
95 weaker magnetic field creates more exposure risk. The development of abnormal cells and mutations, two results of increased radiation, could rise. However, there is no evidence that any mass extinctions or cataclysmic events occurred during
100 past field reversals, so the true extent of a reversed magnetic north cannot yet be known.

28. The main purpose of the passage is to:

    F. inform the public about an impending disaster.
    G. describe a natural phenomenon and its potential effects.
    H. promote the dynamo effect as the most likely source of the Earth's magnetic field.
    J. discuss the importance of iron in scientific study.

29. According to the passage, which of the following would impact the position of iron filings in a lava rock?

    A. The location of magnetic north when the lava rock solidified
    B. The strength of the magnet that attracted the iron filings
    C. The length of time the lava rock was liquefied
    D. The amount of electric current generated by the iron

30. In the passage, the dynamo effect is described as:

    F. a widely-accepted fact.
    G. a hypothesis that is unlikely to be proven.
    H. a mistaken conception scientists used to have.
    J. the leading theory of the cause of the Earth's magnetic field.

31. The passage suggests that the author's attitude toward the potential effects of a global magnetic field reversal is:

    A. skeptical and resigned.
    B. concerned and attentive.
    C. hopeful and fascinated.
    D. relieved and peaceful.

32. It can reasonably be inferred from the passage that the occurrence of abnormal human cells could increase as a result of:

    F. a weaker magnetic field on Earth.
    G. risky electrical systems.
    H. an increase of radiation from Earth's magnetic field.
    J. mutations that cause mass extinctions.

33. In the passage, a component of the dynamo effect that is thought to be critical in generating Earth's magnetic field is:

    A. radioactive decay.
    B. the rotation of the Earth.
    C. volcanic activity.
    D. the periodic reversal of magnetic north.

Part 4
ACT READING

34. The main point of the sixth paragraph (lines 62–78) is for the author to discuss support for the hypothesis that:

    F. the Earth's magnetic field is produced via the dynamo effect.
    G. a weak magnetic field could have devastating effects on our way of life.
    H. a reversal of the Earth's magnetic poles in the next few centuries is possible.
    J. magnetic north is not where scientists would expect it to be.

35. Which of the following statements does the author highlight as a scientific hypothesis that scientists once accepted but is now being questioned?

    A. The Earth's magnetic field is a stable phenomenon.
    B. Venus has an Earth-like magnetic field.
    C. The movement of the Earth's iron core contributes to the Earth's magnetic field.
    D. The reversal of Earth's magnetic field takes thousands of years.

36. In the context of the passage, the comparison of Earth and Venus primarily serves to:

    F. explain why Venus's magnetic field is different from Earth's magnetic field.
    G. provide evidence that factors other than Earth's iron core impact its magnetic field.
    H. highlight the significant difference between the rotation times of the planets.
    J. argue against the importance of Earth's iron core in generating a magnetic field.

Answers and Explanations

Passage I

Suggested Passage Map Notes

¶1: mother (M) understood directions

¶2–3: narrator (N) impatient

¶4–5: M shows N bullet holes

¶6: N thinks of father (F)

¶7: first trip back

¶8: N came to US as kid

¶9: 15+ yrs later, visit Don Lorenzo (DL)

¶10–12: M and DL talk

¶13–14: N smile reminds DL of F

¶15–16: N finally feels connected to F

BIG PICTURE SUMMARY

Main idea: The narrator explains her feelings toward a father who passed away before she was born and a country she left as a young child.

Author's purpose: To describe how her feelings change from impatience and resentment to an acknowledgement of her mother's grief to an unexpected sense of connection with her father.

1. B
Difficulty: Medium
Category: Inference
Getting to the Answer: "It can reasonably be inferred" signals that this is an Inference question. In paragraph 5, the narrator states, "Her voice trailed off, lost in mourning." The word *mourning* indicates that the narrator's mother was very sad about what had happened years ago, which matches (B).

Choices A and C are incorrect because the passage does not give any indication that the narrator's mother forgot what she was going to say or changes her mind about sharing her thoughts; instead, the clues lead to the conclusion that she is too sad to continue her sentence. Choice D is a misused detail; it is the narrator, not her mother, who is described as tired and hungry.

2. H
Difficulty: Low
Category: Detail
Getting to the Answer: "The narrator describes" signals that this is a Detail question. Based on the passage map notes, paragraph 9 is the place to look. Here, the narrator describes Don Lorenzo as a "modest, stately man who was very ill," so (H) is the best match and is correct.

Eliminate F, G, and J because the passage does not attribute those characteristics to Don Lorenzo.

3. B
Difficulty: Low
Category: Detail
Getting to the Answer: "According to the passage" indicates that this is a Detail question. Research the answer in the passage and match it to the correct choice. Paragraph 7 states, "Her brother, my uncle Carlos, was living in the United States and invited her north to start over again," which matches (B).

Choices A, C, and D are incorrect because they misidentify who invited the narrator and her mother to move north.

4. F
Difficulty: High
Category: Function
Getting to the Answer: The clue words "author most likely uses" signal that this is a Function question. Use the information in the passage to predict the importance of the photograph and its description. The narrator states, "I could only picture a worn photograph that my mother always carried, its edges tattered from being touched over and over." The narrator's mother always carried the photograph, which indicates that it was important to her, and the tattered edges are from her mother handling it frequently, which matches (F).

Choice G is a distortion; the narrator's mother did cause the photograph to become worn, but she wouldn't be careless with something so important to her. Eliminate H and J because the passage does not provide information about the narrator handling the photograph as a young child or Don Lorenzo's feelings about the photograph.

Part 4
ACT READING

5. B
Difficulty: Medium
Category: Global
Getting to the Answer: This question is asking about the narrator's view of Nicaragua as a whole, so this is a Global question. The passage begins with the narrator feeling impatient and resentful, and then ashamed of those feelings when she is reminded of the war. She states that she and her mother were "back to visit" and admits that her "Spanish was not quite good enough for me to participate fully," which indicates that she is somewhat reluctantly visiting and does not feel like she fits in perfectly, which matches (B).

Eliminate A because it is opposite; she does not feel it is familiar. Choices C and D are distortions; the narrator does want to feel a connection to her father but does not mention feeling overwhelmed, and while she is hot and uncomfortable, she doesn't talk about hoping that the weather will get better.

6. H
Difficulty: Medium
Category: Inference
Getting to the Answer: The phrase "most strongly suggests" indicates that this is an Inference question, so consider the meaning of the word within the context of the surrounding text. Paragraph 7 states, "My father had fought on the victorious side, so with speeches and ceremonies we were honored, along with other bereft families, for our sacrifice, but the hole in my mother was too big to fill with speeches." The speeches were for families who lost loved ones in the war, but they did not help to heal the narrator's mother's profound grief over losing her husband, which matches (H).

Choices F and G are distortions; the injuries were emotional, not physical, and the passage indicates that the mother had difficulty grieving her husband, not difficulty choosing to leave Nicaragua. Choice J is a misused detail; the damage to the high concrete wall is mentioned at the beginning of the passage, but it is not connected to the discussion about the grief the mother experienced immediately following her husband's death.

7. A
Difficulty: High
Category: Inference
Getting to the Answer: "It can reasonably be inferred" shows that this is an Inference question. The narrator refers to the air fresheners in Uncle Carlos's car as "what most evokes my early childhood," so her earliest childhood memories were of the United States, not Nicaragua. The passage states that the narrator was "too young to remember the journey" to the United States, so she wouldn't have any memories of her life in Nicaragua before she relocated, which matches (A).

Choice B is out of scope because the passage does not include information about her mother's childhood memories. Eliminate C because the narrator does not have vague memories of her father—she does not have any memories of her father. Choice D is tempting because it is possible that the narrator wishes she could remember more of her childhood, but the passage does not provide direct evidence to support this idea; the passage focuses on the narrator's feelings toward a father who died before she was born.

8. J
Difficulty: Easy
Category: Global
Getting to the Answer: The phrase "passage as a whole" means that this is a Global question. Use the passage map notes to consider what the narrator explores in the whole passage. It begins with Nicaragua and how the narrator is unfamiliar with the country. Next the author discusses her father and why she doesn't remember him. Use this to form a prediction, and match to (J).

Choice F is a misused detail. The narrator did discuss her father's military service in paragraph 6, but that was not what the narrator explored throughout the passage. Choice G is out of scope because the passage does not include the story of the narrator's parents' romance. Choice H is also out of scope because the conversation between the narrator's mother and Don Lorenzo, the narrator's father's uncle, does not show any signs of conflict.

9. C
Difficulty: High
Category: Function
Getting to the Answer: The phrase "most likely...to convey" indicates that this is a Function question. Consider how the sentence's meaning would change if that phrase were removed. Without the phrase "or so I imagined," the narrator would be asserting that her father definitely laughed inappropriately and was reprimanded frequently. By including the phrase, she

conveys that she does not know these facts for sure, which matches (C).

Choices A, B, and D are tempting because they are all mentioned in paragraph 15, but they do not correctly explain the specific function of the phrase "or so I imagined."

Passage II

Suggested Passage Map Notes

¶1: modern courtrooms different from ancient, description of ancient

¶2: description of modern, author (au) critical

¶3: strict security rules

¶4: other inhospitable things

¶5: attempt to change for children, Bexar county

¶6: how they changed

¶7: what changed: tech/video

¶8: what changed: comfy waiting room

¶9: au POV: good start but limited

¶10: example: Supreme Court

¶11: au POV: change still possible

BIG PICTURE SUMMARY

Main idea: Unlike those of ancient courts, the architecture and security procedures of modern courtrooms are inhospitable for visitors and intimidating for witnesses.

Author's purpose: To argue that the physical arrangements of modern courtrooms should be reevaluated to make courts more accessible to the public.

---

10. H
Difficulty: Low
Category: Global
Getting to the Answer: Since this question asks for the main purpose, it is a Global question. Refer to your passage notes to answer it. The author opens by claiming that the architecture of modern courtrooms is inhospitable to the public, provides an example of an alternative arrangement, and closes by stating that the current architecture may even undermine the purpose of the court. Choice (H) correctly matches this summary and is correct.

Choice F is outside the scope of the text and is therefore incorrect. The extended example of the Bexar county court redesign focused on making the child witnesses comfortable and did not intend to accommodate "spirited debate." Choice G is a misused detail. Although the author agrees that respect for the authority of the court is an important consideration, the first sentence of the final paragraph of the passage indicates that the author believes the comfort of witnesses and the accessibility of the courts are more important. Choice J is extreme. The Bexar county court redesign did occur in 2003, but the passage never states that this was the first attempt to solve the problem.

11. C
Difficulty: Medium
Category: Function
Getting to the Answer: The phrase in the question, "author likely mentions," identifies this as a Function question. Return to the lines 17–18, but read above and below these lines to find the reason the author used those words. Immediately following the words cited in the question, the author says courtrooms may feel more like "a performance rather than a truth-seeking enterprise," and this criticism sums up the second paragraph's comparison of modern courtrooms with those of ancient times. The author continues in the remainder of the passage to develop the idea that modern courtrooms should be comfortable for witnesses and accessible to the public. Choice (C) is correct.

Choice A is not mentioned in the passage, so it is incorrect. Choice B is a distortion of information presented in the text; although a theater-style arrangement may meet the author's goal, this idea is not discussed in the passage and is not the reason the author used the cited words. Choice D is also a distortion of a detail from the passage. The author does state in the previous lines that the judge's elevated position enables the judge to see the viewers but does not emphasize this as an important consideration for courtroom design.

12. G
Difficulty: Low
Category: Inference
Getting to the Answer: The keyword *inferred* in the question tells you that this is an Inference question. Since you are asked about an unusual word, the

passage will have to provide enough context for you to understand its meaning. Go back to the cited line references and read above and below them to find the definition. Lines 32–34 state that *legalese* is something used by lawyers and that most non-lawyers "have not heard, let alone fully understand" it. This matches (G).

Choices F and J are misused details from the passage. Although the author addresses the need for authority and tradition in the courtroom and uses the architectural terms *ingress* and *molding*, *legalese* is not a word used to describe either of these concepts. Choice H is never mentioned in the passage, so it is incorrect.

13. **C**
Difficulty: High
Category: Inference
Getting to the Answer: The language "Based on the passage" is a clue that this as an Inference question. The correct answer will be supported by the passage but not directly stated. It may also be necessary to support the correct answer by putting information together from different parts of the passage. This question asks about the author's attitude, so begin by identifying that attitude as positive, negative, or neutral. The author uses many positive adjectives to describe the Bexar county specialized courtrooms, such as "protection and entertainment of children," "replete with games and books," "Staff members are...welcoming," and "comfortable." Although the author does state that these changes are "unlikely" to extend to standard courtrooms, the first sentence in the final paragraph indicates that the author believes that changes like these are needed. Choice (C) is correct.

The negative tone of B and D does not match the author's positive view. Eliminate these choices. Choice A is a subtle distortion of the author's concession. The author does state that the special needs of children drove the Bexar County reforms, but the author uses the extended example to illustrate how modern courtrooms can be improved, even if these changes may not be implemented in standard courtrooms. This makes A incorrect.

14. **F**
Difficulty: High
Category: Detail
Getting to the Answer: This as a Detail question, so look for the answer to be stated directly in the passage. Before returning to the text, though, try to put the question into your own words to focus your research. Here you might think, "I need to identify why the use of video was important." The passage map identifies paragraph 7 as the place to research, so reread that paragraph, looking for the answer to the question. Lines 62–66 provide the answer: "The extensive use of video would be expected to allow a participant in any location within the complex to communicate with another participant anywhere else." Choice (F) is correct.

Choice G is a misused detail. The special, comfortable waiting room for children is discussed in the text, but it is not a reason the use of video was important. Choices H and J are not mentioned in the passage, so they are incorrect.

15. **D**
Difficulty: High
Category: Functions
Getting to the Answer: The phrase "in order to" identifies this as a Function question. Return to line 64 and read a little before and after the cited line, looking for an explanation of "within the complex." The sentence that immediately follows the line reference gives the example of a judge using video to transmit the interview of a child from the judge's chambers to other participants in the trial in different locations. Choice (D) is correct.

Choices A and C stem from misused details from the passage. Both relate to details that are mentioned in the passage but have no connection to "within the complex." Choice B is not discussed in the passage, so it is also incorrect.

16. **F**
Difficulty: Medium
Category: Function
Getting to the Answer: The phrase "the author uses" identifies this as a Function question. Refer back to the cited line and read above and below that line researching the idea that the author believes is "unlikely." The answer is found in the phrase immediately following the cited word: "it is unlikely that the design of standard courtrooms will follow suit." This matches (F), the correct answer.

Choices G and J are not mentioned in the passage and are therefore incorrect. Choice H is the opposite of what's stated in the passage; the author states that one of the issues hindering the redesign of courtrooms is the traditions surrounding the profession. The author would believe this idea to be likely, not unlikely.

17. B
Difficulty: High
Category: Function
Getting to the Answer: The keyword phrase "serves to" identifies this as a Function question. Return to the cited lines, read around them, and identify the author's point in that section of the passage. The sentence immediately preceding the context clues identifies the Supreme Court as "the most striking example of hierarchical American courthouse architecture." Unfortunately, this doesn't match any of the choices. Continue to research further up in the passage and identify why the author is using the Supreme Court as an example. From the passage map, the main idea of the previous paragraph is that courts will likely not be redesigned soon because of the traditions and hierarchy of the law. This matches (B).

Choice A is incorrect because instilling respect for the institution is part of the reason the Supreme Court contains these features, but that is not the reason the author mentions them. Choice C is a subtle distortion of information in the passage. Although the passage identifies the Supreme Court as the most prestigious court in the United States, the author does not state that the reason these features were used was to establish that prestige. Choice D is an irrelevant comparison; the text never compares the design of the Supreme Court to that of other American courts.

18. J
Difficulty: Low
Category: Detail
Getting to the Answer: The phrase "According to the author" identifies this as a Detail question. You'll be able to look up the answer in the passage. In the passage map, "most standard courtrooms" are described in the second paragraph, so return to that paragraph and compare the information there to the choices. The "low wall or divider" is mentioned in the second sentence, and the "raised platform for the judge" is mentioned in the third sentence. Choice (J) is correct.

Choice F is half-correct and half-incorrect, and this makes it completely incorrect. Although the platform is mentioned, the children's waiting room is a feature of the Bexar County courtroom, not "most standard courtrooms." Choice G is a misused detail. The forty-four steps and considerable elevation of the justices are features of the Supreme Court, not "most standard courtrooms." Choice H is also half-correct and half-incorrect. The court officers are a feature of "most standard courtrooms," but the red curtains are only mentioned as a feature of the Supreme Court.

Passage III

Suggested Passage Map Notes

¶1: Whorf POV: native language limits thinking

¶2: Ex: Hopi language

¶3: Whorf: Hopis & English = diff descriptions of env

¶4: Whorf's views not well received

¶5: Jakobson (20 yrs later): what must be said vs what can be said

¶6: Deutscher ex: English vs Mandarin

¶7: Deutscher POV: can understand concept w/o needing to include in conversation

¶8: Ex 2: aboriginal language (GY) uses directions to describe location

¶9: Result: always know directions

¶10: author POV: essence of Whorf's thinking correct

BIG PICTURE SUMMARY

Main idea: It is possible that native languages influence the ways humans perceive and describe the world.

Author's purpose: To discuss Whorf's theory and later developments; to illustrate linguistic theories.

19. B
Difficulty: Low
Category: Vocab-in-Context
Getting to the Answer: The phrase "most nearly means" identifies this as a Vocab-in-Context question. Return to the line reference, reread the sentence, and predict a word or phrase that could replace the word *temporal*. The last phrase describes a language that can "distinguish and quantify changes in time." This matches (B). Note that when substituted for *temporal* in

the original sentence, the answer retains the identical meaning of the sentence.

Choice A is incorrect because *temporal* refers to how the language uses the concept of time, not secularism. The passage never discusses the ease of understanding a language, so C is incorrect. Choice D is incorrect because the passage never discusses differences in how languages express secular (worldly) or sacred (holy) concepts.

20. G
Difficulty: Medium
Category: Function
Getting to the Answer: This as a Function question. Return to the cited lines and determine how the example contributes to the main idea of the passage. The sentence immediately preceding the example provides the reason: to show how "People throughout the world are quite capable of thinking about the future and past even if they lack the terminology for it." This matches (G), the correct choice.

The remaining choices are all incorrect because the author's intention is to make the point that the use of incorrect grammar does not mean that the speaker does not understand the concept being discussed.

21. D
Difficulty: High
Category: Inference
Getting to the Answer: The keyword "inferred" identifies this as an Inference question. The correct choice will be supported by the passage but may not be directly stated. Here, the "nuanced conclusion" refers to Jakobson's point of view. Match this information to the choices; choice (D) is correct.

Choice A is a misused detail from the previous paragraph. The "nuanced conclusion" is that of Jakobson, not Whorf. Choice B is not mentioned in the text and is therefore incorrect. The author never discusses "interpreting languages." Choice C is incorrect because Deutscher is not introduced until the following paragraph, so the "nuanced conclusion" cannot be his.

22. H
Difficulty: High
Category: Function
Getting to the Answer: The phrase "primarily functions" identifies this as a Function question. Find the citation in the passage and read around it to determine how the author uses the idea to develop the purpose of the passage. The context clue is found at the end of the sixth paragraph. The passage map identifies that paragraph as containing an example illustrating Deutscher's point of view. Choice (H) is correct.

Choice F is incorrect because, although the author does correct some aspects of Whorf's thinking, that is not the primary function of the cited detail. The first sentence of the final paragraph concedes, "To an extent, then, Whorf was right." Choice G is not discussed in the passage and is incorrect. There is never any attempt to identify "the principal foundation of linguistics." Choice J is incorrect because it is the content of the citation, not the reason the author used it. The purpose of the passage is not to review different concepts of time but to illustrate the different linguistic theories through the examples of statements involving time.

23. D
Difficulty: Medium
Category: Detail
Getting to the Answer: The phrase "According to the passage" is a clue that this might be a Detail question. The answer will be stated directly in the passage, so go back to the text and research. The passage map identifies the sixth and seventh paragraphs as the place to start, so skim them quickly looking for the comparison between English and Mandarin speakers. Lines 66–67 state, "the person [who speaks Mandarin] wouldn't have to articulate timing every time they wanted to tell a story." This matches (D).

Choice A is subtly extreme. The author does present the possibility that Mandarin speakers might think less about time than English speakers but does not definitely state that this is the case. Choice B is not discussed in the text and is therefore incorrect. Choice C is not mentioned in the passage and is incorrect.

24. H
Difficulty: Medium
Category: Detail
Getting to the Answer: "According to the passage" indicates that this is a Detail question. The passage map indicates that Jakobson is discussed in the fifth paragraph, so return to that paragraph and skim, looking for keywords that describe how most people

view his theories. In the first sentence, the adjective *renowned* indicates that Jakobson is famous in his field. Choice (H) is correct.

Choice F is both factually incorrect and extreme. There is no mention in the passage of Jakobson ever being criticized, and *revered* is too strong of a word. *Revered* has a connotation of adoration, and although Jakobson was famous, there is no evidence in the passage that he was adored. Choice G is the opposite of what's stated in the passage. If Jakobson is *renowned*, he is famous for his work and other linguists are not indifferent. Choice J is half-correct, half-incorrect. Jakobson's theories are well-respected, but his character is not discussed in the text.

25. A
Difficulty: High
Category: Detail
Getting to the Answer: The keyword *describes* provides a clue that this as a Detail question. The correct choice will be stated directly in the passage, so start at the line reference but skim the lines above and below for the definition of "linguistic obligation." The beginning of the first sentence in paragraph 8 states that the paragraph will present an example of "linguistic obligation," so skim upward, looking for the definition. The sixth and seventh paragraphs are Deutscher's example and opinion, so continue looking earlier in the passage. In lines 46–48, Jakobson describes the way language shapes our thinking as "determining what we're obligated to think about rather than all that it is possible to think about." This matches (A).

The remaining incorrect choices are not discussed in the text. For B, there is no mention of vocabulary or the issues facing non-native speakers. The author makes no recommendations for further studies as mentioned in C. There is no discussion of "fundamental terms," much less the effect of their poor definition, so D is also incorrect.

26. H
Difficulty: Medium
Category: Function
Getting to the Answer: The phrase "most likely asks" identifies this as a Function question. Start at the lines cited in the question, but since the context clue is a rhetorical question, expect that the author's explanation of the purpose of the question will follow those lines. The answer to the question comes in the following line, "...*it doesn't happen*. Native Guugu Yimithirr speakers...*always* know where north is..." As noted in the passage map, this is another example of language affecting native speakers' understanding of the physical world. Since the word "attribute" means "inherent feature," choice (H) is correct.

Choice F is incorrect because the explanation is provided in the text, so it doesn't fit the passage, and would be more inline with a Detail question than a Function question. Choice G is incorrect because, according to the passage, the Guugu Yimithirr do not experience this problem. Choice J is incorrect because the question is used to illustrate an example, not to modify a theory.

27. A
Difficulty: Low
Category: Function
Getting to the Answer: This as a Function question. Since the question is asking about the final paragraph, start by reviewing the passage map and answering the question, "Why did the author return to Whorf's thesis?" Since the purpose of the passage is to discuss Whorf's theory and later developments, the last paragraph, as noted in the passage map, provides the author's summary: Whorf was fundamentally correct. This matches (A).

Choice B is a subtle distortion of information in the paragraph. The author does not state that Whorf's original theory was completely correct; the second sentence of the final paragraph acknowledges a correction of his view. Similarly, C is too extreme. The author recognizes the weakness in Whorf's theory but opens the paragraph with "To an extent...Whorf was right." Choice D is not mentioned in the passage and is incorrect. No new discoveries are credited to Whorf.

Passage IV

Suggested Passage Map Notes

¶1: Earth's magnetic field—why important

¶2: Origin? dynamo effect

¶3: Venus—iron core, but no mag field

¶4: mag field changes, iron in volcanic rocks

¶5: mag field reversed in past

¶6: now, mag field may reverse w/in a few hundred yrs

¶7: effect of weakened field—elec grid

¶8: effect of weakened field—human health

BIG PICTURE SUMMARY

Main idea: The Earth's magnetic field has many benefits to life on Earth, but it may reverse and cause problems.

Author's purpose: To discuss the Earth's magnetic field and its changes.

28. G
Difficulty: Medium
Category: Global
Getting to the Answer: The keywords "main purpose of the passage" identify this as a Global question. Use the purpose you identified in preparing your passage map as your prediction: to discuss the Earth's magnetic field and its changes. This matches (G), the correct choice.

Choice F is extreme and is incorrect. Although the author is concerned about the potential ill effects of a weakened/reversed magnetic field, the choice's strong language, "impending disaster," does not match the author's more neutral tone. Choice H is both too extreme and too narrow. The author is not "promoting" the dynamo effect; the dynamo effect is presented factually as the most prominent theory for the origin of the magnetic field. Also, this choice does not include any aspects of the magnetic field reversal discussed in paragraphs 4 through 8. Choice J misstates the author's intention in the frequent references to iron in the passage. Iron is always discussed in relation to the Earth's magnetic field, not to its importance in general scientific study.

29. A
Difficulty: Low
Category: Detail
Getting to the Answer: The phrase "According to the passage" provides a clue that this is a Detail question. Use the passage map to find the location of the information in the passage and look up the answer. In the passage map, "iron in volcanic rock" is discussed in paragraph 4. Return there, and find the discussion of the position of iron particles. Lines 49–52 state that "...a lava rock that solidified at a particular point in time will therefore have iron particles oriented in the direction of magnetic north at that time." This matches (A), the correct choice.

Choice B is a distortion of information in the paragraph. The discussion of the magnet and iron filings was an example to illustrate that iron will align with a magnetic field, not a statement that a magnet could be or was used to affect the iron in lava rock. Choices C and D are not mentioned in the passage and are therefore incorrect.

30. J
Difficulty: Medium
Category: Detail
Getting to the Answer: This is a Detail question, so look up the answer in the passage. The dynamo effect is found in paragraph 2 of the passage map. The map states that this paragraph is discussing the origin of the magnetic field: the dynamo effect as "the prominent theory." Choice (J) is correct.

Although the dynamo effect may be *widely accepted* because it is "the prominent theory," it is described as a theory, not a fact, so F is incorrect. The likelihood of the proof of the dynamo theory is never discussed, so G is also incorrect. As "the prominent theory," the dynamo effect is not described as a "mistaken conception" of the past, so H is incorrect.

31. B
Difficulty: Medium
Category: Inference
Getting to the Answer: When a question asks about the author's attitude, consider if you read any emphasis or emotional keywords such as "unfortunately," "remarkable," or "critical concern." This passage did not; the tone is neutral. With that in mind, review the last third of the passage map and, if needed, the last three paragraphs of the text for clues specifically about

the author's attitude toward possible field reversal. The author states in lines 82–85 that "the effects of a reversed magnetic north are worth discussing, especially given that this switch could have profound effects on everyday life." This supports choice (B), the correct choice.

Although some scientists are skeptical that the magnetic field will reverse quickly, this is not the author's opinion, so A is incorrect. There are no positive keywords in the passage that indicate the author is hopeful, so C is incorrect. Finally, the author is concerned, not relieved, making D incorrect.

32. F
Difficulty: Medium
Category: Inference
Getting to the Answer: The passage map identifies paragraph 8 as containing the effects of a weaker magnetic field on human health, so research there to find out if the "abnormal human cells" mentioned in the question are one of those effects. Lines 96–97 mention the abnormal cells as a result of increased radiation, and the previous line identifies the cause of the increased radiation to be the weakening of Earth's magnetic field. Choice (F) is correct.

Although the danger to electrical systems from the weakened magnetic field is discussed in the previous paragraph, it is never described as "risky" or connected to any effect on human health. Choice G is incorrect. Choice H is a distortion of information in the passage and is incorrect. Although the text states that the development of abnormal cells is a result of radiation, that radiation is not from the magnetic field. Choice J is incorrect because it is another distortion of information in the text. "Mass extinctions" are only mentioned as something that has not been seen in conjunction with magnetic field reversals in the past.

33. A
Difficulty: Medium
Category: Detail
Getting to the Answer: This is a Detail question. In addition, the emphasis keyword "critical" indicates that you're looking for a one of the most important aspects of the dynamo effect. The passage map locates the discussion of the dynamo effect in paragraph 2, so return there to research the answer. In line 22, the keyword *compels* identifies a critical component: heat from radioactive decay. This matches (A), the correct choice.

Choice B is a faulty use of a detail from the next paragraph. Although the rotation of the Earth may affect the magnetic field, rotation is not mentioned as a component of the dynamo effect. Choice C is a distortion of information in the passage. The iron in rocks after volcanic activity is used to determine past movement of the magnetic field, but volcanic activity is not a component of the dynamo effect. Choice D is another faulty use of a detail from the passage. Although the passage goes on to discuss the periodic reversal of magnetic north (and this may be a result of the dynamo effect), this reversal is not a component of the generation of the magnetic field. These choices are all incorrect.

34. H
Difficulty: Medium
Category: Function
Getting to the Answer: This question is essentially asking for the main idea of the sixth paragraph. Think about why the author included that paragraph and refer to your passage map. The passage map notes for paragraph 6 read "now, mag field may reverse w/in a few hundred yrs." This matches (H), the correct choice.

For the incorrect choices, F and G are correct details from the passage, but they are not a part of the sixth paragraph since the dynamo effect is discussed in paragraph 2 and the effects of the weakening magnetic field are discussed in the final two paragraphs. Choice J is a distortion of the information presented in paragraph 6. Although the movement of magnetic north is accelerating, the text never suggests that scientists might be wrong about the location of magnetic north.

35. D
Difficulty: Medium
Category: Detail
Getting to the Answer: This is a Detail question. This question can be approached in two different ways. If you noticed that paragraph 6 started with the contrast of an old view with a new one ("It was assumed...however...") and noted that in your passage map, a quick look at either the map or lines 62–66 is enough to lead you to (D), the correct choice. If that information is missing from your passage map, you can also take each choice back to the passage and eliminate the incorrect ones.

Choice A is mentioned in paragraph 4, but it is a hypothetical statement by the author, not a scientific hypothesis that has been revised. Choice B is the opposite of what's stated in the passage; the discussion of Venus in paragraph 3 indicated that unlike Earth, Venus does NOT have a magnetic field. Choice C is an aspect of the dynamo effect discussed in paragraph 2, and although it is a theory, it is well-accepted and has not been questioned.

36. G
Difficulty: High
Category: Function
Getting to the Answer: The keyword phrase "primarily serves" identifies this as a Function question. Consider how the comparison between Earth and Venus contributed to the author's purpose: to discuss the Earth's magnetic field and its changes. According to the passage map, Venus is discussed in paragraph 3 because, like Earth, it has an iron core, but, unlike Earth, it does NOT have a magnetic field. Notice that the first sentence of Paragraph 3 provides the author's reason for including the paragraph: "Other forces also significantly influence the Earth's magnetic field" and that the Earth/Venus comparison will provide an example of one of these forces. Choice (G) is correct.

Choices F and H are a type of common trap choice for Function questions: they relate to the content of the comparison, but not the reason the author included the comparison. Choice F also includes a subtle error: Venus' magnetic field is different from that of Earth because Venus does NOT have a magnetic field. Although the author does highlight the significant difference between the planets' rotation times, the reason the author does so is to indicate a possible influence on Earth's magnetic field, which makes H incorrect. Choice J is the opposite of true: the passage argues for the importance of Earth's iron core in generating the magnetic field, not against it.

[PART 5]

COUNTDOWN TO TEST DAY

[CHAPTER 22]

COUNTDOWN TO TEST DAY

The Week Before the Test
- Focus your additional practice on the question types and/or subject areas in which you usually score highest. Now is the time to sharpen your best skills, not cram new information.
- Make sure you are registered for the test. Remember, Kaplan cannot register you. If you missed the registration deadlines, you can request waitlist status on the test maker's website, **www.act.org**.
- Confirm the location of your test site. Never been there before? Make a practice run to make sure you know exactly how long it will take to get from your home to your test site. Build in extra time in case you hit traffic or construction on the morning of the test.
- Get a great night's sleep the two days before the test.

The Day Before the Test
- Review the methods and strategies you learned in this book.
- Put new batteries in your calculator.
- Pack your backpack or bag for test day with the following items:
  - Photo ID
  - Registration slip or printout
  - Directions to your test site location
  - Five or more sharpened no. 2 pencils (no mechanical pencils)
  - Pencil sharpener
  - Eraser
  - Calculator
  - Extra batteries
  - Non-prohibited timepiece
  - Tissues
  - Prepackaged snacks, like granola bars
  - Bottled water, juice, or sports drink
  - Sweatshirt, sweater, or jacket

Part 5
COUNTDOWN TO TEST DAY

The Night Before the Test
- No studying!
- Do something relaxing that will take your mind off the test, such as watching a movie or playing video games with friends.
- Set your alarm to wake up early enough so that you won't feel rushed.
- Go to bed early, but not too much earlier than you usually do. You want to fall asleep quickly, not spend hours tossing and turning.

The Morning of the Test
- Dress comfortably and in layers. You need to be prepared for any temperature.
- Eat a filling breakfast, but don't stray far from your usual routine. If you normally aren't a breakfast eater, don't eat a huge meal, but make sure you have something substantial.
- Read something over breakfast. You need to warm up your brain so you don't go into the test cold. Read a few pages of a newspaper, magazine, or novel.
- Get to your test site early. There is likely to be some confusion about where to go and how to sign in, so allow yourself plenty of time, even if you are taking the test at your own school.
- Leave your cell phone at home or in your car's glovebox. Many test sites do not allow them in the building.
- While you're waiting to sign in or be seated, read more of what you read over breakfast to stay in reading mode.

During the Test
- Be calm and confident. You're ready for this!
- Focus on the section you're working on at that moment; don't think about previous or upcoming sections.
- Use the methods and strategies you have learned in this book as often as you can. Allow yourself to fall into the good habits you built during your practice.
- Don't linger too long on any one question. Mark it and come back to it later.
- Can't figure out an answer? Try to eliminate some choices and take a strategic guess. Remember, there is no penalty for an incorrect answer, so even if you can't eliminate any choices, you should take a guess.
- There will be plenty of questions you CAN answer, so spend your time on those first!
- Maintain good posture throughout the test. It will help you stay alert.
- If you find yourself losing concentration, getting frustrated, or stressing about the time, stop for 30 seconds. Close your eyes, take a few deep breaths, and relax your shoulders. You'll be much more productive after taking a few moments to relax.
- Use your breaks effectively. During the breaks, go to the restroom, eat your snacks, and get your energy up for the next section.

After the Test
- Congratulate yourself! Then, reward yourself by doing something fun. You've earned it!
- If you got sick during the test or if something else happened that might have negatively affected your score, request a score cancellation form from your test proctor. Visit the test maker's website for more information.
- Your scores will be delivered in a two- to eight-week window after your test.

[PART 6]
PRACTICE TESTS

Part 6
PRACTICE TESTS

How to Score Your Practice Test

The ACT is scored differently from most tests that you take at school. Your ACT score on a test section is not reported as the total number of questions you answered correctly, nor does it directly represent the percentage of questions you answered correctly. Instead, the test makers add up all of your correct answers in a section to get what's called your raw score. They then use a conversion chart, or scale, that matches up a particular raw score with what's called a scaled score. The scaled score is the number that gets reported as your score for that ACT subject test.

You gain one point for every question you answer correctly. You lose no points for answering a question incorrectly OR for leaving a question blank. This means you should ALWAYS answer EVERY question on the ACT—even if you have to guess.

You can use the instructions below to score your practice test. Most importantly, be sure to carefully review the question explanations to get the most out of your practice. Taking practice tests and analyzing your performance is one of the best ways to prepare for the ACT. Your online resources (**kaptest.com/login**) include additional practice tests in the Simulate Test Day section. When you score these online tests, Kaplan provides you with a detailed score report, which can help your review.

GO ONLINE
kaptest.com/login

Score Tracker

1. **Figure out your raw score for each subject test.** Refer to the answer key to determine how many questions you answered correctly. Enter the results below:

RAW SCORES

English: ☐

Math: ☐

Reading: ☐

2. **Convert your raw scores to scaled scores for each subject test.** Locate your raw score for each subject test in the following table. The score in the outside columns indicates your estimated scaled score if this were an actual ACT. Enter your scaled scores in the boxes that follow the table.

Practice Test 1

SCALED SCORE	RAW SCORES			SCALED SCORE
	Test 1 English	Test 2 Mathematics	Test 3 Reading	
36	49–50	44–45	36	36
35	48	43	34–35	35
34	47	41–42	33	34
33	46	40	32	33
32	45	39	31	32
31	—	38	30	31
30	44	37	29	30
29	43	35–36	28	29
28	42	34	27	28
27	41	32–33	—	27
26	40	29–31	26	26
25	38–39	28	25	25
24	36–37	26–27	24	24
23	34–35	24–25	23	23
22	32–33	23	21–22	22
21	30–31	22	20	21
20	28–29	20–21	18–19	20
19	26–27	19	17	19
18	25	17–18	16	18
17	23–24	14–16	15	17
16	22	12–13	14	16
15	20–21	10–11	13	15
14	17–19	7–9	11–12	14
13	16	6	10	13
12	15	5	9	12
11	13–14	4	7–8	11
10	11–12	3	6	10
9	9–10	—	—	9
8	7–8	—	5	8
7	6	2	—	7
6	5	—	4	6
5	4	—	3	5
4	3	1	2	4
3	2	—	—	3
2	—	—	1	2
1	0–1	0	0	1

Part 6
PRACTICE TESTS

SCALED SCORES

English: ☐

Math: ☐

Reading: ☐

3. **Calculate your estimated composite score.** Simply add together your scaled scores for each subject test and divide by three.

ACT Practice Test 1
ANSWER SHEET

ENGLISH TEST

1. Ⓐ Ⓑ Ⓒ Ⓓ
2. Ⓕ Ⓖ Ⓗ Ⓙ
3. Ⓐ Ⓑ Ⓒ Ⓓ
4. Ⓕ Ⓖ Ⓗ Ⓙ
5. Ⓐ Ⓑ Ⓒ Ⓓ
6. Ⓕ Ⓖ Ⓗ Ⓙ
7. Ⓐ Ⓑ Ⓒ Ⓓ
8. Ⓕ Ⓖ Ⓗ Ⓙ
9. Ⓐ Ⓑ Ⓒ Ⓓ
10. Ⓕ Ⓖ Ⓗ Ⓙ
11. Ⓐ Ⓑ Ⓒ Ⓓ
12. Ⓕ Ⓖ Ⓗ Ⓙ
13. Ⓐ Ⓑ Ⓒ Ⓓ
14. Ⓕ Ⓖ Ⓗ Ⓙ
15. Ⓐ Ⓑ Ⓒ Ⓓ
16. Ⓕ Ⓖ Ⓗ Ⓙ
17. Ⓐ Ⓑ Ⓒ Ⓓ
18. Ⓕ Ⓖ Ⓗ Ⓙ
19. Ⓐ Ⓑ Ⓒ Ⓓ
20. Ⓕ Ⓖ Ⓗ Ⓙ
21. Ⓐ Ⓑ Ⓒ Ⓓ
22. Ⓕ Ⓖ Ⓗ Ⓙ
23. Ⓐ Ⓑ Ⓒ Ⓓ
24. Ⓕ Ⓖ Ⓗ Ⓙ
25. Ⓐ Ⓑ Ⓒ Ⓓ
26. Ⓕ Ⓖ Ⓗ Ⓙ
27. Ⓐ Ⓑ Ⓒ Ⓓ
28. Ⓕ Ⓖ Ⓗ Ⓙ
29. Ⓐ Ⓑ Ⓒ Ⓓ
30. Ⓕ Ⓖ Ⓗ Ⓙ
31. Ⓐ Ⓑ Ⓒ Ⓓ
32. Ⓕ Ⓖ Ⓗ Ⓙ
33. Ⓐ Ⓑ Ⓒ Ⓓ
34. Ⓕ Ⓖ Ⓗ Ⓙ
35. Ⓐ Ⓑ Ⓒ Ⓓ
36. Ⓕ Ⓖ Ⓗ Ⓙ
37. Ⓐ Ⓑ Ⓒ Ⓓ
38. Ⓕ Ⓖ Ⓗ Ⓙ
39. Ⓐ Ⓑ Ⓒ Ⓓ
40. Ⓕ Ⓖ Ⓗ Ⓙ
41. Ⓐ Ⓑ Ⓒ Ⓓ
42. Ⓕ Ⓖ Ⓗ Ⓙ
43. Ⓐ Ⓑ Ⓒ Ⓓ
44. Ⓕ Ⓖ Ⓗ Ⓙ
45. Ⓐ Ⓑ Ⓒ Ⓓ
46. Ⓕ Ⓖ Ⓗ Ⓙ
47. Ⓐ Ⓑ Ⓒ Ⓓ
48. Ⓕ Ⓖ Ⓗ Ⓙ
49. Ⓐ Ⓑ Ⓒ Ⓓ
50. Ⓕ Ⓖ Ⓗ Ⓙ

MATHEMATICS TEST

1. Ⓐ Ⓑ Ⓒ Ⓓ
2. Ⓕ Ⓖ Ⓗ Ⓙ
3. Ⓐ Ⓑ Ⓒ Ⓓ
4. Ⓕ Ⓖ Ⓗ Ⓙ
5. Ⓐ Ⓑ Ⓒ Ⓓ
6. Ⓕ Ⓖ Ⓗ Ⓙ
7. Ⓐ Ⓑ Ⓒ Ⓓ
8. Ⓕ Ⓖ Ⓗ Ⓙ
9. Ⓐ Ⓑ Ⓒ Ⓓ
10. Ⓕ Ⓖ Ⓗ Ⓙ
11. Ⓐ Ⓑ Ⓒ Ⓓ
12. Ⓕ Ⓖ Ⓗ Ⓙ
13. Ⓐ Ⓑ Ⓒ Ⓓ
14. Ⓕ Ⓖ Ⓗ Ⓙ
15. Ⓐ Ⓑ Ⓒ Ⓓ
16. Ⓕ Ⓖ Ⓗ Ⓙ
17. Ⓐ Ⓑ Ⓒ Ⓓ
18. Ⓕ Ⓖ Ⓗ Ⓙ
19. Ⓐ Ⓑ Ⓒ Ⓓ
20. Ⓕ Ⓖ Ⓗ Ⓙ
21. Ⓐ Ⓑ Ⓒ Ⓓ
22. Ⓕ Ⓖ Ⓗ Ⓙ
23. Ⓐ Ⓑ Ⓒ Ⓓ
24. Ⓕ Ⓖ Ⓗ Ⓙ
25. Ⓐ Ⓑ Ⓒ Ⓓ
26. Ⓕ Ⓖ Ⓗ Ⓙ
27. Ⓐ Ⓑ Ⓒ Ⓓ
28. Ⓕ Ⓖ Ⓗ Ⓙ
29. Ⓐ Ⓑ Ⓒ Ⓓ
30. Ⓕ Ⓖ Ⓗ Ⓙ
31. Ⓐ Ⓑ Ⓒ Ⓓ
32. Ⓕ Ⓖ Ⓗ Ⓙ
33. Ⓐ Ⓑ Ⓒ Ⓓ
34. Ⓕ Ⓖ Ⓗ Ⓙ
35. Ⓐ Ⓑ Ⓒ Ⓓ
36. Ⓕ Ⓖ Ⓗ Ⓙ
37. Ⓐ Ⓑ Ⓒ Ⓓ
38. Ⓕ Ⓖ Ⓗ Ⓙ
39. Ⓐ Ⓑ Ⓒ Ⓓ
40. Ⓕ Ⓖ Ⓗ Ⓙ
41. Ⓐ Ⓑ Ⓒ Ⓓ
42. Ⓕ Ⓖ Ⓗ Ⓙ
43. Ⓐ Ⓑ Ⓒ Ⓓ
44. Ⓕ Ⓖ Ⓗ Ⓙ
45. Ⓐ Ⓑ Ⓒ Ⓓ

READING TEST

1. Ⓐ Ⓑ Ⓒ Ⓓ
2. Ⓕ Ⓖ Ⓗ Ⓙ
3. Ⓐ Ⓑ Ⓒ Ⓓ
4. Ⓕ Ⓖ Ⓗ Ⓙ
5. Ⓐ Ⓑ Ⓒ Ⓓ
6. Ⓕ Ⓖ Ⓗ Ⓙ
7. Ⓐ Ⓑ Ⓒ Ⓓ
8. Ⓕ Ⓖ Ⓗ Ⓙ
9. Ⓐ Ⓑ Ⓒ Ⓓ
10. Ⓕ Ⓖ Ⓗ Ⓙ
11. Ⓐ Ⓑ Ⓒ Ⓓ
12. Ⓕ Ⓖ Ⓗ Ⓙ
13. Ⓐ Ⓑ Ⓒ Ⓓ
14. Ⓕ Ⓖ Ⓗ Ⓙ
15. Ⓐ Ⓑ Ⓒ Ⓓ
16. Ⓕ Ⓖ Ⓗ Ⓙ
17. Ⓐ Ⓑ Ⓒ Ⓓ
18. Ⓕ Ⓖ Ⓗ Ⓙ
19. Ⓐ Ⓑ Ⓒ Ⓓ
20. Ⓕ Ⓖ Ⓗ Ⓙ
21. Ⓐ Ⓑ Ⓒ Ⓓ
22. Ⓕ Ⓖ Ⓗ Ⓙ
23. Ⓐ Ⓑ Ⓒ Ⓓ
24. Ⓕ Ⓖ Ⓗ Ⓙ
25. Ⓐ Ⓑ Ⓒ Ⓓ
26. Ⓕ Ⓖ Ⓗ Ⓙ
27. Ⓐ Ⓑ Ⓒ Ⓓ
28. Ⓕ Ⓖ Ⓗ Ⓙ
29. Ⓐ Ⓑ Ⓒ Ⓓ
30. Ⓕ Ⓖ Ⓗ Ⓙ
31. Ⓐ Ⓑ Ⓒ Ⓓ
32. Ⓕ Ⓖ Ⓗ Ⓙ
33. Ⓐ Ⓑ Ⓒ Ⓓ
34. Ⓕ Ⓖ Ⓗ Ⓙ
35. Ⓐ Ⓑ Ⓒ Ⓓ
36. Ⓕ Ⓖ Ⓗ Ⓙ

Practice Test 1

English Test

35 Minutes—50 Questions

Directions: In the passages that follow, certain words and phrases are underlined and numbered. In the right-hand column, you will find alternatives for the underlined part. You are to choose the best answer to each question. If you think the original version is best, choose "**No Change.**"

Some questions will ask about part or all of the passage. These questions do not refer to a specific underlined segment. Instead, these questions will accompany a number in a box.

For each question, choose your answer and fill in the corresponding bubble on your answer sheet. Read the passage once before you answer the questions. You will often need to read several sentences beyond the underlined portion to be able to choose the correct answer. Be sure to read enough to answer each question.

PASSAGE I

My Old-Fashioned Father

My father, though he is only in his early 50s, is stuck in his old-fashioned ways. He has a general mistrust of any innovation or technology that he can't immediately

1. Which choice makes the sentence most grammatically acceptable?

   A. **No Change**
   B. ways he has a
   C. ways having a
   D. ways, and still has a

grasp and he always tells us, that if something isn't broken, then you shouldn't fix it.

2. Which choice makes the sentence most grammatically acceptable?

   F. **No Change**
   G. tells us, that,
   H. tells us that,
   J. tells us that

He has run a small grocery store in town, and if you were to look at a snapshot of his back office taken when he opened the store in 1975, you would

3. Which choice makes the sentence most grammatically acceptable?

   A. **No Change**
   B. was running
   C. runs
   D. ran

CONTINUED

see that not much has changed since. He is the most
disorganized person I know and still uses a pencil
and paper to keep track of his inventory. His small office
is overflowing with paper; his filing cabinets have long
since been filled up. The centerpiece of all the clutter
is his ancient typewriter, which isn't even electric.

4. Which choice is least redundant in context?

   F. **No Change**
   G. not be likely to see very much that has changed since.
   H. be able to see right away that not very much has changed since.
   J. not change very much.

5. Which choice is clearest and most precise in context?

   A. **No Change**
   B. possessions.
   C. stuff.
   D. archives.

6. Which choice provides the most vivid description of the state of Father's office?

   F. **No Change**
   G. about to burst with all the various documents, notes, and receipts he has accumulated over the years;
   H. a big mess, with various items in a state of disarray;
   J. cluttered with ephemera;

Because they are no longer being produced, Father's search for replacement typewriter ribbons has become an increasingly difficult task in the past few years. When people ask him why he doesn't upgrade his equipment, he tells them, "Electric typewriters won't work in a blackout. All I need is a candle and some paper, and I'm fine." Little does Father know, however, that the "upgrade" people are speaking of is not to an electric typewriter but to a computer.

Hoping to bring Father out of the Dark Ages, my sister and I bought him a brand-new computer for his fiftieth birthday. Eagerly, we told him about all the new spreadsheet programs that would help simplify his recordkeeping and organize his accounts. Rather than offering us a look of joy for the life-changing gift we had presented him, however, he again brought up the blackout scenario. To Father, this is a concrete argument, although our town hasn't had a blackout in five years, and we only lasted an hour or two.

My father's state-of-the-art computer now serves as a very expensive bulletin board for the hundreds of adhesive notes he uses to keep himself organized. Anon, we fully expect it will completely disappear under the mounting files and papers in the back office.

7. Which choice makes the sentence most grammatically acceptable?

   A. **No Change**
   B. Because they are no longer being produced, Father's task of finding replacement typewriter ribbons has become increasingly difficult in the past few years.
   C. Because they are no longer being produced, replacement typewriter ribbons have become increasingly difficult for Father to find in the past few years.
   D. Having become increasingly difficult to find in the past few years, Father has searched for replacement typewriter ribbons, which are no longer being produced.

8. Which transition word or phrase is most logical in context?

   F. **No Change**
   G. On the other hand,
   H. In addition
   J. Rather,

9. Which choice makes the sentence most grammatically acceptable?

   A. **No Change**
   B. they
   C. that one
   D. he

10. Which choice most effectively maintains the essay's tone?

    F. **No Change**
    G. Sooner or later,
    H. Somewhen,
    J. In the entirely of time's progression,

Part 6
PRACTICE TESTS

PASSAGE II

Du Fu: Poet-Sage

Du Fu, an official of the Tang dynasty, is considered one of the greatest poets in Chinese literary history. Born in 712 CE near Luoyang to a minor scholar-official family, Du Fu spent his early years studying the Confucian classics while also traveling extensively and exploring far and wide throughout China.
₁₁

When he aspired to serve in the imperial government,
₁₂
Du Fu failed the civil service examinations multiple times.

The An Lushan Rebellion of 755 CE marked a turning point in Du Fu's life and poetry. During this tumultuous period, Du Fu saw war tear everything apart, inspiring
₁₃
some of his most renowned works The Ballad of the
₁₄
Army Carts, a poignant commentary on conscription,
₁₄
and *Spring View*, which vividly captures the contrast between nature's beauty and human suffering.

11. Which choice is least redundant in context?

    A. **No Change**
    B. traveling extensively and far and wide
    C. traveling and exploring extensively
    D. traveling extensively

12. Which transition word or phrase is most logical in context?

    F. **No Change**
    G. Although
    H. Because
    J. Whereas

13. Which choice most effectively maintains the essay's tone?

    A. **No Change**
    B. got a front-row seat to war's destruction
    C. saw firsthand how war messes everything up
    D. witnessed the devastating effects of war on society

14. Which choice makes the sentence most grammatically acceptable?

    F. **No Change**
    G. works, The Ballad of the Army Carts,
    H. works: The Ballad of the Army Carts,
    J. works; The Ballad of the Army Carts,

Throughout his itinerant life, Du Fu produced a vast body of work, with approximately 1,450 poems extant. Du Fu's poetry is renowned for its technical mastery, emotional depth, and keen social awareness. His verses cover a wide range of subjects, from political commentary and historical events to personal experiences and observations of nature. Du Fu's influence on Chinese literature has been immense, earning him the title "Poet-Historian" <u>and comparisons to Shakespeare in Western literature</u>. His work continues to be studied and admired by scholars and poetry enthusiasts worldwide.

15. Which choice best illustrates the global significance of Du Fu's literary influence?

   A. **No Change**
   B. and recognition for his contributions to calligraphy
   C. and praise for his contributions to Chinese painting
   D. and acclaim for his travels across China

PASSAGE III

Breaking Baseball's Color Barrier

[1]

A quick perusal of any modern major league baseball team will <u>reveal a roster of players of multiple ethnicities</u> from the farthest reaches of the globe.
[A] Second only to soccer, baseball has evolved into a global sport and a symbol for equality among races.

[2]

Its diversity today presents a stark contrast to the state of the sport over seventy years ago. As late as the 1940s, there existed an unwritten rule in baseball that prevented all but <u>white players from practicing, traveling with and playing ball in</u> the major leagues. This rule was known as the "color barrier" or "color line." [B] The color line in baseball actually predated the birth of the major leagues. Prior to the official formation of any league of professional baseball teams, there existed an organization of amateur baseball clubs known as the National Association of Baseball Players, <u>which was the precursor to today's National League</u>. On December 11, 1868, the governing body of this association had unanimously adopted a rule that effectively barred any team that had any "colored persons" on its roster.

16. Which choice makes the sentence most grammatically acceptable?

   F. No Change
   G. reveal a roster, of players of multiple ethnicities
   H. reveal a roster of players of multiple ethnicities,
   J. reveal a roster of players, of multiple ethnicities,

17. Which choice is least redundant in context?

   A. No Change
   B. white players from participating in
   C. white players from engaging with any team in
   D. white players from being part of a team in

18. If the writer were to delete the underlined portion (adjusting the punctuation as needed), the paragraph would primarily lose:

   F. details about a modern organization.
   G. a detail that shows the writer's opinion of an organization.
   H. information that indicates the importance of an organization.
   J. information that clarifies how one organization is related to another.

However, when baseball started to organize into leagues of professional teams in the early 1880s, the National Association of Baseball Players' decree no longer had any weight, especially in the newly formed American Association. [C] The color barrier was lost and it never reemerged in professional baseball.

[3]

Most baseball historians believe that the first African American to play in the major leagues was Moses "Fleet" Walker. Walker was a catcher for the Toledo Blue Stockings of the American Association between 1884 and 1889. During that time, a few other African Americans, including Walker's brother Weldy, who joined him on the Blue Stockings.

19. Which choice is least redundant in context?
   A. No Change
   B. began collecting information in order to organize
   C. had organizers that wanted to started sorting
   D. implemented a plan to organize

20. Given that all the choices are accurate, which one most effectively leads from its current paragraph to the next paragraph?
   F. No Change
   G. For a brief period in those early years, a few African Americans played side by side with white players on major league diamonds.
   H. Other professional sports also had histories that included segregation and color barriers.
   J. Many white athletes wanted a color barrier implemented in the American Association as soon as the organization began.

21. Which choice makes the sentence most grammatically acceptable?
   A. No Change
   B. were
   C. would be
   D. are

22. Which choice makes the sentence most grammatically acceptable?
   F. No Change
   G. whom had joined
   H. he joined
   J. joined

[D] Unfortunately, this respite from segregation did not last for very long; as Jim Crow laws took their hold on the nation, many of the most popular white ballplayers started to refuse to take the field with their African American teammates. By the 1890s, the color barrier had fully returned to baseball, where it would endure for more than half a century. 24

23. Which transition word or phrase is most logical in context?

A. **No Change**
B. In addition,
C. Therefore,
D. Recently,

24. At this point, the writer is considering adding the following accurate sentence:

   The National Basketball Association had a similar color barrier until it was broken by Earl Lloyd in 1950.

   Should the writer make this addition?

   F. Yes, because it makes it clear that the two organizations faced the same challenges from their beginnings.
   G. Yes, because it indicates that the color barrier was not unique to professional baseball.
   H. No, because it is draws the focus away from the color barrier that returned to baseball.
   J. No, because it fails to provide details about the history of the National Basketball Association's color barrier.

   Question 25 asks about the preceding passage as a whole.

25. The writer wants to add the following sentence to the essay:

   A handful of African Americans played for other teams as well.

   The sentence would most logically be placed at:

   A. Point A in Paragraph 1.
   B. Point B in Paragraph 2.
   C. Point C in Paragraph 2.
   D. Point D in Paragraph 3.

PASSAGE IV

The Dream of the American West

As the sun <u>was slowly rising</u> over the Atlantic
                    26
Ocean and painted New York Harbor a spectacular fiery orange, I started my old Toyota's engine. At this early hour, there was still some semblance of the night's tranquility left on the city sidewalks, but I knew that, as the minutes ticked by, the streets would flood with humanity. I smiled <u>with</u> the thought that soon
                27
all the wonderful chaos of New York City would be disappearing behind me as I <u>embarked on my trip to the
                                                  28
other side of</u> the country.
      28

As the morning sun climbed into the sky, I shuddered with excitement <u>to think that my final stop
                                       29
would be in California, where the sun itself ends its
                          29
journey across America</u>. Like the sun, though, I still had
       29
quite a journey before me.

I had been planning this road trip across the United States for as long as I could remember. In my life, I had been fortunate enough to see some of the most beautiful countries in the world. However, it had always bothered me that although I'd stood in the shadow of the

26. Which choice makes the sentence most grammatically acceptable?

F. **No Change**
G. rising slowly
H. rose slowly
J. continued to rise

27. Which choice makes the sentence most grammatically acceptable?

A. **No Change**
B. along with
C. at
D. all because of

28. Which choice is least redundant in context?

F. **No Change**
G. embarked on this journey across
H. traveled to the other side of
J. traveled across

29. The writer is considering revising this sentence by deleting the underlined portion. If this is done, the paragraph would primarily lose:

A. information about the reasons for the writer's trip.
B. information about the writer's destination.
C. a description of the writer's planned route.
D. a comparison between the sunrise in New York and the sunset in California.

Part 6
PRACTICE TESTS

Eiffel Tower, marveled in the desert heat at the Pyramids
of Giza, I'd never seen any of the wonders of my own country, except those found in my hometown of New York City. All of that was about to change.

As I left the city, the tall buildings began to give way to smaller ones, then to transform into the quaint rows of houses that clustered the crowded suburbs. Trees and grass, then the yellow-green of cornfields and the golden wash of wheat were slowly replacing the familiar mazes of cement and steel. My world no longer stretched vertically toward the sky, it now spread horizontally toward eternity. For two days, I pushed through the wind-whipped farmlands of Mid-America, hypnotized by the beauty of the undulating yet unbroken lines. At night, the breeze from my car would stir the wheat fields to dance beneath the moon, and the silos hid in the

30. Which choice makes the sentence most grammatically acceptable?

   F. No Change
   G. Eiffel Tower and had marveled in the desert heat at the Pyramids of Giza,
   H. Eiffel Tower and marveled in the desert heat at the Pyramids of Giza
   J. Eiffel Tower, and had marveled, in the desert heat, at the Pyramids of Giza

31. Given that all the choices are accurate, which one provides the best transition between the third paragraph and the description of the Midwest in the fourth paragraph?

   A. No Change
   B. In fact, there were changes on the horizon almost immediately.
   C. My excitement hadn't diminished.
   D. I realized that people who lived in other areas might feel the same way about visiting New York.

32. Given that all the choices are accurate, which one provides the most relevant information at this point in the essay?

   F. No Change
   G. appearing before me.
   H. racing past my window.
   J. becoming monotonous.

33. Which choice makes the sentence most grammatically acceptable?

   A. No Change
   B. the sky but it now spread
   C. the sky; it now spread
   D. the sky spreading

shadows, quietly imposing their simply serenity upon
everything.

As the night's shadows gave way to light, there seemed to be a great force rising to meet the reappearing sun. Still, I had no idea what I was looking at. Then, there was no mistaking it. The unbroken lines of Mid-America had given way to the jagged and majestic heights of the Rockies: the gateway to the American West.

34. Which choice makes the sentence most grammatically acceptable?

   F. **No Change**
   G. simple
   H. simplest
   J. simpler

35. Which transition word or phrase is most logical in context?

   A. **No Change**
   B. Even so,
   C. At first,
   D. Eventually,

PASSAGE V

Spiders on Mars?

NASA scientists have unlocked the secrets of the Martian spiders—though these "spiders" aren't actually alive.
[36]

The surface of Mars is marked with peculiar spider-like patterns, with a central pit and radiating channels that extend outward like legs. These "spiders," formally referred to as "araneiform terrain," were first detected by NASA orbiters in 2003. At first a mystery, scientists now know that these terrain features are caused by sunlight as it penetrates Mars' translucent carbon dioxide (CO_2) ice, warming the ground beneath. This process causes the CO_2 ice to sublimate directly into gas, building pressure until it explosively escapes, and carve out channels that resemble spider legs. [39]

For the first time on Earth, in 2024 researchers at NASA's Jet Propulsion Laboratory replicated these formations in a lab. The JPL team used the DUSTIE (Dirty Under-vacuum Simulation Testbed for Icy Environments) chamber to recreate Martian ground conditions. They cooled beds of Martian soil simulant

36. The writer wants to clarify in a playful way that the Martian "spiders" aren't living creatures. Which choice best accomplishes this goal?

F. **No Change**
G. —though these "spiders" are actually called "araneiform terrain."
H. —though thankfully, these "spiders" don't need webs, just a block of dry ice and a little sunshine.
J. **Delete** the underlined portion.

37. Which choice is least redundant in context?

A. **No Change**
B. now know, without a doubt,
C. now know with certainty
D. know

38. Which choice makes the sentence most grammatically acceptable?

F. **No Change**
G. build
H. is building
J. builds

39. If the writer were to delete the phrase "that resemble spider legs" from the preceding sentence (adjusting the punctuation as needed), the sentence would primarily lose:

A. specific information that illustrates the depth of the channels.
B. specific information that conveys the unique and recognizable shape of araneiform terrain.
C. a detail that defends the argument that araneiform terrain deserves its nickname.
D. a detail that clarifies the process that results in araneiform terrain.

CONTINUED

and overlaid it with CO_2 ice. As the ice sublimated, it resulted in gas jets that displaced the soil, creating patterns strikingly like the Martian spiders. The success of this experiment not only proves that the sublimation process created these features on Mars but also gives scientists a way to study them in a controlled environment.

40. Which choice makes the sentence most grammatically acceptable?

F. **No Change**
G. them
H. they
J. its

Part 6
PRACTICE TESTS

PASSAGE VI

Flight of the Concorde

The last of the supersonic Concorde passenger planes, in which were jointly operated by British Airways and Air France, made its final trip across the Atlantic in November of 2003, training the new pilots on the plane's most common flight path. The fleet of Concorde Supersonic Transports had been making routine, intercontinental trips across the Atlantic for almost thirty years. The route was established due in part to the 1973 ban by the U.S. Federal Aviation Administration on supersonic jetliners flying over land.

In addition to making an explosive sound, supersonic booms, caused by the sound waves accumulated by the planes as it breaks the sound barrier, had the potential to damage property.

Flying at a height almost twice of that at which standard passenger airplanes fly, these amazing machines cruised at Mach 2, more than twice the speed

41. Which choice makes the sentence most grammatically acceptable?
    A. No Change
    B. planes, which
    C. planes and
    D. planes,

42. Which choice most clearly builds on the information provided earlier in the sentence about the Concorde's transatlantic journey?
    F. No Change
    G. complying with new regulations established by the U.S. Federal Aviation Administration.
    H. closing an interesting chapter in aeronautic history.
    J. introducing a new route it would be starting.

43. The writer is considering revising the underlined portion to the following:

    a loud

    Should the writer make this revision?
    A. Yes, because the revision reinforces the parallel drawn between the noisiness of the booms and their destructive potential.
    B. Yes, because the revision simplifies the reason that the U.S. Federal Aviation Administration banned supersonic jetliners.
    C. No, because the original word establishes the intensity of the sonic booms, before explaining how destructive they are.
    D. No, because the original word more clearly defines the extent of the U.S. Federal Aviation Administration's ban on supersonic aircraft.

644

CONTINUED →

of sound. In spite of this, a trip, from New York to
                44
London could be made in less than three hours.

Our ears are able to pick up those sound waves
                45
and convert them into what we hear. As air temperature
        45
and pressure decrease with altitude, so does the speed
of sound. An airplane flying at the speed of sound at
sea level is traveling roughly at 761 mph; however,
when that same plane climbs to 20,000 feet, the speed
of sound is only about 707 mph. This is why the

Concordes cruising altitude was so much higher than
        46
that of a regular passenger aircraft: the planes can reach
                                        47
supersonic speeds more easily at higher altitudes. The
        47
awe-inspiring swiftness of the Concorde Supersonic
Transports would leave their spectators breathless, but

44. Which transition word or phrase, if any, is most logical in context?

   F. **No Change**
   G. Nonetheless, a trip
   H. Similarly, a trip
   J. A trip

45. The writer is considering deleting the underlined sentence. Should the sentence be kept or deleted?

   A. Kept, because it contrasts the human experience of sound with the velocity of the Concorde.
   B. Kept, because it emotionally connects the reader to the subject of the essay.
   C. Deleted, because it undermines the essay's claim about the history of supersonic aircraft.
   D. Deleted, because it adds an irrelevant detail to the paragraph's explanation of supersonic flight.

46. Which choice makes the sentence most grammatically acceptable?

   F. **No Change**
   G. Concorde's cruising altitude
   H. Concordes cruise altitude
   J. Concorde's cruise altitude

47. Which choice best maintains the stylistic pattern of descriptions established earlier in the sentence?

   A. **No Change**
   B. these things can really go when they're over the clouds.
   C. their fantastic performance soared with loftier heights.
   D. the higher, the faster.

Part 6
PRACTICE TESTS

would also leave their passengers struggling to hear.
                        —————————————————
                              48
The speed and structure of the aircraft resulted in the cabin being described as "extremely noisy." Though flying in a supersonic Concorde passenger plane is no longer possible, walking through one is. [49] New York City's Intrepid Museum is proud to house one of these (along with Chantilly's Udvar-Hazy Center and Seattle's
——————————————————————————————————————
                              50
Museum of Flight) commercial jetliners.
——————————————
      50

48. Which choice makes the sentence most grammatically acceptable?

   F. **No Change**
   G. its passengers struggling
   H. them struggling
   J. it struggling

49. Which of the following true statements, if added here, would best build on the ideas presented in this paragraph and connect to the final sentence of the essay?

   A. No matter what the year, it is difficult to not be caught up in the majesty and wonder generated by the sight and sound of a Concorde in flight.
   B. If aspiring aeronautical engineers or novice aerophiles are so inclined, they are able to tour a retired Concorde.
   C. Supersonic aircraft have recently fallen out of popularity.
   D. However, pilots are no longer allowed to fly them.

50. The best placement for the underlined portion would be:

   F. where it is now.
   G. after the word *house*.
   H. after the word *jetliners*.
   J. after the word *Museum*.

Mathematics Test

50 Minutes—45 Questions

Directions: Solve each problem, choose the correct answer, and then fill in the corresponding oval on your answer document.

Do not linger over problems that take too much time. Solve as many as you can; then return to the others in the time you have left for this test.

You may use a calculator on this test for any question you choose. However, some questions may be better solved without a calculator.

Note: Unless otherwise stated, you can assume:

1. Figures are NOT necessarily drawn to scale.
2. Geometric figures are two dimensional.
3. The term *line* indicates a straight line.
4. The term *average* indicates arithmetic mean.

1. On her first three geometry tests, Sarah scored an 89, a 93, and an 84. If there are four tests total and Sarah needs at least a 90 average for the four, what is the lowest score she can receive on the final test?

   A. 90
   B. 92
   C. 94
   D. 96

2. In the Venn diagram, circles *M*, *S*, and *H* represent the number of students taking math, science, and history, respectively. How many of the 45 students represented in the diagram do **not** take math?

   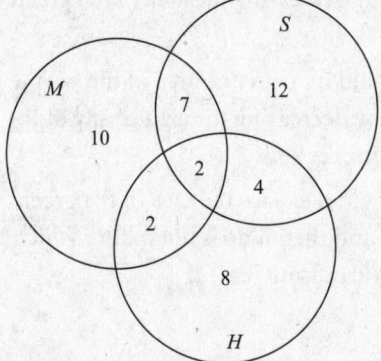

   F. 23
   G. 24
   H. 25
   J. 26

3. Cassie designs a dart board that has exactly 5 regions: red, blue, green, purple, and yellow. She wants a dart to have a 20% chance of landing in each region. She haphazardly throws a dart 600 times at the board. The results of her throws are shown in the table.

Region	Number of times the dart lands in each region
Red	125
Blue	115
Green	150
Purple	92
Yellow	118

Based on the results in this table, one of the following changes would be the best fix. Which one?

A. She should decrease the area of the purple region by increasing the area of the green region.
B. She should increase the area of the purple region by decreasing the area of the green region.
C. She should increase the area of the purple region by decreasing the area of any of the other four regions.
D. She should decrease the area of the green region, and then it does not matter which region's area is increased.

4. In the following figure, $\overline{MN}$ and $\overline{PQ}$ are parallel. Point A lies on $\overline{MN}$, and points B and C lie on $\overline{PQ}$. If $AB = AC$ and $\angle MAB$ has a measure of 55°, what is the measure of $\angle ACB$?

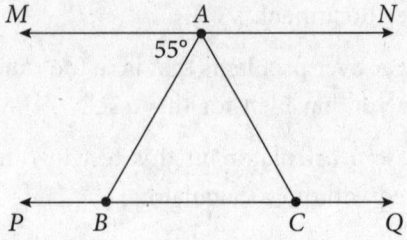

F. 35°
G. 55°
H. 65°
J. 80°

5. Which of the following is a solution to the equation $x^2 - 8x = 8x$?

A. 32
B. 16
C. 8
D. 4

6. Which of the following matrices is equal to the matrix product $\begin{bmatrix} -2 & 0 \\ 1 & -3 \end{bmatrix} \cdot \begin{bmatrix} 2 \\ 2 \end{bmatrix}$?

F. $\begin{bmatrix} -4 & 0 \\ 2 & -6 \end{bmatrix}$

G. $\begin{bmatrix} -4 & 2 \\ 2 & -6 \end{bmatrix}$

H. $\begin{bmatrix} -4 \\ -4 \end{bmatrix}$

J. $\begin{bmatrix} -4 \\ -6 \end{bmatrix}$

7. Roman purchased some hats and balloons for an upcoming party and gave them to the members of his class. Each member of his class received the same number of hats and the same number of balloons. The total number of hats he gave to his class was 10, and the total number of balloons was 35. Which of the following could be the number of people in Roman's class?

   A. 5
   B. 10
   C. 15
   D. 20

8. The yield of a certain crop, in pounds, can be estimated by multiplying the initial number of seeds planted by 20 and then taking the square root of the product. According to this method, what is the estimated yield, in pounds, of the crop when 90 seeds are planted?

   F. $\sqrt{110}$
   G. $30\sqrt{3}$
   H. $30\sqrt{2}$
   J. $90\sqrt{6}$

9. If $2x - 7y = 8$, then $x = ?$

   A. $4 + \frac{7}{2}y$
   B. $4 - \frac{7}{2}y$
   C. $\frac{4 + 7y}{2}$
   D. $\frac{4 - 7y}{2}$

10. Court reporters type every word spoken during trials and hearings so that there is a written record of what transpired. Suppose a certain court reporter can type 3.75 words per second, and a trial transcript contains 25 pages with an average of 675 words per page. If this court reporter typed the transcript at his typical rate, how long was he actively typing?

    F. 1 hour, 15 minutes
    G. 1 hour, 40 minutes
    H. 2 hours, 10 minutes
    J. 2 hours, 30 minutes

11. If $f(x) = 16x^2 - 20x$, what is the value of $f(3)$?

    A. -12
    B. 36
    C. 84
    D. 144

12. Dillon is going to randomly pick a domino from a pile of dominoes that are all facing downward. Of the dominoes in the pile, 48 have an even number of dots on them. He randomly picks a single domino. If the probability that he picks a domino with an even number of dots is $\frac{3}{4}$, how many dominoes are in the pile?

    F. 48
    G. 56
    H. 64
    J. 72

13. In the following triangle, what is the value of cos R?

    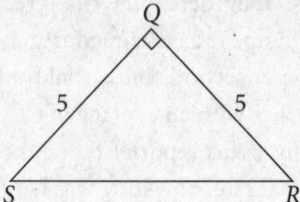

    A. $\dfrac{\sqrt{2}}{6}$

    B. $\dfrac{\sqrt{2}}{5}$

    C. $\dfrac{\sqrt{2}}{2}$

    D. $2\sqrt{2}$

14. Which of the following values, if any, is the x-value of the solution set to the system of equations?

    $$3x - y = 4$$
    $$-6x + 2y = 1$$

    F. 3
    G. 5
    H. 8
    J. There is no such value for x.

15. Which of the following expressions is equivalent to $(x - 6)^3$?

    A. $x^3 - 18x^2 + 108x - 216$
    B. $x^3 - 12x - 216$
    C. $x^3 - 12x + 36$
    D. $x^3 - 216$

16. In a high school senior class, the ratio of girls to boys is 5:3. If there are a total of 168 students in the senior class, how many girls are there?

    F. 100
    G. 105
    H. 147
    J. 152

17. The expression $2y^3 \cdot 3xy^2 \cdot 6xy^2$ is equivalent to which of the following?

    A. $11x^2y^7$
    B. $11x^2y^{12}$
    C. $36x^2y^7$
    D. $36x^2y^{12}$

18. Given $i = \sqrt{-1}$, what is $\sqrt{25} - \sqrt{-36}$?

    F. $5 + 6i$
    G. $5 - 6i$
    H. $i\sqrt{11}$
    J. $11i$

19. A finite arithmetic sequence has five terms. The first term is 4. What is the difference between the mean and the median of the five terms?

    A. 0
    B. 1
    C. 2
    D. 4

20. The sides of a triangle are in the ratio of exactly 15:17:20. A second triangle, similar to the first, has a longest side of length 12. To the nearest tenth of a unit, what is the length of the shortest side of the second triangle?

    F. 15.9
    G. 10.2
    H. 9.0
    J. 7.0

21. In rectangle ABCD shown, segments $\overline{DE}$ and $\overline{AC}$ partition the rectangle into 3 triangles. Given $AD = 45$ centimeters, $AE = 27$ centimeters, and $CD = 60$ centimeters, what is the length, in centimeters, of $\overline{EC}$?

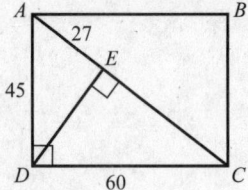

A. 21
B. 48
C. 60
D. 75

22. If an object travels at a speed of 3 feet per second, how many feet does it travel in half an hour?

F. 2,400
G. 3,600
H. 4,200
J. 5,400

23. Let $f(x) = 4e^{2x} - 3$. Which of the following is closest to the value of $f(1)$?

A. -3×10^1
B. -3×10^{-1}
C. 3×10^{-1}
D. 3×10^1

24. Which of the following expresses 50° in radians?

F. $\dfrac{5}{18\pi}$
G. $\dfrac{5\pi}{18}$
H. $\dfrac{18\pi}{5}$
J. $\dfrac{9{,}000}{\pi}$

25. The figure shown represents the function $g(x) = \sqrt{x}$. Suppose $h(x)$ is a transformation of $g(x)$ and is given by the equation $h(x) = \sqrt{x+1} + 3$. Which of the following correctly states the domain and range of $h(x)$?

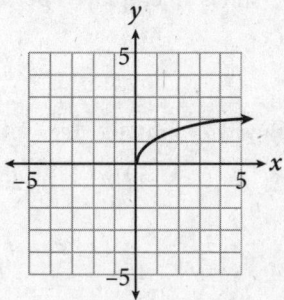

A. Domain: $x \geq -1$; Range: $y \geq 0$
B. Domain: $x \geq -1$; Range: $y \geq 3$
C. Domain: $x \geq 1$; Range: $y \geq -3$
D. Domain: $x \geq 1$; Range: $y \geq 3$

26. For all positive values of a, b, c, and d, when $a^2 + bc = \dfrac{d}{2}$, which of the following expressions is equal to a?

F. $\sqrt{\dfrac{2(d-b)}{c}}$
G. $\sqrt{\dfrac{d-2b}{c}}$
H. $\sqrt{\dfrac{d-2bc}{2}}$
J. $\sqrt{\dfrac{2d-bc}{2}}$

27. The following table shows the results of a study identifying the number of males and females with and without college degrees who were unemployed or employed at the time of the study. If one person from the study is chosen at random, what is the probability that the person is an employed person with a college degree?

	Unemployed	Employed	Totals
Female, degree	12	188	200
Female, no degree	44	156	200
Male, degree	23	177	200
Male, no degree	41	159	200
Totals	120	680	800

A. $\frac{73}{160}$

B. $\frac{10}{17}$

C. $\frac{73}{136}$

D. $\frac{17}{20}$

28. The chord shown in the figure is 8 units long. If the chord is 3 units from the center of the circle, what is the area of the circle?

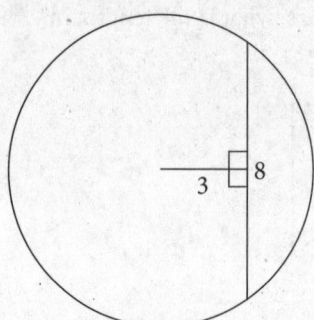

F. 16π

G. 18π

H. 25π

J. 28π

29. Ms. Ruppin is a machinist who works 245 days a year and earns a salary of $51,940. She recently took an unpaid day off from work to attend a bridge tournament. The company pays temporary replacements $140 a day. How much less did the company have to pay in salary by paying the replacement instead of Ms. Ruppin that day?

A. $72

B. $140

C. $196

D. $212

30. In the standard (x, y) coordinate plane, how many points are both 6 coordinate units from the origin and 3 coordinate units from the line $x = 0$?

F. 0

G. 1

H. 2

J. 4

31. In △ABC, if the measure of ∠A is greater than the measure of ∠B, and the measure of ∠B is greater than the measure of ∠C, what is the correct ordering of the side lengths, from least to greatest?

    A. $AC < BC < AB$
    B. $AC < AB < BC$
    C. $AB < AC < BC$
    D. $BC < AB < AC$

32. Of 896 seniors at a certain university, approximately $\frac{1}{3}$ are continuing their studies after graduation, and approximately $\frac{2}{5}$ of those continuing their studies are going to law school. Which of the following is the best estimate of how many seniors are going to law school?

    F. 120
    G. 180
    H. 240
    J. 300

33. In the following figure, lines l and m are parallel and $a = 110$. Which of the following is equal to the sum of b, c, and d?

    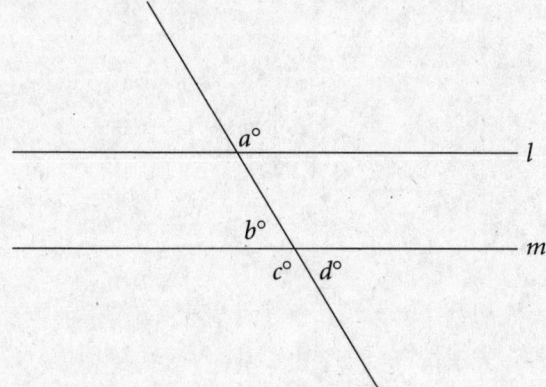

    A. 250
    B. 260
    C. 270
    D. 280

34. The first and seventh terms in a sequence are 1 and 365, respectively. If each term after the first in the sequence is formed by multiplying the preceding term by 3 and subtracting 1, what is the sixth term?

    F. 120
    G. 121
    H. 122
    J. 123

35. On the real number line, how many integers are between $-\frac{72}{7}$ and $\frac{89}{2}$?

    A. 25
    B. 55
    C. 75
    D. 150

36. During a particular experiment, 2 events, A and B, can each occur. Events A and B are mutually exclusive during this experiment. Which of the following probabilities is 1?

    F. $P(A)$
    G. $P(B)$
    H. $P(A)P(B)$
    J. $P(A) + P(B)$

37. The polynomial function defined by $p(x) = x^3 + 5x^2 + 3x - 9$ has $(x - 1)$ as one of its linear factors. What are all of the zeros of p?

    A. -3 and -1
    B. -3 and 1
    C. -1 and 3
    D. 1 and 3

38. The population of fish in a certain pond from 1985 to 1995 is shown. Which of the following years contains the median population for the data?

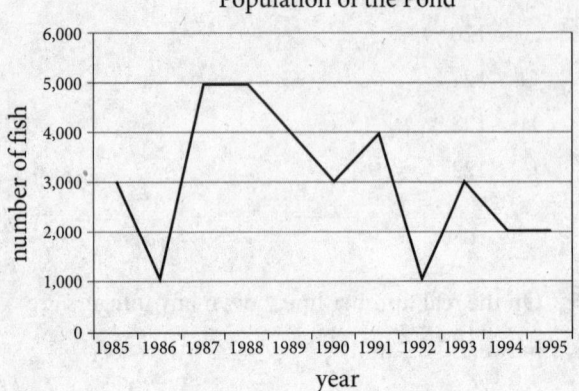

Population of the Pond

F. 1988
G. 1989
H. 1990
J. 1991

39. A polling organization randomly selected 50 people from Town X. The organization asked them how many vacations they had taken in the last year. The table shows the results. Based on these data, for the population of Town X, what is the best estimate of the mean number of vacations taken?

Number of vacations	1	2	3
Number of people	10	35	5

A. 1.9
B. 2
C. 2.9
D. 3

40. Given the equation $\sqrt[3]{x} = y$, where y is a negative number, what must be true of x? x is:

F. an even real number
G. an odd real number
H. a positive number
J. a negative number

41. Given that $1 \leq a \leq 3$, $4 \leq b \leq 9$, and $5 \leq c \leq 11$, what is the least possible value of $\left(\frac{1}{c}\right)\left(\frac{b}{a}\right)$?

A. $\frac{1}{99}$
B. $\frac{4}{33}$
C. $\frac{9}{33}$
D. $\frac{9}{5}$

42. Which of the following data sets has the smallest standard deviation?

F. 0, 1, 9, 10
G. 0, 5, 5, 10
H. 0, 0, 0, 10
J. 10, 10, 10, 10

43. A formula for the volume, V, of a right circular cylinder is $V = \pi r^2 h$, where r is the radius and h is the height. The cylindrical swimming pool shown here is filled completely with water and has a radius of 6 feet and a depth of 4 feet. If 1 cubic foot of water weighs approximately 62.4 pounds, then the weight, in pounds, of the water in the swimming pool is:

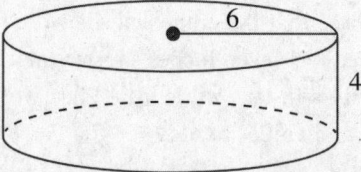

A. less than 20,000.
B. between 20,000 and 25,000.
C. between 25,000 and 30,000.
D. between 30,000 and 35,000.

44. The table gives values of $f(x)$, $g(x)$, and $h(x)$ for all positive integers $x \leq 5$. Given $f(h(g(a))) = 3$ where a is a positive integer less than or equal to 5, what is the value of a?

x	$f(x)$	$g(x)$	$h(x)$
1	5	2	1
2	1	4	3
3	2	1	5
4	4	3	2
5	3	5	4

F. 2
G. 3
H. 4
J. 5

45. The probability distribution of the discrete random variable X is shown in the following table. Based on the probability distribution, what is the expected value of X?

X	Probability $P(X = x)$
10	$\frac{1}{5}$
11	$\frac{1}{10}$
12	$\frac{3}{10}$
13	$\frac{3}{20}$
14	$\frac{1}{4}$

A. 11
B. 12
C. $12\frac{3}{20}$
D. $13\frac{1}{20}$

Part 6
PRACTICE TESTS

Reading Test

40 Minutes—36 Questions

Directions: The Reading Test includes multiple passages. Each passage includes multiple questions. After reading each passage, choose the best answer and fill in the corresponding bubble on your answer sheet. You may review the passages as often as necessary.

Passage I

LITERARY NARRATIVE: This passage is adapted from *The Age of Innocence*, by Edith Wharton (1920).

It was generally agreed in New York that the Countess Olenska had "lost her looks."

She had appeared there first, in Newland Archer's boyhood, as a brilliantly pretty little girl
[5] of nine or ten, of whom people said that she "ought to be painted." Her parents had been continental wanderers, and after a roaming babyhood she had lost them both, and been taken in charge by her aunt, Medora Manson, also a wanderer, who was
[10] herself returning to New York to "settle down."

Poor Medora, repeatedly widowed, was always coming home to settle down (each time in a less expensive house), and bringing with her a new husband or an adopted child, but after a few
[15] months she invariably parted from her husband or quarrelled with her ward, and, having got rid of her house at a loss, set out again on her wanderings. As her mother had been a Rushworth, and her last unhappy marriage had linked her
[20] to one of the crazy Chiverses, New York looked indulgently on her eccentricities, but when she returned with her little orphaned niece, whose parents had been popular in spite of their regrettable taste for travel, people thought it a pity
[25] that the pretty child should be in such hands.

Everyone was disposed to be kind to little Ellen Mingott, though her dusky red cheeks and tight curls gave her an air of gaiety that seemed unsuitable in a child who should still have been in
[30] black for her parents. It was one of the misguided Medora's many peculiarities to flout the unalterable rules that regulated American mourning, and when she stepped from the steamer her family was scandalized to see that the crepe veil she wore for
[35] her own brother was seven inches shorter than those of her sisters-in-law, while little Ellen wore a crimson dress and amber beads.

But New York had so long resigned itself to Medora that only a few old ladies shook their
[40] heads over Ellen's gaudy clothes, while her other relations fell under the charm of her high spirits. She was a fearless and familiar little thing, who asked disconcerting questions, made precocious comments, and possessed outlandish arts, such
[45] as dancing a Spanish shawl dance and singing Neapolitan love-songs to a guitar. Under the direction of her aunt, the little girl received an expensive but incoherent education, which included "drawing from the model," a thing never dreamed
[50] of before, and playing the piano in quintets with professional musicians.

Of course no good could come of this, and when, a few years later, poor Chivers finally died, his widow again pulled up stakes and departed
[55] with Ellen, who had grown into a tall bony girl with conspicuous eyes. For some time no more was heard of them; then news came of Ellen's marriage to an immensely rich Polish nobleman of legendary fame. She disappeared, and when a few years later
[60] Medora again came back to New York, subdued, impoverished, mourning a third husband, and in quest of a still smaller house, people wondered that her rich niece had not been able to do something for her. Then came the news that Ellen's own
[65] marriage had ended in disaster, and that she was herself returning home to seek rest and oblivion among her kinsfolk.

These things passed through Newland Archer's mind a week later as he watched the Countess

Olenska enter the van der Luyden drawing room on the evening of the momentous dinner. In the middle of the room she paused, looking about her with a grave mouth and smiling eyes, and in that instant, Newland Archer rejected the general verdict on her looks. It was true that her early radiance was gone. The red cheeks had paled; she was thin, worn, a little older-looking than her age, which must have been nearly thirty. But there was about her the mysterious authority of beauty, a sureness in the carriage of the head, the movement of the eyes, which, without being in the least theatrical, struck him as highly trained and full of a conscious power. At the same time she was simpler in manner than most of the ladies present, and many people (as he heard afterward) were disappointed that her appearance was not more "stylish"—for stylishness was what New York most valued. It was, perhaps, Archer reflected, because her early vivacity had disappeared; because she was so quiet—quiet in her movements, her voice, and the tones of her voice. New York had expected something a good deal more resonant in a young woman with such a history.

1. The point of view from which the passage is told is best described as that of:

   A. an old acquaintance who knew the Countess as a child.
   B. a much married woman who comes to New York to settle down.
   C. an unidentified but knowledgeable narrator.
   D. an unnamed other relation of Ellen's.

2. The passage as a whole can best be described as an exploration of the:

   F. vicissitudes in the life of an orphan.
   G. condemnation of an eccentric widow.
   H. conflicts between individuality and New York society expectations.
   J. changes from Ellen as a child to Ellen as a divorced adult.

3. The passage most strongly suggests that after the death of Medora's third husband, Ellen did not help her aunt primarily because:

   A. Ellen was no longer wealthy, since her own marriage had failed.
   B. Medora had become embittered because she hadn't heard from Ellen for so long.
   C. Ellen resented the incoherent education she received from her aunt.
   D. receiving help from her niece would interfere with Medora's desire to be eccentric.

4. Based on the passage, Newland Archer can best be described as:

   F. thoughtful and analytical.
   G. likeable but withdrawn.
   H. harsh and unfair.
   J. stylish and gregarious.

5. The author describes which of the following practices as undesirable to New York society?

   A. Playing the piano
   B. Performing Spanish shawl dances
   C. Traveling
   D. Adopting children

6. Which of the following characters learns to do something otherwise unheard of by New York society?

   F. Ellen Mingott
   G. Newland Archer
   H. Medora Manson
   J. Count Olenska

Part 6
PRACTICE TESTS

7. The author most likely includes reference to Medora's mother and Medora's marriage to "one of the crazy Chiverses" (line 20) to:

    A. mention that she had an unhappy childhood.
    B. indicate that her eccentricities were not surprising.
    C. show that she was the perfect person to raise Ellen.
    D. specify that she was a wanderer.

8. The passage suggests that when Ellen returned to New York after the end of her marriage, she was:

    F. vibrant and beautiful.
    G. strong and sure of herself.
    H. somber and defeated.
    J. subdued and impoverished.

9. What does the narrator suggest is a central characteristic of Medora Manson?

    A. Arrogance
    B. Immodesty
    C. Non-conformity
    D. Orthodoxy

Passage II

INFORMATIONAL: This passage discusses challenges facing Florida's two largest economic sectors due to climate change.

Every state in the U.S. relies on at least one or two industries to drive its economic growth. Boasting a top-five economy among the 50 states, Florida thrives on its tourism industry and
5 agricultural production. Recent climate change reports are a cause for concern for the policymakers who want to keep the state on its current upward economic trajectory. How serious are the threats that the state faces, and can anything be done to
10 stave off the effects of climate change before they irreparably damage the Floridian economy?

The National Climate Assessment, a government-mandated report released every four years, references South Florida frequently as
15 a locale that is likely to experience the worsening effects of climate change sooner rather than later. In September 2017, for example, Hurricane Irma wreaked havoc on large swaths of the Florida coastline when it made landfall in the Florida Keys;
20 economists put the price tag for Irma at $50 billion, making it the costliest hurricane in Florida's history. It is estimated that if Irma had made a more direct hit on Miami, Florida's second-most popular tourist destination, the damage would have
25 been closer to $200 billion. Many scientists feel that rising sea levels are making areas like Miami and Orlando increasingly vulnerable to such catastrophic weather events.

Another top tourist attraction in Florida, the
30 Everglades, is already experiencing a reduction in size due to a combination of rising sea levels and serious weather events. Large sections of the Everglades are less than three feet above sea level, and soon many of the low-lying regions will be
35 completely submerged. This does not bode well for the over one million visitors who make the trek to the national park each year nor for the more than $20 million in revenue that the Everglades National Park generates annually. In addition, the sea level
40 rise causes salt water to push further inland and upstream, which endangers not only tourism but also the drinking water of several communities.

CONTINUED

On a peninsula like Florida, it seems ironic that a lack of water could become an issue, but an Environmental Protection Agency report published in 2016 pointed to a lack of irrigation due to warmer temperatures as a potential downside of a longer growing season. Florida relies on groundwater pumped from permeable underground aquifers, and Florida farms consume nearly half of the state's public water supply. Citrus fruits require substantial amounts of irrigation to maintain crop size; a 2003 agriculture study found that a 20% reduction in irrigation resulted in significant losses for citrus crops. The citrus fruit industry in Florida is a $10 billion industry, so any negative trends have a direct impact on Florida's overall economic health.

Climate change has an impact on the livestock side of Florida's agriculture as well as the produce side; although it makes up a smaller portion of Florida's $120 billion in agricultural revenue than the citrus industry, the livestock industry exports cattle, calves, milk, poultry, and eggs both nationally and internationally. One problem that arises with livestock as a result of warmer temperatures is a reduction in productivity because of metabolic disruption caused by heat stress. The livestock industry also relies on the extensive perennial grasslands of the region, which have degraded in quality because of the greater frequency of severe weather events. Additionally, the combination of temperature and rainfall increases have led to greater instances of livestock diseases like the West Nile virus; the increase in humidity leads directly to larger mosquito populations.

With so many challenges facing their state, Floridians are taking a proactive approach to combating some of the consequences of climate change. In Miami, lawmakers are considering some rather unconventional recommendations. For example, a group of Harvard students presented Miami Beach leaders with two unique options to help adapt to rising seas: concrete cisterns strategically placed on roofs throughout the city to capture rainwater, and "sacrificial floors" designed to absorb excess water before it reaches the inhabited floors. Researchers are encouraging the South Florida Water Management District to change their timetable for increasing freshwater flow to the Everglades to maintain the level of freshwater higher than sea level. Farmers are investing in micro-surface and subsurface drip irrigation systems to reduce the overall volume of water needed to maintain their crops and making the move to mixed crop-livestock farms, as studies have shown this farming style to be mutually beneficial to both crops and livestock.

While a complete reversal of the consequences of climate change seems improbable, Floridians can be encouraged by the fact that leaders in their state are taking some pragmatic steps to cope with the changes. Furthermore, as those policymakers look to protect the sectors that have long served as the foundation of Florida's economy, there is also a push to continue to diversify. International trade—Florida is already one of the largest export states—seems an ideal sector to expand with the increasingly globalized nature of economic systems. Despite the challenges, Florida is preparing to weather the storm of climate change as it has weathered so many storms before.

10. The primary purpose of the passage is to:

F. describe how climate change has harmed Florida's land and industries.

G. discuss the threats climate change poses to Florida and how to address them.

H. argue for the implementation of unorthodox means of combating climate change.

J. explain the varied ways in which climate change can impact people's lives.

11. The author most likely references the 2016 Environmental Protection Agency report (lines 45–46) and the 2003 study (lines 53–55) to:

    A. provide specific numerical evidence for the cost of climate change.
    B. counter an argument that contradicts the author's point.
    C. open a discussion about their long-term implications for Florida.
    D. add support for the paragraph's claims from authoritative sources.

12. It can reasonably be inferred from the second paragraph that South Florida:

    F. is a major source of tourism revenue for the state.
    G. is likely to be entirely submerged by rising sea levels.
    H. is more vulnerable to extreme weather than North Florida.
    J. is central to agricultural production in Florida.

13. In the context of the passage, the detail "Florida is already one of the largest export states" (lines 107–108) mainly serves to:

    A. identify one of the main drivers of Florida's economic expansion.
    B. compare Florida's trade balance to that of other states.
    C. explain why expanding Florida's international trade is likely to be effective.
    D. emphasize the benefits of diversifying Florida's economy.

14. The author most likely mentions Hurricane Irma in order to:

    F. give an example of worsening climate change.
    G. illustrate the dangers of rising sea levels.
    H. support designing sacrificial floors to mitigate hurricane damage.
    J. explain the effects of excess rainfall on livestock and insects.

15. According to the passage, how might climate change negatively impact the livestock industry in Florida?

    A. Decreased crop yields would mean less food for the animals.
    B. Higher temperatures would put a strain on the animals' bodies.
    C. Animals exposed to poor weather would be more likely to become ill.
    D. Water shortages would cause the animals to become dehydrated.

16. In the passage, the author makes it clear that the main threat climate change poses to the Everglades is:

    F. contamination; salt water pushed inland will destroy fresh water sources.
    G. submersion; rising sea levels will put lands at low elevations under water.
    H. habitat destruction; extreme weather will degrade the park's lush vegetation.
    J. isolation; changes to the landscape will cut the park off from visitors.

17. The main purpose of the sixth paragraph (lines 77–98) is to:

A. suggest infrastructure adaptations to be applied throughout Florida.
B. summarizes the primary challenges facing Florida's economy due to climate change.
C. explain some of the ways Floridians are planning to address problems caused by climate change.
D. examines how to best direct water supplies in order to compensate for imbalances in rainfall.

18. As used in line 86, the word "sacrificial" most nearly means:

F. expendable.
G. religious.
H. unimportant.
J. deniable.

Passage III

INFORMATIONAL: One of the most enjoyable ways to analyze culture is through music. By analyzing musical styles and lyrics, one can explore quintessential characteristics of particular cultures. Passage A explores the relationship between the central and southern areas of the Appalachian mountain range and country music. Passage B contrasts bluegrass and country music and culture.

Passage A

Country music has its roots in the southern portions of the United States, specifically in the remote and undeveloped backcountry of the central and southern areas of the Appalachian mountain
5 range. Recognized as a distinct cultural region since the late nineteenth century, the area became home to European settlements in the eighteenth century, primarily led by Ulster Scots from Ireland. Early inhabitants have been characterized as
10 fiercely independent, to the point of rudeness and inhospitality. It was in this area that the region's truly indigenous music, now known as country music, was born.

Rooted in spirituals as well as folk music,
15 cowboy songs, and traditional Celtic melodies, country music originated in the 1920s. The motifs are generally ballads and dance tunes, simple in form and accompanied mostly by guitar, banjo, and violin. Though today there are many genres of
20 country music, all have their roots in this mélange of sources.

The term "country" has replaced the original pejorative term "hillbilly." Hillbillies referred to Appalachian inhabitants who were considered poor,
25 uneducated, isolated, and wary; the name change reflects a more accepting characterization of these mountain dwellers.

Hank Williams put country music on the map nationally, and is credited with the movement of
30 country music from the South to more national prominence. Other early innovators include the Carter family, Ernest Tubb, Woody Guthrie, Loretta Lynn, and Bill Monroe, father of bluegrass music.

More recently, Faith Hill, Reba McEntire, and Shania Twain have carried on the tradition.

What might be considered the "home base" of country music is in Nashville, Tennessee, and the legendary music hall, the Grand Ole Opry. Founded in 1925 by George D. Hay, it had its genesis in the pioneer radio station WSM's program *Barn Dance*. Country singers are considered to have reached the pinnacle of the profession if they are asked to become members of the Opry. While noted country music performers and acts take the stage at the Opry numerous times, Elvis Presley performed there only once, in 1954. His act was so poorly received that it was suggested he return to his job as a truck driver.

The offshoots and relatives of country music highlight the complexity of this genre. In a move away from its mountain origins, and turning a focus to the West, honky-tonk music became popular in the early twentieth century. Its name is a reference to its roots in honky-tonk bars, where the music was played. Additionally, Western swing emerged as one of the first genres to blend country and jazz musical styles, which required a great deal of skill and creativity. Some of the most talented and sophisticated musicians performing in any genre were musicians who played in bluegrass string bands, another relative of country music.

Country music has always been an expression of American identity. Its sound, lyrics, and performers are purely American, and though the music now has an international audience, it remains American in its heart and soul.

Passage B

A style of music closely related to country is the similarly indigenous music known as bluegrass, which originated in the Appalachian highland regions extending westwards to the Ozark Mountains in southern Missouri and northern Arkansas. Derived from the music brought over by European settlers of the region, bluegrass is a mixture of Scottish, Welsh, Irish, and English melodic forms, infused, over time, with African-American influences. Indeed, many bluegrass songs, such as "Barbara Allen" and "House Carpenter," preserve their European roots, maintaining the traditional musical style and narratives almost intact. Story-telling ballads, often laments, are common themes. Given the predominance of coal mining in the Appalachian region, it is not surprising that ballads relating to mining tragedies are also common.

Unlike country music, in which musicians commonly play the same melodies together, bluegrass highlights one player at a time, with the others providing accompaniment. This tradition of each musician taking turns with solos, and often improvising, can also be seen in jazz ensembles. Traditional bluegrass music is typically played on instruments such as banjo, guitar, mandolin, bass, harmonica, and Dobro (resonator guitar). Even household objects, including washboards and spoons, have, from time to time, been drafted for use as instruments. Vocals also differ from country music in that, rather than featuring a single voice, bluegrass incorporates baritone and tenor harmonies.

Initially included under the catch-all phrase "folk music," and later referred to as "hillbilly," bluegrass did not come into his own category until the late 1950s, and appeared first in the comprehensive guide *Music Index* in 1965. Presumably it was named after Bill Monroe's Blue Grass band, the seminal bluegrass band. A rapid, almost frenetic, pace characterizes bluegrass tempos. Even today, decades after their most active performing era, The Foggy Mountain Boys members Lester Flatt, a bluegrass guitarist and mandolinist, and Earl Scruggs, known for his three-finger banjo picking style, are widely considered the foremost artists on their instruments.

Partially because of its pace and complexity, bluegrass has often been recorded for movie soundtracks. "Dueling Banjos," played in the movie *Deliverance*, exemplifies the skill required by the feverish tempo of the genre. The soundtrack for *O Brother, Where Art Thou?* incorporates bluegrass and its musical cousins folk, country, gospel, and blues. Bluegrass festivals are held throughout the country and as far away as the Czech Republic. Interactive,

120 often inviting audience participation, they feature performers such as Dolly Parton and Alison Krauss.

Central to bluegrass music are the themes of the working class—miners, railroad workers, farmers. The phrase "high, lonesome sound" was coined to
125 represent the bluegrass undertones of intensity and cheerlessness, symbolizing the hard-scrabble life of the American worker. As with so much of a nation's traditional music, and for better or worse, bluegrass music reflects America.

19. According to Passage A, country music originated:

   A. in the late nineteenth century.
   B. from folk songs, Celtic melodies, and bluegrass music.
   C. in the early twentieth century.
   D. in rural areas of the western United States.

20. As it is used in line 23, the word *pejorative* most nearly means:

   F. traditional.
   G. accurate.
   H. disparaging.
   J. mountain dwelling.

21. Based on Passage A, which of the following would be the most logical place to hear the best of country music?

   A. Honky-tonk bars
   B. Ireland
   C. The Appalachian backcountry
   D. The Grand Ole Opry

22. According to Passage B, the instruments played in bluegrass music are:

   F. both typical and unusual.
   G. derived from African-American influences.
   H. made famous by the piece "Dueling Banjos."
   J. restricted to those used in the Ozarks.

23. In the context of Passage B, the main purpose of the second paragraph (lines 84–97) is:

   A. to provide a comparison of bluegrass music to country music.
   B. to explain the roots of bluegrass music.
   C. to describe how instruments are used in bluegrass music.
   D. to introduce the social traditions of bluegrass culture.

24. It can be inferred from Passage B that laments and high, lonesome sounds both reflect:

   F. the influence of Irish music.
   G. the challenges of American life.
   H. songs sung by Shania Twain.
   J. hillbilly music.

25. Compared to Passage A, Passage B focuses more on:

   A. a specific venue that serves as the modern hub of a musical genre.
   B. the subgenres and variations of a musical style.
   C. a description of a style of music that expresses American identity.
   D. use of a musical genre in contemporary media.

26. Which of the following elements of Passage B is not included in Passage A?

   F. An exploration of the origins of a musical genre
   G. An description of common instruments used by musicians of a musical genre
   H. A discussion of common themes of a musical genre
   J. A mention of how the term "hillbilly" plays into a musical genre

27. It can be inferred that both authors would agree that:

A. country and bluegrass music are popular genres.
B. both genres—country and bluegrass—are showcased at the Grand Ole Opry.
C. music genres can evolve.
D. country and bluegrass music are gaining in acceptance.

Passage IV

INFORMATIONAL: This passage is adapted from an article about the history of artificial satellites.

When the researchers at California Polytechnic university (CalPoly) and Stanford University determined the specifications of the CubeSat design back in 1999, they likely did not realize the full
[5] potential of the miniature satellites. NASA's Mars Cube One (MarCO) mission has provided strong evidence that CubeSats offer many advantages for deep space exploration. The ability to build a large portion of the CubeSat with off-the-
[10] shelf components means that future missions can be more cost-effective. The low cost of the satellites may also allow for more radical scientific experiments to be performed in space.

Experimental radio and antenna designs were
[15] an important part of the mission. The MarCO-A and MarCO-B satellites, affectionately referred to as "Eve" and "WALL-E" by the engineering team, had softball-sized UHF and X-band radios mounted to the main unit. These allowed the satellites, which
[20] were launched into space at the same time as the InSight lander, to send back photos of the landing in under eight minutes. By contrast, the lander itself took over an hour to transmit its successful landing. The same radio and antenna technology
[25] also allowed for more efficient monitoring of the landing process. With only a 40% success rate as of 2017, Mars landings remain notoriously difficult. The data recorded by the MarCO satellites will help future missions.

[30] Even beyond the completion of the Mars mission, engineers like Joel Krajewski, project manager for MarCO, hope to use the data sent back by the satellites to test how long technological systems can withstand the hardships of space. Both units
[35] will continue to relay system data until they cease to function. The successful survival of the two modified satellites could lead to the possibility of longer explorations much deeper into the outer reaches of the universe.

[40] In order to increase the success of the mission, the MarCO team fitted the satellites with some specific modifications. The cameras that MarCO-B

used to take stills of the planet as the satellite approached Mars represent a significantly more economical approach. The consumer-grade cameras highlight the potential for greatly reducing the costs associated with deep space missions. Soon after receipt, images of the Red Planet, along with its moons Phobos and Deimos, were proudly displayed on the NASA website. An elated Cody Colley, mission manager from JPL, happily reported, "WALL-E sent some great postcards from Mars!" It is of note that the entire MarCO project checked in at $18.5 million. Compared to the price tag associated with building and sending a more traditional satellite into space, which can easily reach $100 million, CubeSats represent an unprecedented breakthrough in the financial burden of space exploration.

Cost reductions also mean that it is increasingly possible for science experiments that stood little chance of being greenlighted in the past to make it into deep space via a CubeSat. Several projects already exist in near-Earth orbit, including a 2009 study on antibacterial effectiveness in zero-g, a QuakeSat in 2003 to measure for Extremely Low Frequency (ELF) signals that some scientists believe occur before earthquakes, and the 2015 LightSail 1 mission to test propulsion systems. The ability to travel greater distances into space in an economical manner will no doubt encourage researchers to propose more novel experiments for future missions.

The possibility of linked networks of CubeSats in deep space offers another intriguing proposition. The QB50 project involved the cooperation of over 30 international universities to send CubeSats into near-earth orbit to study temporal and spatial characteristics of the lower thermosphere. Benefits of linked networks include increased flexibility to distribute tasks among the satellites and reduced probability of single-point failure. This kind of redundancy against failure, along with the ability to adapt in real-time, is even more helpful in deep space where the satellites face an incredibly challenging environment.

Since its inception in 1958, NASA has encouraged its researchers, scientists, and engineers to push the limits of existing technology. In building on the work of teams at CalPoly and Stanford, the engineers at NASA have proven that cost-effective CubeSat technology has the potential to exponentially increase scientific experimentation in deep space. As the MarCO team continues to collect data from "Eve" and "WALL-E," the lessons learned will no doubt raise the bar for the vast array of deep space CubeSats to come.

28. In the context of the passage, how does the difference between the MarCO project and a more traditional satellite project mentioned in lines 54–57 relate to the claim that CubeSats are cost-effective?

F. The difference supports the claim.
G. The difference confirms that the claim is true.
H. The difference supports the claim in some ways and does not support the claim in other ways.
J. The difference does not support the claim.

29. According to the passage, the CubeSat was first designed by:

A. Joel Krajewski.
B. Cody Colley.
C. CalPoly and Stanford researchers.
D. NASA scientists and engineers.

30. In the context of the passage, the fourth paragraph primarily serves to:

F. argue for using consumer-grade components wherever possible for future NASA projects.
G. explain how innovative choices in technology led to significant cost reductions for the MarCO satellites.
H. describe the many reasons why the MarCO project was less expensive than comparable satellite projects.
J. praise the superiority of the images the MarCO satellites sent back from Mars.

31. According to the passage, why was the MarCO satellites' experimental communication technology notable?

    A. It transmitted landing data over seven times faster than the previous technology.
    B. It took barely an hour to transmit landing data back to NASA.
    C. Its off-the-shelf components made it much less expensive than other radios.
    D. The radios were unusually space-efficient, being the size of softballs.

32. In the context of the passage, the statement in lines 5–8 mainly serves to:

    F. assert that the MarCO mission was cost-effective.
    G. introduce the idea that CubeSats may bring significant benefits to space exploration.
    H. recount details of the inception of the CubeSat design.
    J. insist that NASA should use CubeSats for all future missions.

33. According to the passage, the InSight lander compared to the MarCO satellites:

    A. can monitor landings more efficiently.
    B. possesses a broader number of experimental radio and antenna designs.
    C. relays information back to Earth with less speed.
    D. is able to land less effectively in difficult Martian conditions.

34. In the context of the passage, the detail that much of a CubeSat can be built with off-the-shelf components provides support for the claim that:

    F. consumer-grade cameras have been included in CubeSat specifications.
    G. miniature satellites have potential to change how scientists design landers.
    H. future missions using CubeSats may be more cost-effective.
    J. CubeSats can more efficiently monitor landing processes.

35. The passage most clearly indicates that the advantages of linked networks of satellites include:

    A. considerable reductions in cost from traditional satellites.
    B. increased adaptability and protection against breakdown.
    C. encouraging international cooperation due to shared ownership.
    D. the possibility of studying previously inaccessible parts of the atmosphere.

36. Based on the passage, the scientists at NASA most likely posted photos from the MarCO satellites on their website because:

    F. they hoped to gain support for future missions.
    G. they wanted to prove that the new satellites were viable.
    H. they needed to satisfy public demands for information.
    J. they were pleased with the success of the mission.

Answer Key

English Test

1. A	11. D	21. A	31. A	41. B
2. J	12. G	22. J	32. F	42. H
3. C	13. D	23. A	33. C	43. C
4. F	14. H	24. H	34. G	44. J
5. A	15. A	25. D	35. C	45. D
6. G	16. F	26. H	36. H	46. G
7. C	17. B	27. C	37. A	47. A
8. F	18. J	28. J	38. G	48. F
9. C	19. A	29. B	39. B	49. B
10. G	20. G	30. G	40. G	50. J

Mathematics Test

1. C	10. F	19. A	28. H	37. B
2. G	11. C	20. H	29. A	38. H
3. B	12. H	21. B	30. J	39. A
4. G	13. C	22. J	31. C	40. J
5. B	14. J	23. D	32. F	41. B
6. H	15. A	24. G	33. A	42. J
7. A	16. G	25. B	34. H	43. C
8. H	17. C	26. H	35. B	44. H
9. A	18. G	27. A	36. J	45. C

Part 6
PRACTICE TESTS

Reading Test

1. C
2. H
3. A
4. F
5. C
6. F
7. B
8. G
9. C
10. G
11. D
12. F
13. C
14. F
15. B
16. G
17. C
18. F
19. C
20. H
21. D
22. F
23. A
24. G
25. D
26. H
27. C
28. F
29. C
30. G
31. A
32. G
33. C
34. H
35. B
36. J

Answers and Explanations

English Test

My Old-Fashioned Father

1. A
Difficulty: Low
Category: Sentence Structure
Getting to the Answer: When a period appears in the underlined portion, check to see if each sentence is complete. Here, each sentence is complete and correct; therefore (A) is correct. Choice B creates a run-on sentence. Choices C and D create sentences that are not concise.

2. J
Difficulty: Medium
Category: Sentence Structure
Getting to the Answer: The ACT tests very specific punctuation rules. If punctuation is used in a way not covered by these rules, it will be incorrect. No commas are required in the underlined selection; (J) is correct. Choices F, G, and H all contain unnecessary commas.

3. C
Difficulty: Medium
Category: Agreement
Getting to the Answer: When a verb is underlined, make sure it places the action properly in relation to the other events in the passage. This passage is written primarily in the present tense; *runs*, (C), is the correct answer here. Choices A and B use verb tenses that do not make sense in context. The past tense verb in D is inconsistent with the rest of the passage.

4. F
Difficulty: Medium
Category: Conciseness
Getting to the Answer: Very rarely will a correct answer choice of a Conciseness question be significantly longer than the original selection. You can eliminate G and H, both of which are wordier than the original. Choice J may be tempting because it's shorter than the underlined selection, but it changes the meaning of the sentence; the back office, not the reader, is what hasn't changed. Choice (F) is correct.

5. A
Difficulty: Medium
Category: Development
Getting to the Answer: When asked for the most precise choice, examine the context of the underlined portion. In this case, the old-fashioned father runs his grocery store, so it is logical that he will keep track of the items he is selling. Choice (A), *inventory*, meaning "a list of goods in stock," is very specific, but check the other choices for a more specific term. Choices B and C are incorrect because they are less specific, so eliminate them. Choice D, *archives*, means "collection of historical documents," which is not an accurate description of what a grocery store would stock. The correct choice is (A).

6. G
Difficulty: Medium
Category: Development
Getting to the Answer: When the question stem presents you with a specific goal, pick the choice that addresses the goal. In this case, the question is asking for "a vivid description" of the office. Look for the choice that evokes a picture with specific details. Choice (G) is correct; it contains the most specific details, mentioning "documents, notes, and receipts." All the other choices use more general terms.

7. C
Difficulty: High
Category: Agreement
Getting to the Answer: When the underlined portion is an entire sentence and it asks about grammar, check for punctuation errors. In this case, though, the punctuation in every choice is correct. Notice that the sentence contains a modifying introductory phrase; that is a clue that the question could be testing modifiers. Make sure that the noun that is closest to the modifying phrase is the logical noun. In A and B, it is not logical for Father's search or Father's task, respectively, to be no longer produced; eliminate both. It is logical for the replacement typewriter ribbons to be no longer produced, as in correct choice (C). On test day, move on, but for practice, D is incorrect because it is not logical for Father to have become increasingly difficult to find.

Part 6
PRACTICE TESTS

8. F
Difficulty: High
Category: Organization
Getting to the Answer: When a transition word or phrase is underlined, make sure it properly relates the ideas it connects. The underlined word is the transition between the gift of the computer and the information about ways a computer could be helpful. The second sentence is a continuation of the first, so you can eliminate G and J, both of which suggest a contrast. Choosing between (F) and H is a little more difficult, but remember that new errors may be introduced in answer choices. Choice H, *In addition*, would be acceptable if it were followed by a comma, but as written, it's incorrect. Choice (F) is correct.

9. C
Difficulty: Low
Category: Agreement
Getting to the Answer: When a pronoun is underlined, check to see whether it agrees with its antecedent. In this case, it's a singular blackout that only lasted an hour or two, so predict that the correct answer would be *it*. However, there is no answer choice that matches, so eliminate. Choices A and B are both plural, so they are both incorrect. The blackout is a thing, not a person, so eliminate D and choose (C), which correctly refers to a particular blackout.

10. G
Difficulty: Medium
Category: Style and Tone
Getting to the Answer: Since this question is testing the essay's tone, identify whether the passage is written in a formal tone or casual tone. This passage is written from a first person point of view and relates a humorous story about the narrator's father and his refusal to adopt new technology. The tone is casual. All the choices given mean *eventually*, so choose the one that is the most casual and conversational. The idiom in (G), *Sooner or later*, is the most casual of the choices, so that is the correct answer. Choice F (*Anon*) and H (*Somewhen*) are both archaic terms for *eventually* and are incorrect. Eliminate J because *In the entirely of time's progression* is extremely formal.

Du Fu: Poet-Sage

11. D
Difficulty: Low
Category: Conciseness
Getting to the Answer: The underlined portion is redundant, as the phrases "traveling extensively" and "exploring far and wide" repeat the same idea. Choice B is similarly wordy, and Choice C is repetitive because "traveling" and "exploring" overlap. Choice (D) is the most concise and clear, avoiding unnecessary repetition while conveying the intended meaning. Thus, (D) is correct.

12. G
Difficulty: Medium
Category: Organization: Transitions
Getting to the Answer: When a transition word is underlined, check to see if it properly relates the ideas it connects. The sentence discusses Du Fu's aspiration to serve in the imperial government and his repeated failures on the civil service examinations. Only choice G properly establishes a contrast between his aspiration and his setbacks. Thus, (G) is correct. Choice F suggests a time relationship, which does not fit the contrast implied by the sentence. Choice H implies causation, incorrectly suggesting that his aspirations caused his failure. Choice J sets up a comparison but does not accurately convey the relationship between aspiration and failure.

13. D
Difficulty: Medium
Category: Style and Tone
Getting to the Answer: Since this question is testing the essay's tone, identify whether the passage is written in a formal or casual tone. The passage, focused on Du Fu's artistic contributions and the context of his experiences, is written in a formal tone. Therefore, the correct choice should reflect this formal tone. Choice (D), "witnessed the devastating effects of war on society," is the most formal and objective option, making it the best fit. Thus, choice (D) is correct. Choice A, "saw war tear everything apart," is more casual and dramatic, which does not align with the formal tone of the passage. Similarly, choice B, "got a front-row seat to war's destruction" uses informal language and an idiomatic expression that is not suitable for the essay's tone. Choice C, "saw firsthand how war messes everything up," is also too informal.

14. H
Difficulty: Low
Category: Sentence Structure
Getting to the Answer: Here, the phrase beginning with "inspiring some of his most renowned works" introduces a list of specific works that further explain or illustrate the preceding clause. A colon is the correct punctuation because it introduces or clarifies information directly related to the earlier statement. Choice (H) is correct. Using a comma is incorrect because commas cannot introduce a list following an independent clause. A semicolon is also incorrect because semicolons are used to join two independent clauses, not to introduce a list. Finally, omitting punctuation altogether would create a run-on sentence.

15. A
Difficulty: Low
Category: Development
Getting to the Answer: The best choice that illustrates the global significance of Du Fu's literary influence would be "and comparisons to Shakespeare in Western literature." This comparison shows how big of an impact Du Fu had on Chinese literature by comparing him to Shakespeare, one of the most famous writers in Western literature. It places Du Fu on a global scale, suggesting that just as Shakespeare shaped English literature, Du Fu had a huge effect on Chinese poetry. This connection also helps readers who may not know much about Chinese literature understand how significant Du Fu's work is. Thus, (A) is correct. Choices B, C, and D do not focus on Du Fu's influence as a writer. "Recognition for his contributions to calligraphy" and "praise for his contributions to Chinese painting" are about other art forms, not his writing. "Acclaim for his travels across China" talks about his personal life instead of his literary impact.

Breaking Baseball's Color Barrier

16. F
Difficulty: Low
Category: Sentence Structure
Getting to the Answer: Peek at the answers to identify the specific grammar being tested. All the choices have commas added. No commas are needed in the underlined portion, so choice (F) is correct. Choices G, H, and J all include unnecessary commas, so they should be eliminated.

17. B
Difficulty: Medium
Category: Conciseness
Getting to the Answer: In Conciseness questions, finding the shortest way to express the original information is key. Eliminate A because it is wordier than the remaining choices. Choices C and D may be tempting because they are shorter than the underlined selection, but they still add the idea of being on a team, instead of simply participating in the major leagues. Choice (B) is correct.

18. J
Difficulty: Medium
Category: Development
Getting to the Answer: The underlined phrase shows how the National Association of Baseball Players was part of the history of today's National League. Choice (J) matches this and is correct.

Choice F is a distortion; the phrase mentions today's National League but does not include any details. The writer does not express an opinion about the National Association of Baseball Players, so choice G is incorrect. Choice H is outside the scope of the essay because the writer doesn't discuss the importance of either organization.

19. A
Difficulty: Low
Category: Conciseness
Getting to the Answer: Very rarely will a correct answer choice of a Conciseness question be significantly longer than the original selection. Eliminate B and C. Choice D may be tempting, but *implemented a plan* still has more words than *started*. Choice (A) is correct.

20. G
Difficulty: High
Category: Organization
Getting to the Answer: This question asks for a transition sentence connecting the second and third paragraphs. The second paragraph discusses the history of the color barrier in early professional baseball, while the third paragraph identifies the first African American professional baseball player in the major leagues. The correct answer will connect these ideas, and only (G) does so.

Choice F is incorrect because it actually contradicts statements in paragraph 3. Choice H is irrelevant to the paragraph because it discusses other professional sports. Choice J is incorrect because the white athletes didn't refuse to play with their African American teammates until nearly 5 years later.

21. A
Difficulty: Low
Category: Agreement
Getting to the Answer: When an underlined portion includes a verb, always check that it agrees with the subject and that it is consistent with the verb tenses around it. The subject is the first African American to play in the major leagues, which is singular. Eliminate both B and D. The verb tense needs to past tense, so (A) is the correct answer. Eliminate C because it is a form of future tense.

22. J
Difficulty: Low
Category: Sentence Structure
Getting to the Answer: The underlined portion includes a pronoun, so check to see if it agrees with the antecedent. The pronoun appears to be correct, but looking at the sentence as a whole, the pronoun should not be there. Having *who*, *whom*, or *he* creates a sentence fragment, so eliminate choices F, G, and H. Choice G is also incorrect because it's an objective pronoun acting as a subject of the phrase that follows it. Choice (J) is correct.

23. A
Difficulty: Low
Category: Organization
Getting to the Answer: A transition word or phrase must logically connect what follows it to what precedes it. The sentence before the underlined portion explains how some African Americans played for the Blue Stockings. The sentence following states that *this respite . . . did not last very long.* A contrast keyword is needed, so choice (A) is correct. The remaining choices do not have contrast keywords. Choice B is a connection keyword. Choice C is a cause-and-effect keyword. Choice D is a connection keyword that signals a development within a timeline.

24. H
Difficulty: High
Category: Development
Getting to the Answer: When asked if a writer should add a sentence, start by asking if the answer is yes or no. The new sentence should not be added because it changes the focus of the paragraph. Eliminate F and G. Choice (H) is correct because it describes why the sentence should not be added.

25. D
Difficulty: Medium
Category: Organization
Getting to the Answer: To decide where to place the new sentence, think about what information is in it. The new sentence explains that some African Americans *played for other teams*. So it would best fit in the paragraph that discusses African American players and a team. Paragraph 3 is a match, so (D) is correct.

The Dream of the American West

26. H
Difficulty: Medium
Category: Agreement
Getting to the Answer: Verbs in a compound should be in the same tense. The compound verb in this clause is "was . . . rising . . . and painted." These verbs do not match, so F is incorrect. Since the second verb is in the past tense, the first should be as well. Choice (H) is correct. Choice G uses the gerund verb form without the necessary helping verb. Choice J is unnecessarily wordy.

27. C
Difficulty: Medium
Category: Agreement
Getting to the Answer: Although all four answer choices form idioms that would be correct in some contexts, one smiles *at* someone or something. Choice (C) is correct.

28. J
Difficulty: Medium
Category: Conciseness
Getting to the Answer: When you don't spot an error in grammar or usage, look for errors in style. Choice F is a wordy way of saying *traveled across*. Choices G and H are unnecessarily wordy as well. Choice (J) is the most concise and is correct.

29. B
Difficulty: Medium
Category: Development
Getting to the Answer: Use your Reading skills for questions like this one that asks for the development of a detail. The underlined portion tells us that the writer's journey will end in California. Choice (B) is correct. The underlined selection does not mention the reasons for the writer's trip, describe the route, or make any comparisons, so A, C, and D are incorrect.

30. G
Difficulty: Medium
Category: Sentence Structure
Getting to the Answer: Use commas in a list or series only if there are three or more items. Since the writer only mentions two places she has been, the first comma here is incorrect; eliminate F. Choice (G) corrects this without introducing any additional errors. Choice H eliminates the incorrect comma but removes the one at the end of the selection, which is needed to separate the introductory clause from the rest of the sentence. Choice J does not address the error and introduces unnecessary commas.

31. A
Difficulty: Medium
Category: Organization
Getting to the Answer: To identify the most effective transition, you'll need to read both paragraphs. Paragraph 3 is about how the author has traveled to foreign countries but, within the United States, only knows New York City. Paragraph 4 describes their drive through the Midwest. The text as written takes the reader from New York City (*tall buildings*) to the less populated areas, leading to the description of the cornfields. Choice (A) is the best option here. Choice B misstates the passage; the cornfields didn't appear *almost immediately*, but gradually. Choices C and D do not provide an appropriate link between the two paragraphs.

32. F
Difficulty: Medium
Category: Development
Getting to the Answer: When you're asked to identify the *most relevant* choice, use context clues. The paragraph is about the change the author experiences as they drive from New York across the country. That contrast is clear in the passage as written, so (F) is correct. Choices G and H do not relate to the paragraph's topic. Choice J is opposite; the writer describes many different settings, which is the opposite of *monotonous*.

33. C
Difficulty: Medium
Category: Sentence Structure
Getting to the Answer: As written, the sentence is a run-on sentence. Choice A is incorrect. There are a number of ways to correct a run-on, but only one answer choice will do so without introducing any additional errors. Each of the clauses in this sentence is independent; (C) corrects the run-on by replacing the comma with a semicolon. Choice B omits the comma that must be paired with the coordinating conjunction *but*. Choice D distorts the intended meaning of the sentence. It makes it sound as if the sky, not the author's world, is spreading horizontally toward eternity.

34. G
Difficulty: Medium
Category: Agreement
Getting to the Answer: When a single adverb is underlined, you are most likely being tested on idioms. Determine what is being modified. The underlined portion modifies the noun *serenity*, so it should be an adjective. Eliminate F. Choices H and J compare this serenity to other states of being, but there is no such comparison in the passage. Choice (G) is correct.

35. C
Difficulty: Medium
Category: Organization
Getting to the Answer: When a transition word or clause is underlined, determine the relationship between the ideas being connected. Look at the relationship between the sentences in this paragraph. The ideas are presented chronologically—that is, in the order in which they happened. Choice (C), *At first*, is the best transition into this series of events. Choices A and B imply contradiction or qualification, which is incorrect in context. Choice D implies the conclusion of a series of events or period of time, and is, therefore, incorrect.

Spiders on Mars?

36. H
Difficulty: Low
Category: Development
Getting to the Answer: The question specifically asks for a choice that meets two goals: the choice must communicate that the "spiders" aren't alive and the choice must be playful in tone. The only choice that does both is (H), which is correct. Choices F and G lack a playful tone, so they are incorrect. Deleting the underlined portion does not clarify that the spiders aren't alive, so J is also incorrect.

37. A
Difficulty: High
Category: Conciseness
Getting to the Answer: The phrase "least redundant" indicates this is a Conciseness question. The correct answer will include all essential information in the fewest number of words, so start with the shortest choice. However, D is incorrect, even though it is the shortest choice. The phrase "at first a mystery" sets up a contrast with the present understanding, and adding "now" clarifies that the mystery has been solved. By leaving out "now," the sentence loses this essential information. The correct answer is (A). Choices B and C are longer without containing any new essential information, so they are both incorrect.

38. G
Difficulty: Medium
Category: Agreement
Getting to the Answer: A glance at the answer choices tells you the issue being tested is verbs. The underlined verb is part of a list, and all items in a list must be parallel in structure. Check the other two items in the list, *sublimate* and *carve*, and choose the verb form that matches; (G), *build*, is correct. Choices F, H, and J do not maintain the parallel structure.

39. B
Difficulty: Medium
Category: Development
Getting to the Answer: To determine what the paragraph would lose, first determine what the function of the underlined portion is. The phrase "that resemble spider legs" evokes a mental picture of exactly what this kind of terrain looks like using an image everyone understands. The best match is (B), the correct answer. Choice A is out of scope; there is no discussion in the text of how deep the channels are. Choice C is a distortion; the text does not present any argument for or against the nickname given to this terrain. Finally, whether the underlined portion is included will not affect the factual description of the process through which araneiform terrain is created, so D is incorrect.

40. G
Difficulty: Medium
Category: Agreement
Getting to the Answer: When a pronoun is underlined, identify the antecedent, which is the noun to which the pronoun refers. In this case, the antecedent is *beds*. The pronoun that agrees must be the objective plural pronoun *them*; (G) is correct. It may be tempting to select F, *it*; however, the prepositional phrase "of Martian soil simulant" is modifying the main noun, *beds*, and thus is not grammatically the antecedent. Choice H is incorrect because *they* is the subjective case, but the pronoun needed is the object of *overlaid*. Choice J, *its*, is the possessive form of *it*, which is incorrect.

Flight of the Concorde

41. B
Difficulty: Medium
Category: Sentence Structure
Getting to the Answer: The answer choices contain various ways that clauses may be connected. Note that there is a second comma after 2003, and the phrase between the two commas contains nonessential information that should be offset. Eliminate choices A and C. It does not make sense that two operating entities would physically be in the last of planes, so eliminate D. Choice (B) is correct: *which* is a pronoun for the planes that were operated by the two firms.

42. H
Difficulty: Low
Category: Revising Text
Getting to the Answer: Since the question asks about the preceding details, read them carefully. The last plane is making its final transatlantic flight. Predict that the correct answer will add additional details about this: something about the end of this journey. Choice F is incorrect. Pilots are not mentioned, and new ones would be an illogical addition to the information. Eliminate J for a similar reason: nothing new has been referenced. Eliminate choice G because regulations have not been mentioned yet. Choice (H) fits the prediction, building on the idea of the closing that this flight represents.

43. C
Difficulty: Medium
Category: Revising Text
Getting to the Answer: For a Revising Text question, be mindful of answer choices that do not add to (or take away from) the passage. In this case, you need to determine whether "explosive" is the best adjective for this sentence. The sentence explains why there was a ban on supersonic jets over land: the sonic booms were disruptive and potentially dangerous. The existing words emphasize the severity of the booms. Choice (C) is correct. The words should be kept; so A and B are incorrect. While the words should not be replaced, choice D is incorrect beause it is about the ban, not the sonic booms.

44. J
Difficulty: Low
Category: Organization: Transitions
Getting to the Answer: For Transition questions, identify how to best connect the two ideas. The first sentence states that the planes fly very high and very fast. The second sentence is an example of that. Since none of the given transition words signals that an instance of the speed will be given, choice (J) is correct.

45. D
Difficulty: High
Category: Revising Text
Getting to the Answer: When reviewing the necessity of keeping a sentence within a passage, ask yourself how the sentence supports the author's purpose and if anything would be lost if it is removed. While the passage does include scientific information as it relates to the sound barrier, this sentence shifts the focus from planes to people. Additionally, if it were removed, the passage would not lose any relevant or essential information. Choice (D) is correct. Choices A and B are incorrect; the sentence should be cut. Because the sentence doesn't take away from the author's purpose, choice C is incorrect.

46. G
Difficulty: High
Category: Modifiers
Getting to the Answer: Note that the answer choices include pronouns with apostrophes, so this question is testing modifiers. Eliminate choices F and H because neither correctly reflect the Concorde's possession of the *altitudes*. Next, eliminate choice J because *cruise*, which is either a noun or verb, cannot modify *altitudes*. Choice (G) is correct because verbs with an *-ing* suffix can be used as adjectives.

47. A
Difficulty: Medium
Category: Style and Tone
Getting to the Answer: For a Style and Tone question, reflect on the author's purpose and word choice. This is a informational text with plain, formal language. Look for the phrase that doesn't clash with the passage. Eliminate choices B and D because the language is informal and unspecific. Eliminate choice C because it's more dramatic than the author's style. Choice (A) is correct.

48. F
Difficulty: Low
Category: Pronouns
Getting to the Answer: Note that the answer choices all contain pronouns. As indicated in the first clause, *Concorde* is plural (*their*); therefore, choices G and J are incorrect. Choice H would create ambiguity: to which noun would *them* belong? It could be either the spectators or the Concorde; however, it is neither. Choice (F) is correct.

49. B
Difficulty: High
Category: Introductions and Conclusions
Getting to the Answer: Similar to the approach with Transitions, if you're tasked with connecting two parts

of an essay, begin by identifying the ideas that are being connected. The first two sentences of the paragraph are about people's impression of the planes: awe-inspiring and really loud. The third sentence informs the reader that they could still walk though one. The final sentence identifies where the retired planes may be found. Predict the correct sentence adds detail about who would visit the planes and why. Choice (B) is correct. Incorrect choice A introduces an impossibility: the Concorde is no longer flying. Choice C detracts from the author's idea: that it would be fun to tour a Concorde. Choice D is irrelevant: the paragraph makes no mention of pilots.

50. J
Difficulty: Low
Category: Sentence Structure
Getting to the Answer: For clarity, a parenthetical phrase should be next to what it's explaining or qualifying. Since the phrase is adding information about a different museum, it should be placed after *Museum*. Choice (J) is correct.

Mathematics Test

1. C
Difficulty: Medium
Category: Statistics and Probability
Getting to the Answer: When a question about averages involves a missing value (here, the final test score), it often helps to think in terms of the sum instead. For Sarah's exam scores to average at least a 90, they must sum to at least $90 \times 4 = 360$. She already has an 89, a 93, and an 84, so she needs at least $360 - (89 + 93 + 84)$, which gives $360 - 266 = 94$ points on her final test. Choice (C) is correct.

2. G
Difficulty: Low
Category: Statistics and Probability
Getting to the Answer: You are told that there are 45 total students. To find the students who do not take math, subtract away all of the numbers in the *M* circle: $45 - 10 - 7 - 2 - 2 = 24$. Choice (G) is correct.

3. B
Difficulty: Medium
Category: Statistics and Probability
Getting to the Answer: If Cassie throws a dart 600 times and wants the probability of landing on each region to be 20%, then she wants it to land on each different region $600(0.20) = 120$ times. The red, blue, and yellow regions are fairly good approximations to this number, but the green and purple are way off. To make each region about 120, the green should be decreased and the purple should be increased. That matches (B).

4. G
Difficulty: Medium
Category: Geometry
Getting to the Answer: This is a pair of parallel lines cut by a transversal, but this time, there's also a triangle thrown into the mix. Begin with segment $\overline{AB}$. This is a transversal, so $\angle MAB$ and $\angle ABC$ are alternate interior angles and $m\angle MAB = m\angle ABC = 55°$. Because triangle ABC is isosceles with $\overline{AB} = \overline{AC}$, $m\angle ACB$ is also 55° (base angles of an isosceles triangle have equal measures). Choice (G) is correct.

5. B
Difficulty: Medium
Category: Algebra
Getting to the Answer: Quadratic equations (equations with an x^2 term in them) are usually best solved by factoring. Before you factor, make sure to set everything equal to zero. Here, $x^2 - 8x = 8x$ becomes $x^2 - 16x = 0$.

$$x^2 - 16x = 0$$
$$x(x - 16) = 0$$
$$x = 0 \text{ or } x - 16 = 0$$
$$x = 0 \text{ or } x = 16$$

Only 16 appears as an answer choice, so (B) is correct.

6. H
Difficulty: Medium
Category: Number and Quantity
Getting to the Answer: To multiply two matrices, the sizes (# of rows by # of columns) must match in a certain way. Here, the size of the first matrix is 2×2 and the size of the second is 2×1. If you multiply a 2×2 matrix by a 2×1 matrix (which is possible

Practice Test 1
Answers and Explanations

because the middle dimensions match), the result will be a 2 × 1 matrix (the outer dimensions when the sizes are written as a product). This means you can eliminate F and G, which are all 2 × 2 matrices. To multiply the matrices, multiply each element in the first row of the first matrix by the corresponding element in the second matrix and add the products. Then repeat the process using the second row of the first matrix:

$$\begin{bmatrix} -2 & 0 \\ 1 & -3 \end{bmatrix} \cdot \begin{bmatrix} 2 \\ 2 \end{bmatrix} = \begin{bmatrix} -2(2) + 0(2) \\ 1(2) + (-3)(2) \end{bmatrix} = \begin{bmatrix} -4 \\ -4 \end{bmatrix}$$

Choice (H) is correct.

7. A
Difficulty: Medium
Category: Algebra
Getting to the Answer: You are trying to find the total number of people in Roman's class, so let this be x. The 10 hats were evenly divided among the x members of his class. Since you cannot have fractional people, $\frac{10}{x}$ must be a whole number. Using similar logic, $\frac{35}{x}$ must also be a whole number. In other words, x must divide evenly into both 10 and 35. The only number in the answer choices that does this is 5, so (A) is correct.

8. H
Difficulty: Medium
Category: Number and Quantity
Getting to the Answer: Follow the directions given in the question. First, take the number of seeds (90) and multiply it by 20 to obtain 90(20) = 1,800. Then take the square root. Since $\sqrt{1,800}$ does not appear in the answer choices, simplify this expression:

$$\sqrt{1,800} = \sqrt{900}\sqrt{2}$$
$$= 30\sqrt{2}$$

Choice (H) is correct.

9. A
Difficulty: Low
Category: Algebra
Getting to the Answer: This question asks you to isolate x. Get x on one side of the equal sign and everything else on the other side using inverse operations:

$$2x - 7y = 8$$
$$2x = 8 + 7y$$
$$x = \frac{8}{2} + \frac{7y}{2}$$
$$x = 4 + \frac{7}{2}y$$

Choice (A) is correct.

10. F
Difficulty: Medium
Category: Number and Quantity
Getting to the Answer: Whenever multiple rates are given, pay very careful attention to the units. As you read the question, decide how and when you will need to convert units. Use the factor-label method as needed. The answer choices are given in hours and minutes, so start by converting the given typing rate from words per second to words per minute:

$$\frac{3.75 \text{ words}}{1 \text{ second}} \times \frac{60 \text{ seconds}}{1 \text{ minute}} = \frac{225 \text{ words}}{1 \text{ minute}}$$

Next, find the number of words in the 25-page transcript:

$$\frac{675 \text{ words}}{1 \text{ page}} \times 25 \text{ pages} = 16,875 \text{ words}$$

Finally, let m be the number of minutes it takes the court reporter to type the whole transcript. Set up a proportion and solve for m:

$$\frac{225 \text{ words}}{1 \text{ minute}} = \frac{16,875 \text{ words}}{m \text{ minutes}}$$
$$225m = 16,875$$
$$m = 75$$

Because 75 minutes is not an answer choice, convert it to hours and minutes: 75 minutes = 1 hour, 15 minutes, making (F) the correct answer.

11. C
Difficulty: Low
Category: Functions
Getting to the Answer: When given a function and a value of x, plug in the number value for each x in the equation and simplify. Make sure you follow the order of operations:

$$f(x) = 16x^2 - 20x$$
$$f(3) = 16(3)^2 - 20(3)$$
$$= 16(9) - 60$$
$$= 144 - 60 = 84$$

Choice (C) is the answer.

12. H
Difficulty: Medium
Category: Statistics and Probability
Getting to the Answer: Probability is the number of desired outcomes divided by the total number of possible outcomes. Here, you're given the probability $\left(\frac{3}{4}\right)$ and the number of desired outcomes (48). You're looking for the total number of possible outcomes (the number of dominoes in the pile). Let d represent the number of dominoes in the pile. Set up an equation using the definition of probability and the given information:

$$P(\text{even \# dots}) = \frac{\text{\# with even \# dots}}{\text{total \# dominoes in pile}} = \frac{3}{4}$$

$$\frac{3}{4} = \frac{48}{d}$$
$$3d = 192$$
$$d = 64$$

Choice (H) is correct.

13. C
Difficulty: Medium
Category: Geometry
Getting to the Answer: Because $\overline{QS} = \overline{QR}$, triangle QRS must be a 45°-45°-90° triangle and the hypotenuse is $5\sqrt{2}$. Remember that $\cos = \frac{\text{adjacent}}{\text{hypotenuse}}$. Therefore:

$$\cos R = \frac{5}{5\sqrt{2}}$$
$$= \frac{1}{\sqrt{2}}$$
$$= \frac{1}{\sqrt{2}} \times \frac{\sqrt{2}}{\sqrt{2}} = \frac{\sqrt{2}}{2}$$

Choice (C) is correct.

14. J
Difficulty: Medium
Category: Algebra
Getting to the Answer: Look carefully at the two equations. If you multiply the first one by −2, then you arrive at something that looks almost identical to the second:

$$-2(3x - y = 4)$$
$$-6x + 2y = -8$$

But they are not exactly the same! The first equation shows that $-6x + 2y = -8$, while the second shows that $-6x + 2y = 1$. The same expression cannot equal two different things at the same time. Therefore, this system of equations has no solution. Choice (J) is correct.

15. A
Difficulty: Medium
Category: Algebra
Getting to the Answer: The expression $(x - 6)^3$ is equivalent to $(x - 6)(x - 6)(x - 6)$. Begin by simplifying $(x - 6)(x - 6)$:

$$(x - 6)(x - 6) = x^2 - 6x - 6x + 36$$
$$x^2 - 12x + 36$$

Then, multiply this result by the remaining $(x - 6)$ term.

$$(x^2 - 12x + 36)(x - 6) = x^3 - 6x^2 - 12x^2 + 72x + 36x - 216$$
$$= x^3 - 18x^2 + 108x - 216$$

Choice (A) is correct.

16. G
Difficulty: Medium
Category: Number and Quantity
Getting to the Answer: To find the number of girls in the senior class, use the given ratios. The ratio of girls to boys is 5:3, so the ratio of girls to the total number of seniors is 5:(3 + 5), or 5:8. Call g the number of girls in the senior class. Set up a proportion and cross-multiply to solve for g:

$$\frac{5}{8} = \frac{g}{168}$$
$$8g = 840$$
$$g = 105$$

There are 105 girls in the senior class, which is (G).

17. C

Difficulty: Low
Category: Number and Quantity
Getting to the Answer: The signs (multiplication dots) between these terms say to *multiply*. Be careful not to leave any parts out or multiply by any part more than once. First, multiply the number parts together: $2 \cdot 3 \cdot 6 = 36$, which immediately eliminates A and B. Then, x times x is x^2. Finally, multiply the y's to get $y^3 \cdot y^2 \cdot y^2 = y^{3+2+2} = y^7$. Choice (C) is correct. Remember that you're counting the number of y's that are being multiplied, so add the exponents.

18. G

Difficulty: Medium
Category: Number and Quantity
Getting to the Answer: Simplify this expression piece by piece. Begin by rewriting $\sqrt{25}$ as 5. Then rewrite $\sqrt{-36}$ as $\sqrt{36}\sqrt{-1}$. The first square root simplifies to 6, and the second simplifies to i. Therefore, the entire expression is equal to $5 - 6i$. Choice (G) is correct.

19. A

Difficulty: High
Category: Statistics and Probability
Getting to the Answer: This question hinges on the fact that in arithmetic sequences you add the same number each time to get to the next term. Here, you don't know what that number is, so call it n. The five terms in the sequence are:

$$4$$
$$4 + n$$
$$4 + n + n$$
$$4 + n + n + n$$
$$4 + n + n + n + n$$

For example, for $n = 1$ this sequence would look like this:

$$4$$
$$5$$
$$6$$
$$7$$
$$8$$

These terms are already listed in ascending order, so the median is the middle term, which is $4 + n + n$, or $4 + 2n$. The mean is the sum of all the terms divided by the number of terms:

$$\frac{4 + (4 + n) + (4 + 2n) + (4 + 3n) + (4 + 4n)}{5} =$$

$$\frac{20 + 10n}{5} = \frac{5(4 + 2n)}{5} = 4 + 2n.$$ Thus, the mean and the median have the same value, so the difference between them is equal to 0. Choice (A) is correct.

You could arrive at this result more quickly by realizing that if the numbers in a sequence are evenly spaced, the mean will always be equal to the median because the distribution is symmetrical.

20. H

Difficulty: Medium
Category: Geometry
Getting to the Answer: Similar triangles have equal angles and proportional sides. Be sure to keep track of which side is proportional to which—the longest side of one triangle goes with the longest side of the other triangle, and so on. Use the given ratio and the fact that the longest side of the second triangle has length 12 to set up a proportion comparing the longest sides of both triangles and the shortest sides of both triangles:

$$\frac{12}{20} = \frac{x}{15}$$
$$20x = 12(15)$$
$$20x = 180$$
$$x = 9$$

Since $9 = 9.0$, choice (H) is correct.

21. B

Difficulty: High
Category: Geometry
Getting to the Answer: There are multiple ways to work this question. One way is to note that angle *DEC* is given as a right angle, so angle *AED* must also be a right angle. Use the Pythagorean theorem ($a^2 + b^2 = c^2$) to solve for the missing side *ED* in triangle *ADE*. Remember that c always represents the hypotenuse of the right triangle.

$$a^2 + b^2 = c^2$$
$$27^2 + b^2 = 45^2$$
$$729 + b^2 = 2{,}025$$
$$b^2 = 1{,}296$$
$$b = 36$$

Now apply the Pythagorean theorem again to triangle *DEC*. Remember that *ED* = 36.

$$a^2 + b^2 = c^2$$
$$36^2 + b^2 = 60^2$$
$$1{,}296 + b^2 = 3{,}600$$
$$b^2 = 2{,}304$$
$$b = 48$$

Choice (B) is correct.

If you remember the common Pythagorean triple 3-4-5, you can speed things up considerably. In triangle *ADE*, 27-36-45 is the same as 9(3-4-5). Similarly, in triangle *DEC* 36-48-60 is 12(3-4-5). Always keep an eye out for multiples of Pythagorean triples.

22. J
Difficulty: Medium
Category: Number and Quantity
Getting to the Answer: To keep the units organized, use the factor-label method. Remember that half an hour is equal to 30 minutes:

$$30 \text{ min}\left(\frac{60 \text{ sec}}{1 \text{ min}}\right)\left(\frac{3 \text{ ft}}{1 \text{ sec}}\right) = 5{,}400 \text{ ft}$$

Choice (J) is correct.

23. D
Difficulty: Medium
Category: Functions
Getting to the Answer: The constant *e* is approximately 2.718. Therefore, the function can be rewritten as $f(x) \approx 4(2.718)^{2x} - 3$. The question asks for the value of $f(1)$, so replace *x* with 1 and simplify using your calculator:

$$f(1) \approx 4(2.718)^{2(1)} - 3$$
$$\approx 4(2.718)^2 - 3$$
$$\approx 4(7.380) - 3$$
$$\approx 29.55 - 3$$
$$\approx 26.55$$

The number 26.55 is close to 30, or 3×10^1. Choice (D) is correct.

24. G
Difficulty: Medium
Category: Number and Quantity
Getting to the Answer: To convert from degrees to radians, use the conversion factor $\pi \text{ radians} = 180°$. Align the ratio so that the unwanted units cancel out:

$$50°\left(\frac{\pi \text{ radians}}{180°}\right) = \frac{50\pi \text{ radians}}{180} = \frac{5\pi \text{ radians}}{18}$$

Choice (G) is correct.

25. B
Difficulty: High
Category: Functions
Getting to the Answer: The fastest route to the correct answer here (because you're given a graph of the parent square root function) is to write the domain and range of $g(x)$ and then adjust the values based on the transformation. The *x*-values of the curve shown in the graph begin at 0 and extend to the right indefinitely, so the domain is $x \geq 0$. The transformation $(x + 1)$ shifts the graph to the left 1 unit, so the domain of $h(x)$ is $x \geq -1$. Eliminate C and D. Likewise, the *y*-values of the curve shown in the graph begin at 0 and extend upward indefinitely, so the range is $y \geq 0$. The transformation $(+3)$ shifts the graph up 3 units, so the range of $h(x)$ is $y \geq 3$. This means (B) is correct.

Note that you could also quickly sketch the graph of $h(x)$ to find its domain and range. The graph would look like the dashed curve below:

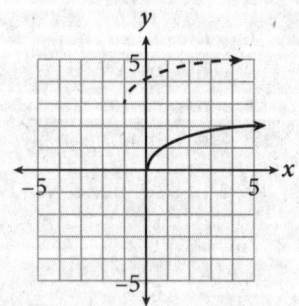

Practice Test 1
Answers and Explanations

26. H
Difficulty: Medium
Category: Algebra
Getting to the Answer: Isolate a using inverse operations:

$$a^2 + bc = \frac{d}{2}$$
$$a^2 = \frac{d}{2} - bc$$
$$a^2 = \frac{d}{2} - \frac{2bc}{2}$$
$$a^2 = \frac{d - 2bc}{2}$$
$$a = \sqrt{\frac{d - 2bc}{2}}$$

Choice (H) is correct.

27. A
Difficulty: Medium
Category: Statistics and Probability
Getting to the Answer: Recall that Probability $= \frac{\text{desired}}{\text{total}}$. Identify which pieces of information from the table you need. The question asks for the probability that a randomly chosen person from the study is employed and has a college degree, so you need the total of both females and males with college degrees who are employed compared to all the participants in the study. There are 188 employed females with a college degree and 177 employed males with a college degree for a total of 365 employed people with a college degree out of 800 participants, so the probability is $\frac{365}{800}$, which reduces to $\frac{73}{160}$, (A).

28. H
Difficulty: Medium
Category: Geometry
Getting to the Answer: Recall that the area formula for a circle is Area $= \pi r^2$. So to find the area, you must find the radius first. The given chord is perpendicular to the line segment from the center of the circle, so that line segment must also be its bisector. This allows you to add the following measures to the figure:

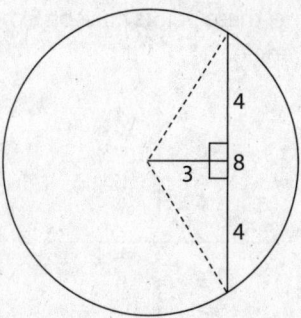

The two right triangles have legs 3 and 4, so they are both 3-4-5 right triangles with hypotenuse 5. This hypotenuse is also the radius of the circle, so plug 5 into the circle area formula and simplify:

$$A = \pi r^2$$
$$= \pi (5)^2$$
$$= 25\pi$$

Choice (H) is correct.

29. A
Difficulty: Low
Category: Number and Quantity
Getting to the Answer: Make sure you solve for what the question is asking. Incorrect answer choices will often be other parts of the question or steps along the way. Ms. Ruppin earns $\frac{\$51,940}{245} = \$212$ per day. The company will save $\$212 - \$140 = \$72$ by paying the replacement instead, which is (A). Note that D is Ms. Ruppin's pay and B is the replacement's pay.

30. J
Difficulty: Medium
Category: Geometry
Getting to the Answer: Draw a picture to visualize the situation. You are asked to find points that are 3 coordinate units away from the line $x = 0$, which is the same as the y-axis.

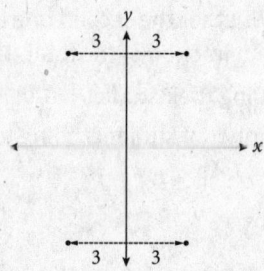

At the same time, these points must be 6 coordinate units away from the origin.

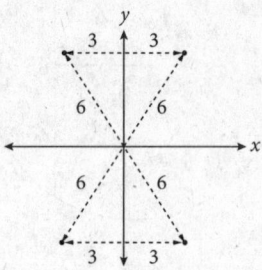

There are 4 points that satisfy these criteria, one in each quadrant, so (J) is correct.

31. C
Difficulty: Medium
Category: Geometry
Getting to the Answer: Draw a quick sketch to visualize the situation.

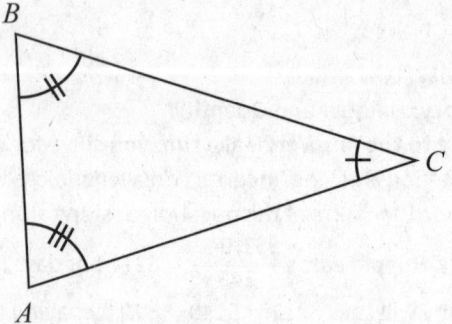

In a triangle, the longest side is opposite the greatest angle. Since ∠A is the greatest angle, the side opposite it, BC, must be the longest side. Eliminate choices A and D. Using similar logic, ∠B is the second greatest angle so AC is the second longest side. Choice (C) is correct.

32. F
Difficulty: Medium
Category: Number and Quantity
Getting to the Answer: When given two ratios, make sure you check whether the second one is a fraction of the first group or a fraction of the total. The number of students continuing their studies = $\frac{1}{3}(896) \approx 299$. Of that 299, the number of students going to law school is $\frac{2}{5}(299) \approx 120$, which is (F).

33. A
Difficulty: Low
Category: Geometry
Getting to the Answer: If two parallel lines are cut by a transversal, all acute angles are equal and all obtuse angles are equal. If a is 110, then the corresponding angle below it has the same measure. Recall that all of the angles in a straight line sum to 180 degrees. This allows you to conclude the following.

$110 + d = 180 \rightarrow d = 70$

$b + c = 180$

$b + c + d = 180 + 70 = 250$

Choice (A) is correct.

Alternatively, since all of the angles around a point sum to 360 degrees, $a + b + c + d = 360$. Since $a = 110$, $110 + b + c + d = 360$ and $b + c + d = 250$. Again, (A) is correct.

34. H
Difficulty: Medium
Category: Number and Quantity
Getting to the Answer: Because you're looking for the sixth term of the sequence, call the sixth term x. Every term in this sequence is formed by multiplying the previous term by 3 and then subtracting 1, so the seventh term must be formed by multiplying the sixth term, x, by 3, and then subtracting 1; in other words, the seventh term is equal to $3x - 1$. Because the seventh term is 365, you have $365 = 3x - 1$. You can solve for x by adding 1 to both sides of the equation and then dividing by 3. The result is $x = 122$, which is (H).

35. B
Difficulty: Medium
Category: Number and Quantity
Getting to the Answer: First simplify the fractions, using your calculator if necessary. Since $-\frac{72}{7} \cong -10.29$ and $\frac{89}{2} = 44.5$, you are being asked how many integers are between -10.29 and 44.5. An integer is a whole number. To find the smallest integer greater than -10.29, round down to -10. Similarly, find the greatest integer smaller than 44.5 by rounding down to 44. To determine how many numbers are between these two, subtract: $44 - (-10) = 54$. You are probably reasonably confident that (B) is the correct answer, and

indeed it is. But why is it 55 instead of 54? Visualize it like this. From -10.29 to 0, there are 10 integers. From 0 to 44.5, there are 44 integers. But you must also include 0 itself! Therefore, there are $10 + 44 + 1 = 55$ total integers.

36. J
Difficulty: Low
Category: Statistics and Probability
Getting to the Answer: The words "mutually exclusive" mean that if one event happens, the other can't happen. In other words, A completely "excludes" B, and vice versa. In this experiment, only two events can occur. Since A and B have no "overlap," A and B together comprise the entire universe of possibilities for this experiment. This means that $P(A) + P(B) = 1$. Choice (J) is correct.

37. B
Difficulty: High
Category: Algebra
Getting to the Answer: If $(x - 1)$ is a factor of $p(x)$, then the function can be written in the form $p(x) = (x - 1)(x - m)(x - n)$. Plugging $x = 1$ into the function gives the following:

$$p(1) = (1 - 1)(1 - m)(1 - n)$$
$$= (0)(1 - m)(1 - n)$$
$$= 0$$

This means that $x = 1$ is one of the "zeros" of the function because plugging it in makes the function equal to zero. Eliminate A and C.

To decide between (B) and D, plug in the numbers in the answer choice and see which one makes $p(x) = 0$. Since positive numbers are easier to work with, start with D and try $x = 3$:

$$p(3) = 3^3 + 5(3)^2 + 3(3) - 9$$
$$= 27 + 5(9) + 9 - 9$$
$$= 27 + 45$$
$$= 72$$

This does not work, so (B) must be correct. On test day, you would stop here but for the record:

$$p(-3) = (-3)^3 + 5(-3)^2 + 3(-3) - 9$$
$$= -27 + 5(9) - 9 - 9$$
$$= -27 + 45 - 18$$
$$= 0$$

38. H
Difficulty: Medium
Category: Statistics and Probability
Getting to the Answer: The median is the middle value when the data is ordered from least to greatest. There are 11 total years, so the median will be the 6th term. Begin by arranging the data:

1,000, 1,000, 2,000, 2,000, 3,000, 3,000, 3,000, 4,000, 4,000, 5,000, 5,000

The median is thus 3,000. The years 1985, 1990, and 1993 all had populations of 3,000, but the only one of these years in the answer choices is 1990. Choice (H) is correct.

39. A
Difficulty: Medium
Category: Statistics and Probability
Getting to the Answer: Recall that

Average $= \dfrac{\text{sum of terms}}{\text{\# of terms}}$. However, the answer is not as simple as $\dfrac{1 + 2 + 3}{3}$ or $\dfrac{10 + 35 + 5}{50}$. The data is presented as a frequency table: 10 people took 1 vacation, 35 people took 2 vacations, and 5 people took 3 vacations. You must take into account both the number of vacations and the number of people who took these vacations.

To do so, calculate the total number of vacations taken by multiplying the rows of the table together. Then divide by the total number of people, 50.

$$\text{Average} = \frac{1(10) + 2(35) + 3(5)}{50}$$
$$= \frac{10 + 70 + 15}{50}$$
$$= \frac{95}{50}$$
$$= 1.9$$

Choice (A) is correct.

40. J
Difficulty: Medium
Category: Number and Quantity
Getting to the Answer: If $\sqrt[3]{x} = y$, then $x = y^3$. If y is a negative number, then y^3, or $y \times y \times y$, is also a negative number. You can prove this to yourself by picking a number like -2: $-2 \times -2 \times -2 = -8$. Choice (J) is correct.

Part 6
PRACTICE TESTS

41. B
Difficulty: High
Category: Number and Quantity
Getting to the Answer: To find the least possible value of the product of two fractions, you must minimize the value of each fraction. Recall that you can make a fraction smaller in two ways: increase its denominator or decrease its numerator. For the quantity $\frac{1}{c}$, the numerator is fixed. Therefore, the only way to decrease its overall value is to increase its denominator. The question says that $5 \leq c \leq 11$, so the largest that c can be is 11. Therefore, the smallest that $\frac{1}{c}$ can be is $\frac{1}{11}$. Using similar logic, the expression $\frac{b}{a}$ attains its minimum when b is small and a is large. Using the constraints in the question, this makes $\frac{b}{a} = \frac{4}{3}$.

Therefore, the minimum possible value of $\left(\frac{1}{c}\right)\left(\frac{b}{a}\right) = \left(\frac{1}{11}\right)\left(\frac{4}{3}\right) = \frac{4}{33}$. Choice (B) is correct.

42. J
Difficulty: Medium
Category: Statistics and Probability
Getting to the Answer: Intuitively, standard deviation measures the "spread" of a data set. Data sets whose points are closely clustered around the mean have small standard deviations, while data sets whose points are widely dispersed from the mean have large standard deviations. Choice (J) is a data set composed solely of 10s. There is thus no "distance" between each data point and the mean, so the standard deviation is 0. This is as small as it is possible to be, so (J) is correct.

43. C
Difficulty: Medium
Category: Geometry
Getting to the Answer: Start by finding the volume of the swimming pool: $V = \pi r^2 h = \pi(6)^2(4) = \pi(36)(4) = 144\pi$ cubic feet. To find the weight of the water in the pool, multiply the pool's volume in cubic meters by the weight of 1 cubic foot: 144π cubic feet $\times$ 62 pounds per cubic feet $= 8{,}928\pi$ pounds. Because the answer choices consist of large ranges of numbers, you can estimate the volume by rounding π to the nearest whole number, which is 3. Using 3 as an estimate for π, $8{,}928\pi$ pounds is approximately 26,784 pounds, making (C) correct.

44. H
Difficulty: Hard
Category: Functions
Getting to the Answer: You are given that $f(h(g(a))) = 3$ and are asked to find a. This is a lot of parentheses to unravel, so it may help to say that $h(g(a)) = m$ and rephrase the question as $f(m) = 3$. In other words, what value do you need to plug into the f function to yield 3? According to the table, this is 5. Since you made $m = h(g(a))$, you now know that $h(g(a)) = 5$. This is still a lot to process, so apply the same logic to say that $n = g(a)$ and rewrite this equation as $h(n) = 5$. So what value do you need to plug into the h function to yield 5? The table says that $n = 3$. Again, since you made $n = g(a)$, you now have $g(a) = 3$. Do one final check in the table to see that $a = 4$. Choice (H) is correct.

45. C
Difficulty: Medium
Category: Statistics and Probability
Getting to the Answer: The expected value of a random discrete variable is the weighted average of all possible values that the variable can take on. The weights are determined by the probability distribution. To find the expected value, multiply each possible value by its given probability and then add the products:

$$E(X) = \frac{1}{5}(10) + \frac{1}{10}(11) + \frac{3}{10}(12) + \frac{3}{20}(13) + \frac{1}{4}(14)$$
$$= 2 + \frac{11}{10} + \frac{36}{10} + \frac{39}{20} + \frac{14}{4}$$
$$= \frac{40}{20} + \frac{22}{20} + \frac{72}{20} + \frac{39}{20} + \frac{70}{20}$$
$$= \frac{243}{20} = 12\frac{3}{20}$$

Choice (C) is correct.

Practice Test 1
Answers and Explanations

Reading Test

Passage I

Suggested Passage Map Notes

¶1: Countess Olenska (CO) no longer pretty

¶2: CO 1st in NY as little girl adopted by aunt Medora (M)

¶3: M repeatedly widowed, NY accepting of M's eccentricities

¶4: All kind to Ellen (E) [aka CO], M not follow mourning rules

¶5: E was well-liked, fearless child; E's odd edu.

¶6: E married Polish nobleman, ended in disaster

¶7: NY expected CO to be more stylish and vibrant

BIG PICTURE SUMMARY

Main idea: Ellen Mingott as a child and Countess Olenska as an adult did not fit New York society's expectations of her.

Author's purpose: To portray how a character changed from childhood to adulthood and the influences that shaped her.

---

1. C
Difficulty: Medium
Category: Global
Getting to the Answer: This is a Global question, asking about the passage as a whole. A quick review will show that though several characters are named, none is in the position to narrate the entire story. An identified narrator, seemingly privileged to all the action, explains the story from beginning to end. This matches choice (C). Choice A refers to Archer, but he speaks only of Ellen as a child and as a widowed Countess; he does not comment on events in between. Choice B is a misused detail. The much married woman would be Medora Manson, who is not telling the story. Choice D is also a misused detail. The narrator mentions "her other relations," (lines 40–41), but they then drop completely out of the story.

2. H
Difficulty: High
Category: Global
Getting to the Answer: "The passage as a whole" indicates that this is a Global question, so go back to the main idea, which is that Ellen did not fit society's expectations. She is described as a "fearless and familiar little thing, who asked disconcerting questions" (lines 42–43), indicating a child of strong individuality. However, when she returned to New York after her disastrous marriage, "many people (as he heard afterward) were 'stylish'—for stylishness was what New York most valued" (lines 85–88) and New Yorkers were disappointed that she was not more "resonant" (line 92). Both as a child and as an adult, Ellen, Countess Olenska, defied New York society's expectations, which matches choice (H). Choices F and J are incorrect because they omit any mention of society expectations, and choice G is incorrect because it focuses on Medora Manson, not on the passage as a whole.

3. A
Difficulty: Medium
Category: Inference
Getting to the Answer: To answer Inference questions, you will have to go beyond what is directly stated in the passage. However, the correct answer choice will be supported by evidence from the passage, so make sure you make a prediction that has solid textual support. You can predict, based on lines 56–67, that Ellen was unable to help her aunt because her own marriage to the immensely rich Polish nobleman "had ended in disaster." Choice (A) matches this prediction. Choice B is a distortion; since both Medora and Ellen left New York, their communication over the years is unknown. Choice C is a distortion; while the author tells you that Ellen had an incoherent education, nothing in the passage suggests that she resented this. Choice D is a distortion; though the passage makes it clear that Medora was eccentric, this is in no way related to receiving help from her niece.

4. F
Difficulty: Medium
Category: Inference
Getting to the Answer: Predicting an answer is particularly important for Inference questions like this. Make sure you can support your prediction with

K 685

information in the passage. Lines 68–70 suggest that Newland has spent time thinking about Ellen, and lines 74–93 all describe Newland's observations of Ellen. Newland is not disappointed that Ellen is not as "stylish" as others expected (lines 85–87). You can predict that Newland has thoughtfully considered Ellen, reaching conclusions that differ from those of his peers. Choice (F) matches this prediction. Choice G is out of scope; it might seem reasonable to conclude that Newland is likeable, but the passage does not provide any evidence to directly support this. Also, there is nothing to suggest that he is withdrawn. Choice H is opposite; Newland concludes that Ellen is "full of a conscious power" (lines 82–83), which is a positive rather than a "harsh" assessment, especially in contrast with others' determination that Ellen has lost her looks and is unstylish. Choice J is a distortion; Newland's observation that Ellen is not as stylish as New York society might expect says nothing about his own stylishness, nor does the author ever describe Newland's level of sociability.

5. C
Difficulty: Medium
Category: Detail
Getting to the Answer: Remember that the correct answer to Detail questions will be directly stated in the passage. Your notes should guide you as you locate specific references to the details in question. Line 24 mentions Ellen's parents' "regrettable taste for travel" in the context of lines describing what the people of New York thought. Predict something like "travel." Choice (C) matches this prediction. Choice A is a misused detail; Medora does teach her niece to play the piano, but nothing in the passage suggests that this was undesirable. Choice B is a misused detail; Spanish shawl dances are described as "outlandish," but this is within the context of Medora and Ellen's eccentric, but accepted, behaviors. Choice D is a misused detail; while Medora often adopted children, this is never described as undesirable.

6. F
Difficulty: Low
Category: Detail
Getting to the Answer: Detail questions like this one are straightforward, but it can sometimes be difficult to find exactly where in the passage the relevant information comes from. Make sure that you are answering the specific question being asked, so that other details don't distract you. Medora teaches Ellen "drawing from the model" (line 49), which is described as "a thing never dreamed of before," so predict Ellen, Countess Olenska. Choice (F) matches your prediction. Choice G is out of scope; Newland is not described as having learned anything at all, let alone something controversial. Choice H is a distortion; Medora teaches Ellen, but the passage does not mention Medora learning anything herself. Choice J is a distortion; Count Olenska is only mentioned indirectly as the rich nobleman whom Ellen marries. The passage makes it clear that Ellen is Countess Olenska; don't be fooled by this initially tempting, but incorrect, choice.

7. B
Difficulty: Medium
Category: Function
Getting to the Answer: Locate where the author mentions Medora's mother and read the next few lines. The author writes that "her mother had been a Rushworth," (line 18), that Medora married "one of the crazy Chiverses" (line 20), and that because of these two conditions, "New York looked indulgently on her eccentricities" (lines 20–21). In other words, given her mother and her marriage, people were not surprised by Medora's unconventional life, which matches (B). There is no support for A, so it is out of scope. Choice C is opposite; New Yorkers "thought it a pity that the pretty child should be in such hands" (lines 24–25), and D is true but not relevant to Medora's eccentricities.

8. G
Difficulty: Medium
Category: Inference
Getting to the Answer: The answer to an Inference question must have unstated support in the passage, so review the last paragraph, which discusses Ellen's return to New York. While admitting that "her early radiance was gone" (lines 75–76), Archer also notes her "sureness in the carriage of the head" (line 80) and "full of a conscious power." (lines 82–83). In other words, she was strong and sure of herself, as choice (G) states. Choice F references Ellen as a child, not an adult, and choice H is counter to Archer's description of the Countess at the dinner party. Choice J is a misused detail. It is Medora, not Ellen, who is described as subdued and impoverished.

9. C

Difficulty: Medium
Category: Inference
Getting to the Answer: Make sure you have good evidence for your prediction, and the correct answer choice will be easy to find. Line 21 mentions Medora's *eccentricities*, line 31 mentions her *peculiarities*, and line 44 mentions the *outlandish arts* that Medora teaches Ellen. From these descriptions, you can predict that Medora is unconventional or eccentric. Choice (C) matches this prediction. Choice A is out of scope; although Medora does not adhere to conventions, as indicated by lines 31–32, there is nothing to suggest that this is attributable to arrogance. Choice B is a distortion; the description of the short veil that Medora wore to her brother's funeral in lines 34–36 might suggest immodesty, but the author makes clear that this is evidence of Medora's willingness to flout social conventions and never mentions any immodest dress or behavior. Choice D, which means following established practice, is opposite; you are told in lines 31–32 that one of her peculiarities is to "flout the unalterable rules that regulated American mourning."

Passage II

Suggested Passage Map Notes

¶1: climate change threat to FL economy: tourism + agriculture

¶2: S. FL hurricane damage (tourism)

¶3: Everglades

¶4: not enough water for citrus farms

¶5: livestock industry

¶6: plans to deal w/ problems

¶7: more prep, diversify economy

BIG PICTURE SUMMARY

Main idea: Potential dangers to Florida's tourism and agriculture industries from climate change and ways Floridians plan to address them.

Author's purpose: To describe how climate change is likely to impact Florida's economy.

10. G

Difficulty: Medium
Category: Global
Getting to the Answer: This is a Global question because it asks for the purpose of the passage as a whole. Review your passage map and predict that the passage describes probable challenges to Florida's economy due to climate change and how the state is preparing to meet those challenges. The correct answer is (G).

Choice F is a distortion; while the passage does occasionally mention harm that has already occurred, it is primarily focused on future issues. Choice H is both out of scope and extreme; combating climate change itself is not addressed in the passage, and the author doesn't argue for any particular course of action. Choice J is also out of scope; the passage is focused on economic impacts, not on multiple ways climate change can impact people's lives.

11. D

Difficulty: High
Category: Function
Getting to the Answer: The wording "author most likely references . . . to" identifies this as a Function question. Examine the surrounding text to understand why the author includes these references. The paragraph discusses how lack of water could harm agriculture; the EPA report explains how water shortages could come about, and the study demonstrates the impact of insufficient water on citrus crops. Predict that both provide support from scientific sources for the paragraph's main idea. The correct answer is (D). This choice doesn't match the exact wording of the prediction, but correct answer choices rarely will. Look for the choice that matches the general idea of the prediction rather than its specific wording. In this case, (D) includes supporting the main idea, and most readers are likely to find scientific studies and reports authoritative; thus, (D) fits the prediction even without exactly matching it.

Choice A is true of the study but not the EPA report, while C is true of the EPA report but not the study, so both are incorrect. Nothing in the paragraph is countering an argument, so B is also incorrect.

Part 6
PRACTICE TESTS

12. F
Difficulty: Medium
Category: Inference
Getting to the Answer: The phrase "reasonably be inferred" is a clue that this is an Inference question. Research what the second paragraph says about South Florida. It lost a great deal of money as a result of a hurricane, which could have been far worse if Miami, "Florida's second-most popular tourist destination" (lines 23–24), had been directly hit. You can predict that the area generates a lot of money from tourism. Choice (F) is correct. Choice G is extreme; while the paragraph mentions rising sea levels as a concern, it does not suggest that South Florida is likely to become submerged. Choice H is out of scope; the passage does not discuss northern Florida at all. Finally, J is incorrect because there is no evidence in the paragraph linking South Florida with agricultural production.

13. C
Difficulty: Medium
Category: Function
Getting to the Answer: The phrase "serves to" in the question stem indicates that this is a Function question. Read around the lines in question for context to determine why the author includes this detail. The paragraph states that policymakers want to diversify Florida's economy and international trade seems like a good way to do so. Predict that the fact that Florida already exports a great deal provides a reason *why* policymakers see this as a suitable area to expand. The correct answer is (C).

Choice A is extreme; although the passage makes clear that exports are important to Florida's economy, it does not suggest that they are a primary driver of expansion. Choice B is out of scope; the passage does not compare Florida's trade balance with any other state. Finally, D is a distortion; while the paragraph does explain the importance of diversification, that is not the purpose of this detail.

14. F
Difficulty: Low
Category: Function
Getting to the Answer: The phrase "in order to" signals a Function question. The passage map shows that Hurricane Irma would be discussed in paragraph 2, where it serves as an example of "the worsening effects of climate change" (lines 15–16). This matches choice (F). Rising sea levels refer to the Everglades, making G a faulty use of detail. The hurricane does not support sacrificial floors, which is in paragraph 6, thus incorrect, and it is a "combination of temperature and rainfall increases" (line 73), which affects the health of livestock and the increase in mosquitoes, making J incorrect.

15. B
Difficulty: Low
Category: Detail
Getting to the Answer: The phrase "According to the passage" shows that this is a Detail question. The fifth paragraph discusses issues facing the livestock industry, including heat stressing the animals, loss of grasslands, and increased insect-borne diseases. Choice (B) matches the first of these and is correct.

Choice A is a misused detail; while the passage predicts reduced crop yields, it says nothing about these crops being used to feed livestock. Choice C is a distortion; the passage says that animals are likely to get sick because of increased mosquito populations, not because of the weather itself. Choice D is a misused detail similar to A; while water shortages may occur, the passage does not discuss their impact on the livestock industry.

16. G
Difficulty: Medium
Category: Detail
Getting to the Answer: "The passage makes clear" shows that this is a Detail question. Use your passage map to find where the passage discusses the Everglades and identify how climate change threatens it. Using paragraph 3, predict that the Everglades is likely to become submerged since much of it is barely above sea level. Choice (G) is correct.

Choice F is extreme; while paragraph 3 does mention salt water pushing inland and endangering fresh water sources, it does not say that this will totally destroy these sources. Choice H is a misused detail; the fifth paragraph mentions degradation of grasslands but not in reference to the Everglades. Choice J is a distortion; although paragraph 3 predicts problems for visitors, it does not suggest they will be entirely cut off from the park.

Practice Test 1
Answers and Explanations

17. C
Difficulty: Low
Category: Function
Getting to the Answer: This question asks for the purpose of a paragraph, which requires an understanding of both the paragraph itself and how it fits into the passage as a whole. Thus, this is a Function question. While the passage so far has described problems raised by climate change, paragraph 6 discusses some potential solutions to these problems. Choice (C) is correct. Choice A is a misused detail; only some of the paragraph is about infrastructure adaptations. Choice B is incorrect because this paragraph has moved on from describing the problems. Finally, D is a distortion; while parts of the paragraph involve directing water supplies, it does not refer to imbalances in rainfall.

18. F
Difficulty: Medium
Category: Vocab-in-Context
Getting to the Answer: To understand the meaning of a word in context, read to see how it fits with the surrounding information. The entire phrase is "sacrificial floors," which are "designed to absorb excess water before it reaches the inhabited floors" (lines 87–88). Thus, those floors would be given up for the sake of saving higher floors on which people are living. In other words, they are "expendable," which matches choice (F) (line 86). Choice G plays on the association of sacrifice with religion, but does not fit into the passage. The fact that sacrificial floors are being suggested as a solution to the problem of rising seas means that they have the possibility to be important, making H incorrect. "Deniable" means *capable of being contradicted*, which doesn't make sense in the sentence and is thus incorrect.

Passage III

Suggested Passage Map Notes

Passage A

¶1: Country music (C) born in central & southern Appalachians

¶2: Originated from multiple sources

¶3: The term "country" replaced "hillbilly"

¶4: Hank Williams 1st to take country national; artists

¶5: Nashville, TN = country home w/ Grand Ole Opry (1925)

¶6: C relatives = honky tonk, Western Swing

¶7: C expresses Am. identity

Passage B

¶1: Bluegrass (B) origin and description

¶2: B diff. from C: highlight 1 musician at a time, diff. instruments, vocal harmonies

¶3: own category in late 1950s, named after Bill Monroe's band

¶4: today: movies, festivals

¶5: B themes = working class; reflects Am.

BIG PICTURE SUMMARY

Passage A

Main idea: Country music is an American musical genre with a rich history.

Author's purpose: To describe the origins and history of country music.

Passage B

Main idea: Bluegrass music is related to but distinct from country music, with its own cultural niche.

Author's purpose: To explain what makes bluegrass music unique.

19. C
Difficulty: Medium
Category: Detail
Getting to the Answer: Review your passage map to locate this detail; both the first and second paragraphs have a substantial amount of information about the roots of country music, so making a prediction might be difficult. Use elimination and check each choice against those paragraphs. Eliminate A as a misused detail; the text states that the area from where country music originated was recognized in the late nineteenth century, not that country music itself dates from then. Eliminate B as a distortion and a misused detail; country music did not have roots in bluegrass. Passage B examines the connection between bluegrass music and country music in detail. Choice (C) is correct; paragraph 2 states "country music originated in the 1920s," which is the early twentieth century. On test day, choose the answer and move on, but for practice, D is distortion; country music began in southern areas, not western ones.

20. H
Difficulty: High
Category: Vocab-in-Context
Getting to the Answer: As with all Vocab-in-Context questions, use the surrounding clues to define the word in question. The word appears in paragraph 3, where the original term "hillbillies" is used to describe "Appalachian inhabitants who were considered poor, uneducated, isolated, and wary." The more accepting word "country" has replaced "hillbillies," indicating that *pejorative* is a negative word, an adjective used to highlight the negative characteristics described in the paragraph. This matches (H), since "disparaging" means *belittling*, or *bad*. Choice F is a synonym for *original* rather than a word that means *negative*. Choice G is out of scope, as the author never expresses that the negative view is accurate, and J refers to where the people live rather than fitting the context of describing the term (i.e., it is not a "mountain-dwelling" term).

21. D
Difficulty: Medium
Category: Inference
Getting to the Answer: The answer to an Inference question is supported by the passage. However, because all answer choices are in the passage, be careful to assess each one in terms of the actual question asked. A look at your notes or a quick scan of the passage should provide enough information to make a prediction about where to find the best country music. Match that prediction to the correct answer. Choice (D) is correct; in paragraph 5, the author writes "Country singers are considered to have reached the pinnacle of the profession if they are asked to become members of the Opry." To hear the best music, it makes sense to go to the place where those at the pinnacle, or top of their field, perform. Choice A is a misused detail; one would hear honky-tonk music, a derivative of country, but not country music itself, in these bars. Choice B is a misused detail; Ireland is the original home of the Ulster Scots, many of whom settled in Appalachia. Choice C is a misused detail; though country music had its origins in the mixture of music created in Appalachia, the author does not state that it is the place to hear the best music.

22. F
Difficulty: Medium
Category: Detail
Getting to the Answer: Locate the paragraph in which bluegrass instruments are described, and match those descriptions with the correct answer choice. Your notes point to only one paragraph in which musical instruments are mentioned. Scan the answer choices, then reread the information in that paragraph to determine which answer choice characterizes the information given. Choice (F) is correct; musical instruments are described in the second paragraph and include typical ones such as "banjo, guitar, mandolin, bass, harmonica, and Dobro (resonator guitar)." But the paragraph goes on to include far less typical ones, such as "household objects, including washboards and spoons," which are not usually considered musical instruments, but are sometimes included in a bluegrass band. Choice G is a misused detail; African-American influences are provided as one more source of the bluegrass genre but instrumentation is not referenced. Choice H is a misused detail; this is an example of a bluegrass piece used in a movie soundtrack. Choice J is out of scope; the reference to the Ozark mountains concerns the origin of bluegrass but has nothing to do with a description of musical instruments.

23. A
Difficulty: Medium
Category: Function
Getting to the Answer: A question that asks about the main purpose of a paragraph is a Function question. Review your passage note about paragraph 2 of Passage B: the paragraph is about the ways that bluegrass music is different than country music. The transition keyword *unlike* that starts the first sentence is also a clue that this paragraph is contrasting bluegrass music and country music. Match to (A), the correct choice. An explanation of the roots of bluegrass is in the first paragraph, not the second; incorrect choice B is a misused detail. Choice C is too narrow in scope. The paragraph also describes other differences, so C is incorrect. Choice D is out of scope; the paragraph never discusses the social traditions of bluegrass culture.

24. G
Difficulty: Medium
Category: Inference
Getting to the Answer: Locate the paragraphs that mention *laments* and "high, lonesome sound," and consider what the author means by including these two details. The reference to *laments* is in the first paragraph and the reference to "high, lonesome sound" in the last paragraph are examples of "the hard-scrabble life of the American worker," which matches (G). Choice F is out of scope; the elements mentioned in the question stem do not necessarily reflect Irish music; bluegrass has multiple sources. Choice H is a misused detail; Shania Twain is an example of a country singer and is mentioned in Passage A only. Choice J is a misused detail; though bluegrass was originally called "hillbilly," this is the name for the genre, not the theme.

25. D
Difficulty: Medium
Category: Global
Getting to the Answer: Since the question is asking about the focus of a whole passage, this is a Global question. However, it might be difficult to predict since the question is so broad. Refer to your passage notes as needed to eliminate answers. Eliminate A since it is Passage A, not B, that discusses the Grand Ole Opry as the home of country music. Eliminate B because the sixth paragraph in Passage A discusses the musical relatives of country music, which is far more than the passing mentions in Passage B. Eliminate C because both passages describe a music style that expresses American identity. That leaves (D) as the correct answer, but for the record, it is correct because Passage B devotes the fourth paragraph to how bluegrass is played in today's movies.

26. H
Difficulty: Medium
Category: Global
Getting to the Answer: Because the question asks about elements of the passages, it is a Global question. Because the question is broad, though, use your passage notes and elimination. Eliminate F, G, and J because both passages discuss these elements. The first paragraph of each discusses the origins, as described in F; the second paragraph in each discusses instruments, and the third paragraph in each discusses the term "hillbilly." Only Passage B discusses themes in its last paragraph; select choice (H), which is correct.

27. C
Difficulty: Medium
Category: Inference
Getting to the Answer: When looking for something on which both authors would agree, first determine what each one actually states in the passage, then consider what must be true based on those statements. The evolution, or gradual change, in music, as with anything else, must start from somewhere, so look to the parts of each passage that detail the genesis of the music genres, then consider the progression from there. Choice (C) is correct; both authors detail the various music sources that became either country or bluegrass. In the first passage, the author mentions "folk music, cowboy songs, and traditional Celtic melodies," and in the second passage, the author refers to "Scottish, Welsh, Irish, and English melodic forms, infused, over time, with African-American influences." Both authors affirm that the two music genres are "indigenous." Thus, it must be true that both country and bluegrass music have evolved from their various roots to become American music, supporting agreement on the fact that music can evolve. Choice A is out of scope; each passage mentions how its particular music genre is popular (as explained in the next sentence in the explanation—the Czech festivals and international growth), but both authors don't describe why *both* genres are popular. Choice B is a misused detail; the Grand Ole Opry showcases country music only, not bluegrass. Choice D is out of scope; the passages don't each discuss both genres.

Passage IV

Suggested Passage Map Notes

¶1: CubeSats good for space exploration

¶2: improved radios; InSight

¶3: testing for longer missions

¶4: consumer cameras → less expensive

¶5: less expensive → more experiments possible

¶6: linked networks

¶7: CubeSats improve future space exploration

Part 6
PRACTICE TESTS

BIG PICTURE SUMMARY

Main idea: CubeSats offer many advantages for exploration and experimentation in deep space.

Author's purpose: To describe the benefits of using CubeSats.

---

28. F
Difficulty: Low
Category: Function
Getting to the Answer: Since this question is asking about how a detail relates to a claim, it is a Function question. Review the lines in the question stem and determine how they relate. The difference is that the MarCO project cost less than a traditional satellite project. This is evidence that supports the claim that CubeSats are cost-effective; match to (F). Choice G is extreme; no evidence in a scientific endeavor *proves* a claim. Choices H and J are both opposites and thus are incorrect.

29. C
Difficulty: Low
Category: Detail
Getting to the Answer: The phrase "According to the passage" marks this as a Detail question. Think about where in the passage you might find the original designers of the CubeSat and use your notes to help. The first sentence states that researchers at California Polytechnic and Stanford Universities "determined the specifications of the CubeSat design." This matches (C).

Choices A, B, and D all refer to other people in the passage who made use of the CubeSats, but who were not the original designers. NASA used the design for the MarCO mission, for which Joel Krajewski was a project manager and Cody Colley was a mission manager.

30. G
Difficulty: Medium
Category: Function
Getting to the Answer: The phrase "serves to" in the question stem indicates that this is a Function question. Review your notes to identify the purpose of the fourth paragraph and predict that it describes how using commercially available cameras made the satellites less expensive. Choice (G) is correct.

Choice F is extreme; the author is not arguing for using off-the-shelf components "wherever possible." Choice H is too broad; the paragraph describes only one reason why the project was less costly. Choice J is a misused detail; although the paragraph does briefly praise the images, that is not its main purpose.

31. A
Difficulty: Medium
Category: Detail
Getting to the Answer: The words "According to the passage" identify this as a Detail question. Use your notes to find where the passage discusses communication technology. Research paragraph 2 and predict that the satellites' radios and antennae were faster and more efficient. The correct answer is (A).

Choice B is incorrect because it describes the InSight lander's communication technology. Choice C is incorrect because it describes the MarCO satellites' cameras, not their radios. Choice D is incorrect because, although the passage mentions that the MarCO radios are the size of softballs, it does not discuss whether the radios were unusually small.

32. G
Difficulty: Low
Category: Function
Getting to the Answer: The phrase "serves to" in the question stem is your clue that this is a Function question. Review the referenced lines, which state, "NASA's MarsCube One (MarCO) mission has provided strong evidence that CubeSats offer many advantages for deep space exploration." Note the similarity to the big picture summary; this is the main idea of the passage, which is that CubeSats offer many advantages to space exploration. Match to (G), the correct choice.

Choices F is incorrect because though the author is likely to agree that the MarCO mission was cost-effective, that is not the purpose of this sentence. Choice H is incorrect because the first sentence in the passage serves that function, not the second. Choice J is extreme: there is no support that the author *insists* that CubeSats should be used for *all* missions.

33. C
Difficulty: Medium
Category: Detail
Getting to the Answer: You can easily tell that this is a Detail question because of the phrase "According to the passage" in the question stem. As indicated in the passage notes, the second paragraph contains the comparison between the InSight lander and the MarCO satellites. In lines 21–24, the passage says that the InSight lander communicated more slowly than the MarCO satellites, so use this as your prediction. Match to (C), the correct answer. Choices A and B both describe the MarCO satellites, not the InSight lander; they are incorrect. Choice D is out of scope; there is no information about the landing efficacy of the InSight lander.

34. H
Difficulty: Medium
Category: Function
Getting to the Answer: The phrase "support for the claim" is the clue that this is a Function question asking which claim the given detail about "off-the-shelf components" supports. Both paragraphs 1 and 4 contain information about components, so check those locations for the question stem keyword "off-the-shelf." Lines 8–11 contain a direct reference: "The ability to build a large portion of the CubeSat with off-the-shelf components means that future missions can be more cost-effective." Predict "future missions could be cheaper," which matches the correct answer (H). Choice F is incorrect because it is not a claim; it is another detail that might support the same claim as the detail mentioned in the question. Choice G is a distortion; the text mentions landers only in the context of comparing communication speeds, and never makes a claim about their design. Choice J is a misused detail; the experimental radio and antenna technology made the InSight's landing process more efficient, but there is no support that these components were off-the-shelf.

35. B
Difficulty: Medium
Category: Detail
Getting to the Answer: "The passage most clearly indicates" wording marks this as a Detail question. Consult your notes to find that the passage discusses linked satellite networks and their advantages in the sixth paragraph. You can predict that these networks are flexible and less likely to fail. Choice (B) is correct.

Choice A is a misused detail; while the passage does say that CubeSats are less expensive, that is not an advantage of linked networks specifically. Choice C is incorrect because there is no evidence that the international cooperation mentioned was a result of the satellite network. Choice J is incorrect because the passage does not suggest that the thermosphere was previously inaccessible or that linked networks of satellites were necessary to study it.

36. J
Difficulty: Medium
Category: Inference
Getting to the Answer: The phrasing "Based on the passage . . . most likely" are a clue that this is an Inference question. In the fourth paragraph, where the passage discusses posting mission photos, it describes the scientists as proud and elated. You can predict that they were happy about how well the satellites did. This matches choice (J).

Choices F, G, and H are all out of scope; there is no evidence to suggest that the scientists had anything to prove or any demands to satisfy, and while they may have hoped to gain support, this is not stated in the passage.

ACT Practice Test 2
ANSWER SHEET

ENGLISH TEST

1. Ⓐ Ⓑ Ⓒ Ⓓ
2. Ⓕ Ⓖ Ⓗ Ⓙ
3. Ⓐ Ⓑ Ⓒ Ⓓ
4. Ⓕ Ⓖ Ⓗ Ⓙ
5. Ⓐ Ⓑ Ⓒ Ⓓ
6. Ⓕ Ⓖ Ⓗ Ⓙ
7. Ⓐ Ⓑ Ⓒ Ⓓ
8. Ⓕ Ⓖ Ⓗ Ⓙ
9. Ⓐ Ⓑ Ⓒ Ⓓ
10. Ⓕ Ⓖ Ⓗ Ⓙ
11. Ⓐ Ⓑ Ⓒ Ⓓ
12. Ⓕ Ⓖ Ⓗ Ⓙ
13. Ⓐ Ⓑ Ⓒ Ⓓ
14. Ⓕ Ⓖ Ⓗ Ⓙ
15. Ⓐ Ⓑ Ⓒ Ⓓ
16. Ⓕ Ⓖ Ⓗ Ⓙ
17. Ⓐ Ⓑ Ⓒ Ⓓ
18. Ⓕ Ⓖ Ⓗ Ⓙ
19. Ⓐ Ⓑ Ⓒ Ⓓ
20. Ⓕ Ⓖ Ⓗ Ⓙ
21. Ⓐ Ⓑ Ⓒ Ⓓ
22. Ⓕ Ⓖ Ⓗ Ⓙ
23. Ⓐ Ⓑ Ⓒ Ⓓ
24. Ⓕ Ⓖ Ⓗ Ⓙ
25. Ⓐ Ⓑ Ⓒ Ⓓ
26. Ⓕ Ⓖ Ⓗ Ⓙ
27. Ⓐ Ⓑ Ⓒ Ⓓ
28. Ⓕ Ⓖ Ⓗ Ⓙ
29. Ⓐ Ⓑ Ⓒ Ⓓ
30. Ⓕ Ⓖ Ⓗ Ⓙ
31. Ⓐ Ⓑ Ⓒ Ⓓ
32. Ⓕ Ⓖ Ⓗ Ⓙ
33. Ⓐ Ⓑ Ⓒ Ⓓ
34. Ⓕ Ⓖ Ⓗ Ⓙ
35. Ⓐ Ⓑ Ⓒ Ⓓ
36. Ⓕ Ⓖ Ⓗ Ⓙ
37. Ⓐ Ⓑ Ⓒ Ⓓ
38. Ⓕ Ⓖ Ⓗ Ⓙ
39. Ⓐ Ⓑ Ⓒ Ⓓ
40. Ⓕ Ⓖ Ⓗ Ⓙ
41. Ⓐ Ⓑ Ⓒ Ⓓ
42. Ⓕ Ⓖ Ⓗ Ⓙ
43. Ⓐ Ⓑ Ⓒ Ⓓ
44. Ⓕ Ⓖ Ⓗ Ⓙ
45. Ⓐ Ⓑ Ⓒ Ⓓ
46. Ⓕ Ⓖ Ⓗ Ⓙ
47. Ⓐ Ⓑ Ⓒ Ⓓ
48. Ⓕ Ⓖ Ⓗ Ⓙ
49. Ⓐ Ⓑ Ⓒ Ⓓ
50. Ⓕ Ⓖ Ⓗ Ⓙ

MATHEMATICS TEST

1. Ⓐ Ⓑ Ⓒ Ⓓ
2. Ⓕ Ⓖ Ⓗ Ⓙ
3. Ⓐ Ⓑ Ⓒ Ⓓ
4. Ⓕ Ⓖ Ⓗ Ⓙ
5. Ⓐ Ⓑ Ⓒ Ⓓ
6. Ⓕ Ⓖ Ⓗ Ⓙ
7. Ⓐ Ⓑ Ⓒ Ⓓ
8. Ⓕ Ⓖ Ⓗ Ⓙ
9. Ⓐ Ⓑ Ⓒ Ⓓ
10. Ⓕ Ⓖ Ⓗ Ⓙ
11. Ⓐ Ⓑ Ⓒ Ⓓ
12. Ⓕ Ⓖ Ⓗ Ⓙ
13. Ⓐ Ⓑ Ⓒ Ⓓ
14. Ⓕ Ⓖ Ⓗ Ⓙ
15. Ⓐ Ⓑ Ⓒ Ⓓ
16. Ⓕ Ⓖ Ⓗ Ⓙ
17. Ⓐ Ⓑ Ⓒ Ⓓ
18. Ⓕ Ⓖ Ⓗ Ⓙ
19. Ⓐ Ⓑ Ⓒ Ⓓ
20. Ⓕ Ⓖ Ⓗ Ⓙ
21. Ⓐ Ⓑ Ⓒ Ⓓ
22. Ⓕ Ⓖ Ⓗ Ⓙ
23. Ⓐ Ⓑ Ⓒ Ⓓ
24. Ⓕ Ⓖ Ⓗ Ⓙ
25. Ⓐ Ⓑ Ⓒ Ⓓ
26. Ⓕ Ⓖ Ⓗ Ⓙ
27. Ⓐ Ⓑ Ⓒ Ⓓ
28. Ⓕ Ⓖ Ⓗ Ⓙ
29. Ⓐ Ⓑ Ⓒ Ⓓ
30. Ⓕ Ⓖ Ⓗ Ⓙ
31. Ⓐ Ⓑ Ⓒ Ⓓ
32. Ⓕ Ⓖ Ⓗ Ⓙ
33. Ⓐ Ⓑ Ⓒ Ⓓ
34. Ⓕ Ⓖ Ⓗ Ⓙ
35. Ⓐ Ⓑ Ⓒ Ⓓ
36. Ⓕ Ⓖ Ⓗ Ⓙ
37. Ⓐ Ⓑ Ⓒ Ⓓ
38. Ⓕ Ⓖ Ⓗ Ⓙ
39. Ⓐ Ⓑ Ⓒ Ⓓ
40. Ⓕ Ⓖ Ⓗ Ⓙ
41. Ⓐ Ⓑ Ⓒ Ⓓ
42. Ⓕ Ⓖ Ⓗ Ⓙ
43. Ⓐ Ⓑ Ⓒ Ⓓ
44. Ⓕ Ⓖ Ⓗ Ⓙ
45. Ⓐ Ⓑ Ⓒ Ⓓ

READING TEST

1. Ⓐ Ⓑ Ⓒ Ⓓ
2. Ⓕ Ⓖ Ⓗ Ⓙ
3. Ⓐ Ⓑ Ⓒ Ⓓ
4. Ⓕ Ⓖ Ⓗ Ⓙ
5. Ⓐ Ⓑ Ⓒ Ⓓ
6. Ⓕ Ⓖ Ⓗ Ⓙ
7. Ⓐ Ⓑ Ⓒ Ⓓ
8. Ⓕ Ⓖ Ⓗ Ⓙ
9. Ⓐ Ⓑ Ⓒ Ⓓ
10. Ⓕ Ⓖ Ⓗ Ⓙ
11. Ⓐ Ⓑ Ⓒ Ⓓ
12. Ⓕ Ⓖ Ⓗ Ⓙ
13. Ⓐ Ⓑ Ⓒ Ⓓ
14. Ⓕ Ⓖ Ⓗ Ⓙ
15. Ⓐ Ⓑ Ⓒ Ⓓ
16. Ⓕ Ⓖ Ⓗ Ⓙ
17. Ⓐ Ⓑ Ⓒ Ⓓ
18. Ⓕ Ⓖ Ⓗ Ⓙ
19. Ⓐ Ⓑ Ⓒ Ⓓ
20. Ⓕ Ⓖ Ⓗ Ⓙ
21. Ⓐ Ⓑ Ⓒ Ⓓ
22. Ⓕ Ⓖ Ⓗ Ⓙ
23. Ⓐ Ⓑ Ⓒ Ⓓ
24. Ⓕ Ⓖ Ⓗ Ⓙ
25. Ⓐ Ⓑ Ⓒ Ⓓ
26. Ⓕ Ⓖ Ⓗ Ⓙ
27. Ⓐ Ⓑ Ⓒ Ⓓ
28. Ⓕ Ⓖ Ⓗ Ⓙ
29. Ⓐ Ⓑ Ⓒ Ⓓ
30. Ⓕ Ⓖ Ⓗ Ⓙ
31. Ⓐ Ⓑ Ⓒ Ⓓ
32. Ⓕ Ⓖ Ⓗ Ⓙ
33. Ⓐ Ⓑ Ⓒ Ⓓ
34. Ⓕ Ⓖ Ⓗ Ⓙ
35. Ⓐ Ⓑ Ⓒ Ⓓ
36. Ⓕ Ⓖ Ⓗ Ⓙ

English Test

35 Minutes—50 Questions

Directions: In the passages that follow, certain words and phrases are underlined and numbered. In the right-hand column, you will find alternatives for the underlined part. You are to choose the best answer to each question. If you think the original version is best, choose "**No Change**."

Some questions will ask about part or all of the passage. These questions do not refer to a specific underlined segment. Instead, these questions will accompany a number in a box.

For each question, choose your answer and fill in the corresponding bubble on your answer sheet. Read the passage once before you answer the questions. You will often need to read several sentences beyond the underlined portion to be able to choose the correct answer. Be sure to read enough to answer each question.

PASSAGE I

Thomas Edison, Tinfoil Cylinders, and Digital Music

[1]

Thomas Edison first recorded sounds on tinfoil cylinders in the 1870s. Since then, formats for recording music have come and gone at a breakneck pace.

1. Which choice makes the sentence most grammatically acceptable?
   A. **No Change**
   B. formats for recording music have come and gone,
   C. formats for recording music, have come and gone
   D. formats, for recording music have come and gone

Innovation in recording music has been constant, and the popularity and lifespan of the newest format have always been transitory.
2

Those first tinfoil cylinders, which were addressed
3
as a miracle in their day, quickly progressed to wax cylinders, then hard plastic cylinders and, within a decade, were replaced by the next "miracle," the gramophone disc record.

[2]

[A] The vinyl phonograph record, which sounded better, kicked the gramophone to the curb in the 1940s. [B] This new-fangled format dominated the music landscape for the next 30 years but eventually fell into obsolescence. The vinyl record being no longer
4
mass-marketed to the public. For that matter, neither is its successor, the 8-track cartridge of the 1970s. [C] However, DJs and those who mix popular music still uses and appreciates the vinyl record format, keeping it
5

2. Which choice provides the most effective transition from the first two sentences of the paragraph to the rest of the paragraph?

F. No Change
G. Edison was responsible for a variety of other inventions as well, including key achievements in the development of motion pictures.
H. The telephone was also invented in the 1870s, though its heyday lasted longer than Edison's cylinders.
J. Unfortunately, recordings made with the tinfoil cylinders suffered from poor quality.

3. Which choice is clearest and most precise in context?

A. No Change
B. hailed
C. saluted
D. signaled

4. Which choice makes the sentence most grammatically acceptable?

F. No Change
G. record, having been
H. record is
J. record,

5. Which choice makes the sentence most grammatically acceptable?

A. No Change
B. use and appreciates
C. uses and appreciate
D. use and appreciate

from falling into oblivion. [6]

[3]

Someone who witnessed the rise and fall of the cassette tape may not have been surprised that the compact disc experienced a similar spiral toward its own particular doom. [D] However, sound quality did not drive this change. This time, the driving force was
                                                                                                                              7

something different the quality of the player itself.
              8

[4]

A standard audio compact disc can store only about 700 megabytes worth of digital data, or about an hour of songs. In contrast, modern technological devices, such as smartphones and tablets, can have up to an impressive 1 terabyte of storage space. This has transformed the experience of listening to songs. Compared to the hour's worth of songs stored on a CD, a 1-terabyte device can

6. At this point, the writer is considering adding the following true sentence:

   Similarly, they have saved the 8-track tape and a more recent recording format, the cassette tape.

   Should the writer make this addition?

   F. Yes, because it adds details relevant to the focus of the passage.
   G. Yes, because it reinforces the passage's main argument.
   H. No, because it distracts from the passage's main topic of vinyl records.
   J. No, because it weakens the passage's main argument.

7. Which choice most effectively maintains the essay's tone?

   A. **No Change**
   B. spiral toward its own doom.
   C. progression toward a negative ending.
   D. progression toward an ending that was less than ideal.

8. Which choice makes the sentence most grammatically acceptable?

   F. **No Change**
   G. different;
   H. different:
   J. different,

store a notable mass of musical data on a gadget about
               9
the size of an old cassette tape.

[5]

Has the summit in the climb toward better ways to play recorded music been reached? Such a bold statement will surely prove shortsighted when the next "miracle" in music arrives.

9. Which choice provides the most vivid description of a smartphone's storage capabilities?

A. **No Change**
B. two years' worth of uninterrupted music
C. an impressive quantity of songs
D. the equivalent of many CDs' worth of musical data

Question 10 asks about the preceding passage as a whole.
---

10. The writer is considering adding the following sentence to the essay:

> Though the gramophone record's disc shape proved to have longevity, the gramophone record itself did not.

If the writer were to add this sentence, it would most logically be placed at:

F. Point A in Paragraph 2.
G. Point B in Paragraph 2.
H. Point C in Paragraph 2.
J. Point D in Paragraph 3.

PASSAGE II

Conservation Technology and the BearID Project

Biologists and organizations working to protect endangered and threatened species utilize conservation technology to monitor those same species. Some of the technology being employed include tracking collars and tags, camera traps, and genomics, and drones. Currently, the BearID Project is developing a deep learning system that works with camera traps, videos, and personal photos to help track brown bears. [12]

Traditionally, biologists tracking brown bears used physical and behavioral characteristics, such as size, fur color, scars, fishing styles, and aggression to observe individual bears. Many of these characteristics have been unreliable as identifiers because they can change. For example, size and shape can fluctuate

11. Which choice makes the sentence most grammatically acceptable?

   A. **No Change**
   B. endangered and threatened species,
   C. endangered, and threatened species
   D. endangered, and threatened species,

12. At this point, the writer is considering adding the following true sentence:

   > Two Silicon Valley engineers started the BearID Project because they were studying deep learning while also watching the livestream of bears fishing for salmon in Katmai National Park.

   Should the writer make this addition here?

   F. Yes, because it makes it clear that bears are poorly understood.
   G. Yes, because it shifts the essay back to the main topic, the motivation for using camera traps and drones.
   H. No, because it isn't relevant to the use of technology in conservation projects.
   J. No, because it doesn't specify whether the brown bear is a threatened or endangered species.

13. Which choice is clearest and most precise in context?

   A. **No Change**
   B. align
   C. associate
   D. distinguish

over the summer and fall months as bears gain weight in preparation for winter and hibernation.

To improve the identification of specific bears, the creators of BearID have developed a software system that uses facial recognition algorithms and machine learning to differentiate individual bears. The biologists have collected hundreds of images to upload into the software; this helps BearID classify each imaged bear. While BearID has successfully identified particular bears using their facial characteristics, its accuracy is only 84 percent. The project engineers are making adjustments as they work to improve its accuracy.

14. The writer is considering revising the underlined portion to the following:

when bears gain weight

Given that the information is accurate, should the writer make this revision?

F. Yes, because the revision reveals one reason why the biologists wish to track bears' weight.
G. Yes, because the revision offers additional details about the bears' diet.
H. No, because the revision lacks the clarity and specificity of the original phrase.
J. No, because the revision suggests that changes in body shape can only happen as the bear matures.

15. Which choice makes the sentence most grammatically acceptable?

A. **No Change**
B. have succeeded in identifying
C. is identifying
D. identifies

PASSAGE III

The Toughest Task in Sports

I've often heard that the hardest single act in all of sports is to hit a major league fastball. I'm not going to deny that hitting a ball traveling at upwards of 95 miles per hour is a daunting task, but I can think of something even tougher than taking a major league at-bat: stopping a crank shot in lacrosse.

Lacrosse is often referred to as "the fastest sport on two feet." The game is often <u>brutal</u>, and the best players
16
normally possess a bit of toughness and a bit of finesse. Using sticks known as "crosses" to pass a hard rubber ball back and forth through the air, players on two teams sprint around a field; <u>they then attempted</u> to set
17
up a shot on the opposing team's goal. As in hockey or soccer, the only thing that stands between the ball and the goal is the goalkeeper. Using just his body and his crosse, the goalie must protect the six-foot by six-foot goal from being penetrated by a ball that is less than eight inches in circumference.

A regulation lacrosse ball is almost an inch narrower than a regulation baseball, with an unstitched, smooth rubber surface. The fastest baseball pitch was clocked at 105.1 mph <u>on record</u>, though the average pitching speed
18
is in the low nineties. In men's lacrosse, because the crosse acts as a lever, the fastest crank shots on

16. Which choice is clearest and most precise in context?

   F. **No Change**
   G. stringent
   H. austere
   J. heartbreaking

17. Which choice makes the sentence most grammatically acceptable?

   A. **No Change**
   B. they must attempt
   C. we must attempt
   D. we then attempted

18. The best placement for the underlined portion would be:

   F. where it is now.
   G. after the word *fastest*.
   H. after the word *pitch*.
   J. after the word *clocked*.

Part 6
PRACTICE TESTS

<u>goal, can</u> reach more than 110 mph. Even at the high
       19
school level, crank shots of more than 90 mph are not

uncommon.

19. Which choice makes the sentence most grammatically acceptable?

A. **No Change**
B. goal, can,
C. goal can
D. goal can,

Unlike a baseball pitcher <u>that</u> throws his fastball from a
                            20
fixed position on the mound, a lacrosse player may

20. Which choice makes the sentence most grammatically acceptable?

F. **No Change**
G. which
H. who
J. whom

shoot from anywhere on the field. [21] To make the

21. The writer is considering adding a comma and the following information to the end of the preceding sentence:

   which is usually grass.

Should the writer make this addition?

A. Yes, because it allows the reader to picture the field.
B. Yes, because it adds a detail that supports the rest of the sentence.
C. No, because it distracts from the focus on the game.
D. No, because it weakens the claim in the following sentence.

goalie's job even more <u>absurd</u>, a lacrosse player may
                        22
shoot from over his shoulder, from his side, or drop his

stick down and wind up from the ground.

22. Which choice is clearest and most precise in context?

F. **No Change**
G. insurmountable
H. harrowing
J. difficult

Like hitting a major league fastball, stopping a crank shot in lacrosse is tough.[23]

Both of these endeavors, however, require[24] the same set of skills. One must possess superlative athleticism, great hand-eye coordination, and catlike quickness. Above all, one must be fearless.

23. Given that all the choices are accurate, which one provides the best transition from the preceding paragraph to this paragraph?

A. **No Change**
B. The combination of these unknown variables makes stopping a crank shot in lacrosse tougher than hitting a major league fastball.
C. Though baseball is less challenging than lacrosse, both sports require tremendous skill and dedication from athletes.
D. There is little question that stopping a crank shot in lacrosse is among the toughest tasks an athlete can face.

24. Which choice makes the sentence most grammatically acceptable?

F. **No Change**
G. requires
H. required
J. would have required

Question 25 asks about the preceding passage as a whole.

25. Suppose that the writer had wanted to write an essay comparing the strategies used by baseball pitchers and lacrosse goalies. Would this essay fulfill the writer's goal?

A. Yes, because the writer compares both sports throughout the essay.
B. Yes, because the writer details the challenges that lacrosse goalies face.
C. No, because the writer does not provide any specific details about baseball pitchers.
D. No, because the writer focuses on comparing the difficulty of hitting a ball pitched by a major league pitcher to the difficulty of blocking a crank shot in men's lacrosse.

PASSAGE IV

The Handsome Bean

[26] On the ground floor of the apartment building where I live, the Handsome Bean coffee shop is almost always bustling with customers. Across the street from the building is the neighborhood Little League field. [27]

The Handsome Bean often <u>sponsors</u> a local team.
              28

26. Given that all the choices are accurate, which one most effectively introduces the main subject of the passage?

   F. Many coffee shops are more than just restaurants; they are places where the local community gathers.
   G. Although it is generally cheaper to make one's own coffee, going to a coffee shop can be a pleasant and rewarding experience.
   H. The first coffee shops were established in Western Europe in the late 17th century.
   J. In cities, it is not uncommon to rent an apartment above a business.

27. Given that all the choices are accurate, which one provides the most effective transition between the previous sentences of this paragraph and the last sentence of this paragraph?

   A. During the warm months, the shop sets up outdoor tables on the sidewalk, and the chatter of conversation mixed with the aroma of coffee often floats in through my window to wake me in the mornings.
   B. Next to the Handsome Bean is a used bookstore, and the two shops share many of the same customers.
   C. During the games, the coffee shop offers a discount to parents whose children are competing across the street.
   D. It is a pleasure to have as a neighbor a business that children and adults enjoy so much.

28. Which choice makes the sentence most grammatically acceptable?

   F. **No Change**
   G. had sponsored
   H. was a sponsor of
   J. supported

Over the past few years, I have become friends with Mary, the owner of the shop. The store's main counter is a century-old antique that Mary bought and restored to its original condition, and the photos that adorn the back wall depict our town during the 1920s and 1930s. My favorite detail of the shop, however, is the original tin ceiling. One afternoon, I noticed a name camouflaged within the ornate design: Harvey. I pointed it out to Mary, and she said the original owner of the building was named Harvey Wallaby. Her guess was that he had probably written it there more than 70 years ago. [31] That night after the coffee shop had closed, Mary and I etched our names into the ceiling right next to Harvey's, hoping that our names would similarly be discovered in the far-off future.

On Friday nights, the Handsome Bean has live entertainment, usually in the form of a band or a poetry reading. I am shocked by the performances that transpire within its cozy walls.

[1] The clientele of the coffee shop is as varied as the selection of flavored brews. [2] In the mornings, the Handsome Bean is abuzz with the 9-to-5 crowd stopping

29. Which choice most effectively leads the reader into the topic of this paragraph?

A. No Change
B. Mary, the shop's owner, has a great appreciation for history.
C. The Handsome Bean has only been open for a couple of years, but the owner, Mary, has taken great care to make it look like it has been there for decades.
D. Before Mary, the shop's owner, opened the Handsome Bean, the space had been unoccupied for six months.

30. Which choice most effectively maintains the essay's tone?

F. No Change
G. depict our place clearly
H. illustrate our town
J. illustrate our city

31. The writer is considering deleting the sentence below from the passage:

   Her guess was that he had probably written it there more than 70 years ago.

If the writer were to delete this sentence, the essay would primarily lose:

A. an additional detail about the building that houses the coffee shop.
B. a depiction of the action taken by Mary and the writer.
C. an emphasis on the original owner's influence.
D. a description of the shop's interior.

32. Which choice is clearest and most precise in context?

F. No Change
G. perplexed
H. amazed
J. flabbergasted

Part 6
PRACTICE TESTS

in for some java before heading off to work. [3] During the day, the tables are home to local artists lost in their thoughts and cappuccinos. [4] The evening finds the Handsome Bean filled with bleary-eyed college students loading up on caffeine so they can cram all night for their upcoming exams or finishing their research papers
                                                       33
with looming due dates. [5] Then there's me, sitting in the corner, maybe talking to Mary or reading the paper, smiling at the thought that the best cup of coffee in town is found right beneath my bedroom window. [6] In the afternoons, a group of high school students stops by having an ice cream cone or an egg cream. 35
  34

33. Which choice makes the sentence most grammatically acceptable?

  A. **No Change**
  B. finish
  C. finishes
  D. finalizing

34. Which choice is clearest and most precise in context?

  F. **No Change**
  G. to have
  H. taking
  J. to take

35. For the sake of logic and coherence, Sentence 6 should be placed:

  A. where it is now.
  B. before Sentence 2.
  C. before Sentence 4.
  D. before Sentence 5.

PASSAGE V

A Starlet of the Genes

In 2008, <u>associate biology professor John Finnerty</u> began spending his days researching *Nematostella vectensis*—colloquially called the starlet sea anemone—a creature that shares 80% of its genes with those that are also found in humans.

<u>This includes one of the genes associated with breast cancer.</u>

N. vectensis are <u>the size of a grain of rice.</u> Initial comparisons conducted between the human genome and those of the fruit fly and the nematode have indicated limited similarities. This makes the finding for *N. vectensis*, when compared with that of vertebrates, appealing to scientists. *N. vectensis* are deemed evolutionarily basal, or closer to the root of a phylogenetic tree, so to have a significant number of shared genes that underlie human disease is a breakthrough.

36. Which choice makes the sentence most grammatically acceptable?
    F. No Change
    G. associate, biology professor, John Finnerty,
    H. associate biology professor, John Finnerty,
    J. associate biology professor John Finnerty,

37. If the writer were to delete the underlined sentence, the paragraph would primarily lose:
    A. a contrasting perspective to John Finnerty's theories about the evolution of the starlet sea anemone.
    B. a statement that clarifies a previous detail about *N. vectensis*' ability to regenerate damaged limbs.
    C. evidence that the starlet sea anemone has been the focus of Finnerty's research for some time.
    D. information emphasizing why the *N. vectensis*' genes are so interesting to biologists.

38. Given that all the choices are accurate, which one best helps the sentence introduce the main focus of the paragraph?
    F. No Change
    G. not the first invertebrate to have its genome sequenced and compared with that of humans.
    H. believed to be native to the east coast of North America.
    J. an aquatic animal of the phylum Cnidaria.

The <u>morphology, or the structure,</u> of a living creature, of *N. vectensis* is relatively basic. Tiny and translucent, they have a bulbous base, a long contracting column in the middle, and an oral disc at the top, which has a mouth ringed with two circles of tentacles.

However, <u>their complexity is not elementarily simple.</u> They are able to regenerate damaged and severed body parts within a series of days. Understanding the *N. vectensis* genetic regenerative capabilities is one of the first steps in improving human longevity.

39. Which choice makes the sentence most grammatically acceptable?

    A. **No Change**
    B. morphology, or the structure
    C. morphology or the structure,
    D. morphology or the structure

40. Which choice is least redundant in context?

    F. **No Change**
    G. the sophistication of the *N. vectensis* is complicated.
    H. their intricacy is more than rudimentary.
    J. *N. vectensis* are not so simple.

PASSAGE VI

My Cousin Nicola

My father and his two younger brothers emigrated from Italy to New York in the early 1970s. Only their older sister Lucia, who was already married, <u>clung</u> in
                                                                                41
their small home <u>town, this village</u> lies in the
                        42
shadow of Mount Vesuvius. Growing up in America, my cousins and I were as close as brothers and sisters, but we hardly <u>known</u> our family across the Atlantic.
                                    43
When I was a young child, my parents and I went to Italy to visit Aunt Lucia and her family for a week. I first met my cousin Nicola then. I remember that we were not only about the same age, but we also got along well. <u>Then</u> because
                  44

41. Which choice is clearest and most precise in context?

    A. **No Change**
    B. hovered
    C. remained behind
    D. held on

42. Which choice makes the sentence most grammatically acceptable?

    F. **No Change**
    G. town, it can be seen where it
    H. town it
    J. town that

43. Which choice makes the sentence most grammatically acceptable?

    A. **No Change**
    B. knew
    C. had knew
    D. been known

44. Which transition word is most logical in context?

    F. **No Change**
    G. And
    H. But
    J. Also

I being so young, I remember little else. I hadn't seen him again up until this last summer.

   Nicola decided that he wanted to join the Italian Air Force after finishing high school. Before beginning his service, though, he wanted to travel for a bit.

He had never been to America, even though so many of his relatives live here, but he had been to England already. When the rest of the cousins heard the news, they were ecstatic.

   Two weeks later, we picked Nicola up at JFK Airport. The moment I saw the acoustic guitar slung over his shoulder, I knew he and I would get along just fine. None of them plays an instrument, and I always thought that I was the only musician

in the family (even though some relatives have lovely singing voices). I was happy to find out I was wrong.

45. Which choice makes the sentence most grammatically acceptable?

   A. **No Change**
   B. I, who was
   C. I was
   D. I,

46. Given that all the choices are accurate, which one provides the most relevant information about Nicola's travel plans at this point in the essay?

   F. **No Change**
   G. He had never been to America, so he called my father and asked if he could come spend the summer with us in New York.
   H. He had never been to America, which is most easily reached from Italy by plane.
   J. Because it was expensive for his whole family to travel overseas, Nicola had never been to America before.

47. Which choice makes the sentence most grammatically acceptable?

   A. **No Change**
   B. us
   C. the Americans
   D. my American cousins

48. Which choice is least redundant in context?

   F. **No Change**
   G. in the family, which has at least 20 members that I know of.
   H. in the family.
   J. DELETE the underlined portion (ending the sentence with a period).

Throughout that summer, Nicola and I shared the gift of music. Taught to him as a child before she passed away in Italy, I was taught by him the Italian folk songs of our grandmother more importantly. On the night before Nicola returned to Italy, my father threw a big party for all of the relatives.

Nicola and I played the folk songs of our grandmother's country for the American side of our family. When we were done, my Uncle Vittorio had a tear in his eye. In the music and our singing, Nicola and I brought the beautiful country back to him.

49. Which choice makes the sentence most grammatically acceptable?

A. **No Change**
B. Teaching him as a child before she passed away, our grandmother in Italy more importantly taught to me many of the Italian folk songs.
C. Teaching him as a child, more importantly, by our grandmother in Italy, I was taught by him many Italian folk songs.
D. More importantly, however, he taught me many of the Italian folk songs our grandmother in Italy had taught him as a child before she passed away.

Question 50 asks about the preceding passage as a whole.

---

50. Suppose the writer's primary purpose had been to write a personal narrative that emphasizes the value of family. Would this passage accomplish this purpose?

F. Yes, because it shows how connecting with distant family can be meaningful.
G. Yes, because it shows how much closer the narrator is to Nicola than to his American cousins.
H. No, because the narrator and Nicola are not closely related.
J. No, because the passage does not mention any family members besides Nicola.

Mathematics Test

50 Minutes—45 Questions

Directions: Solve each problem, choose the correct answer, and then fill in the corresponding oval on your answer document.

Do not linger over problems that take too much time. Solve as many as you can; then return to the others in the time you have left for this test.

You may use a calculator on this test for any question you choose. However, some questions may be better solved without a calculator.

Note: Unless otherwise stated, you can assume:

1. Figures are NOT necessarily drawn to scale.
2. Geometric figures are two dimensional.
3. The term *line* indicates a straight line.
4. The term *average* indicates arithmetic mean.

1. For all nonzero values of x and y, which of the following expressions is equivalent to $-\dfrac{48x^3y^9}{6x^2y}$?

   A. $-8xy^8$
   B. $-8x^3y^9$
   C. $-8x^6y^{10}$
   D. $-54xy^8$

2. The degree measures of the 3 angles of the triangle shown are expressed in terms of x. What is the value of x?

   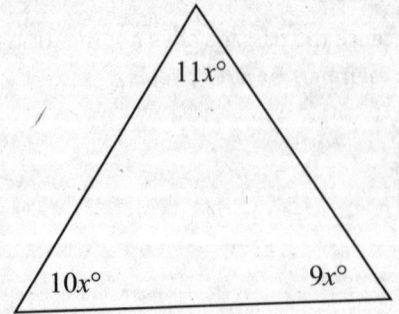

   F. 6
   G. 12
   H. 24
   J. 30

3. A 1,900-milliliter water cooler will be used to fill empty cups. Each full cup will contain 120 milliliters of water. This water cooler will fill at most how many cups full of water?

   A. 14
   B. 15
   C. 16
   D. 17

4. Of the 60 pieces played by a certain orchestra this year, 5% were composed after 1950. Of those pieces **not** composed after 1950, 20 were concertos. How many pieces that were **not** composed after 1950 were **not** concertos?

   F. 20
   G. 27
   H. 30
   J. 37

5. On his 18th birthday, Kurt opens a retirement account. Kurt begins by depositing $1,000. For each successive birthday until he turns 25, he deposits $100 less than the amount deposited for the previous birthday. This is the only money deposited into the account. What is the total amount of money Kurt will have deposited into the account up to and including his 25th birthday?

   A. 4,700
   B. 4,900
   C. 5,200
   D. 5,400

6. Which of the following matrices is equal to $\begin{bmatrix} 1 & -7 \\ -3 & 6 \end{bmatrix} + \begin{bmatrix} -5 & -4 \\ 2 & 9 \end{bmatrix}$?

   F. $\begin{bmatrix} -19 & -67 \\ 27 & 66 \end{bmatrix}$
   G. $\begin{bmatrix} -4 & -11 \\ -1 & 15 \end{bmatrix}$
   H. $\begin{bmatrix} -4 & -11 \\ -5 & 15 \end{bmatrix}$
   J. $\begin{bmatrix} 5 & -7 \\ -4 & 11 \end{bmatrix}$

7. Nick and Rusty are tarring a roof. They started with 10 gallons of tar. On the first day, Nick used $2\frac{1}{2}$ gallons of tar and Rusty used $\frac{3}{4}$ gallons of tar. How many gallons of tar were left when they completed their first day of tarring?

   A. $5\frac{3}{4}$
   B. $6\frac{1}{4}$
   C. $6\frac{3}{4}$
   D. $7\frac{1}{4}$

8. What is the slope of the line that passes through the points $(-10, 0)$ and $(0, -6)$?

   F. $-\frac{5}{3}$
   G. $-\frac{3}{5}$
   H. $\frac{3}{5}$
   J. $\frac{5}{3}$

9. The lengths of corresponding sides of 2 similar right triangles are in the ratio 5:7. The hypotenuse of the larger triangle is 84 inches long. How many inches long is the hypotenuse of the smaller triangle?

   A. 80
   B. 60
   C. 100
   D. 117.6

10. The hypotenuse of right triangle ABC is 18 feet. The cosine of $\angle A$ is $\frac{4}{5}$. How long, in feet, is $\overline{AC}$?

    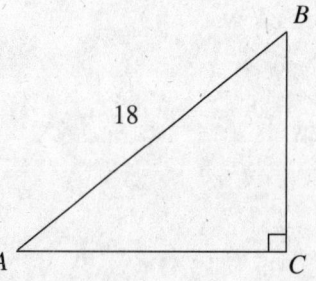

    F. 15.2
    G. 14.4
    H. 13.9
    J. 12.6

11. In rectangle ABCD, E is the midpoint of $\overline{CD}$. What is the length, in units, of $\overline{AD}$?

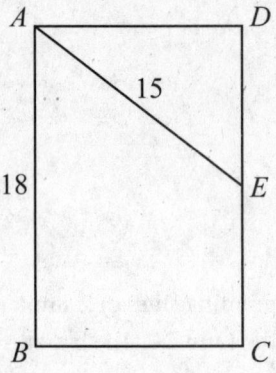

A. 9
B. 12
C. 18
D. 20

12. What is the sum of the 2 solutions of the equation $x^2 - x - 56 = 0$?

F. -56
G. 0
H. 1
J. 15

13. A ladybug stands in the bottom left corner of a chessboard. It moves at a rate of 2 squares per minute. It walks for 3 minutes up the chessboard and then turns and walks for 2 minutes to the right. If its starting position can be modeled by the coordinate point (0, 0), where each square on the chessboard represents one coordinate unit, at what point is the ladybug located after these two moves?

A. (4, 4)
B. (4, 6)
C. (6, 4)
D. (6, 6)

14. What value of x makes the equation $-\frac{1}{125} = -5^x$ true?

F. -3
G. 3
H. 25
J. 625

15. The equation $E = mc^2$ describes the relationship between energy, E; matter, m; and the speed of light, c. Which of the following gives c in terms of e and m?

    A. $\sqrt{\dfrac{E}{m}}$

    B. $\sqrt{\dfrac{m}{E}}$

    C. $\dfrac{E}{m}$

    D. $\dfrac{m}{E}$

16. On a certain afternoon, Mrs. McGrady receives a text notification every 14 minutes and an email notification every 21 minutes. At a certain instant, both notifications pop up at the same time. How many minutes elapse until both notifications next pop up at the same time?

    F. 7
    G. 35
    H. 42
    J. 294

17. The perimeter of a certain square is 60 inches. What is the area of this square, in square inches?

    A. 15
    B. 30
    C. 225
    D. 360

18. Every year at a factory, 90,000 tons of grain are required to make 150,000 tons of bread. How many tons of grain are required to produce 6,000 tons of bread?

    F. 3,600
    G. 10,000
    H. 25,000
    J. 36,000

19. Which of the following statements describes the total of the first n terms of the arithmetic sequence below?

    $$1, 3, 5, 7, 9, \ldots$$

    A. The total is always equal to 25 regardless of n.
    B. The total is always equal to $2n$.
    C. The total is always equal to $3n$.
    D. The total is always equal to n^2.

20. Meri read 96 pages in 2 hours and 40 minutes. What was Meri's average rate in pages per hour?

    F. 26
    G. 30
    H. 36
    J. 40

21. Among a group of 30 stray cats, 14 are male, 11 are orange, and 8 are both orange and male. How many of the 30 cats are neither orange nor male?

    A. 3
    B. 6
    C. 13
    D. 16

22. On his first four 100-point tests this quarter, a student has earned the following scores: 52, 70, 76, and 79. What score must the student earn on the fifth 100-point test in order to earn an average test grade of 75 for all five tests?

    F. 69
    G. 70
    H. 91
    J. 98

CONTINUED

Part 6
PRACTICE TESTS

23. A circle in the standard (x, y) coordinate plane is tangent to the x-axis at 4 and tangent to the y-axis at 4. Which of the following is an equation of the circle?

    A. $x^2 + y^2 = 4$
    B. $x^2 + y^2 = 16$
    C. $(x - 4)^2 + (y - 4)^2 = 16$
    D. $(x + 4)^2 + (y + 4)^2 = 16$

24. Set A contains 7 consecutive even integers. If the average of Set A's integers is 46, which of the following is the smallest integer of Set A?

    F. 36
    G. 38
    H. 40
    J. 42

25. A movie theater offers two types of membership plans for frequent viewers. Plan A costs $30 per month plus $5 per movie ticket. Plan B has no monthly fee but charges $8 per movie ticket. After how many movie tickets in a month will the costs of Plan A and Plan B be the same?

    A. 8
    B. 10
    C. 12
    D. 14

26. The radius of a circle is increased so that the radius of the new circle is triple that of the original circle. How many times larger is the area of the new circle than that of the original circle?

    F. $\frac{1}{3}$
    G. 3
    H. 6
    J. 9

27. If $f(x) = 2(x + 7)$, then $f(x + c) = $?

    A. $2(x + 7) + c$
    B. $2x + c + 7$
    C. $2x + c + 14$
    D. $2x + 2c + 14$

28. For real numbers x and y such that $-2 \leq x \leq 2$ and $y \geq 8$, the expression $\frac{x}{x - y}$ can have which of the following values?

    F. -1
    G. $\frac{1}{6}$
    H. $\frac{1}{2}$
    J. 1

29. If $f(x) = \frac{1}{3}x + 13$ and $g(x) = 3x^2 + 6x + 12$, which expression represents $f(g(x))$?

    A. $x^2 + 12x + 4$
    B. $x^2 + 2x + 17$
    C. $x^2 + 2x + 25$
    D. $x^2 + 2x + 54$

30. If $a = 6c + 7$ and $b = 3 - 2c$, which of the following expresses a in terms of b?

    F. $a = \frac{16 - b}{3}$
    G. $a = \frac{17 - b}{2}$
    H. $a = 16 - 3b$
    J. $a = 25 - 12b$

31. Erin hiked a small mountain over the course of a day. She began at 7 a.m. at an altitude of 4,000 feet. As she climbed the mountain, Erin climbed at a constant speed during each one-hour interval. She finished her hike back at 4,000 feet at 1 p.m. Erin's altitude, as a function of time, is shown in the following graph. Which graph best represents the absolute value of the velocity that Erin traveled, in vertical feet per hour?

(Note: Ignore acceleration and deceleration at the beginning and end of each one-hour interval.)

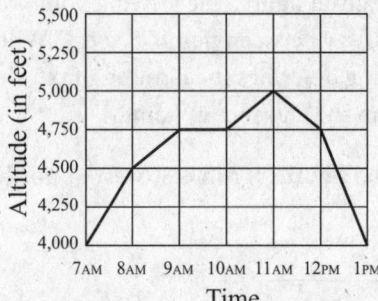

A.
B.
C.

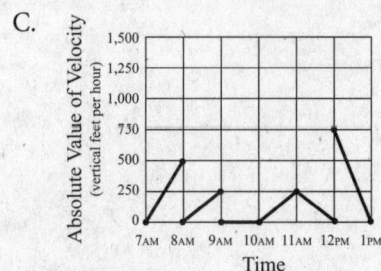

D.

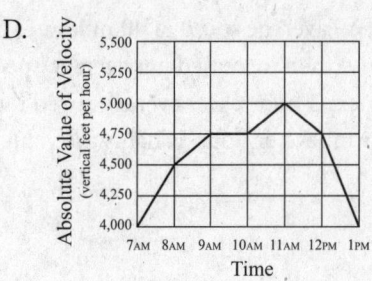

32. The function $f(x) = 0.5 \sin(2x)$ is graphed as shown over the domain $[0, 2\pi]$. What is the period of the function?

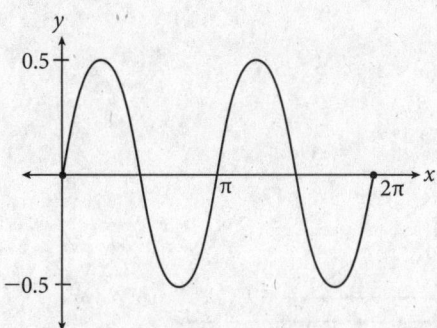

F. $\dfrac{\pi}{4}$

G. $\dfrac{\pi}{2}$

H. π

J. 2π

33. For all x, where $x \neq -1$, which of the following is equivalent to $\dfrac{x^2 - 5x - 6}{x + 1} + x + 1$?

A. $x - 5$

B. $2x - 5$

C. $\dfrac{2x - 5}{x + 1}$

D. $\dfrac{x^2 - 4x - 5}{x + 1}$

34. Assume m and n are nonzero integers such that $m > 0$ and $n < 0$. Which of the following *must* be negative?

F. $-n^m$

G. $-mn$

H. m^n

J. $n - m$

Part 6
PRACTICE TESTS

35. Liza drove at an average speed of 40 miles per hour for 2 hours and then increased her average speed by 25% for the next 3 hours. Her average speed for the 5 hours was r miles per hour. What is the value of r?

    A. 45
    B. 46
    C. 47
    D. 48

36. What is the perimeter of triangle ABC graphed in the coordinate plane?

    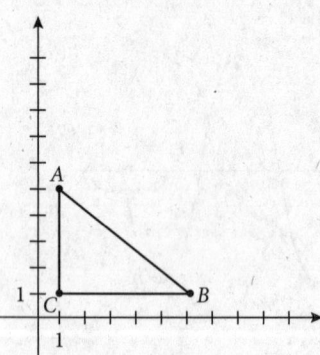

    F. $\sqrt{41}$
    G. 10
    H. $9 + \sqrt{41}$
    J. $10 + \sqrt{61}$

37. Which of the following is the solution set for all real numbers x such that $x - 2 < x - 5$?

    A. The empty set
    B. The set containing all negative real numbers
    C. The set containing all nonnegative real numbers
    D. 0

38. Triangle ABC is reflected across the y-axis to create the image $A'B'C'$ in the standard (x, y) coordinate plane. If the coordinates of point A are (v, w), what are the coordinates of point A'?

    F. $(v, -w)$
    G. $(-v, w)$
    H. $(-v, -w)$
    J. (w, v)

39. A zoo has the shape and dimensions, in yards, shown in the given figure. The viewing point for the giraffes is halfway between points B and F. Which of the following describes the location of the viewing point from the entrance at point A?

    (Note: The zoo's borders run east/west or north/south.)

    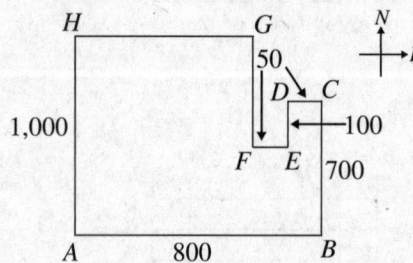

    A. 400 yards east and 350 yards north
    B. 400 yards east and 500 yards north
    C. 750 yards east and 300 yards north
    D. 750 yards east and 350 yards north

40. In complex numbers, where $i^2 = -1$, what is the simplified form of the expression $\dfrac{(2i + 2)^2}{(2i - 2)^2}$?

    F. $\dfrac{i}{4}$
    G. $\dfrac{4}{i}$
    H. 1
    J. -1

41. If $\log_7 7^{\sqrt{7}} = x$, then x is between which of the following pairs of consecutive integers?

    A. 0 and 1
    B. 2 and 3
    C. 4 and 5
    D. 6 and 7

42. If $f(x) = 3^{3x+3}$ and $g(x) = 27^{\left(\frac{2}{3}x - \frac{1}{3}\right)}$, for what value of x does the graph of $y = f(x)$ intersect the graph of $y = g(x)$?

    F. -4
    G. $-\frac{7}{4}$
    H. $-\frac{10}{7}$
    J. 2

43. The sides of an acute triangle measure 15, 13, and 11 inches. The measure of the largest angle A of the triangle is a solution to which of the following equations?

    A. $15^2 = 11^2 + 13^2 - 2(11)(13)\sin A$
    B. $15^2 = 11^2 + 13^2 - 2(11)(13)\cos A$
    C. $11^2 = 13^2 + 15^2 - 2(13)(15)\sin A$
    D. $11^2 = 13^2 + 15^2 - 2(13)(15)\cos A$

44. Which of the following sets of numbers has the property that the sum of any two numbers in the set is also a number in the set?

    I. The set of even integers
    II. The set of odd integers
    III. The set of prime numbers

    F. I only
    G. III only
    H. I and II only
    J. I and III only

45. If an integer is randomly chosen from the first 50 positive integers, what is the probability that an integer with a digit of 3 is selected?

    A. $\frac{1}{10}$
    B. $\frac{7}{25}$
    C. $\frac{3}{10}$
    D. $\frac{2}{5}$

Part 6
PRACTICE TESTS

Reading Test

40 Minutes—36 Questions

Directions: The Reading Test includes multiple passages. Each passage includes multiple questions. After reading each passage, choose the best answer and fill in the corresponding bubble on your answer sheet. You may review the passages as often as necessary.

Passage I

LITERARY NARRATIVE: This passage is adapted from the novel *My Doggie and I* by R.M. Ballantyne.

I possess a doggie—not a dog, observe, but a doggie. If he had been a dog I would not have presumed to intrude him on your notice. A dog is all very well in his way—one of the noblest of
5 animals, I admit, and preeminently fitted to be the companion of man, for he has an affectionate nature, which man demands, and a forgiving disposition, which man needs—but a dog, with all his noble qualities, is not to be compared to a
10 doggie.

Freely admit that you don't at once perceive the finer qualities, either mental or physical, of my doggie, partly owing to the circumstance that he is shapeless and hairy. The former quality is not
15 attractive, while the latter tends to veil the amiable expression of his countenance and the luster of his speaking eyes. But as you come to know him he grows upon you; your feelings are touched, your affections stirred, and your love is finally evoked.
20 As he resembles a doormat, or rather a scrap of a very ragged doormat, and has an amiable spirit, I have called him "Dumps." I should not be surprised if you did not perceive any connection here. You are not the first who has failed to see it; I never saw it
25 myself.

When I first met Dumps, he was scurrying towards me along a sequestered country lane. It was in the Dog Days. Dust lay thick on the road; the creature's legs were remarkably short though
30 active, and his hair being long he swept up the dust in clouds as he ran. He was yelping, and I observed that one or two stones appeared to be racing with, or after, him. The voice of an angry man also seemed to chase him, but the owner of the voice
35 was at the moment concealed by a turn in the lane, which was bordered by high stone walls.

Rabies, of course, flashed into my mind. I grasped my stick and drew close to the wall. The hairy whirlwind, if I may so call it, came wildly on,
40 but instead of passing me, or snapping at my legs as I had expected, it stopped and crawled towards me in a piteous, supplicating manner that at once disarmed me. If the creature had lain still, I should have been unable to distinguish its head from its
45 tail; but as one end of him whined, and the other wagged, I had no difficulty.

Stooping down with caution, I patted the end that whined, whereupon the end that wagged became violently demonstrative. Just then the owner
50 of the voice came round the corner. He was a big, rough fellow, in ragged garments, and armed with a thick stick, which he seemed about to fling at the little dog, when I checked him with a shout—

"You'd better not, my man, unless you want your
55 own head broken!"

You see, I am a pretty well-sized man myself, and, as I felt confidence in my strength, my stick, and the goodness of my cause, I was bold.

"What d'you mean by ill-treating the little dog?"
60 I demanded sternly, as I stepped up to the man.

"A man may do as he likes with his own, mayn't he?" answered the man, with a sulky scowl.

"A 'man' may do nothing of the sort," said I indignantly, for cruelty to dumb animals always
65 has the effect of inclining me to fight, though I am naturally of a peaceable disposition. "There is an Act of Parliament," I continued, "which goes by the honored name of Martin, and if you venture to infringe that Act I'll have you taken up and
70 prosecuted."

While I was speaking I observed a peculiar leer on the man's face, which I could not account for. He appeared, however, to have been affected by my threats, for he ceased to scowl, and assumed a
75 deferential air as he replied, "Well, sir, it do seem rather hard that a man's head should be broken for kindness."

"Kindness!" I exclaimed, in surprise.

"Ay, kindness, sir. That there animal loves me,
80 it do, like a brother, and the love is mutual. We've lived together now—off an' on—for the matter of six months. Well, I get employment in a factory about fifteen miles from here, in which no dogs is allowed. Of course, I can't give up that employment,
85 sir, can I? Neither can my doggie give up his master that he's so fond of, so I'm obliged to leave him in the charge of a friend, with strict orders to keep him locked up till I'm fairly gone. Well, off I goes, but he manages to escape and runs after me. Now,
90 what can a feller do but drive him home with sticks an' stones, though it do get to my heart to do it? But if he goes to the factory, he's sure to be shot, or dragged, or drowned, or something; so you see, sir, it's out of pure kindness I'm chasing him."

95 I confess that I felt somewhat doubtful of the truth of this story; but, in order to prevent any expression of my face betraying me, I stooped and patted the dog while the man spoke. It received my attentions with evident delight. A thought suddenly
100 flashed on me:

"Will you sell your little dog?" I asked.

1. The passage suggests that the narrator views his "doggie" as different than a "dog" in that his "doggie":

   A. may be less impressive at first sight.
   B. is older than a puppy but not a dog.
   C. is forgiving of humans, no matter what.
   D. is a majestic creature, both handsome and good-natured.

2. According to the passage, which of the following accurately describes Dumps?

   F. His eyes are dull, and his body is shapeless.
   G. Observers are quickly struck by his wise demeanor.
   H. He has kind-looking eyes that are often hidden behind his hair.
   J. His abundant hair gives him the appearance of a well-groomed carpet.

3. Based of the passage, Dumps's running in lines 26–46 can best be describe as:

   A. a leisurely pace, stopping to sniff the grass.
   B. desperate in manner, looking for help.
   C. compelled by immobilizing terror.
   D. fetching a stick as part of his favorite game.

4. As it is used in line 53, *checked* most nearly means:

   F. prevented.
   G. square patterned.
   H. verified.
   J. assaulted.

5. The author places the word *man* in quotes (line 63) in order to:

   A. compare the narrator's recognition of the dog owner's large size to his own stature.
   B. indicate that the narrator is ironically agreeing with the dog owner's assertion.
   C. signal that the narrator is attempting to start a violent fight with the dog owner despite his typically peaceful nature.
   D. imply that the narrator considers the dog owner inhumane regarding his treatment of animals.

Part 6
PRACTICE TESTS

6. The narrator most clearly indicates that the dog's owner stops scowling because:

    F. after listening to the narrator, he decides that the dog is unlikely to bite the narrator.
    G. he shifts his concern away from his dog's behavior to anxiety about being late for his job at the factory.
    H. he is concerned about the narrator's mention of breaking the law and wants to make a better impression.
    J. the narrator has stopped threatening to hit the dog with a stick and is offering to help.

7. The attitude of the narrator throughout the passage as a whole can best be described as:

    A. considerate and wanting the reader to think well of him.
    B. argumentative about how pets are commonly perceived.
    C. fearful that the reader will disagree with his unorthodox views.
    D. deceptive in order to gain a favorable opinion from the reader.

8. Based on the passage, the dog owner's explanation as to why chasing the dog with a stick is actually a demonstration of kindness can best be expressed by the statement:

    F. the dog belongs to the owner, so the owner is entitled to treat the dog as he chooses.
    G. the owner cannot take the dog to his factory job, but the dog escapes and runs after him so he must drive the dog back.
    H. dogs love running after thrown sticks, and this activity will provide the dog with exercise before the owner goes to work at the factory.
    J. the men who work at the factory have a record of mistreating animals, especially dogs.

9. It can most reasonably be inferred that the narrator doubts the dog owner's story because:

    A. the owner is so eager to sell the dog that the narrator doubts he really cares for it.
    B. the narrator cannot believe that a man with his temperament could hold down a job.
    C. it seems unlikely that the dog would actually be harmed as the owner claims.
    D. the owner seems to claim he loves the dog only after being threatened with legal prosecution.

Passage II

INFORMATIONAL: The following two passages were written in the early 1990s and present two viewpoints about the ways that the public responds to the results of scientific research.

Passage A

The way that people in present-day industrial societies think about science in the modern world actually tends to cultivate the very unscientific perception that science supplies us with unquestionable facts. If there is one unquestionable fact about science, it is that science is inherently uncertain. Research consists not so much of a search for truth as a search for some degree of certainty in an uncertain world. Every research study, every experiment, and every survey incorporates an extensive statistical analysis that is meant to be taken as qualifying the probability that the results are consistent and reproducible. Yet policy makers, public relations interests, and so-called experts in the popular media continue to treat the results of every latest study as if they were surefire truths.

History is filled with examples of the fallibility of scientific certainties. From the medieval monks who believed the sun orbited around Earth and the world was only 4,000 years old, to the early twentieth-century scientists who thought that X-rays were a hoax and that exploding a nuclear bomb would set off a chain reaction that would destroy all matter in the universe, it has been demonstrated repeatedly that science deals primarily with possibilities and is subject to the same prejudices as other kinds of opinions and beliefs. Yet statistics are complicated, and in our need to feel that we live in a universe of predictable certainties, it is tempting to place our faith in the oversimplified generalities of headlines and sound bites rather than the rigorous application of probabilities. Ironically, even though the intent of science is to expand the realm of human knowledge, an unfounded prejudice stemming from a desire for scientific constancy can actually discourage inquiry.

Science serves an important practical function; predictability and reproducibility are vital to making sure that our bridges remain standing, our nuclear power plants run smoothly, and our cars start in the morning so we can drive to work. When these practicalities become everyday occurrences, they tend to encourage a complacent faith in the reliability and consistency of science. Yet faced with so many simple conveniences, it is important to remember that we depend on the advance of science for our very survival. With progress expanding into those gray areas at the boundaries of scientific exploration, caution and prudence are just as important as open-mindedness and imagination. As technological advances engage increasingly complex moral questions within fields such as pharmaceutical developments, indefinite extension of life, and the potential for inconceivably potent weapons, an understanding of the limitations of science becomes just as important as an understanding of its strengths.

Passage B

While it is important that scientific knowledge be taken into consideration in significant matters of public interest, such consideration must be tempered with critical rigor. In the early days during the ascendance of science as a practical discipline, the public was inclined to view every new advance and discovery with a healthy skepticism. In the late 19th century, when Italian astronomer Giovanni Schiaparelli first detected seas and continents on the planet Mars, many people balked at the idea of Earth-like topography on the Red Planet. Just a few decades later, when fellow Italian astronomer Vincenzo Cerulli provided evidence that the seas and continents Schiaparelli observed were merely optical illusions, public disbelief proved to be entirely appropriate.

Since then, the historic tendency of the public to question scientific findings has unfortunately been lost. Yet in present-day industrial societies, and especially where public policy is at issue, response to scientific research needs more than ever to pursue an informed, critical viewpoint. Who performs a research study, what kind of study it is, what kinds of review and scrutiny it comes under, and what interests support it are every bit as important as a study's conclusions.

Studies of mass media and public policy reveal that, all too often, scientific findings presented to the public as objective and conclusive are actually funded at two or three degrees of removal by corporate or political interests with a specific agenda related to the outcome of those findings. For example, some critics question the issue of whether a study of the effectiveness of a new drug is more likely to produce favorable results when the study is funded by the pharmaceutical company that owns the drug patent. In cases where such findings conflict with the interests of the funding parties, analysts sometimes wonder if information was repressed, altered, or given a favorable public relations slant in order to de-emphasize dangerous side effects. Some critics of company-funded studies argue that the level of misrepresentation included in such studies borders on immoral.

Part of the problem grows from the public's willingness to place blind faith in the authority of science without an awareness of the interests that lie behind the research. Public officials then, in turn, may sometimes be too willing to bend in the face of public or private political pressure rather than pursuing the best interests of the constituency. Issues such as genetics, reproductive health, and preventative care are particularly fraught with political angst. Where the safety of individuals is at stake, a precautionary principle of allowing for unpredictable, unforeseen negative effects of technological advances should be pursued. It is the duty of active citizens in a free society to educate themselves about the real-world application of risk-assessment and statistical analysis, and to resist passive acceptance of the reassurances of self-styled scientific authorities. The most favorable approach to policy decisions based on realistic assessments finds a middle ground between the alarmism of political "Chicken Littles" and the recklessness of profit-seeking risk takers.

10. According to Passage A, policy makers consider the results of studies:

F. with concern.
G. as unquestioned truth.
H. as debatable.
J. as false.

11. According to Passage A, the author believes that trust should be placed in:

A. the generalized application of scientific headlines.
B. discouraging scientific inquiry.
C. viewing scientific results as possibly incorrect.
D. the predictable certainty of the universe.

12. As it is used in line 44, the word *complacent* most nearly means:

F. conceited.
G. dangerous.
H. unquestioned.
J. dissatisfied.

13. According to Passage B, which of the following is an example of a scientific discovery greeted with skepticism by the public?

A. A pharmaceutical study funded by drug patent holder
B. Schiaparelli's detection of continents on Mars
C. The statement that x-rays are a hoax
D. Darwin's theory of evolution

14. In the context of Passage B, the main point of the first paragraph (lines 59–74) is for the author to explain:

F. a new scientific hypothesis.
G. a historical contrast.
H. a public policy generality.
J. the underlying cause of an issue.

15. The author references "Chicken Littles" in line 123 in order to:

    A. point out that poultry are notoriously easy to frighten.
    B. praise politicians for their favorable policy decisions.
    C. accuse unrealistic policy makers of being motivated by financial gain.
    D. compare some politicians to scaremongers.

16. What can reasonably be inferred that the author of Passage A believes is the biggest obstacle to reaching the solution described by the author of Passage B in lines 115–120 ("It is the duty . . . authorities")?

    F. Policy makers are too willing to bend to public pressure when it comes to regulating scientific research.
    G. The interests that fund research are the same interests that stand to profit by favorable results, making impartiality impossible.
    H. Statistics are too abstract when compared with the concrete evidence of technological conveniences.
    J. Unanswered ethical questions are increasingly coming under scrutiny at the forefront of our most advanced scientific research.

17. Both passages refer to which of the following?

    A. Present-day industrial societies
    B. Early twentieth-century scientists
    C. Critics of company-funded studies
    D. Significant matters of public interest

18. According to Passage B, which of the following is an example of the "fallibility of scientific certainties" (lines 18–19) mentioned in Passage A?

    F. Medieval monks who believed the sun orbited around Earth
    G. People who balked at the idea of Earth-like topography on Mars
    H. Issues such as genetics, reproductive health, and preventative care
    J. Early twentieth-century scientists who thought that x-rays were a hoax

CONTINUED

Passage III

INFORMATIONAL: This passage is adapted from a Wikipedia article titled "Walter Scott."

Born in Edinburgh in 1771, the young Walter Scott survived a childhood bout of polio that would leave him lame in his right leg for the rest of his life. After studying law at Edinburgh University,
5 he followed in his father's footsteps and became a lawyer in his native Scotland. Beginning at age 25, he started dabbling in writing, first translating works from German, then moving on to poetry. In between these two phases of his literary career, he
10 published a three-volume set of collected Scottish ballads, *The Minstrelsy of the Scottish Border*. This was the first sign of his interest in Scotland and history in his writings.

After Scott had founded a printing press, his
15 poetry, beginning with *The Lay of the Last Minstrel* in 1805, brought him great fame. He published a number of other poems over the next ten years, including the 1810 popular *Lady of the Lake*, portions of which (translated into German) were
20 set to music by Franz Schubert. Another work from this time period, *Marmion*, produced some of Scott's most quoted (and often misattributed) lines, such as

  Oh! what a tangled web we weave
25 When first we practise to deceive!

In 1814, when Scott's press became embroiled in financial difficulties, he set out to write a successful (and profitable) work. The result was *Waverley*, a novel that did not name its author. It
30 was a tale of the last Jacobite rebellion in the United Kingdom, the "Forty-Five," and the novel met with considerable success. There followed a large number of novels in the next five years, each in the same general vein. Mindful of his reputation as a poet,
35 he maintained the anonymity he had begun with *Waverley*, always publishing the novels under a name such as "Author of Waverley" or attributed as "Tales of . . ." with no author. Even when it was clear that there would be no harm in coming out into the
40 open, he maintained the façade, apparently out of a sense of fun. During this time, the nickname "The Wizard of the North" was popularly applied to the mysterious best-selling writer. His identity as the author of the novels was widely rumored, and
45 in 1815, Scott was given the honour of dining with George, Prince Regent, who had wanted to meet the "Author of Waverley."

In 1820, Scott broke away from writing about Scotland with *Ivanhoe*, a historical romance set in
50 twelfth-century England. It, too, was a runaway success and, as he did with his debut novel, he unleashed a slew of books along the same lines. As his fame grew during this phase of his career, he was granted the title of Baronet, becoming Sir
55 Walter Scott. At this time, he organized the visit of King George IV to Scotland. When the King visited Edinburgh in 1822, the spectacular pageantry Scott had concocted to portray the King as a tubby reincarnation of Bonnie Prince
60 Charlie resulted in tartans and kilts becoming both fashionable and symbols of national identity.

Beginning in 1825, Scott fell into dire financial straits again, and his company nearly collapsed. That he was the author of the novels became general
65 knowledge at this time as well. Rather than declare bankruptcy, he placed his home, Abbotsford House, and income into a trust belonging to his creditors, and proceeded to write his way out of debt. He kept up his prodigious output of fiction (as well
70 as producing a biography of Napoleon Bonaparte) through 1831. By then his health was failing, and he died at Abbotsford in 1832. Though not solvent by then, his novels continued to sell, and he made good on his debts from beyond the grave. He was
75 buried in Dryburgh Abbey, fittingly nearby a large statue can be found of William Wallace—one of Scotland's great historical figures.

Scott was responsible for two major trends that carry on to this day. First, he popularized the
80 historical novel: an enormous number of imitators (and imitators of imitators) would appear in the nineteenth century. It is a measure of Scott's influence that Edinburgh's central railway station, opened in 1854, is called Waverley Station. Second,
85 his Scottish novels rehabilitated Highland culture after years in the shadows that followed the Jacobite rebellions.

Scott was also responsible, through a series of pseudonymous letters published by the *Edinburgh Weekly News* in 1826, for retaining the right of Scottish banks to issue their own banknotes, which is reflected to this day by his continued appearance on the front of all notes issued by the Bank of Scotland.

19. The main purpose of the passage is to:

    A. theorize about the ability of historical novels to successfully rehabilitate a country's culture.
    B. present the success of Sir Walter Scott's novels as being due to his decision to anonymously publish.
    C. introduce Sir Walter Scott's successful writing career and subsequent cultural impact.
    D. compare the success of Sir Walter Scott's writing career with his financial struggles.

20. It can most reasonably be inferred from the passage that the author believes that Sir Walter Scott is an important historical figure because:

    F. Scott degraded Scottish culture by parodying the wearing of tartans and kilts.
    G. the novels that Scott published were flattering of Scottish culture.
    H. the first serious analysis of Scotland's history was written by Scott.
    J. Scottish culture has been dismissed for many years until Scott's novels made it acceptable again.

21. The main purpose of the third paragraph (lines 14–25) is to:

    A. clarify how Sir Walter Scott was able to posthumously pay his debts.
    B. show that Sir Walter Scott was very interested in collaborating with Franz Schubert.
    C. explain how different Sir Walter Scott's first novel was from that of his later works.
    D. summarize the influence of the poetical works Sir Walter Scott published.

22. Based on the passage, the phrase *Wizard of the North* (line 42) is most likely meant to be read:

    F. literally; the anonymous author was a person with magical abilities from the North.
    G. literally; the anonymous author was a character from a Scottish fairy tale.
    H. figuratively; the anonymous author was a person highly skilled in writing about Scottish history.
    J. figuratively; the anonymous author had entranced a large audience with the history a Northern country.

23. Based on the passage, regarding his debts, Sir Walter Scott's attitude can best be described as:

    A. accepting.
    B. resentful.
    C. despondent.
    D. irresponsible.

24. As it is used in line 7, the phrase *started dabbling* most nearly refers to the way Sir Walter Scott:

    F. demonstrated short, superficial interest in a literary career.
    G. engaged in diverse acts of composition.
    H. proposed new interpretation of historical works.
    J. signaled an aptitude for advanced legal studies.

25. According to the passage, what event led directly to Sir Walter Scott becoming a popular writer during the 1800s?

   A. His father was a lawyer in Scotland.
   B. He founded a printing press.
   C. He published *The Lay of the Last Minstrel*.
   D. His work *Lady of the Lake* was translated into German.

26. Based on the passage, Sir Walter Scott's reputation after his death can most nearly be described as one that is:

   F. consistently favorable.
   G. increasingly popular.
   H. ultimately forgotten.
   J. deeply blemished.

27. The passage indicates that, compared to the novels initially written by Sir Walter Scott, the novels he published after his established anonymous success were:

   A. less formal: they focused on using more common language.
   B. less serious: they focused on love and relationships.
   C. more personal: they were meant to mirror Scott's own life.
   D. more factual: they were inspired by Scottish history.

Passage IV

INFORMATIONAL: The following is adapted from Wikipedia articles titled "Lemur" and "Ring-tailed Lemur."

Lemurs are part of a suborder of primates known as prosimians, and make up the infraorder Lemuriformes. This type of primate was the evolutionary predecessor of monkeys and apes
5 (simians). The term "lemur" is derived from the Latin word *lemures*, which means "spirits of the night." This likely refers to many lemurs' nocturnal behavior and their large, reflective eyes. It is generically used for the members of the four
10 lemuriform families, but it is also the genus of one of the lemuriform species. The two flying lemur species are not lemurs, nor are they even primates.

Lemurs are found naturally only on the island of Madagascar and some smaller surrounding islands,
15 including the Comoros (where it is likely they were introduced by humans). While they were displaced in the rest of the world by monkeys, apes, and other primates, the lemurs were safe from competition on Madagascar and differentiated into a number of
20 species. These range in size from the tiny 30-gram pygmy mouse lemur to the 10-kilogram indri. The larger species have all become extinct since humans settled on Madagascar, and since the early twentieth century the largest lemurs reach about seven
25 kilograms. Typically, the smaller lemurs are active at night (nocturnal), while the larger ones are active during the day (diurnal).

All lemurs are endangered species, due mainly to habitat destruction (deforestation) and hunting.
30 Although conservation efforts are underway, options are limited because of the lemurs' limited range and because Madagascar is desperately poor. Currently, there are approximately 32 living lemur species.

35 The ring-tailed lemur is a relatively large prosimian, belonging to the family Lemuridae. Ring-tailed lemurs are the only species within the genus *Lemur* and are found only on the island of Madagascar. Although threatened by habitat
40 destruction and therefore listed as vulnerable by the IUCN Red List, ring-tailed lemurs are the most

populous lemurs in zoos worldwide; they reproduce readily in captivity.

   Mostly grey with white underparts, ring-tailed
45 lemurs have slender frames; their narrow faces are white with black lozenge-shaped patches around the eyes and black vulpine muzzles. The lemurs' trademark, their long, bushy tails, are ringed in black and white. Like all lemurs, ring-tailed lemurs
50 have hind limbs longer than their forelimbs; their palms and soles are padded with soft, leathery skin and their fingers are slender and dexterous. On the second toe of their hind limbs, ring-tailed lemurs have claws specialized for grooming purposes.

55   The very young animals have blue eyes while the eyes of all adults are a striking yellow. Adults may reach a body length of 46 centimeters (18 inches) and a weight of 5.5 kilograms (12 pounds). Their tails are longer than their bodies, at up to 56
60 centimeters (22 inches) in length.

   Found in the southwest of Madagascar and ranging farther into highland areas than any other lemur, ring-tailed lemurs inhabit deciduous forests with grass floors or forests along riverbanks
65 (gallery forests); some may also inhabit dry, open brush where few trees grow. Ring-tailed lemurs are thought to require primary forest (that is, forests that have remained undisturbed by human activity) in order to survive; such forests are now being
70 cleared at a troubling rate.

   While primarily frugivores (fruit-eating), ring-tailed lemurs will also eat leaves, seeds, and the odd insect. Ring-tailed lemurs are diurnal and primarily arboreal animals, forming troops of up
75 to 25 individuals. Social hierarchies are determined by sex, with a distinct hierarchy for each gender; females tend to dominate the troop, while males will alternate between troops. Lemurs claim a sizable territory, which does not overlap with those
80 of other troops; up to 5.6 kilometers (3.5 miles) of this territory may be covered in a single day's foraging.

   Both vocal and olfactory signals are important to ring-tailed lemurs' communication: 15 distinct
85 vocalizations are used. A fatty substance is exuded from the lemurs' glands, which the lemurs run their tails through; this scent is used by both sexes to mark territory and to challenge would-be rivals amongst males. The males vigorously wave their
90 tails high in the air in an attempt to overpower the scent of others.

   The breeding season runs from April to June, with the female fertile period lasting for only a day. Gestation lasts for about 146 days, resulting in a
95 litter of either one or two. The young lemurs begin to eat solid food after two months and are fully weaned after five months.

28. The main purpose of the passage is to:

   F. relate lemurs' classification, location, status, and characteristics, specifically those of the ring-tailed lemur.

   G. compare the severity of the endangered status of lemurs to that of other primates.

   H. present a theory about why females tend to dominate the troops of ring-tailed lemurs.

   J. introduce ring-tailed lemurs as an example of a endangered species that has responded positively to conservation efforts.

29. The main idea of the third paragraph (lines 28–34) is that:

   A. ring-tailed lemurs experience challenges when breeding in captivity.

   B. wild lemur populations are limited to Madagascar and some of its surrounding islands.

   C. all lemurs are endangered because of deforestation and hunting.

   D. lemur communications include both vocal and olfactory signals.

30. In the passage, male ring-tailed lemurs waving their tails vigorously is cited as an example of:

   F. an olfactory communication.
   G. a vocal communication.
   H. a visual communication.
   J. a tactile communication.

31. As it is used in line 73, the word *odd* most nearly means:

   A. strange.
   B. unusual.
   C. eerie.
   D. occasional.

32. According to the passage, why are ring-tails the most populous species of lemurs in zoos?

   F. They inhabit deciduous forests, which make the lemurs' capture relatively easy.
   G. They have no difficulty giving birth in a zoo environment.
   H. Their attractive appearance makes them popular with patrons.
   J. Their eating preferences are easily accommodated.

33. Based on the passage, the author would most likely agree that the rate at which primary forests are being cleared is "troubling" (line 70) because:

   A. it is causing significant soil erosion in the lemurs' primary habitat.
   B. valuable hardwoods are being destroyed.
   C. lemurs' predators inhabit the cleared area.
   D. lemurs need to live in primary forests to survive.

34. The author most likely mentions "infraorder Lemuriformes" to:

   F. contend that simians are the evolutionary predecessors to prosimians.
   G. explain the evolutionary relationships between lemurs and other primates.
   H. indicate why flying lemur species are not considered to be lemurs.
   J. suggest that lemurs are predominantly nocturnal.

35. It can reasonably be inferred from the second paragraph (lines 13–27) that:

   A. the pygmy mouse lemur is diurnal.
   B. the larger species of lemur were hunted for their fur.
   C. the indri lemur is extinct.
   D. lemurs are descended from monkeys.

36. According to the passage, which animal would have blue eyes?

   F. A very young pygmy mouse lemur
   G. An adult indri lemur
   H. A very young ring-tailed lemur
   J. An adult ring-tailed lemur

Answer Key

English Test

1. A	11. A	21. C	31. A	41. C
2. F	12. H	22. J	32. H	42. J
3. B	13. D	23. B	33. B	43. B
4. H	14. H	24. F	34. G	44. H
5. D	15. A	25. D	35. C	45. C
6. F	16. F	26. F	36. F	46. G
7. B	17. B	27. C	37. D	47. D
8. H	18. H	28. F	38. G	48. H
9. B	19. C	29. C	39. B	49. D
10. F	20. H	30. F	40. J	50. F

Mathematics Test

1. A	10. G	19. D	28. G	37. A
2. F	11. B	20. H	29. B	38. G
3. B	12. H	21. C	30. H	39. C
4. J	13. B	22. J	31. A	40. J
5. C	14. F	23. C	32. H	41. B
6. G	15. A	24. H	33. B	42. F
7. C	16. H	25. B	34. J	43. B
8. G	17. C	26. J	35. B	44. F
9. B	18. F	27. D	36. H	45. B

Part 6
PRACTICE TESTS

Reading Test

1. A
2. H
3. B
4. F
5. D
6. H
7. A
8. G
9. D
10. G
11. C
12. H
13. B
14. G
15. D
16. H
17. A
18. G
19. C
20. J
21. D
22. J
23. A
24. G
25. C
26. F
27. B
28. F
29. C
30. F
31. D
32. G
33. D
34. G
35. C
36. H

Answers and Explanations

English Test

Thomas Edison, Tinfoil Cylinders, and Digital Music

1. A
Difficulty: Low
Category: Sentence Structure
Getting to the Answer: When a comma is placed in a sentence, be sure that it's serving a purpose. Comma usage follows specific rules, and knowing these rules will help you to determine when commas should, or should not, appear in a sentence. The sentence is correct as written, (A). Choice B incorrectly separates the prepositional phrase "at a breakneck pace" from the verb it describes. Choices C and D both incorrectly insert a comma between the subject "formats" and the verb phrase "have come and gone."

2. F
Difficulty: Low
Category: Organization
Getting to the Answer: This question asks for a transition between the first two sentences and the fourth sentence of the paragraph. The first two sentences deal with Edison's invention of tinfoil cylinders in the 1870s and the rapid rate of change in sound recording technology since then. The fourth describes the initial popularity of the cylinders and the subsequent popularity of other sound recording formats. The correct answer should link these sentences together. Choices G and H digress into discussions of other technological breakthroughs; eliminate. Choice J laments the "poor quality" of the tinfoil cylinders, but this sentiment contrasts inappropriately with the cylinders being described as a *miracle* at the beginning of the next sentence. Eliminate. Choice (F) refers to constant innovation and change in music recording technology, which links the ideas in sentences 1 and 2 with the specific details in sentence 4. It is correct.

3. B
Difficulty: Medium
Category: Development
Getting to the Answer: This sentence deals with the perception of the tinfoil cylinders as a *miracle*. Only choice (B) correctly conveys the idea that people referred to the cylinders as miracles. The other choices are incorrect because they create the nonsensical implication that people were talking to or getting the attention of the cylinders.

4. H
Difficulty: Medium
Category: Sentence Structure
Getting to the Answer: The *-ing* verb form cannot be the predicate (main) verb in a sentence. As written, this sentence is a fragment. Choice (H) corrects this by providing a predicate verb without introducing any additional errors. Choices G and J do not address the error.

5. D
Difficulty: Medium
Category: Agreement
Getting to the Answer: A compound subject joined with *and* requires a plural verb form. The subject here is "DJs and those," so the two verbs need to be in the plural form. Choice (D) is correct. Choice A uses two singular verbs. Choices B and C make one verb plural but not the other.

6. F
Difficulty: Medium
Category: Development
Getting to the Answer: When asked whether a writer should add a new sentence, note the context surrounding the proposed addition. The passage focuses on changes in music-playing technology, so the new information is relevant, adding an interesting detail. Eliminate H and J. The passage does not make an argument, so G is incorrect. Choice (F) correctly states the reason for making the addition.

7. B
Difficulty: High
Category: Style and Tone
Getting to the Answer: This question asks you for the answer that best matches the essay's tone. Consider that the essay often uses descriptive, playful, and extreme language, including phrases such as "breakneck pace," "kicked . . . to the curb," and "falling into oblivion." Choice (B) matches this tone and is correct. Choice A is similar to B but includes unnecessary

wording that adds nothing to the meaning; this makes it incorrect. Choice C is too vague and too neutral to match the established tone; it is incorrect. Choice D is pointlessly wordy and thus incorrect.

8. **H**
Difficulty: High
Category: Sentence Structure
Getting to the Answer: Colons are used to introduce or emphasize a brief definition, explanation, or list. The information after the underlined selection serves as an explanation of the "something different" to which the writer refers. Choice (H) correctly places a colon before this information. Choice F uses no punctuation, which makes the sentence ungrammatical and hard to understand. Choice G incorrectly uses a semicolon between an independent clause and an explanatory phrase. Choice J uses a comma, which makes the clause parenthetical; this is incorrect because the information is necessary for the sentence.

9. **B**
Difficulty: Medium
Category: Development
Getting to the Answer: The correct answer will do the best job of describing a smartphone's storage capabilities in an evocative way. Choice (B) specifically refers to "two years' worth" of music and even invites the reader to imagine listening to it *uninterrupted*; this vivid description is correct. The other choices are less evocative, using general wording such as *notable*, *impressive*, and *many* without implying a specific scenario.

10. **F**
Difficulty: Medium
Category: Organization
Getting to the Answer: Look for the portion of the essay that contains details related to this sentence. The first mention of the gramophone comes at the end of Paragraph 1, and the start of Paragraph 2 explains how the gramophone record was replaced by the vinyl phonograph record. The new sentence introduces the idea that the gramophone record's popularity did not last, so the beginning of Paragraph 2 is the most logical placement. Choice (F) is correct. Choice G awkwardly segues back to the gramophone after the topic has shifted to the vinyl phonograph record; it is incorrect. Choices H and J both come long after the essay has finished discussing the gramophone; both are incorrect.

Conservation Technology and the BearID Project

11. **A**
Difficulty: Medium
Category: Sentence Structure
Getting to the Answer: The underlined portion appears to be correct. Check the other choices to see which elements change in order to identify the issue tested; B, C, and D all include unnecessary commas that attempt to offset a parenthetical phrase. The underlined portion includes essential information and should not be offset with commas. Choice (A) is correct.

12. **H**
Difficulty: High
Category: Development
Getting to the Answer: When asked if a sentence should be added, consider the context. Adding the sentence at the end of the paragraph often indicates a conclusion for the paragraph or a transition to the next paragraph. The writer's new sentence accomplishes neither goal and should not be added. Eliminate choices F and G. Choice (H) is correct because the new sentence adds information about the creators of BearID, not about the use of technology in conservation. Choice J is incorrect because it offers an incorrect reason for rejecting the sentence.

13. **D**
Difficulty: Medium
Category: Precision
Getting to the Answer: The correct answer will be the best match to the context. The underlined portion is in a sentence that discusses how the scientists track bears. The next sentence discusses how the characteristics are unreliable as *identifiers*, so the prediction should be something like "identify." Choice (D) matches the prediction. Choice A doesn't match the context because the biologists are not trying to just watch the bears. Choice B doesn't match the context; *align* means "arrange in a straight line." Choice C doesn't match the context because it means to "connect" or "partner."

14. **H**
Difficulty: Medium
Category: Development
Getting to the Answer: The suggested revision seems more concise, but it eliminates important information from the passage. Therefore, the revision should not be made; eliminate F and G. (H) is correct.

The revision should not be made because the suggested phrase would lose the clarity and specificity of the original phrase. Choice J is incorrect because the passage discusses seasonal changes, not maturation.

15. **A**
Difficulty: Low
Category: Agreement
Getting to the Answer: The underlined portion includes a verb, so check that it agrees with the subject and aligns with the verb tense of other verbs in the essay. The subject is BearID, which is singular. Eliminate B. Before looking at the verb tense, be sure any changes made do not change the meaning of the phrase. Choices C and D both remove the concept of success included in the underlined phrase, which is essential to the original sentence. Eliminate C and D. Therefore, choice (A) is correct.

The Toughest Task in Sports

16. **F**
Difficulty: Medium
Category: Agreement
Getting to the Answer: The paragraph depicts lacrosse as an intense physical challenge. This matches (F). Choice G means to have strict rules, which is not the same thing as being physically demanding. Choice H refers to a simple, unluxurious way of life. This does not describe lacrosse. Emotions are not mentioned in the paragraph, so J is out too.

17. **B**
Difficulty: Medium
Category: Agreement
Getting to the Answer: A pronoun and a verb are underlined, so you have several things to check. First, make sure that the pronoun has a clear antecedent and is used consistently. Then, make sure that the verb agrees with its subject and is in the correct tense. The pronoun *they* correctly refers to the *players*, but this paragraph is written in the present tense (*is*, *possess*, *stands*, *sprint*). Choice A incorrectly uses the past tense, so the present tense *attempt* in (B) is correct. In the context of the paragraph, the author is not included among those playing lacrosse, so the pronoun *we* in choices C and D is incorrect.

18. **H**
Difficulty: Medium
Category: Sentence Structure
Getting to the Answer: Put modifiers directly next to what they are intended to modify. What is "on record?" The pitch is. Choice (H) is correct. All of the other choices separate the modifier from the word it is modifying.

19. **C**
Difficulty: High
Category: Sentence Structure
Getting to the Answer: If you're not sure how to approach a tough Punctuation question, try boiling the sentence down to its basics. Eliminate the introductory phrase and dependent clause from this sentence, and you're left with "the fastest crank shots on goal, can reach 110 mph." The subject is "crank shots," and the verb is "can reach." There should not be a comma separating them, so (C) is correct. The sentence should read "the fastest crank shots on goal can reach 110 mph." Choice A treats "the fastest crank shots on goal" as a nonessential phrase, but the sentence does not make sense without it. Choice B inserts two commas, treating "can" as nonessential. However, "can" is a necessary part of the verb phrase "can reach." Choice D places the comma between the two verbs in the verb phrase, which will never be correct.

20. **H**
Difficulty: Medium
Category: Agreement
Getting to the Answer: On the ACT, "that" and "which" refer to things, not people. Eliminate F and G. The word "who" is used when the relative pronoun is the subject of the clause. Since the baseball pitcher is the one performing the act of throwing, (H) is correct. Choice J is incorrect because "whom" is used when the relative pronoun is an object, not a subject.

21. **C**
Difficulty: Low
Category: Development
Getting to the Answer: When asked if a writer should add new information, first consider whether it is relevant. The information about the composition of the field is not relevant to the point about the difficulty of stopping a lacrosse shot. Eliminate A and B. Choice (C) accurately describes the irrelevance of the new information, so it is correct.

Part 6
PRACTICE TESTS

22. J
Difficulty: High
Category: Development
Getting to the Answer: When the answer choices are all single words with similar meanings, you are likely being tested on Precision. Choose the word that best describes the challenging job of the goalie. Choice F does not fit; to be *absurd* is to be ridiculous or meaningless, which does not characterize the goalie's job. Choice G is incorrect because a task cannot be *more* insurmountable. If it is *insurmountable*, the task cannot be done, and there is no way to have a higher degree of that failure. A *harrowing* event is deeply disturbing. While the goalie's job is challenging, we do not get a sense that the narrator is disturbed by the job. Rather, the narrator seems in awe of lacrosse goalies. Thus, H is incorrect. Choice (J), *difficult*, accurately describes the goalie's job.

23. B
Difficulty: Medium
Category: Organization
Getting to the Answer: When asked to connect paragraphs, be sure you read through them, considering both subject matter and tone. The keyword *however* in the second sentence of the final paragraph tells you that there must be some sort of contrast between the first and second sentences. The second sentence also refers to "Both of these endeavors," so the sentence in question should discuss both hitting a major league pitch and blocking a crank shot. Only (B) meets both of these requirements. Choices A and C do not provide the contrast indicated by "however." Additionally, the slang phrase "is tough" in A is inconsistent with the tone of the rest of the passage. Choice D does not mention hitting a major league pitch, making "Both of these endeavors" in the second sentence illogical.

24. F
Difficulty: Medium
Category: Agreement
Getting to the Answer: Get in the habit of matching verbs with their subjects. Since the subject of the underlined verb is the plural *Both*, this sentence is correct as written, (F). Choice G is singular and does not agree with the plural subject *Both*. Choice H changes the verb to the past tense, but the passage is in the present tense. Choice J uses the conditional *would have*, but there is nothing conditional or hypothetical about the writer's opinion.

25. D
Difficulty: Medium
Category: Development
Getting to the Answer: This type of question requires you to determine the main idea of the passage. In the first paragraph, the writer argues that stopping a crank shot in men's lacrosse is even tougher than taking a major league at-bat. All of the following details support this position. Choice (D) correctly identifies the main idea of the passage. The "Yes" choices A and B are both automatically out because the passage does not go into any depth about the strategies employed by baseball pitchers. Choice C is incorrect because the passage provides details in Paragraph 3 about the speeds achieved by baseball pitchers.

The Handsome Bean

26. F
Difficulty: Medium
Category: Development
Getting to the Answer: When you are asked to introduce the main subject of the passage, you need to read significantly beyond the question marker to gather some context. The first paragraph describes the Handsome Bean and mentions that it sponsors a local Little League team. The second paragraph describes how the author and the owner have become friends. The third paragraph mentions how the Handsome Bean features local music and poetry performances. Clearly this coffee shop is interested in more than just selling as much coffee as possible; it is actively involved in the community. Choice (F) is correct. Choices G, H, and J are incorrect because they do not explore the relationships between the coffee shop and its clientele.

27. C
Difficulty: Medium
Category: Development
Getting to the Answer: You are asked to create a transition to the last sentence of the paragraph. The previous sentence describes how the coffee shop is across the street from a Little League field. The last sentence says that the Handsome Bean often sponsors a team. Choices A, B, and D interrupt the logical flow between these ideas by inserting irrelevant information. Only (C) correctly maintains the connection between coffee and baseball.

28. F
Difficulty: Low
Category: Agreement
Getting to the Answer: Use context to determine the correct form of a verb. The verbs in this paragraph are in the present tense: *come, stay, is,* and *offers*. The present tense *sponsors* is correct, so no change is needed and (F) is correct. Choice G uses the past perfect *had sponsored*, incorrectly suggesting that the coffee shop sponsored the Little League team before another past event. Choices H and J use the past tense, which is inconsistent with the rest of the paragraph.

29. C
Difficulty: Medium
Category: Development
Getting to the Answer: You need to select the sentence that best introduces the topic of the paragraph, so you must read the paragraph to understand what you are introducing. The paragraph describes the antique décor of the coffee shop—its "century-old" counter, the photos from the 1920s and 1930s, and the "original tin ceiling." Choice (C) effectively leads into this description by explaining that the owner wants the shop to "look like it has been there for decades." Choice A focuses on the friendship between the writer and Mary; this doesn't connect with the details of the antique counter, old photos, and original tin ceiling. Choice B is too general; (C) provides a more specific reason for the decorating decisions Mary has made. Choice D explains that the space was vacant before the Handsome Bean opened, but this doesn't introduce the description of the décor.

30. F
Difficulty: Medium
Category: Style and Tone
Getting to the Answer: The tone of this passage is friendly and informal. Therefore, the figurative language "illustrates" is out of place. Eliminate H and J. Choice G is both vague (what "place?") and wordy ("clearly" is not needed). Therefore, (F) is correct.

31. A
Difficulty: High
Category: Development
Getting to the Answer: To answer this type of question, focus on the function of the sentence. What purpose does it serve in the paragraph? The sentence provides the reader with the information that the building is at least 70 years old. Therefore, if the sentence were deleted, you would lose information about the age of the building. Choice (A) is correct. Choice B refers to Mary and the writer etching their names in the ceiling, but the sentence does not describe this action. Choice C relates the sentence to the influence of the original owner; however, the time at which Harvey etched his name has little to do with his influence on Mary, the writer, or anyone else. Choice D treats the sentence as a description of the interior of the coffee shop, but no description of the ceiling is given in this sentence.

32. H
Difficulty: Medium
Category: Precision
Getting to the Answer: All of the answer choices have similar basic meanings but very different tones. The author has had a positive experience with the coffee shop performances, so eliminate F, which has a negative connotation. The author is not confused in any way, so G and J are also out. This leaves (H), which correctly describes a feeling of happy surprise.

33. B
Difficulty: Medium
Category: Sentence Structure
Getting to the Answer: Elements in a compound must be parallel in structure. The conjunction *or* creates a compound: students load up on caffeine "so they can cram all night . . . or finishing their research papers." Choice (B) makes the two verbs, *cram* and *finish*, parallel. Choices C and D do not address the parallelism error.

34. G
Difficulty: Medium
Category: Precision
Getting to the Answer: The word "take" implies obtaining something by force. Since the students are presumably not criminals and pay for their ice cream, eliminate H and J. Idiomatically, one stops by "to have" something, not "having" something, so (G) is correct.

35. C
Difficulty: Medium
Category: Organization
Getting to the Answer: When you need to add or move information, read the new information into the passage at the suggested points to determine its

Part 6
PRACTICE TESTS

logical placement. The paragraph describes different customers at the coffee shop throughout a typical day, starting in the morning and ending in the evening. This sentence talks about customers who come to the coffee shop in the afternoon, so it should be placed between Sentence 3, which talks about daytime customers, and Sentence 4, which describes customers in the evening. Choice (C) is correct. Choices A and D both place the information about customers in the afternoon after information about customers in the evening. Choice B places the information about afternoon customers before the information about morning customers.

A Starlet of the Genes

36. F
Difficulty: High
Category: Sentence Structure
Getting to the Answer: When the only thing unique about the answer choices is the commas, begin by identifying what information may be parenthetical, or nonessential, to the sentence. Both the title and the name of the biologist are essential information. Choice (F) is correct. Choice G has multiple unnecessary commas. Incorrect choice H puts the professor's name as parenthetical information and removes the subject from the sentence, creating a grammatical error. Choice J creates a modifier error; "associate biology professor" does not logically modify a year.

37. D
Difficulty: Medium
Category: Development
Getting to the Answer: This question asks you to identify why the underlined sentence is important to the paragraph. The sentence makes the connection that not only does the anemone share a significant percentage of genes with humans, but also that one of them is associated with a prominent human disease. The correct answer should touch on the importance of this observation. Eliminate choice A: neither a contrasting theory nor the anemone's evolution are mentioned. Eliminate choice B because the regenerative capabilities are not mentioned *previously*; they are introduced later in the passage. Eliminate choice C because, although the passage does indicate that the professor has been studying them for a while, the underlined sentence does not reference that. Choice (D) is correct.

38. G
Difficulty: Medium
Category: Development
Getting to the Answer: Since the question directs you to find the choice that best supports the paragraph's main idea, begin by identifying it. The next sentences state that "Initial comparisons... limited similarities" and that *N. vectensis* was "appealing to scientists". The paragraph ends by adding that the "shared genes are a breakthrough". The main idea is that researchers are excited about the anemone's genome because it matches the human genome better than have others. Choice (G) is the only choice to reference two key points of the main idea: genomes and comparisons. Choice F is incorrect because the sizes of the invertebrates are not mentioned, nor are they relevant to the main idea. Choices H and J are both incorrect because they include irrelevant details.

39. B
Difficulty: High
Category: Sentence Structure
Getting to the Answer: A glance at the answer choices shows that this question is testing parenthetical elements, specifically the correct usage of commas to offset nonessential information—if there is any. Check the sentence for any other punctuation. There is a comma between *creature* and *of N. vectensis*. Because the clause at the end of the sentence is not a complete idea, there must be another comma to offset nonessential information. Eliminate D and A. Choice (B) is correct because it accurately offsets the definition of the term *morphology*. Choice C is incorrect because it would illogically imply that morphology and structure are two separate nouns, rather than morphology being described as "the structure of a living creature".

40. J
Difficulty: Low
Category: Conciseness
Getting to the Answer: For questions testing redundancy, eliminate answer choices that repeat an idea. Choice F is incorrect because *complexity* and *not simple* communicate the same idea. Eliminate H for the same reason. Choice G is incorrect because *sophistication* and *complicated* have very similar meanings. Choice (J) is correct.

My Cousin Nicola

41. C
Difficulty: Medium
Category: Development
Getting to the Answer: Context always reveals the correct answer to Precision questions. The paragraph describes how Lucia did not immigrate to America with the rest of the family but stayed in Italy. As written, "clung" is too strong. It suggests that she stubbornly refused to go even when she asked, but you do not know anything about her background or motivations. Eliminate D for the same reason. Choice B describes what helicopters, not people, do, so it is also incorrect. Choice (C) is an action appropriate for a person and maintains the neutral tone, so it is a perfect fit.

42. J
Difficulty: Medium
Category: Sentence Structure
Getting to the Answer: Independent clauses should either be joined by a semicolon or connected with a coordinating conjunction; otherwise, one of the clauses must be made subordinate. As written, the sentence is a run-on. None of the answer choices offers a semicolon or a comma and a coordinating conjunction, but (J) makes the second clause dependent by using *that*. Choices G and H do not address the run-on error.

43. B
Difficulty: Medium
Category: Agreement
Getting to the Answer: Use context to determine the appropriate verb tense. This sentence uses the simple past tense *were* and doesn't indicate any time shift, so the simple past tense *knew* makes the most sense. Choice (B) is correct. Choice A uses the past participle *known* without the necessary helping verb *had*. Choice C incorrectly uses *had knew*; the correct form is *had known*. Choice D uses *been known* without the necessary helping verb *had*; it also creates a sentence that is grammatically incorrect.

44. H
Difficulty: Medium
Category: Organization
Getting to the Answer: Look at the relationship between the sentence before the underline and the sentence that contains the underline. The previous sentence discusses how the narrator remembers getting along well with Nicola. The sentence with the underline describes how the narrator remembers little else. This is a contrast between the things the narrator *does* remember with the things that he *does not*. Therefore, the contrast word in (H) is correct. Choices G and J are both continuation words, which do not match the context. Choice F describes a sequence in time, which also does not fit the scenario.

45. C
Difficulty: Medium
Category: Sentence Structure
Getting to the Answer: The *-ing* form can serve several functions. When used as a verb, it requires a helping verb to be correct. *I being* is grammatically incorrect, so eliminate A. Choice (C) substitutes the finite verb form *was*. Choice B creates a grammatically incorrect sentence, and D omits the verb altogether.

46. G
Difficulty: Medium
Category: Development
Getting to the Answer: The question asks you to select the sentence that gives the most relevant information about Nicola's travel plans. Only (G) does so; he intends to spend the summer with his family in New York. Choice F mentions Nicola's trip to England, which is out of scope. Choice H provides general information about the easiest way to travel from Italy to America, but it doesn't tell you anything about Nicola's specific plans to visit America. Choice J also focuses on the past, explaining why Nicola had not previously come to America; this doesn't match the question stem's request for information about Nicola's travel plans.

47. D
Difficulty: High
Category: Agreement
Getting to the Answer: When a pronoun is underlined, first determine to what or whom it refers. In this case, the reference is unclear. The last plural noun is *musicians*, but that refers to the narrator and Nicola, who do play instruments. Eliminate A. Choice B clearly refers to the narrator and Nicola, so it should also be eliminated. Choice C is ambiguous: to which Americans does the sentence refer? Choice (D) correctly identifies the group mentioned earlier in the paragraph: the narrator's American cousins.

Part 6
PRACTICE TESTS

48. H
Difficulty: Medium
Category: Conciseness
Getting to the Answer: The shortest answer isn't always correct—J omits a phrase necessary for the rest of the sentence to make sense. Choices F and G include information irrelevant to the topic of the writer meeting Nicola. That leaves (H), which eliminates the irrelevant information without distorting the logic of the sentence.

49. D
Difficulty: Medium
Category: Agreement
Getting to the Answer: As a general rule, descriptive phrases modify the nouns that immediately follow them. As written, this sentence tells us that *I* was "Taught to him . . . before she passed away in Italy." Choice A is incorrect. Choice (D) is the most concise and logical version of this sentence. Choice B incorrectly suggests that the grandmother, not Nicola, taught the songs to the writer. Choice C is garbled; the introductory phrase makes it sound like the writer taught the songs to Nicola, but the main clause says that Nicola taught the author the songs.

50. F
Difficulty: Medium
Category: Development
Getting to the Answer: When asked about the purpose of the passage as a whole, consider its topic and tone. The narrator describes a personal experience getting to know his cousin from Italy. The tone is positive, emphasizing their similarities and ending with a scene in which family members are touched emotionally by the singing of family folk songs. Thus, the passage accomplishes the stated purpose; eliminate H and J. Choice G is a distortion; the differences between Nicola and the narrator's American cousins are not the reason the essay accomplishes the stated purpose. Thus, (F) is correct.

Mathematics Test

1. A
Difficulty: Low
Category: Number and Quantity
Getting to the Answer: Simplify this expression one piece at a time. First, divide -48 by 6 to obtain -8. Next, reduce the exponents. Remember that $\frac{x^a}{x^b} = x^{a-b}$. In other words, when you have one exponent divided by another, you subtract the exponents. Applying this rule to the *x* terms gives $\frac{x^3}{x^2} = x^1 = x$. Using similar logic, the *y* terms become $\frac{y^9}{y} = \frac{y^9}{y^1} = y^8$. Put everything together to obtain $-8xy^8$. Choice (A) is correct.

2. F
Difficulty: Low
Category: Geometry
Getting to the Answer: Recall that all of the interior angles of a triangle sum to 180 degrees. Here, $10x + 11x + 9x = 180$. This simplifies to $30x = 180$, or $x = 6$. Choice (F) is correct.

3. B
Difficulty: Low
Category: Number and Quantity
Getting to the Answer: To find out how many 120 milliliter cups a 1,900-milliliter water cooler can fill, divide 1,900 by 120: $\frac{1,900}{120} \cong 15.83$. Be careful! If about 15.83 cups can be filled, then the greatest number of complete cups that can be filled is 15, not 16. Choice (B) is correct. In this context, rounding up would be a mistake.

4. J
Difficulty: Medium
Category: Number and Quantity
Getting to the Answer: Work through the given information one step at a time. The question says that 5% of the 60 total pieces were composed after 1950. This means that $60(0.05) = 3$ pieces were composed after 1950. Of the 57 pieces that were **not** composed after 1950, 20 are concertos. The question asks how many pieces from this group were **not** concertos, which is $57 - 20 = 37$. Choice (J) is correct.

Practice Test 2
Answers and Explanations

5. C
Difficulty: Hard
Category: Number and Quantity
Getting to the Answer: Work through the scenario step by step. On his 18th birthday, Kurt deposits $1,000. Each birthday after that, he deposits $100 less. It may help to make a table to visualize what is happening.

Birthday	Deposit
18	$1,000
19	$900
20	$800
21	$700
22	$600
23	$500
24	$400
25	$300

Add up all of the money in the right column to obtain $5,200. Choice (C) is correct.

6. G
Difficulty: Medium
Category: Number and Quantity
Getting to the Answer: To add two matrices, add componentwise. In other words, add the two numbers in the top left position of each matrix, the two numbers in the top right position of each matrix, and so on.

$$\begin{bmatrix} 1 & -7 \\ -3 & 6 \end{bmatrix} + \begin{bmatrix} -5 & -4 \\ 2 & 9 \end{bmatrix} = \begin{bmatrix} 1-5 & -7-4 \\ -3+2 & 6+9 \end{bmatrix}$$
$$= \begin{bmatrix} -4 & -11 \\ -1 & 15 \end{bmatrix}$$

Choice (G) is correct.

Notice that you do not need to add all the numbers in the matrices to arrive at the correct answer. Since all the numbers in the bottom left are different in the answers, you only need to add those to find the correct one: $-3 + 2 = -1$. This appears in choice (G) only.

7. C
Difficulty: Low
Category: Number and Quantity
Getting to the Answer: To determine how many gallons of tar are left after the first day, subtract the amount that Nick and Rusty use from the starting amount of 10 gallons. Remember that you need a common denominator when subtracting fractions.

$$10 - 2\frac{1}{2} - \frac{3}{4}$$
$$= \frac{10}{1} - \frac{5}{2} - \frac{3}{4}$$
$$= \frac{40}{4} - \frac{10}{4} - \frac{3}{4}$$
$$= \frac{27}{4}$$
$$= 6\frac{3}{4}$$

Choice (C) is correct.

Alternatively, you could convert $2\frac{1}{2}$ into 2.5 and $\frac{3}{4}$ into 0.75 and subtract these numbers from 10: $10 - 2.5 - 0.75 = 6.75$. Since 6.75 is equivalent to $6\frac{3}{4}$, again (C) is correct.

8. G
Difficulty: Low
Category: Algebra
Getting to the Answer: Use the slope formula to find the slope of the line given two points:

$$m = \frac{y_2 - y_1}{x_2 - x_1}$$
$$= \frac{-6 - 0}{0 - (-10)}$$
$$= -\frac{6}{10}$$
$$= -\frac{3}{5}$$

Choice (G) is correct.

Part 6
PRACTICE TESTS

9. B
Difficulty: Medium
Category: Geometry
Getting to the Answer: Similar triangles have proportional corresponding sides. The side ratio between the two triangles is given as 5:7, and the hypotenuse of the larger triangle is given as 84. Set up a proportion to find the hypotenuse of the smaller triangle.

$$\frac{5}{7} = \frac{x}{84}$$
$$7x = 420$$
$$x = 60$$

Choice (B) is correct.

10. G
Difficulty: Medium
Category: Geometry
Getting to the Answer: Most of the trigonometry on the ACT revolves around the definitions of sine, cosine, and tangent. The acronym SOHCAHTOA tells you that cosine is adjacent over hypotenuse. Let x be the length of $\overline{AC}$, the adjacent side.

$$\cos A = \frac{\text{adjacent}}{\text{hypotenuse}}$$
$$\frac{4}{5} = \frac{x}{18}$$
$$5x = 72$$
$$x = 14.4$$

Choice (G) is correct.

11. B
Difficulty: Medium
Category: Geometry
Getting to the Answer: Since the figure is a rectangle, $\overline{AB}$ is the same as side $\overline{CD}$. Point E is the midpoint of $\overline{CD}$, so $\overline{ED} = 9$. To find the missing length $\overline{AD}$, use the Pythagorean theorem.

$$a^2 + b^2 = c^2$$
$$9^2 + b^2 = 15^2$$
$$81 + b^2 = 225$$
$$b^2 = 144$$
$$b = 12$$

Choice (B) is correct.

Alternatively, if you recognized that 9-12-15 is a multiple of the common Pythagorean triple 3-4-5, you could have arrived at this result even faster.

12. H
Difficulty: Medium
Category: Algebra
Getting to the Answer: Whenever you see a quadratic equation, determine if you can factor it. Look for two numbers that multiply to the constant term (-56) and add to the coefficient of the x term (-1). The pair -8 and 7 works perfectly.

$$(x - 8)(x + 7) = 0$$

Find the solutions by setting each expression in parentheses equal to 0 and solving.

$$x - 8 = 0 \quad x + 7 = 0$$
$$x = 8 \quad x = -7$$

The question asks for the sum of the solutions, which is $8 + (-7) = 1$. Choice (H) is correct.

13. B
Difficulty: High
Category: Geometry
Getting to the Answer: Right now, the ladybug is located at (0, 0). It walks for 3 minutes in a vertical direction, and its speed is 2 squares per minute. This means that it travels $3(2) = 6$ squares vertically. Using similar logic, it travels $2(2) = 4$ squares to the right. In the coordinate system, x represents movement to the left or right and y represents movement up or down. Therefore, the ladybug stops at point (4, 6). Choice (B) is correct.

14. F
Difficulty: Medium
Category: Number and Quantity
Getting to the Answer: Perhaps the simplest way to approach this question is to plug each answer choice in for x and use your calculator to see which one makes -5^x equal to $-\frac{1}{125}$. Doing so reveals that (F) is correct.

You can also solve for x using algebra by rewriting $\frac{1}{125}$ in base 5.

$$-\frac{1}{125} = -5^x$$
$$\frac{1}{125} = 5^x$$
$$\frac{1}{5^3} = 5^x$$
$$5^{-3} = 5^x$$
$$-3 = x$$

Again, (F) is correct.

15. A
Difficulty: Medium
Category: Algebra
Getting to the Answer: Use inverse operations to isolate for c in the given equation.

$$E = mc^2$$
$$\frac{E}{m} = c^2$$
$$\sqrt{\frac{E}{m}} = c$$

Choice (A) is correct.

16. H
Difficulty: Medium
Category: Number and Quantity
Getting to the Answer: Text notifications pop up every 14 minutes, and email notifications pop up every 21 minutes. List out when the next few notifications occur to help visualize the situation.

$$\text{Text} = 14, 28, 42, 56, \ldots$$
$$\text{Email} = 21, 42, 63, \ldots$$

The two notifications will pop up at the same time every 42 minutes. Choice (H) is correct. This is equivalent to finding the least common multiple of 14 and 21.

17. C
Difficulty: Low
Category: Geometry
Getting to the Answer: To find the perimeter of a shape, add up all of its sides. In a square, all sides are equal, so call a side x. You are told that the perimeter of the square is 60 inches, so $x + x + x + x = 60$, or $4x = 60$. Solving for x gives $x = 15$. The area of a square is side times side, so the area of this square is $15 \times 15 = 225$ square inches. Choice (C) is correct.

18. F
Difficulty: Medium
Category: Number and Quantity
Getting to the Answer: Set up a proportion relating grain to bread. Solve for x, the tons of grain required to produce 6,000 tons of bread.

$$\frac{90{,}000 \text{ grain}}{150{,}000 \text{ bread}} = \frac{x \text{ grain}}{6{,}000 \text{ bread}}$$
$$\frac{9}{15} = \frac{x}{6{,}000}$$
$$54{,}000 = 15x$$
$$3{,}600 = x$$

Choice (F) is correct.

19. D
Difficulty: Medium
Category: Functions
Getting to the Answer: Picking Numbers works well here. Test the sum for $n = 2, 3, 4,$ and 5 terms to see if a pattern emerges. If $n = 2$, the sum is $1 + 3 = 4$. If $n = 3$, the sum is $1 + 3 + 5 = 9$. If $n = 4$, the sum is $1 + 3 + 5 + 7 = 16$. If $n = 5$, the sum is $1 + 3 + 5 + 7 + 9 = 25$. For this particular sequence, the sum is equal to the square of n. Therefore, the correct answer is (D).

20. H
Difficulty: Medium
Category: Number and Quantity
Getting to the Answer: The word "per" means "divide." To get Meri's rate in pages per hour, take the 96 pages and divide by the time, in hours. The time is given as 2 hours and 40 minutes. Forty minutes is $\frac{2}{3}$ of an hour (40 minutes divided by 60 minutes), so you can express Meri's time as $2\frac{2}{3}$ hours, or $\frac{8}{3}$ hours:

$$\frac{96 \text{ pages}}{\frac{8}{3} \text{ hour}} = 96\left(\frac{3}{8}\right)$$
$$= \frac{288}{8}$$
$$= 36$$

Choice (H) is correct.

Part 6
PRACTICE TESTS

21. C
Difficulty: Medium
Category: Statistics and Probability
Getting to the Answer: Questions that involve overlapping sets can be approached by making a table. Let the rows represent Male or Not Male and the columns denote Orange or Not Orange. The totals of each row and column are shown on the margins. The grand total of 30 is in the bottom right corner.

	Orange	Not Orange	Total
Male	8		14
Not Male			
Total	11		30

Now fill in the blanks of the table. One way is to start with the rows to find that there are 6 Not Orange and Male cats (14 − 8), and then there are a total of 19 Not Orange cats (30 − 11). Now fill in the needed column, 6 Not Orange Male cats plus x Not Orange Not Male cats equals a total of 19 Not Orange cats. Solve for an answer of 13 cats that are neither orange nor male. Choice (C) is correct. You could also fill in columns first and then the row needed. The complete table is:

	Orange	Not Orange	Total
Male	8	6	14
Not Male	3	13	16
Total	11	19	30

If you prefer not to use a table, you can get the answer by subtracting the number of cats that are both orange and male (8) from the sum of male (14) and orange cats (11): 14 + 11 − 8 = 17. Then subtract this number from the total number of cats: 30 − 17 = 13. Again, (C) is correct.

22. J
Difficulty: Medium
Category: Statistics and Probability
Getting to the Answer: The average is equal to the sum of the terms divided by the number of terms. Let x be the fifth test score. Plug the given information into the average formula,

average = $\frac{\text{sum of terms}}{\text{number of terms}}$, and solve for x:

$$75 = \frac{52 + 70 + 76 + 79 + x}{5}$$

$$75 = \frac{277 + x}{5}$$

$$375 = 277 + x$$

$$98 = x$$

Choice (J) is correct.

23. C
Difficulty: High
Category: Geometry
Getting to the Answer: The word "tangent" means "touching." If the circle is tangent to the y-axis at 4, it touches the y-axis at $y = 4$. Similarly, if the circle is tangent to the x-axis at 4, it touches the x-axis at $x = 4$. Drawing a sketch to visualize the situation could be helpful.

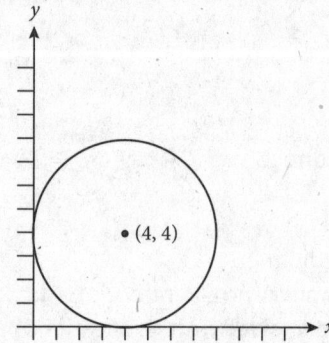

According to the sketch, the center of the circle is at (4, 4), and the radius is 4. In the standard form of a circle, $(x − h)^2 + (y − k)^2 = r^2$, the center is at (h, k), and the radius is r. Plug in the information from the sketch to obtain $(x − 4)^2 + (y − 4)^2 = 4^2$, or $(x − 4)^2 + (y − 4)^2 = 16$. Choice (C) is correct.

24. H
Difficulty: Medium
Category: Statistics and Probability
Getting to the Answer: Because the integers in Set A are consecutive, their average must equal their median. In a set of 7 integers, the median is the fourth term. To find the smallest term, count backward from 46: 46, 44, 42, 40. Choice (H) is correct.

You could also Backsolve. Starting with (H), if 40 is the smallest integer of Set A, then the next six consecutive integers must be 42, 44, 46, 48, 50, and 52. Since for

746

consecutive integers the average is the same as the median, the average of these 7 integers is 46. This matches the information in the question. Again, (H) is correct.

25. B
Difficulty: Medium
Category: Algebra
Getting to the Answer: Create equations to model the situation. Let x represent the number of movie tickets. Plan A costs $30 per month plus $5 per ticket, so it costs $30 + 5x$ dollars. Plan B simply charges $8 per movie ticket, so it can be represented by $8x$ dollars. The question asks when the costs of Plan A and Plan B will be the same, so set the two equations equal to each other and solve for x:

$$30 + 5x = 8x$$
$$30 = 3x$$
$$10 = x$$

Choice (B) is correct.

26. J
Difficulty: Medium
Category: Geometry
Getting to the Answer: The area of a circle is $A = \pi r^2$, where r represents the radius. Let x represent the radius of the original circle. This circle has an area of $A = \pi x^2$. Let $3x$ represent the radius of the new larger circle. It has an area of $A = \pi(3x)^2 = \pi(9x^2) = 9\pi x^2$.

Now, divide the two areas to find out how many times larger the area of the new circle is compared to the area of the original circle.

$$\frac{\text{area of new circle}}{\text{area of original circle}} = \frac{9\pi x^2}{\pi x^2} = 9$$

Choice (J) is correct.

27. D
Difficulty: Medium
Category: Functions
Getting to the Answer: To solve this question with the notation of $f(x + c)$, replace x with $x + c$ in the function f.

$$f(x + c) = 2((x + c) + 7)$$
$$= 2(x + c + 7)$$
$$= 2x + 2c + 14$$

Choice (D) is correct.

28. G
Difficulty: High
Category: Number and Quantity
Getting to the Answer: One way to answer this question is to use the given constraints on x and y to construct a range of possible values for the expression $\frac{x}{x - y}$. Begin by testing the "extreme" points. If $x = -2$ and $y = 8$, then $\frac{x}{x-y} = \frac{-2}{-2-8} = \frac{-2}{-10} = \frac{1}{5}$. If $x = 2$ and $y = 8$, then the expression becomes $\frac{2}{2-8} = \frac{2}{-6} = -\frac{1}{3}$. Since $y \geq 8$ and you are subtracting y in the denominator, a larger y value will yield a number smaller than $\frac{1}{5}$ and larger than $-\frac{1}{3}$. For example, if $x = 2$ and $y = 9$, then $\frac{x}{x-y} = \frac{2}{2-9} = -\frac{2}{7}$. Therefore, the correct answer will be between the values of $-\frac{1}{3}$ and $\frac{1}{5}$. The only answer choice with this property is (G), $\frac{1}{6}$.

To further convince yourself, you can plug two numbers within the question's constraints, $x = -2$ and $y = 10$, into the expression $\frac{x}{x-y}$ to get $\frac{1}{6}$.

29. B
Difficulty: Medium
Category: Functions
Getting to the Answer: With nested functions, work from the inside out. Substitute the entire expression for $g(x)$ for x in the function f and simplify:

$$f(g(x)) = \frac{1}{3}(3x^2 + 6x + 12) + 13$$
$$= x^2 + 2x + 4 + 13$$
$$= x^2 + 2x + 17$$

Choice (B) is correct.

30. H
Difficulty: High
Category: Algebra
Getting to the Answer: The phrase "a in terms of b" means that you are looking for the value of a and that b terms will appear in your answer. Both equations have a c term, so you can isolate for c in one equation and then substitute it into the other equation.

Begin by rearranging the second equation to get c in terms of b.

$$b = 3 - 2c$$
$$b + 2c = 3$$
$$2c = 3 - b$$
$$c = \frac{3-b}{2}$$

Now substitute this value of c into the first equation.

$$a = 6c + 7$$
$$a = 6\left(\frac{3-b}{2}\right) + 7$$
$$a = 3(3-b) + 7$$
$$a = 9 - 3b + 7$$
$$a = 16 - 3b$$

Choice (H) is correct.

31. A
Difficulty: Medium
Category: Functions
Getting to the Answer: The question states that during each one-hour interval, Erin traveled at a constant speed. Speed is the slope of each one-hour interval. Therefore, the line showing her speed should remain constant (horizontal) within each one-hour interval. The only graph that does this is (A). All other graphs show a change in speed during each interval, which suggests an acceleration or deceleration. These are movements at speeds that are not constant.

32. H
Difficulty: Medium
Category: Functions
Getting to the Answer: The *period* of a repeating function is the distance along the *x*-axis required for the function to complete one full cycle. For a sine curve, this means one full wave (one up "bump" and one down "bump"). This happens between 0 and π, which means the period is π. Choice (H) is correct.

33. B
Difficulty: Medium
Category: Algebra
Getting to the Answer: To simplify the given expression, look for factors in the fraction term that will cancel. Use the denominator as a hint as to how to factor the numerator. Note that you cannot simply cancel the $x + 1$ in the denominator with the $x + 1$ at the end of the expression.

$$\frac{x^2 - 5x - 6}{x+1} + x + 1 = \frac{(x+1)(x-6)}{x+1} + x + 1$$
$$= x - 6 + x + 1$$
$$= 2x - 5$$

Choice (B) is correct.

34. J
Difficulty: High
Category: Number and Quantity
Getting to the Answer: The notation $m > 0$ means that m is a positive number. Similarly, $n < 0$ means that n is a negative number. Pick numbers for m and n and plug them into each answer choice to decide whether the expression must be positive or negative. Keep in mind that m and n can be even or odd.

First, let $m = 2$ and $n = -2$. Plug these values into the answer choices and eliminate the ones that do not yield a negative result.

F: $\quad -n^m = -(-2)^2$
$\quad\quad\quad = -(4)$
$\quad\quad\quad = -4$
$\quad\quad$ Keep.

G: $\quad -mn = -(2)(-2)$
$\quad\quad\quad = 4$
$\quad\quad$ Eliminate.

H: $\quad m^n = 2^{-2}$
$\quad\quad\quad = \frac{1}{2^2}$
$\quad\quad\quad = \frac{1}{4}$
$\quad\quad$ Eliminate.

(J): $\quad n - m = -2 - 2$
$\quad\quad\quad = -4$
$\quad\quad$ Keep.

Now try some odd numbers. Let $m = 3$ and $n = -3$. Plug these numbers into F and J and see which one is negative.

$$F: -n^m = -(-3)^3$$
$$= -(-27)$$
$$= 27$$
Eliminate.

$$(J): n - m = -3 - 3$$
$$= -6$$
Keep.

Choice (J) is correct.

35. B
Difficulty: High
Category: Number and Quantity
Getting to the Answer: This question revolves around the distance formula, $d = rt$. Liza drove at 40 miles per hour for 2 hours, for a total of $40(2) = 80$ miles. If she increased her speed by 25%, then she increased her speed by $0.25(40) = 10$ miles per hour. Her new speed was thus $40 + 10 = 50$ miles per hour. She drove at 50 miles per hour for the next 3 hours, for a total of $50(3) = 150$ miles.

Liza went 80 miles and then 150 miles, for a total of 230 miles. She drove for 2 hours and then for 3 hours, for a total of 5 hours. Rewrite $d = rt$ as $r = \frac{d}{t}$ to find her average rate for the trip. Plugging in the values above gives $\frac{230 \text{ miles}}{5 \text{ hours}} = 46$ miles per hour. Choice (B) is correct.

36. H
Difficulty: Medium
Category: Geometry
Getting to the Answer: To find the perimeter of a shape, add up all its sides. Use the given coordinate plane to help you. Side AC extends vertically from (1, 1) to (1, 5). You can find its length by subtracting its y-coordinates: $5 - 1 = 4$. Use similar logic to see that side CB is 5. Plug these values into the Pythagorean theorem to find the length of hypotenuse AB.

$$a^2 + b^2 = c^2$$
$$4^2 + 5^2 = c^2$$
$$16 + 25 = c^2$$
$$41 = c^2$$
$$\sqrt{41} = c$$

Finally, add up all these sides to obtain $4 + 5 + \sqrt{41}$, or $9 + \sqrt{41}$. Choice (H) is correct.

37. A
Difficulty: Medium
Category: Algebra
Getting to the Answer: Solve the inequality and then think about which answer choice describes the solution. Subtracting x from both sides yields $-2 < -5$. When is -2 less than -5? Never. What set has no solutions? The empty set. Choice (A) is correct.

38. G
Difficulty: Medium
Category: Geometry
Getting to the Answer: Draw a triangle and flip it over the y-axis to help you visualize the situation. Choose coordinates to represent A and see what happens to those coordinates. For example:

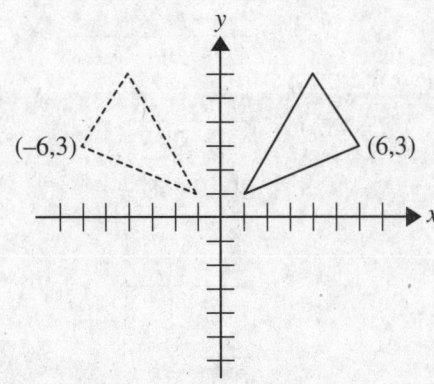

The y-coordinate stays the same, and the x-coordinate goes from positive to negative. This means that (v, w) will become (−v, w). Choice (G) is correct.

39. C
Difficulty: High
Category: Geometry
Getting to the Answer: Set up a coordinate system to compare points B and F. Because you're trying to find the distance relative to A, make A (0, 0). Then B is at (800, 0). Use the labeled distances to find the x-value of F, which is 700 (AB − DC − FE), and the y-value of F, which is 600 (CB − DE). This means that F is at (700, 600).

The lookout point is the midpoint of B and F, so use the midpoint formula, $\left(\dfrac{x_1+x_2}{2}, \dfrac{y_1+y_2}{2}\right)$:

$$\left(\dfrac{800+700}{2}, \dfrac{0+600}{2}\right) = (750, 300)$$

Using these coordinates, the lookout is 750 yards to the right (east) of point A and 300 yards up (north). Choice (C) is correct.

40. J
Difficulty: High
Category: Number and Quantity
Getting to the Answer: Write the squared binomials as repeated multiplication, FOIL, and replace i^2 with −1 whenever it appears:

$$\dfrac{(2i+2)^2}{(2i-2)^2} = \dfrac{(2i+2)(2i+2)}{(2i-2)(2i-2)}$$

$$= \dfrac{4i^2+4i+4i+4}{4i^2-4i-4i+4}$$

$$= \dfrac{4i^2+8i+4}{4i^2-8i+4}$$

$$= \dfrac{4(-1)+8i+4}{4(-1)-8i+4}$$

$$= \dfrac{-4+8i+4}{-4-8i+4}$$

$$= \dfrac{8i}{-8i}$$

$$= -1$$

Choice (J) is correct.

41. B
Difficulty: High
Category: Number and Quantity
Getting to the Answer: Rewrite the logarithmic equation as an exponential equation and solve. The equation $\log_7 7^{\sqrt{7}} = x$ is equivalent to $7^x = 7^{\sqrt{7}}$. The bases are the same, so the exponents must be equal. This means that $x = \sqrt{7} \approx 2.65$, which lies between 2 and 3. Choice (B) is correct.

Alternatively, if you recognized the rule $\log_b(b^x) = x$, you could arrive at $\sqrt{7} = x$ even more quickly.

42. F
Difficulty: High
Category: Functions
Getting to the Answer: The graphs of two functions intersect when their two function expressions are equal. Set the functions equal to each other and solve for x.

$$f(x) = g(x)$$

$$3^{3x+3} = 27^{\left(\frac{2}{3}x - \frac{1}{3}\right)}$$

Since $27 = 3^3$, you can rewrite this equation as follows:

$$3^{3x+3} = 3^{3\left(\frac{2}{3}x - \frac{1}{3}\right)}$$

This simplifies to $3^{3x+3} = 3^{2x-1}$. Now that the bases are equal, set the exponents equal to each other and solve for x:

$$3x + 3 = 2x - 1$$
$$x + 3 = -1$$
$$x = -4$$

Choice (F) is correct.

43. B
Difficulty: High
Category: Geometry
Getting to the Answer: The solution depends on knowing the Law of Cosines. Think of it as an extension of the Pythagorean theorem. In a triangle with sides a, b, c, and opposite angles A, B, C, the Law of Cosines states the following.

$$c^2 = a^2 + b^2 - 2ab \cos C$$

The question asks for the measure of the largest angle. Since the largest angle is opposite the largest side, the largest side 15 must be on the left side of the equation. Eliminate C and D. As its name suggests, the Law of Cosines features the cosine function, not the sine function, so (B) is correct.

44. F
Difficulty: High
Category: Number and Quantity
Getting to the Answer: Picking Numbers is the best way to approach this question. Choose a pair of numbers from each set and add them together. In Set I, if you add 2 and 4, you get 6. Adding 12 and 8 gives you 20. Adding −2 and 8 gives you 6. Because each sum is a member of the set of even integers, Set I seems to be true.

For Set II, adding 3 and 5 yields 8, which is not an odd integer. Therefore, Set II is not true.

Finally, if you add two primes, say 2 and 3, you get 5. That example is true. If you add 3 and 5, however, you get 8, which is not a prime number. Therefore, only Set I has the desired property. Choice (F) is correct.

45. B
Difficulty: High
Category: Statistics and Probability
Getting to the Answer: Recall that Probability = $\frac{\text{desired}}{\text{total}}$. The probability of choosing an integer with a digit of 3 is therefore the number of integers with a digit of 3 divided by 50. The integers 3, 13, 23, 30, 31, 32, 33, 34, 35, 36, 37, 38, 39, and 43 are the only integers less than 50 with 3s in them. There are 14 different total integers with this property, so the probability is $\frac{14}{50}$ or $\frac{7}{25}$. Choice (B) is correct.

Reading Test
Suggested Passage Map Notes

¶1: dog vs. doggie

¶2: describes doggie look; doggie grows on you; called "Dumps"

¶3: meeting Dumps: dog running; angry man

¶4: afraid of dog, but dog whines

¶5: owner wants to hurt dog

¶6–9: argue about dog

¶10: narrator threatens owner

¶11–12: owner changes and claims kindness to dog

¶13: owner story: loves dog, got new job, dog escapes, must drive dog back

¶14–15: narrator doubts story, offers to buy dog

BIG PICTURE SUMMARY

Main idea: Despite his rough appearance, Dumps the doggie evokes affection. The author met Dumps when the dog was running from his possibly abusive former owner.

Author's purpose: To describe his dog, his affection for his dog, and the circumstances under which he first met his dog.

1. A
Difficulty: High
Category: Inference
Getting to the Answer: Review the narrator's discussion of dogs in paragraph 1. In paragraph 2, the narrator notes that people may not initially notice his doggie's "finer qualities," but they will see his "amiable spirit" after getting to know him. Predict that while both dogs and the narrator's doggie are companionable, the main distinction is that his doggie must be less initially appealing; this matches (A). Choice B is incorrect because the narrator never discusses the relative ages of any dog or doggie. Choice C is incorrect because a "forgiving disposition" (lines 7–8) is attributed to dogs, while the correct answer must reflect a trait of his doggie. Likewise, D reflects the narrator's description of dogs in paragraph 1.

Part 6
PRACTICE TESTS

2. H
Difficulty: Medium
Category: Detail
Getting to the Answer: List the characteristics of Dumps before looking at the answer choices. The narrator states that his "finer qualities" are not obvious but goes on to describe his other features in lines 11–25. Predict: Dumps is mangy-looking, but friendly. This matches (H). Choice F is incorrect because his eyes are described as having a "luster" rather than being "dull." Choice G is the opposite; the narrator claims "you don't at once perceive" his mental qualities. Choice J is a distortion because while the dog is certainly hairy, he resembles a "ragged doormat" rather than something "well-groomed."

3. B
Difficulty: Medium
Category: Inference
Getting to the Answer: Consider the scene in paragraphs 3–4. Dumps is described as "active," "yelping," and running so quickly that he was kicking up stones. The narrator also notes hearing "the voice of an angry man." Though the narrator expects the dog to "snap" at him, the dog instead approaches him in a "piteous" manner. This matches (B). Choice A does not match the description of a dog running "wildly." Choice C is too extreme; the dog is trying to escape the "angry man," but he is running away, so he is clearly not so upset that he is "immobilized." Choice D is a distortion: the narrator states in the next paragraph that the owner "seemed about to fling" a "thick stick" at the dog (lines 52–53), not toss a stick in a playful manner.

4. F
Difficulty: Low
Category: Vocab-in-Context
Getting to the Answer: The dog's owner is ready to throw a stick at the dog, so the narrator "checks" him by shouting a threat. The narrator is trying to stop the owner from hurting the dog, so predict "checked" means stopped. This matches (F), "prevented." The scene has nothing to do with a square patterned design, G, and the narrator is not merely "verifying" something, H, but shouting to prevent an act of violence. "Assaulted," J, is too extreme for a verbal response and lacks the necessary connotation of preventing the throw.

5. D
Difficulty: High
Category: Function
Getting to the Answer: When stopped, the owner scowls and claims that "A man may do as he likes with his own." The narrator responds with indignation, showing the owner and the reader that animal welfare is important to him. The word "man" is emphasized to indicate that the narrator is using it sarcastically; he does not think the owner is acting like a "man" at all, which matches (D). Choice A is a misused detail; the narrator does refer to the other man as "big" in paragraph 5, but he is not using the word "man" to describe the other man's size. Instead, he is using it to question his humanity. Choice B is opposite, as the narrator does not agree with the owner, answering him "indignantly." Choice C is a distortion. Although the narrator states that "cruelty" to animals "has the effect of inclining me to fight," his actions are not physical.

6. H
Difficulty: Low
Category: Detail
Getting to the Answer: In lines 61–62, the owner initially responded to the narrator's words with a "sulky scowl." In response, the narrator mentions an Act of Parliament and makes a threat. At this, the owner stops scowling, seeming "to have been affected by my threats." The owner was worried about the narrator's threats of prosecution, (H). Choice F is out of scope; the owner never seems worried that the dog will bite, and the dog has been behaving kindly toward the narrator since running up to him. Choice G is incorrect because the owner does not discuss his factory job until a later paragraph and never mentions being late to work. Choice J distorts the passage: the owner, not the narrator, was about to throw a stick at the dog.

7. A
Difficulty: High
Category: Global
Getting to the Answer: Consider the narrator's tone and comments directed toward the reader. Although the introduction might appear to be argumentative, the narrator includes comments to the reader in lines 2–3 and lines 22–25 that display a thoughtful attitude. He will later explain his behavior in lines 65–66: "I am naturally of a peaceable disposition." Clearly, the narrator doesn't want the reader to think him a brute. This tone matches (A). Choice B is opposite; the narrator is

mindful of the reader, though he argues with the dog owner in the passage. Choice C is extreme; the narrator never expresses fear that anyone will disagree with his views about dogs, doggies, or animal welfare. Choice D is also extreme. The narrator seems to desire the reader to have a favorable opinion of him, but nothing suggests that he is so concerned that he's misrepresenting the events.

8. **G**
Difficulty: Medium
Category: Inference
Getting to the Answer: Locate the paragraph that contains the owner's explanation about "kindness" (lines 79–94) and review his story. To prevent the dog from following him to the factory, the owner chases him home "out of pure kindness." This matches (G). Choice F is a misused detail; the owner does make this claim in lines 61–62, but this is before he's trying to explain his behavior toward the dog as kindness. Choice H is out of scope, as no mention is made of playing fetch, and the owner even admits that the throwing of "sticks an' stones" is meant to drive the dog home. Choice J is a distortion. While the owner does claim that the dog might be harmed at the factory, he does not claim that the men at the factory "have a record" of these types of actions in the past.

9. **D**
Difficulty: High
Category: Inference
Getting to the Answer: In lines 79–94, the owner explains his motivation for his treatment of the dog. After hearing this, the narrator is "somewhat doubtful of the truth of this story." The narrator had just seen the owner mistreating his dog, despite his claims, and his initial "scowl" morphs to a "deferential air" (line 75) as soon as the narrator threatens to have him arrested for his behavior. It seems that the owner is putting on an act to avoid prosecution, (D). Choice A is out of scope; the passage concludes before the purchase of the dog is discussed, so we don't know anything about the owner's eagerness. The narrator calls the owner "big" and "rough" (lines 50–51) but never questions his employability, B, only his treatment of animals. Choice C is a distortion; the narrator's suspicion of the story stems from the owner's contradictory actions and behaviors, not his assumptions about conditions at the owner's workplace.

Suggested Passage Map Notes

Passage A

¶1: Present-day people think science is unquestionable

¶2: History shows that science is not always correct

¶3: People think science remains constant, but questioning leads to progress

Passage B

¶1: Historically people were skeptical about science

¶2: Scientific research should be questioned

¶3: Pharma. company studies should be scrutinized

¶4: Policy decisions should be based on balance of faith and doubt

---

BIG PICTURE SUMMARY

Passage A

Main idea: The public misunderstands scientific research as supplying unquestionable certainties rather than probabilities because science seems predictable in everyday life.

Author's purpose: To argue that scientific research is subject to uncertainties, possibilities, and limitations.

Passage B

Main idea: The current public is not critical enough of scientific research, especially as it is applied to public policy.

Author's purpose: To argue for better public knowledge about the background of scientific studies and a middle-of-the-road approach to applying research to public policy.

---

10. **G**
Difficulty: Low
Category: Detail
Getting to the Answer: The first mention of policy makers is at the end of the first paragraph, where the author writes that they "treat the results of every latest study as if they were surefire truths." In other words, they accept the results without question, which matches (G). Choices F, H, and J are opposites.

11. C
Difficulty: Medium
Category: Detail
Getting to the Answer: The phrase "According to the passage" is a clue that this is a Detail question. The answer can be found in the passage, but there will not always be a word-for-word match between the answer choices and the passage's text. Choice A is incorrect. In lines 30–32, the author states that "it is tempting to place our faith in the oversimplified generalities of headlines." The word *tempting* shows that this is the opposite of what the author believes. Eliminate A. Choice B can likewise be eliminated. "(A)n unfounded prejudice stemming from a desire for scientific constancy can actually discourage inquiry" indicates that the author does not believe in discouraging scientific inquiry. Choice (C) is correct. In advocating "the rigorous application of probabilities," the author allows for uncertainty in scientific results. Choice D is given as a reason for the tempting belief in answer choice A. Eliminate it as well.

12. H
Difficulty: Medium
Category: Vocab-in-Context
Getting to the Answer: The word *complacent* follows examples of predictable events, including a car starting and a power plant running without problems. Since we assume these events will always be the same, we become used to them and don't question them at all. In the same way, we have a "a complacent faith in the reliability and consistency of science" and assume that study results are always correct. Choice (H), "unquestioned," is a synonym for *complacent*. All other choices are incorrect definitions based on the context provided.

13. B
Difficulty: Medium
Category: Detail
Getting to the Answer: Lines 68–69 state that "many people balked" at Schiaparelli's ideas about features on Mars; (B) matches this prediction and is correct. Alternatively, you could scan through the passage looking for each of the answer choices and eliminate those that were accepted by the public. Choice A is questioned by "some critics," who we cannot assume are the general public. Choice C is in Passage A, not Passage B, and choice D isn't in the passage at all. That leaves (B) as the correct answer.

14. G
Difficulty: Medium
Category: Function
Getting to the Answer: Use your passage notes to help predict an answer for a Function question that refers to an entire paragraph. The first paragraph of Passage B outlines the way that skepticism toward science has changed over time. Choice (G) matches the function of paragraph 1. Choice F is out of scope; no new hypothesis is introduced in this paragraph. Choice H is a misused detail; paragraph 2 introduces the issue of public policy, but this question asks specifically about paragraph 1. Choice J is a misused detail; underlying causes are discussed in the third paragraph, not the first.

15. D
Difficulty: Medium
Category: Function
Getting to the Answer: The passage speaks about finding "a middle ground" between "alarmism" and "recklessness." "Chicken Little" refers to a fable in which Chicken Little famously cries that the sky is falling, even though it is clearly not. Even if you don't know the fable, the words "alarmist" and "recklessness" indicate a negative characterization of some politicians. Thus, eliminate choice B, which is positive. Though the word "chicken" is used, the sentence is not about chickens but about politicians. Eliminate choice A. Policy makers motivated by profits refers to risk-takers, not alarmists, so choice C is incorrect. Chicken Little's cries are scares about impending doom, as is, according to the author, "the alarmism of political 'Chicken Littles'" (lines 122–123), so (D) is correct.

16. H
Difficulty: High
Category: Inference
Getting to the Answer: Keeping track of each author's primary viewpoints or beliefs can help you to more quickly evaluate and eliminate answer choices. Passage B describes a solution in which people understand enough about science to assess its reliability for themselves, but Passage A claims that people don't do this because they desire a world of certainties. The contrast between striving for more knowledge and clinging to easy beliefs is captured in (H). Choice F is a distortion; the actions and attitudes of policy makers don't prevent people from becoming better educated. Choice G is a misused detail; Passage B discusses the

difficulties of obtaining impartial results, but this is not relevant to the question. Choice J is out of scope; the author of Passage A discusses ethical questions, but this is not related to the solution specified in Passage B.

17. A
Difficulty: Low
Category: Detail
Getting to the Answer: Remember that the answers to Detail questions are always stated directly. By turning first to the passages, you can accurately predict the correct answer and not be misled by misused details. Passage A includes the phrase "present-day industrial societies" in the first sentence, and Passage B mentions "present-day industrial societies" in the second paragraph. Choice (A) matches your research. Choice B is a misused detail; this phrase is from paragraph 2 in Passage A. Choice C is a misused detail; this is included in paragraph 3 in Passage B. Choice D is a misused detail; this is mentioned in the first paragraph of Passage B only.

18. G
Category: Detail
Difficulty: Medium
Getting to the Answer: Prediction is key in Detail questions. Incorrect answer choices will often reference other details erroneously. In paragraph 2, the passage directly states "In the late 19th century, when Italian astronomer Giovanni Schiaparelli first detected seas and continents on the planet Mars, many people balked at the idea of Earth-like topography on the Red Planet," which shows the fallibility, or inaccuracy, of a scientific certainty. Use this as a prediction. Choice (G) matches the prediction. Choice F is a misused detail; this example is mentioned in Passage A, not Passage B. Choice H is a distortion; the author of Passage B discusses this in paragraph 4, but these are not examples of the fallibility of scientific certainties. Choice J is a misused detail; this example is mentioned in Passage A, not Passage B.

Suggested Passage Map Notes

¶1: Walter Scott (S) born in Scotland in 1771, wrote Scottish ballads

¶2: S's poetry brought fame

¶3: 1814, S anonymously started writing novels (ex: *Waverley*) for $

¶4: 1820, S wrote *Ivanhoe*; became Baronet; made tartans & kilts popular

¶5: to clear debt, wrote for $ until his death in 1832

¶6: S (1) popularized historical novel, (2) rehabilitated Highland culture

¶7: S responsible for Scottish banks retaining right to issue own banknotes

BIG PICTURE SUMMARY

Main idea: Sir Walter Scott faced highs and lows throughout his writing career, which included writing poetry and historical fiction that popularized his native Scotland.

Author's purpose: To describe the career and influence of author Sir Walter Scott.

19. C
Difficulty: Medium
Category: Global
Getting to the Answer: This question focuses on the big picture. Identifying the author's purpose as part of the big picture summary can help you form predictions and more quickly work through questions like these. Predict that the correct choice will match your passage notes: the author's purpose was to provide information about Scott's success and influence. This matches choice (C), the correct answer. Choice A is a distortion: the author provides an example—not a theory—of the impact of novels. Choice B is a distortion: the passage states that "Even when it was clear that there would be no harm in coming out . . . he maintained the façade". Choice D is a distortion; although Scott had financial difficulties, the passage is not comparing them with his writing career.

20. J
Difficulty: Medium
Category: Inference
Getting to the Answer: Use your passage notes and big picture summary to determine why the author would believe that Scott is important. In the last paragraphs of the text, the author credits Scott as the reason that tartans and kilts became popular and why Scottish banks retain banknote-issuing rights. Predict that the author would say that Scott was important for revitalizing an appreciation of Scotland's culture and autonomy. This matches (J), the correct answer.

Choice F is opposite: the author dignified tartans and kilts by making them part of an important ceremony and reconnecting them to cultural identity. While Scott's novels were flattering of Scottish culture, it was his efforts in connecting people with Scottish culture and encouraging Scotland's autonomy that had the most historical influence. Therefore, choice G is incorrect. Choice H is a distortion; Scott wrote novels, not serious analyses of Scottish history.

21. D
Difficulty: Medium
Category: Function
Getting to the Answer: Use your passage notes to help predict an answer for a Function question that refers to an entire paragraph. This paragraph lists the poetry that Scott published and the fame that came with it. Predict that the main purpose is to show how his publishing his poetry affected his career. Eliminate A; it is a misused detail from paragraph 5. Eliminate B because it is out of scope: though Schubert set one of Scott's poems to music, Scott's feelings about the collaboration are not mentioned. Choice C can be eliminated; this is a misused detail from paragraph 4. Choice (D) is correct: it summarizes the influence it had on Scott (fame) and the influence it had on others.

22. J
Difficulty: High
Category: Function
Getting to the Answer: When determining if a word or phrase is being used literally or figuratively, determine its function, or role, in the sentence or paragraph. The passage asserts that it was "popularly applied to the mysterious best-selling writer" (lines 42–43). Eliminate choices F and G, because nothing implies that this wizard was either actually magical or fictional.

Choice H is tempting, so review (J) to see which choice is best supported by the text. There's nothing in the paragraph that explicitly states that Scott is "highly skilled in writing about Scottish history," but there are many context clues to show that readers were "entranced" by the author: "successful (and profitable) work" (line 28), "met with considerable success" (lines 31–32), and the previously quoted phrases. Choice (J) is correct: the term is used figuratively to convey the extent to which the public was enamoured with the anonymous author.

23. A
Difficulty: Medium
Category: Inference
Getting to the Answer: The author writes that Sir Walter Scott refused to declare bankruptcy, insisting on putting his home and income into a trust that would eventually pay back his creditors completely. Similarly, he resumed writing when he faced financial struggles toward the end of his life, and that those debts were paid off from a trust after he passed away. Predict that he was committed to paying back his debts. Choice (A) is the closest match and is correct. There is no evidence in the passage that he was "inclined toward ill will" (resentful), as in B; depressed, as in C; or lacking a sense of responsibility, as in D.

24. G
Difficulty: High
Category: Vocab-In-Context
Getting to the Answer: After becoming a lawyer, Scott *started dabbling* in two ways: *first* in translating other's writings and *then* in writing his own poetry. Predict that *started dabbling* means something similar to "began experimenting with new things." This matches (G) and is correct. Choice F is incorrect because *short, superficial*, which means "shallow," are the opposite of his long-term commitment to writing. Choice H is incorrect because nothing in the text implies that his translations or poetry are *new interpretations*. Incorrect choice J is unrelated to the writing in which *he started dabbling*.

25. C
Difficulty: Medium
Category: Detail
Getting to the Answer: Remember that the answers to Detail questions are always specifically stated. By using your passage map, you can accurately predict the correct answer and not be misled by misused details. Paragraph 2 notes that poetry brought Scott fame,

so look there for the specific event. Lines 15–16 states that "his poetry, beginning with *The Lay of the Last Minstrel* . . . brought him great fame". This matches correct choice (C). Choices A, B, and D all misuse details. If choice B was tempting, note that it wasn't until *after* he founded the printing press and released his work in 1805 that his fame began.

26. F
Difficulty: Hard
Category: Inference
Getting to the Answer: This question asks about Scott's reputation after his death. Since the overall structure of the passage is chronological, it is likely that the answer will come toward the end. The last three paragraphs give evidence of Scott's continued popularity: you read that his novels continued to sell after his death, eventually covering his debts; that Edinburgh's central railroad station was named after his first successful novel; and that his picture is on Scottish currency today. Predict that his reputation is still positive. Choice (F) matches the prediction. There is no evidence in the text that suggests that his popularity has increased, considering the high popularity experienced during his life. Choice G is incorrect. Choice H is opposite; the passage clearly states that Scott's novels continued to sell well after his death. Choice J is a distortion; though his debts were unpaid and he was imitated, nothing implies these damaged Scott's reputation.

27. B
Difficulty: High
Category: Detail
Getting to the Answer: Using your passage notes, identify which paragraph will have specifics about the novels he published after his debut series of novels. The first sentence in paragraph 4 reveals that Scott *broke away* from his previous setting and content: writing a historical romance set in 12th-century England. Further, the passage states (lines 51–52) that "he unleashed a slew of books along the same lines". This matches (B), which is the correct answer. Choice A is out of scope; language is never mentioned. Choices C and D are both opposite of what the passage indicates.

Suggested Passage Map Notes

¶1: Lemur (L) part of suborder of primates, nocturnal; flying lemurs not primates

¶2: L found on Madagascar, larger are nocturnal, smaller are diurnal

¶3: All L species are endangered b/c deforestation and hunting

¶4: Ring-tailed lemur (RTL) most populous L in zoos

¶5: RTL physical characteristics

¶6: RTL baby v. adult characteristics

¶7: RTL live in forests or open brush, require primary forests

¶8: RTL behavior, territory

¶9: RTL communication

¶10: RTL breeding

BIG PICTURE SUMMARY

Main idea: Several species of lemurs inhabit Madagascar and are endangered. The characteristics of ring-tailed lemurs in particular are described.

Author's purpose: To describe the classification, location, status, and characteristics of lemurs, particularly the ring-tailed lemur.

28. F
Difficulty: Medium
Category: Global
Getting to the Answer: Global questions ask about the main idea or main purpose of the *entire* passage. Wrong answers are often outside the scope of the passage or are too specific when compared to the entire passage. Don't forget to complete a big picture summary, because this summary will help you to predict the answers to main idea and main purpose questions. Checking the big picture summary indicates that the main purpose is to offer information about lemurs and, specifically, ring-tailed lemurs. Choice (F) is a match. Choice G is incorrect because, while the writer did mention lemurs' endangered status, there was no comparison to the status of other primates. Choice H is incorrect because the writer did not include a theory of female dominance in lemur troops.

Choice J is incorrect because it distorts the information in the passage. Conservation efforts are being made, but there's no indication there is a positive response to those efforts.

29. C
Difficulty: Low
Category: Function
Getting to the Answer: Research the passage carefully to interpret the context correctly. Look for the main idea of paragraph 3 by checking the passage notes. Paragraph 3 focuses on why lemurs are endangered. Choice A is opposite; in captivity, ring-tailed lemurs reproduce easily. Choice B is a misused detail; paragraph 2 discusses their locations, not paragraph 3. Choice (C) paraphrases the main idea of paragraph 3 and is correct. Choice D is a misused detail; vocal and olfactory communications for one species of lemurs are mentioned in paragraph 9.

30. F
Difficulty: Medium
Category: Detail
Getting to the Answer: Taking good notes and marking the passage will help you on Detail questions that lack line references. From your notes, you should see that lemur communication is mentioned in paragraph 9. The writer states that "males vigorously wave their tails high" to attempt to make their scent stronger than others' scents. Look for this among the choices. Choice (F) matches your prediction. Choice G is a distortion; the author does reference "*vocal*" communication, but it is not connected to the tail waving. Choices H and J are out of scope; the author doesn't offer visual or tactile communications.

31. D
Difficulty: Medium
Category: Vocab-in-Context
Getting to the Answer: Since *odd* is a common word, it's important to think about it in the specific context of what the author has written. The author uses the word when describing what ring-tailed lemurs usually eat—fruit, leaves, and seeds, plus an insect every now and then. Thus, *odd* refers to *occasional*, as (D) says. All other answer choices are possible definitions of *odd*, but none make sense in the sentence.

32. G
Difficulty: Medium
Category: Detail
Getting to the Answer: The answers to Detail questions are stated directly in the passage—you can find the answer with research. This point is fairly obscure, and may not be reflected in your notes. If you have to, skim for *zoo*, which appears in paragraph 4. The author states that ring-tailed lemurs are the most populous lemurs in zoos and follows that by writing "they reproduce readily in captivity." Use that as your prediction. Choice F is out of scope; the author doesn't make such a contention. Choice (G) is a good paraphrase of the text referenced above. Choice H is out of scope; the author does not make this point. Choice J is a distortion; the author addresses *foraging*, but not in connection with zoos.

33. D
Difficulty: Medium
Category: Inference
Getting to the Answer: When given a line reference, move quickly and read at least that entire sentence to discern context. The author indicates that lemurs need to live in primary forests to survive. The clearing will likely endanger the lemurs' continued survival. Look for a match to this idea. Choices A and B are out of scope; the author does not refer to either statement. Choice C is also out of scope; the author doesn't reference such predators here. Choice (D) matches the research above.

34. G
Difficulty: Medium
Category: Function
Getting to the Answer: Function questions are answered by looking for why something is included in the passage. Referencing your passage notes can give you context. The question asks why the author mentions the infraorder Lemuriformes. This leads you to the first paragraph, which discusses lemurs in general and how they are related to other primate species. You may be unsure exactly what the function of the scientific name is, so compare this paragraph to the choices. Choice F is opposite; prosimians are the predecessors of simians. Choice (G) is correct because it describes the context of the scientific name. Paragraph 1 states that lemurs represent the *evolutionary predecessor* of monkeys and apes, a paraphrase of what you see here. Choice H is a distortion; at the end of paragraph 1, the author clearly states that flying lemur

specie are not actually lemurs but doesn't explain why. Choice J is a misused detail; lemurs being nocturnal is mentioned in paragraph 2, not paragraph 1.

35. C
Difficulty: Medium
Category: Inference
Getting to the Answer: You need to "read between the lines" to find the correct answer. But don't make too great a logical leap. Check your notes for the second paragraph, and read it again if necessary. The question is very open-ended, so work through the choices and compare them to the information in the paragraph. Choice A is opposite; the author states that the pygmy mouse lemur is the smallest species and that smaller species are typically nocturnal, not diurnal. Choice B is out of scope; the author does not discuss why certain species of lemur have become extinct. Choice (C) works. The author writes that the indri was the largest lemur. The next sentence states that "the larger species" are all extinct. Therefore, you can infer that the indri is extinct. Choice D is opposite; in paragraph 1, you learn that lemurs are described as evolutionary *predecessors* of monkeys, meaning monkeys are descended from them.

36. H
Difficulty: Medium
Category: Detail
Getting to the Answer: To determine which lemur would have blue eyes, look in the passage notes. There's no note about eye color, but both paragraphs 5 and 6 discuss physical characteristics, which can include eye color. Paragraph 6 mentions that very young ring-tailed lemurs have blue eyes. (H) is the correct answer. Choices F and G are misused details; a pygmy mouse and an indri lemur were mentioned to show the size range for lemur species, not to discuss their eye color. Choice J is contradicted by paragraph 6—ring-tailed adults have yellow, not blue, eyes.